96

DICTIONARY
OF INDIAN TRIBES
OF THE AMERICAS

Cover Design:
MANDELLA

The Mandella symbolizes the Indian shield of good luck. With this shield they believed they would be protected, and by having them in their homes, it would bring prosperity, good health and happiness.

DICTIONARY
OF INDIAN TRIBES
OF THE AMERICAS

SECOND EDITION

VOLUME

I

**ABABCO
–CUNA**

AMERICAN INDIAN PUBLISHERS, INC.
177F Riverside Avenue
Newport Beach, CA 92663

Editor and Publisher
CISCO

Associate Editor
GAIL HAMLIN-WILSON

Principal Staff Writer
JAN ONOFRIO-GRIMM

Art and Production
THOMAS F. GILLE

Editorial Associate
NANCY K. CAPACE

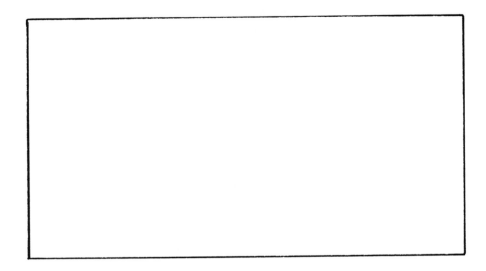

PUBLISHER'S FOREWORD

The first edition of DICTIONARY OF INDIAN TRIBES OF THE AMERICAS (1980) contained 476 entries. This new edition adds 678 for a total of 1,154.

The number of illustrations and maps has also increased several-fold.

Each entry has been reviewed and when appropriate updated and expanded with the aid of current references and research.

DICTIONARY OF INDIAN TRIBES OF THE AMERICAS continues to be the only major general reference on native peoples to cover the entire Western Hemisphere.

We have believed from the beginning that the growing trend toward "Pan Indianism" should encompass territory as well as cultural and other ethnic considerations.

This position is well supported by the policy of the founders of the Museum of the American Indian (New York), to include exhibits from the Aleutians to the southernmost reaches of the hemishere. A tour of the museum gives a truly comprehensive and most graphic experience of the history of the related continents since the initial migration and habitation of the Western Hemisphere from Siberia in the distant past.

The recent quincenteniary commemeration of the European settlers arrival has further emphasized the relevance of relationships throughout the area.

Note should be made of the decision by our editors to forgo the use of foreign language accents and diacritics in the words contained in this presentation (as was also the case in the first edition.)

These volumes are intended to give comprehensive coverage of the peoples native to the Americas with special consideration to the needs of general library users.

For those scholars requiring more detail, many sources are available or in process.

First, one might consider the bibliographical references cited following most entries in this dictionary. They have been selected as being most directly related to the subject and available in most large public or academic libraries. Many of these references themselves have extensive bibliographies (e.g., Hodge, *Handbook of Indians North of Mexico*; Swanton, *The Indian Tribes of North America*; Steward, *The Indians of South America*.)

The primary bibliographical reference covering North and Meso- America is *Ethnographic Bibliography of North America;* edited by Timothy J. O'Leary (1975) five vols., based on editions originated and edited by George Peter Murdoch.

A companion to this is *Ethnographic Bibliography of South America,* (1963) also edited by O'Leary.

Both were published by Human Relations Area Files (New Haven, Connecticut.)

The North America edition covers the region north of the northern boundries of Meso America (the area of "high cultures" in Mexico and Central America. It contains nearly 40,000 entries seperated into fifteen culture areas.

The regional divisions also provide the arrangement basis for the in process *Handbook of North American Indians* being published by the Smithsonian Institution. This work, when completed, will contain twenty volumes. A number of volumes are now in print (1992) with final completion estimated by the end of the decade.

It will be the definitive source for scholarly reference on the geographic areas covered, containing a vast quantity of statistics written largely by authoritative academics. Since it is not arranged alphabetically, but rather by culture area, considerable searching may be required for assembling data on a particular tribe or nation.

We believe DICTIONARY OF INDIAN TRIBES OF THE AMERICAS can serve as a first-source instrument in the quest for information; complimated by supplementary data from the other sources.

It is also to be noted that, as we go to press, Ted Turner has announced an ambitious project to further document the history of native America, to be presented in a variety of media forms.

We wish to gratefully acknowledge the contributions of many persons, organizations, and instituions that have made available facilities and material for these volumes.

The Publisher,
December, 1992

INITIAL MIGRATION PATTERNS

Crossing the land-bridge through the Bering Strait, ancestors of Native Americans are assumed to have followed routes along fertile valleys bordering mountain ranges throughout the continents in populating the hemisphere.

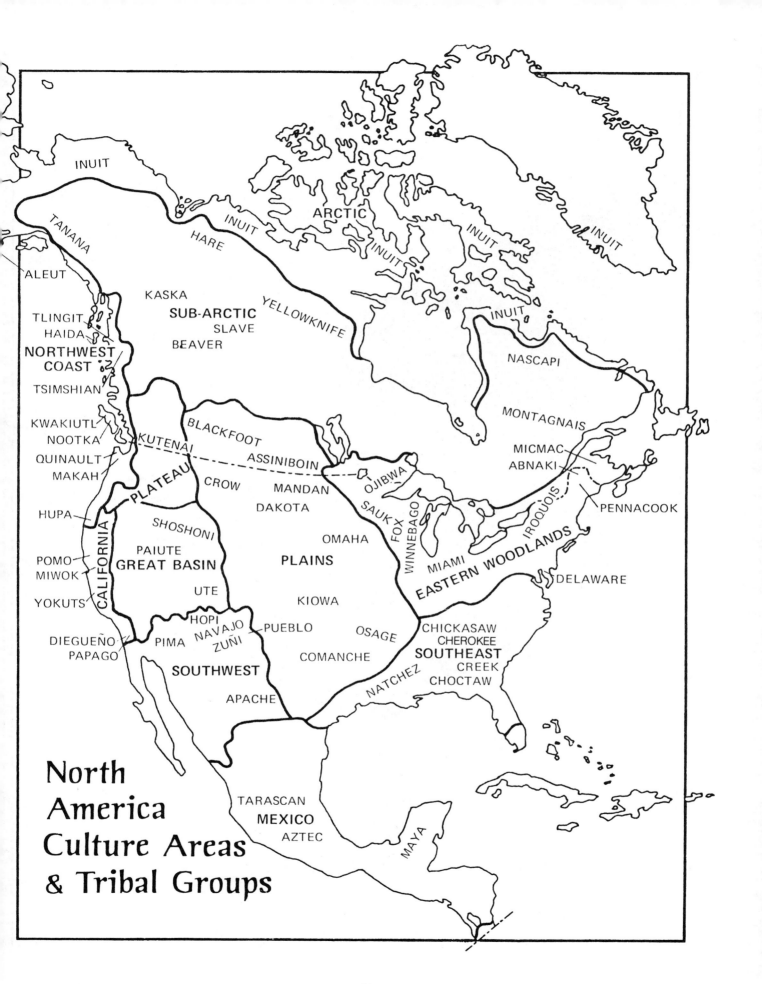

INUIT

ARCTIC

TANANA

HARE

INUIT

INUIT

INUIT

INUIT

INUIT

ALEUT

KASKA

SUB-ARCTIC

YELLOWKNIFE

INUIT

TLINGIT

HAIDA

SLAVE

**NORTHWEST
COAST**

BEAVER

NASCAPI

TSIMSHIAN

MONTAGNAIS

KWAKIUTL
NOOTKA

BLACKFOOT

KUTENAI

ASSINIBOIN

MICMAC
ABNAKI

QUINAULT
MAKAH

CROW

MANDAN

OJIBWA

PLATEAU

PENNACOOK

DAKOTA

SAUK

HUPA

SHOSHONI

OMAHA

FOX
WINNEBAGO

IROQUOIS

POMO
MIWOK

PAIUTE
GREAT BASIN

PLAINS

MIAMI

EASTERN WOODLANDS

CALIFORNIA

UTE

DELAWARE

YOKUTS

KIOWA

HOPI

PUEBLO

CHICKASAW
CHEROKEE

DIEGUEÑO
PAPAGO

PIMA

NAVAJO
ZUÑI

OSAGE

SOUTHEAST

CREEK

SOUTHWEST

COMANCHE

NATCHEZ

CHOCTAW

APACHE

North
America
Culture Areas
& Tribal Groups

TARASCAN
MEXICO

AZTEC

MAYA

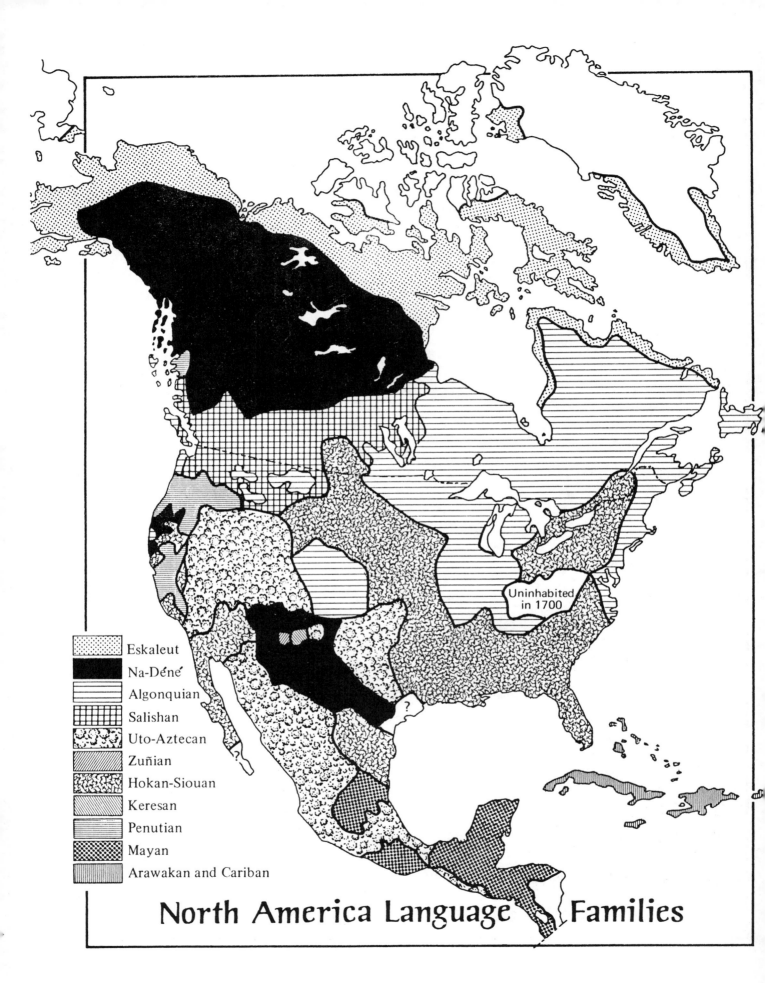

North America Language Families

Legend:
- Eskaleut
- Na-Déné
- Algonquian
- Salishan
- Uto-Aztecan
- Zuñian
- Hokan-Siouan
- Keresan
- Penutian
- Mayan
- Arawakan and Cariban

Uninhabited in 1700

Culture Areas and Tribal Locations South America

CIBONEY
TAINO
MOSQUITO
CARIBBEAN SEA
TAINO
CIBONEY
CARIB
INCA
CUNA
JIRAJARA
ARMA
TIMOTÉ
QUIMBAYA
CHIBCHA
CARA
PURUHA
PALTA
JÍVARO
CARIB
PALICUR
CARIB
MURA
MUNDURUCÚ
ARARA
TIMBIRA
TUPINAMBA
PARINTINTIN
CANELLA
SHAVANTE
SHERENTE
INCA
CONIBO
BAURÉ
MOJO
PARESSÍ
SIRIONÓ
BORORO
TUPINAMBA
URU
AYMARÁ
ZAMUCO
MBAYA
ATACAMEÑO
GUARANÍ
PAYAGUA
DIAGUITA
HUARPE
ABIPÓN
GUAYAKÍ
CHARRUA
QUERANDÍ
PUELCHE
PACIFIC OCEAN
ATLANTIC OCEAN
TEHUELCHE
CHONO
ALACALUF
ONA
YAHGAN

Chiefdoms of Central America and the Caribbean

Irrigation civilizations of the Central Andes

Farmers and pastoralists of the Southern Andes

Tropical forest village farmers

Marginal nomadic hunters and gatherers

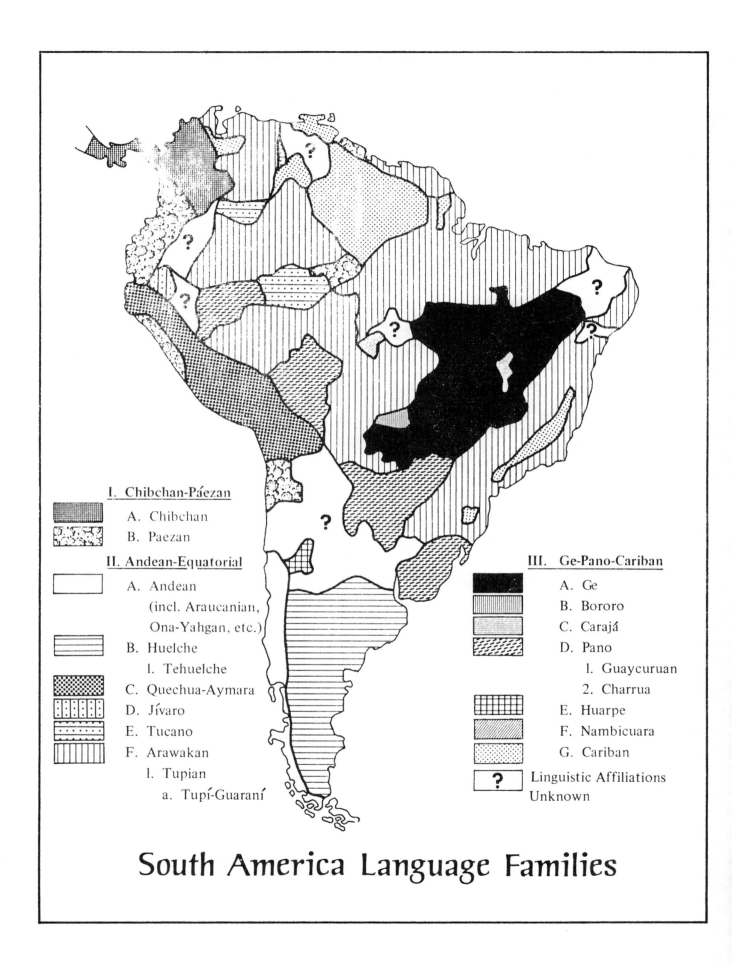

I. Chibchan-Páezan

- A. Chibchan
- B. Paezan

II. Andean-Equatorial

- A. Andean
  (incl. Araucanian,
  Ona-Yahgan, etc.)
- B. Huelche
  1. Tehuelche
- C. Quechua-Aymara
- D. Jívaro
- E. Tucano
- F. Arawakan
  1. Tupian
     a. Tupí-Guaraní

III. Ge-Pano-Cariban

- A. Ge
- B. Bororo
- C. Carajá
- D. Pano
  1. Guaycuruan
  2. Charrua
- E. Huarpe
- F. Nambicuara
- G. Cariban

? Linguistic Affiliations Unknown

South America Language Families

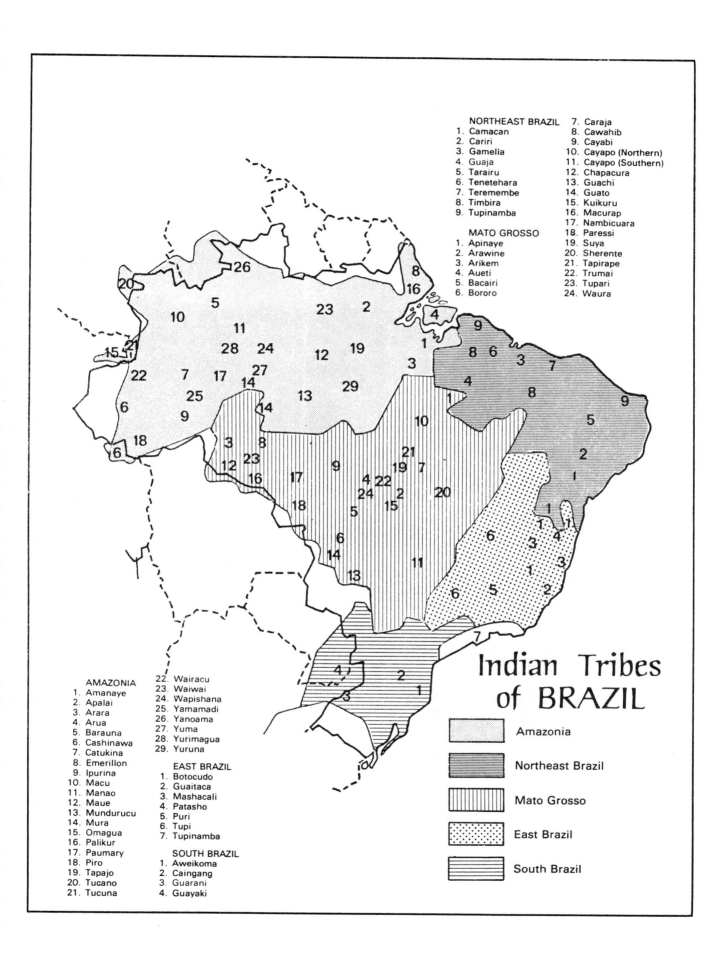

Indian Tribes of BRAZIL

NORTHEAST BRAZIL
1. Camacan
2. Cariri
3. Gamella
4. Guaja
5. Tarairu
6. Tenetehara
7. Teremembe
8. Timbira
9. Tupinamba

MATO GROSSO
1. Apinaye
2. Arawine
3. Arikem
4. Aueti
5. Bacairi
6. Bororo
7. Caraja
8. Cawahib
9. Cayabi
10. Cayapo (Northern)
11. Cayapo (Southern)
12. Chapacura
13. Guachi
14. Guato
15. Kuikuru
16. Macurap
17. Nambicuara
18. Paressi
19. Suya
20. Sherente
21. Tapirape
22. Trumai
23. Tupari
24. Waura

AMAZONIA
1. Amanaye
2. Apalai
3. Arara
4. Arua
5. Barauna
6. Cashinawa
7. Catukina
8. Emerillon
9. Ipurina
10. Macu
11. Manao
12. Maue
13. Mundurucu
14. Mura
15. Omagua
16. Palikur
17. Paumary
18. Piro
19. Tapajo
20. Tucano
21. Tucuna
22. Wairacu
23. Waiwai
24. Wapishana
25. Yamamadi
26. Yanoama
27. Yuma
28. Yurimagua
29. Yuruna

EAST BRAZIL
1. Botocudo
2. Guaitaca
3. Mashacali
4. Patasho
5. Puri
6. Tupi
7. Tupinamba

SOUTH BRAZIL
1. Aweikoma
2. Caingang
3. Guarani
4. Guayaki

Amazonia

Northeast Brazil

Mato Grosso

East Brazil

South Brazil

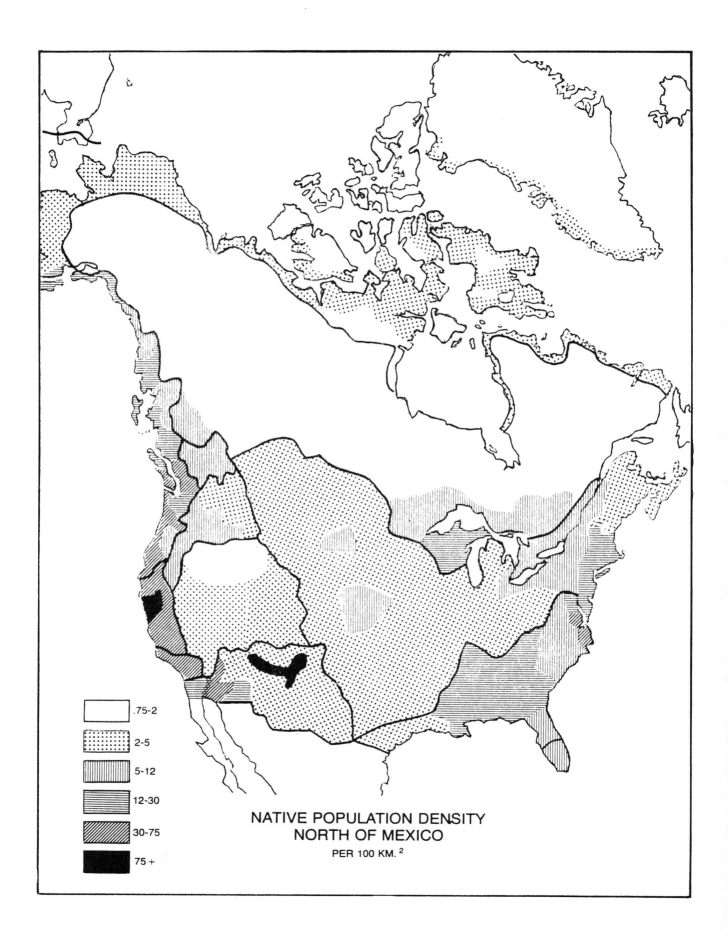

NATIVE POPULATION DENSITY
NORTH OF MEXICO

PER 100 KM.^{2}

.75-2

2-5

5-12

12-30

30-75

75 +

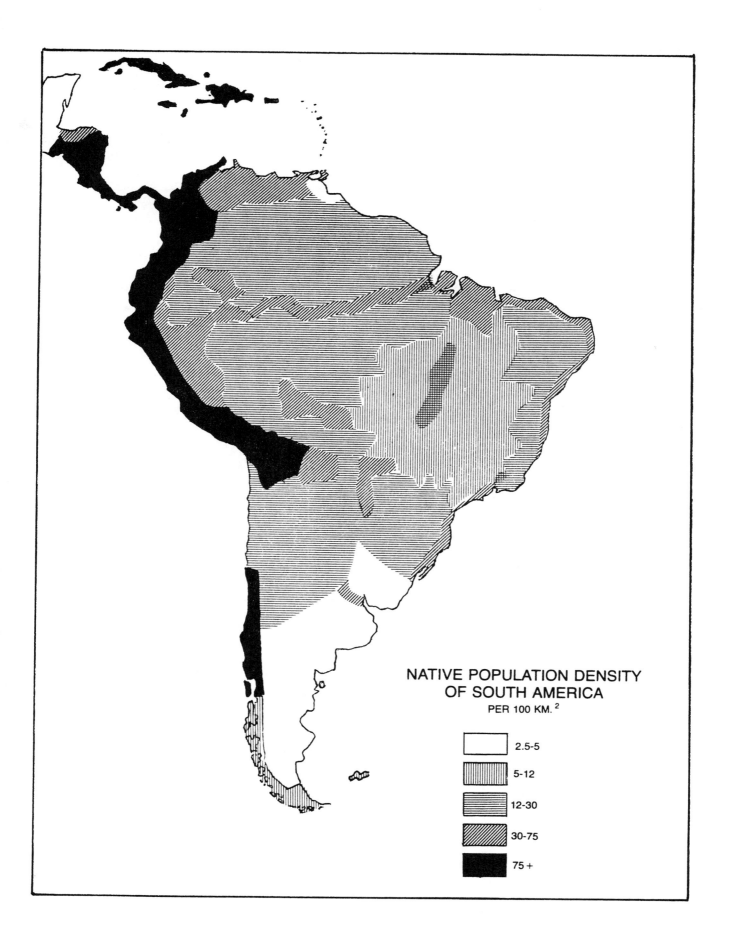

NATIVE POPULATION DENSITY
OF SOUTH AMERICA

PER 100 KM. ^{2}

	2.5-5
	5-12
	12-30
	30-75
	75 +

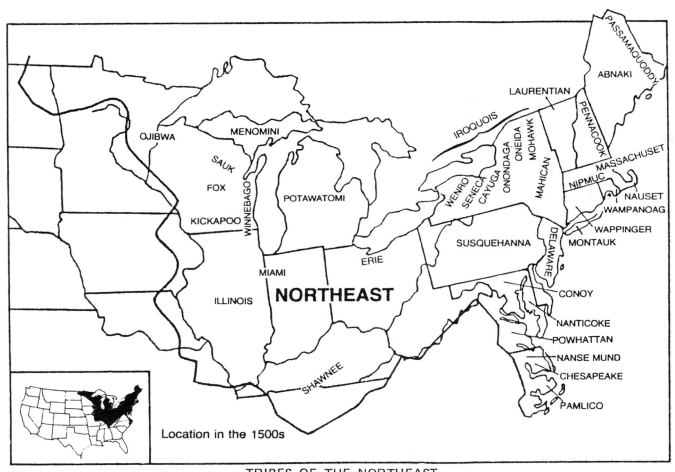

Location in the 1500s

TRIBES OF THE NORTHEAST

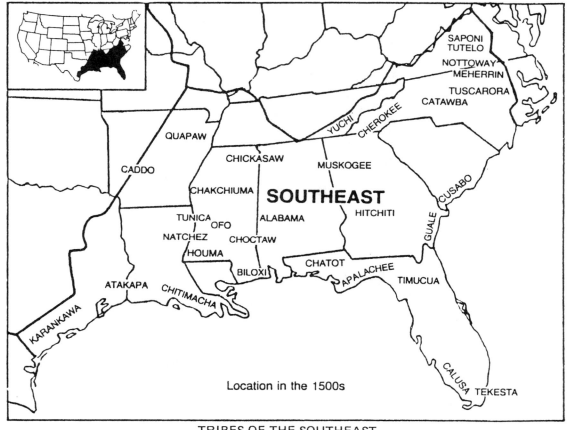

Location in the 1500s

TRIBES OF THE SOUTHEAST

xiv

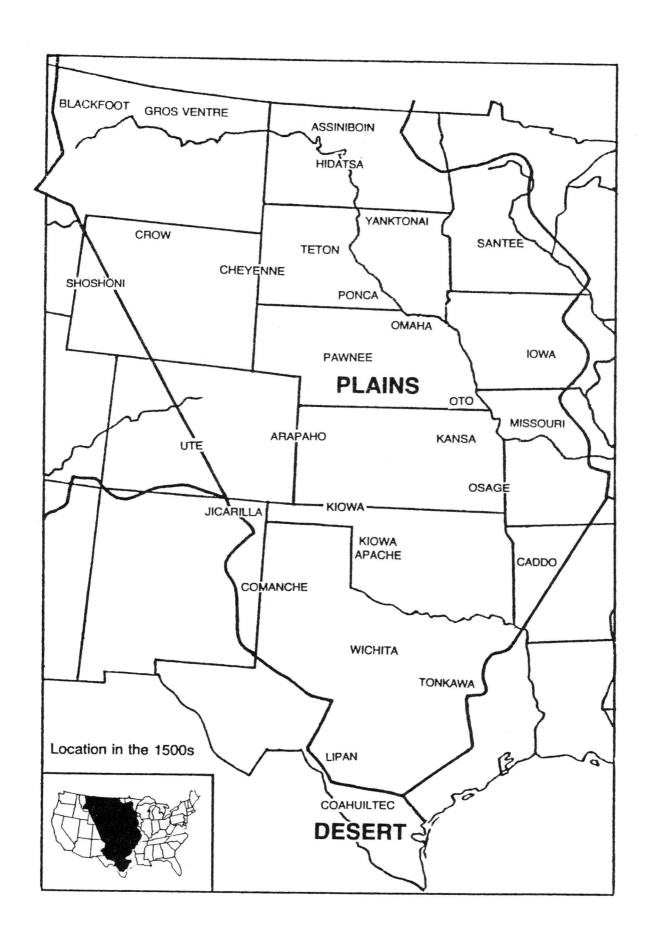

BLACKFOOT GROS VENTRE

ASSINIBOIN

HIDATSA

YANKTONAI

CROW

SANTEE

TETON

CHEYENNE

SHOSHONI

PONCA

OMAHA

IOWA

PAWNEE

PLAINS

OTO

MISSOURI

UTE

ARAPAHO

KANSA

OSAGE

JICARILLA

KIOWA

KIOWA
APACHE

CADDO

COMANCHE

WICHITA

TONKAWA

Location in the 1500s

LIPAN

COAHUILTEC

DESERT

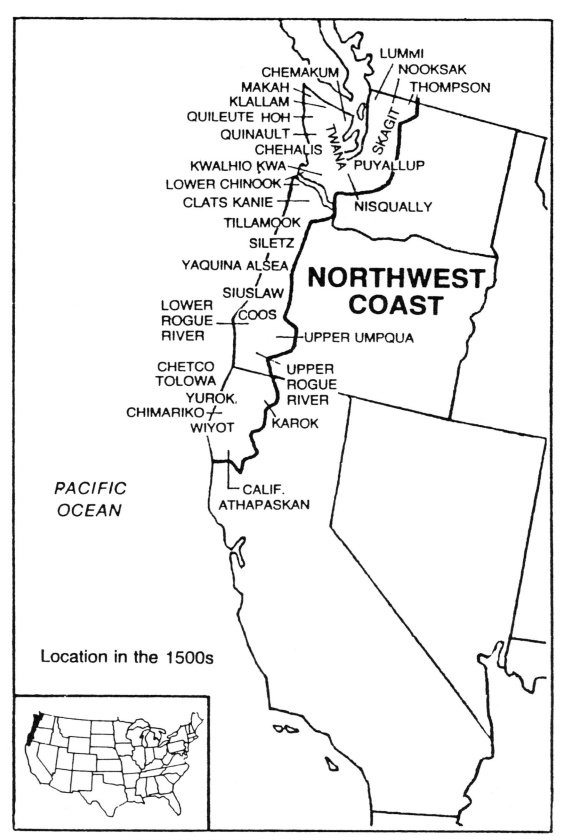

TRIBES OF THE NORTHWEST COAST

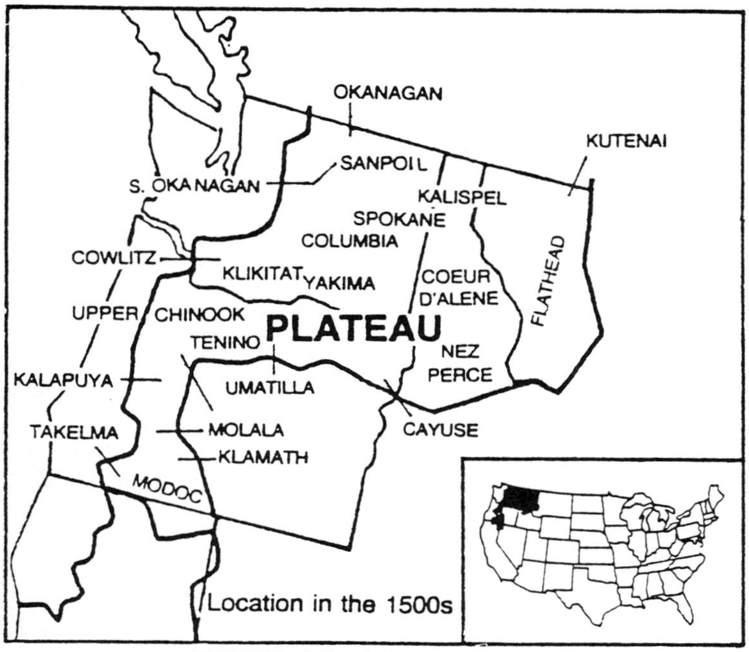

TRIBES OF THE PLATEAU

OKANAGAN
KUTENAI
SANPOIL
S. OKANAGAN
KALISPEL
SPOKANE
COLUMBIA
COWLITZ
KLIKITAT YAKIMA
COEUR D'ALENE
UPPER CHINOOK
FLATHEAD
TENINO
NEZ PERCE
KALAPUYA
UMATILLA
TAKELMA
MOLALA
CAYUSE
KLAMATH
MODOC

PLATEAU

Location in the 1500s

TRIBES OF THE PLATEAU

TRIBES OF THE GREAT BASIN

NORTHERN PAIUTE
WASHO

GREAT BASIN

SOUTHERN PAIUTE
CHEMEHUEVI
SERRANO
CAHUILLA
KAMIA
EAST DIEGUENO

Location in the 1500s

TRIBES OF THE GREAT BASIN

TRIBES OF CALIFORNIA 1500

SHASTA
ACHOMAWI
WINTU
ATSUGEWI
YUKI
MAIDU
POMO
NISENAN
WAPPO
COAST MIWOK
COSTANOAN
MIWOK
ESSELEN
SALINAN
W. MONO
TUBATULABAL
KAWAIISU
CHUMASH
GABRIELINO
LUISENO
WEST DIEGUENO

CALIFORNIA

Location in the 1500s

TRIBES OF CALIFORNIA 1500

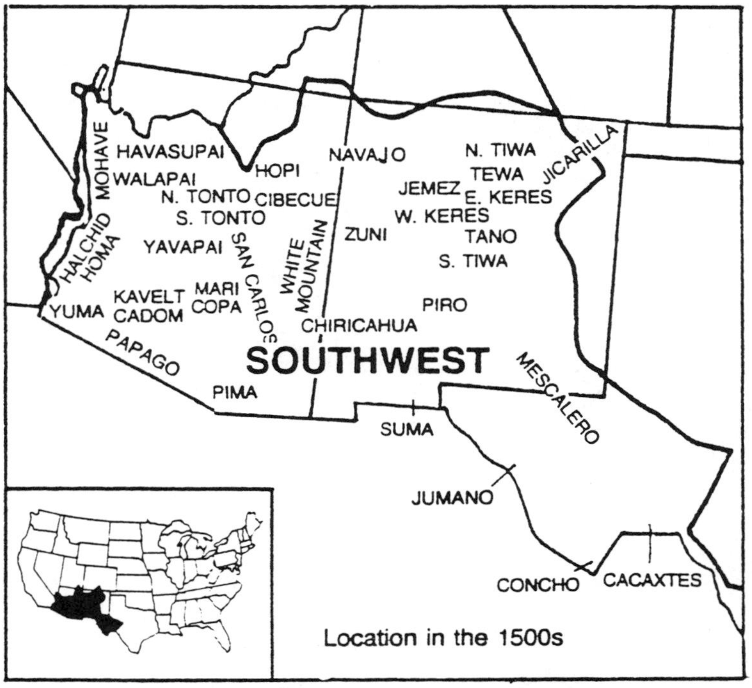

TRIBES OF THE SOUTHWEST

MOHAVE
HAVASUPAI
HOPI
NAVAJO
N. TIWA
JICARILLA
WALAPAI
TEWA
HALCHID HOMA
N. TONTO
CIBECUE
JEMEZ
E. KERES
S. TONTO
W. KERES
YAVAPAI
SAN CARLOS
WHITE MOUNTAIN
ZUNI
TANO
S. TIWA
YUMA
KAVELT CADOM
MARI COPA
PIRO
CHIRICAHUA
PAPAGO
SOUTHWEST
MESCALERO
PIMA
SUMA
JUMANO
CONCHO
CACAXTES

Location in the 1500s

TRIBES OF THE SOUTHWEST

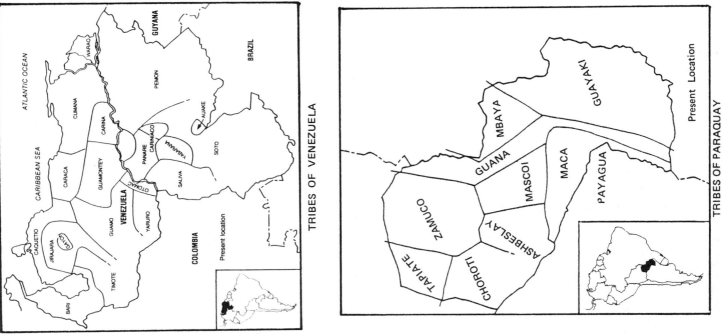

TRIBES OF VENEZUELA

TRIBES OF PARAQUAY

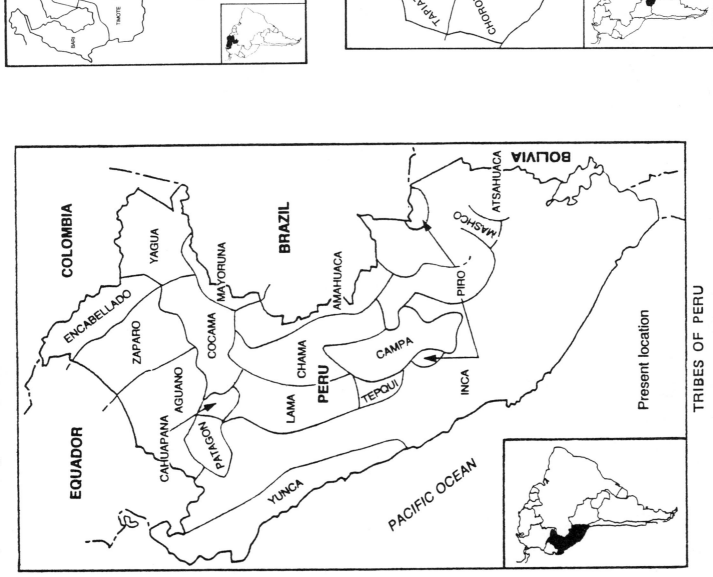

TRIBES OF PERU

xviii

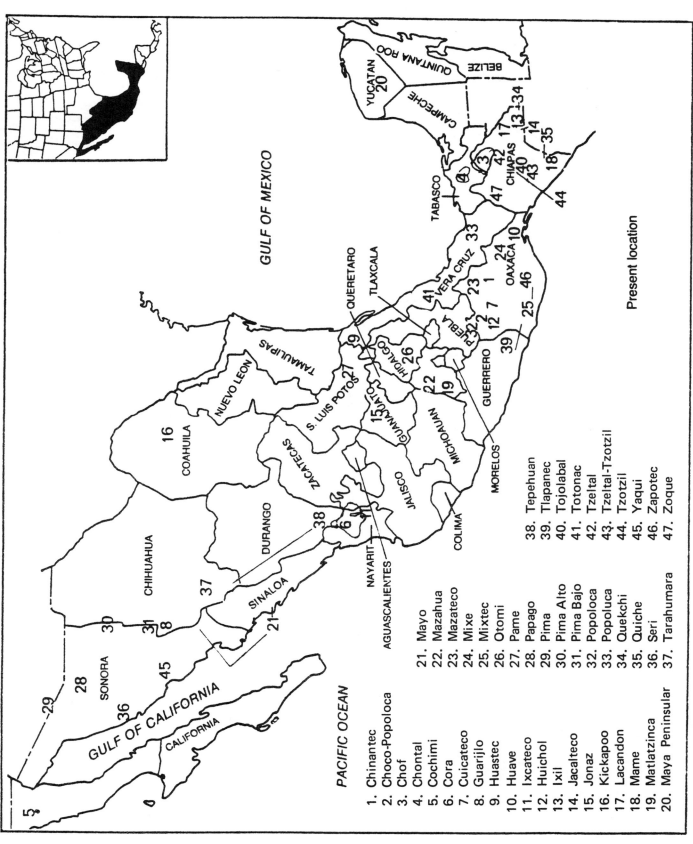

PACIFIC OCEAN

1. Chinantec
2. Choco-Popoloca
3. Chol
4. Chontal
5. Cochimi
6. Cora
7. Cuicateco
8. Guarijilo
9. Huastec
10. Huave
11. Ixcateco
12. Ixil
13. Jacalteco
14. Jonaz
15. Kickapoo
16. Lacandon
17. Mame
18. Matlatzinca
19. Maya Peninsular
20. Maya Peninsular

21. Mayo
22. Mazahua
23. Mazateco
24. Mixe
25. Mixtec
26. Otomi
27. Pame
28. Papago
29. Pima
30. Pima Alto
31. Pima Bajo
32. Popoloca
33. Popoluca
34. Quekchi
35. Quiche
36. Seri
37. Tarahumara

38. Tepehuan
39. Tlapanec
40. Tojolabal
41. Totonac
42. Tzeltal
43. Tzeltal-Tzotzil
44. Tzotzil
45. Yaqui
46. Zapotec
47. Zoque

Present location

INDIANS IN MEXICO

GULF OF MEXICO

GULF OF CALIFORNIA

xix

INTRODUCTION

THE INDIAN PEOPLES

We are the Ancient People;

Our father is the Sun;

Our mother, the Earth,

where the mountains tower

And the rivers seaward run;

The stars are the children of the sky,

The red men, of the plain;

And ages over us both had rolled

Before you crossed the main;

For we are the Ancient People,

Born with the wind and rain.

EDNA DEAN PROCTOR

THE ANCIENT PEOPLE remain in their home-lands of North, Central, and South America. True, many are gone today, but the American Indian is not vanishing and many peoples remain to form a link with the ancient past. One need consider only the vast reaches of the American continents, areas where many different languages were spoken in pre-Columbian times and where many culturally different peoples had their being. From the polar ice cap of the northwest Greenland Inuit (Eskimo) to the bleak reaches of the Ona and Yahgan peoples at the southern tip of South America, through plain, fjord, and desert to the tropical forests of the Orinoco and Amazon river basins, are scenes of diversity, adjustments, and adaptations to differing ecological and environmental conditions.

ANCIENT TRADITIONS

In the United States alone, many ancient traditions are still viable and more than one hundred fifty Indian languages are spoken. The Hopi rec-reates his traditional rain plea while the Seminole continues to pole his pirogue through the eerie wa-ters of the Everglades. In the Arctic, the Inuit sea hunters manipulate their kayaks through the icy waters off the Arctic shores, while the Jivaro in South America trek through quicksand- infested swamps.

Interestingly, throughout so vast an area, the cultures may differ markedly or, again, may be wholly similar. One may look, for example, at the northern Californian Yurok, Karok, and Hupa, where even an expert museum specialist cannot differentiate their baskets and tools from each other, yet whose languages are totally mutually unintelligble. Or, on a broader basis, a relation-ship may be noted through a geographic sweep of Shoshonean-speakers in the Great Basin of North America, including the various Ute and Paiute peoples, whose culture is among the most basic of those found in the New World, and whose language relates to the Aztec, possessors of a major world civilization.

In so great a land mass, there are processes of culture, changes over time, inventions, diffusions, varying environmental impacts, and technological achievements. It can be stated that the beginnings lie in a two-fold ecological adaptation--a sub- arc-tic and Arctic hunting pattern found in northern North America, and a temperate, tropical, and sub-tropical seed- gathering adjustment with mild modifications between.

CULTURE AREA CLASSIFICATION

There are those groups which retained the hunt-ing base as opposed to those seed-gatherers who found their way into agriculture, controlling na-ture instead of being controlled by it. Thus the hunters and gatherers appear in prehistoric times at the edges of the New World; the farmers on the other hand, are located centrally, in a middle American focus which spreads both north and south.

It would seem almost impossible, therefore, to classify the complex cultural varieties of the Americas into some cohesive whole. Diversity, both linguistic and cultural, appears as a keynote. To treat the local or isolated segments of the Na-tive Americans is to engender chaos. It is, however, possible to evaluate man in the New World in the ecological-environmental aspect and also to note that certain cultural patterns recur within given regions and areas. This gives rise to a concept of culture area, a convenient peg on which to hang ordered data. In a given region, commonality of adaptation, the similar utilization of natural resources, suggest a common history and a consequent means of observing parallel and related development. Thus the delineation by the U.S. anthropologist Alfred L. Kroeber of the North American continent in terms of cultural and natural areas may elucidate this problem. Kroeber lists seven major sub- divisions with eighty-four subareas. The major areas include: (1) the Arctic Coast, (2) the North, consisting of an Eastern sub-Arctic (Algonkin) and a Western (Athapascan), area (3) the Northwest Coast, (4) the Intermediate and Intermontane Areas, including the Plateau, the Great Basin, and California. For the east, Kroeber envisioned a total configuration of which the Plains forms a part. This area, (5) the East, includes the Plains, the Prairie, the Great Lakes, the Ohio Valley, the Atlantic Coast, and the Southeast. Area (6) is the Southwest, while area (7) is represented by Mexico and Central America. Kroeber's subareas are quite detailed, offering a precision indicative of the manifold variation of native American cultures.

The classification of North America by U.S. anthropologist Harold E. Driver, on the hand is a refinement of Kroeber's, suggesting a diversity rather than temporal depth, and utilizing the culture area concept as a convenient mode of ordering rather than an ecological classification. He lists seventeen major areas: (1) the Arctic, western, (2) the Arctic, central and eastern, (3) the Yukon sub-arctic, (4) the McKenzie sub-Arctic, (5) the Eastern sub-Arctic, (6) the Northwest Coast, (7) the Plains, (8) the Prairie, (9) the East Great Lakes and St. Lawrence to the Gulf, inclusive of the Atlantic Coast, (10) California, (11) the Great Basin, (12) Baja California, (13) Oasis Southwest (14) the Plateau, under Driver's classification, (15) Northeast Mexico, (16) Mesoamerica, (17) the Circum- Caribbean. The Antillean and Circum-Caribbean area has, however, been sacrificed, causing a severe loss in its historical relationship between the Southeast and the cultures of the tropical forests of South America.

NEW WORLD ETHNOGRAPHY

Archaeological records offer little beyond the material. Religion, social or political organization, and language can perhaps be in some measure inferred, but it is not until a precise ethnographic description of native cultures is made available that a picture can be obtained of native America as it was on the eve of contact and in the period immediately following it. European contact brought about rapid changes in some areas. There was the hispanicization of Latin America, and all the social and religious change that this implied. In the

North American Plains and the pampas (vast grassy plains) of South America the horse was re-introduced. This animal, evolving in the New World, migrated to Asia and became extinct in its homeland. Domesticated by Asians and Europeans, and transferred to Indian groups, as in the Plains, after 1700, it paved the way for the development of equestrian societies of a special kind. But without considering at length the changes which post-Columbian contact effected, it can be said that the various native areas possessed their own precise forms and orientations which persisted and, to some degree, still persist. A tribe-by-tribe analysis is clearly too laborous; rather is it possible to examine areas where there is commonality of shared tradition. To the ethnographer, these are culture areas, implying common historical roots, shared traditions, and similar ecological focus. Compared with each other from the point of view of modes of subsistence, material objects and inventions, art and technology, and familial, societal, political, and religious organizations, the distinctiveness of each area emerges sharply. The delineation of culture areas offers a convenient way to pin- point the cultural achievements of the various Amerindian peoples as they were on the eve of discovery and shortly thereafter.

ARCTIC AND SUB-ARCTIC

The Inuit (Eskimo) Area

Perhaps eighty-five thousand Inuit and Aleut, the native peoples of the Aleutian archipelago, were spread from south Alaska along the coasts of the Arctic Ocean to Greenland. Subsistence was based mainly on sea mammals, the seal, the walrus, in the west whales, and on the tundra (i.e. the vast treeless plains of the arctic regions) caribou. The Inuit made many inventions enabling them to exist effectively in their environment. Tailored skin and fur clothing, harpoons, the stone lamp, and effective boats and sleds attest to the interst of these cultures in the material. The Inuit house was only rarely of snow blocks. In the western Arctic, sod houses were used, coursed-stone in Greenland. Small settlements or encampments were the rule. Lacking political organization as such, the Inuit, stressed family and kinship as a means of holding a community together. In other words, a group was often one of demonstrably related people. Marriage was always across group lines, and served to expand the horizons of all-important kinship cooperation. Inuit religion was not out of keeping with a hunting culture where relations to animals were primary. The thought was that animals allowed themselves to be captured by magic. Each hunter had rituals to perform for effective hunting. A second element in religion was shamanism--the presence of a curer to treat the illnesses resulting from having given offense to the world of animal spirits. Inuits had an elaborate mythology, some of it connected to Asia. The Inuit, remarkably similar in both language and culture across the wide expanses of the Arctic, lack tribes as such; various local designations are employed.

The Interior Sub-Arctic

Different from the Inuit the estimated one hundred ten thousand peoples of the interior of Alaska and northwest Canada traditionally concentrated on caribou hunting and trapping. In the main the groups lived in the boreal (northern) forest and at the tundra edge. In Alaska and Canada, Na-Dene (Atahapascan) was spoken, but the cultural type shades off into the eastern regions of Canada where Algonquian languages are spoken. Divided into socio-economic bands between which marriages occurred, the various peoples of the area--Tanana, Hare, Slave, Kaska, Beaver, Yellow-Knife--existed as tribes by virtue of dialect difference. A band might have an informal leader, a chief hunter, but again, kinship and hunting territory provided the basis for group identity. The Athapascans wore tailored skin clothing, lived in tents and windbreaks, often covered with snow, invented the snowshoe, and made extensive use of *babiche,* or caribou rawhide, for making netting, containers, and lines for the caribou impound. Food was meat, often pounded with berries and fat and then dried. Shamans existed, as among the Inuit, and the principal ceremonial, in addition to hunting magic, was the girls' puberty rite, when girls, having been secluded for a year, were declared marriageable. These interior peoples resemble the original settlers to the New World the most closely.

The Northwest Coast

From southeastern Alaska to northwestern California is a narrow strip of coastal land characterized by high mountains, which come directly down to the sea. Valleys, fjords, beaches, and islands were settled by groups drawn to the sea, who were mainly dependent on salmon and other fish. The workable cedar of Alaska and British Columbia provided material for the elaborated development of housing, tools of wood, and especially of art forms. The Northwest Coast, with its crests, sometimes erroneously called totems, had a most elaborate series of social forms, strict regulations about marriage, and paid great attention to

wealth. Wealth was assembled by various social groups for the purpose of distribution to others. Until comparatively recently a man validated his rights to a title, to a house, or to inheritance at great give-away feasts known as *potlatches.* Houses were ornate, made gabled, with split cedar planks, often with the owner's coat-of-arms in the form of an upright "totem pole." Chiefs existed, but their function was rather ceremonial than political, they being men of high title in an elaborated system of rank, at the bottom of which were war captives held as slaves. The culture was thus highly competitive and wealth oriented, the basis of wealth being simply the vast array of goods which this rich culture offered. Curing shamans were known, as well as sorcerers, but the basis of religion lay in such features as the greeting of the first salmon of the year, impersonations, and reenactments of mystical experiences with animal spirits whose presence underlay the social system which was based on clan or descent. Many diverse languages were spoken in the area by its estimated one hundred twenty-seven thousand inhabitants. Typical and well known tribes were the Tlingit, Haida, and Tsimshian in the north, the Kwakiutl and Nootka in the center, and the various tribes of Puget Sound, such as the Quinault and Makah. In Northwestern California such groups as the Yurok and Hupa offer a variation on the theme of the more northerly culture.

WESTERN NORTH AMERICA

Gathering, rather than hunting, formed the mainstay of life for three sub-areas located generally in the inter-montane regions of the western part of the North American continent.

The Plateau

The forty-eight thousand people of the upper reaches of the Columbia and Fraser river systems fished for salmon at upstream spawning places, hunted deer, and gathered a wide variety of roots. They lived in small villages with brush and mat houses, emphasized simple biological family relationships, and had chiefs, who were mainly spokesmen and peace-makers. Like the inhabitants of other western regions, the people of the Plateau did not possess an especially elaborate material culture. Okanagan and Sanpoil are well known tribes.

The Great Basin

Small bands of variously constituted gathering groups ranged through the deserts of Nevada, Utah, and adjacent states. Theirs was a desert adaptation. They appear to reflect the seed-gathering focus of the earliest migrants. They collected pine nuts and juniper berries, and engaged in limited hunting, especially of rabbits. The various Shoshoni, Paiute, and Ute, as well as others in the deserts, numbered an estimated twenty-seven thousand.

California

In the California central valley and the nearby foothills the staple food was the local acorn. This was gathered by women, stored in the ubiquitous basketry, leached, and pounded for food. The dependable food supply created separatistic and permanent villages, leading to a remarkable isolation of groups from each other. House types, social organization, and language varied considerably across the area, but the mode of life was essentially the same. Native California tended toward the spokesman chief, shamanism, and to festivals in which impersonation of the ancestral dead played an important role. The latter may have been an importation from the rich culture of the Southwest. The area was the most densely populated in North America north of Mexico, with an estimated one-hundred thirty- three thousand inhabitants in 1700, or even double this number. The most eleborated development of art in the entire western area lay in basketry.

Some representative tribes are the Shasta, Maidu, Miwok, Pomo, Yokuts, Mohave, and Digueno.

The Plains

This area, one of the most fully analyzed in native North America, came into its own after 1700, with the introduction of the horse from Europeans. An estimated one hundred twenty-five thousand people were spread from the Mexican border to southern Canada and from the Rockies to the lands fronting the Mississippi. The high, or western plains, seemingly originally Basin in type, changed with the advent of the horse. In the east, along the river systems, a modified agriculture had begun. Thus the non-farming and wholly equestrian Blackfoot, Crow, Assiniboin, Dakota, Cheyenne, Kiowa, and Comanche contrasted in their life-style with the agricultural Mandan, Omaha, Osage, and many others. This is the popular stereotyped area of the American Indian with its tipis, feather headdresses, buckskin, beads, and buffalo robes. Despite these features which run with some uniformity across the Plains, there was considerable difference in detail, both in material items and social structure. All groups hunted

bison (buffalo) but the farmers left permanent settlements to do so, while the equestrian groups tended toward a nomadism within a defined territory, breaking up into bands but coming together for great communal hunts. For most the bison was the mainstay of life. The theme of war ran through all of Plains cultures, high status being achieved by military success. This in turn gave rise to "soldier" societies, clubs, and grades to which warriors belonged. These differed in type from tribe to tribe. In religion, all men, and some women, sought a spiritual guardian, a mystic supernatural experience. Ceremonials involved the display of "bundles," wrapped amulets developed in visions, brought out for communal or tribal good. Victory and vengeance celebrations were common, one of the latter being the famous Sun Dance. Languages were much varied, reflecting the movement of many different peoples into the area.

The Southwest

The Southwest is marked by intensive agriculture. The peoples included the various Pueblo Indians, such as Hopi, Zuni, Taos, and many others, who raised maize and its associated plants under desert conditions. The Pueblos, inhabitants of permanent towns, possess a rich prehistory. It is possible, for example, to trace the beginnings of agriculture among these peoples from 700 B.C. out of a wild seed gathering complex not unlike that of the geographically similar Basin. The peoples of the Pueblos show a high degree of social complexity, stressing aspects of kinship as well as of tribal or national concepts. The Pueblos stressed a degree of communalism, at least to the extent of emphasizing group rather than individualized activity. Shamanistic practices appeared but, unlike the northern development, the Pueblo emphasized curing by a group of practitioners. Maize, beans, and squashes formed the mainstay of diet; hunting was a secondary activity. Ritual overlay much of Pueblo activity, with various religious societies, priesthoods, and officials to carry on the ceremonials of agriculture. Rain-making and rain symbolism, masked impersonation of rain beings and ancestors, and underground ceremonial chambers known as *kivas*, reflected the stress on the religious modes of these societies.

A somewhat different agricultural focus in seen in regions of the Southwest outside of the Pueblo area. In southern Arizona were the Pima and Papago, themselves descendants of the founders of another agricultural focus. They stressed ranch type life with brush dwellings rather than the stone and adobe of the Pueblo. The invading Navajo and Apache, speaking Athapaascan in contrast to the diverse languages of the rest of the area, borrowed numerous elements of culture from the Pueblos but never became intensive agriculturalists. Other smaller enclaves also appear in the area, but none are so strongly oriented to maize cultivation. The area as a whole extends, again in terms of Pueblo influences, well down into desert Mexico. As many as one hundred thousand inhabited the area at the time of contact, although prehistoric populations may have been considerably higher in number.

EASTERN AREAS

Eastern Woodlands (The Eastern Maize Area)

A modified agricultural complex spread from the upper Midwest of the United States to the Atlantic seaboard. Always a marginal area, it was rather the Southeast which provided the agricultural focus. Further to the north, in eastern Canada, climactic limitations begin, causing the area to fade off into an eastern sub-arctic phraisng, not unlike that of interior Alaska-Canada. The cultures of the area began to change shortly after the settlement of New England from Europe, since displacement of populations began to occur. Midified farming was practiced where possible, for example around the Great Lakes, down the St. Lawrence, and into New England. It was, however, never wholly integrated, suggesting that the area is marginal to a Southeastern center. The use of birch bark for containers, housing, and canoes, was well-known. War was important, but became more so after contact, and with the invasion from the south of the people known as Iroquois, whose political league and war machine began to modify the nature of the area. The Chippewa (Ojibwa) were non-agricultural, but began to plant wild rice without cultivation, an incipient form of farming. Here was the area of the Happy Hunting Ground and the Great Spirit, both possibly from European hearsay contact. The Mide, a form of secret society, provided a social and ceremonial base for group activity. Representative groups were the Chippewa, Winnebago, Sauk, Fox, and Miami, and, on the Atlantic coast, such peoples as the Delaware, Pennacook, Abnaki, and Micmac, and in interior Quebec, the Montagnais-Naskapi.

Southeast

The Southeast, also an area of intensive agriculture, has deep prehistoric roots and a clear affinity to Mexico. Characterized by mounds, palisades, a fully fledged maize complex, the intensive use of tobacco, hunting, and the use of poi-

sons, this area suggests not only Mexican by trans-Caribbean South America influences as well. The area appears to have peaked and declined even before European contact. Both among the Iroquois, in intruded southeastern people in the north, and among such typical groups in the Southeast as the Creek, Choctaw, Chickasaw, Natchez, and others, the stress was laid on political orgainization. Here was a strong system of matrilineal descent, meaning that clan membership and rights to political office passed to the individual from his mother's side. The Creek, and especially the Iroquois, developed political leagues with war and peace chiefs, exchange of ambassadors, and unity for peace and war. The societies were complex in terms of the various kinds of social associations, priesthoods, and ritual groups. Noteworthy in the area, and diffusing to the north as well, was the lacrosse game, a ball game reflecting not only the preoccupation with war but also a world renewal ritual. The sub-tropical aspect of the area gave agriculture a quite different pattern than in the Southwest. Hominy (corn macerated in lye), succotash (a dish of corn and beans), and persimmon bread were known. Hunting was also more widely practiced than in the Southwest. The entire area, from Washington to Nova Scotia, from the St. Lawrence to the Gulf of Mexico, had a large and diverse aboriginal population, one in excess of four hundred thousand. It does not, however, show the density of native California.

Mexico

South of the Rio Grande and southward to Central America is a great range of cultures, from the high civilizations of the Maya, Toltec, Olmec, and Aztec to the gatherers of the deserts of the north. A rich history, populations in excess of millions, although varying from time to time through the long periods, and numerous inventions, especially of agriculture, make Mexico the high point of any survey of the New World cultures. The Mexican civilizations, along with those in South America, such as the Inca of Peru, are comparable to those of the Old World. It seems clear that north of the Rio Grande only tribal cultures existed; Mexico and South America represented the pinnacle of New World development.

INDIAN ORIGINS IN THE AMERICAS

Within an area of essentially common culture, whether a subarea or a major geographic region, lived the various peoples of the Americas. Convention has desigated these as "tribes," although the word has very little actual meaning. It should be made clear that the cultures of the American Indians permitted little or no generalization as to what made up a group, a "tribe." Although real property, in the sense of precise land ownership, never assumed great importance anywhere in the Americas, there were some groups with a strong national sense who did identify with a defined territory. Some were tribes in the political sense, while others saw themselves united with their fellow tribesmen only informally, on the basis of language and community of culture rather than because of unifying political institutions. There is a considerable range between the simple socio-economic band and the elaborate political federation. The circumstances of the locality and of the culture area must obviously be taken into account. Tribes existed because of common language, common culture and social organization, commmon territory and, in some instances, common residence in town or village. All such factors are variously operative.

The American continents were peopled by men out of Asia. Beginning perhaps as early as forty thousand years ago, small groups of migrants made their way from the interior of Asia to northeastern Siberia, across the Bering Straits, and so into Alaska. These movements took place in the geologic period known as the Pleistocene (Ice Age). The movements of ice and animals very likely provided the motivation for migration by men.

A human adaptation to a hunting mode of life generally implies small population segments. Contemporary hunters on a similar subsistence level never form large groups. Such must have been the case with the first migrants to the New World; many small units, socio-economic bands, can be envisioned, following game, moving gradually eastward and southward as the presence of ice permitted, and thus gradually filtering into the American continents. Nor would such movements have been limited to a single time period. Human antiquity in the New World can be determined in several different ways. The artifacts of man may be found in association with the bones of animals now extinct, of a wide array of Pleistocene fauna such as the mastodon and mammoth, extinct species of elk, musk-oxen and deer, and--further to the south--camels and horses. The glaciers themselves with their associated climactic variations also provide a time perspective. While such dates are relative, and although there may be some disagreement among archaeologists as to the initial time of man's arrival into the Americas, most are agreed that by twenty-five thousand years ago the ancestry of the American Indian was well established in both North and South America. Ice-free

corridors directed human movement both east of the Rockies and along the mountain chains of the west.

Thus the picture which emerges is that of small hunting groups adapted to boreal (northern) conditions. The initial stages of cultural development of these first Americans have been identified as Mesolithic (a transitional period of the Stone Age when the dog first appeared), to use an archaeological category out of an Old World context, correlated with use of tools of stone. These took the form of dart points, there being as yet no bow and arrow, as well as of stone scrapers and awls. The tool assemblage suggests dependence on animal skins for shelter and clothing. It seems evident that there were many such movements of hunters over a long period of time, and continuing until relatively recently.

As migratory movements took place back and forth in the New World, a mixture of populations occurred. Adaptation occurred in local areas and genetically transmitted physical traits emerged in various regions. The Inuit, apparently one of the last comers to the Americas, shows a capacity, unquestionably based on natural selection, to adapt a cold, while the same processes may be said to operate in the adaptations to altitude in Peru and Bolivia. Basically Mongoloid, with Australoid admixtures, and possibly with other human varietal types as well, the American Indians consist of many "races." Physical types differ greatly from each other, localized gene pools creating tall and rangy types as against short and stocky groups. But hair and nasal form suggest the basic Mongoloid increment. Skin color, usually brownish, is still highly variable. The "red" Indian is actually a misnomer, stemming from Sebastian Cabot's description of the Beothuk at the time of his discovery of Newfoundland in 1497. This extinct group smeared the body with a mixture of bear grease and red ochre as mosquito protection, giving a decidedly red appearance.

"Lost tribes and sunken continents" leave room for rather fascinating speculation, but concrete evidence is lacking. Mexico and Peru, for example, developed extraordinarily high civilizations, suggesting to some that ancient Egyptian influences may have made themselves felt. Yet, despite recent claims to the contrary, it seems unlikely that ancient Egypt had the seacraft or the ability to navigate in uncharted waters. Such contact, moreover, could have occurred very late in time, too late in fact to have materially changed the bent toward high civilization already in existence in Middle America. Finally, if there were contact with the Old World affecting the American Indians, one would expect the presence of some Eastern or Asiatic traits. The New World never had the wheel, for example, made almost no use of domesticated animals, and possessed an array of food plants totally different from those in Eurasia or Africa. That there could have been pre-Columbian contact between Polynesia and the south American mainland is by no means unlikely. This, along with any other contact real or imagined, occurs too late in time to have significance in the growth of the New World cultures.

LANGUAGES OF THE AMERICAS

Further evidence of the fact that there was not one but rather many waves of migration into the Americas is attested by the presence of many different and mutually unintelligible languages among the American Indians. It is known that languages change through time. The various migrants very likely spoke different languages which changed over a long period, thus accounting for the great linguistic diversity. As nearly as can be judged, none of the American Indian languages has relatives in the Old World, and therefore represent distinct native American developments. With the exception of the Maya of Yucatan and Guatemala, and to some degree the Aztecs of the Valley of Mexico, no American people developed writing. But it would be rank error to assume that because a language is not written it is slovenly or debased. The American Indians generally stressed oratory and stylistic elegance in speech. It is equally wrong to think of the many Indian languages as "dialects." Dialects there were, to be sure, local varieties of single languages, but each language stands out with remarkable distinctness.

Considering that many languages are gone, a result of population decimation in some areas, it is somewhat difficult to say how many actual languages there were in 1492. About two thousand seems a reasonable estimate. Of these, between six hundred and eight hundred were spoken in the area which was to become the United States. Greater linguistic diversity appears in South America, where extensive linguistic work is still being undertaken.

Just as the Romance languages of Europe spring from an earlier Latin, and are thus demonstrably closely related to each other, so also are there language families in the native Americas. When relationships, based on similar grammatical structure and cognate vocabulary, can be shown, a speech family is suggested, a common ancestor from which a group of languages, by no means necessarily mutually intelligible, can be said to descend. There are numerous such major families in the New World. Not only may a comparative analysis of related languages show movement and migration within the continent, but it can also be suggested that the various groups of migrants to the New World brought with them separate and unrelated languages from which modern tongues descended. It is to be emphasized that the structures of the various speech groups may differ remarkably from one another; it is clear that there was no one common base. To say that one native American language in one speech family may differ as much from another as English differs from Chinese is not far wrong.

Some of the major language groupings of North America--by no means all--can be readily delineated and listed:-

1. Algonquin (Algonkin). Ranging through eastern Canada and the United States, the Algonquin languages have an extremely wide distribution. Groups of languages in the southeastern United States once classed as Caddoan and Muskogean are now recognized to be Algonquian, as are some remnants found in Central America. These are all remotely related to Algonquian and suggest considerable time depth. There are also islands of Algonquian speakers in the Plains (Cheyenne) and in California (Yurok, Wiyot).

2. Eskaleut (Inuit Eskimo and Aleut) are widely spread along the far northern fringes of the American continent. Inuit is virtually mutually intelligible from central Alaska to Greenland. Prehistoric evidence shows a recency of Inuit movements across the Arctic. Southwestern Inuit and Aleutian form another but related series of languages.

3. Uto-Aztecan (Aztec-Tanoan). These languages are spoken in the Great Basin and segments of the Southwest and have relatives in Mexico. Aztec (Nahuatl) shows northern affinities which point to a northern origin for the famous inhabitiants of the Valley of Mexico.

4. Na-Dene (Athapascan). This group of languages may be one of the last to have introduced into the American continent. Originally spoken in northwest Canada and interior Alaska, related languages are also found on the southeastern Alaskan coasts. Groups of Athapascan-speakers pushed into the American Southwest approximately between A.D. 700-1000 and are represented there today by such groups as the Navajo and Apache.

5. Hokan-Siouan (Hokan-Coahuiltecan). This phylum (group of languages related more remotely than those of a family or stock) consists of rather diverse groups of languages which may stem from an original strain. Yet the affinities between the Hokan groups (California, Lower Colorado, Texas Coast, possibly Iroquoian), Coahuiltecan (Gulf languages), and Siouan (Plains) are less easily discerned.

6. Other languages. Other linguistic groupings exist which lend themselves to classification. The small pueblo of Zuni, for example, seemingly possesses its own language, one related to any other. The Penutian languages of the western United States, the Salishan groups in Puget Sound, pose problems of classification. The same problems become apparent in Central and South America. In these areas, the latter especially, where less intensive study has been made, the problem is if anything more complex.

As an important consideration with respect to the native American languages, it should be noted that mode of life, general society, and culture are by no means consistent among groups with the same or related languages. Uto-Aztecan, for example, was spoken by one of the elaborated civilizations of Mexico and at the same time by the simplest desert peoples of Nevada and Utah. The famous pueblos of Arizona and New Mexico generally show a common culture but are linguistically very diverse. Thus the Hopi speak Shoshoshean, a branch of Uto-Aztecan, but Zuni is wholly separate in language, as are the Keresan peoples of the Rio Grande, while the Tanoan pueblos or towns, even if related to Hopi in an Uto-Aztecan or Aztec-tanoan family, are far removed from Shoshonean patterns.

THE AMERICAS-

Differences and Similarities

There would seem to be a basic sameness among the hunters of both American continents. At the margins, the extremes of both North and South America, one found the small band, a socio-economic group of driving game to the kill, depending on the skins for clothing and housing, using darts thrown with an atlatl (a spear-throwing board), as well as cordage, nets, and carefully shaped points of stone. Not until later did the bow and arrow appear. But this similarity was reflected too in a theory of a world in harmony, one peopled with spirits of animals. But hunting patterns were in contrast with those of agriculture.

The discovery in Middle America of the ancestry of maize (Dea mays), along with other plants of the so-called maize complex, various squashes, and the common kidney bean, suggests the movement away from the hunting base. American agriculture, indeed, is unique. Not until post-Columbian times did the rest of the world enjoy the benefits of maize, the potato (from highland South America), manioc, or the now universal tobacco. American Indian agriculture is distinctive in its lack of major domesticated animals, its dependence on the digging stick rather than the plow, and the basic simplicity of its irrigation techniques. Yet it was this distinctive mode of farming which permitted the rise of civilizations paralleling anything the Old World had to offer. Given the distinctiveness of New World agriculture, it seems clear that no influences from the Old World could have been significantly felt in pre-Columbian times.

The classic civilization of the Maya may be contrasted with other refinements in both North and South America. Mayan influences in Mexico reached the Aztecs and their precursors, while in the south, the Inca state was preceded by those of the Nazca, Chimu, and Tihuanaco. Similarly, the Chibcha of Columbia lent their goldsmithing art both to Middle America and to peoples further south.

These areas and epochs of brilliance, already partly in decline by the time of the arrival of the conquering Spanish, suggest the importance of agriculture in the New World. If one considers relations between the New World peoples, these were manifest not so much in political or social contact, but rather in the ways in which ideas and culture traits spread from group to group. Given the underlying hunting focus with its overlay of maize farming, it can be seen how agriculture, for example, spread both north and south from a Middle American center. It became increasingly attenuated in each direction. In what is now the Southwestern United States, for example, the Pueblo Indians still retained an intensive agriculture, but as one moves up the Mississippi into the Missouri and Ohio basins, farming begins to fade gradually. Where the central American exploited a great variety of products--cotton, manioc, potatoes, tomatoes, avocados, and chocolate, along with the basic corn cluster--the peoples of what are now the Gulf States, or those of Bolivia and Paraguay, were modified farmers, relying only on the basic maize elements, together with the ubiquitous tobacco. Thus, in viewing Central America, the Mayan empire's legacy of art, mathematics, and astronomy stands renowned throughout the world, yet these peoples were basically settled farmers. The civilization of the Mayas stands as perhaps the cultural apex of the two Americas, and certainly the epitome of the ancient American world.

After the fall of these "Greeks of the New World," unrest among the city-states of central southern Mexico occurred in the centuries after A.D. 600. The Toltecs, a people driven from their own homeland on the Pacific coast of Mexico, founded the first real empire in the New World. Prior to A.D. 1000, they had conquered the Maya country in Guatemala and Yucatan. After the Mayan abandonment of their cities and their subsequent move to Yucatan, Mayan culture enjoyed a renaissance under Toltecan influence. A magnificent classic of cohesive acculturation is evidenced by their city, Chichen-Itza.

The growth of corn and beans and the craft of pottery which were their complement had diffused throughout nearly all of the northern regions wherever climactic conditions allowed. The ancestors of the Pima-Papago in Arizona living in an irrigated desert built ball courts for a sacred game derived from the Maya to the south. The Golden Age of the Pueblos dawned in New Mexico, Arizona, Utah, and Colorado. From the Gulf of Mexico to Wisconsin, and from New York to Nebraska and Kansas, earthwork mounds and walls were constructed, further suggestive of a basic idea diffused from a Mexican center. Some of these were ceremonial burial monuments, while others were fortifications, altars, or platforms for temples. Ideas traveled to the woodland peoples of the north as well as to settled seed-gatherers. Meanwhile, the use of the bow and of moccasins spread southward.

Again, the similarities of cultures may be seen in Mexico and Peru. Both shared irrigation and farming. Both built ceremonial cities, temple mounds, and pyramids, and both societies had divine-kings or priest-kings. Pottery styles and even some similar religious ideas, such as the jaguar-feline cult, were shared. Differences are evidenced, however, by Andean metalworking and corn-growing having begun nearly one thousand years earlier. These were the people who built in stone--temples and pyramids in Mexico, large fortifications in the Andean domain. They introduced terracing, as well as the digging stick and the hoe. The Inca excelled in their art of weaving. The white potato, sweet potato, quinine, rubber and pineapple were all part of Andean life. The Andean world enjoyed a prosperity rich in animal domestication, the hair of the llama and apaca being used

for weaving. By approximately A.D. 1200, the Incas emerged victorious in their region, and by 1492 controlled an empire that extended from northern Ecuador to central Chile and covered a large part of South America.

In the north, Mexico, by 1492, was nearly totally conquered by the Aztecs. By 1516, Cortes as well as the horse had invaded the North American continent. At this time, a conservative estimate of nearly five hundred to one thousand different languages were spoken in North America, and in South America, an even greater number. In America north of Mexico very few of the villages, tribes, kingdoms, or confederacies had any knowledge of the conflicts going on south of them.

Meanwhile, in the Greater Southwest of what is now the United States, the Papagos and the Pimas lived in the near-dry river valleys of southern Arizona. Both were descendants of the earlier Hohokam. Both peoples shared with the Indians of Central America and Mexico the same clay figurines, snake and bird designs, ball courts, and copper ceremonial bells, but with one major addition. They were the first known etchers in the world. The Hohokam decorated with their delicate etchings sea shells found where the Gila River meets the Salt River. They shared some of the technology of irrigation with the great civilizations of Mexico, but unlike them stressed a democratic form of political organization.

Northeast of the Hohokam and centralized in what is now called the "Four Corners" of New Mexico, Colorado, Utah, and Arizona, live the people still known as the Pueblos. They too lived in houses built over the dug-out floors, although the houses themselves were entirely above ground, and were built of log, adobe, and stone. By A.D. 600 to 700 they had emerged as pottery workers and had adopted a variation of the intensive agricultural patterns of Mexico--modes of subsistence which they still practice today. Amongst the Pueblo, moderation was, and still is, the rule of life. Here, indeed, is the stress on social and religious harmony which was characterized by Ruth Benedict as "Apolllonian"--a communalistic focus in which the individualism characteristic of so many other Amerindian groups was suppressed. Among the various Pueblos, the Hopi and Zuni, and others on the Rio Grande, still continue at the present time to invoke the beings of rain, masked dancers impersonating the denizens of the spirit world who represent the communal element of good, symbolizing the successful raising of agricultural products in an arid environment.

The people in the lower Mississippi Valley were a mixture of nations with different customs and different languages. They were all agricultural farmers and used the hoe to raise the same crops. They all roamed the same woodland regions to kill bear and buffalo (bison). They glided along the same rivers in the same kinds of dugout canoes. They made art objects in materials ranging from wood and mica to copper, and traded for goods of pipestone, shell, and metal all stretches from the Rocky Mountains to the Atlantic Ocean.

The first white men entering this region found numerous tribes, but they also found some fifty villages joined in a confederacy. In the Southeast were the Ocheese Creek and the Creek confederacy. West of the Creeks were the Chickasaws, on the site of what is now Memphis, Tennessee, who had a river port on the Mississippi. These, together with the Choctaw and Seminole, as well as the Cherokee who were later during the administration of U.S. president Andrew Jackson, formed the "civilized tribes." Near them, too, were the Natchez. This tribe was wholly unique in North America, possessing a "king" called the "Great Sun." Natchez laws pertaining to marriage and descent were intricate, involving a complex system of descent through the female line, and a shifting series of social classes.

In the wooded lake regions of the northeast lived the various Algonquian speakers. These groups raised corn as far as the climate permitted. Their trade goods were represented as volcanic glass from the Rockies to Ohio, and their tobacco moved from Virginia to the St. Lawrence. Their copper was used from Canada to South Carolina. Some of the bands formed confederacies and held power over other groups. Their descent systems ranged from patrilineal or matrilineal to organized clans.

Prior to the advent of the white man, peace usually reigned amongst these peoples, except for occasional raids on each other for loot, glory, revenge, or captives. Their greater fears were of famine, the gods, or invasion by spirits. They enjoyed a life style rich in color, emotion, and pageantry, centered around the village.

Further northward, throughout Maine, across the black spruce forest area, and into the plains around Hudson Bay, the Algonquian peoples roamed. The Abnaki of Maine shared a linguistic kinship with the Algonquian peoples around the Great Lakes region. In the hundreds of miles of territory between the two, however, lay the Iroquois world, representing another language group in culture. It was the Iroquois who, settling in New York state and adjacent Ontario and Quebec, had formed the famous Iroquois league, consisting of five tribes--the Cayuga, Mohawk, Oneida, Onondaga, and Seneca--

who together constituted one of the significant political federations in native North America. Perhaps this is as close as any people in the world have come to a matriarchate, a rule by women. It was the women who ratified the selection of chiefs and who possessed the power to depose them. The Iroquois strength lay in its federation for mutual aid and conquest, in its strongly maternal focus, and in its bicameral political organization. An upper and lower house of sachems, the varying chiefs of the league, seems in retrospect to have presaged the development in the United States of a two-house political system.

During the first third of the seventeenth century, the French intrusion into what is now Canada resulted in the institutionalization of the interrelationship between Indian and European based on the fur trade. The Indians possessed great woodland skills--traveling on snowshoes over winter snows, using light, roomy, birchwood canoes with ample man-power to paddle them, and, above all else, using their knowledge of river-to-lake and overland pathways to gain additional fur pelts. The French also benefited the Indian with their pots-that-hung-over-the- fire, bolts of bright cloth, metal kinves and hatchets, and warm blankets of wool.

The French also brought gunpowder and firearms. The Huron and their allies aligned themselves with the gunpowder and the French. By 1650, the Seneca and the Mohawk had broken the five- nation truce to invade the Huron. The resulting chaos and bloodshed left the Huron nation devastated, and warfare spread to the Neutral confederacy.

Along the frontier, wanderers filled the land. More colonists arrived, pushing Indian states into further quarrels and conflicts, but where the borderland of nations remained unbroken, the settlers remained aloof. It was time, however, in which traditions were destroyed, and famine and devastation were widespread. The power of the once-proud ancient peoples of the Americas was being undermined by the peoples from Europe.

From one end of the Americas to the other, the American Indians nevertheless continued to endure--as they still do. But by the beginning of the twentieth century, in the United States alone, the Indian peoples had shrunk to two hundred fifty thousand--less than one-third the nummber estimated to have inhabited this area before the coming of Columbus. By 1975, it is expected that their numbers will have increased to seven hundred thousand. Canada now has more than one hundred sixty thousand Indians, while in Latin America there are thousands more who refer to themselves as Indian. In the U.S., Indians form less than one-half of one percent of the population, while in Columbia, Bolivia, Peru, and Guatemala they make up forty to fifty percent, apart from millions more who are of mixed ancestry.

In North America, during the Indians' darkest epoch--the 1870s to the 1920s--hunger was the monolithic reality, while at the same time they were confined to reservations, forbidden religious activities, and subjected to shame and humiliation over their heritage. Once proud and spirited peoples were reduced to merely killing time on reservations.

In South America, apart from the regions of high civilization, such as those of the Inca and Chibcha, marginal peoples lived in the Amazon-Orinoco basin, while, far to the south lived the dwellers of the pampas (vast grassy plains) of what is now Argentina and of the fjorded reaches of the southern Pacific coast down to Tierra del Fuego. At the same time, in the interior, beyond the mountains of Peru and Bolivia, live groups little seen by outsiders even today. The tropical forests of South America show a primary dependence on agriculture, with corn as the staple represents a synthesis deriving from diverse Indian cultures. Many of them are, however, drawn from the Plains area, such as the Plains-type war dance, the war bonnet, and the Plains modes of dancing. Inter-tribal visiting and intermarriage is on the increase, and by the mid-1970s it seems that in the future the Pan-Indian movement might acquire a greater political significance than it has had in the past.

The Ancient People do still live...

ROBERT F. SPENCER

ABABCO

(U.S.; Md.) An eastern Algonquian tribe or sub-tribe. Although mentioned in the original records of 1741 (Bacon, Laws of Maryland, 1765) in connection with the Hutsawaps and Tequassimoes as a distinct tribe, they were probably only a division of the Choptank. This name is not mentioned in John Smith's narrative of his exploration of Chesapeake Bay. The band lived on Choptank River, Maryland, and in 1741 the Colonial government confirmed them in the possession of their lands on the south side of that stream, in Dorchester County, near Secretary Creek. By 1837 the entire tribe to which they belonged had dwindled to a few individuals of mixed Indian and African blood.

BIBLIOGRAPHY-

● HODGE, FREDERICK WEBB. Handbook of American Indians North of Mexico. Washington: Smithsonian Institution: BAE Bulletin No. 30: U.S. GPO, 1907.
● MURDOCK, GEORGE P. Ethnographic Bibliography of North America. New Haven, CT: Human Relations Area Files Press, 1975.
● SWANTON, JOHN R. The Indian Tribes of North America. Smithsonian Institution: BAE Bulletin No. 145: U.S. GPO, 1952.

ABIPON

(South America; Chaco) An extinct Indian tribe, lived in the southern Chaco area of the Bermejo River and spoke a Guaycuruan language. They began to appear in literature only at the beginning of the 17th century.

According to Alfred Metraux, a Swiss ethnographer, they were divided into three language groups: the Yaaukaniga (Water People), the Nakaigetergehe (Forest People), and the Riikahe (People of the Open Country). The Toba and Mocovi Indians called them Callaga. They were known also as Ecusgina, Quiabanaite, and Frentones. Others identify them with the Mepene, another tribe from the Bermejo River area, but this relationship is doubtful.

Prehistory. There is little archaelogical evidence of the Abipon, as is the case for most of the Chaco Indians. It is accepted, however, that in the prehistoric past most of the Chaco Indians, including the Abipon, were nomadic bands of food collectors, fishermen, and hunters. Each band was composed of a few extended families who practiced magic rites through shamanistic

activities: they celebrated puberty rites for girls and initiation ceremonies for boys. They used nettled bags but had no basketry, weaving, or pottery. Metraux assumed that they dressed in pointed skin cloaks and lived in flimsy communal houses. By the time the Europeans came in contact with them in the 16th century, they were, in many ways, acculturated by both the Andean and

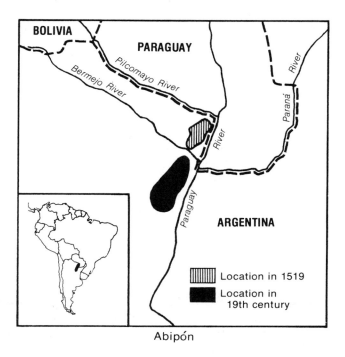

Abipón

the Amazonean cultures, and agriculture, pottery, and other important new features were known by most Chaco Indians.

Tribal history. The Abipon first became well known following the publication, in 1784, of a complete description of their culture by Martin Dobrizhoffer, a Jesuit missionary. By the end of the 16th century, Jesuit missionaries had visited the Abipon, intending to convert them and other tribes. One of these early missionaries wrote a grammar and a vocabulary of the Abipon and Toba languages.

The Abipon originally lived in the northern area of the lower Bermejo River. In the 17th century, they expanded toward the south, especially after they acquired the horse from the Spaniards and other Chaco Indians, such as the Calchaqui. As horsemen they became more aggressive and more effective warriors, first fighting against other Indian groups, and later making alliances with some of them. After the beginning of the 18th century, they began to fight specifically against the Spanish settlements of the southern Chaco area, reaching to the Santa Fe zone near the Parana River.

By 1700, the Abipon, together with other horsemen tribes of the Guaycuruan family of Chaco Indians *(e.g., the Mocovi and some groups of the Toba,)* became warriors. They raided and expanded into a vast area, ranging from the middle Bermejo River in the north to Santa Fe in the south, and from Cordoba in the west to the Parana River in the east. In his almost 20 years of living with the Abipon during the mid-18th century, Dobrizhoffer stated that they endangered the most important Spanish settlements, including Santiago del Estero and Cordoba, and raided Corrientes and Santa Fe. By the mid-18th century, the Abipon began to be missionarized by the Jesuits, especially after the Mocovi accepted Jesuit missionaries. The first Abipon mission was founded in 1748 at San Jeronimo, which later became the city of Reconquista. In the following two years, new Abipon missions were founded at Concepcion and San Fernando. The Rosario mission on the Paraguay River was established in 1763.

The Mocovi and the Toba, former allies of the Abipon, now became their enemies and raided their missions. This warfare continued even after the expulsion of the Jesuits from the Spanish territories in the 1770s. When the missions ended, the Abipon began to migrate and again moved throughout the Chaco area, returning to the bush or passing to the left bank of the Parana River, where they joined marauder bands or became part of guerilla armies, like that of Artigas, a famous Abipon leader.

Because of continuous warfare with the Spanish, the Mocovi, and the Toba, and later with the Paraguayans and Argentines along the frontier, on were almost extinct by the middle of the 19th century. The few who remained lived with the modern Chaco population or with the Mocovi and Toba Indians.

Tribal culture. After the Abipon obtained the horse, they almost abandoned their farming practices and adopted a form of restricted nomadic horse culture, often obtaining food through hunting or looting wild cattle. They combined this way of life with collecting wild plant food, fishing for seasonal water life in the Bermejo River, and hunting other animals. Fishing was carried out primarily during two or three months of the year, chiefly on an individual basis. But hunting, being more of a group activity, was done

Abipón hunting party. Abipón men generally hunted with bows and arrows and spears. From Dobrizhoffer.

on horseback. The normal range of game animals included rhea, guanaco, deer, peccary and, especially, wild cattle and horses. A natural division of labor was based on sex and age.

The Abipon usually roasted meat on a spit or boiled it. They believed that the properties of an animal were transmissible to those who ate its flesh. They used to season their food with the ashes of different plants, and sometimes they stored and preserved food. They used some cooking utensils, calabash containers, shell or horn spoons, and mortars dug out of palm.

The Abipon had domesticated dogs, chickens and, in some cases, baby otters, but the most important domesticated animals in historical times were cattle and horses. These animals were often stolen from the Spanish settlements or from other Indians. The Abipon never became real herdsmen; they slaughtered most of the cattle for tribal needs and then simply replenished the stock by raiding excursions. Nevertheless, they had to find suitable pastures because their economy relied almost totally upon their social structure, which eventually combined the democratic features of primitive food collecting bands with incipient forms of a military aristocracy based on rank differences.

The Abipon lived in crude houses, usually constructed by women from small tree trunks, branches, leaves, and grass. Generally, groups of related families lived in long communal houses which were merely a series of small huts linked together end to end without internal partitions. They camped under bulrush mats laid on a flimsy framework of sticks or stretched on the lower branches of a tree.

In the 18th century, after the introduction of sheep, the Abipon dressed in woolen blankets. Jaguar-skin jackets were a prized possession of men. Women travelling on horseback often protected themselves with rhea feathers. Men usually covered their head with bird skins and used wooden lip plugs. Both men and women usually had their forehead shaved. They depilated themselved by rubbing their faces with hot ashes and then removed the body hair with a pair of flexible tweezers. The Abipon, especially the women, were profusely tattooed.

For transportaion, Abipon women placed all their possessions, mats, tent poles, children, and pets in large peccary-skin bags suspended from the backs of the horses they rode. When crossing a river, everything was put on a boat made of deer or cow hide, with up-curved edges. In the historic period, the Abipon, like all the Chaco Indians, had pottery as well as gourds for containers. The bow and arrow was used heavily by the Abipon along with quivers and spears. Once they became warrior horsemen, the lance became their principal defensive weapon, although they also used bolas, slings, pellet bows, and armor.

Trade was always active among the Chaco tribes. For example, the Abipon used to barter their horses and cattle for spears or iron tools

Three Abipón men wearing skin cloaks. Drawing from the book by Martin Dobrizhoffer, *An Account of the Abipónes, an Equestrian People of Paraguay,* 3 Volumes, published in 1822 (1st edition in Latin, 1784).

Abipón on horseback. Horses were introduced by the Spanish in the 17th century. From Dobrizhoffer.

from the Paisan of the middle Bermejo River. The game obtained by hunting or food gathering was shared by all the members of an extended family. Clothes and tools, however, were personal possessions.Others could borrow these items freely, but only for a short time.Horses, cattle, and sheep eventually became personal property and were earmarked or branded.

The Abipon were among the most warlike of the Chaco Indians. They were feared by their neighbors and the Spaniards alike. They were among the few Indian tribes of South America that challenged Spanish domination and repeatedly defeated the Europeans.They usually fought a guerilla-type war.

The Abipon developed a complex marriage ritual, and they held commemorative ceremonies on the graves of their dead. They believed that dangerous ghosts would linger around a camp. Certain species of ducks were considered to be ghosts. They had both male and female shamans, who conjured spirits and recaptured lost souls.

When Dobrizhoffer studied the Abipon in the mid-18th century, he estimated their population at about 5,000.At the peak of the missionization in 1776, there were about 2,000 Abipon in the four Jesuit missions.By the mid-19th century, they had disappeared as a tribe.

BIBLIOGRAPHY-

● STEWARD, JULIAN H. Handbook of South American Indians. 7 Vols., Washington, DC: U.S. Govt. Printing Office, 1946-59.

ABNAKI

(U.S.; Maine- Canada; Quebec) is the name used for a group of coastal Algonquian tribes that lived in those areas that are now Maine, eastern Quebec, and the Canadian Maritime Provinces.The name--more correctly, Wabnaki, from *wabun* ("light) and *a-ka dik*("land")--means people from the eastland or land of sunrise.The Puritans called these people Tarratines. The name Abnaki is also applied more narrowly to a tribe that formerly lived along the Kennebee River in Maine and now reside in Quebec on Odank Reserve near the St. Francis River, at Becancour near Trois Rivieres, and further north at Cacouna.

The Abnaki group includes the Penobscot of Penobscot Bay and the Penobscot River; the Passamaquoddy at Passamaquoddy Bay; the Malecite of St. John's River; the Micmac of the coast of New Brunswick, Nova Scotia, Prince Edward Island, Cape Breton, and Newfoundland; and the Abnaki tribe proper.The Malecite and Passamaquoddy together were sometimes called

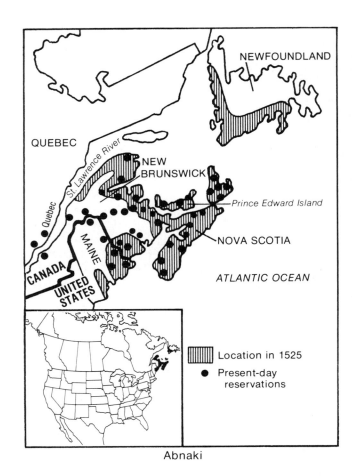

Abnaki

the Etchemin.The Pennacock of New Hampshire are sometimes classed with the Abnaki group on linguistic grounds, although in culture they may have been somewhat closer to more southerly Algonquian-speaking tribes. In historic times the Penobscot, Passamaquoddy, Malecite, and Micmac joined together into a political unit termed the Abnaki Confederacy.

Language and culture. Some linguists consider Eastern Abnaki (Penobscot) and Western Abnaki (St. Francis) to be two distinct languages, with a complex history resulting from the absorption of speakers of other dialects.Nevertheless, recent findings indicate that all the Abnaki tribes had one and the same language.The Micmac, however, have a more diversified dialect. All the Abnaki speak related Algonquian languages.

In precontact and early colonial times, Abnaki political organization did not go beyond the level of the hunting band. Each band respected the hunting territories of every other band. These small bands generally hunted and trapped moose, elk, beaver, otter, muskrat, and other animals during the winter months upstream along the watercourses.In the summer, they fished for alewives, shad, and salmon, and gathered shellfish along the lower courses of the streams and along the seacoast. They also harvested wild plants and perhaps such products as maple sugar. At the time of European contact, the Malecite and some other groups were growing maize (corn), fertilizing the fields by placing one or two surplus fish near the roots of the plants. Tobacco may also have been grown or received in trade from tribes to the south. The office of chief has always been regarded with deep respect and honor among the Abnaki. The British and the French tried to belittle the place of the chief or, at times, tried to manipulate him into persuading his people to sign over land to the foreigners. But the Indians, for the most part, maintained their strong sense of respect for the position of the chief.

Religious beliefs focused on numerous supernatural beings-- (*e.g.*, the god of the forest, the god of thunder and lightning, etc.) One of the most prominent gods was Glooskap (abbreviated from Gelowasid-skidup, meaning "good man") who was believed to have created man by shooting at ash trees with his bow and arrow; the Indians came out of the bark of these trees. The Abnaki believed that Glooskap was capable of doing extraordinary good things to the bad spir-

Scene from a legend about Glooskap. Drawing from a book by Charles G. Leland, *Algonquin Legends of New England,* 1884.

its. They believed that he was an example for them of how they were to live, much as Christians believe in Jesus Christ. Animal tricksters, in the form of badgers, rabbits, raccoons, wolverines, and lynxes, were also prominent in Abnaki mythology. Although the Abnaki legends have come to be regarded as fairy tales, each one had a meaning and a message about life.

With the Europeans, beginning in the 16th century, came the fur trade, a development that increased the importance of beaver trapping in the Abnaki economies and led to social changes. Family hunting and trapping territories became more formalized; boundaries were marked by natural landmarks such as rivers, brooks, trees, and hills and, in some cases, perhaps by blazing marks upon trees. Territories were inherited through the male line. Larger and more permanent settlements developed along the major rivers, with both summer residences and established villages. Houses were conical, covered with birch bark or woven mats; each was occupied by several families. The houses had holes in the top to let out smoke from cooking fires. The bark mats lining the wigwam could be rolled up and moved to other locations, perhaps when the Indians left an area for hunting or warring, or when they moved to the ocean to collect shellfish. In winter, the Abnaki lined their wigwams with bear or deer furs for insulation from the cold. Some of the villages were enclosed in palisades--upright walls built of logs to protect the village from outsiders, and each contained a large, oblong council house.

Iron received in trade began to displace stone,

Three Passamaquoddy with Father Vermilljou *c.* 1860-75. The French established missions among the Abnaki to convert them to Christianity.

Micmac bark lodge photographed about 1875. Most Abnaki houses were made of birch bark and were conical in shape.

bone, wood, bark, and antler in arrowheads, tomahawks, axes, knives, kettles, and other implements.Guns began to displace bows and arrows. Imported beads replaced shell ornaments, and European clothing replaced native furs.Birchbark canoes, however, remained the major mode of transportation.The structure of the family bands, each named after a land or sea animal, also became more formalized, and the chief became, in addition to being a leader in the hunt and in war, the commmercial representative of the band in the fur trade.Christian rites and beliefs were adopted, sometimes subordinating aboriginal ones, but noteliminating them entirely. Polygyny and shamanism, opposed by the missionaries, gradually declined.

Finally, pressure from Iroquois (particularly Mohawk) attacks and European incursions led to the formation of the Abnaki Confederacy, which was similar to the League of the Iroquois. Within the Abnaki group, the delegates of each tribe had equal influence in the councils.According to some observers, however, the Penobscot were considered the leading members and were referred to as "our elder brothers" by the others. By the mid- 18th century, the Abnaki made peace with the Mohawks and established an alliance with them and with neighboring Algonquian tribes led by the Ottawa, an alliance that lasted some 100 years.

History. The Abnaki tribes may have encountered Norse visitors as early as AD 1000, but continuous contact with whites (French and British fishermen at first) did not begin until the 16th century.In 1604, Samuel de Champlain visited several Abnaki bands, and friendly relations were established with the French.French missions were successful in making converts to Christianity among these groups. English settlement of their area began about this time, but ill-treatment of the Abnaki, including kidnapping and enslavement, gained their enmity.Much land was signed over to Englishmen, the Indians probably believing that they were agreeing to share their lands, not to sell them. As a result, the French succeeded in attracting Abnaki support in their dispute with the English over territory, and they provided weapons for the Abnaki to use against the English.

The Abnaki proper and some others gradually withdrew from Maine to Canada and, after King Philip's War (1675-76), many of the survivors fled theirhomeland, settling eventually at St. Francis in Quebec.The withdrawal was essentially completed after the outbreak of the French and Indian War in 1755. From there, they continued to fight the New England settlers until 1759, when an English force attacked and burned St. Francis and killed some 200 men, women, and children.The end of French power in North America generally ended the hostilities between the Abnaki and the British.The Penobscot, Passamaquoddy, and Malecite had remained in their traditional lands, and in 1749, the Penobscot made peace with the English and accepted fixed bounds.Many of the Penobscot and Passamaquoddy now live on reservations in Maine.The Micmacs concluded a peace with the English in 1760, but disputes lasted until 1779.

Population figures. The Abnaki, including the Penobscot and Passamaquoddy, may have numbered about 3,000 in 1600.Contact withEuropeans brought a decline in population. The introduction of new diseases (amongthem smallpox, tuberculosis, and syphilis), alcohol, the depletion of food resources, and the replacement of balanced food resources and balanced native diet with European-imported foods contributed to their losses. Intertribal conflict fostered by the fur trade,war with the English, and, in general, a social decline further lessened their numbers.About 800 Abnaki lived in Quebec (at Odank, Becancour, and Cacouna) in 1962.In the MaritimeProvinces in the mid- 1970s, there were about 5,000 Abnaki--including 2,000 Malecite and 3,000 Micmac--in New Brunswick; 5,000 Micmac in Nova Scotia; 1,000 Micmac in Prince Edward Island; and 400 Micmac in Newfoundland.More than 1,000 Passamaquoddy and 800 Penobscot Indians were enrolled as tribal members in Maine in 1969. They were legally wards of the state and were untaxed.

(see map page XIV)

BIBLIOGRAPHY-
● CAMPBELL, T. J. Pioneer Priests of North America, 1642-1710. New York, NY: The America Press, 1908-1911.
● DE SCHWEINITZ, EDMUND. The Life and Times of David Zeisberger. Philadelphia, PA: J. B. Lippincott & Co., 1870.
● HODGE, FREDERICK WEBB. Handbook of American Indians North of Mexico. Washington: Smithsonian Institution: BAE Bulletin No. 30: U.S. GPO, 1907.
● MURDOCK, GEORGE P. Ethnographic Bibliography of North America. New Haven, CT: Human Relations Area Files Press, 1975.
● SCHOOLCRAFT, HENRY R. History of the Indian Tribes of the U.S. Philadelphia, PA: J.B. Lippincott & Co., 1857.
● SHEA, JOHN G. Catholic Missions among the Indian Tribes of the U.S. New York, NY: E. Dunigan & Bros., 1854.

-----Discovery and Exploration of the Mississippi Valley. New York, NY: 1852.
● SPECK, FRANK G. Penobscot Man: The Life History of a Forest Tribe in Maine. Philadelphia: University of Pennsylvania Press, 1940.
● SWANTON, JOHN R. The Indian Tribes of North America. Smithsonian Institution: BAE Bulletin No. 145: U.S. GPO, 1952.
● TRIGGER, BRUCE G., AND STURTEVANT, WILLIAM C. Handbook of North American Indians. vol. 15, Washington: Smithsonian Institution, 1978.
● WISSLER, CLARK. Indians of the United States. Four Centuries of Their History and Culture. New York, NY: Harper & Bros., 1907.

ACAXEE

(Mexico; Durango and Eastern Sinaloa) are a Middle American People. Inhabiting a fairly isolated region, the Acaxee never were influenced by the great civilizations of Mexico. The Acaxee language appears to be part of the Uto-Aztecan family, and there is no known native writing system.

Culture. The Acaxee fall into the culture area of northwest Mexico. The rugged landscape of the area is characterized by high mountains of the Sierra Madre Occidental and by barrancas (ravines) several thousand feet in depth. Northwest Mexico is not a unitary culture area but a collection of the barrancas. Because of the limited influx of the Spanish Jesuit missionaries, with the end of Spanish rule and with the absence of strong central government in Mexico, the northwest area today is a blend of Spanish and Indian cultures. At one time, the Acaxee were spread throughout the general area of the Sierra Madre Occidental, with a population center surrounding the present town of Topia in Durango. In the mid-1970s, the only remnants of the true Aztec were in the Tamazula area of Durango.

The social structure of the Acaxee is not clear. It does appear to have been based on lineage, with the existence of some form of sodality most likely based on sex. Polygyny was practiced, and there may have been infanticide.

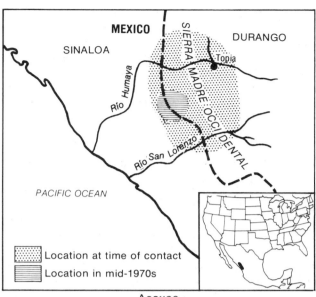

Acaxee

The leader of a tribe had very limited power, except in the case of a war leader whose abilities were recognized and submitted to. Warfare and cannibalism were central to Acaxee life. Because there was no political tribal head, disputes between individuals were settled by clan feuds and could be both inter- and intra-tribal. War could be waged either through organized community bands of warriors or through small parties. If an enemy's body was captured, it would be ceremonially cooked and eaten. The first serving would go to the village idol and the next to the man who had done the killing. Combat weapons included the bow and arrow, the spear, sling, an obsidian-edged wooden sword, and a basketry shield. Although warlike, the Acaxee welcomed visitors and strangers to their villages with great ceremony and would always offer any food at hand.

The Acaxee dwellings were built around an interior court. The outer walls often had small openings for shooting arrows. Each village had separate communal dwellings for men and women. The Acaxee wore few clothes. The major article of dress was a shirtlike smock, woven usually of maguey fiber and occasionally of cotton, cinched around the waist with a cord belt to which was attached a tassel. Braided long hair and pierced noses were popular for both men and women. Curing of diseases and healing wounds were accomplished by bleeding and by blowing or sucking a wound. Acaxee dead were buried in a fetal position in a cave or hollow rock.

The Acaxee were an agricultural people who developed the limited fields of the barrancas and often cultivated areas high into the mountains. The main crops were beans, maize (corn), chili, and calabashes, with some cotton cultivation. Wild mountain honey was collected, and a kind of wine was made from the agave plant. In general, salt was a rare commodity in this region, and usually it was used for trade. The diet was supplemented with some venison and fish, caught by damming an area of a stream and then poisoning the water above the dam.

The Acaxee religion is quite intricate and centers around warfare and agriculture. Based on idols and fetishes, the religion included a creator, called Neyuncame or Mayuncame, a war god, and several other defined deities. The idols, called *tesaba*, ranged from the community idol (always inherited by the "chief,") which could predict the best time for and the outcome of a war or reveal who had killed a member of the village, to personal idols that either could be acquired or inherited. A kind of shaman-priest intermediary was utilized in consulting the more important deity idols. Each idol had an altar and was made of stone or wood, often roughly carved in human or animal shapes. The ceremonies surrounding the more importanat idols, especially the war idol, included fasting and dancing. Certain trees were worshipped as agriculture idols, and the bones of past enemies were utilized in the planting ceremonies.

When not involved with warfare, the Acaxee participated in a number of games including foot races and a kind of ball game the Spanish missionaries called *pelota de ule*. The game was played on an intricately prepared field which served as the center of any Acaxeecommunity. Preceeded by a quasi-religious ceremony, a game could be played between members of a village or with other villages. A ball about the size of a soccer ball and weighing about 2 1\2pounds could be touched only by the buttocks and right shoulder.

History. The early history of the Acaxee people is dominated by their geographic isolation. They were more a series of small tribes isloated in the lowlands of the barrancas and separated by the mountains of the Sierra Madre Occidental. They escaped any influence from the flux of Mexico's great civilizations. With no political, social, or cultural center or authority, the pre- Columbian history of the Acaxee settles around their incessant feuding. With the Spanish Conquest of Mexico in the 16th century, Jesuit priests began to enter northwestern Mexico. The Acaxee resented and resisted the Spanish, and in 1603 they revolted against the Spanish presence. The Acaxee tribes joined one another in preparing an organized resistance that included a number of ambushes and attacks. The revolt was put down, and in time the Acaxee became employed

in the mines opened by the Spanish. In the 1600s, the Acaxee population in the mission settlements reached some 8,000. With the intermingling of Spanish and Indian cultures over time, only a few people of pure Acaxee stocks survived, but the population of clearly Acaxee descended people grew to 40,000 by the early 20th century.

BIBLIOGRAPHY-

● BOWDITCH, CHARLES. P. Mexican and Central American Antiquities, Calendar Systems and History. Washington, DC.: Bureau of American Ethnology- Bulletin 28: U.S. GPO, 1904.
● SWANTON, JOHN R. The Indian Tribes of North America. Smithsonian Institution: BAE Bulletin No. 145: U.S. GPO, 1952.
● THOMAS, CYRUS. Indian Languages of Mexico and Central America and Their Geographical Distribution. Bureau of American Ethnology Bulletin 44: Washington, D. C.: U.S. GPO, 1911.

ACCOHANOC

(U.S.; Va.) was a tribe of the Powhatan Confederacy that was scattered from its home on the Accohanoc River in Virginia by 1833. The Accohanoc had intermarried with the black population and were probably driven off by whites following the unsuccessful revolt of slaves led by Nat turner in 1831. In 1608, the Accohanoc reportedly had 40 warriors.

BIBLIOGRAPHY-

● HODGE, FREDERICK WEBB. Handbook of American Indians North of Mexico. Washington: Smithsonian Institution: BAE Bulletin No. 30: U.S. GPO, 1907.
● MURDOCK, GEORGE P. Ethnographic Bibliography of North America. New Haven, CT: Human Relations Area Files Press, 1975.
● SWANTON, JOHN R. The Indian Tribes of North America. Smithsonian Institution: BAE Bulletin No. 145: U.S. GPO, 1952.

ACHAGUA

(South America; Venezuela-Columbia) are a tropical forest people comprised of small tribes scattered throughout an area of generallylow population density. The name Achagua is the designation for the language spoken by these tribes; it is a member of the Maipurean subdivision of the Arawakan family of South American languages. No native writing system was developed. Scholars have divided the Achagua into various sub- groups of differing numbers and designations, but there seems to be no general agreement as to such subdivisions.

Economy and social organization. The Achagua are among the tropical forest farming peoples of South America and, as such, have had a clearly defined tropical forest culture. Those few tribes living in the arid plains of eastern Columbia followed more of a nomadic life. The Achagua seem to be located mainly around the confluenceof the Meta and Orinoco rivers. At their height, they stretched as far as the present state of Zamora, Ecuador, and were most populous in the present Venezuelan states of Bolivar and Guarico.

Achagua society was organized in terms of patrilineal descent, with authority defined by kinship, age, and sex.Marriages were exogamous, and polygyny was fostered. A man sought three or four wives, each with equal legal status and her own field to cultivate.A totemic system of patrilineal groups named after various animals--including the bat, jaguar, fox, and serpent-- dominated the social-political structure. A village was surrounded by a palisade, composed of one or more totemic groups, and governed by a cacique (chief).The cacique had very few priviledges, except that a group of "vestal virgins," whom he could take as concubines, was at his disposal.Each totemic group maintained a circular communal dwelling, known to have been large enough to hold up to 500 people, a men's clubhouse called a *daury,* and a separate house for cooking.Infanticide among firstborn daughters was practiced in the belief that only a male may inherit the rights and priviledges of another male within the totemic group.In general, women were not allowed to enter the *daury,* and they could not participate in most ceremonies.

The main crops of the Achagua were bitter cassava (manioc), beans, and maize. Fish, turtles, turtle eggs, and game were important dietary staples, but agriculture, carried out by the women, was always more important than hunting.Although the women did the farming, the men cleared the fields and were responsible for all hunting and fishing as well as for gathering wild foods.Basketry, done by the men, was well developed, and some ceramics are evident, but most utensils were calabash vessels made by the women. Although hammocks and women's skirts were made of netted hemp or bast by the women, there was no true weaving. Dugout canoes and pole rafts were used for river transportation, and trade was carried out with strings of beads and with oil from a fruit called *abay.* An alcoholic beverage known as *berria* was made from cassava fermented with honey and water.

The Achagua were often raided by the neighboring Chibcha, to the west, but they seldom ever launched their own forays into non-Achagua territories.In warfare, they utilized bows and arrows and basketry shields. Unlike most South American peoples, the Achagua sometimes poisoned their arrows with curare.

Religion. The Achagua religion recognized a supreme god, called Cuaigerry.Among the other recorded gods are: Cuisiabirri, the god of fire; Pruvisana, the god of earthquake; Guarrana min-

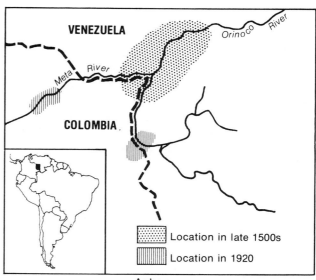

Achagua

ari, the god of cultivated fields; Baraca, the god of riches; Achacato, the god of fate and madness; and the two demons Tanafimi and Tanasuru.The worship of lakes also was practiced. Although idols were not employed, the gods were represented by dance masks worn by the men, who alone could participate in religious ceremonies. The only group ritual for the entire community centered around the death ceremony.Participants delivered speeches about thedeceased for three to four days, after which the body was buried in a hole dug in the center of the house.Ancestor worship was quite prominent.Shamanism and witchcraft were practiced.Yopa snuff, a narcotic, was used in divination, and dreams were considered capable of predicting the future.Curses were believed to be powerful enough to kill an enemy at a distance.The Achagua had a flood myth, according to which some Indians escaped a great flood by climbing tothe top of a high mountain.They maintained a legend that sometime in their past they had fought with a tribe of huge women known as the Amazons.

History. There is no early independent history of the Achagua people aside from their numerous encounters with the Chibcha.A series of small tribes occupying a region of low population density, the Achagua had no centralized authorities or political structures. Their recorded history basically is that of their interactions with the Jesuit missionaries who began to subdue the area at the end of the 16th century.In the early 17th century, most of the Achagua were brought into mission villages where, due to disease and continued attacks by the Chibcha, their numbers rapidly declined.The remnants of the Achagua that remained in the hinterlands continually moved farther into the Cordillera Oriental of

Columbia and into the forests of southern Venezuela as Spanish and Portugese civilization encroached upon their territories.Those Achagua established in mission villages soon became involved with farming and cattle ranching introduced by the Jesuits. In time, these Achagua were acculturated to European customs.Since the 17th century, the Achagua language has all but completely disappeared, and tribal religion has been replaced by Roman Catholicism.

BIBLIOGRAPHY-

● STEWARD, JULIAN H. Handbook of South American Indians. 7 Vols., Washington, DC: U.S. Govt. Printing Office, 1946-59.

ACHOMAWI

(U.S.; Calif.) is the name of an Indian tribe also known as the Pit River Indians. Linguistically classified with the Hokan family, they occupied the entire Pit River drainage basin to its confluence with the Sacramento River.

Early white settlers named the Pit River for the numerous pits encountered on game trails adjacent to its banks, and later extended the name to the Indians of the river region.The Indians refer to themselves as Ees ("the people").The term Achomawi bears some resemblance in pronunication to the correct designation of the tribe, Ah-Jum-Ma-We ("from the river").

Some scholarly observers, noting a variety of differences influenced by environment and geographical isolation, have reported that the only-commmon bond among the Achomawi was their language.

Tribal territorial possessions generally extended east from Mt. Shasta to Mt. Vida on the Warner Range, from Mt. Vida south along the crest of the Warners to Emerson Peak, thence southwesterly encompassing Eagle Lake, and then west to Mt. Lassen and north to Mt. Shasta.Tribal boundaries, however, had little significance because of the total autonomy of the several bands that comprised the tribe. Settlement boundaries and hunting and fishing areas were jealously guarded against all intrusions, including those of neighboring tribesmen.

Tribal culture. To the west, along the lower Pit River, cultural activity was similar to the California Valley culture, with salmon and acorns comprising the basic economy.Settlements were comparatively permanent. To the east, salmon and acorns, were nonexistent, and there is evidence of the influence of the neighboring Northern Plains and Great Basin cultures. Basic economies and settlement activities revolved around hunting and the harvesting of plant crops, which required seasonal migrations from a permanent winter camp.

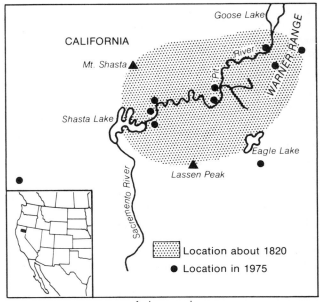

Achomawi

Each of the bands had basic social, political, and economic units, based on a blood group and involving a large family.The importance of family independence was founded upon an extremely important basic attitude of the Achomawi.Relationship by blood and, to a much lesser degree, by marriage was and is held as a sacred bond on which a relative gives or expects friendship, hospitality, and help.

Perhaps by design, the independence of each tribal settlement precluded permanent allegiance to adjacent tribal settlements. It was not unusual for a settlement to ignore one neighboring group while exercising friendly relationships with others.

The independence of each self-contained settlement contributed to the lack of strong tribal ties and, to some degree, encouraged hostilities within tribal segments.Marriages were often arranged to reduce intratribal friction, but success was usually only temporary.

Local leadership was generally provided by the eldest male of the "family." Although he directed the daily activities of the settlement and advised his people as a patriarch, his position was purely civil in nature and without complete authority. Final and important decisions were made by a council composed of sub- families within the settlement. The services of shamans, possessed of unusual powers and in short supply, were the only commodity shared without question among the Achomawi bands.

All segments of the tribe developed extensive folklore. Legends depict a beginning when all living creatures communicated freely, and relate a struggle between forces of evil and good.

Old Yokuts woman pounding acorns. Like many of their neighbors, the Achomawi depended upon acorns as a source of food.

Coyote led the forces of evil, while Silver Fox provided the leadership for good.

Religion, with some variations, was common to all. There was a supreme being, the Provider of all things and events. Depending upon various harvest and other special occasions, rituals for a variety of purposes were practiced in all seasons. Individuals were recognized to have a physical and a spiritual being, and it was important to develop both. Thus, the individual participated in community activities to develop physically, but his spiritual development remained an individual effort. One needed to find his own "medicine" to assist him in communicating with the spirit world. Great importance was placed on the spirits of the dead, which could be called upon for assistance or, if offended, could be the source of tragedy. Boys acquiring the status of manhood sought their identity alone, in specified locations, while girls achieved the status of women through elaborate ceremonies.

Achomawi philosophy recognizes a purpose in nature for all things. Unnecessary waste or harm could provoke bad luck or worse. Earth was the mother of all things and, having the same mother, all things were respected as an integral part of the whole.

Achomawi artistry is evidenced in song, legend, and basketry. In each, history was pre-served, joy and sorrow were shared, and reverence was perpetuated.

Exquisitely chipped obsidian knives and ceremonial pieces were among the items traded with coastal tribes for strings of shell discs and dentilla. Both tribesmen and strangers on trade missions were treated as special guests.

Technology consisted primarily of the development of survival techniques and tools in a seasonally harsh environment. Whether it was hunting or fishing, or a complex method of preparing some marginal food, the methodology used, under the circumstances, left little room for improvement.

Tribal history. The first recorded contact between the Achomawi and the white man occurred in 1828, when a contingent of trappers led by Alexander R. McLeon entered Pit River country. Between 1828 and 1836, several trapping expeditions entered the Pit River area without incident. But exploring expeditions, beginning with that of John C. Fremont in 1840, were less than welcome. With the discovery of gold in California and the establishment of emigrant routes through Pit River country, competition for resources provoked active hostilities. Between 1848 and 1868, numerous military engagements with army regulars and volunteers were recorded.

In 1868, the conquest of the Achomawi was completed. History is brutal in describing the near total destruction of the tribe during the period of settlement that followed. In his autobiography, Gen. George Crook described the Achomawi as "noted all over the Pacific coast as being amongst the very worst. They had the reputation of being warlike, fierce, and wild." Hubert H. Bancroft, a 19th century historian of the American West, wrote: "The inhabitants were a bolder, braver people, who would not tamely submit to every indignity."

By 1853, several hundred Achomawi had been herded onto Round Valley Indian Reservation in Mendocino County, California. After the turn of the century, a half dozen 20-acre parcels of nearly worthless land were purchased for the establishment of rancherias for home sites. In 1939 the XL Indian Reservation was established for 20 families. Perhaps five percent of the tribe lived on trust lands in the mid-1970s. The balance of the 2,000 remaining tribesmen suffered from all the indignities of being landless and unrecognized.

Since 1920, several attempts to organize the Achomawi have failed. Tragically, the tribe continues to be haunted by historical differences and distrust. Bitter intratribal rivalries absorb energies that might otherwise be diverted to constructive endeavors, while the tribe and its heritage slowly die.The uniqueness of the tribe, while providing advantages in earlier times, has largely contributed to its frustrations and demise as a conquered people.The tribe numbered 980 in 1970.

BIBLIOGRAPHY-

● HUMFREVILLE, J. LEE. Twenty Years among our Hostile Indians. New York, NY: Hunter & Co.
● SWANTON, JOHN R. The Indian Tribes of North America. Washington: Smithsonian Institution: BAE Bulletin No. 145: U.S. GPO, 1952.
● WHEELER-VOEGELIN, ERMINIE. Pitt River Indians of California. New York, NY: Garland Publishing, Inc., 1974.
● YARROW, DR. H. C. A Further contribution to the Study of the Mortuary Customs of the North American Indians. Washington, DC: 1st Annual Report, Bureau of Ethnology, 1881.

ACOLAPISSA

(U.S.; La., Miss.) was a tribe that lived in what is now southern Louisiana, and possibly Mississippi, around 1700. Their name was apparently derived by French chroniclers from the Choctaw phrase *hakla pisa*("those who listen and see"). Many variations of the name exist, a common variation being Colapissa. The Acolapissa reportedly lived four leagues (about 10-18 miles) from the mouth of the Pearl River when the French arrived in 1699, moved west to the north side of Lake Pontchartrain a few years later, and by 1722 had settled on theeast side of the Mississippi River, 13 leagues (about 30-60 miles) above New Orleans.The Acolapissa inhabited the Southeastern cultural area, and their life was much like that of the Choctaw, with whom they shared an almost identical Muskogean language.

French chroniclers reported the following picture of Acolapissa culture: the Indians hunted deer, bear, and buffalo, gathered fruit and nuts, fished from canoes using many hooks and lines, and probably grew corn. They shaved using the ashes of shells and hot water.Women and girls tattooed their arms and faces.Religious life involved worship morning and evening before a round temple that held the carved figures of frogs, snakes, and other animals.

Bits of Acolapissahistory were also recorded. The tribe was raided by English and Chickasaw slave hunters shortly before the French came, and was later ravaged by an epidemic.Upon French request, they accepted the Natchitoches into their homeland in the early 1700s, but attacked them for an unrecorded reason in 1714.About 1730, they joined the French military effort against the Natchez. By 1739, the Acolapissa had disappeared as a tribe, a reduced number having merged with the Houma.Liquor brought by the French may have contributed to the disruption of the tribe.

In 1699, the population of the Acolapissa was estimated to be 150-300 men; in 1722, 200 men; and in 1739, combined wiith the Houma, 900-1000 men.

BIBLIOGRAPHY-

● HODGE, FREDERICK WEBB. Handbook of American Indians North of Mexico. Washington: Smithsonian Institution: BAE Bulletin No. 30: U.S. GPO, 1907.
● MURDOCK, GEORGE P. Ethnographic Bibliography of North America. New Haven, CT: Human Relations Area Files Press, 1975.
● SWANTON, JOHN R. Indian Tribes of the Lower Mississippi Valley and Adjacent Coast of the Gulf of Mexico. Washington, DC: Bureau of Ethnology, 1911.
-----The Indian Tribes of North America. Smithsonian Institution: BAE Bulletin No. 145: U.S. GPO, 1952.

ACOMA

(U.S.; New Mex.) is the name of the westernmost Keresan- speaking group of Pueblo Indians who occupy a 357-foot-high mesa, about 80 miles west of Albuquerque.Their traditional village and religious center, known as Acu, is one of the oldest continuously occupied settlements in the western United States. The 256,000-acre Acoma Reservation, located in the Cebolleta mesa region of Valencia County, is dotted with juniper and pinion trees and includes grazing lands and irrigated fields along the San Jose River.

Origins of the name. Acoma tribal accounts indicate that the name of Acu originated sometime after the tribal group's last prehistoric migration from the village of Katsima, or "Enchanted Mesa." When the people approached the new mesa, which they felt was the center of the world, the chief shaman gazed up at its heights and called in a loud voice, *"ako!"* A voice or an echo answered, and the shaman asked the group what they had heard. Dissension arose because some thought they heard the voice say

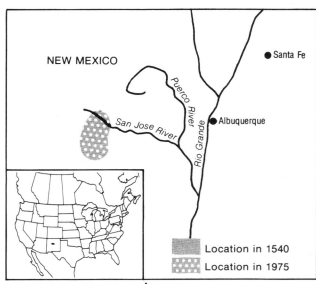

Acoma

yuko (go away") while others thought they heard the voice say ako, which supported their decision to settle on te mesa. Those that heard *yuko* migrated to the south, and the group that heard *ako* stayed and established the present village of Acu.

The Zuni, tribal neighbors to the west, refer to Acoma as H'akukya (from *acu* and the Zuni, locative *kya*). The Laguna, a related tribe to the east, know Acoma as Acu. The 16th-century Spanish Franciscan Acoma explorer Fray Marcos de Niza mentioned Acoma as Acu, although he did not visit the village. In 1540, Capt. Alvarado of the Spanish conquistador Coronado's army referred to Acu as Acuco. The contemporary name of Acoma is, then, a variant of the original call of *ako* by the chief shaman.

It is difficult to focus upon the cultural boundaries of the Acoma specifically, as they are part of the Keresan linguistic group. Found in seven Indian pueblos, the Keresan speakers are spread out into eastern and western groups, separated by approximately 100 miles from one extreme point to another. The term Keresan is an Anglicized form of *queres,* the name given to the linguistic group by the Spaniards.

Tribal structure. There are five kivas in existence in Acoma. They differ in construction from those in most pueblos in that they are ceremonial rooms within the communal houses. Edward S. Curtis, in *The North American Indian* (1926), lists the names of the existing kivas as: (1) Shutyuni-tsi ("Squash Seed Room"), Hamish ("Jemez") Katsina; (2) Haimata-tsi ("Hopi") Katsina; (3) Shosk'a-tsi ("Dust Room") Hoapichani Katsina, a personage with one side of the face yellow, the other side red; (4) K'oshkasi-tsi ("Cold Room"), the name of this personage referring to two upright eagle-feathers, one at each side of the head; and (5) Totakori-tsi ("Turkey-call Room"), Wayosa ("Duck Room") Katsina, the name deriving from the discovery of a flock of turkeys roosting in the rafters during the kiva's construction. In addition, Curtis also mentions the ceremonial chambers of the two surviving shaman societies. They are the kivas for the Flint Shamans and the Fire Shaman.

Every Acoma male traditionally joins one of the kiva groups. Female participation is limited to initiation rites. Traditionally, women are not permitted to progress within the ceremonial organization.

The clan system is similar to that of other Pueblo Indians in that it is matrilineal and exogamous and has special social, political, and religious significance. By the early 1920s only 9 of the 23 clans listed by Curtis existed. These were the Kochinish-yaka ("Yellow Corn"), Kukanish-yaka ("Red Corn"), Kasheshi-yaka ("White Corn"), Koishkash-yaka ("Blue Corn"), Hakani ("Fire"), Tyani ("Deer"), Hooka ("Dove"), Sii ("Ant), and Tyantsi (Pinon). Several others were approaching extinction.

The cacique, or chief, who holds life tenure, is the most important individual in Acoma. Always also the head of the Kuts-hanu ("Antelope people"), he is responsible for the annual selection and appointment of all other tribal officers. The dual system of officers includes the ceremonial appointments of the Tsatyohochani ("country chief") with the title of Masah-we, the second war chief with the title of Spatyi-muty ("Mockingbird Boy"). In addition, there are ten appointed assistant war chiefs.

The civil government of Acoma, established during the Spanish period, includes the *tah-pu-pu* ("governor"), *tinyeute* ("lieutenant-governor", from the Spanish *teniente*), the assistant lieutenant-governor, and three *pishkari* (from the Spanish *fiscales*).

Religious beliefs. The important deities of Acoma are female. Nowtsityi, the Mother-Creator, or Iatiku, is the supreme being. Her younger sister, Ure-se-te, is part of a dual godhead. A structure of lesser deities includes Mah-sa-we and his twin brother Uyu-ye-wi who, as good and courageous warriors, serve the tribal leaders and teachers.

Stories of creation and origin begin with the mythological past when the Earth existed in its present form and all the people lived in darkness in the underworld. At a location in the indistinct north known as *shi-pa-pu,* Badger burrowed upward to create a hole large enough for the people to pass through from the underworld on a rainbow bridge. As each woman passed up through the hole, Mah-sa-we gave her a name, thereby establishing the Acoma clans. The first woman to emerge was given the name Osafa ("Sun").

The people then migrated southward to the "White House." The Mother-Creator gave them instructions in purification, prayer-stick making, and curing. Songs for the sacred ceremonies and models of sacred altars were given to the people. Dissension within the groups that lived at "White House," however, became rampant. The Mother-Creator gave each group a different language; those with similar languages migrated in different directions. The Acoma went southward again, temporarily settling in several areas until they reached Katsima, the "Enchanted Mesa." From Katsima they moved on to Acoma Mesa, upon which they established the present village of Acu.

History. Archaelogical evidence indicates that the Acoma village of Acu was established no

An Acoma woman with an *olla*, a large earthenware jar common to the southwestern U.S., on her head. She was photographed by Adam Clark Vroman in 1899.

later than AD 1250. It was first mentioned in written documents by Fray Marcos de Nisa in 1539, and the following year the town was visited by the Spanish army of Colorado. The early Spanish chronicles mentioned the defensive strength of the mesa-top town and estimated its size at about 200 households.

Antonio de Espejo visited Acu in 1583 and was impressed by the town's size and the distant cultivated fields. The colonizer of New Mexico, Juan de Onate, visited the mesa in 1598. Hostilities between the Acoma and the Spanish began with a battle between soldiers and warriors in December 1598, in which the Indians were victorious. The next month, January 1599, a force of 70 Spaniards returned to "avenge" the deaths of their fellows. During the course of the three-day battle, about 1,500 members of the tribe were killed and Acu was partially burned.

The first Roman Catholic mission and church were established at Acoma by Fray Juan Ramirez in 1629. The church building was replaced by the present structure in 1699.

The Acoma, then about 1,500 strong, successfully participated in the Pueblo Revolt against the Spanish in 1680. Largely because of their isolated, defensive location, they resisted an attempt to reconquer them in 1696, but submitted to Spanish rule on July 6, 1699. By 1760, fewer than 1,100 persons lived at Acoma, and in 1782 the mission's status was reduced to that of a *vista* of nearby Laguna.

The Spanish grant of 1689 allocated 94,159 acres to the Acoma. This was confirmed by the U.S. government in 1858, and the reservation was established in 1928. Since that time, land has been acquired by the Acoma through purchase or rented acreage. In 1902, the population of Acoma numbered only 566, but by 1969 it had grown to 1,920.

The importance of Acu as the main population center of Acoma has waned. The summer villages of Acomita and McCartys are of recent construction. An inadequate water supply in old Acu and a desire to reside closer to the cultivated and grazing lands surrounding the mesa were factors that led to Acoma to establish the newer villages. Family houses are still maintained in Acu, but the tribal headquarters has been removed to Acomita.

Economy. The Acoma people have long been agriculturally oriented, with emphasis placed on farming and livestock herding. They cultivated wheat, corn, beans, and alfalfa mainly on irrigated land, although dry-farming was also practiced. These activites are still important, despite the recent abandonment of these activities by many families. There are several small retail stores owned by the Acoma, and some mining for clay, obsidian, and coal. Tourism centers around Acu and the Spanish mission building. Ceramic handicrafts have taken on a renewed importance in recent years because of the development of marketing outlets.

The basic economic unit has shifted from the communal clan orientation to that of the nuclear family. The migration of working-age men and, in some cases, of entire families away from the reservation has also had profound results. Benjamin J. Taylor and Dennis J. O'Connor cited this in their study, *Indian Manpower Resources in the Southwest* (1969).

Cultural change. Among the non-Indian influences on Acoma life, the Roman Catholic Church, the ranchers, and the railroads have been primary contributors to change. As in other pueblos, Roman Catholicism and other Christian churches have grown stronger as the Acoma religion has weakened. The efforts of the church toward the suppression of Acoma ceremonies were first felt about 1692. The post-1692 period saw the development of secrecy aimed at the exclusion of non-Indians from ceremonial activities. Many aspects of Acoma religion were forced underground but not out of existence.

Contemporary Acoma rites are a combination of various Acoma celebrations conveniently fitted into the Roman Catholic rites and calendar of liturgical activities. Although the Roman Catholic priest may celebrate mass for the dead, Acoma prayers to pave the way for the departed to be received by his or her creator will have already been offered. A child may receive both baptism by the priest and the purification or baptismal rite of the Acoma. The Acoma people are devoted to their own religion and its observances. With few exceptions, however, they participate in Roman Catholic rituals with but a vague understanding of their origin or meaning. Acoma religious ceremonies, still performed in Acu, include the winter solstice, the summer rain dance, the harvest dance, and the St. Stephen's Fiesta (September 2).

The rancher or cowboy is very evident in Acoma life. Rodeo events are highly popular. Western (cowboy) clothing is the most popular dress of the Acoma men, horsemanship is highly prized, cattle raising is one of the major activities on the Acoma lands, and Western music and movies are popular. In essence, the tough outdoor style of life portrayed in the image of the cowboy fits well with the Acoma perception of their own life concepts.

The Santa Fe Railroad has had direct influence upon the Acoma economy because it supported the first mass migration of Acoma men from the reservation. The company offered jobs and technical training as railroad mechanics, electricians, and painters. It has hired and provided skilled technical training for approximately half the working-age, male population of the reservation. The Santa Fe Railroad may have been the single most important factor in facilitating the change of attitudes toward education and job training from the time of its advent into the Acoma lands.

Contemporary conditions remain complex at Acoma. The advantages of various government and other agencies outside the pueblo are steadily becoming more obvious, but the people continue to resist any efforts to assimilate them into the American mainstream. While they have accommodated much of what is non-Indian to the surface, they have steadfastly refused to succumb to influences outside their own patterns of thought and lifestyle. In the mid-1970s, Acoma remains one of the more conservative of the Keresan people. The Acoma numbered 4,408 in 1970 (2,464 in Laguna and 1,944 in Acoma.)

BIBLIOGRAPHY-

● CURTIS, NATALIE. The Indians' Book; An offering by the American Indians of Indian lore, musical and narrative, to form a record... New York, NY: Harper & Bros., 1907.
● FORREST, EARLE R. Missions and Pueblos of the Old Southwest, Their Myths, Legends, Fiestas, and Ceremonies. Glendale, CA: The Arthur H. Clark Co., 1929.
● HODGE, FREDERICK WEBB. Handbook of American Indians North of Mexico. Washington: Smithsonian Institution: BAE Bulletin No. 30: U.S. GPO, 1907.
● LA FARGE, OLIVER. The Changing Indian. University of Oklahoma Press, 1942.
● LOWERY, WOODBURY. The Spanish Settlements Within the Present Limits of the U.S., 1513-1561. New York, NY: 1901.
● MINGE, WARD ALAN. Acoma, Pueblo in the Sky. Albuquerque, NM: University of New Mexico Press, 1976.
● MURDOCK, GEORGE P. Ethnographic Bibliography of North America. New Haven, CT: Human Relations Area Files Press, 1975.
● PALMER, ROSE A. The North American Indians, An Account of the American Indians North of Mexico. New York, NY: Smithsonian Institution Series, Inc., 1929.
● SEDGEWICK, MRS. WILLIAM T. Acoma, The Sky City: A Study in Pueblo-Indian History and Civilization. Cambridge: Harvard University Press, 1927.
● STEVENSON, JAMES. Illustrated Catalogue of the Collections obtained from the Indians of New Mexico and Arizona in 1879. Washington, DC: 2nd Annual Report, Bureau of Ethnology, 1883.
● STIRLING, MATTHEW W. Origin Myth of the Acoma and Other Records. Washington, DC: Bureau of American Ethnology Bulletin 135, 1942.
● STANTON, JOHN R. The Indian Tribes of North America. Smithsonian Institution: BAE Bulletin No. 145: U.S. GPO, 1952.
● UNDERHILL, RUTH. First Penhouse Dwellers of America. New York, NY: J. J. Augustin Publisher, 1938.
● WISSLER, CLARK. Indians of the U.S. Four Centuries of Their History and Culture. New York, NY: Doubleday, Doran & Co., 1940.

ACUERA

(U.S.; Fla.) The meaning of the name is unknown (acu signifies "and" and also "moon"). The tribe belonged to the Timucuan or Timuquanan linguistic division of the Muskhogean linguistic family. They were located near the headwaters of the Ocklawaha River in Florida. The Acuera were first noted by De Soto in a letter written at Tampa Bay to the civil cabildo of Santiago de Cuba. According to information transmitted to him by his officer Baltazar de Gallegos, Acuera was "a large town...where with much convenience we might winter," but the Spaniards did not in fact pass through it. While they were at Ocale, however, they sent to Acuera for corn. The name appears later in Laudonniere's narrative of the second French expedition to Florida, 1564-65 (1586), as a tribe allied with the Utina. It is noted sparingly in later Spanish documents, but we learn that in 1604 there was an encounter between these Indians and Spanish troops and that there were two Acuera missions in 1655, San Luis and Santa Lucia, both of which had disappeared by 1680. The inland position of the Acuera is partly responsible for the few notices of them.The remainder of the tribe was probably gathered into the "Pueblo de Timucua," which stood near St. Augustine in 1736, and was finally removed to the Mosquito Lagoon and Halifax River on Volusia County, where Tomoka River keeps the name alive.Specific population information for this tribe is not known.See *Utina* for general population reference.

BIBLIOGRAPHY-

● SWANTON, JOHN R. The Indian Tribes of North America. Smithsonian Institution: BAE Bulletin No. 145: U.S. GPO, 1952.

ADAI: *See* CADDO.

AGLEMIUT

(U.S.; Alaska) was an Inuit (Eskimo) tribe that apparently lived on the southwest coast of Alaska between the Nushagak and Ugashik rivers, and eastward to the highlands which the borders of present-day Katmai National Monument partly encompass. Ethnologists reported that, at the beginning of the 20th century, the Aglemiut hunted walrus and occasionally whales, carved ivory skillfully, and, although accepting Christianity, still adhered to native beliefs and customs.

BIBLIOGRAPHY-

● HODGE, FREDERICK WEBB. Handbook of American Indians North of Mexico. Washington: Smithsonian Institution: BAE Bulletin No. 30: U.S. GPO, 1907.
● MURDOCK, GEORGE P. Ethnographic Bibliography of North America. New Haven, CT: Human Relations Area Files Press, 1975.
● SWANTON, JOHN R. The Indian Tribes of North America. Smithsonian Institution: BAE Bulletin No. 145: U.S. GPO, 1952.

AGOMIUT

(Canada; Greenland) was an Inuit (Eskimo) tribe that inhabited the northeastern shore of Baffin Island. Ethnologists reported that, in the early 20th century, they hunted seals, white shales, and narwhals, used sledges for transportation on land, and were in contact with the natives of Ellesmere Island and the Iglulirmiut, through whom they may have traded with tribes on mainland North America. The Agomiut reportedly were divided into the Tununirmiut and the Tununirusirmiut.

BIBLIOGRAPHY-

● HODGE, FREDERICK WEBB. Handbook of American Indians North of Mexico. Washington: Smithsonian Institution: BAE Bulletin No. 30: U.S. GPO, 1907.
● SWANTON, JOHN R. The Indian Tribes of North America. Smithsonian Institution: BAE Bulletin No. 145: U.S. GPO, 1952.

AGUANO

(South America; Peru) are a relatively small and isolated tribe of the inhospitable montana area

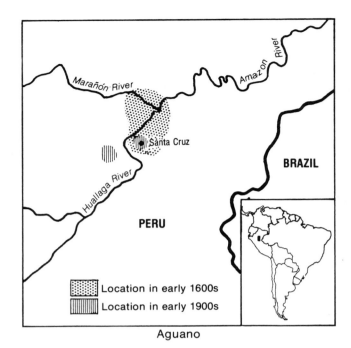

Location in early 1600s
Location in early 1900s

Aguano

whose numbers have steadily diminished to the point of virtual extinction since the first influx of Europeans in the 16th century. Aguano also may be rendered as Uguano, Aguanu, and Awano. The Spanish called them the Santa Crucino.

Language and culture. The original language of the Aguano people is not known but may have been of the Arawakan family. Sometime in the 16th century, they adopted the Quechan language of the Quechumaran family. There is no native writing system that was used.

The Aguano were divided into two subgroups: the Seculusepa and the Chilicagua, and the Meliquine and the Tivilo. Spread throughout the montana region of Peru, their chief area encompassed the lower Huallaga and the Maranon rivers down to the Samiria River; they are not easily categorized as to culture type. The montana is tropical rain forest but, unlike the forests of the Amazon, has a very rugged terrain with small swift streams and numerous isolated tribes. Although the Aguano cultivated some foods, fish and other river life, as well as some wild plants, were
very important to their diets. They were not a nomadic people, but their farming was somewhat peripheral.

Because of the topographic nature of montana, the early Spanish soldiers and missionaries, whose records serve as the primary source of information about many tribal cultures, did not have easy access to the Aguano areas. There is little concrete archaeological information on the pre-Columbian Aguano, and thus their cultural origins are not clear. The Aguano community was composed of usually one, occasionally more, patrilineal family of 15 to 30 people housed in one structure. Not until the missionary period (1630-1830) were they collected in a few large villages. The typical dwelling was approximately 60 feet by 17 feet with a system of beams and rafters supporting the roof. As in the case of many south American tribes, bitter cassava (manioc) was a dietary staple along with corn (maize) and peanuts. Because of the abundant stream and river life, fish caught with a dip net, turtles, turtle eggs, and other river mammals were particularly important. Ceramic pots were used for cooking and storage. Although the Aguano could make dugout canoes, this may have been an acquired skill. A modest people, they soon adopted European dress but continued to file their incisors to points as a form of adornment.

A vaguely shamanistic religion was practiced, with the shaman serving as intermediary. The narcotic *guayasa,* made into a drink, was often used in religious ceremonies. In warfare, especially against the neighboring Chamicura and Jivaro, blowguns were employed and scalps were taken as trophies. Belts were made from the hair, and scalps were hung from leg bands.

There does not seem to have been any particular social structure beyond that defined by patrilineal descent. The role of the tribal "chief" is at best vague, although there was some organization geared to warfare. The shaman was loosely defined, and both shaman and individual tribespeople used the *guayusa* drink. With their settlement into the mission villages, much of their own culture wa rapidly lost.

History. A general history of the Aguano people is difficult to construct, largely because of the characteristics of the montana region, where the tribes, including the Aguano, were rather isolated, with no overall central organization or any apparent hierarchy. Described as a fierce people by the earliest Spanish missionaries, their primary enemies were the Chamicura and the Jivaro. Nothing precise is known of their pre-Columbian intertribal contact except for these traditional enmities. For the most part, their known history involves the interplay between the Jesuit mission
aries and Spain over the control and utilization of the native population.

The Aguano were first noticed seriously in the early 1600s because of their continuing conflict with the Chamicura, which was considered counterproductive to the promulgation of Christianity and the use of the Indian peoples in the service of Spain. About 1653, after a tentative peace was established between the two tribes, many of the Aguano people entered mission vil-

lages established by the Jesuits where, strangely enough, they settled with the Chamicura. An epidemic soon reduced their numbers to about 1,000. The incessant epidemics in the New World, usually caused by European diseases, reduced the general population of South America drastically during the 16th century and continued to do so throughout the missionary period.

The Aguano, now with the support of the Chamicura, continued to fight the Jivaro, who militarily were far superior to the Aguano. Because of these wars and because of continued epidemics, their population continued to decrease. Like all nativepeoples of South America, the Aguano were employed on the ranches, farms, and mines of the Spanish and Portugese. Under the influence of European culture and with the steady decline of their population, which was concentrated in a village at Santa Cruz on the Huallaga River, the Aguano ceased to be a distinct cultural entity.With the beginning of the national period in South America after 1830, white settlers began to push farther along the Huallaga and Maranon rivers, forcing the remaining nonvillage Aguano farther into the hinterlands. By 1859, the village population had been reduced to about 300.In the early 1900s, only 100 clearly identified Aguano were alive, and these people were close to being assimilated completely into the general culture.Today it is difficult to determine if any truly Aguano people still exist. *(see map page XVIII)*

BIBLIOGRAPHY-

● STEWARD, JULIAN H. Handbook of South American Indians. 7 Vols., Washington, DC: U.S. Govt. Printing Office, 1946-59.

AHANTCHUYUK.

(U.S.; Oreg.) Also called French Prairie Indians, by early settlers; and Pudding River Indians, by various authors.
The significance of the tribe's name is unknown. They belonged to the Kalapooian linguistic stock. The tribe was located on or near the Pudding River, in Oregon, which empties into the Willamette from the east about 10 miles south of Oregon City. Specific population information for this tribe is not known. See *Calapooya* for general population reference.

BIBLIOGRAPHY-

●HODGE, FREDERICK WEBB. Handbook of American Indians North of Mexico. Washington: Smithsonian Institution: BAE Bulletin No. 30: U.S. GPO, 1907.
●SWANTON, JOHN R. The Indian Tribes of North America. Smithsonian Institution: BAE Bulletin No. 145: U.S. GPO, 1952.

AHTENA

(U.S.; Alaska; Canada) are a tribe that have lived on the Copper River in the southeastern part of present-day Alaska at least since the late 18th century.

Name and location. The name *ahtena* means "ice people." There are approximately ten other tribal names that are still being used within the tribe. These reveal characteristics about the groups named, such as where they came from or how they came to their present locations.

The Ahtena tribe lives in the Western or Yukon part of the Subarctic culture area, which includes most of Alaska and Canada below the Arctic Circle. There appear to be divisions within the tribe. Chitina is the furthest village down the Copper River. People from this village are called Ahtna'ht'aene ("lower people"). People from Copper Center through Gakona are called Dan'ehwt'aene ("upper people") by the Ahtna'ht'aene, and those from Chistochina to Mentasta are known as Tatl'ahwt'aene ("the people from the upper most part of the Copper River").

Lieut. Henry J. Allen, who explored the Copper River area in 1885, observed a two-part division of the tribe. He gave the name Midnusky to those living on the Copper river from its mouth to the Tazlina River and also to those on the Chitina River and its branches; he gave the name Tatlatan to those on the Copper River above the Tazlina.

Language and culture. Whether it is an Athapascan language itself or an isolated branch of the Na-Dene family was not known in the mid-1970s. There are three dialects in the Ahtena language: the upper, the central, and the lower. These dialects differ only in the pronunciation of word prefixes--*e.g.,* "I will walk" is *kosya'* in the lower dialect and *txosya'* in the upper dialect.

An alphabet for the Ahtena language was developed in 1973, with the help of Dr. Michael Kraus, Jeff Leer, and Jum Kari from the University of Alaska. It has 39 letters with 27 consonants, 5 short vowels, and 4 long vowels. In the mid-1970s, a noun and verb dictionary with approximately 5,000 entries was being compiled, and the language was being taught in two schools and all seven Ahtena villages.

Information detailing changes in the territory occupied by the Ahtena is not available. Their territory may have decreased since 1905, when reports indicated they had two more villages than at present.

Visitors to the Ahtena before 1905 reported that the Ahtena fished and hunted for food. Guns were scarce, and hunters shot moose and caribou

Ahtena

principally with bows and arrows. The Ahtena wore parkas and one-piece boots and trousers, decorating their clothes with beads, fringe, and porcupine quills. The Ahtena also traded once a year, exchanging beads, cotton prints, and tobacco obtained from coastal tribes for furs and copper from interior tribes. They sometimes travelled in skin-covered boats bought from traders or coastal tribes.

The Ahtena reportedly lived in small settlements of one or two houses. The houses had underground rooms where the Ahtena could take steam baths. In addition, hunters often built temporary shelters for protection while on trips. Each village had a *tyone* (headman, *skillies* (officials who were usually related to the headman), and at least one shaman. The tribe's social structure reportedly allowed for a servant class and polygamy. Entertainment centered around the potlatch, a ritualized feast that lasted for at least three days.

History and contemporary situation. It is not known when the Ahtena or their ancestors came to present-day Alaska. Between 1796 and 1884, they reportedly drove off five Russian exploring parties and killed several explorers and a trader. U.S. expeditions, under Lieut. W.R. Abercrombie in 1884 and Lieut. Henry J. Allen in 1885, explored the area, apparently without incident. Allen reported visiting Ahtena villages on the Copper River and its tributaries.

In the mid 1970s, the Ahtena still caught fish and dried them in the summer, and hunted moose and caribou in the fall. Game was becoming more scarce, however, and the people had begun to

An Ahtena family shown, in this 1910 photograph, standing in front of their home.

look for other means of livelihood. Traditional potlatches continued to be the most popular entertainment, although some of the young people had lost aspects of the traditional culture. Stories about culture, tradition, and legends told by the elderly Ahtena were being preserved on tape recordings and transcribed for use in educating the young in the traditional culture.

At last record, the Ahtena population living in the basin of the Copper River numbered 300.

● ALLEN, HENRY T. Atnatanas: Natives of Copper River, Alaska. Annual Report of the Board of Regents of the Smithsonian Institution, Part 1, 1886 (published in 1889).
● HANABLE, WILLIAM S., AND WORKMAN, KAREN W. Lower Copper and Chitina River: A Historic Resources Study. Alaskan Division of Parks, Dept. of Natural Resources, 1974.
● HODGE, FREDERICK WEBB. Handbook of American Indians North of Mexico. Washington: Smithsonian Institution: BAE Bulletin No. 30: U.S. GPO, 1907.
● MURDOCK, GEORGE P. Ethnographic Bibliography of North America. New Haven, CT: Human Relations Area Files Press, 1975.
● SWANTON, JOHN R. The Indian Tribes of North America. Smithsonian Institution: BAE Bulletin No. 145: U.S. GPO, 1952.

AIS

(U.S.; Fla.) was a major tribe that apparently dominated the southeastern area during the 17th and early 18th centuries. The tribe later disappeared, perhaps migrating from its homeland.

The Ais, also called the Aiz or Jece, spoke a Muskogean language. They probably lived along the present-day Indian River, with their principal village near Indian River Inlet. It is believed that they lived only along the coast.

The Ais obtained most of their food by fishing, using long spears, and by gathering foods such as fruits. Living in huts built with saplings and covered with thatched palmetto leaves, they travelled in dugout canoes that were poled or paddled. One three-day ritual, probably of a religious nature, involved feasting and dancing. The Ais chief was held in high esteem.

The Ais are thought to have been dominated by the Calusa to the west, and themselves to have dominated coastal tribes to the north and south. In the early 1600s, the Ais were friendly with the Spanish, but there is no evidence to indicate that they were subdued by them or converted to Christianity.

BIBLIOGRAPHY-

● BOLTON, HERBERT E. Athanase de Mezieres and the Louisana-Texas Frontier, 1768-1780. Cleveland, OH: The Arthur H. Clark Co., 1914.
● HODGE, FREDERICK WEBB. Handbook of American Indians North of Mexico. Washington: Smithsonian Institution: BAE Bulletin No. 30: U.S. GPO, 1907.
● MURDOCK, GEORGE P. Ethnographic Bibliography of North America. New Haven, CT: Human Relations Area Files Press, 1975.
● SWANTON, JOHN R. The Indian Tribes of North America. Smithsonian Institution: BAE Bulletin No. 145: U.S. GPO, 1952.

AIVILIRIMIUT

(U.S.; Alaska) is the name of a central Inuit (Eskimo) tribe that lived on the north shore of Judson Bay from Chesterfield Inlet to Fox Channel. In the early 20th century, they hunted deer, musk-oxen, seal, and walrus, and they fished for trout and salmon. Their name means "people of the walrus place."

BIBLIOGRAPHY-

● HODGE, FREDERICK WEBB. Handbook of American Indians North of Mexico. Washington: Smithsonian Institution: BAE Bulletin No. 30: U.S. GPO, 1907.
● MURDOCK, GEORGE P. Ethnographic Bibliography of North America. New Haven, CT: Human Relations Area Files Press, 1975.
● SWANTON, JOHN R. The Indian Tribes of North America. Smithsonian Institution: BAE Bulletin No. 145: U.S. GPO, 1952.

AKOKISA

(U.S.; Tex.) was a tribe of the general area of Galveston Bay that is now extinct.

Variations of the name Akokisa ("river people") include Accokesaw and Han. The tribe lived primarily along the Trinity and San Jacinto rivers in present-day Texas and probably spoke a language of the Atakapan group. They were identified by some scholars as one of the tribes that had contact with the 16th century exploratory party led by Cabeza de Vaca. In 1805, the Akokisa hunted deer and bear, fished, gathered fruit and, possibly, farmed to a limited extent. It is thought that their government had no chief over the whole tribe and that they lived in semi-permanent villages.

Spanish and the French. A Spanish mission and presidio were established in Akokisa territory during the 1700s, but neither lasted long. It is believed that an epidemic of 1777-78 and the disruptive influence of white colonization contributed to the dispersal of the tribe in the 19th century.

ALABAMA

(U.S.; Tex.) are a Muskogean tribe of the Creek Confederacy who formerly dwelt in southern Alabama and now live on a state reservation in Polk County, Texas, together with the Coushatta tribe, with whom they are closely related. Intermarriage has been extensive, and the Indians of that reservation are known as the Alabama-Coushatta.

The Alabama name has had many variants in history, with over 30 being used in Frederick W. Hodge's *Handbook of American Indians North of Mexico* (1912). Alibamu is the name chosen by Hodge to designate the tribe. There are at least two versions of the derivation of the name; one is that it is from *abibamy* (Q*place of rest"), which the tribe used to identify a refuge from enemy tribes behind the Chattahooche River in the southeastern U.S.; another is that the name is from the Choctaw *alba ayamule* ("I open the thicket").

Language and culture. The Alabama Indians spoke the Muskogean dialect of the Coushatta (Koasati). They were within the Creek Confederacy: Muscogee and Hitchiti.

Alabama is an ancient tribe, and little is known of their culture except that they generally followed most of the customs of the Creek, though there were some exceptions. Marriage outside the clan was the rule. Descent was in the female line. They did not punish adultery with death, as was the Creek law. Each clan within the tribe was advised by a matriarch, and the tribe was governed by a council of clan representatives who elected a chief, or *miko*. The council appointed a warchief, the *tustenuggi*.

Each Alabama town had a ceremonial center comprised of a rotunda, a square of earth, and a chunkey yard. The circular rotunda was covered with fine bark daubed with mud, and was used for meetings and on ceremonial occasions. The square ground-the fair weather counterpart of the rotunda-consisted of a central plaza with four cabins, which were oriented to the four cardinal directions, surrounding the plaza. It lay beyond the rotunda's entrance, which faced the east. Opposite the rotunda was the yard used for playing chunkey, a variant of the hoop and pole game. Posts used for burning captives stood in the yard, as did a tall post bearing the town's emblem.

Early Alabama villages were defended by wooden stockades. The journals of the Spanish explorer Hernando de Soto described the village of Ullibahali as being enclosed with a large timber fence coated with mud inside and outside and equipped with holes for archers.

History. When De Soto explored the southeast in 1541, the town he referred to as Alibamo was in what is now central Mississippi. Little more is known of the location of the Alabama until 1701 when the French entered Mobile Bay. Jean Baptiste le Moyne, sieur de Bienville, the French governor of Louisiana, found "on the banks and many adjacent islands, places abandoned by the savages on account of war with the...Alibamos." The French built Fort Toulouse in 1717 and established relative peace. When Fort Toulouse was abandoned in 1783, a part of the tribe removed to the banks of the Mississippi about 60 miles above New Orleans. This band numbered about 120, including 30 warriors. Subsequently, the tribe moved to western Louisiana and, in 1890, some were still living in Calcasieu Parish, Louisiana, others among the Creek Nation in Indian Territory (now Oklahoma), and about 200 in Polk County, Texas.

During the first half of the 19th century, the Congress of the Republic of Texas granted two leagues of land along the Trinity River to both the Alabama and the Coushatta tribes. White settlers took this land, however, and the Indians were again landless until 1854 when, upon the recommendations of Gen. Sam Houston, the state of Texas bought approximately 1,280 acres of land for the Alabama tribe, which had diminished to 340 members. Houston also tried to have 640 acres of land granted to the Coushatta tribe, but the legislature never purchased the land. Some

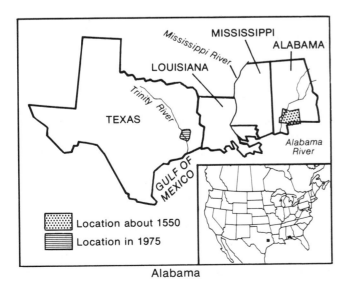

MISSISSIPPI
ALABAMA
LOUISIANA
Mississippi River
Trinity River
TEXAS
Alabama River
GULF OF MEXICO

Location about 1550
Location in 1975

Alabama

Council house of the Alabama Indians. Drawing is from the *Bureau of American Ethnology Annual Report*, 42 (1928).

Coushatta, by marriage and by special permission of the Alabama, came to live with the Alabama on their land. The majority of the Coushatta, however, moved to Louisiana, near Kinder.

The Alabama and the Coushatta lived for 74 years on this original 1,280-acre tract without assistance from either state or national governments. The forest land is poor, however, and the Indians' food supply consisted primarily of game from the Big Thicket, a large forested area adjacent to the reservation. When this unlicensed hunting became prohibited, disease and hunger diminished the tribe by half.

In 1928, both state and federal funds were appropriated in an effort to relieve the plight of the Indians. The U.S. government bought 3,071 acres of land adjoining the original tract, to be held in trust for the Alabama and the Coushatta living on the reservation. In 1954, the U.S. government relinquished its trusteeship of all lands and other assets pertaining to the Indians, and Texas assumed full responsibility.

By the mid-1970s, the Alabama-Coushatta Indian Reservation was one of the few Indian reservations in the United States that was exclusively under state control and was the only Indian reservation in Texas. Until 1965, management authority was vested in the Board of Texas State Hospitals and Special Schools in the Tribal Council, which managed and administered the affairs of the reservation. The creation of such a body, within the structure of state government, to deal exclusively with Indian affairs was largely the result of the efforts of the Big Thicket Association, a group of prominent and public-spirited citizens dedicated to the preservation of the Big Thicket wilderness. This group also advocated legislation that would add an additional 3,000 acres to the reservation and create a Big Thicket State Park.

Population figures for the Alabama-Coushaffa tribe were about 450 in 1969; in the Coushaffa Community, they numbered 196 in 1966.

BIBLIOGRAPHY-

● DEBO, ANGIE. The Road to Disappearance. Norman, OK: University of Oklahoma Press, 1941.
● EGGLESTON, GEORGE CARY. Red Eagle and the Wars with the Creek Indians of Alabama. New York, NY: 1878.
● FOLSOM-DICKERSON, W. E. S. The White Path. San Antonio, TX: The Naylor Co., 1965.
● HODGE, FREDERICK WEBB. Handbook of American Indians North of Mexico. Washington: Smithsonian Institution: BAE Bulletin No. 30: U.S. GPO, 1907.
● HOLMES, W. H. Aboriginal Pottery of the Eastern U.S. Washington, DC: 20th Annual Report, Bureau of Ethnology, 1903.
-----Prehistoric Textile Fabrics of the U.S., derived from impressions on pottery. Washington, DC: 3rd & 13th Annual Report, Bureau of Ethnology, 1884, 1896.
● MURDOCK, GEORGE P. Ethnographic Bibliography of North America. New Haven, CT: Human Relations Area Files Press, 1975.
● PICKETT, ALBERT JAMES History of Alabama, and incidentally of Georgia and Mississippi. Charleston, WV: Walker & James, 1851.
● STRAIT, NEWTON A. Alphabetical List of Battles, 1754-1900: War of the Rebellion, Spanish-American War... Washington, DC: 1900.
● SWANTON, JOHN R. The Indian Tribes of North America. Smithsonian Institution: BAE Bulletin No. 145: U.S. GPO, 1952.
● THOMAS, CYRUS. Report on Mound Explorations. Washington, DC: 12th Annual Report, Bureau of Ethnology, 1894.

ALACALUF

(South America; Chile) are an almost extinct canoe- using tribe which formerly inhabited the islands of the Chilean coast fron the Gulf of Penas southward to Tierra des Fuego. In 1950, they occupied two settlements, the larger northern one at Puerto Eden on Wellington Island, and the smaller one in the region around La Rinconada, south of Punta Arenas. By 1955, there were only 68 surviving Alacaluf.

The name "Alacaluf" may come from the Yahgan term *innalum aala kaluf,* meaning "western men with mussel-shell knives." Variant forms

of the name include Halawulup, Alakaluf, Alacal-
ouf, Alaculuf, Alaculoof, Alucaluf, Alukoeluf,
Alooculoof, Alookooloop, Alukulup, Alokolup,
Alikhoolip, Alikuluf, and Alikoolif.

The archipelagoes of southern Chile formerly
frequented by the tribes are isolated, on the east
by the mountains and ice fields of the mainland
and of Tierra del Fuego, by a difficult channel to
the north, and by the southern Pacific Ocean to
the west and south. Heavy rainfall, often more
than 120 inches a year in places, results in a
dense vegetation which, together with the difficulty of the local topography, discouraged land
travel, leading the Alacaluf to rely on canoes and
boats. While the region rarely receives sunshine,
and thick clouds hang low as they move in from
the west, temperatures are usually moderate (the
annual mean is about 40' F) with relatively little
seasonal or daily fluctuation.

Physically, Alacaluf are believed to be related to the Yahgan of the Tierra Fuego region,
with whom they share many cultural traits, and to
the now extinct Chono, who lived on the islands
to the north of the Alacaluf. While the Alacaluf
language may be loosely grouped with that of the
Yahgan, it is nevertheless a distinct linguistic
family. It is unclear whether the now lost Choco
tongue was an Alacalufan dialect or a separate
language.

Social and economic organization. The
largest social unit recognized among the Alacaluf
is the family. No clans or other tribal subdivisions are recognized, nor are there any chiefs, although the advice of the oldest person is
occasionally sought. Families sometimes go
hunting with other families related to them by
blood, but otherwise they do not congregate with
others except under special circumstances, such
as shipwreck or the stranding of a whale.

The Alacaluf do not practice agriculture.
They have traditionally subsisted by food-gathering, moving along the beaches in search of shellfish, sea lions, and sea birds--a diet that they
supplement with porpoises, fish, birds' eggs,
land game, berries, and seeds. Otter and copyu,
which were formerly hunted, have now grown
scarce, as has the huemal, a small deer. The shellfish are either gathered at low tide, speared from
canoes, or brought to the surface by swimmers
who sometimes dive down 30 feet to dislodge
their catch. Birds caught include penguins, cormorants, flightless steamer ducks, blue petrels,
and red-billed oyster catchers. Parrots are not
killed, as it is believed that to do so will bring on
bad weather. The dog is the only domesticated
animal, and it is used in hunting otters and other
prey. Hunting weapons include shellfish spears
and poles, net traps, clubs, and harpoons.

Alacaluf

In the mid-20th century, the northern settlements of the Alacaluf used dugout canoes from
12 to 16 feet long, while many of the southern
group used chalupas (boats) obtained by trade.
Both types of craft are propelled by oars and/or
a sail made of canvas or sacking; they are steered
wth a paddle.

The Alacaluf originally used canoes made of
bark, but these were replaced in the latter part of
the 18th century by plank boats. By the end of
World War I, both plank boats and bark canoes
had become things of the past, having been replaced by the modern type of dugout canoe,
which has driftwood planks nailed to the gunwales to prevent objects in the boat from falling
out.

The usual form of Alacaluf habitation is an
oval or round hut. These huts have a framework
made from saplings that have been bent into
arches, the framework then being covered with
sea lion skins; bark, sacking, or ferns are also

used as a covering when sea lion skins are lacking. Each hut is warmed by a fire, built on an oval-shaped hearth in the center of the interior. The hut's doorway is protected by fern fronds, which form a type of curtain. Among the southern Alacaluf, tipis are now in use.

Life style ceremonies and beliefs. Although children receive affection, they are to a great extent left to their own devices, especially after they can walk. Experience is regarded as the best teacher--even when it is a question of learning that flames can burn. Initiation ceremonies for youths coming to the age of manhood include building of a special house and teaching the youths to sing the Whale Song. There are no particular sexual restrictions before marriage, but after marriage infidelity by a wife may be punished by a beating.

There are no particular marriage ceremonies: The husband usually moves in with his wife's family. Polygamy is unusual, but it is not forbidden. A husband had been known to have been married to two sisters, or to a mother and daughter.

When a death occurs, all those in the settlement paint their faces black, and the property of the deceased, except for his canoe and certain other valuables, is burned. The body is buried, if the terrain permits; otherwise it is placed in a cave or at the base of cliff; sometimes it is hidden in the forest. Reports of cannibalism among the Alacaluf, based on unreliable evidence, are generally discounted.

There is a belief in the spirit and in a life after death. One authority, Martin Gusinde, reported in 1925 that the Alacaluf believed in a single supreme creator-god, named Xolas, who sends a soul into the body of each newborn child and reclaims the soul at death. Shamanistic methods are used to help cure illness. Many Alacaluf beliefs are associated with the weather--*e.g.,* that bad weather is caused by a flock of parrots flying overhead, or that good weather results from ashes being thrown onto the water. The Alacaluf are said to be vague in measuring time, making only a few elementary distinctions, such as those between winter and summer or between yesterday and tomorrow.

In former times, the Alacaluf are believed to have numbered several thousand, although this is unsure. As mentioned earlier, they reportedly numbered no more than 68 in 1955. Substantial contact between the southern Alacaluf and whites first began when, with the arrival of steam navigation, a lighthouse service was established along the Straits of Magellan in the 19th century and, later, when a coaling station was established in Munoz Gamero Bay soon after 1900. The northern Alacaluf only came into regular contact with whites in the 1930s. Early contacts with whites (called "cristianos" by the Alacaluf) were friendly, but later became characterized by distrust. The southern group has been the most adversely affected by associations with whites, having suffered both physically and culturally in consequence. In 1961, it was reported that the Alacaluf at Puerto Eden almost all spoke Spanish and that they had adopted "official" Spanish names, although continuing to speak Alacaluf and to use their own names among themselves. In the early 1970s, it seemed that prospects for the survival of the Alacaluf as a separate group were poor and that they were likely, like their former neighbors the Chono, either to die out or else to become absorbed into other groups.

BIBLIOGRAPHY-

● STEWARD, JULIAN H. Handbook of South American Indians. 7 Vols., Washington, DC: U.S. Govt. Printing Office, 1946-59.
● SWANTON, JOHN R. The Indian Tribes of North America. Smithsonian Institution: BAE Bulletin No. 145: U.S. GPO, 1952.

ALEUT

(U.S.; Alaska) are a people living in the Aleutian Islands (the island chain that separates the Bering Sea to the north from the Pacific Ocean), in the Pribilof Islands in the Bering Sea, and in the western part of Alaska. The Aleut are closely related to the Inuit (Eskimo), from whom they diverged about 4,500 years ago, and share with them many basic physical, cultural, and linguistic traits.

Population figures. As a result of the expeditions of Vitus Bering, a Dane in the service of the imperial Russian government, the Russians first came into contact with the Aleut in the earlier part of the 18th century. At that time, the Aleuts numbered about 25,000. Under Russian domination, their numbers declined so drastically, however, that by the end of the 18th century they numbered only about 2,000. The Aleut have remained relatively stable in numbers since then, despite intermixture with peoples of European origin. In 1867, the Russians sold the Aleutians and rest of Alaska to the United States. In the 1970s, the Aleuts numbered approximately 1,300, of whom roughly 500 lived on the Aleutian Islands and in Alaska, about 500 lived on the Aleutian Islands and in Alaska, about 500 in the Pribilof Islands further north, and about 300 on the Soviet-administered Commander Islands (Komandorskiye Ostrova_), which are the westernmost extension of the Aleutian Island chain, lying about 110 miles off the coast of Kamchatka in Siberia.

At last report, approximately 2,300 Aleut were living on the Alaska Peninsula and Aleutian Islands, and a small group was living on the Commander (Komandorskii) Islands of the Soviet Union.

Tribal name. According to one account, the name "Aleut" is derived from the islanders' name for a heavenly creator, Aleuksta-Agudax. Another supposition is that the name is derived from the word *aliat* (meaning "island") used by the Chakchi (the Inuit living on Diomede Island in the Bering Strait). The name came into general usage at the time of the Russian contact in the 18th century. The Aleut call themselves "Unung'un," which, like the word "Inuit" to which it may be related, means "people."

Location and climate. The Aleutian Islands, numbering about 69 (14 large and 55 small), are divided, from east to west, into five main groups--the Shumagin, Fox, Andreanof, Rat, and Near islands. At the time of the coming of the Russians in the 1740s, almost every one of the 69 islands was inhabited. During the period of the Russian occupation, two changes took place. Firstly, as a result of the reduction in the Aleut population, by 1831 only 16 islands remained inhabited. Secondly, whereas the Pribilof and Commander islands were uninhabited at the time of the Russian arrival, they were subsequently colonized with Aleuts.

In recent times, only nine of the Aleutian Islands themselves remained inhabited--Unga in the Shumagin Islands, Atka in the Andreanof Islands, Attu in the Near Islands, and Sanak, Akun, Sedanka, Unalaska, and Umnak in the Fox Islands. In addition, there remain Aleut settlements at Belkofski and Morzhovoi bays near the tip of the Alaska Peninsula.

The islands themselves are volcanic, and are rugged and treeless, being covered only with grass or sedges. They extend over some 30 degrees of latitude in a giant arc which trends first to the southwest and then swings to trend northwest. They consist of the partially submerged peaks of the Aleutian Range, which begins on the Alaskan Peninsula, and lie directly along the Circum-Pacific Belt, an earthquake zone that corresponds to a line of volcanic fissures. On the mainland, the Aleutian Range contains some of the largest volcanoes in the world, while on the islands most of the active volcanoes are found on the northern side of the chain.

The Aleutian climate is rainy, windy, and foggy, but the temperature is fairly uniform, ranging from an average mean of about 28' F in January to 48' F in August.

Major groups and neighbors. The Aleut are separated into two groups speaking slightly different dialects: the Unalaskans, inhabiting the Shumagin and Fox Islands and the settlements on

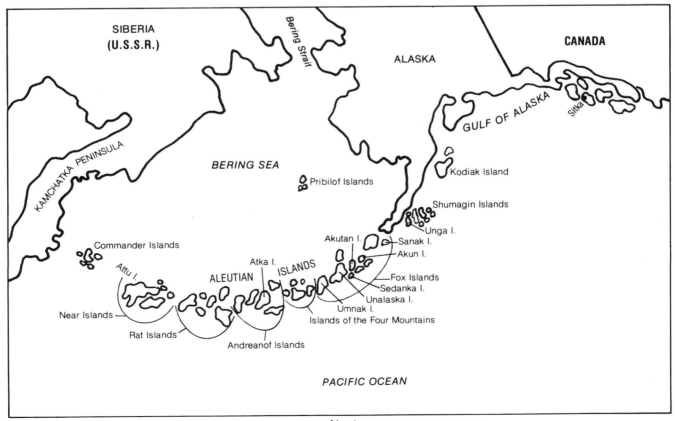

Aleut

the Alaskan Peninsula, and the Attuan-speaking Atkans, inhabiting the Andreanof and Near Islands. The Atkans formerly also inhabited the Rat Islands, but these are now uninhabited. The eastern neighbors of the Aleut have traditionally been two Inuit groups: the Aglemiut, who inhabit the upper part of the Alaskan Peninsula and Nushagak Bay, an inlet of Bristol Bay to the north; and the Kaniagmiut (Koniaga), who inhabit Kodiak Island and other neighboring islands, all lying to the east of the Alaskan Peninsula, as well as the adjacent coast of the peninsula. (The 18th-century Russians mistook the inhabitants of Kodiak Island for Aleut).

Physical despription. Today, very few Aleut are of unmixed Aleutian descent, having intermixed with peoples of European descent over the past century and more. In 1741, G.W. Steller, a naturalist with the second Russian expedition, described the Aleut living on the Shumagin Islands in the following terms:

They are of medium stature, strong and stocky, yet fairly well proportioned; and with very fleshy arms and legs. The hair of the head is glossy black and hangs straight down all around the head. The face is brownish; a little flat and concave. The nose is also flattened, though not particularly broad or large. The eyes are as black as coals, the lips, prominent and turned up. In addition, they have short necks, broad shoulders, and their body is plump, though not big bellied.

He might also have added that they have an epicanthic eye fold (a prolongation of a fold of the skin of the upper eyelid over the inner angle of the eye, a characteristic also known as Mongolian fold) and small hands and feet.

Economy. The Aleut are a people of the sea; they are hunters and gatherers, rather than agriculturalists. Traditionally, they have hunted sea otters, which they harpoon from bidarks (skin-covered boats resembling kayaks), as well as sea lions, seals, walrus (in the eastern islands), and whales. Whales were usually hunted by two bidarks, the whales being killed with poisoned lances. The poison used was aconite, made from the roots of the monkshood (*Aconitum napellus*). It was placed on the stone blade of each lance. The use of the poison was, however, a closely guarded secret; it was told, instead, that human fat from corpses was used to grease the harpoon heads.

Among the many fish caught are salmon, cod, flounder, herring, trout, and even an occasional shark. To catch them, the Aleut use fish spears, lines, dip nets, siene nets, and, in rivers, dams and weirs.

The birds hunted include ptarmigan, many kinds of duck (including the eider duck, which is valued for its down), geese, cormorant and puffin. In catching birds, bolas are sometimes used. The bola is a kind of sling, at the end of which are four to six cords about 30 inches long, each with a stone tied to its end. When the bola is thrown at a bird in flight, the cords spread out, and when one touches the bird, the other cords wrap around it, bringing it down to the ground. Birds are also caught by bird darts, which are thrown from a throwing board--a length of wood that extends the thrower's arm and permits a surer aim.

In some regions, other animals such as bear, caribou, and reindeer are hunted. The Arctic fox, once numerous, is now becoming scarce. In the Pribilof and Commander islands, fur seals are hunted in summer, all local adult Aleut males being obliged to participate in the hunt. The seals are clubbed into insensibility, after which their throats are cut and their skins taken.

In addition to the above, the Aleut also gather mollusks, sea urchins, and, on land, various kinds of berries.

Boats. Traditionally, the Aleut have used two kinds of skin boats, the bidarka and the *igilax*. The bidarka--called *igyax* or *igax* by the Aleut-- originally had only one or two hatches (*e.g.,* it was built to carry only one or two persons), but the Russians introduced a three-hatch bidarka which permitted one or more passengers to be carried. After the introduction of firearms, the two-hatch bidarka was used for shooting expeditions, one of the two men in it firing the gun, and the other steadying the boat against the recoil. The *igilax* (*nigalax* in the Attu dialect) has now disappeared. It resembled the Inuit umiak, being a craft 30 feet long, capable of carrying from 30 to 40 people. In the 1970s, the use of the motorboat was common.

"Canoes of Oonalashka [Unalaska]," after a drawing by John Webber, 1778, showing Aleuts paddling one-hatch and two-hatch bidarkas.

Basketry and other crafts. The Aleut women are renowned for their fine basketry, woven from grasses. Among the grasses used, the wild barley and wild pea are favored. The grass threads are of different tints, usually varying from green to yellow. The basketry is sometimes plaited into a kind of filigree work and covered with silk embroidery.

The Aleut also used stone, bone, ivory, and driftwood for fabricating various objects in daily use. Bone was used for fishhooks, harpoon-heads, wedges, and other objects; stone, usually andesite, was used for the blades of knives, arrows, darts, and other tools and weapons, as well as for lamps. Knowledge of metal predated the arrival of the Russians, and iron knives and hatches were in use. These may have come from European or Japanese shipwrecks, or they may have been obtained by trade with peoples on the American mainland.

Clothing. The traditional clothing worn by the Aleut resembles that of the Inuit. Both men and women wear, or used to wear, a long shirtlike garment. Those worn by the men are made of the skins of birds with especially tough and water-resistant skins, such as puffins, cormorants, and guillemots, while those of the women are made from sea otter or seal skins. The skins of young eagles are used to make downy parkas for young children. In rainy weather, or while afloat, a waterproof and hooded ornament called the Kamleika has also customarily been worn. It is rated with tufts of feathers, and is translucent. An elongated hunting helmet was worn by the men; conical in shape, it projected forward over the eyes. Sometimes a wooden visor, open at the top, was worn instead. Such helmets and visors were often elaborately decorated. The Aleut of the Andreanof Islands, and perhaps those further west, habitually went barefoot, but on islands to the east of these, fur stockings and leather boots were often in use.

Villages and homes. Aleut villages are invariably located on the coasts, the interior of the islands remaining uninhabited. Former village sites can easily be located by the dense green growth of vegetation that occurs there, as well as by the presence of planes usually associated with men.

Originally, Aleutian houses were long communal buildings as much as 240 feet in length and about 40 feet wide. They were sunk deeply into the ground and covered over with earth, so that the early Russians considered them more as caves than as houses. Driftwood timbers and whale bones formed the framework for the walls and roof supports, after which the roof was covered with poles overlaid with dry grass and sod. En-

Aleut women at the entrance to their barabara in Cheinoffoke Village, Unalaska Island, 1890.

trance was gained through an opening in the roof (there was often more than one such opening), after which one climbed down a notched pole or log which served as a ladder. Sometimes as many as 150 people lived in a single house of this type. The later form of a house, called the barabara, is a much smaller single-family dwelling. Like the older dwellings, it is sunk into the ground, but not so deeply, having the entrance in the side. The roof is covered with sod. Modern houses, built by the government, are usually of wooden frame construction.

The barabara, like the older houses, is heated and lighted with stone or bone lamps. These are bowl-shaped, have wicks made of grasses, and use seal, sea lion, or whale blubber for fuel.

Burial practices and folk medicine. In former times, the Aleut had three ways of disposing of the dead--by burial in the ground, by cremation, and by cave burial. Burial in the ground took place in burial pits in which the bodies were placed in a sitting position. Cremation was used for the most part for women, children, and slaves. In cave burial, the men of particular importance, such as noted whalers, were mummified.

The Aleut have a traditional folk medicine, and a knowledge of the medical uses of certain herbs. They possess a remarkable knowledge of anatomy, resulting from their experience in disecting the bodies of sea mammals, and often undertake post mortem examinations to determine the cause of death.

Religion. In religion, the Aleut adhere to the Green Orthodox Church, to which faith they were converted by the Russian missionary Verniaminov (for whom a volcano on the Alaskan Peninsula is named), who lived among the Aleuts of Unalaska from 1824 to 1834. Much of his influence was gained by his putting an end to the cruel and barbaric treatment of the Aleut by Russian traders and others. Among other things, he devised a written language for the Aleut, in the Russian script, and his influence among them was so great that it resulted in the virtually total obliteration--at least in public practice--of the old Aleut customs, ceremonies, beliefs, and institutions.

Previously, the Aleut had held the belief that light was the source of life, and that, consequently, they should rise at dawn and spend all the daylight hours awake. They also believed that running water in general, and sea water in particular, were sacred. Thus, they bathed in the sea at all seasons, and sea bathing took place before all special events, as well as in times of crisis.

Recreation. For diversion, the Aleut play a number of games, including a number of throwing and catching games, cat's cradle, and chess. Chess is played at high speed and on a board with 56 squares instead of 64. The moves are the same as in orthodox chess, but the disposition of the pieces at the beginning of play differs (see the attached diagram). The telling of tales is also popular, but this is regarded as tribal tradition, and not only as a personal art. Thus, an expert narrator will begin his tale with the words: "This is the work of my country."

Language. The language of the Aleut is a branch of the Eskimo-Aleut language family. Apart from the Unalaskan and Attuan dialects, a third dialect was also formerly spoken, but by the 1970s, it was virtually extinct. In the Aleutian and Pribilof islands, less than 1,000 Aleut still speak their language, while in the Commander Islands less than 100 do so. As mentioned, the language is written in the Russian script.

Early history. Whereas in earlier times, and especially during the period of the Russian occupation, there was a question as to whether the Aleut originated in Asia or in North America, the physical, cultural, linguistic, and archaelogical evidence available in the mid-1970s indicated that paleo-Aleuts had their origins in the Alaskan Peninsula. The oldest known Aleut culture existed around 6000 BC, samples having been found in northwest Alaska.

After their settlement in the Aleutian islands in about 2000 BC, the Aleut engaged in warfare not only with their neighbors but also with each other. Lances and bows and arrows were the principal weapons of offense, and wooden shields and body armor made of wooden slats were the principal means of defense. Persons taken prisoner in these conflicts were enslaved. Aleut war expeditions were launched against the Inuit of Kodiak Island as well as against the Aglemiut Inuit living on Bristol Bay in Alaska, and attacks against the Aleut from these same peoples were fought off, presumably with varying success. Among the Aleut themselves, those of Unimak Island fought with those of the Shumagin group, the Alaskan Peninsula, and the islands of Unalaska, Akin, Akutan and Umnak. Hostilities also took place between the Aleut of Unalga, Umnak, and islands further west, and those of Unalaska.

Under Russian rule. In 1741, a Russian expedition consisting of two ships -- captained respectively by Aleskey Chirikov and Vitus Bering --sailed eastward from Kamchatka in Siberia on a voyage that resulted in their discovery of the Aleutians. On their return, the Russians took back with them sea otter, fox, and fur seal skins. News of the "fur islands" attracted numbers of *promyshlenniki,* the fur hunters of Siberia, who spread throughout the Aleutians from Bering Island in the Commander group to Kodiak off the Alaskan coast. Possessing firearms, they were able to dominate the Aleut villages, seizing the women and obliging the men to go hunting. The most cruel measures were taken in reprisal, hundreds being slaughtered to avenge the death of a single Russian. An Aleut uprising against the Russians, which spread from the Alaskan mainland as far west as Umnak was suppressed with ferocious cruelty by Soloviev and other Russian traders, after which all resistance ceased. As a result of these events, the Aleut population was decimated, and many islands became uninhabited after the Russians removed the populations from them in order to exercise administrative control more effectively. Subsequently, the population was further reduced by wholesale epidemics of smallpox, measles, and pneumonia, one of the worst being the smallpox epidemic of 1838-39, which resulted in the death of half the population of Alaska.

Under Russian rule, the Aleuts were systematically set to work gathering furs and skins; as the resources became depleted, they were sent further afield. In 1794, for example, about 1,000 Aleuts in 500 bidarkas were sent to Yakutat in southeast Alaska to hunt sea otter. Such encroachments on the territory of others led to reprisals, and hundreds of Aleuts were killed by Tlingit warriors when the Tlingit attacked Sitka on Baranof Island in southeast Alaska in 1802.

Under U.S. rule. After the purchase of Alaska by the United States in 1867, American fur hunters entered the area. Whereas the Russian system of exploiting the fur trade included measures of control and conversation, the Americans engaged in the indiscriminate slaughter of sea otters and fur seals. In the absence of effective governmental supervision, they were joined in their activities by fur traders from Canadian, Japanese, and Russian ships, so that the fur seals became endangered and the sea otters virtually extinct. In 1910, however, the U.S. government intervened, subsequently concluding treaties with the other nations concerned, and in consequence both species began once more to increase.

In 1942, during World War II, the Japanese attacked the islands. Attu and Kiska, at the western end of the island chain, were occupied, and the inhabitants were deported to Japan. In the following year, the Japanese were driven from Attu by U.S. troops after three weeks of hard fighting, after which the Japanese abandoned Kiska. The population of some other islands were temporarily evacuated to the American mainland by the U.S. Navy at about this time. Since World War II, there has been a permanent U.S. military presence in the islands. The Aleut peoples of the Alaskan mainland, the Aleutians, and the Pribilof Islands became U.S. citizens when Alaska attained statehood in 1958.

In 1971, the Aleut who had one quarter or more native blood were included in the provisions of the Alaska Native Claims Settlement Act (q.v.), which extinguished native land titles in return for making available 40 million acres and a cash settlement to native regional and village corporations.

BIBLIOGRAPHY-

●HODGE, FREDERICK WEBB. Handbook of American Indians North of Mexico. Washington: Smithsonian Institution: BAE Bulletin No. 30: U.S. GPO, 1907.
●HRDLICKA, ALES. The Aleutian and Commander Islands and Their Inhabitants. Philadelphia: The Wistar Institute of Anatomy and Biology, 1945.
● MURDOCK, GEORGE P. Ethnographic Bibliography of North America. New Haven, CT: Human Relations Area Files Press, 1975.
●SWANTON, JOHN R. The Indian Tribes of North America. Smithsonian Institution: BAE Bulletin No. 145: U.S. GPO, 1952.

ALGONKIN

(Canada; Ontario, Quebec, Newfoundland) refers to a number of related Canadian Indian bands that are collectively called the Algonkin. This term should not be confused with the Algonquian family, which refers to the widespread language group in eastern and central Canada, along the north Atlantic seaboard, and in the western Great Lakes region in the United States. The name Algonquian, however, comes from the tribal group, the Algonkin, which are one component member of the language family. At the time of first white contact, the Algonkin lived in the Ottawa Valley in Quebec and Ontario. Between the 17th and 18th centuries, the Algonkin were dispersed by other Indian groups as well as by white settlers, and suffered great losses because of disease and other effects of white contact. Living in a densely wooded, mixed coniferous and deciduous forest region, their culture reflected their environment: the Algonkin fished, hunted, trapped, and practiced marginal horticulture.

Tribal name. The meaning of the word Algonkin is not entirely clear. The most recent suggestion is that it is derived from the Malecite word *elekomokwik* which means "they are our relatives (or allies)." An earlier suggestion attributed the word to the Micmac *algoomeaking* "at the place of spearing fish and eels (from the bow of a canoe)."

Samuel de Champlain was the first to record the word and wrote it in Algoumequian. In 1632, Algonquian appeared in the *Jesuit Relations* for the first time. The names that the Algonkin give themselves and the names that other Indian groups have for them, however, are very different. The Algonkin call themselves *omamiwininiwak* and *anisinabeg*. The Huron called them Aqanaques; the Iroquois called them Adirondacks; and the Western Abnaki call them Wesogenak. *The Handbook of American Indians North of Mexico,* edited by F.W. Hodge (1907), spells the name Algonkin, gives other variants in spelling, and provides reference as to first appearance of these forms.

Social and cultural boundaries and subdivisions. The Algonkin occupy a marginal position between the Subarctic and Northeastern culture areas. Harold Driver places them in the eastern Subarctic Culture Area. A.L. Kroeber puts them, along with the Ojibwa and the Ottawa to the west, in the Northern Great Lakes Culture Area. He separates them from groups immediately to the north, the Eastern Subarctic, and from Iroquoian-speaking neighbors. This made the Algonkin divergent in many ways from their Eastern Subarctic neighbors to the north.

Specifically, the Algonkin were boarded on the southeast by the Huron, and on the east by the Montagnais and the Tete de Boule, and--although the 17th-century boundaries are not distinct--by the Cree on the north, and on the west and southwest by the Ottawa, with whom the Algonkin merged culturally and linguistically.

The historical Algonkin of the 17th century consisted of the following related bands: the Wescarini on the Rouge, the Petite- Nation and the Lievre rivers in Quebec; the Matouwescarini in the Madawaska Valley in Ontario; the Keinoche between Pembroke and Renfrew, On-

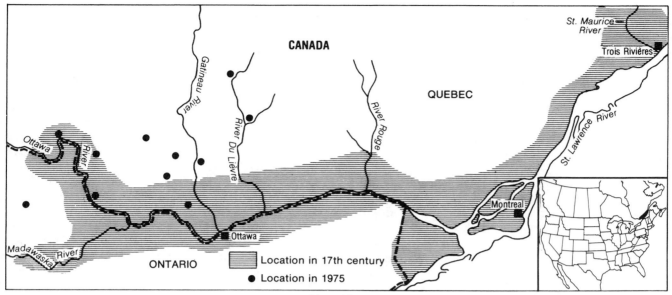

Algonkin

tario, in the Muskrat Lake region; the Kichesipirini on Morrison Island, Quebec, a small island in the Ottawa River off Allumette Island; the Otaguottouemins in the upper valley of the Kichesipirini; and the Onontchataronon on the South Nation River in eastern Ontario. The territory occupied by the Algonkin in the 17th century was from roughly the St. Maurice River in Quebec, to the area in Ontario drained by the Ottawa River and its tributaries.

Language. As previously stated, the Algonkin are members of the widespread Algonkin language family. They speak dialects of a language shared with the Ojibwa, the Saulteaux, and the Ottawa. Neighboring bands along this chain from Ojibwa to Algonkin speak mutually intelligible dialects, although culturally the groups are given different "tribal" designations.

Summary of tribal history. (16th and 17th centuries.) The earliest European accounts of the Algonkin, which date from 1603, found them at Tadoussac. Here, with other Algonkin groups, they were celebrating a victory feast over the Lower St. Lawrence Iroquoians that they had ousted from the region. The struggle between the Lower St. Lawrence Iroquoians and the Algonkin, along with their allies -- other Algonkin-speaking groups in the east - - had been going on for at least 30 years.

Before 1570, However, Algonquians and the Lower St. Lawrence Iroquoians appear to have lived together on friendly terms. The 30-year war was likely precipitated because the Iroquoians wanted to carry out trade directly with the French and not through the Algonquian groups who, at that time, were acting as middlemen.

Champlain came up the Ottawa River into Algonkin territory in 1613 and identified the 17th-century bands given above. He found the Kichesipirin on Morrison Island living in constant fear of Iroquois (Mohawk) attacks. The Algonkin were allies of the Huron, and both were traditional enemies of the Iroquois. The enmity between the Iroquois and the Huron was felt in Algonkin territory because the Algonkin provided the Huron with European goods, for which they received in exchange corn, hemp nets, and wampum. Because the Iroquois occupied the St. Lawrence River above the Ottawa, the Algonkin, with their strategically advantageous position on the Ottawa River, provided not only the closest, but also the safest route to Lake Huron for the French.

The Huron-Algonkin alliance was extremely beneficial to the Algonkin, and they attempted, however unsuccessfully, to keep the French from trading with the Huron. The presence of armed Frenchmen travelling through Algonkin country to trade with the Huron, however, led to a brief period of peace in the 1620s, when the Iroquois, who had been spurred on by the Dutch to hijack the fur fleets on the Ottawa River, now hesitated to attack the Algonkin. This lull in fighting led to another direction in the quest for furs.

To better their position, the Algonkin, with their access to furs from more northern groups, attempted to assume trade links with the Dutch at Fort Orange. The Mohawk, nevertheless, would not permit this competition, and in the 1630s and early 1640s, the Mohawk and the Algonkin were again at war. At this time, the superior Mohawk control of arms led to the ousting of the southernmost Algonkin from the Ottawa Valley. These Algonkin were forced to find asylum with the more inaccessible Algonkin bands to the north and west.

Peace proposals were begun in 1645 by the French, on behalf of the several Algonkin-speaking groups and the Iroquois. But the Algonkin found themselves ultimately at a disadvantage, as the Iroquois were now permitted to hunt at the southern edge of Algonkin territory. The following year, the Mohawk invaded Algonkin territories.

Raids weakened the Algonkin, and the assistance sought from neighboring Algonquian groups brought little success. Between 1650 and 1675, the Algonkin temporarily left the Ottawa Valley. Some went to the Lake Saint John region of Quebec; others went to Trois Riveres and to the Sulpician Fathers' mission at Montreal. Around the end of the 17th century, the Algonkin at Trois Riveres amicably gave their hunting grounds to the south of the St. Lawrence to the Abnaki, another Algonquian group.

(18th and 19th centuries.) The Great Peace between the French, their Algonquian allies, and the Iroquois was established in 1701. From this time on, the Algonkin carried on extensive trade with Albany. In 1704, a mission for the Algonkin was established by the French at Ste-Anne-debout-de-l'ile. In 1721, another mission was established for the Christian Ioquois, the Nipissing, and the Algonkin at Lake of Two Mountains--the present Oka Reserve near Montreal. The Two Mountains Algonkin were not cultivators at this time, but were living from the profit of furs, which they continued to obtain in winter by hunting and trapping on family hunting grounds on the Upper Ottawa River.

The 19th century brought considerable movement of Algonkin groups once more. As early as 1807, some Lake of Two Moutains Algonkin and Timiskaning had dispersed northward to Golden Lake, Ontario, and a reserve was established for them in 1870. In 1830 Algonkin from Trois Riveres moved to Lake of Two Mountains. Other Lake of Two Mountain Algonkin settled at Maniwaki (River Desert), where a reserve was established in 1854. Many of the remaining Algonkin left Lake of Two Mountains after 1868. Other Algonkin reserves established in Quebec were at Argonaut, Barrierre Lake, Grand Lake Victoria, Kipewa, Lake Simon, Long Point, Timiskaming, and Wolfe Lake. Many Algonkin lived off reserves on the River du Lievre and the Ottawa.

Tribal culture The way of life of the Algonkin at the time of first writings usually failed to specify which Algonquian group they were discussing under the heading Algonkin. Moreover, since the writers had religious and economic motives in mind, the description of aboriginal traits were irrelevant in such contact situations.

William Penn's treaty with the Algonkin

The descriptions by 20th-century writers, too, are not necessarily representative of the early Algonkin. During the 19th century, the Algonkin had borrowed much from the tribes farther north, who were more thoroughly Subarctic in character.

Seventeenth century Canadian anthropologists, Bruce Trigger and Gordon Day, , suggested that the Algonkin bands likely were patrilineal clans. A patrilineal clan consisted of a number of families related to one another through males who married women from outside the clan. Each of these clans may have formed a village at favored fishing spots during the warmer months. In winter, they dispersed or sent out hunting parties to obtain deer, beaver, moose and, in some districts, caribou as well. A 1761 description of these family hunting grounds coincides closely to what F.G. Speck's informants still remembered in 1913. Family tracts were delineated by such natural boundaries as lakes and rivers. Trespass on another's hunting ground was avoided. Fear of witchcraft revenge was the most widespread sanction against violation of trespass. If, however, a family was badly in need of food, permission was often given to the man to hunt in the territory of another. Game, moreover, was consistently preserved: pregnant female animals or those with young were not killed; attempts were made to permit the game to replenish itself in a given tract if it was in danger of extinction. Speck refers to this as "farming" of game.

Those 17th-century Algonkin who lived in close proximity to the St. Lawrence Iroquois grew some crops where the soil was suitable. The dense wooded areas were cleared by burning the trees and undergrowth, and here corn, beans, squash, and after French contact, peas were planted. These crops, however, provided only a minimal amount of food requirements.

The Algonkin also shared a number of traits from contact with the Huron. Among these was the hemp net. With the hemp net, the Algonkin fished through holes in the ice in winter. Moreover, the Algonkin ate dogs on special occasions. They entertained guests in the Huron manner--*i.e.,* hosts served their guests, but did not themselves eat the food they had prepared. At council, tobacco was smoked before any discussion began. The graves of prominent persons were covered with painted wooden structures called grave houses. The largest of these were seven feet long and four feet wide. At one end a wooden figure was attached, representing the deceased.

Descriptions of 20th-century writers show that the Algonkin shared many traits identified with Algonquian-speaking peoples to the north. For

Algonkin Indians in aboriginal dress, from *Works of Samuel de Champlain*, edited by H. P. Biggar (1929).

example, in terms of cosmology and religion, the Algonkin believed in a supreme being who was owner of everything. In addition, their mythology tells of a trickster-transformer culture hero called Wiskedjak who spent his life going about wherever there were Indians. He teased and played tricks, but because he was so humorous, the Algonkin liked to have him around. Moreover, he had the power to make everything in nature respond to him. Another supernatural being was the Windigo, a man-eating creature who roamed through the woods, devouring all humans in sight. Not to be forgotten was Paguk, a skeleton who made great rattling and squeaking noises. His presence was an omen that some friend would become lost. Finally, there were the Pugwudgininiwug, a race of powerful little men.

All men, if they were to be successful hunters, needed a guardian spirit. These were obtained through the dream vision quest. The shaman, or religious practitioner, was simply a man who had more power than the ordinary hunter. This power, too, was obtained from one or more guardian spirits. Using the shaking tent, the shaman or conjuror, through clairvoyance, could determine such causes of illness as sorcery and taboo violation. He could also cure illnesses resulting from sorcery.

Practically all hunters knew some form of divination; some knew scrying and others knew scapulamancy. The latter is one ritual performed to discover where game was to be found or to identify the species of game. A charred shoulder blade or scapula is read like a map to direct the hunter where to hunt, or like a drawing to see what kind of animal he would get. In addition, a number of omens were recognized; a white animal was a sign of bad luck, while a dwarfed animal foretold misfortune.

Items of material culture made by the Algonkin, too, were common to much of the Subarctic: birchbark canoe, snowshoe, toboggan, rectangular bark hunting camp, birchbark container, clothing of deer and moosehide, and cradle board, to name a few.

Contemporary tribal situation The survivors of the Algonkin, all of whom have considerable white intermixture, either live on reserves mentioned above, have intermarried with whites and live largely off reserve, or have intermarried with other tribal groupings and live on reserves which are not considered Algonkin. These include: the Iroquois at Oka and Gibson; the Cree at Manowan, Weymontachie, Obedjiwan, and Abitibi; the Montagnais at Lake St. John; and the Ojibwa (Ottawa) on Georgian Bay and Lake Ontario. Depending upon location and resources available, the present-day Algonkin work as truck gardeners, hunters, guides, and trappers. Many Algonkin women have married white trappers, lumbermen, and pioneer farmers, both in the past and at present. Their descendants have assimilated with the whites who originally displaced and dispersed the Algonkin from their traditional hunting territories.

Population figures It is possible that at the time of first white contact, the Algonkin may have numbered between 3,000 and 4,000 persons. On January 1, 1970, the Algonkin bands in Quebec had the following populations: Argonaut, 2; Barrierre Lake 214; Grand Lake Victoria 192; Kipawa 111; Lake Smon 371; Long Point 269; River Desert 946; Timiskaming 384; and Wolfe Lake 58. In Onatrio the Gold Lake band had a population of 475. In addition there were approximately 2,500 persons of Algonkin descent distributed through the Ottawa Valley but unaffiliated with any band. The population of the Algonkin has shown a slight increase since 1900.

BIBLIOGRAPHY-
● BARAGA, REV. FREDERIC. A Dictionary of the Otchipwe Language, explained in English... (part II) This language is spoken by the Chippewa, Ottawa, Potawatomi and Algonkins. Cincinnati, OH: Printed for Jos. A. Hemann, Publisher of the Wahrheitsfreund, 1853.
● BLAIR, EMMA HELEN. The Indian Tribes of the Upper Mississippi Valley and Region of the Great Lakes, as described by Nicolas Perrot, French Commandant in the Northwest... Cleveland, OH: The Arthur H. Clark Co.
● CAMPBELL, T. J. Pioneer Priests of North America, 1642-1710. New York, NY: The America Press, 1908-1911.
● HODGE, FREDERICK WEBB. Handbook of American Indians North of Mexico. Washington: Smithsonian Institution: BAE Bulletin No. 30: U.S. GPO, 1907.
● MURDOCK, GEORGE P. Ethnographic Bibliography of North America. New Haven, CT: Human Relations Area Files Press, 1975.
● PALMER, ROSE A. The North American Indian, An Account of the American Indians North of Mexico. New York, Smithsonian Institution Series, Inc., 1929.
● PARKMAN, FRANCIS. The Jesuits in North America in the Seventeenth Century, Boston, MA: Little, Brown & Co., 1867.
● POUND, ARTHUR. Johnson of the Mohawks. A Biography of Sir William Johnson, Irish Immigrant, Mohawk War Chief..., New York, NY: The Macmillan Co., 1930.
● SHEA, JOHN G. Catholic Missions among the Indian Tribes of the U.S. New York, NY: E. Dunigan & Bros., 1854.
● SWANTON, JOHN R. The Indian Tribes of North America. Smithsonian Institution: BAE Bulletin No. 145: U.S. GPO, 1952.
● TRIGGER, BRUCE G., AND STURTEVANT, WILLIAMS C. Handbook of North American Indians. vol. 15, Northeast. Washington D.C: Smithsonian Instution, 1978.
● VANDIVEER, CLARENCE A. The Fur-Trade and Early Western Exploration. Cleveland, OH: The Arthur H. Clark Co., 1929.
● VERWYST, P. CHRYSOSTOMUS. Life and Labors of Rt. Rev. Frederic Baraga, First Bishop of Marquett, MI... Milwaukee, WI: M. H. Wiltzuis & Co., 1900.
● WISSLER, CLARK. The American Indian, An Introduction to the Anthhropology of the New World. New York, NY: Douglas C. McMurtrie, 1917.
-----Indians of the U.S.: Four Centuries of Their History and Culture. New York, NY: Doubleday, Doran & Co., 1940.
● WITTHOFT, JOHN. Green Corn Ceremonialism In The Eastern Woodlands. Ann Arbor, MI: University of Michigan Press, 1949.
● YOUNG, EGERTON R. Algonkin Indian Tales. New York, NY: Fleming H. Rovell Co.

ALGONQUIAN FAMILY

(U.S.; Canada, Colo. to Newfoundland) Adapted from the name of the Algonkin tribe, this linguistic stock formerly occupied a more extended area than any other in North America. Their territory reached from the east shore of Newfoundland to the Rocky Mts. and from Churchill River to Pamlico sd. The east parts of this territory were separated by an area occupied by Iroquoian tribes. On the east, Algonquian tribes skirted the Atlantic coast from Newfoundland to Neuse River; on the south, they touched on the territories of the eastern Siouan, southern Iroquoian, and the Muskhogean families; on the west, they bordered on the Siouan area; on the N.W. on the Kitunahan and Athapascan; in Labrador, they came into contact with the Eskimo; in Newfoundland, they surrounded three sides of the Beothuk. The Cheyenne and Arapaho moved from the main body and drifted out into the Plains. Although there is a general agreement as to the peoples which should be included in this family, information in regard to the numerous dialects is too limited to justify an attempt to give a strict linguistic classification; the data are, in fact, so meager in many instances as to leave it doubtful whether certain bodies were confederacies, tribes, bands, or clans, especially bodies which have become extinct or can not be identified. Early writers have frequently designated settlements or bands of the same tribe as distinct tribes. As in the case of all Native Americans, travelers observing part of a tribe settled at one place and part at another have frequently taken them for different peoples, and have signified single villages, settlements, or bands with the title "tribe" or "nation," named from the locality or the chief. It is generally impossible to discriminate between tribes and villages throughout the greater part of New England and along the Atlantic coast, for the Indians there seem to have been grouped into small communities, each taking its name from the principal village of the group or from a neighboring stream or other natural feature.   In many instances, it is impossible to determine whether these groups were insubordinate to some real tribal authority or of equal rank and interdependent, although still allied. Since true tribal organization is found among the better known branches and can be traced in several instances in the eastern division, it is presumed that it was general. A geographic classification of the Algonquian tribes follows:

Western division, comprising three groups dwelling along the east slope of the Rocky Mts.: Blackfoot confederacy, composed of the Siksika, Kainah, and Piegan; Arapaho and Cheyenne.

Northern division, the most extensive one, stretching from the extreme N. W. of the Algonquian area to the extreme east, chiefly North of the St. Lawrence and the Great Lakes -- including several groups which, because of insufficient knowledge of their linguistic relations, can only partially be outlined: Chippewa group, embracing the Cree (?), Ottawa, Chippewa, and Missisauga; Algonkin group, comprising the Nipissing, Temiscaming, Abittibi, and Algonkin.

Northeastern division, embracing the tribes inhabiting East Quebec, the Maritime Provinces, and East Maine: the Montagnais group, composed of the Nascapee, Montagnais, Mistassin, Bersiamite, and Papinachois; Abnaki group, comprising the Micmac, Malecite, Passamaquoddy, Arosaguntacook, Sokoki, Penobscot, And Norridgewock.

Central division, including groups that resided in Wisconsin, Illinois, Indiana, Michigan, and Ohio: Menominee; the Sauk group, including the Sauk, Fox, and Kickapoo; Mascouten; Potawatomi; Illinois branch of the Miami group, comprising the Peoria, Kaskaskia, Cahokia, Tamaroa, and Michigamea; Miami branch, composed of the Miami, Piankashaw, and Wea.

Eastern division, embracing all the Algonquian tribes that lived along the Atlantic coast south of the Abnaki and including several confederacies and groups as the Pennacook, Massachuset, Wampanoag, Narraganset, Nipmuc, Montauk, Mohegan, Mahican, Wappinger, Delawares, Shawnee, Nanticoke, Conoy, Powhatan, and Pamlico.

As the early settlements of the French, Dutch, and English were all within the territory of the eastern members of the family, they were the first aborigines north of the Gulf of Mexico to feel the blighting effect of contact with a superior race. As a rule, the relations of the French with the Algonquian tribes were friendly, the Foxes being the only tribe against whom they waged war. The English settlements were often engaged in border wars with their Algonquian neighbors, who continually pressed farther toward the interior by the advancing white immigration and, for a time, kept up a futile struggle for the possession of their territory. The eastern tribes, from Maine to Carolina, were defeated and their tribal organization broken up. Some withdrew to Canada, others crossed the mountains into the Ohio valley, while a few bands located on reservations by the whites, only to dwindle and ultimately become extinct. Of many of the smaller tribes of New England, Virginia, and other eastern states, there are no living representatives. Even the languages of some are known only by a few words mentioned by early historians, while some tribes are known only by name. The Abnaki and others who fled into Canada settled along the St. Lawrence under the protection of the French, whose active allies they became in all subsequent wars with the English down to the fall of the French power in Canada. Those who crossed the Allegheny Mts. into the Ohio valley, together with the Wyandot and the native Algonquian tribes of that region, formed themselves into a loose confederacy, allied first with the French, and afterward with the English, against advancing settlements, and with the declared purpose of preserving the Ohio River as the Indian boundary. Wayne's victory in 1794 put an end to the struggle, and at the treaty of Greenville in 1795, the Indians acknowledged their defeat and made the first cession of land west of the Ohio. Tecumseh and his brother, Ellskwatawa, instigated by British intriguers, again aroused the western tribes against the U.S. a few years later, but the disastrous defeat at Tippecanoe in 1811 and the death of their leader broke the spirit of the Indians. In 1815 those who had taken part against the U.S. during the War of 1812 made peace with the Government; then began the series of treaties by which, within thirty years, most of the Indians of this region ceded their lands and removed west of the Mississippi.

A factor which contributed greatly to the decline of the Algonquian ascendency was the power of the Iroquoian confederacy which, by the beginning of the 17th century, had developed a power destined to make them the scourge of the other Indian populations from the Atlantic to the Mississippi and from Ottawa River in Canada to the Tennessee. After destroying the Huron and the Erie, they turned their power chiefly against the Algonquian tribes, and before long, Ohio and Indiana were nearly deserted, with only a few villages of Miami remaining here and there in the northern portion. The Algonquian tribes fled before them to the region of the upper lakes and the banks of the Mississippi, and only when the French had guaranteed them protection against their deadly foes did they venture to turn back toward the east.

The central Algonquians are tall, averaging about 173 cm.; they have the typical Native American nose, heavy and prominent, somewhat hooked in men, flatter in women; their cheek bones are heavy; the head among the tribes of the Great Lakes is very large and almost brachycephalic, but showing considerable variation; the face is very large. The Atlantic coast Algonquians can hardly be determined from living individuals, as no full-bloods survive, but skulls found in old burial grounds show that they were tall, their faces not quite so broad, the heads much more elongated and remarkably high, resembling in this present the Inuit, and suggesting the possibility that along the New England coast, there may have been some mixture with that type. The Cheyenne and Arapaho are even taller than the central Algonquians; their faces are larger, their heads more elongated. It is worth noting that in the region in which the mounqd builders' remains are found, rounded heads prevailed, and in 1905 the population of the region were also more round-headed, perhaps suggesting fusion of blood.

Religion. Religious beliefs of the eastern Algonquian tribes were similiar in their leading feaures. Their myths are numerous. Their deities, or *manitus,* including objects animate and inani-

mate, were many, but the chief culture hero -- he to whom the creation and control of the world were ascribed --was substantially the same in character, although known by various namesamong different tribes. As Manibozho, or Michabo, among the Chippewa and other lake tribes, he was usually identified as a fabulous great rabbit, bearing some relation to the sun. This identification with the great rabbit appears to have prevailed among other tribes, being found as far south as Maryland. Brinton (Hero Myths, 1882) believes this mythological animal to have been merely a symbol of light, adopted because of the similarity between the Algonquian words for rabbit and light. Among the Siksika, this chief beneficient deity was known as Napiw, among the Abnaki as Ketchiniwesk, among the New England tribes as Kiehtan, Woonand, Cautantowit, etc. It was he who created the world by magic power, peopled it with game and the other animals, taught his favorite people the arts of the chase, and gave them corn and beans. But this deity was distinguished more for his magical powers and his ability to overcome opposition by trickery, deception, and falsehood than for benevolent qualities.

The objects of nature were deities as well: the sun, the moon, fire, trees, lakes, and various animals. Respect was also paid to the four cardinal points. There was a general belief in a soul, shade, or immortal spiritual nature not only in man but in animals and all other things, and in a spiritual abode to which the soul went after the death of the body, in which the occupations and enjoyments were supposed to be similar to those of this life. Priests, or conjurers, called medicine men by the whites, played an important part in social, political, and religious systems. They were supposed to possess influence with spirits or other agencies, which they could bring to their aid in prying into the future, inflicting or curing disease, etc.

Descent. Among the tribes from south New England to Carolina, including especially the Mohegan, Delawares, the people of the Powhatan confederacy, and the Chippewa, descent was reckoned in the female line; among the Potawatomi, Abnaki, Blackfeet, and probably most of the northern tribes, in the male line. Within recent times, descent has been paternal the Menominee, Sauk and Fox, Illinois, Kickapoo, and Shawnee. Although it has been stated that descent was anciently maternal, there is not satisfactory proof of this. The Cree, Arapaho, and Cheyenne are without clans or gentes. The gens or clans were usually governed by a chief, who in some cases was installed by the heads of other clans or gentes. The tribe also had its chief, usu-

Religious dance of the Algonquian

ally selected from a particular clan or gens, though the manner of choosing a chief and the authority vested in him varied somewhat in the different tribes. There was the peace chief, whose authority was not absolute, and who had no part in the declaration of war or in carrying it on, the leader in the campaign being one who had acquired a right to the position by noted deeds and skill. In some tribes the title of chief was hereditary, and the distinction between a peace chief and a war chief was not observed. The chief's powers among some tribes, as the Miami, were greater than in others. The government was directed in weighty matters by a council, consisting of the chiefs of the clans or gentes of the tribe. It was by their authority that tribal war was undertaken, peace concluded, territory sold, etc.

Food The Algonquian tribes were mainly sedentary and agricultural, probably the only exceptions being those of the cold regions of Canada and the Siksika of the Plains. The Chippewa did not formerly cultivate the soil. Maize was the staple native food product, but the tribes of the region of the Great Lakes, particularly the Menominee, made extensive use of wild rice. The Powhatan tribes raised enough maize to supply not only their own wants, but those of the Virginia colonists for some years after the founding of Jamestown, and the New England colonists were more than once relieved from hunger by corn raised by the natives.

In 1792, Wayne's army found a continuous plantation along the entire length of the Maumee from Ft. Wayne to Lake Erie. Although depending chiefly on hunting and fishing for subsistence, the New England tribes cultivated large quantities of maize, beans, pumpkins, and tobacco. It is said they understood the advantage of fertilizing, using fish, shells, and ashes for this purpose. The tools they used in preparing the ground and in cultivation were usually wooden spades or hoes, the latter being made by fastening a shell, shoulder blade of an animal, or a tortoise shell to a stick handle.

It was from the Algonquian tribes that the whites first learned to make hominy, succotash, samp, maple sugar, johnnycake, etc. Gookin, in 1674, thus describes the method of preparing food among the Indians of Massachusetts: "Their food is generally boiled maize, or Indian corn,

The manner of their fishing, by John White

They make also a certain sort of meal of parched maize. This meal they call 'nokake.'"

Their pots were made of clay, somewhat egg-shaped; their dishes, spoons, and ladles of wood; their water pails of birch bark, doubled up so as to make them four-cornered, with a handle. They also had baskets of various sizes in which they placed their provisions; these were made of rushes, stalks, corn husks, grass, and bark, often ornamented with colored figures of animals. Mats woven of bark and rushes, dressed deer-skins, feather garments, and utensils of wood, stone, and horn are mentioned by explorers. Fish were taken with hooks, spears, and nets, in canoes and along the shore, on the sea and in the ponds and rivers. They captured without much trouble all the smaller kinds of fish, and, in their canoes, often dragged sturgeon with nets stoutly made of canada hemp (DeForst, Hist. Inds. Conn, 1853). Canoes used for fishing were of two kinds--one of birch bark, very light, but liable to overset; the other made from the trunk of a large tree.

Clothing. was composed chiefly of the skins of animals, tanned until soft and pliable, and sometimes ornamented with paint and beads made from shells. Occasionally they decked themselves with mantles made of feathers over-lapping each other as on the back of the fowl. The dress of the women consisted usually of two arti-cles, a leather shirt, or undergarment, ornamented with fringe, and a skirt of the same material fastened round the waist with a belt and reaching nearly to the feet; moccasins were of soft dressed leather, often embroidered with wampum. The men usually covered the lower part of the body with a breech- cloth, and often wore a skin mantle thrown over one shoulder. The women dressed their hair in a thick, heavy plait which fell down the neck, and sometimes ornamented their heads with bands decorated with wampum or with a small cap. Higginson (New England's Plantation, 1629) says: "Their hair is usually cut before, leaving one lock longer than the rest." The men went bareheaded, with their hair fantas-tically trimmed, each according to his own fancy. One would shave it on one side and leave it long on the other; another left an unshaved strip, 2 or 3 inches wide, running from the forehead to the nape of the neck.

Housing. The typical Algonquian lodge of the woods and lakes was oval, and the conical lodge, made of sheets of birch-bark, also occurred. The Mohegan, and to some extent the Virginia Indi-ans, constructed long communal houses which ac-commodated a number of families. The dwellings in the north were sometimes built of logs, while those in the south and parts of the west were con-

mixed with kidney beans, or sometimes without. Also, they frequently boil in this pottage fish and flesh of all sorts, either new taken or dried, as shad, eels, alewives, or a kind of herring, or any other sort of fish. But they dry mostly those sorts before mentioned. These they cut in pieces, bones and all, and boil them in the aforesaid pot-tage. I have wondered many times that they were not in danger of being choked with fish bones; but they are so dexterous in separating the bones from the fish in their eating thereof that they are in o hazard. Also, they boil in this frumenty all sorts of flesh they take in hunting, as venison, beaver, bear's flesh, moose, otters, raccoons, etc., cutting this flesh in small pieces and boiling it as aforesaid. Also, they mix with the said pot-tage several sorts of roots, as Jerusalem arti-chokes, and groundnuts, and other roots, and pompions, and squashes, and also several sorts of nuts or masts, as oak acorns, chestnuts, and wal-nuts; these husked and dried and powdered, they thicken their pottage therewith. Also, sometimes, they beat their maize into meal and sift it through a basket made for that purpose. With this meal they make bread, baking it in the ashes, covering the dough with leaves. Sometimes they make of their meal a small sort of cakes and boil them.

structed of saplings fixed in the ground, bent over at the top, and covered with movable matting, thus forming a long round-roofed house. The Delawares and some other eastern tribes, preferring to live separately, built smaller dwellings. The manner of construction among the Delawares is thus described by Zeisberger: "They peel trees, abounding with sap, such as lime trees, etc., then cutting the bark into pieces of 2 or 3 yards in length, they lay heavy stones upon them, that they may become flat and even drying. The frame of the hut is made by driving poles into the ground and strengthening them by cross beams. This framework is covered, both within and without, with the above- mentioned pieces of bark, fastened very tight with bast or twigs of hickory, which are remarkably tough. The roof runs up to a ridge, and is covered in the same manner. These huts have one opening in the roof to let out the smoke and one in the side for an entrance. The door is made of a large piece of bark without either bolt or lock, a stick leaning against the outside being a sign that nobody is at home. The light enters by small openings furnished with sliding shutters." The covering was sometimes rushes or long reed grass. The houses of the Illinois are described by Hennepin as being "made like long arbors" and covered with double mats of flat flags. Those of the Chippewa and the Plains tribes were circular or conical, a framework covered with bark among the former, a frame of movable poles covered with dressed skins among the latter. The villages, especially along the Atlantic coast, were frequently surrounded with stockades of tall, stout stakes firmly set in the ground. A number of the western

The town of Pomeioc

Algonquian towns are described by early explorers as fortified or as surrounded with stockades of tall, stout stakes firmly set in the ground. A number of the western Algonquian towns are described by early explorers as fortified or as surrounded with palisades.

In no other tribes north of Mexico was picture writing developed to the advanced stage that it reached among the Delawares and the Chippewa. The figures were scratched or painted on pieces of bark or on slabs of wood. Some of the tribes, especially the Ottawa, were great traders, acting as chief middlemen between the more distant Indians and the early French settlements. Some of the interior tribes of Illinois and Wisconsin made but little use of the canoe, traveling almost always afoot; while others who lived along the upper lakes and the Atlantic coast were expert canoemen. The canoes of the upper lakes were of birch-bark, strengthened on the inside with ribs or knees. The more solid and substantial boat of Virginia and the western rivers was the dugout, made from the trunk of a large tree. The manufacture of pottery, though the product was small, except in one or two tribes, was widespread. Judging by the number of vessels found in the graves of the regions occupied by the Shawnee, this tribe carried on the manufacture to a greater extent than any other.

Mortuary Customs. The usual method of burial was in graves, each clan or gens having its own cemetery. The mortuary ceremonies among the eastern and central tribes were substantially as described by Zeisberger. Immediately after death the corpse was arrayed in the deceased's best clothing and decked with the chief ornaments worn in life, sometimes having the face and shirt painted red, then laid on a mat or skin in the middle of the hut; weapons and other personal effects were placed about it. After sunset, and also before daybreak, the female relations and friends assembled around the body to mourn over it. The grave was dug generally by old women; inside it was lined with bark, and, when the corpse was placed in it, four sticks were laid across, and a covering of bark placed over these; then the grave was filled with earth.

An earlier custom was to place in the grave the personal effects or those indicative of the character and occupation of the deceased, as well as food, cooking utensils, etc. Usually the body was placed horizontally, although among some of the western tribes, as the Foxes, it was sometimes buried in a sitting posture. It was the custom of probably most of the tribes to light fires on the grave for four nights after burial. The Illinois, Chippewa, and some of the extreme western tribes frequently practiced tree or scaffold burial. The bodies of the chiefs of the Powhatan confederacy were stripped of the flesh and the skeletons were placed on scaffolds in a charnel house. The Ottawa usually placed the body for a short time on a scaffold near the grave previous to burial. The Shawnee, and possbily one or more of the southern Illinois tribes, were accustomed to burying their dead in box-shaped sepulchers made of undressed stone slabs. The Nanticoke, and some of the western tribes, after temporary burial in the ground or exposure on scaffolds, removed the flesh and reinterred the skeletons.

The eastern Algonquian tribes probably equaled the Iroquois in bravery, intelligence, and physical powers, but lacked their constancy, solidity of character, and capability of organization, and do not appear to have appreciated the power and influence they might have wielded by combination. The alliances between tribes were generally temporary and without real cohesion. There seems, indeed, to have been some element in their character which rendered them incapable of combining in large bodies, even against a common enemy. Some of their great chieftains, as

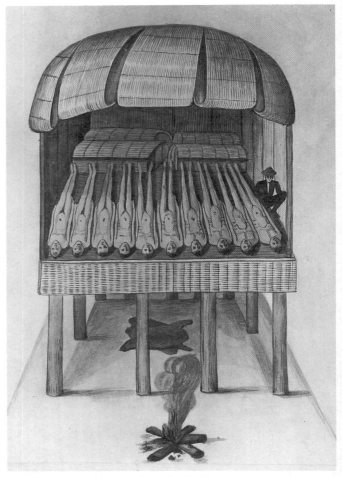

Algonquian burial house

Philip, Pontiac, and Tecumseh, attempted at different periods to unite the kindred tribes in an effort to resist the advance of the white race; but each in turn found that a single great defeat disheartened his followers and rendered all his efforts fruitless, and the former two fell by the hands of deserters from their own ranks.

The Virginia tribes, under the able guidance of Powhatan and Opechancanough, formed an exception to the general rule. They presented a united front to the whites, and resisted for years every step of their advance until the Indians were practically exterminated. From the close of the Revolution to the treaty of Greenville (1795), the tribes of the Ohio valley also made a desperate stand against the Americans, but in this they had the encouragement, if not the more active support, of the British in Canada as well as of other Indians. In individual character, many of the Algonquian chiefs rank high, and Tecumseh stands out prominently as one of the noblest figures in Indian history.

ALLIKLIK

(U.S., Calif.) The Alliklik belonged to the California group of the Shoshonean division of the Uto-Aztecan linguistic stock, their closest relatives probably being the Serrano. They were located on the upper Santa Clara River. Some of their villages included Akavavi Kashtu, Kamulus, and Etseng. The Alliklik, together with the Serrano, Vanyume, and Kitanemuk, numbered 3,500 in 1770 and 150 in 1910. In the census of 1930, 361 southern California Shoshoneans were counted. They numbered about 400 in recent times.

BIBLIOGRAPHY-

●SWANTON, JOHN R. The Indian Tribes of North America. Smithsonian Institution: BAE Bulletin No. 145: U.S. GPO, 1952.

ALSEA

(U.S.; Oreg.) were one of several northwest coast Indian tribes occupying the Oregon coast in the past 500 years; they are now virtually extinct. They held a rugged region of mountains, seashore, and estuary, which was dominated by the Pacific Ocean to the west and the coast range of mountains on the east. They lived in a land that yielded an abundance of fish, game and plant foods.

Name, territory, and language. The origin of the name Alsea is unclear and its meaning is unknown. Clatsop Indian informants told Lewis and Clark in 1805-06 that the Indians of Oregon's central coast were the Ulseah. John McLoughlin of the Hudson's Bay Company noted a river in their homeland as the Alique in a letter in 1828.

In 1835 Michel La Frambose, a fur trapper, referred to them as the Aleya. Duflot de Mofras listed these people in 1841 as the Alsiias. After linguistic work with them in 1900, Livingston Farrant asserted that their name was the corruption of Alsi, their aboriginal name.

The Alsea are classed in the Northwest Coast culture area. Although they lacked some of the refinements and artistry of the tribes farther north, they used plank houses and dugout canoes, valued wealth, held slaves, and followed basic culture patterns of north Pacific peoples. Like the Indians on the Columbia River Estuary, the Alsea practiced head deformation. Philip Drucker, who worked with two of the last linguistic informants of the tribe, concluded: "The picture is one of a small nation dwelling in an isolated spot along the coast--an eddy in the swirling current of North Pacific culture."

The Alsea are frequently listed with the Yaquina, the tribe occupying the coastline and estuary to the north. These two groups shared a common culture, mythology, and geographical setting. Their language possessed minor dialectic differences. Fur trappers, however, distinguished between them. Lewis and Clark noted the Yorickone north of the Alsea. LaFramboise called them the Tacoon. After working with both groups in the 1880s, the linguist J. Owen Dorsey differentiated between them.

The Alsea territory included the entire watershed of the Alsea and Yachats rivers and reached from the crest of the Coast Range to the Pacific. The tibe held the coastline south of ten Mile Creek below Cape Perpetua and north to the vicinity of Seal Rock. This region was made part of the Siletz Reservation in 1856. From 1859 to 1875 the Alsea, who then lived mostly along the shores of Alsea Bay, were under the Alsea subagency with headquarters at Yachats Prairie. All of these lands were opened to white settlement in 1875 by executive order. Some Alsea survivors relocated on the greatly reduced Siletz Reservation to the north.

The Alsea belonged to the Yakonan language family. It includes the Yaquina, Siuslaw, Lower Umpqua, and the yet more distantly related Miluk Coos and Hanis Coos of the south coast of Oregon. North of the Alsea resided the Siletz and Tillamooks, who were Salishan-speakers. The distribution of the Yakonan-speakers along so large part of the shore and their hold on key village sites suggests their early presence in the region. The prehistory of these people is largely unknown, for there has been only one partial scientific excavation in their homeland.

Tribal culture. Fishing, especially for salmon, was the principal subsistence activity of the

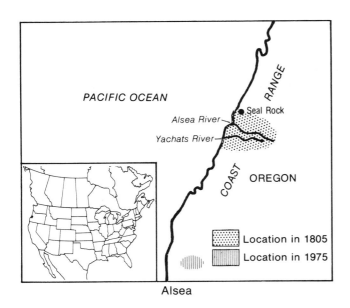

Alsea

Alsea. Three different runs of salmon from summer to late fall enabled the Alsea to secure sufficient supplies for year-round needs. They supplemented their diet with flounder, eel, trout, and smelt. The Alsea were exclusively estuary fishermen and did not fish in the sea. They employed salmon harpoons with detachable heads of barbed bone or horn. They constructed cylindrical traps, conical sack dip nets, and clubbing platforms for use on the pole wires that they built into the estuary.

Hunting and gathering were secondary activities that added variety to their diet. Some Alsea men perhaps never hunted; others sought elk, deer, and smaller game. They frequently took the larger mammals in pitfalls. They speared or shot beaver, caught quail and grouse in traps, and shot ducks and geese. Although the ethnographic literature is silent on their hunting of marine mammals, archaeological excavations by Oregon State University at Seal Rock in 1972 and 1974 uncovered large amounts of sea lion and seal remains in a village midden.

Gathering was largely, if not exclusively, women's work. They took crabs, clams, cockles, snails, piddocks, and other marine crustaceans and mollusks. They picked berries and gathered acorns in the Coast Range. The acorns were mixed with salmon eggs to make a bitter food. They dug the roots of ferns and skunk cabbage. Women were also the principal preparers and preservers of food. They cooked some fish and game over the coals of the fire, boiled some in wooden troughs or boxes, and prepared great amounts of foods in earthen ovens for celebrations. They dried or smoked much of the fish the men took from the bay and rivers.

The Alsea lived in semi-subterranean plank houses that they dug four or five feet into the earth, lined with cedar boards, framed with poles, and covered with cedar planks supporting a gabled roof of overlapping boards. Their sleeping platforms ran around the walls, while a cooking area, two or three feet below, filled the center of the house. The women covered the earth floors with tule mats and baskets of household goods. Although two or three families might share the same house, there were no partitions. These people erected temporary matshelters at fishing camps, and possessed two types of simple sweathouses.

Because their homeland was heavily forested, the Alsea preferred water travel. They favored the Chinook dugout canoe which they obtained by trade. They made a smaller canoe with uniform bow and stern, thwarts, and vine maple gunwales to withstand constant paddling. Even in this arduous labor, the Alsea made little use of stone. Their adzes and chisels were usually of bone or yew wood. They made their bows of yew and backed them with sinew.

Both men and women wore fringed skirts of bark or grass before white contact. Most Alsea donned rain capes in the winter, though the men often went naked in mild weather. Women plaited their hair in two braids; the men wore theirs in one. Both sexes decorated their bodies with red paint and ornaments, especially dentalia shells, which the men sometimes wore in their ears and nose.

The Alsea valued wealth and accorded social distinction by a man's holdings of dentalia, clamshell beads, other pelts, or slaves. Riches, however, meant little difference in general living conditions. Almost all shared the same foods and life. Elders arranged marriages and concluded these arrangements by purchase of the bride. Residence was patrilocal. Conflicts in Alsea society were technically to end with payment of goods. Feuds festered in spite of "blood money", and were often renewed by allegations of the evil work of a shaman.

Shamanism was the main religious and ceremonial activity of the Alsea. Novices gained their powers on spirit quests and through dreaming. The labors of the shaman for curing, perhaps their most common assignment, involved singing, dancing, sleight of hand, and sucking. Observers sometimes pounded a pole on the roof boards as accompaniment. The Alsea also had bone whistles, wooden flutes, and wooden disk buzzers to play on these occasions. The shaman might sing and dance to bring in the salmon run, ritually bathe mourners after a burial, or assist in divining the future.

The life cycle of the Alsea included a feast at age five days, the piercing of the nose and ears in infancy, the bestowing of a name, a strict taboo in "first fruits," and puberty observances. Some boys went on spirit quests at puberty. All girls had a special five-day confinement at the time of the first menstruation. That event was not thereafter viewed as critical. Alsea women were not secluded each month, but did forgo heavy labor. At death, these people dressed the body in its finest clothing, bound it in mats and placed it in a canoe near the village.

Tribal history. The treacherous bar of the Alsea River precluded close examination of these people's lands by maritime explorers. Whites first entered the domain of the Alsea in the late 1820s, when Hudson's Bay Company fur trappers spied out the region. They found few furs and generally avoided the area for the next two decades. In the early 1850s, pioneers from the Willamette Valley settled on the headwaters of the Alsea River. Nathan Scholfield hiked up the coast to the Yachats River in the summer of 1854 and made brief notes on the Indians. The Alsea ceded their lands in a treaty in the summer of 1855; that treaty was never ratified. Executive orders nevertheless placed their lands in the Siletz Reservation from 1856 to 1875.

The Alsea remained peaceful in spite of white incursions in their property. They, however, protested the government decision of 1875 to throw open the region to whites. William, one of their chiefs, said that spring: "This is our land. We live on our own land. Our children live there...Never have we done wrong to the whites. Never have we killed a white man. Why do the whites have sick hearts for our land?" The Alsea were shoved aside. Some of them removed to the Siletz Reservation and, under the allotment agreement of 1892, filed on properties. There they labored as farmers or worked as fishermen and loggers. Some of the Alsea descendants were plaintiffs in the case *Alsea Band of Tillamooks et al. v. The United States.* Although Congress had recognized their land claims in 1888 and 1893, the U.S. Court of Claims did not act until 1945. The Alsea and other bands of the north- central Oregon coast were awarded $1.3 million for 1.1 million acres. In 1951, the U.S. Supreme Court disallowed any interest on this sum, which had been fixed at estimated 1855 land prices. Congress terminated the Alsea in 1956.

Population figures for the tribe are sketchy. Lewis and Clark estimated 150 people in 1805. The 1864 census of the Alsea subagency enumerated 150 Alsea. In 1910 the census found 29, though in 1913 the linguist Leo J.

Frachtenberg located only 5 Alsea on the Siletz Reservation. It is likely that Alsea descendants were enumerated under other designations through intermarriage with whites and other tribes on the Siletz Reservation.

The Alsea were a small tribe occupying a strikingly beautiful land. Their myth tales, revolving around Suku, Black Bear, Beaver, and other cultural figures, taught the young the values of the tribe and entertained those weary of the long winters. For centuries they lived in the remote foothills of Oregon's Coast Range. The sea gave them the salmon, the rain, and the winds.

BIBLIOGRAPHY-

● BANCROFT, HUBERT HOWE. The Native Races of the Pacific States of North America. San Francisco, CA: (Vol. 1, Wild Tribes), 1874.
● DRUCKER, PHILIP. "Contributions to Alsea Ethnography." University of California Publications in American Archaeology and Ethnology. vol. 35, 1939.
● HODGE, FREDERICK WEBB. Handbook of American Indians North of Mexico. Washington: Smithsonian Institution: BAE Bulletin No. 30: U.S. GPO, 1907.
● ROYCE, CHARLES C. Indian Land Cessions in the U.S. Washington, DC: 18th Annual Report, Bureau of Ethnology, 1896- 97.
● SWANTON, JOHN R. The Indian Tribes of North America. Smithsonian Institution: BAE Bulletin No. 145: U.S. GPO, 1952.

AMAHAMI

(U.S.; Mo.) A former distinct Siouan tribe, long since incorporated with the Hidatsa; q.v. also the name of their village. Along with the Hidatsa, they claimed to have formerly constituted one tribe with the Crows. Their language, however, indicated closest affinity with the Hidatsa, differing but slightly from it, although they occupied a separate village and long maintained separate tribal organization. They were recognized as a distinct tribe by Lewis and Clark in 1804, but had practically lost their identity 30 years later. In Lewis and Clark's time, their village was at the mouth of Knife River, North Dakota, and was one of three, the other two being Hidatsa, which for many years stood on the banks of that stream. Their strength was estimated at 50 warriors. After the epidemic of 1837, all or the greater part of the survivors joined the Hidatsa and were merged with that tribe. Lewis and Clark state that they had been a numerous and prosperous agricultural tribe which once divided the upper Missouri valley, West of the Dakota group, with the Arikara, Mandan, and Hidatsa, the remains of the old towns of these four tribes being visible on every prairie terrace along the river for 600 miles. The remnants of all four were found by Matthews (Ethnog. Hidatsa, 13, 1877) at Fort Berthold, numbering fewer than 2,500.

BIBLIOGRAPHY-

● HODGE, FREDERICK WEBB. Handbook of American Indians North of Mexico. Washington: Smithsonian Institution: BAE Bulletin No. 30: U.S. GPO, 1907.
● SWANTON, JOHN R. The Indian Tribes of North America. Smithsonian Institution: BAE Bulletin No. 145: U.S. GPO, 1952.

AMAHUACA

(South America; Peru) is a panoan-speaking tribe of the Peruvian montana, living along the headwaters of the Ucayali, Juruna, and the Purus rivers in the Amazon Basin. Called *bipitineri* (a large but timid rodent) by the Piro Indians because of their passive nature, the Amahuaca are also known as the Amawaka, Ipitinere, and Sayaco. Their culture is decidedly panoan, with occasional indications of influence from the Arawakan Indians to the north.

History. Tribal tradition says that the first Amahuaca settlements were founded on the headwaters of the Purus river and later moved to the upper reaches of the Sepahua. When first encountered in 1686 by the Dominican priest Manuel Biedma, they were scatttered throughout the southern Amazon Basin in eastern Peru. During the late 19th century, slave raids carried out by the rubber barons forced the Amahuaca away from the Ucayali Basin into the Amazon forests, and by 1910 they were confined to the area between the headwaters of the Jurua River in the north and those of the Piedra River in the south. Until the 1950s, the Amahuaca continued to live as jungle nomads in autonomous groups of three or four families. In 1953, two missionaries, Robert L. Russell and Bryan Burtch, arrived in the Peruvian military garrison at Puesto Vardero and began the task of gathering the Amahuaca into a community. They succeeded to some degree, and by the mid 1960s, Varadero comprised the largest settlement of Amahuaca in Peru-- about 17 families.

Culture. As they did in the days when enemies, especially slavers, travelled by water, the Amahuaca live in open-ended huts built inland from nearby rivers. Directly behind the huts, land for a *chacra* (garden plot) is cleared. Sugarcane, sweet potatoes, squash, peanuts, cotton, watermelon, and corn (maize), one of the major staples, are grown. The other staple of Amahuaca life, cassava (manioc), is grown in a separate *chacra.* While these *chacras* are the sole responsibility of the women--the men only clear the land for planting--the men will often maintain another *chacra* for growing tobacco and arrowcane, used for making hunting arrows. A second set of *chacras,* for use during the rainy

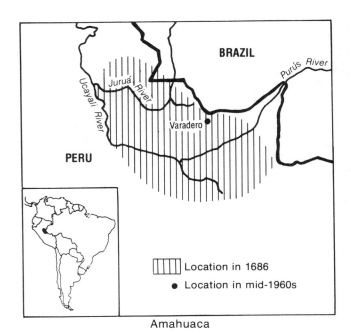

Amahuaca

season, is maintained some distance from the hut. Corn is stored in graneries built behind the huts.

Besides bearing the responsibility for agricultural production, women grind the corn (using a wooden mortar on a pestle made from a slab of rock), make clay pots, collect water and firewood, spin thread for weaving clothes and hammocks, cook, and rear the children. Men make arrows and hunt for fish and game. Like other Panoan Indians, the men may mimic an animal's sound in order to get within bow-and-arrow range. Childrens' games center around adult tasks: thus, a small boy makes a miniature bow and arrow to shoot bugs and leaves. Infantacide, especially of female children, is accepted.

Notable among the Amahuaca is a lack of both decorative art and ritual. Pots are not decorated, and arrows only slightly. Woven cloth used to make skirts for the women is plain, and the *tembetas* (lip ornaments, whose original purpose was probably to serve as an amulet) are made from tin. Personal decoration is limited to geometric designs made on the face and body with *achiote* (orange) or *huito* (black fruit dyes. Tattooing has all but disappeared. Only when a man is going to kill an enemy does he use the black dye over his entire body. Dancing and singing are spontaneous, not ritualisic. Musical instruments consist of a recorder, a bark trumpet, and a string bow that is strummed with a palm leaflet.

There are no birth, puberty, marriage, warfare, or hunting rites, no professional shamans, and no organized mythology. The creation myth, which exists in several versions, tells of the creation of the first Amahuaca couple, although not of the

Two Amahuaca of the Amazon River drainage area playing musical bows.

world. It includes stories of flood, fire, and earthquake, and of the culture hero Rantanga, who taught the survivors to hunt, to make bows, arrows, and axes, and to fish, make pots, and cultivate corn. He then died and went to heaven from where, when he clears his *chacra,* thunder is heard on earth.

Ceremonies are confined to harvest festivals, funerals, and gatherings at which *ayahuasca* (an hallucinogenic drug) is taken. Corn and banana festivals are celebrated irregularly; they tend to be directed toward the maturation of the children rather than the growth of the crops. Funerals center around the cremation of the dead. The dead person's ashes are mixed with corn soup and drunk by members of his family either to absorb the dead person's powers or to banish his spirit. The *ayahuasca* parties are restricted to men. After taking the drug, the men may spend several nights in succession singing and talking with *yoshi* (the souls of dead people, animals, and trees). *Yoshi* have an anthropomorphic nature and may be malevolent (like those of the anaconda, electric eel, carrion eagle, puma, ocelot, cayman, porpoise, or rattlesnake), friendly (like that of the king vulture), or simply mischievous (like that of a human being). Under the influence of *ayahuasca,* the men talk to the *yoshi,* who are made friendly by the presence of the drug, and occasionally ask for help in the healing of a sick person.

Neither Rantanga nor the *yoshi,* however, assume godlike qualities, and the belief in these supernatural beings is tempered by a pragmatic acceptance of day-to-day accidents and other misfortunes.

Future prospects. The attempts to civilize and, more than occasionally, to exploit the Amahuaca by missionaries and slave traders, from the 17th to the early 20th centuries, have given way to similar attempts by modern-day missionaries and entrepreneurs. Under the guise of "civilizing" the Amahuaca, missionaries prepare them for economic acculturation and assimilation, which has resulted in a loss of their Indian heritage and identity. Entrepreneurs, on the other hand, place the Amahuaca in the centuries-old patron-peon relationship, keeping them indebted and isolated. Of the original estimated 5,000 to 8,000 Amahuaca, 3,000 survived in 1927; 1,500 in 1940; and about 500 in 1970. Unless the economic and cultural identities of the Amahuaca are made compatible instead of mutually exclusive, they are not likely to survive the 20th century. *(see map page XVIII)*

BIBLIOGRAPHY-

● STEWARD, JULIAN H. Handbook of South American Indians. 7 Vols., Washington, DC: U.S. Govt. Printing Office, 1946-59.

AMANAYE

(South America; Brazil) are a Tupi-speaking tribe located between the present-day Brazilian cities of Belem (at the mouth of the Amazon River) and Brasilia, on the Pindare, Gurupi, Capim, and Moju rivers, and along the eastern bank of the Tocantins. Known as the Manaye or Amanyaye among themselves (possibly from the Guarani word meaning "an association of people"), they are also known as Manaye, Manazewa, Amanajo, Manajo, and Manaxo. In the only published description of them, Algot Lange refers to them as the Ararandeuraras.

Between 1755 and 1767, when they were expelled from South America, the Jesuits managed to establish *reducciones* (mission settlements where Christianity and economic self-sufficience were taught); there the Amanaye lived peacefully. During the next 100 years, references to members of the Amanaye group place them along the Tocantins, Moju, and Pindare rivers. No Amanaye settlement, however, was comprised of more than 60 people until 1872, when the Anauera Mission, with 200 Amanaye, was founded by Father Candido de Heremence. After killing Father Candido in 1873, the group fled to the Ararandeua River region, some of them adopting the river's name, others calling themselves Turiwa. In 1911, a group of 300 Amanaye were reported living on the Ararandeau River, and in 1913, Algot Lange visited a settlement of them on the Moju consisting of 26 houses.

Like other Tupi tribes, the Amanaye practice a slash-and-burn form of agriculture, cultivating cassava (manioc), cotton, and tobacco. The cotton is woven on simple wooden looms into skirts

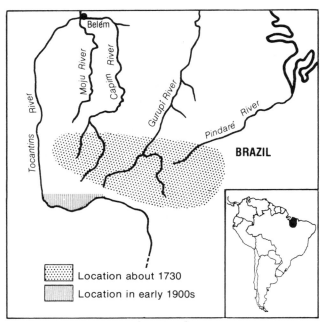

Amanayé

for the women and string belts for the men. The cassava is made into farina, the tribe's dietary staple. Tobacco is smoked by the men and is also used to cement friendly relations. Men use bows and arrows and stone axes to hunt. A nut placed under an arrowhead gives off a whistling noise as the arrow goes through the air. Canoes made of felled tree trunks are used for transportation, but no mention is made in the existing literature about the use of them for fishing. Decorative arts are apparently nonexistent. Mention is made in Lange's work of a clay cooking pot, but potting is carried on only for practical purposes.

Because of the scarcity of prolonged contact with the Amanaye, little is known of their social or political organization. It would appear that each settlement is autonomous, that intermarriage with other peoples is fairly common, and that no religious cults exist. Lange, however, does indicate that one man, acting as a shaman, held some influence over the tribe's actions as a whole. The only musical instrument known is a large drum.

One ritual--the ant ordeal--common to Tupi Indians, is carried out by the Amanaye. To prove their fortitude, a commodity deemed necessary for a successful marriage, young men endure the biting of captured and caged tocandeira ants for a specified period of time.

No accurate population figures are available for the Amanaye, but the acceptance of miscegenation would seem to indicate that their extinction as a distinct tribe is inevitable.

BIBLIOGRAPHY-

● STEWARD, JULIAN H. Handbook of South American Indians. 7 Vols., Washington, DC: U.S. Govt. Printing Office, 1946-59.

AMEDICHE

(U.S.; Tex.) A tribe, probably Caddoan, that lived about 68 leagues West of Natchitoches, in East Texas. La Harpe stated that in 1714-16 they were at war with the Natchityoches, and that the Spaniards had established a settlement among them a few years previously, but soon abandoned it.

BIBLIOGRAPHY-

● HODGE, FREDERICK WEBB. Handbook of American Indians North of Mexico. Washington: Smithsonian Institution: BAE Bulletin No. 30: U.S. GPO, 1907.
● SWANTON, JOHN R. The Indian Tribes of North America. Smithsonian Institution: BAE Bulletin No. 145: U.S. GPO, 1952.

AMIKWA

(U.S.; Wis.) An Algonquian tribe found by the French on the North shore of Lake Huron, opposite Manitoulin id., where they were located in the Jesuit Relations at various dates up to 1672. Bacqueville de la Potherie (Hist. Am. Sept., 1753) says that they and the Nipissing once inhabited the shores of Lake Nipissing, and that they rendered themselves masters of all the other nations in those quarters until disease made great havoc among them, and that Iroquois compelled the remainder of the tribe to betake themselves, some to the French settlements, others to Lake Superior and to Green Bay of Lake Michigan. In 1740, a remnant had retired to Manitoulin id. Chauvignerie, writing in 1736, says of the Nipissing: "The armorial bearings of this nation are, the heron for the Achague or Heron tribe, the beaver for the Amekoes, the birch for the Bark tribe." The reference may possibly be to a gens only of the Nipissing and not to the Amikwa tribe, yet the evidently close relation between the latter and the Nipissing justifies the belief that the writer alluded to the Amikwa as known to history. They claimed in 1673 to be allies of the Nipissing.

BIBLIOGRAPHY-

● HODGE, FREDERICK WEBB. Handbook of American Indians North of Mexico. Washington: Smithsonian Institution: BAE Bulletin No. 30: U.S. GPO, 1907.
● SWANTON, JOHN R. The Indian Tribes of North America. Smithsonian Institution: BAE Bulletin No. 145: U.S. GPO, 1952.

ANADARKO

(U.S.; Okla., Tex.) A tribe of the Caddo confederacy whose dialect was spoken by the Kadohada cho, Hainai, and Adai. The earliest mention of the people is related by Biedma (1544), who writes that Moscoso in 1542 led his men during their southward march through a province that lay east of the Anadarko. The territory occupied by the tribe was S. W. of the Kadohadacho. Their villages were scattered along Trinity and Brazos Rivers, Texas, higher up than those of the Hainai, and do not seem to have been visited so early as theirs by the French. A Spanish mission was established among the Anadarko early in the 18th century, but was soon abandoned. La Harpe reached an Anadarko village in 1719, and was kindly received. The people shared in the general friendliness for the French. During the contentions of the latter with the Spaniards, and later with the English throughout the 18th century, the Anadarko suffered greatly. They became embroiled in tribal wars; their villages were abandoned; and those who survived the havoc of war and the new diseases brought into the country by the white people were forced to seek shelter and safety with their kindred toward the N. E. In 1812 a village of 40 men and 200 souls was reported on Sabine River. The Anadarko lived in villages, having fixed habitations similar to those of the other tribes of the Caddo confederacy, to whom they were evidently also similar in customs, beliefs, and clan organization. Nothing is known definitely of the subdivisions of the tribe, but that such existed is probable from the fact that the people were scattered over a considerable territory and lived in a number of villages. They are now incorporated with the Caddo on the allotted Wichita reservation in Oklahoma. The town of Anadarko perpetuates the tribal name. They are living in a Federal trust area in west-central Oklahoma and numbered 1,207 in 1970.

BIBLIOGRAPHY-

● DEBO, ANGIE. The Road to Disappearance. Norman, OK: University of Oklahoma Press, 1941.
● FOREMAN, GRANT. Advancing the Frontier, 1830- 1860. Norman OK: University of Oklahoma Press, 1933.
-----Pioneer Days in the Early Southwest. Cleveland, OH: The Arthur H. Clark, Co., 1926.
● GRINNELL, GEORGE BIRD. The Fighting Cheyennes. New York, NY: Chas. Scribner's Sons, 1915.
● HARMON, DEWEY. Sixty Years of Indian Affairs, Political, Economic, and Diplomatic, 1789-1850. Chapel Hill, NC: University of North Carolina Press, 1941.
● HODGE, FREDERICK WEBB. Handbook of American Indians North of Mexico. Washington: Smithsonian Institution: BAE Bulletin No. 30: U.S. GPO, 1907. Washington, DC: 17th Annual Report, Bureau of American Ethnology, (Pt. 1, 1895-96) 1898.
● MURDOCK, GEORGE P. Ethnographic Bibliography of North America. New Haven, CT: Human Relations Area Files Press, 1975.
● RICHARDSON, RUPERT NORVAL. The Comanche Barrier to South Plains Settlement, A century and a half of savage resistance... Glendale, CA: The Arthur H. Clark, Co., 1933.
● SWANTON, JOHN R. The Indian Tribes of North America. Smithsonian Institution: BAE Bulletin No. 145: U.S. GPO, 1952.

ANDAQUI

(South America; Colombia) According to *Velasco*, the Andaqui left the headwaters of the Magdalena River in 1564 in their flight from the conquerors who had settled in Timana and, having traveled on the Fragua and Pescado Rivers, went eastward down the mountains to the jungle of the Caqueta River and broke up into several groups. Their numbers decreased gradually and, in 1851, only 630 survived, but their hostility to other tribes and to the whites had not abated. In this warlike attitude, they closely resemble the *Pijao*, and make the ethnographic details we possess very interesting. Some authors, beginning with Felipe Perez (1862), have maintained that the culture found archaeologically in San Agustin is attributable to the Andaqui, and that the stone statues found there were made by them. Archaeological excavations have proved, however, that subsequent to the period to which the statues belong, the territory was occupied by an altogether different people, who must have been the Andaqui.

Castellvi classifies the Andaqui linguistically in the *Chibcha-Aruacan* family, *Aruaco* subgroup. In the opinion of a historian (Garcia Borrero, 1935), the Andaqui had 27 communities, which, however, included the *Timana* and the Yalcon neither of which has yet been well identified.

The only known fact about Andaqui ethnology of the time of the Conquest is that they used very large spears, as reported by *Velasco*. Their culture was not described until 1854, when they still kept aloof from the Spanish culture and clung to their ancient customs.

They farmed and hunted. All the members of a group came together to plant both bitter and sweet manioc (cassava), yams, maize, and sugarcane. They ate fruits, especially pineapple and the custard apple, a certain worm, snails, ants, and a large wood borer (comejen grande), and drank chicha. They used a vegetable poison to hunt animals. The wooden spear was their favorite weapon.

The women raised wild animals and sold them for silver coins which they worked into triangular earrings.

In recent times the special industry has been the extraction of oil from the "milpesos" palm. Hunting and war are the principal occupations of the cacique, assisted by a deputy or second in command of a group. These rites are performed as follows (Albis, 1934):

In preparing for an attack on the Witoto, the deputy captain takes his men to hunt animals, while the women prepare chicha and "caguana." Upon their return, the hunters adorn themselves, dance, and drink chicha, and then go to their houses. The following day they catch "conga" ants, whose bite causes fever, and place them in a palm-leaf mat so that their heads stick out. The captain's wife picks up the mat and lets the ants bite her husband on his legs to make him strong, on his breast to make him brave, on his face to prevent him from sleeping, and on the chin to make him silent. The captains then make the ants bite the back and legs of the women, so that young *Witoto* prisoners will be diligent helpers. Afterward, the captains each eat three ants mixed with water. If they have pains, the hunt will be successful. After this, the captain, carrying a turtle shell, speaks to the women, admonishing and scolding them, and then retires to a separate house where he holds a conference with his men, forecasting the probable outcome of the fight and exhorting the men to avenge those who may be killed by the *Witoto*. That night they hold ritual dances and mimic animals. Two balsa-wood images are placed at the door of the main building and two Indians must pierce them with their spears while running. These two Indians are whipped after their feat by all those present. At dawn, they plant a pole in the middle of the yard or square, pour water around it, and dance there until they have made mud, and then spend the day gathering food for the departing warriors. In order to be strong and to capture many young *Witoto*, each warrior has to place an arm in a bag full of "yuco" ants until it is thoroughly bitten. Upon departing, the captain gives his wife a knotted hemp cord (a kind of quipu). She unties a knot every night and thus knows when to expect him back and on what day the fight will take place. The day of the battle, she remains in the hut where the hunters stayed the first day; otherwise they will be unable to capture any *Witoto* children. With other women, she waits there 3 days for the men to return. Then, after leaving there a *"araraita,"* a palm branch, the women return to their homes to prepare more chicha. If the expedition is successful, the men return with great demonstrations of joy. But if it fails, they hit everything and bemoan their luck. The captain's principal wife unbraids her husband. After a community meal, all go home and resume their occupations.

Menstruating women throughout this area remain in a special house weaving hemp. They may have no visitors. At the end of the period, they bathe and return to their dwellings.

At childbirth, a woman must remain at home three months, while her husband stays in his hammock, refraining from labor and dieting, lest his child die. After three months, the parents anoint themselves and child with "jagua" fruit and resume normal life.

BIBLIOGRAPHY-

● STEWARD, JULIAN H. Handbook of South American Indians. 7 Vols., Washington, DC: U.S. Govt. Printing Office, 1946-59.

ANGMAGSALINGMIUT

(Canada; Greenland) A tribe of Inuit on the east coast inhabiting the fiords of Angmagsalik, Sermilik, and Sermiligak. According to Rink, the total population was 413 in 1886. A Danish mission and commercial station on Angmagsalic fiord is the most northerly inhabited place on the East coast. Each Angmagsalingmiut village consists of a single house, which has room for 8 or 10 families. Holm (Ethnol. Skizz.af Anmagsalikerne,1887) names 8 villages on the fiord, with a total population of 225. Notwithstanding their isolation, the people, according to Nansen, are among the most vigorous of the Inuit.

BIBLIOGRAPHY-

● HODGE, FREDERICK WEBB. Handbook of American Indians North of Mexico. Washington: Smithsonian Institution: BAE Bulletin No. 30: U.S. GPO, 1907. Smithsonian Institution: BAE Bulletin No. 145: U.S. GPO, 1952.

AMEDICHE

(U.S.; Tex.) A tribe, probably Caddoan, that lived about 68 leagues west of Natchitoches, in east Texas. La Harpe stated that in 1714-16, they were at war with the Natchityoches, and that the Spaniards had established a settlement among them a few years previously, but soon abandoned it.

BIBLIOGRAPHY-

● HODGE, FREDERICK WEBB. Handbook of American Indians North of Mexico. Washington: Smithsonian Institution: BAE Bulletin No. 30: U.S. GPO, 1907. America. New Haven, CT: Human Relations Area Files Press, 1975.
● SWANTON, JOHN R. The Indian Tribes of North America. Smithsonian Institution: BAE Bulletin No. 145: U.S. GPO, 1952.

APACHE

(U.S.; Southwest.) Apache was the name applied to six culturally and linguistically related tribes of the North American Southwest, many of whom were fierce warriors and experts in desert survival. They raided surrounding Indian tribes and white settlers almost constantly for four centuries (the late 15th century to the late 19th century), often driven by economic necessity. Although now associated with territory in Arizona and New Mexico, the Apache homeland once extended north into Colorado and Kansas and south into Mexico. Information describing their tribal divisions and cultural similarities is frequently contradictory.

Name. The name Apache is derived from the Zuni word for "enemy" and was used by the Spaniards to denote the tribe. At first there was much confusion among the Europeans about who exactly were the Apache. and the name was applied to many non Apache people. The confusion arose because the Apache did not think of themselves as a single, unified tribe. and there was no word in their language to designate the entire tribe. They simply referred to themselves as "the people" in the dialect of their particular band, such as *ndee* (White Mountain), *nnee* (San Carlos) or *dine'* (Navajo).

Origins of the Apache. The Apache are the descendents of Athapascan-speaking peoples. It is not known exactly where those Athapascan-speaking people emigrated from originally or just when they first arrived in the Western Hemisphere, but they probably came from Asia by way of Siberia, across the Bering Strait, and into the New World more than 2,000 years ago. There is some evidence to show that most of these early Athapascan people moved south into what is now the state of Montana, then after a long period they divided into three major groups. One group, called the Northern Athapascans, moved back to the north into Canada and Alaska where their descendants still live today. Another group moved west to the northern Pacific coast of the United States. The third group, called the Southern Athapascan, moved far to the south to become the ancestors of the modern Apache and Navajo people.

The Southern Athapascans may have entered the southwestern United States a thousand years or more ago, probably having travelled down the eastern slopes of the Rocky Mountains. Along the way, some groups settled on the Great Plains, while others continued in a southerly direction into the Texas and New Mexico area as far south as northern Mexico. Other groups moved west into what is now Arizona. Although all of these groups shared a basic culture, they eventually developed into seven different divisions. These divisions were the six Apache tribes - the Kiowa Apache, the Lipan, the Jicarilla, the Mescalaro, the Chiricahua, and the Western Apache - and the Navajo.

Tribal divisions. The Jicarilla Apache lived in the northern region of New Mexico. The Lipan Apache. similar culturally to the Jicarilla, were more mobile: they first inhabited eastern New Mexico and western Texas, but were later forced southward into what is today Mexico by the Comanche. The Mescalero Apache lived in south-central New Mexico with territory extending into the Big Bend region of Texas and south into Mexico. The Chiricahua inhabited mainly the Chiricahua Mountains of southeastern Arizona, although their territory extended also into southwestern New Mexico and parts of Chihuahua, Mexico. The Western Apache lived in east-central Arizona.

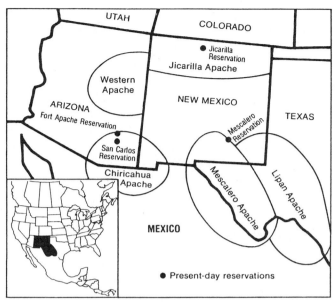

Apache

The Kiowa Apache and the Navajo are special cases. The Kiowa Apache lived in the region between the Platte River and the northern border of New Mexico. They were an Apache tribe only in language, their culture being nearly identical to that of the Kiowa, Plains tribe. The Navajo people settled over a large area where the four states of Arizona, Colorado, Utah, and New Mexico meet. Their culture change so much. especially after contact with Europeans in thought of as being closely related to the Apache, although their languages are still very similar.

It is impossible to say precisely when the Western Apache reached their present.home in what is now the east-central part of Arizona, but a study of the folk tales and legends of the Apache, Pueblo, and Pima peoples and examination of long abandoned prehistoric ruins provide reason to believe that they first settled in the Rio Grande Valley, moved sometime after 1200, and were living along the Little Colorado River and on the Mogollon Rim in Arizona in the 1300s and 1400s. Also, according to Western Apache clan legends, all but three clans came from the north to where they are now living. As the Western Apache moved gradually from the Rim area southward into east-central Arizona, they separated into five major groups according to geographic location. These five groups, allowing for some disagreement among sources, were the White Mountain, the Cibicue, the San Carlos, the Northern Tonto, and the Southern Tonto.

The remaining Apache tribes are sometimes referred to as the Eastern Apache. When they began occupying those territories previously mentioned as their traditional homes is not known. Some bands were living along the Dismal River in Kansas as late as 1700. As a result of the Apache Wars, that ended in 1886, many of the Eastern Apache were uprooted several times, and the territory of all the tribes was greatly reduced by the U.S. government.

Language. The traditional language of the six Apache tribes is Apachean, a branch of the Athapascan can language that linguistically links the Apache tribes to Athapascan-speaking Indians in Canada, Alaska, and along the Pacific coast. There are minor differences in the dialects spoken by the different Apache tribes.

Political and social organization. With the exception of the Kiowa Apache, who will not be further considered in this article, the Apache tribes were characterized by a number of social, political, and cultural similarities. Apache political organization was informal. From the bottom up, the units of Apache organization were the single family, extended family, group, band, and tribe. The Apache are gregarious people, and they dislike living alone or far removed from their relatives. Several single family units usually camped together, comprising an extended family, or "family cluster." Several related family clusters constituted a local group.

Apache woman, photographed c. 1905, holding a baby in a cradleboard. The elliptical frame is of bent wood and has transverse pine laths. The hood is of reeds, arched and tied, and is decorated with pendants of beads and shells.

Each family unit in a family cluster had its own dwelling, ate at its own fire, and owned its own tools and utensils, but the work, apart from the immediate household chores, was generally shared by all members of the extended family. The women went out in groups to gather food, wood, and water, and the men formed parties for raiding and hunting. Raiding parties were also formed by the group. The group was the largest political unit that had a definite leader, who was chosen by demonstrated abilities rather than heredity. When, rarely, all the groups belonging to a band assembled to mount a raid the most influential group leader took charge. There was a vaguely defined allegiance to the tribe, but no tribal organization.

Cultural patterns. The Apache tribes were also different in some respects. The differences developed from variations in their environments and contacts with other tribes. Some observers see a broad cultural division between the Western and the Eastern Apache based, it would appear on the amount of dependence on farming and on kinship systems. The Western Apache farmed most extensively, growing corn, beans, squash, and gourds to supply an estimated 20-25 percent of their food. Their language and culture were more heavily influenced by the Navajo than by the other tribes. Descent among the Western Apache was traced through the mother, and socially they were organized by clans which controlled areas of farm land and were the basis of war parties and some ceremonies. The Eastern Apache, on the other hand, were more influenced by the Plains culture than by the Navajo. They relied less on farming, purportedly traced descent through both father and mother, and did not have a clan system.

The simple picture presented by this broad division is, however, complicated by scattered similarities between Western and Eastern groups and by differences among the Eastern tribes. For example, both the Chiricahua (Eastern Apache) and the Western Apache lived in wickiups, domed shelters built with a framework of saplings covered with brush and bear grass. The Jicarilla, another Eastern tribe, engaged in farming practices similar to those of the Western Apache. Each of the Eastern tribes had its own cultural peculiarities. The Jicarilla Apache culture reflected a split influence-their buffalo hunting and tipis were similar to those of the Plains Indians, while their ceremonies and farming were similar to those of the Pueblo. The Chiricahua were perhaps the most nomadic Apache. The Lipan were apparently a branch of the Jicarilla but, like the Chiricahua, did little farming. The Mescalero lived mostly by hunting and gathering. Their chief staple food, for which they were named, was the mescal or agave, which they prepared by steaming on hot rocks for

Chiricahua wickiup at Fort Sill, Oklahoma, photographed in 1897.

a day or more in huge pits, the largest 20 feet across by 5 feet deep. The Mescalero had Plains elements in their culture and, like the Jicarilla, they lived in tipis.

Raiding and warfare. Raiding and warfare were important to most Apache groups. Young men were taught that aggressiveness, courage, and physical prowess were ideal traits. The Apache were expert in the military arts of camouflage and ambush, having the ability to hide themselves where there was little cover but clumps of dry grass. They could go for long periods of time without food or water, and they could read natural signs and trails that no other eye could see. After the horse became available, they used it to good advantage, both to extend their effective range and to befuddle pursuers.

The favorite weapons of the Apache were the bow and arrow, the lance, and the war club. They also used shields made from cowhide or horsehide. Bows were made of mulberry wood, arrows of cane and hardwood, and war clubs of rawhide sewn around a stone. The lance was often held under the arm, the shaft steadied in both hands. The Apache continued to use the bow and arrow for many years after the gun was introduced to the Southwest. Powder and lead for the guns were difficult to obtain, and bow and arrow could be fired much faster than most early rifles.

Crafts. The Apache did not make much pottery because clay utensils are heavy, fragile, and unsuited to nomadic life. The Apache were expert, however, in the dressing of buckskin and the making of baskets. Apache women made bowls, storage jars, burden baskets, and pitch-covered water jars from willow cottonwood, and sumac.

Shallow baskets, some with colorful, spiraling designs, were often used during ceremonies to hold corn pollen. Buckskin was fashioned into breechcloths, shirts, and the upper sections of moccasins, (the soles were made of elkhide).

In the mid-1970s, the old crafts were practiced in varying degrees. Basketmaking had already died out because metal and plastic containers were inexpensive and basketmaking for sale to tourists did not produce much income. The Western Apache still make a few burden baskets and waterjars, however, and the Jicarilla and Mescalero also produce a few baskets. Buckskin clothing is rare, but buckskin moccasins most of which are sewed with sinew in the traditional way are still produced.

Marriage and divorce. Traditional marriages among the Apache were accomplished through preliminary negotiations and an exchange of gifts. The bride and groom then moved in together without further ceremony. Divorce was obtainable by either partner through a simple and unmistakable ritual. The wife would place her husband's

White Mountain Apache, Coyotero band man and woman in heavily decorated clothing photographed prior to March 1888.

belongings outside the house while he was away, or the husband would leave to go hunting and not come back. An Apache man could marry several wives, although this practice was usually limited to the wealthy. Because the Apache couple lived in close contact with many relatives, there were elaborate rules governing kinship relationships. An Apache man, for example, could not talk to, look at, or be in the same room with his mother-in-law. It was permissible to marry sisters.

Religious life. Religion was an integral part of Apache life. In the Apache concept of the universe, the earth was female; her hair was the trees and plants, and her bones were the rocks and mountains. The sky was male, lying over the earth to shelter and protect her. The sun was also male and of great importance as the giver of life. The supreme deity, Usen, was considered to be a spirit without form and was often represented by the sun. White Painted Woman, known to the Navajo as Changing Woman, was the major Apache female deity and was represented by the moon. She had control over fertility and long life.

The four directions were prominent in all religious rituals, songs, prayers, and sand paintings. East and west were male, north and south female. The sacred colors were associated with the four directions; east was associated with black, south with blue, west with yellow, and north with white. East was the most holy and powerful of the four.

There were many lesser powers in the Apache concept of the universe, including the Water People and various animal and plant people. The Apache believed that power existed throughout the natural universe and that this power could be utilized by man. Anyone could pray, using traditional ritual or spontaneously, to any power. Some ceremonies were traditional and could not be changed or added to, while others developed as a result of direct, personal contact with the power. Knowledge of the traditional ceremonies was acquired through ceremonial payment to a person who possessed knowledge of that ceremony. Some of the minor ceremonies might last for only half an hour, while others could require a full four days and nights.

The shaman, or medicine man, who conducted the ceremonies knew all of the songs and prayers perfectly, and he possessed the necessary charms and ritual equipment to perform them properly. Such equipment may have included corn meal, pollen, eagle feathers, turquoise, black jet, and white shell. Most ceremonies were performed to bring rain and insure good crops, or to prevent or cure sickness. Although a ceremony might be conducted for a single individual, others present could also benefit from it. Except for certain protective ceremonies performed in the spring, when lightning and snakes and other poisonous creatures were prevalent, the Apache had no ceremonial calendar. Supernatural power could be used for evil purposes by witches, who were widely feared by the Apache.

Among the most important of the supernatural beings were the *ga'ns,* or mountain spirits. These were people who long ago had lived on earth and went away in search of eternal life, free from pain and sickness. They now live in certain sacred places in the mountains. The Apache called on the *ga'n* to help and protect them. Masked and painted dancers reresented the *ga'n* in various religious ceremonies, the best known of which is the girl's puberty ceremony, still frequently performed by the Western Apache.

Another important element in Apache religious life was the treatment of the dead. They were buried immediately, and their possessions were burned; the mourners then underwent elaborate purification rituals. These actions were all to protect the living from the ghosts of the dead.

Cultural changes. Several aspects of Apache culture changed over the years. The most important was probably the subsistence economy of the tribes. At first, all Apache were hunters and gatherers. Then farming and, after the availability of the horse, raiding contributed significantly to the subsistence of certain tribes. In the mid-1970s, farming, herding, wage employment, and tourism were all important elements in the Apache economy, although some food was still collected by hunting and gathering. The Apache political system had been completely revamped, largely under the stimulus of the Indian Reorganization Act of 1934. The Apache are no longer governed by local headmen but by democratically elected tribal councils. Education, clothing, and housing all show a great deal of acculturation to white society. Most houses, for example, are permanent, often constructed of brick or concrete block, and are furnished with electric appliances.

Other aspects of Apache culture are more of a blend between white and Indian. The Apache language is widely spoken along with English. Marriage and divorce are still often performed in the traditional manner, although they now require the additional legalization of the state. Medical healing is accomplished variously by Western medical practices and traditional ceremony. Christian churches have been added to the reservations, but a deep belief in the traditional spirits persists and is still expressed in religious ceremonies.

Apache history. The most popularized aspect of Apache tribal history has been the period of the Apache Wars, which lasted from about 1860 until 1886. During these wars, the Apache proved themselves the equal of any fighting force the U.S.

government could muster. Apache chiefs, among them Cochise, Mangas Coloradas, and Juh, came to the fore. as superb leaders and military tacticians. Thousands of men, women, and children lost their lives as a result of these wars. Material losses were enomrous. The end result of these wars was the confinement of the Apache tribes on reservations. For many Chiricahua, this final "freedom" begrudged to them by the government was preceded by years in federal prisons. But this popularized period of Apache history was preceded by hundreds of years of interaction with neighboring Indian tribes, the Spanish, the Mexicans, and then the Americans, and was followed by a much shorter but nonetheless significant period of acculturation which has brought the Apache to their present status.

The Pre-European Period. Knowledge of Apache history before the late 1500s is based mostly on archaeological and ethnologieal speculation. The Apache may have arrived in the Southwest as early as AD 1000. More definite evidence places them in Arizona, Colorado, and New Mexico by the end of the 1500s, when the Spanish began to move northward into the New Mexican region in increasing numbers. The Apache then, as throughout their history, were divided into a large number of small, independent bands. Some of these bands would be scattered or decimated by the wars with Indian, Spanish, and American adversaries that almost constantly troubled Apache history.

The Apache became great traders prior to the arrival of the Spanish. Favored trading partners were the Pueblo Indians, including the Taos, Tewa, and Zuni, with whom the Apache maintained peaceful relations, except when their economic interests clashed. The Apache also traded with tribes throughout the Rio Grande watershed, exchanging buffalo robes and other leather products from their territory in the southern Great Plains for turquoise, corn (maize), cotton, coral, and shells. Their implacable enemies were the Pawnee, a Plains tribe, and such Arizona tribes as the Pima and the Sobaipuri.

Early Spanish contact. Until the 1600s, the Apache had no real quarrel with the white man, and they saw the Spanish only infrequently. The first, apparently, to make contact with the Apache were Alvar Nunez Cabeza de Vaca and three companions, explorers who wandered through Apache territory in southern Texas in 1535 after escaping from tribes along the Texas coast. Later, Spanish explorers lured by the wealth of the fabled Seven Cities of Cibola penetrated Apache territory. They included Don Francisco Vaisquez de Coronado, who travelled all the way to present day Kansas in 1540-41, along the way meeting the Lipan and

other Plains Apache. A year earlier, Melchior Diaz had brought the first horses into Apache territory while on a reconnoitering expedition hands of the southernmost Apache tribes, and use of the horse was spreading northward to other groups. In the coming years, the horse would importantly extend the range of Apache raiders, making them more equal opponents to the Spanish.

By the end of the 1500s, incidents causing friction between the Apache and the Spanish had begun to accumulate. Lipan and Mescalero had probably come in contact with, if not been captured by, Spanish slaving parties sent north by Mexican mine owners; other Apache had been unwillingly pressed into service as guides; and the Spanish had disrupted some of the Apache trade connections, sometimes by wholesale slaughter like that of Acoma Pueblo in 1599. In 1598, New Mexico was made a Spanish colony and, during the next century under a succession of Spanish governors, Apache-Spanish relations deteriorated into outright war. In 1627, a party of Lipan Apache on a peaceful mission to Santa Fe were captured, and some were killed. Throughout New Mexico, the Apache refused conversion to Christianity, causing the Mexican governors to declare them "heathen enemies" who could legally be sold into slavery. Slave parties against the Apache were sent out by Gov. Luis de Rosas after 1639, and the policy was continued under later governors.

The attack on the peaceful Lipan and the slave raids incited the Apache tribes to widespread and unremitting raiding against Spanish settlements, both to protect themselves and to supplement their economy. By 1680, hatred between the Spanish and the Apache had become so fierce that the latter apparently helped plan and carry out the revolt of the Pueblo Indians, an uprising that may have left more than 400 Spanish dead in the initial attacks and caused the temporary abandonment of New Mexico by the Spanish. The successful Spanish attempt to retake the colony in the 1690s, in which they were aided by the Pima, Sobaipuri, and other tribes inimical to the Apache, left many Apache bands along the Mexican border decimated

18th century. During the 1700s, the war between the Spanish and the Apache continued. Its intensity was increased by an influx of Comanche, who came south into Apache territory from Wyoming to capture horses. These fierce warriors drove the Lipan and other Plains Apache south of their buffalo food source, and they were forced to depend increasingly upon raids against the Spanish in Mexico for food. The Comanche disruption of the Apache economy also contributed to dissension between Apache tribes and their former allies and, in some areas, Apache bands stepped up their raids against the Pueblo tribes. The Spanish took advantage of the intertribal warfare. By the late 1700s, they had enlisted the Comanche, Pueblo, and Ute as their allies against the Apache. Many Apache bands were destroyed or absorbed by neighboring bands in the ensuing wars. The Spanish poured more troops into New Mexico and lured some Apache bands into peace by supplying them with food and liquor. No single chief could bind all the Apache to peace. By the end of the 1700s, however, the Spanish tactic of subjugating individual Apache bands by subsidizing them, combined with the increase in troop strength of the Spanish and their Indian allies, brought a measure of quiet to the New Mexican colony.

The Mexican Period. Unfortunately, the quiet did not last long. In 1821, Mexico won its independence from Spain, and the uneasy peace that the Spanish authorities had finally established with the Apache broke down, in part because the subsidization was too costly. The Mexicans replaced it with a bounty system: for every Apache scalp - of man, woman, or child - the Mexicans paid the bearer cash. The old warfare broke out anew and soon became directed at Americans as well, some of whom decided to augment their hunting and trapping income with the scalp bounty. In one notorious incident that occurred in 1835 or 1836, an American trader, James Johnson, killed about 20 friendly Apache with a howitzer concealed beneath a pile of trade goods.

Contemporary Conditions. In the 1970s, the Apache tribes maintained strong ties to their past through language and religion, but in dress, schooling, economy, and political organization they were acculturated to the white way of life. Government was by democratically elected councils. All four reservations brought in money through a variety of tribal or privately owned businesses, ranging from timber and mineral industries to banks and motels. Many Apache wage earners were working both on and off reservations. Cattle herding was important among the Western Apache, and several Apache tribes earned money through tourism. Despite many successful economic ventures, however, a large percentage of the Apache were unemployed, ranging from a low of 40 percent on the San Carlos Reservation to a high of 69 percent on the Mescalero Reservation in 1969.

Apache population figures are inexact. Estimates place the Apache population m 1680 at 5,000, in 1903 at 6,000, and in the 1970s at between 11,000 and 15,000.

Despite their unemployment problems, the Apache have managed to establish thriving industries, accept a degree of white acculturation, and still hold on to essential aspects of their old

A painting of Cochise, hereditary chief of the Central Chiricahua band of the Apache.

culture, an important achievement in a period when knowledge of the old Indian ways has become a prized possession.

Apache Wars. The fierce 26-year (1860-86) culmination of the confrontation between the Apache Indian and U.S. and Mexican military forces, effectively ended the Indian resistance to the white mans' takeover in the Southwest.

The Apache-Navajo were an active, virile Athapascan people still in the aggressive stage of their evolution and scarcely settled in the arid Southwest when Europeans encountered and came to blows with them. Spanish-Apache hostilities commenced probably in the 17th century. Although initially the Apache were friendly with the U.S. Americans, warfare broke out almost inevitably, given the aggressive natures of both peoples; it arose first with scalp-hunter lawlessness and excesses. It became exacerbated during the U.S. Civil War (1861-65) by two unnecessary incidents, one involving Cochise, hereditary chief of the Central Chiricahua, the other involving Mangas, Coloradas, the greatest Apache leader of record and chief of the Chiricahua. As U.S. military forces occaisionally chased the Apache into Mexico, so Mexican units sometimes penetrated into the United State - e.g., in 1855. 1862., 1870, and 1880 - although each nation proscribed mili-

Mangas Coloradas

ary operations by the other within its own territory more often than permitting them. This situation added to the border unrest that Apache raids generated.

Cochise and Mangas Coloradas: 1861-74. In 1860 some Apache, probably Pinals, raided the John Ward ranch in the Sonoita Valley. Arizona, stealing oxen and kidnaping a boy who later became a famed interpreter and scout known as Mickey Free. Lieut. George N. Bascom and his unit confronted Cochise in Apache Pass in the Chiricahua Mountains, demanding return of the child and stock. Cochise apparently had nothing to do with the raid but promised in to try to secure their return. His pledge proved unsatisfactory and a trap was laid. Cochise daringly escaped into the hills, though three of his colleagues, perhaps relatives, were seized. Cochise in turn captured several whites. Upon the arrival of Capt. B. J. S. D. Irwin at Apache Pass in February 1861 with three captured Coyotero Apache and a large soldier force under Lieut. Isaiah N. Moore, Cochise became alarmed and killed his prisoners, while army officers hanged theirs at Irwin's insistence. This event precipitated 10- year war between Cochise's Chiriccahua and Arizona troops and settlers with devastating results, compounded by the withdrawal of army units from Arizona in the face of a Confederate Army threat to the Rio Grande Valley.

Lieut. Col. John R. Baylor of the Confederate Mounted Rifles occupied "Arizona" (i.e. New Mexico and Arizona below the 34th parallel) in mid-1861, proclaimed himself governor, and instantly came to war with the Apache. principally Mimbreno, and Central Chiricahua, losing about 100 men in scattered engagements. He issued his famous order to exterminate the Apache by treachery, this in part leading to his own downfall.

Col. James H. Carleton moved in from the West Coast with his 1,800-man California Column, and in July 1862 ran into an ambush at Apache Pass, which was laid by Cochise with help from Mangas Coloradas who was reportedly wounded in the engagement Casualties were light on either side, but the action is one of the most famed in Southwestern Indian wars and led to the establishment of Fort Bowie overlooking the springs in the pass and designed to protect them from Indians.

Carleton, in the face of continuing Mimbreno and Chiricahua activity, mimicked Baylor and on October 12, 1862, ordered that all Apache men were to be killed wherever found; his intransigence prolonged Indian hostility for several years. Adding fuel was the murder of Mangas Coloradas on January 18, 1863, at Fort McLane, New Mexico, on Carleton's implied directive and by Brig. Gen. Joseph R. West's more or less explicit instructions. This and succeeding acts of white treachery were long lasting in effect and are still remembered by the Apache.

Mangas was succeeded in leadership of the Eastern Chiricahua by Delgadito, or Tudeevia, a warlike chief of great ability and sagacity. He was killed shortly, and Victorio and Loco then gradually emerged into leadership.

The Mescalero Apache east of the Rio Grande, meanwhile, had engaged in no major operations against the Americans, although they had participated in countless raids into Mexico and numerous others north of the border that cumulatively exhausted the patience of Carleton and others. Carleton ordered Col. Christopher (Kit) Carson in late 1862 to operate remorselessly against the Mescalero, and by March 1863 most had been herded to Carleton's abortive reservation for the Navajo and Apache at Bosque Redondo, near Fort Sumner, New Mexico. The remainder continued in hostility with waning effectiveness or joined the Mimbreno-Chiricahua. The Mescalero ceased to exist as a potentially hostile force to be reckoned with. The Bosque Redondo endeavor became a debacle, so the Mescalero who had been collected there filtered away and returned to their own country to live by raiding. After Carleton's removal from New Mexico, they were granted their present reservation near Fort Stanton. In Arizona, most of the populous White Mountain (Coyotero) Apache remained virtually unmolested and generally at peace with the whites.

Lieut. Charles E. Drew, named agent to the Mimbreno in the summer of 1869, soon contacted and persuaded them to accept a rationing system and cease depredations. In 1871 Vincent Colyer, secretary of the U. S. Board of Indian Commissioners, charged with implementing the peace program of the administration of Pres. Ulysses S. Grant (18d9-77), selected a reservation at Fort Tularosa, New Mexico, for the Mimbreno, but after two years of dissatisfaction they were moved to Ojo Caliente (Warm Springs), New Mexico, where they remained until the mid-1870s. Gen. 0. 0. Howard, meanwhile, had visited Cochise in the Dragoon-Chiricahua mountain region of southeastern Arizona and persuaded him to accept a large reservation on the Mexican border, with Thomas-J. Jeffords as agent. Cochise died, apparently of cancer, in 1874.

Juh and Geronimo: 1878-86. The Chiricahua Reservation enabled Cochise's young men and Mimbreno warriors to continue their heavy raids into Mexico and was one of the reasons for implementation of the "concentration policy," by which most Apache and some peripheral tribes were to be gathered at San Carlos, Arizona, purportedly also in the interests of economy, control, and implementation of a civilizing process. Gen. George Crook, assisted by such chiefs of scouts as Al Sieber, Archie McIntosh, and Dan O'Leary, had cleared most of Arizona of Indians hostile toward whites by 1874. The concentration policy was then embarked upon; it proved to be a disaster.

Pushed onto the San Carlos Reservation with its indigenous Apache were the Yavapai in 1875, most of the White Mountain Apache in 1875, most of the Central Chiricahua in 1876, and the Mimbreno in 1877. But important leaders, including Juh, the most able of all, remained in Mexico where they had fled as concentration proceeded. Victorio found he could not endure San Carlos and withstand his enemies there, and so he broke out in the summer of 1877, surrendered at Fort Wingate, New Mexico, and was removed temporarily to Ojo Caliente. When it was sought to return him to San Carlos, he broke out again, surrendering eventually at the Fort Stanton Reservation. From here, believing mistakenly that he was to be arrested, he broke out for the last time, in August 1879, and precipitated a major war. Following a dazzling series of operations, he was trapped in October 1880 by a Mexican force under Lieut. Col. Joaquin Terrazas in the Tres Castillos Mountains and destroyed, but not until he had generated turmoil in New Mexico, Arizona, Texas, and Mexico and caused Juh and other Southern

A watercolor painting of Juh, the most able of all the Apache leaders. No photograph of him is known to have been taken.

Chiricahua, numerous Mescalero, and warriors of various tribes to rally to him. Juh and Geronimo eventually surrendered and were taken to San Carlos, while Victorio's chief subordinate, aged Nana, led a spectacular raid across southern New Mexico in the summer of 1881.

Meanwhile, unrest mounted among the Apache remaining at the San Carlos and Fort Apache reservations in Arizona, becoming personified in a medicine man-ghost dancer, Noch-ay-del-klinne, whom the whites suspected of fomenting discord and perhaps rebellion. Col. Eugene Asa Carr was directed by Indian agent Joseph C. Tiffany in August 1881 to "arrest or kill" the Apache. At Cibecue Creek, Arizona, scouts seeking to arrest the medicine man mutinied and precipitated an action in which Noch-ay-del- klinne was slain, whites suffered losses, Fort Apache was attacked, and a nucleus of Indians remained out.

More serious was the resulting bolt of the Juh-Geronimo faction for Mexico where they regained their traditional stronghold, though leaving behind Loco and the bulk of the Mimbreno. In April 1882, Juh engineered a spectacular raid on San

Geronimo

blistering raid by Chatto, a young Chiricahua warrior, provided him an excuse; the capture of Peaches, one of Chatto's men familiar with the Sierra Madre stronghold, supplied him with a guide. In the spring of 1883, with nearly 200 Apache scouts and token white support, Crook penetrated the almost unexplored region and in one of the most remarkable expeditions in frontier history contacted the Indians and persuaded them to return to the reservation. The final bands came in by the spring of 1884. With this, virtually all of the Apache were at peace for the first time in many years.

Juh died in a fall near Casas Grandes, Mexico, in November 1883, and Geronimo was left as the principal war leader of the Chiricahua-Mimbreno; he came into San Carlos with his people following Crook's expedition.

In mid-May 1895, the bored and restless Chiricahua on the Fort Apache Reservation became drunk on tiswin, a fermented beverage of the Indians of the Southwest. Lieut. Britton Davis, their overseer, failed in his attempt to contact Crook about the difficulty and some of the suspicious Apache bolted under Geronimo and Chihuahua, a ranking chief, regaining the sanctuary of the Sierra Madre where they successfully eluded capture, although approximately one-fifth of the U.S. Army was assigned to guard waterholes, patrol the U.S.-Mexican border, and search for them. Under the raider Josanie, or Ulzana, they even conducted a sweep through Arizona and New Mexico, causing numerous white casualties, although the principal body of Apache remained in Mexico.

On January 10, 1886, Capt. Emmet Crawford was mortally wounded in the Sierra Madre when attacked by Mexican irrelgulars while awaiting an anticipated surrender of Geronimo, and the Apache were frightened away for two more months. In late March, Crook met with Geronimo, Chihuahua, and the other resisters at Canyon de los Embudos, just below the Arizona-Sonora, Mexico, line and secured their promise to surrender. Chihuahua and his band actually did surrender. After Crook had left for Fort Bowie, however a bootlegger named Tribolet, probably working in the interests of the "ring" of contractors and others whose affairs would best be served by continuing hostilities, got Geronimo and the others drunk and frightened them off with tales of atrocities likely to be perpetrated upon them if they gave themselves up. A group of 20 men, 13 women, and 6 youngsters bolted. Crook, dismayed by this unexpected event, resigned and Philip Sheridan, commander of the army, named Brig. Gen. Nelson A. Miles to succeed him.

Miles, convinced that army regulars were more trustworthy than the Apache scouts upon whom

Carlos from which Loco and several hundred Mimbreno were led or driven south toward Mexico through a net of searching troops. Enroute they engaged in three sharp clashes with their pursuers. The last, with Mexican forces under Col. Lorenzo Garcia, caused major losses, though principally of noncombatants. This outstanding operation was directed not by Geronimo, as is sometimes alleged, but by Juh, although Geronimo accompanied him. Juh had conducted a similar action to rescue Victorio from southern New Mexico in 1880, while Geronimo never revealed the capacity either to conceive of or to execute such an expedition. A considerable nucleus of Apache, capable of wreaking untold havoc among scattered settlers of the Southwest, were now gathered in the Sierra Madre. Following destruction of the band of resisters formed after the Cibecue operation at the Battle of Big Dry Wash in July 1882, Crook was returned to the Arizona command. He set about immediately to solve the knotty problem of the Apache in Mexico.

He secured special permission from Mexican officials to enter that nation "in hot pursuit," and a

Crook had depended, spent months fruitlessly searching for Geronimo deep in the Mexico mountains. Although he wore out his men, he accomplished little until he altered his tactics and adopted his predecessor's methods. Miles heard that Geronimo had established contact with Mexican civilian authorities at Fronteras, in northern Sonora, and hastily dispatched Lieut. Charles B. Gatewood and Apache scouts there. The Mexicans believed Geronimo had surrendered to them on August 4, 1886, but had withdrawn into the mountains pending ratification of his capitulation by higher authorities. Gatewood contacted Geronimo and learned that he had no intention of turning himself over to the Mexicans but would consider surrender to the Americans. Geronimo accompanied Gatewood and, later, Capt. Henry W. Lawton to Skeleton Canyon in southeastern Arizona, where he met Miles early in September and surrendered formally on September 4. He and his people, like Chihuahua's band, were shipped to Florida to join the rest of the Chiricahua-Mimbreno in exile; the bulk of the tribe moved east on September 7 from Fort Apache via Holbrook, Arizona, arriving at Fort Marion on September 20.

Although a few Apache, such as the Apache Kid and Massai, continued to roam the mountainous Southwest for several years, conducting minor raids, the Apache wars were effectively concluded with the surrender of Geronimo. But the toll of the Apache Wars was heavy. From 1866 to 1886, hundreds of Apache died in the conflicts; 137 soldiers and 12 officers were killed outright, while numerous others were mortally wounded; and perhaps thousands of civilians in the United States and Mexico also perished. In addition, millions of dollars were lost through raids or were expended for military use to counter them. Few native peoples gave such an impressive account of themselves, certainly in view of their limited numbers the nature of their warfare, and their sporadic mode of operation.

Geronimo and other Apache prisoners after their surrender to U.S. forces on September 4, 1886, while in transit from Arizona to Florida. Sitting in the front row are (left to right) Fun and Perico, half-brothers of Geronimo; Nahche; Geronimo; Chappo, the son of Geronimo; and Chappo's wife.

(See also;CHIRICAHUA APACHE; JICARILLA APACHE; KIOWA APACHE; LIPAN APACHE; and MESCAL APACHE.)

BIBLIOGRAPHY-

● ALSOP, T. J. Memorial and Affidavits Showing Outrages Perpetrated by the Apache Indians in the Territory of Arizona, During the Years 1869-1870. San Francisco, CA: Francis & Valentine, 1871.
● ALTSHELER, JOSEPH A. Apache Gold. New York, NY: D. Appleton & Co., 1913.
● ARBEITER, REV.VINCENT. How Apache Indians Live. In The Indian Sentinel, March, 1937.
● ARIZONA HISTORICAL REVIEW. Lt. Charles B. Gatewood, 6th U.S. Cavalry, and the surrender of Geronimo. AZ: No. 1, v. 4, (pp 29- 44, 1931.
● ARIZONA WRITERS' PROJECT. The Apache. Arizona Highways, Nov., 1941.
● BALDWIN, GORDON C. The Warrior Apaches. Tucson, AZ: Dale Stuart King, 1965.
● BARNES, WILL C. The Apache's Last Stand in Arizona. AZ: Arizona Historical Review III, no. 4, pp 36-59, 1931.
● BLEEKER, SONIA. The Apache Indians, Raiders of the Southwest. New York, NY: Morrow, 1951.
● BOURKE, JOHN G. An Apache Campaign. New York, NY: Charles Scribner's Sons, 1886.
-----Medicine-men of the Apache. Washington: 9th Annual Report, Bureau of Ethnology, pp. 443-603, 1892.
● COYLER, VINCENT. Peace with the Apaches of New Mexico and Arizona. Washington: Govt. Printing Office, 1872.
● COZZENS, S. W. The Marvellous Country; or, Three Years in Arizona and New Mexico, The Apache's Home, and a Complete History of the Apache Tribe... Boston, MA: 1875, 1926.
● CREMONY, JOHN C. Life Among the Apaches. San Francisco, CA: A Roman & Co., 1868.
● CRUSE, THOMAS. Apache Days and After. ID: The Caxton Printers, Ltd., 1941.
● CURTIS, NATALIE. The Indians' Book; An offering by the American Indians of Indian Lore, Musical and Narrative. New York, NY: Harper & Bros., 1907.
● DAVIS, BRITTON. The Truth about Geronimo. New Haven, CT: Yale University Press, London: Humphrey Milford: Oxford University Press, 1929.
● DOWNEY, FAIRFAX. Indian-Fighting Army. New York, NY: Scribner's Sons, 1941.
● EASTMAN, ELAINE GOODALE. Pratt, The Red Man's Moses. Norman, OK: University of Oklahoma Press, 1935.
● EMORY, H. Notes of Military Reconnoissance, from Ft. Leavenworth, in Missouri, including part of the Arkansas, Del Norte, and Gila Rivers. Washington: Wendall and Van Benthuysen, 1848.
● EVERETT, DALE EDWARD. The Indians of the Southwest; a century of development under the U.S. Norman, OK: University of Oklahoma Press, 1949.
● FOREMAN, GRANT. Advancing the Frontier. Norman, OK: University of Oklahoma Press, 1933.
● GOODWIN, GRENVILLE. The Social Organization of the Western Apache. Chicago, IL: The University of Chicago Publications in Anthropology, Ethnological Series; University of Chicago Press, 1942; reprinted The University of Arizona Press, 1969.
-----White Mountain Apache Religion. American Anthropologist, v. 40, no. 1, p.24.
● HEBARD, GRACE RAYMOND. Sacajawea, a Guide and Interpreter of the Lewis & Clark Expedition... Glendale, CA: The Arthur H. Clark, CO., 1933.
● HODGE, FREDERICK WEBB. Handbook of American Indians North of Mexico. Washington: Smithsonian Institution: BAE Bulletin No. 30: U.S. GPO, 1907.
● HUMFREVILLE, J. LEE. Twenty Years among our Hostile Indians. New York, NY: Hunter & Co.

● JACKSON, HELEN HUNT. A Century of Dishonor; A Sketch of the U.S. Government's Dealings with Some of the Indian Tribes. New York, NY: Harper & Bros., 1881; Boston, MA: Little, Brown & Co., 1909.
● KENOI, SAMUEL E. A Chiricahua Apache's Account of the Geronimo Campaign of 1886. NM: New Mexico Historical Review, 13, (pp. 360-386), 1938.
● LA FARGE, OLIVER. The Changing Indian. Norman, OK: University of Oklahoma Press, 1942.
● LOCKWOOD, FRANK C. The Apache Indian. New York, NY: The Macmillan Co., 1938.
● MAILS, THOMAS F. The People Called Apache. Englwood Cliffs, NJ: Prentice Hall, Inc., 1974.
● MAZZANOVICH, ANTON. Trailing Geronimo. Los Angeles, CA: Gem Publishing Co., 1926.
● PALMER, ROSE A. The North American Indians, An Account of the American Indians North of Mexico. New York, NY: Smithsonian Institution Series, Inc., Vol. 4, 1929.
● REAGAN, ALBERT B. Plants Used by the White Mountain Apache Indians of Arizona. WI: Wisconsin Archeologist, July, 1929.
● RICHARDSON, RUPERT NORVAL. The Comanche Barrier to South Plains Settlement, A Century and a Half of Savage Resistance to the Advancing White Frontier. Glendale, CA: The Arthur H. Clark, Co., 1933.
● RISTER, CARL COKE. Border Captives, The Traffic in Prisoners by Southern Plains Indians, 1835-1875. Norman, OK: University of Oklahoma Press, 1940.
● SCHOOLCRAFT, HENRY R. History of the Indian Tribes of the U.S.; Their Present Condition and Prospects, and a Sketch of Their Ancient Status. Philadelphia, PA: J. B. Lippincott & Co., 1857.
● SHEA, JOHN G. Catholic Missions Among the Indian Tribes of the U.S. New York, NY: E. Dunigan & Bros., 1854.
● SONNICHSEN, CHARLES LELAND. The Mescalero Apaches. Norman, OK: University of Oklahoma Press, 1958.
● STURDEVANT, WILLIAM C. Handbook of North American Indians Washington, D. C.: Smithsonian Institution, Vol. 10, 1983.
● SWANTON, JOHN R. The Indian Tribes of North America. Smithsonian Institution: BAE Bulletin No. 145: U.S. GPO, 1952.
● THOMAS, ALFRED BARNABY. Forgotten Frontiers, A Study of the Spanish Indian Policy of Don Juan Bautista de Anza, Governor of New Mexico, 1777-1787, from the original documents in the Archives of Spain, Mexico, and New Mexico translated into English. Norman, OK: University of Oklahoma Press, 1932.
● UNDERHILL, RUTH M. First Penthouse Dwellers of America. New York, NY: J. J. Augustin Publisher, 1938.
● WISSLER, CLARK. Indians of the U.S., Four Centuries of Their History and Culture. New York, NY: Doubleday, Doran & Co., Inc., 1940.
● WOODWARD, ARTHUR. Plateau. John Bourke on the Arizona Apache (V. 16 no. 2, Oct.), 1943.

APALACHEE

(U.S.; Fla.) is an extinct tribe who inhabited the northwestern area between the Aucilla and Apalachiola rivers above Apalachee Bay. They spoke a Muskogean language.

Well back in prehistoric times, culture trait complexes began spreading into the southeastern U.S. from the comparatively advanced Indian peoples of Mexico. On the archaeological level, the most obvious of these complexes was the construction of temple mounds, with a concomitant decline of interest in burial mounds. About AD 1300, there was an actual movement of advanced

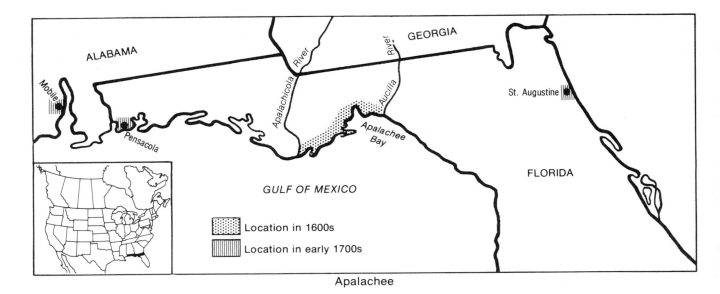

Apalachee

whose coming revolutionized south- eastern Indian culture, emerged into the light of history as
the Muskogeans--the Creek, Hitchiti, Choctaw,
Alabama, Apalachee, and some lesser groups.

Name, location, and language. The name
Apalachee probably is from Choctaw *a'pala-
chi,* meaning "on the other side." The Choctaw
held the country west of Pensacola Bay, while the
Apalachee were, presumably, the people on the
other side of the Bay. Although there are many variant spellings of the name Apalachee, the tribe
should not be confused with the Apalachiola, who
were Hitchiti living near Apalachee territory.

Originally, the area of Apalachee settlement
may have extended from Pensacola Bay to the
Aucilla River. In early historic times, however,
these Indians were concentrated between the
Apalachicola and the Aucilla rivers.

Their political subdivisions are poorly known.
In October 1539, the Spanish explorer Hernando
de Soto crossed the Aucilla and encountered the
Apalachee towns of Ivitachuco and Calahuchi
before he finally reached Iniahica, reportedly the
most important Apalachee settlement. These three
towns were aligned between the Aucilla and
Ochlockonee rivers, not far south of the present
Georgia border. Farther north, beyond the Flint
River, was the province of Capachequi, supposedly subject to Apalachee. Its inhabitants may
have been Hitchiti.

Quite early in the prehistoric period, the territory of the Apalachee was greatly reduced. These
Indians were converted to Roman Catholicism
about 1600 and were concentrated around a string
of missions. They continued to prosper, and in
1655 the Apalachee, numbering about 6,000 to
8,000, resided in eight towns, each with a mission.
In 1703-04 they were nearly wiped out by about 50

South Carolina militia and 1,000 Creek mercenar-
ies under Col. James Moore. The approximately
600 survivors were captured and resettled near
new Windsor, South Carolina, on the Savannah
River. A few Apalachee escaped to Pensacola, and
they subsequently removed to Mobile, Alabama.
Others sought safety with the Spanish at St.
Augustine, Florida.

At the outbreak of the Yamasee War, the New
Windsor band joined the Lower Creek. They
gradually returned to their old country, settling at
scattered localities from St. Marks to Pensacola.
In 1763, the Pensacola and Mobile bands united,
emigrating to the Red River of Louisiana along
with some Taensa and the Pakana band of the
Creek. In time, the Red River band died out, some
of its members uniting with other tribes, or else
going to Oklahoma with the Creek.

Linguistically, the Apalachee formed a separate
group within the Muskogean division of the
Muskogean stock (in the terminology of John R.
Swanton, an important U.S. ethnologist who died
in 1958). Judging from what has been preserved of
Apalachee words and place-names, the language
was close to Choctaw, and perhaps even closer to
Miccosukee, the only surviving Hitchiti language.
In any event, Apalachee similarities are more to
Choctaw and Miccosukee than to Creek.

Cultural and historical notes. From about 400
to 1300, the Weeden Island Phase occupied the
Florida Gulf coast from Pensacola Bay to
Charlotte Harbor. The coming of the ancestral
Apalachee broke the Weeden Island culture area in
two. The Weeden Island Phase passed into the Fort
Walton Phase in the area of direct Apalachee
settlement. Farther south, it passed into the Safety
Harbor Phase, which was merely Apalachee-in-
fluenced. The Englewood Phase, at the extreme

southern end of the former Weeden Island area, may represent minimal influence from the Apalachee.

At the opening of historic times, the Apalachee were typically Muskogean. Their social and religious life was organized around a temple mound with its priest-chief. Religious emphasis was more on the present, on a living priesthood, not so much on the hereafter or the expenditure of labor on grave goods. The priest-chief wielded considerable secular power and could conscript men from a wide area to construct temple mounds. Like most other Southeastern tribes, the Apalachee kept blacks as slaves.

Probably because of an unpleasant experience in 1528 with the Spanish explorer Panfilo de Navarez, the Apalachee were hostile to De Soto and later Spanish explorers.

An Apalachee Indian of the Fort Walton Period (c. 1300-1650 AD). The reconstruction is based on archaeological and ethnographical data. Significant details include a Muskogean scalp lock; minimal clothing; bone beads and a shell gorget; shell ear-pins; large, heavy bow; stone axe with rectanguloid blade; and jar and cazuela bowl of Fort Walton incised pottery. The ears of corn and a pumpkin indicate agriculture, the basis of Apalachee economy. Apalachee religious life centered around temple mounds (background) during this period.

Apalachee economy was based on the usual Southeastern crops: corn (maize), beans, peas, squash, and pumpkins. Corn was important, and two crops of it were raised each year. De Soto encountered one Apalachee town with a great quantity of dried venison. Reference was also made to dried plums among these Indians. Wild fruits, berries, and mollusks were gathered.

The Apalachee had fairly long trade routes, as shown by trade goods (mostly pottery) on archaeological sites. Much trade was with the Timucua of northern Florida.

Both the French and the Spanish believed that the Apalachee mined a great deal of gold in their country. This mistaken belief led the gold-bearing Apalachian Mountains to be named for Indians who never lived near them.

Not much is known about the nonmaterial culture of the Apalachee, for it was rapidly altered when they were missionized. The Leon-Jefferson Phase, which succeeded the Fort Walton, is the tangible remains of missionized Apalachee. A small wattle-and-daub church replaced the temple mound, and a Roman Catholic priest replaced the priest-chief. The Indians were forbidden arms or warfare and were encouraged to raise corn in fields surrounding the church. Peaches, cattle, pigs, and horses were also raised.

Apalachee mission sites have yielded aboriginal pottery, Spanish olive jars, and glazed Hispano-Mexican wares. Interesting vessels are those combining Apalachee and Spanish ceramic techniques. Sites have also yielded flint projectile points, limestone discs, iron tools, and a few weapons, nails, locks, horse trappings, and beads, along with Roman Catholic religious paraphernalia such as rosaries, a crucifix, a censer, and an altar stone.

Population. Apalachee population probably was between 6,000 and 7,000 in the 1600s. It had declined to about 2,000 at the end of the century. In the early 1700s, most Apalachee were killed or captured. In 1715, there were 638 of these Indians at New Windsor. There were over 100 near Pensacola in 1718; about 100 at Mobile in 1725; 87 around the St. Augustine missions in 1726; 41 around these missions in 1728; and only 14 warriors on the Red River in 1805. The tribe has since become extinct.

BIBLIOGRAPHY-

● FAIRBANKS, CHARLES H. Ethnohistorical Report on the Florida Indians. New York, NY: Garland Publishing, Inc., 1974.
● HODGE, FREDERICK WEBB. Handbook of American Indians North of Mexico. Washington: Smithsonian Institution: BAE Bulletin No. 30: U.S. GPO, 1907.
● MILLING, CHAPMAN. Red Carolinians. Chapel Hill, NC: University of North Carolina Press, 1940.
● MURDOCK, GEORGE P. Ethnographic Bibliography of North America. New Haven, CT: Human Relations Area Files Press, 1975.

● SWANTON, JOHN R. The Indian Tribes of North America. Smithsonian Institution: BAE Bulletin No. 145: U.S. GPO, 1952.
● WISSLER, CLARK. Indians of the U.S., Four Centuries of Their History and Culture. New York, NY: Doubleday, Doran & Co., 1940.

APALACHICOLA.

(U.S., Ala., Fla., Ga.) They were also called Talwa lako or Italwa lako, or "big town," the name given by the Muskogee Indians, as well as Palachicola or Parachukla, contractions of Apalachicola. The meaning comes from Hitchiti "Apalachicoli" or Muskogee "Apalachicolo," signifying "People of the other side," with reference probably to the Apalachicola River or some nearby stream. This tribe, which was of the Muskhogean linguistic stock, spoke the Atsik-hata or Hitchiti language, and also included the Hitchiti, Okmulgee, Oconee, Sawokli, Tamali, Mikasuki, Chiaha, and possibly the Osochi. Very early, this tribe lived on the Apalachicola and Chattahoochee Rivers, partly in Alabama. Sometime after 1715, they settled in Russell County, on the Chattahoochee River where they occupied at least two different sites before moving with the rest of the Creeks to the other side of the Mississippi.

The following names of towns or tribes were given by a Tawasa Indian, Lamhatty, to *Robert Beverley, 1722* and may well have belonged to the Apalachicola: Auledley, Ephippick, Sonepah, and perhaps Socsosky (or Socsosky). The census of 1832 returned two distinct bodies of Indians under the synonyms Apalachicola and Talwa lako.

According to Muskogee legend, the ancestors of the Muskogee encountered the Apalachicola in the above-mentioned region when they entered the country, and were at first disposed to fight with them, but soon made peace. According to one legend, the Creek Confederacy came into existence as a result of this treaty. Spanish documents of the seventeenth century are the earliest in which the name appears. It is used both as the name of a town (as early as 1675) and, in an extended sense, for all of the Lower Creeks. This fact, Muskogee tradition, and the name Talwalako all show the early importance of the people. They were on more friendly terms with the Spaniards than the Muskogee generally and, hence, were fallen upon by the Indian allies of the English and carried off, either in 1706 or 1707. They were settled on Savannah River opposite Mount Pleasant, at a place which long bore their name, but in 1716, just after the Yamasee War, they retired into their old country and established themselves at the junction of Chattahoochee and Flint Rivers. Later, they moved higher up the Chattahoochee and lived in Russell County, Alabama, remaining in the general neighborhood until they moved to new homes in the present Oklahoma in 1836-40. There they established themselves in the northern part of the Creek Reservation, but presently gave up their ceremonial ground and were gradually absorbed in the mass of Indians about them.

In 1715, just before the outbreak of the Yamasee War, there were said to be two settlements of this tribe with 64 warriors and a total population of 214. A Spanish census of 1738 also gave two settlements with 60 warriors in one and 45 in the other; a French census of 1750, more than 30 warriors; a British enumeration of 1760, 60; one of 1761, 20; an American estimate of 1792, 100 (including the Chiaha); and the United States Census of 1832, a total population of 239 in two settlements.

The tribal name has become noted in various ways. The Apalachicola River, Apalachicola Bay, and the name of the county seat of Franklin County, Florida, are derived from this tribe. The Spaniards applied their name to the Lower Creeks generally, and they were also noted as one of the tribes responsible for the formation of the Confederation.

BIBLIOGRAPHY-

● SWANTON, JOHN R. The Indian Tribes of North America. Smithsonian Institution: BAE Bulletin No. 145: U.S. GPO, 1952.

APALAI

(South America; Amazon River area.) is a small tribe of the tropical forest area north and west of the delta of the Amazon River. Their last known contact with the outside world occurred in the early 1930s.

The cultural area of the Apalai is bounded in a rough semicircle by the Orinoco and Amazon rivers, and on the east by the Atlantic Ocean. Apalai were reported living along the middle and lower Paru River in 1916-17 and reportedly were still on the Paru in the 1930s. Before 1926, they may also have lived along the Jari and Curua rivers, and at various times along other rivers and creeks northwest of the Amazon Delta.

Few scientists have studied the Apalai, apparently none exclusively. Information must be gleaned from scattered reports, the most recent dating from 1931. Apalai life seemed to be similar to that of all tropical forest tribes. The tribe was loosely organized, united by similar culture, territory, and language. Settlements were small, numbering between 15 and 150 people, and were governed by informally chosen headmen who reportedly obtained counsel from mature married men at drinking bouts.

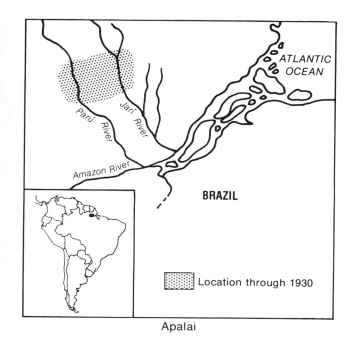

Apalai

The Apalai grew root crops, such as cassava (manioc), and corn, using slash-and-burn techniques and moving their fields every four to ten years. They gathered insects, fruit, honey, and reptiles, probably hunted small animals with bows and arrows and spears, and may have caught fish with poison, traps, and hooks and lines. They believed spirits inhabited all living things and had shamans who performed puberty rituals and curing ceremonies. For recreation they engaged in singing, dancing, and drinking parties with others in nearby villages. The only distinctive features of Apalai life that have been recorded were the patrilocal living system (in which a married couple lived in the husband's home village) and the custom of painting house pots or walls.

There are no records mentioning the Apalai before 1590. They seem to have had infrequent contact with English, Dutch, Portugese, and Spanish traders or missionaries after 1590. Relations were generally friendly. The Europeans may have introduced loincloths, metal implements, and some Christian religious concepts to the natives.

In the mid-1970s, the tribal area was still remote; if the Apalai existed, they apparently had few visitors and had escaped by non-Indians.

BIBLIOGRAPHY-

● STEWARD, JULIAN H. Handbook of South American Indians. 7 Vols., Washington, DC: U.S. Govt. Printing Office, 1946-59.

APIACA

(South America; Brazil) are a people of the northern Mato Grosso region of Brazil, until recently thought to be extinct, who survive only as a small remnant-population, which is largely assimilated into the New-Brazilian culture. The remaining Apiaca families live along the middle Tapajos River, along a limited stretch of the Canuma River with the Mundurucu people, and along the lower Juruena River. Their territory was formerly between the junction of the Arinos and Juruena rivers, from the 11th parellel northward. Their native culture belongs to the Tapajos-Madeira culture area of Brazil, and their native language belongs to the Tupi group. Soon after their first contact with Neo-Brazilians, the Apiaca language received several elements of the Lingua Geral, a Tupi-based trade jargon. Today, Mundurucu (another Tupi language) or Portugese is generally spoken in preference to the Apiaca language. These people have always been known by the name "Apiaca."

Tribal culture. The earliest records show that the Apiaca had extensive cultivated fields. Planting was probably done by women, who raised bitter and sweet cassava (manioc), corn (maize), cara, yams, sweet potatoes, magorito, peanuts, beans, lima beans, pumpkins, cotton, and, by 1848, watermelons. Planting and harvesting were communal activities. Brazil nuts were among the wild foods collected. Early sources do not mention any domestic animals, but by the mid-19th century, the Apiaca had dogs, pigs, chickens, ducks, and other birds. Peccaries, tapirs, and capybaras were hunted, and fish were caught in baskets set at the bottom of weirs across the mouths of streams. Both hunting and fishing were cooperative efforts.

Apiaca settlements were formerly along the river shores and usually consisted of a single, very large house surrounded by a clearing. The huts were rectangular, with rounded ends, and were covered with thatched roofs; the walls were made of palm or bark. Cotton hammocks, made of either net or coarse fabric, were hung inside, along the walls. Large bark canoes provided transportation along the waterways. Strips of creeper were woven into baskets, trays, sieves, and supports for various vessels, and ceramic pots, pans, and dishes were manufactured. Cloth hammocks, armbands, and flour bags were woven. Musical instruments included drums, rattles, and bamboo trumpets. Weapons consisted of bows and arrows, spears with bamboo prints, and short war clubs. Weapons and ornaments were the only forms of private property. Iron tools obtained from Europeans were greatly valued, and the Apiaca sometimes stole them from whites.

Each Apiaca communal hut constituted a settlement and had one or more chiefs. The chieftaincy was transmitted from father to son or, in the absence of a direct heir, to the nearest relative. The

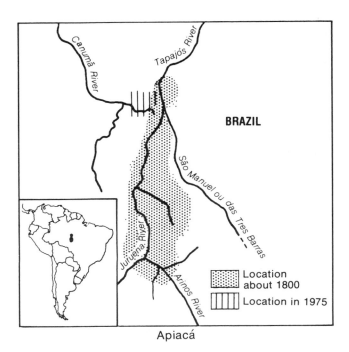

Apiacá

chief was unique in being allowed as many as three wives, but in normal times his authority was exercised unobtrusively. In wartime and in dealings with foreigners, however, he assumed great authority, as evidenced by his distinctive ornaments, which included a feather diadem, a large, white, shell collar, and a large belt of black beads and human teeth.

A mother was confined for only one day after childbirth, and children were raised in an atmosphere of affection. Boys were tattooed by women using thorns, the process being completed at the age of 14 when a rectangle was tattooed around the mouth, symbolizing that the boy could eat human flesh. Facial tattoos consisted of lines from each ear to the nose, mouth, and chin, while designs on the body illustrated war and hunting feats. Women were tattooed after marriage, the design consisting of a rectangle on the chin, with a band running to the ears. The Apacia, except for their chief, were monogamous and married at the age of 14. Divorce was permitted, with children going to the father in such a case. The dead were burned in shallow graves under their hammocks in their houses; bones were exhumed after a year and were later buried in the original grave.

The Apiaca warred regularly with their neighbors, who included the Tapanyuna, the Nambicuara, the Parintintin (Cawahib), and others, for the purpose of avenging former affronts. War expeditions consisting of 200 to 300 warriors were undertaken after the harvest, but only if the shamans predicted victory. Several villages might cooperate under the leadership of a chief. Cannibalism--eating of prisoners and those killed in battle, often with elaborate ceremony--was practiced as late as 1848.

According to mid-19th century sources, the Apiaca believed in a god who created the sky and the earth and who showed his anger in thunder and lightning. Shamans were greatly respected and foretold the future by entering trances and speaking with spirits. They treated the sick by blowing on the patient, sucking the affected part of the body, and washing the patient in a herb bath.

Tribal history. The first records mentioning the Apiaca date from 1791 and 1805, although these Indians may have encountered Europeans in 1747. They established peaceful relations with two European expeditions in 1812. In 1818 and 1819, several Apiaca visited Cuiaba, where their reports of mineral wealth led to an unsuccessful European expedition in search of gold and diamonds. In the mid-19th century, pressure from the Neo-Brazilians led many of the tribe to migrate to the Sao Manoel River, where they became known as the Pari-bi-tete. By 1895, only a remnant of this group survived: they were relatively acculturated and dependent on Neo-Brazilian rubber gatherers for their subsistence. In 1902, the Collectoria Estadoal to Mato Grosso was established, and an Indian attack on the office resulted in reprisals that killed many Apiaca. Some survivors were taken into protection and allowed to live at the Collectoria. In the 1970s, the remnant of the Apiaca living along the Tapajos River were endangered by a new road that was supposed to go through their area, and plans were being made to offer them refuge in the Xingu National Park in Brazil.

In early 19th-century records, the Apiaca are said to have totaled 16,000 persons. In 1819, a single village of 1,500 was observed. In 1848, their number was estimated at 2,700. By 1912, however, only 32 survived and, by the mid-20th century, they were relatively acculturated. Apiaca are known to be living along the Tapajos River.

BIBLIOGRAPHY-

● STEWARD, JULIAN H. Handbook of South American Indians. 7 Vols., Washington, DC: U.S. Govt. Printing Office, 1946-59.

APINAYE

(South America; Brazil) A tribe of the Mato Grosso region, they consider themselves an offshoot of the Timbira people, who live to their east. In fact, the Apinaye are sometimes known as the Western Timbera, and their separation from the Eastern Timbira probably dates back several centuries. The tribal name first appears in written records in 1783 as Pinare and Pinage, and later the form Apinage predominates. Other variant names are Oupinagee, Afotige, Uhitische, Utinsche, Otoge, and Aoge.

Tribal culture. The Apinaye culture is considered part of the Tocantins-Xingi culture area of Brazil. Their territory comprised a triangle between the Tocantins River and the lower Araguaia River, extending southward to about 6 30'. This land had been almost entirely taken over by Neo-Brazilians, and in the mid-1970s, the Apinaye inhabited a few small settlements within their former territory. The Apinaye language is a Timbira dialect and is thus part of the Northwestern Ge (or Je) group. Basic primers in the language, prepared by linguists, were available in the mid-1970s.

Apinaye settlements are situated on the open, high steppe near brooks that provide their water. The houses are rectangular, palm-thatched, gable-roofed huts and are grouped in a rough circle around a plaza. Each village is autonomous, and each has a chief and a counselor; there was probably never a tribal or paramount chief. The chief enjoys a few prerogatives and was formerly aided by a council of elders. The counselor's duty is to promote preservation of traditional customs.

Apinaye's society is divided into two pairs of moieties (subdivisions) in ceremonial affairs. Membership in the Kolti and Kolri moieties is conferred by personal names that each individual receives at birth. (The village chief always belongs to the Kolti moiety.) Membership in the Ipognotxoine ("people of the house of periphery") moieties is conferred on each child at the age of ten by "marks" given by a formal friend.

The Apinaye were formerly seminomadic hunters and gatherers for part of each year, returning regularly to semipermanent villages to harvest the cassava (manioc) and corn (maize) that they had planted before the hunt. As the Neo-Brazilians encroached on their hunting territory, the Apinaye came to depend more on farming. Men cut down trees and burn over the clearing, and both sexes plant, weed, and harvest the crops (bitter and sweet cassava, corn, sweet potatoes and yams). Hunting--for deer, ostriches, armadillos, and tapirs--is done by the men, using bows and arrows, guns, and grass fires, while gathering is done by women. Fish are caught with imported hooks, shot with bows and arrows, or poisoned and then gathered in scoop nets. Domestic animals, which were not kept formerly, now include dogs, pigs, chickens, horses, and cattle. Apinaye men make weapons and musical instruments and plait mats, bags, and permanent baskets; women manufacture gourd bottles and bowls and provisional baskets, know scoop nets, and spin cotton.

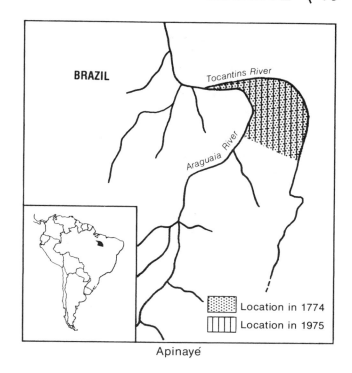

Apinayé

During a woman's pregnanacy and her child's infancy, both parents observe food taboos and other regulations to protect the child. Infants are decorated with pigment to promote growth and with various bone, wood, and other objects to prevent or cure disease. Girls help their mothers in household or farming chores from an early age, and most girls marry before puberty. Males pass through four age classes: boys who have not been initiated, warriors from about 15 to 25 years of age, mature men, and elders. The elaborate male initiation formerly took more than a year to complete, but it is now shorter and may disappear. Men cannot marry until initiation is complete, and after marriage the husband resides with his wife's family. Marriage is always monogamous. The dead are buried in graves in a communal cemetery, but baptized Indians are buried separately.

The sun and moon are the major deities in Apinaye religion and figure large in Apinaye myth. The sun is superior to the moon and is regarded as the creator or father of mankind; he is asked to protect crops and to cure illness, and he may appear in dreams and visions. The moon, also considered male, is invoked to promote the growth of plants. Men, animals, and plants are all believed to possess a soul that leaves the body soon after death. The souls of men continue to dwell on the earth and, unless offended, are generally well disposed toward the living. Nevertheless, the Apinaye, except for their shamans, try to avoid contact with them. Disease is believed to result from soul loss, intrusion of alien souls, or sorcery.

History and population figures. Although from early historic times the Apinaye had a reputation as peaceable people, they did conduct warfare for blood revenge, and there are traditions of enmity with various of their Indian neighbors. The Apinaye's first contact with Europeans probably occurred in the latter half of the 17th century, but the first definite record of such contact dates from 1774. Soon after that, the Apinaye began to raid settlers downstream along the Tocantins for their iron tools. As a result of these attacks, military posts were established along the river, and from 1797, contact was continuous. This produced more conflict, however. The Apinaye killed several soldiers who had been destroying their farms and, in return, the Indian villages were destroyed. In 1816, a European settlement was established in Apinaye territory by Antonio Moreira. The following year, the tribe was struck by a smallpox epidemic. In 1818, they were reported as peaceable and helpful to travellers, but in the following years they became involved in dispute between Moreira and Jose Maria Belem, leader of a rival settlement. In the Brazilian struggle for independence in 1823, they furnished the Brazilians with 250 warriors, and at the skirmish at the Ilha de Botica they helped to defeat the Portugese. The first Christian mission in an Apinaye village was founded in 1843, but missionaries have had little success in converting the Indians.

Throughout the 19th and 20th centuries, the Apinaye, like other Brazilian Indians, have been subject both to Neo-Brazilian efforts to exterminate them and appropriate their land and to the decimating effects of epidemics of European-introduced diseases. In recent years, their problems have also included the loss of their old customs, migration out of their own community, alcoholism, and malnutrition.

In 1824, the population of the Apinaye was estimated to be 4,200, living in four villages ranging in size from 500 to 1,400 people. Warfare with whites and with other Indians rapidly reduced this number. In 1859, the total population was estimated at 1,800 to 2,000; in 1897 at 400; and in 1937 at 160. By the 1960s, some 210 Apinaye were living in two villages in the extreme north of the state of Goias, where they were in close contact with Neo-Brazilians and were integrated into the regional economy. The establishment of an Apinaye reservation was under consideration in the mid-1970s.

BIBLIOGRAPHY-

● STEWARD, JULIAN H. Handbook of South American Indians. 7 Vols., Washington, DC: U.S. Govt. Printing Office, 1946-59.

ARANAMA

(U.S.; Tex.) was a small agricultural tribe formerly located on and near the south coast; the tribe was extinct by 1843. According to one Spanish chronicler, they were for a time hostile to whites. Before they disappeared, they had relocated farther from the coast along the San Antonio River and possibly numbered 125 people.

BIBLIOGRAPHY-

● HODGE, FREDERICK WEBB. Handbook of American Indians North of Mexico. Washington: Smithsonian Institution: BAE Bulletin No. 30: U.S. GPO, 1907.
● MURDOCK, GEORGE P. Ethnographic Bibliography of North America. New Haven, CT: Human Relations Area Files Press, 1975.
● SWANTON, JOHN R. The Indian Tribes of North America. Smithsonian Institution: BAE Bulletin No. 145: U.S. GPO, 1952.

ARAPAHO

(U.S.; Great Plains) are an Algonquian-speaking tribe that occupied a central position on the North American Great Plains. Like the other tribes in that region, they were skilled horsemen and brave fighters, but they were especially noted for their highly organized ceremonial life and symbolic decorative arts.

Tribal name. The name "Arapaho" seems to have been applied by American trappers early in the 19th century. It may derive from the Crow In-

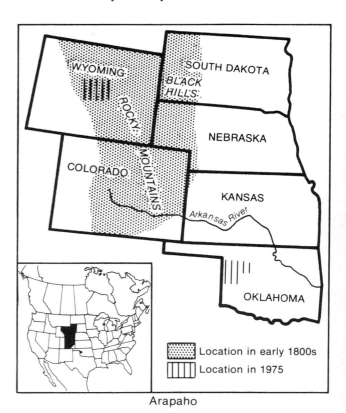

Arapaho

Arapaho village in Whitewood Canyon, Wyoming, in the 1870s or 1880s. The tipis face east and are protected by the foothills.

dian word *ara-pa-ho,* meaning "lots of tattoos," although it has also been suggested that it comes from the Pawnee word *larapihu,* meaning "trader." Earlier, traders on the Missouri River knew the Arapaho by either the Ojibwa term *kananavish* or the French-Canadian term *gens de vache,* both of which mean "buffalo people."

Spelling of the tribal name varies. "Arapaho" is encountered most often in the ethnographic literature and is the spelling used by the southern division of the tribe. "Arapahoe," however, has also been used and is the spelling adopted by the northern branch. Here, "Arapaho" is used except when referring to specific corporate bodies.

Social and cultural boundaries. Despite the well-known 19th- century association with the Cheyenne, the Arapaho seem to be most closely related to the Gros Ventre (Atsina) of the Northern Plains. The latter two tribes speak mutually intelligible dialects of the same language and share many features of social and ceremonial organization. Throughout the historic period, however, they have dwelt apart from each other and have usually been regarded as separate tribes.

Today the Arapaho are in two divisions, one in Wyoming and the other in Oklahoma, as a result of circumstances attending their placement on reservations. These divisions are separate political entities and have adopted somewhat differently to twentieth century life.

Territory. When first contacted by the white man, the Arapaho ranged the area from west of the Black Hills southward along the eastern edge of the Rockies to the Arkansas River. Their western boundary was roughly the Continental Divide, but their eastern boundary was indefinite until defined by the Treaty of 1851 as lying somewhat east of the present Colorado-Kansas border. The Arapaho were thus a mountain, as well as a plains, people, frequenting the sheltered valleys of the foothills in winter, the well-watered mountain parks in late summer, and descending to the plains for the great tribal buffalo hunts of early summer and late fall. As white settlers displaced them in the Colorado Rockies, some Arapaho were increasingly found further out on the plains on either side of the Arkansas River, though other bands managed to stay about the upper reaches of the North Platte.

Although the Arapaho may at some remote date have lived in settled villages and raised corn, they have always been known to the white peoples as horse-using Plains nomads, fully dependent on the buffalo. In material culture they resembled other Plains tribes, making use of the tipi for shelter, the travois for transport, and animal hide for clothing and containers.

Decorative arts. The Arapaho excelled in the decoration of leather items, using porcupine quill or bead embroidery in combination with fringe and pendants of hair, elk teeth, or hoof tips. Designs were geometrical and symbolic. The quilling of robes and tipi ornaments was done ceremonially and was supervised by certain old women who owned medicine bags. Rawhide containers, shields, and sometimes tipis were decorated with painted designs in bright colors.

Hunting and gathering. Arapaho men often hunted buffalo cooperatively, killing animals with lances or bows and arrows. The great tribal hunts were policed by one of the men's age- societies. Individual hunting was permitted when game was plentiful. Surplus meat was dried and stored for winter use, some being pounded with chokecherries and fat to make pemmican. Deer, elk, and bighorn were also hunted, and some small animals and birds, as well as dogs, were occasionally eaten. Prairie turnip, chokecherry, and some other wild plant foods supplemented the meat diet.

Social organization. An individual's life took place within a framework of custom and social relations designed to assure health and long life. The extended family, consisting of several related nuclear families who always pitched their tipis close together, was the unit of residence, and all its members had a part in socializing the child. Women of this group shared in outdoor fireplace and meat drying rack, and they cooperated in such tasks as slicing meat and tanning hides. Young children were watched by older siblings or grandparents, and older children played, boys and girls apart, in imitation of adult activities. At night, old people told stories that not only entertained their audiences but instructed them in tribal traditions and ways of behaving.

The hunting band was made up of a small number of extended families allied by kinship, marriage, or common interest. There were from eight to ten of these bands, which were called by nicknames. Throughout most of the year they wandered independently, being small enough to exploit the resources of game and pasturage in an area, and large enough to defend themselves against attack.

A woman usually married late in her teens and a man in his middle twenties. A man could have more than one wife, usually marrying two or more sisters. A woman earned recognition through her industry, skill at quilling or beading, and participation in the ceremonies of the one woman's society, the Buffalo Lodge. She could also be a doctor and have supernatural power.

Southern Arapaho woman in buckskin dress photographed c. 1910. The dress is trimmed with beadwork, cowrie shells, and metal tinklers.

A man's life was molded by the age-society system. There were eight societies, each with its own dance and/or ceremony, and they were ranked from low to high on the basis of age and ceremonial importance. In order from youngest and lowest, they were: Fox, Star, Tomahawk, *Biitaha? awu?,* Crazy, Dog, Grey- Heads, and Water Sprinkling Old Men. A man and his age-mates joined the Fox society at about age 15, and they moved on through the older societies as they advanced in age. A man, however, had to seek supernatural power to qualify for the two highest societies, whose members were the tribe's ceremonial leaders.

Leadership was a function of the society system, with men in older societies having authority over men below them. Band leaders were usually heads of large extended families and belonged to middle-level societies. There were no head chiefs as such, but some men combined ceremonial authority with great personal influence and were regarded as tribal chiefs.

Ceremonies, religion, and medicine. The major ceremony was the Sun Dance. The Arapaho version of this ceremony was the most elaborate on the Plains. There was a three-day secret session called the Rabbit Lodge, followed by a four-day public ceremony held in a large brush enclosure. The Arapaho called the Sun Dance the "Offerings Lodge," for in their view the dancers made offerings of their bodies by enduring hunger, thirst, and fatigue in return for supernatural blessings for the whole tribe.

Religion included belief in a mysterious, all-pervasive power called "Man Above,' to whom prayers were directed. The more sacred object was the Flat Pipe, which had been given to the Arapaho at creation and linked them to the supernatural world. A sacred wheel was also important, especially among the southern Arapaho, and was used in the Sun Dance.

Serious illness and injuries were treated by doctors, often in sweathouses, with singing, praying, shaking of rattles, and administering of herbal medicines. Most old people had family medicines for treating such ailments as skin rash, diarrhea, fever, and toothache.

When a death occurred, the surviving relatives cut their hair and put on old clothes. The women, especially, wailed loudly and sometimes lightly gashed their arms or legs with a knife. The body was buried in a grave dug in nearby sandhills, and a horse was usually killed over it. Mourning lasted a year and was ended with a face-painting ceremony and feast.

19th century. In the early 1880s, the Arapaho were one of the tribes who traded horses to the Cheyenne and other tribes at the great intertribal gatherings held near the Black Hills and elsewhere

Arapaho preparing for the Sun Dance. Photograph by James Mooney (1893).

on the Plains. Later, the Arapaho and Cheyenne became military allies as well as trading partners. The Arapaho were usually friendly with the Kiowa, Kiowa Apache, and Comanche; they were almost always at war with the Ute, Shoshoni, and Pawnee. The Arapaho resented the presence of white trappers in their territory and killed a few of them, but they ususally met white traders in peace and allowed some posts to be built in their country. Although they were generally peaceful toward official representatives of the United States, they saw nothing wrong in raiding the wagon trains on the Santa Fe Trail. Eventually they participated in hostilities against the white settlers when they saw their lands and way of life threatened.

The Arapaho made their first treaty with the United States at Fort Laramie in 1851, when the Arapaho and Cheyenne title to a vast tract lying between the North Platte and Arkansas rivers was recognized. White settlement of Colorado, however, occurred rapidly after the discovery of gold there in 1858, and treaties were made at Fort Wise, Kansas, in 1862 and on the Little Arkansas River in 1865, in an attempt to move the Indians to reservations away from the settlements. Neither of these treaties was effective, and a more comprehensive attempt to resolve the troubles on the Plains was made at peace councils held at Medicine Lodge Creek in Kansas in 1867 and at Fort Laramie, Wyoming in 1868.

At Medicine Lodge, the southern bands of Arapaho and Cheyenne signed a treaty ceding their former lands and accepting a reservation in Indian Territory. From then on the southern Arapaho remained at peace as a tribe.

The northern bands signed a treaty at Fort Laramie, but were asked to join their kinsmen on the Indian Territory reservation or settle with the Sioux or Crow tribe on their reservations in the north. None of these choices were satisfactory, and for some years the northern Arapaho were fragmented, some groups associating independently with the northern Cheyenne, Sioux, and Gros Ventre, and others coming for a time to Indian Territory. Finally, the northern Arapaho signed an agreement in 1876 in which they ceded their lands and agreed to move south. Many of them, however, sickened in Indian Territory, and they resolved to return to the north. In 1878, the government permitted them to settle on the Wind River Reservation in Wyoming, near their former enemies, the Shoshoni.

By 1880, the buffalo were gone and the Arapaho were dependent upon government rations while they learned other ways of making a living. The southern Arapaho were made to take 160-acre allotments in 1891, and the rest of their reservation was opened to white settlement in 1892. There emerged a "checkerboard" settlement pattern, with Indian lands being interspersed with tracts owned by whites. Over the years, the amount of

Little Raven

The northern Arapaho were also taught to farm, but had little success since their lands required irrigation and were better suited to grazing than the raising of crops. They remained in very poor condition for many years and finally, in the 1930s, the government shifted its emphasis to stock raising as an economic pursuit. Since 1940, a cooperative enterprise, the Arapahoe Ranch, has successfully been producing cattle for the market, though the profits, which are also distributed on an annual per capita basis, make up only a small portion of any individual's income. Many northern Arapaho work in construction and agricultural enterprises of the area, and some find employment with the tribe or Bureau of Indian Affairs. Serious economic problems persist, however, and are the major concern of the tribal business council.

Contemporary situation   Today the southern Arapaho are organized with the southern Cheyenne as the Cheyenne-Arapaho Tribes of Oklahoma, while the northern Arapaho are included in a similar body, the Shoshone and Arapahoe Tribes. Both groups of Arapaho see themselves culturally as one people, but politically as separate entities, each with its own resources and economic concerns. The Arapaho language is still spoken, especially in Wyoming, though the number of fluent speakers is decreasing. The Flat Pipe still exists and is cared for by a northern Arapaho family. It is still reverenced by all Arapaho, who see it as representative of their survival as a tribe.

The Sun Dance continued to be held in Wyoming every July, and many Oklahoma Arapaho go there to participate. New religious forms have appeared. The Ghost Dance of 1890 was accepted by many Arapaho of both divisions, and they helped spread it to other tribes. The peyote religion became popular around 1900 and is still an important avenue of worship. It now has legal recognition as the Native American Church. Many Arapaho have also joined Christian churches, the Roman Catholic and Episcopalian denominations redominating in the north, and the Mennonite and Baptist in the south.

The age-society system, out of place in rapidly changing times, ceased to function soon after allotment. The authority of the chiefs in tribal affairs faded as business committees, composed of elected members, replaced them as official tribal governing bodies.

In both Wyoming and Oklahoma, the Arapaho participate in the dances and powwows that are so much a feature of modern Indian life. Costumes based on traditional clothing styles and featuring elaborate beadwork and featherwork are reserved mainly for these occasions. Not surprisingly, the styles of singing, costuming, and dancing of the two divisions are somewhat different, as each is

land in Indian ownership has steadily declined as Indian tracts have been sold to non-Indians, and many of the remaining Indian tracts are now owned by many heirs of an original allottee.

20th century. Many southern Arapaho became fairly successful at subsistence farming, and a few achieved moderate success at marketing crops on a small scale. Frame houses were built and by World War I, the outward style of life was much like that of their rural white neighbors. The Indian farmers, however, were at a disadvantage in the market, and with the decline in farm prices they came to depend more and more for their livelihood on the income derived from leasing their lands to white farmers. Today only a handful of individuals farm on a market scale, and most depend on income from wage labor, in combination with lease money, for their living. A few individuals derive some income from oil and gas leases on their lands.

The northern Arapaho received individual allotments of 160 acres each in 1907, but the remaining reservation lands remained intact. This unallotted portion, by far the largest part, is owned by the Arapaho and Shoshoni tribes who divide the income from a number of natural resources, mainly oil and gas leases, equally. The Arapaho share is then distributed in annual per capita payments to all enrolled members of the tribe.

influenced more in these matters by neighboring tribes than by any formal tribal style.

Population During the 19th century, Arapaho population was usually estimated at between 2,500 and 3,500 by persons who had any firsthand reports of them. Following 1880, the population of both divisions seems to have declined until about the mid-1920s. Since that time, population has increased rapidly. In 1968 there were approximately 2,200 southern Arapaho and 2,725 northern Arapaho. About one-third of these lived away from the reservation or former reservation area.

Increasingly, the Arapaho are making conscious efforts to preserve their language and certain aspects of their former culture. At the same time, tribal leaders encourage the young to seek higher education and work to broaden the employment base for tribal members. (see map page XV)

BIBLIOGRAPHY-

● CURTIS, NATALIE. The Indians' Book: An offering by the American Indians of Indian Lore... New York, NY: Harper & Bros., 1907.
● DORSEY, GEORGE A. The Arapaho Sun Dance, the Ceremony of the Offerings Lodge. Chicago, IL: Field Columbia Museum Publication 76, 1903.
-----Traditions of the Arapaho. Chicago, IL: Collected under the auspices of the Field Columbia Museum of Natural History, 1903.
● EASTMAN, ELAINE GOODALE. Pratt, The Red Man's Moses. Norman, OK: University of Oklahoma Press, 1935.
● ELKIN, HENRY. The Northern Arapaho of Wyoming. New York, NY: D. Appleton-Century Co., 1940.
● FISHER, M. C. On the Arapaho, Kiowa, and Comanche. London, Journal of the Ethnological Society, 1869.
● FOREMAN, GRANT. Advancing the Frontier, 1830-1860. Norman, OK: University of Oklahoma Press, 1933.
-----Pioneer Days in the Early Southwest. Cleveland, OH, The Arthur H. Clark Co., 1926.
● GABRIEL, RALPH HENRY. The Pageant of America: the Lure of the Frontier... New Haven, CT: Yale University Press, 1929.
● HARMON, GEORGE DEWEY. Sixty Years of Indian Affairs, Political, Economic, and Diplomatic, 1789-1850. Chapel Hill, NC: University of North Carolina Press, 1941.
● HEBARD, GRACE RAYMOND. Sacajawea, A Guide and Interpreter of the Lewis & Clark Expedition, With An Account of the Travels... Glendale, CA: The Arthur H. Clark, Co., 1933.
● HEBARD, GRACE RAYMOND., E. A. BRININSTOOL. The Bozeman Trail; Historical Accounts of the Blazing of the Overland Routes into the Northwest, and the Fights with Red Cloud's Warriors. Cleveland, HO: The Arthur H. Clark Co.
● HODGE, FREDERICK WEBB. Handbook of American Indians North of Mexico. Washington: Smithsonian Institution: BAE Bulletin No. 30: U.S. GPO, 1907.
● HUMFREVILLE, J. LEE. Twenty Years Among Our Hostile Indians. New York, NY: Hunter & Co.
● KROEBAR, ALFRED L. The Arapaho. Bulletin of the American Museum of Natural History, v. 18, 1902-1907.
● MURDOCK, GEORGE P. Ethnographic Bibliography of North America. New Haven, CT: Human Relations Area Files Press, 1975.
● PHILLIPS, PAUL C. Forty Years on the Frontier, As Seen in the Journals and Reminiscences of Granville Stuart. Cleveland, OH: The Arthur H. Clark Co., 1925.
● RISTER, CARL COKE. Border Captives, The Traffic in Prisoners by Southern Plains Indians, 1835-1875. Norman, OK: University of Oklahoma Press, 1940.
-----The Southwestern Frontier - 1865-1881. Cleveland, OH: The Arthur H. Clark Co., 1928.
● ROYCE, CHARLES C. Indian Land Cessions in the U.S. Washington: 18th Annual Report, Bureau of American Ethnology, 1896-97, pt. 2), 1899.
● SCHOOLCRAFT, HENRY R. History of the Indian Tribes of the U.S.; Their Present Condition and Prospects... Philadelphia, PA: J. B. Lippincott & Co., 1857.
● SWANTON, JOHN R. The Indian Tribes of North America. Smithsonian Institution: BAE Bulletin No. 145: U.S. GPO, 1952.
● TRENHOLM, VIRGINIA C. The Arapahoes, Our People. Norman, OK: University of Oklahoma Press, 1970.
● WELLMAN, PAUL I. Death on the Prairie, The Thirty Years' Struggle for the Western Plains. New York, NY: The Macmillan Co., 1934.
● WHEELER, COL. HOMER W. Buffalo Days: Forty Years in the Old West... Indianapolis: The Bobbs-Merrill Co.
● WISSLER, CLARK. Indians of the U.S., Four Centuries of Their History and Culture. New York, NY: Doubleday, Doran & Co., 1940.

ARARA

(South America; Brazil) is a name that has been applied to several Brazilian Indian groups of the tropical forest culture area; the relationships between the groups are not clear. In 1820 Arara were reported to be living along the lower Madeira River and between the Madeira and the Tapajos rivers. In 1853, a tribe called Arara, perhaps migrants from the Madeira region, appeared along the lower Xingu River. The latter group later moved to the woodlands between the Xingu and Tocantins rivers. The Arara are also referred to as the Apeiaca, Apiaca, Apingui, and Pariri; they called themselves Opinadkom or Opinadkom. Some of the surviving groups called Arara are known to speak a Carib language; the linguistic affiliations of others are unknown, although some may speak Tupu languages.

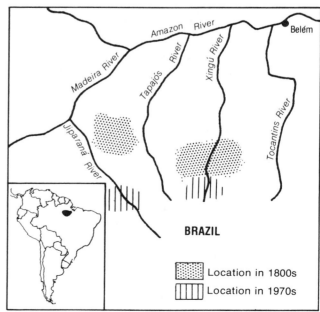

Arara

Arara culture. It is not clear whether the Arara grew cassava (manioc), corn (maize), and other crops, as neighboring tribes did. At the time of the first reported contacts with Europeans, the Arara were nomadic--although they had probably been more settled previously--and their nomadism may have caused a reduction in their material culture. Because the Arara, when they first arrived at the Tocantins River, used only turtles as a medium of exchange, the Neo-Brazilians assumed that the Arara did not farm. While some bands may have given up planting entirely, some Arara farm clearings were found at the headwaters of the Curua River. Furthermore, the Arara owned cotton objects and had words in their language for corn, tobacco, potatoes, and cassava. Hunting, collecting, and fishing must also have been important subsistence activities.

At least some Arara bands made palm-fiber hammocks. Before contact, neither men nor women wore clothing. Their hair, which was brown and wavy, was worn long, and the braids of the women often reached their knees. Personal ornaments included nose pendants, brightly colored diadems of parrot and other feathers, braided cotton forehead bands decorated with feathers and ending in two long strings, necklaces of seeds and bones, cotton arm bands, bracelets made from armadillo claws. The face was tattooed at puberty using genipa stain; two vertical lines were drawn from the eye down to the curve of the lower jaw. The nasal septum and earlobe were pierced to allow the insertion of ornaments.

The Arara are said to have lacked the canoe when first contacted by Neo-Brazilians, although in the late 19th century, the Arara along the Madeira were reported to have canoes made from elastic pieces of bark stiffened in the middle and lightly laced at the ends. Each canoe could hold four persons. The Arara manufactured carrying bags of interlaced palm-fiber cord, basketry, and crude pottery; and they sometimes used the dorsal carapace of a turtle as a vessel. Their tools included stone axes and chisels made of the teeth of the agouti, a rodent native to the area. Their weapons included lances with long bamboo points, powerful bows more than four feet long, and arrows, often decorated, with toothed bamboo points. A perforated nut was commonly placed under the arrowhead, perhaps to keep the arrow from penetrating too far, and feathers were sewn to the arrow shaft.

The Arara fought other tribes intermittently. As war trophies, they took and preserved the scalp (including the ears), the skin of the face, the skull, the teeth, and even the entire skin of the enemy.

Tribal history. In the late 18th and early 19th centuries, the Arara were living in the lower Madeira region, where they were reported by Europeans to be a fierce tribe that made the area unsafe for travellers and missionaries. They were said to have driven the Mundurucu Indians from the region some time before the Portugese Conquest in the 16th century. The Arara later moved to the forests on the right shore of the river and may have migrated or extended eastward to the Xingu. At any rate, a people called "Arara" by the Neo-Brazilians appeared on the lower Xingu in 1853. (They may have come from a tributary of the right bank of the Xingu, having been driven from there by the Cayapo Indians.) In 1861-62 these Arara--343 adults and an unknown number of children--moved downstream and established peaceful contact with the Neo-Brazilian rubber gatherers, but they soon disappeared from the area. In the 1880s, Arara were living west of the Xingu, from the mouth of the Iriri river southward. From the 1890s until they disappeared in 1918, this group was forced to move regularly, suffering persecution by the rubber tappers and conflict with the Shipaya Indians.

Another band of Arara, numbering about 30 in 1917, settled on the right bank of the Pacaja do Xinu River, where they worked and fought the Assurini Indians for the Neo-Brazilians. Some of these Arara may have survived at least into the 1930s.

In 1869, some 500 Arara appeared on the west bank of the Iowe Tocantins, to be followed by other, smaller groups. None survive today. In 1910 or 1911, another band of Arara, under the name of Parari, sought refuge from the Paracana Indians with the Neo- Brazilians of the Pacaja de Portel region. Of these, too, none survive today.

The Arara decline, like that of other Brazilian Indians, can be attributed to warfare with other tribes and, more importantly, to persecution by Neo-Brazilians and decimation by diseases introduced by Europeans. In the 1970s, Indians known as Arara were living on the Jiparana River, at the mouth of the Agua Azul River. Some were working near the town of Rondonia. About 40 were in contact with Neo-Brazilians. Uncontacted groups east of the Jiparana were called by the same name, but it is not known whether they represent the same tribe. Arara groups along the northern edge of the Xingu region have had both peaceful and hostile contacts with Neo-Brazilians in the 20th century. They have been reported along the Anapu, Bacaja, and Jacunda rivers and near the towns of Altamira and Portela, which they visit occasionally.

In late 1970, some 200 Arara living along the Penetacua River, near the route of the Trans-

Amazonica Road, were contacted by government "pacification" terms; by 1972, only about 50 were reported as surviving, and these had abandoned their village and were wandering along the highway in very poor condition.

BIBLIOGRAPHY-

● STEWARD, JULIAN H. Handbook of South American Indians. 7 Vols., Washington, DC: U.S. Govt. Printing Office, 1946-59.

APPOMATTOC

(U.S.; Va.) A tribe of the Powhatan confederacy formerly living on lower Appomattox River. They had 60 warriors in 1608, and were of some importance as late as 1671, but were extinct by 1722. Their principal village, which bore the same name and was on the site of Bermuda Hundred, Prince George County, was burned by the English in 1611. Appomatox was also one of the terms applied to the Matchotic, a later combination of remnants of the same confederacy. Along with other subtribes of the owhatan confederacy, they spoke in Alqonquian language. Population figures in 1968 for Powhatan descendents numbered 1,350.

BIBLIOGRAPHY-

● HODGE, FREDERICK WEBB. Handbook of American Indians North of Mexico. Washington: Smithsonian Institution: BAE Bulletin No. 30: U.S. GPO, 1907.
● SWANTON, JOHN R. The Indian Tribes of North America. Smithsonian Institution: BAE Bulletin No. 145: U.S. GPO, 1952.

ARAUCANIAN

(South America; Argentina, Chile) one of the larger and more important native peoples of South America, includes different sub-ethnic groups, some of which are now extinct. Once a relatively large population spread extensively over the southern region of South America, in the mid-1970s they were reduced to only two closely related ethnic groups--the Mapuche of southern Chile and the neighboring Argentinian Araucanians of southwestern Neuquen province, Argentina.

The name "Araucanian" was applied to the entire people, rather than to the sub-ethnic groups, each of which had its own name (e.g., Mapuche). The general name has also been used to designate the language, which is substantially of the Andean- Equatorial language family. The more appropriate name for the Araucanian language, and especially the language of the Mapuche, however, is Mapudungun. The name "Araucanian" is not their own, nor is it an Indian name, but is one imposed by the Spanish conquerors. The famous 16th-century Spanish warrior-poet Alonso de Ercilla y Zuniga was the first author to use the term "Araucana"--in his epic poem *La Araucana.* The origin of the term, however, is not certain. Some

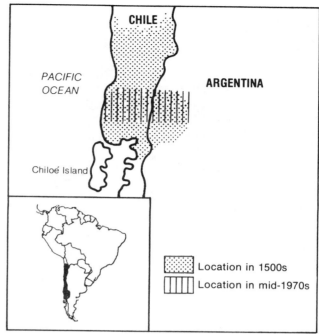

Araucanians

scholars believe that it was derived from the Hispanization of the Indian name Rauco ("muddy water"; from *raqo* or *rau,* "clay," and *ko* or *co,* "water")for the region that is now Arauco province, Chile. Others believe that it was derived from the Quechua names Aucas or Poromaucas (from *purum,* "wild enemy," and *auka,* "rebel") given by the Incas to the population south of the Maipo river in central Chile, whom they failed to conquer.

During the Inca and Spanish conquests, the Araucanians inhabited central-south Chile, from south of Choapa River to northern Chiloe Island. They were divided into three geographically contiguous ethnic groups--the Picunche (*pikun,* "north," and *che,* "people"), the Mapuche (*mapu,* "earth," and *che,* "people"), and the Huilliche (*huilli,* "south," and *che,* "people"). The three names were given to the groups by the Mapuche, who were geographically located in the middle of the region and considered themselves the "people of the earth." Later, other ethnic groups to the east were apparently incorporated into the Araucanian people, such as the Pehuenche ("pinon-eater people") of the cordillera region and at least part of the Puelche of the other side of the cordillera.

One of the earliest Spanish writers to mention the Araucanian people was Goicueta in 1558. Other chroniclers and historians from the 16th and 17th centuries and many explorers and historians from the 18th and 19th centuries also mention them. One of the most important sources is the report of 1673 by Francisco Nunez de Pineda y Bascurian of his long captivity.

Araucanian girls of Temuco, Chile, wearing crosses and other silver ornaments.

Men harvesting grain

Araucanian culture It is difficult to define traditional Araucanian culture because so many changes have taken place in the last 500 years. Araucanian prehistoric and pre-Inca culture can be classified as that of a simple slash-and-burn agricultural tribal society, based on large, and mostly patrilineal families (there were also matrilineal-extended families) with very little political cohesion in the tribe. There was lineage or tribal ownership of land and possibly of llama herds as well. The traditional culture of the Araucanians that is best known is that of the Mapuche- Huilliche from the historical period of Spanish colonial and Chilean independent times. Small differences would arise in a discussion of the Picunche or the Araucanized Peheunche and Puelche.

Economy. The aboriginal Mapuche-Huilliche subsistence economy was based principally on cultivated plants. They also relied on collecting wild seeds and hunting and fishing, emphasizing one or another of these complementary activities. Their diet was, nevertheless, predominantly vegetarian. They domesticated the llama and possibly guinea pigs and a sort of aboriginal chicken or duck. They occasionally used llama meat, but raised the animals mostly for their wool.

Araucanian staple crops were corn (maize) and potatoes. Other important crops--inlcuding beans, squash, chili peppers, and quinoa--were cultivated in relatively permanent fields which were from time to time left fallow. In historical times, plants brought from Europe were added and wheat became the main staple crop. From the Europeans, the Araucanians also adopted the plow and domesticated animals such as cattle, horses, sheep, goats, mules, and pigs.

Food was stored indoors in bins or woven, basket-like graineries, and outdoors in bins in elevated platforms. Meals were usually prepared by women. They smoked and sun-dried meat, boiled or roasted corn, made corn flour for bread or beverages, and combined corn flour with meat and vegetables in soups and stews. They also ate many types of beans and potatoes. Horsemeat was often consumed.

Aboriginal travel was usually by overland trails, goods being transported in fiber bags by human carriers, llamas and, later on, horseback. When horse transportation was not feasible, transportation on water was carried out on balsas (rafts), plank boats, or dugout canoes. The Mapuche-Huilliche manufactured pottery, stonework, baskets, ropes, and nets, and also produced woodwork and fine woven textiles from llama, and later from sheep, wool. Hammered gold and copper metallurgy was known from prehistoric times, and in colonial times, silversmithing was added. The manufactures were produced in the households, mostly by women; later some specialists, such as silversmiths, appeared. Trade was developed usually through the exchange of gifts and barter, and it became an important activity only in historic times, with the development of cattle-and-horse-raising, hunting, or looting. The cattle and horses were traded in large quantities with the Spaniards, and later with the Chileans.

The aboriginal property system was communal in the tribe or lineage, especially in relation to land and animals. With the importance of cattle-and-horse-trading in historical times, a type of private property held by the household head, or more often by the *lonkos* (chief), was developed. This property was based on animals, and land remained communal. Those chiefs who managed to accumulate wealth in animals became known as *ullmens*. There were few other differences between Mapuche households.

The simple pole-and-thatch dwellings of the Araucanians were usually isolated from each other and never formed villages. There were only a few houses for the large family household, which was organized in an exogamous patrilineage with patrilocal residence. Inheritance was also patrilineal. The residential group cooperated in clearing land, planting, and harvesting; most of these agricultural activities were done by women. There were other cooperative activities of the lineage of the tribe, the best known of which was the *mingako* system of collective labor for building a house, cultivating land, etc. Usually, the *lonko* invited the other parties for the *mingako* and initiated the work.

Political and social structure. The Araucanian political system was characterized by a lack of cohesiveness. Each household was led by the head of its extended family or lineage, and depended very little on the tribal *lonko*. Only in late historical times did the authority of *lonkos* and *ullmens* increase. During times of war, a tribal confederation arose under the leadership of some of the more important chiefs. A council advised the *lonkos* and maintained a sort of military democracy. At their peak of political cohesion, probably in the late 18th and 19th centuries, the Mapuche developed a diffuse form of chiefdom. By that time, a weak and incipient social stratification based on kinship status and wealth had developed.

Polygyny was once widespread, especially among the *lonkos* and *ullmens*. The principal wife had more authority than the others and ran the household. Sororate marriage (of a widow to her dead husband's brother), and marriages of brothers from one household to sisters of another were practiced to different degrees. Bride price was important, and it usually was accompanied by bride capture of a more dramatized than real nature. Conflicts between the Mapuche-Huilliche tribes, lineages, or households were settled through blood feud. There was no real warfare between the aboriginal Mapuche-Huilliche for the conquest of land. Only with the long Araucanian Wars did they engage in organized warfare, becoming skillful cavalrymen with great mobility and striking power. The Mapuche-Huilliche took captives in war whom they usually killed, displaying their heads as war trophies. Captives were, however, occasionally adopted or used in a kind of forced labor.

Religion. The patrilineal and generational systems of the Mapuche closely paralleled the hierarchial framework of their gods. Usually described as old people, the gods were believed to

be invisible and to have rather specific and limited powers. Their religion was polytheistic, with many gods categorized as major; minor and lesser deities had ethnic, regional, and lineage importance. Probably the most important major gods were Nillatun, a major agricultural-fertility rite through which contact was made with the gods.

The Mapuche believed in ancestral spirits--especially of their ancestral *lonkos*, founders of the lineages, and military leaders--who usually walked the earth in the company of the sons of the gods. They also believed in evil spirits such as Kalku, the sorcerer-witch, and Wekufe, the malevolent force, which usually assumed animal forms. These evil forces were closely related by the Mapuche to misfortune and illness, which were usually fought through shamanistic activities. In Araucanian aboriginal culture the shaman, or *machi*, was generally a man whose role was passed from father to son. In modern times, however, the role of *machi* was increasingly assigned to women. The most important magic ceremony performed by a shaman was the Machitun. During the ceremony, the shaman stayed close to or stepped on his carved pole, called a *rehue*, and beat his drum, or *kultrum*. Although *machis* used to participate also in the Nillatun ceremony, they must not be confused with the *nillatufe*, who was the ritual head of the ceremony.

In the aboriginal conception of the afterworld, the dead were believed to enter a spirit world in which existence paralleled that on earth. Death was accompanied by a complex mourning and burial ritual that included the tearing of hair, the driving away of evil spirits, a shamanistic autopsy, and partial preservation of the corpse. All this was accompamied by ceremonial wailing. The

Araucanian women performing the pillantun rite accompanied by her drum, or kultrum.

Araucanian pole-and-thatch dwelling.

relatives and friends of the dead person gathered together and drank a fermented beverage called-*mudai*. The burials were in cists or stone-lined graves; later, a canoe was sometimes used.

The Picunche. The traditional culture of the Mapuche- Huilliche described above was similar to that of the northern Picunche. There is no doubt that the Picunche were slightly more advanced. They were the only Araucanian group to practice irrigation in their much more effective agriculture, and they also probably relied more on llama-herding. The Picunche utilized more metal artifacts, had a well-developed pottery and basketry tradition, and used weapons including lances, pikes, spear throwers, and bows. Their settlement pattern, although not one of real villages, was one of larger clusters of houses than those of the Mapuche, who usually lived in isolated dwellings. Picunche houses were generally rectangular, had thatched roofs and wattle- and-daub walls, and were usually situated along rivers and streams or near easily irrigated land. Close to these hamlets were their cemeteries of mound burials. The political system of the Picunche was more affected by Inca influence. By the time of the conquest of the Picunche by the Spanish under Pedro de Valdivia, the democratic Araucanian system had begun among the Picunche. Social stratification and status differentiation had developed, especially under the strong leadership of Michimalongo, the chief who came close to defeating the Spanish army in the mid-16th century.

Araucanized groups. The Pehuenche, who were Araucanized during the 16th and 17th centuries, lived in the cordillera and the intercordilleran valleys east of the Mapuche-Huilliche region. Their acceptance of the Araucanian language and culture was marked by certain specific differences. The staple food of the Pehuenche was the *pehuen* or pinon, the fruit of the Araucanian pine (*Araucaria imbricata*). From that wild fruit, which was stored for a period of about four to five years, they made bread, beverages, and other foods. Horticulture was almost absent; the growing of apple trees was a late development. Pehuenche dwellings were constructed of horse and cattle hides. They apparently used a type of snowshoes during the winter.

The cordilleran people, usually called Chiquillanes, lived farther north, to the east of the Picunche area. Mixed with the Puelche, they were Araucanized by the Pehuenche when they moved north in the early 18th century. The Pehuenche and Mapuche had also Araucanized the western Puelche by that time. During the 18th and early 19th centuries, the Mapuche dominated most of the Argentinian pampas, hunting and capturing wild horses and cattle, or looting them from other Indians or Spanish settlements. They Araucanized the Puelche, or Pampas Indians, and even part of the northern Patagonian Tehuelche. At the same time, they acculturated themselves to the Argentinian pampas, becoming more nomadic and basing their subsistence on the raising, hunting, and looting of cattle and horses. At the end of the Araucanian Wars in the late 19th century, the mixed Araucanized population of Mapuche-Pehuenche-Puelche-Northern Tehuelche formed the modern Argentinian Araucanians, who never lost contact with their Mapuche-Huilliche brothers on the other side of the cordillera.

Origins. The ethnic origins of the Araucanian groups can be traced through archaeology. In the central zone of Chile-- *i.e.*, the habitat of the Picunche--three prehistoric agro- pottery levels or phases can be distinguished. They are, from the oldest to the most recent, the Molloid phases, the polychrome ceramic phases (with black-on-orange local pottery), and the local Incaic phases. The three were diffused and expanded in different time periods and with diverse limits of influence toward the southern, or Mapuche-Huilliche, habitat.

With its early cultural phases, the first level seems to correspond to a basic agro-pottery stratum, by which came a process of acculturation from the area of Chile immediately to the north. It shows influences from the Molle culture of that area which, it seems, introduced agriculture into the central zone in the second half of the first millenium AD. This influence continued toward the south, bringing the agricultural revolution there by the end of the first millenium AD, first in the central zone and later in the southern zone. Later local developments and influences came from the neighboring northern Diaguita cultural phases. All the Araucanian cultural elements crystallized during this prehistoric period when the ethnologenesis of the Araucanian groups began.

At the time of the Inca conquest, a separation and differentiation of the Araucanians took place. The northern ethnic group of the Picunche was conquered and integrated into the socioeconomic structure of the Inca empire. The other two more southern groups--the Mapuche and Huilliche--tenaciously resisted, however, and maintained themselves as independent tribal society.

The Spanish period. At the time of the Spanish conquest in the mid-16th century, the Araucanian population numbered about 1,000,000 persons. As a result of the destruction of the Inca Empire by the Spanish conquistadores, the separate regions of the former empire, such as the central zone of Chile, remained disunited and, in fact, independent. An interregnum of autonomy lasted for decades in the Picunche area, until the new Spanish conquest took place in this zone. The Picunche resisted the Spaniards, but they were eventually conquered and subjugated. Forced manual labor was imposed upon them, especially in the initial decades, for the extraction of precious metals to enrich far away Spain. This process was "legal" status through the law encomienda, in which Indian labor was granted by the Spanish king. Only later was the indigenous labor force channeled into agricultural and cattle-raising activities that soon supplanted the encomienda in the form of the hacienda system of large landholdings. Many Picunche ran away to the south and integrated into the Mapuche-Huilliche groups, which could not be defeated by either the Incas or the Spaniards. Other Picunche mixed with the Spanish population, which led to the appearance of the Chilean mestizo population, especially in the rural areas of the central zone. By the beginning of the independent period in the early 19th century, the Picunche had completely disappeared as a separate ethnic group.

The so-called Araucanian Wars, which began soon after the Spanish invasion, became a struggle between the Mapuche and the Spaniards. Some Huilliche were integrated into the Mapuche and eventually merged with them. Isolated Picunche groups and individuals also fled to the Mapuche area and were incorporated into this ethnic group. The captives that the Mapuche obtained from the Spanish adventurers, werecriminals, and deserters.

The Spaniards' prime purpose in the Araucanian Wars was to obtain captives to replace or increase the servile manual labor force. The vicissitudes of the sporadic wars produced a notable ethnic transformation of the Mapuche and their socioe-

Mapuche-Huilliche hockey game of the early 17th century. From the book by Alonso Ovalle, *Histórica relación del reyno de Chile* (1646).

conomic and cultural structures. There also developed a form of permanent contact and cohabitation between the two warring sectors. This was possible because the wars, although occurring over an extraordinarily long time span, were basically limited to a few short periods of total war, followed by years of tacit armistice intermittently interrupted by small skirmishes or guerilla struggles and harrassments.

The most important of these confrontations during colonial times were probably the long and terrible battles at the end of the 16th century, especially in 1598, when the Indians defeated the Spaniards, destroyed most of their settlements along the frontier area, and killed the governor, Martin Garcia de Loyola. Other important periods of the wars were the 1640s, 1720s, 1740s, and 1760s. During the Chilean war of independence against the Spaniards in the early 19th century, the Mapuche tried to take advantage of the situation. Some tribes fought with the Spanish army against the Chileans, and other tribes fought with the Chileans against the Spaniards.

In the course of appproximately three centuries, from the mid- 16th to the mid-19th century, the Mapuche went through the extraordinary process of territorial and ethnic expansion, as well as one of notable cultural contact, acculturation, and ethnic mixture. Outside of the integration and mixture with the rest of the related Araucanian groups in Chile, and with groups of Spaniards and Creoles, the Mapuche, enclosed on three sides, expanded toeard the Andean Mountains and beyond. There they struggled against other indigenous groups--such as the Pehueneche of the mountains, the Puelche of the eastern slopes of the Andes and the Argentinian pampas, and the Tehuelche of the Patagomian pampas--all of withwhom they either mixed with or Araucanized. More than the tactical necessities of mobile guerila war, this eastern Mapuche expansion followed the development of a commercial cattle exchange which grew, in spite of everything, between the competing sectors of the Mapuche and the Spaniards, and later the Chileans.

The Mapuche adopted and adapted numerous important features of the Spanish material culture. The horse was used not only for war but also for agriculture and cattle-raising, for commerce, for food, and even in religious rites. Metal arms and instruments, firearms, alcohol, numerous artifacts and instruments of daily life, silver work, clothing, elements of the Roman Cathloic religion, and Spanish values were also introduced into Mapuche life. The activities of the missionaries, some of whom entered Araucanian territory as early as the mid-16th century, were important. From 1593 until their expulsion in 1768, the Jesuit missions systematically operated. They were replaced by the Capuchins in the late 19th century. After the 1870s, the Salesians worked among the Argentinian Araucanians, and the Protestant missions from Europe and North America added their efforts toward converting the Indians.

The post-colonial period. After the independence of Chile was achieved in 1813, a few clashes between the Mapuche and the Chilean army occurred. Especially active were the decades of the 1850s and 1860s during the period of Chilean territorial expansion under Col. Hernandarias de Saavedra. The last uprising of the Mapuche was in the early 1880s, when they tried to take advantage of the concentration of the Chilean armed forces in the distant north during the War of the Pacific between Chile, Peru, and Bolivia. The Mapuche were finally defeated in 1883, and the great Araucanian Wars came to an end. The Araucanians of the pampas were defeated by the Argentinian army in the battles in 1879. They were then concentrated in the western Neuquen territory of Argentina.

After the final struggles of the Araucanian Wars, the Chilean government tried to concentrate the Mapuche on Indian reservations. These efforts began in the 1860s, as a product of territorial expansion. In 1866, the central government in Santiago approved the first law for the establishment of Indian reservations. It was only with the law of 1884, after the final military subjugation of the Mapuche, however, that it was really possible to initiate the reservation system.

This system was part of the process of expansion of Chilean capitalism in the last decades of the 19th century. That expansion reached out toward the rich mining sector of the north after the successful expansionist War of the Pacific, toward the Pacific Ocean with the take-over of Easter Island, and toward the southern part of the country through the submission of the Mapuche. In the south, the intention was not only to create, new cities and industries and to expand the national market but especially to expand the *latifundio* or hacienda system. This was done at the expense of the best Mapuche land, which was expropriated by the state and sold to the landowners, who often directly took over the land at any price and by any means. The Mapuche were reduced to living only on their reservations.

The modern period of the history of the Mapuche began with the installation of the reservation system in Chile, the defeat of the Araucanians and their allies on the pampas, and their concentration in Neuquen province, Argentina, in the early 1880s. Although not formally or legally a reservation system like its counterpart in Chile, the policy in Argentina did actually reduce the Araucanians to specific territorial areas.

The early reservation period. With the establishment of the reservation system, the economic, social and cultural structure of Mapuche-Huilliche society changed rapidly. Although land continued to be held communally, it was now property of the reservation with a property title, or *titulo de merced,* granted in the name of the reservation chief. Under this system, the political position of the chiefs, which had greatly weakened, partially regained its strength. Their authority was limited, however, because they did not have any juridicial or administrative powers derived from the Chilean state. Internal authority by the chiefs on the reservations, therefore, was weak. Community leadership was often assumed by others such as the *machi,* the Mapuche schoolmaster, the Christian Mapuche priest, or simply a "richer" Mapuche or a natural leader of the community. Despite these challenges to traditional authority, the reservation continued to function as a sociopolitical unit that was not taken over by the expansionist hacienda system of the landowner class, and it preserved the existence of its indigenous community.

The subsistence economy of the Mapuche continued to play a dominant role on the reservations, where there was a man/land ratio of about six hectares. The production of the Mapuche peasant was much like that of other Chilean farmers, but patterns of distribution and consumption continued to be different. The Mapuche sowed wheat and raised cattle on small farms. Only a small part of their products, however, reached the markets, most of the produce being destined for internal consumption. The various Mapuche crafts were also developed largely for their own consumption and for bartering with their neighbors, with only a small portion reaching the tourist market.

The subsistence economy did not remain outside or on the periphery of the national economy, however. Intermediaries introduced Mapuche products into the national markets, accruing large profits for themselves while encouraging the maintenance of the subsistence level on the reservations. This intensive exploitation of the Araucanians was two-fold--it directly maintained a reserve of cheap manual labor for the large estates and it indirectly decapitalized the Indians by presenting their products on the market at the cheapest price. In this way, the commercialization of native products, especially wheat and cattle, actually increased the Indians' poverty and dependence.

During the first 50 years of the reservation system, the level of Mapuche scholarship was minimal and illiteracy was common. Primary school instruction, rather than being state-supported, was fundamentally private, provided by Roman Catholic or Protestant churches. The Mapudungun language and the values of Mapuche culture, although obviously modified, were preserved to a great extent during the period. Instead of accepting the culture of the larger, dominant society, the Mapuche developed a true resistance culture, strengthening their ethnic identity as a defense against racial discrimination. Mapuche social mobility in the larger society during the early period of the reservation system was minimal. Social conflict generally acquired the character of racial conflict and appeared as a struggle of the Mapuche against the Huinca mestizo, as well as against the exploitive class.

The modern reservation period. In the second and modern period of the reservation system, all the symptoms of the breakdown of this system dis

appeared, sharpening its internal and external contradictions. With the continuing expansion during the 20th century of the large estate or hacienda system, the reservation system lost more land and became more dependent upon the former. These processes led to a decrease and concentration of communal lands and to overpopulation of the reservations and subdivisions of the remaining communal land. The man/land ratio was reduced to only about two hectares. Thus, divided communities were formed with the encouragement of the larger society. In the undivided communities, a trend developed toward internal, de facto subdivisions of communal land among the reservation families and, in fact, to the end of communal property. Only a legal and formal communal holding was retained, continuing in effect the early title granted to the chiefs during the first period of the reservation system.

Production continued fundamentally in a familiar form--each separate family cultivated a certain number of hectares--with only a limited surface area remaining for communal cultivation. Thus, small parcels of land, or minifundia, were introduced into the reservations, and the large native ownership of land, which was communal during the early period, ended in modern times with the appearance of small family properties. The so-called minifunda system modified the Mapuche attitude toward the land from that of a communal and cooperativist view to the petty bourgeois mentality of small peasant ownership.

Another consequence of this most contradictory situation was the substantial increase in migration from the reservation to the large haciendas, thus increasing the quantity of Mapuche tenants and day-laborers in the cities where jobs were available in public works or agricultural industries. This migration produced a breakdown of family and kinship ledership, throwing the entire Mapuche culture and identity system into profound crisis. At the same time, the hacienda system in Chile also broke down, creating growing economic crisis and the rise of social conflict between the peasantry (including the Mapuche) and the landowner class.

The process of disintegration was halted by the agrarian reform that took place in the 1960s and early 1970s. The agrarian structure was greatly changed, affecting the Indian communities as well as the dominant society. It is true that the Mapuche did not profit much from agrarian reform, but they did become integrated into the Chilean peasant class and they gained in both their social and their ethnic consciousness. They continued their centuries-old struggle in the mid-1970s in a new form, now desiring just economic and social participation in Chilean society. The Mapuche continue to

Araucanians near Lake Ranco, Chile.

maintain their culture, although not without modification, and to keep their ethnic identity.

Of a total population of more than 9,000,000 in the Republic of Chile, the Mapuche numbered more than 500,000 during the mid- 1970s. They lived principally in the large area between the Laja River and the Gulf of Relocavi that included Chile's seven southern provinces. The majority of the Mapuche were concentrated in Cautin, Malleco, and northern Valdivia provinces. Of the 3,040 indigenous reservations that existed in the seven provinces, two- thirds were located in Cautin. In Cautin and Malleco provinces, the Mapuche constituted three-fourths of the rural population of less than 50,000--less than one-tenth of their own total population--was concentrated in the larger cities of Santiago, Concepcion, and Temuco.

In the early 1960s, the land operated by the Mapuche totaled 566,000 hectares, 343,000 hectares of which were in Cautin. Most of the Mapuche lived on their reservations, but others were independent small landowners, tenant farmers, or day laborers in rural or urban areas. Some also incorporated in agrarian reform areas as workers on the *asentamientos* established by agrarian reform.

There are no census figures available for the Argentinian Araucanians after they were concentrated in the Neuquen province in 1880. According to the Argentinian census of 1947, the total population of Neuquen was about 85,000 and of these no more than 3,500 were considered Araucanian. In the mid-1970s, probably no more than 10,000 Araucanians lived in Neuquen or elsewhere in Argentina. They were more acculturated to the Argentinians than their Mapuche brothers were to the Chileans, although they continued to maintain their culture and ethnic identity.

BIBLIOGRAPHY- See ARAUCANIAN WARS.

ARAUCANIAN WARS

were the series of military confrontations from the 16th to the 19th centuries through which the Araucanian Indians of South America sought to maintain their independence from the Inca, the Spanish, and the governments of Chile and Argentina.

According to legend, the emperor Topa Inca Yupanqui conquered Araucania in the latter part of the 15th century and exacted tribute from the northern Araucanian Indians. Although no formal data exist to prove that the Inca conquered the entire Araucanian group, the recurrence of certain animal motifs and of similar geometric designs on pottery and in weaving have led scholars to assume substantial contact between the two cultures.

What is certain is that the Araucanians never achieved the higemony and cohesion of social institutions that made the Inca a nation.

When the Spanish entered what is now Chile in the 16th century, they found large numbers of Indians living in tribal units and warring among themselves. The conquistadores concluded that conquest would be a relatively simple affair. They were soon to discover otherwise; the indecisive and bloody warfare between Spaniards and Araucanians, which earned the captaincy--general of Chile the epitaph *cementerio de los espanoles* ("graveyard of the Spaniards"), continued for more than three centuries.

16th century. On February 12, 1541, Pedro de Valdivia, the first governor of Chile, founded what is now the capital city of Santiago, six months later the Araucanians destroyed it. Spanish reinforcements were sent from Peru, and a century characterized by incessant raiding and subsequent retaliatory punitive expeditions began. Ignoring the Spanish crown's Royal Decree of December 4, 1528--in which use of Indians as beasts of burden, personal servants, or work slaves, as well as the exiling of Indians, were prohibited--de Valdivia and the majority of his 16th-century successors moved into Araucania, placing captives under the encomienda system. An encomienda was normally a trust granted by the Spanish crown in a conquistador, by which the conquistador acquired the right to tribute from a native community in exchange for supporting a priest, Christianizing the natives, etc. De Valdivia went beyond this practice of a right to tribute. He supported a right to personal services, whereby Indians held in encomienda were turned over to officials who had been rewarded with *mercedes* (land grants) as work slaves or occasionally were taken off for use on public works.

Concepcion was founded by de Valdivia in February 1550; it was lost to the Araucanians in an uprising led by Caupolican in 1553, in which de Valdivia was killed. Francisco de Villagra retook Concepcion, only to lose it in 1554 to the forces of Lautoaro (the Indian leader immortalized in Alonso de Ercilla y Zunigra's epic poem *La Araucana*). Caupolican was defeated by Garcia Hurtado de Mendoza's forces in 1557 and was killed the following year. Lautaro was also killed in battle in 1557.

Relations with the Spanish were then quiet until the Araucanians killed Don Pedro de Avendano, the man who had killed Caupolican, in 1561. De Villagra, now the governor, sent his brother Pedro on a punitive expedition. A new *toqui* ("leader"), Colo-Colo, defeated the Spanish forces, killed the governor's brother, and began the siege of Fort Arauco. The Indians suffered defeat at the hands

Araucanian and Tehuelche horsemen. Acquisition of horses and better weapons by the Araucanians aided them in withstanding the Spanish.

of Lopez Bernat de Marcado in 1564, and again in 1565 by the largest Spanish army of the period (400 soldiers and 800 Indian auxilliaries). The pattern of intermittent, seemingly futile warfare which was to prevail for almost 200 years was established; it was characterized by successes and defeats for both sides, by parleys and peace treaties, by defensive and offensive tactics.

By the end of the 16th century, the Araucanians had learned to use horses, had improved their weapons (although they still depended on spears, as guns were not readily available), and had perfected their guerilla and counterespionage tactics. Instead of simply attacking and retreating, they began to burn settlements to the ground and steal livestock. Occasionally, an Indian would allow himself to be captured by the Spaniards, gather logistic information, and, if possible, escape and return to his countrymen. The language expanded to include war vocabulary: words like *lineo cona* ("war parties") and *namuntu cona* ("infantry") appeared. *Toquis* began to work together, and tribal war gave way to a broader social war. This occurred in the 1598 uprising led by Paillamachu, in which not only free Araucanians but also allies from the Picunche and Huilliche Araucanian groups, who worked in the mines and fields, participated. As a result, 500,000 animals (horses, catle, goats, sheep, and pigs) were taken, more than 50 churches burned and, in Valdivia, 700 Spaniards were killed or wounded and 18,000 pesos worth of goods stolen from the church.

The Spaniards reacted by developing a counter-strategy. They began using encomiendas and *mitas* (the equivalent of the encomienda, referring specifically to mining) to redistribute the indigenous population. They no longer thought in terms of conquering all of Araucania, but rather of holding their own settlement line. Finally, they developed mobile fighting units copied after those of the Indians. To some degree, this new strategy accounted for the fact that early in the 17th century, of the 100,000 Araucanians left in Chile, 90 percent lived south of the Bio-Bio River.

17th century. The 17th century was marked by a distinct change in tenor. The voices of the missionary priests were heard, and in some instances, they prompted changes in governmental policy.

In 1601, Gov. Alonso de Ribera Figueroa took the reins of power in Chile. His *plan de Concepcion,* which he attempted to put into practice, provided for a fortified settlement line that was to move slowly south, "colonizing" Araucania. This was the first time that colonization, instead of conquest, was suggested. In 1605, Gov. Alonso Garcia Ramon, de Ribera Figueora's successor, attended the Conference of Theologians and Doctors held in Lima, Peru members of the conference decided that the Araucanians were rational human beings and that forced labor should be ended. When he arrived in Chile, Garcia Ramon had with him Father Luis de Valdivia, a friar who spoke Mapudungun, the language of the Mapuche group of Araucanians. A short-lived peace treaty between the Spaniards and the Araucanians was signed.

Frustrated by reports of continued fighting, Philip III of Spain on May 26, 1608, decreed that non-Roman Catholic Indians could once again be enslaved. Gov. Luis Merlo de la Fuente enforced this policy for Chile in 1610. At this point, Father Luis rebelled. He negotiated directly with both the King and the Council of the Indies concerning the Indian problem. He asked that the Bio-Bio River be made a demarcation line between Spanish and Araucanian territories, that only missionaries be allowed to go into Araucania, and that all Araucanian prisoners be pardoned. In short, he asked for a fresh start and three years to carry out his colonization program.

The crown in May 1610, and Father Luis returned to Chile. There, in 1612, he met with *toqui*-Utablame at Paicavi. The experiment began, somewhat shakily, and lasted until 1621 when a new governor, Pedro Osores de Ulloa, and the new Spanish monarch, Philip IV, withdrew support from Father Luis. During this eight- year period, the number of ranches in Araucania rose from 6 to 72 and tithes from 80 to 4,000 per year. Only eight Spaniards were killed (in contrast with more than 40 between 1606 and 1612).

The remainder of the century was marked by the same fighting that had marred the previous one. The Peace of Quillin (1641, ratified by the crown in 1643) was broken in 1655 when another coordinated Indian rebellion was raised in reaction to the blatant slave trade of Indians that was subsidized by Gov. Antonio de Acuna y Cabrera.

18th and 19th centuries. The 18th and 19th centuries were characterized by a series of peace talks in Chile, by Araucanian expansion into Argentina, and by Spanish retaliation. During the previous two centuries, relations between the Araucanians and the native peoples of the Argentine pampas had been based on trade. The former bought horses; the latter, woven goods. In the 18th century, however, assimilation of the Argentine Indians by the Araucanians began in force. In the records of a meeting of the *cabildo* (town council) of Buenos Aires on December 23, 1709, there is mention of Araucanians having been seen on the pampas. Three months later, the records indicate concern bordering on alarm with reference to the large number of *indios aucaes* to be found in Argentina. The rapid encroachment of the Araucanians on the pampas is reflected in the fact that by 1750, Mapudungun was the dominant language of the Indians of Argentina.

Raiding by the Araucanians in Argentina reached its peak during the 1820s. But in 1833, Juan Manuel de Rosas, better known for his dictatorial powers than for his role as peacemaker, negotiated a treaty with the Indians that lasted until his fall from power in 1852. A southern demarcation line, which Indians could not cross without permission from the military, was established, and each cacique (chief) was provided foodstuffs and tobacco for his people. Between 1852 and 1873, when de Rosas died, *toqui* Calfucura led the Araucanians in numerous raids. The national government retaliated with bloody punitive expeditions which resulted in the decimation of Argentina's Indian population. Under the military leadership of Gen. Julio A. Roca, between 1879 and 1883, the conquest of the pampas was finally and firmly consummated. The remaining Indians were forced into Patagonia.

In Chile during this period, 16 peace treaties were negotiated. The more noteworthy include that of Negrete (February 13, 1726), which reiterated the freedom of Indians; of Tapihue (1746), which prohibited alliance with Argentine Indians; of Macimiento (1764), by which the Araucanians agreed to settle in towns; of Negrete (1771), which provided for disarmament for both sides; of Loquilmo (January 3, 1784), which gave Araucanians the right to trade freely and provided for the establishment of four annual trade fairs; and again of Negrete (1793), in which Ambrosio O'Higgins negotiated a peace that lasted well into the 19th century. *Malones* ("raids") continued to occur in Chile, but less frequently and with fewer far-reaching implications. It was as though the consolidated social Araucanian Wars had given way once again to independent tribal war. During the wars for independence and the civil war of the 1850s, Araucanians fought on both sides.

Two final uprisings of Araucanians occurred, in 1869-70 and in 1881. The former was initiated when the government's reservation policy of 1866 (superseding the 1853 law which forbade sale of Indian lands) allowed sale of unclaimed Indian land to immigrants. The latter occurred for much the same reason. Both were quickly subdued, and on January 1, 1883, the last peace talks between the native and non-native populations of Chile were held at Villarrica. The Araucanians were forced onto reservations in southernmost Chile and were stripped of any political autonomy.

BIBLIOGRAPHY-
● STEWARD, JULIAN H. Handbook of South American Indians. 7 Vols., Washington, DC: U.S. Govt. Printing Office, 1946-59.

ARAVAIPA

(U.S.; Ariz.) are an Apache band living in the southeastern area who were nearly decimated by the Camp Grant Incident in 1871. Before the Apache wars of the late 19th century, they were farmers and warriors from the Aravaipa Creek region of southeastern Arizona. By the mid-1970s, federal decrees, economic pressures, and intermarriage had scattered the remaining members of the band over the San Carlos and Fort Apache reservations in east-central Arizona, largely erasing their identity as a band.

History. The name Aravaipa (Arivaipa) comes from a Pima word meaning "girls." The band apparently came to Arizona after the mid-16th century and became less nomadic than most Apache bands; they turned to gathering mescal and raising corn.

As friction in Arizona grew between the Apache and the whites, the Aravaipa became a target for Indian-haters. In 1863, the California Volunteers, headquartered at nearby Camp Grant, murdered 58 of the 70 Aravaipa living near the creek. Further raids drove the band away from their homes along the creek. Some, led by the noted warrior Eskiminzin, hid in the nearby mountains. Others went north to White Mountain Apache territory or west to Fort Goodwin. In February 1871, the Tuscon Committee of Public Safety massacred 125 unarmed Indians, including 117 women and children, near Camp Grant. Eskiminzin took the remnants of the band back into the mountains and, in 1872, agreed to reservation settlement. For the next seven years, the band was shifted between the San Carlos and Fort Apache reservations, while the U.S. Army determined the most efficient way to administer them. In 1879, they were given their choice between the two reservations. Eskiminzin and about 40 followers chose fertile land near the border of San Carlos Reservation. After building adobe homes and fencing their ranches, they were displaced by white settlers in 1883 when the reservation line was changed. Shortly thereafter, the entire group was imprisoned by Gen. Nelson A. Miles for allegedly aiding a fugitive, but they were later released to find new homes.

Contemporary situation. By the mid-1970s, the maximum population estimate for Aravaipa on both reservations was less than 300, with approximately twice as many living on San Carlos Reservation as on Fort Apache. Only 32 persons could be directly traced to Aravaipa lineage through land records. The majority of Aravaipa on both reservations worked for the federal or tribal government, in the timber industry, or were unemployed. There were no activities on either res-

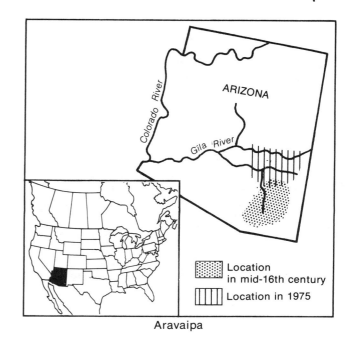

Location in mid-16th century
Location in 1975

Aravaipa

ervation to unite the Aravaipa as a band, and consciousness of former Aravaipa unity was gradually disappearing.

BIBLIOGRAPHY-

● WELLMAN, PAUL I. Death in the Desert. The Fifty Years' War for the Great Southwest. New York, NY: Macmillan Co., 1935.

ARAWAK

(South America) is a term that refers to native peoples of the Greater Antilles and South America who spoke languages of the Arawakan linguistic group.

The terms "Arawak" and "Arawakan" are used in at least four ways: historical, archaeological, ethnographic, and linguistic.

Historical, archaeological, and ethnographic. In a historical context, the terms are applied primarily to the indigenous inhabitants of the Greater Antilles whom Columbus encountered on his voyages of discovery in the late 15th century, and secondarily to assorted indigenous groups scattered along the coastline of northeastern South America. In archaeological discussions, the terms refer to a horizon comprised of boat- shaped pottery, large house construction, rather intensive horticulture, spear throwers to the exclusion of the bow and arrow, and certain religious figurines (*Cemi*), which occur throughout the Caribbean islands and, to a much lesser extent, on the Circum-Caribbean littoral.

Ethnographic usage reverses the historical and archaeological meanings, for Arawak society has completely disappeared from the islands. Today,

Arawak

groups calling themselves Arawak--or called such by other Indians or non-Indians--are found only in the coastal and near interior parts of the countries of Guyana, Surinam, and French Guiana. In Indian districts of these countries, the word *locono* ("the people") is used synonomously with the pidginized "Arawak" as a group label. Since most Arawak are bilingual in English or Dutch (if they retain their indigenous language at all), they use these terms interchangeably. In this article the same practice is adopted in sections dealing with Arawak ethnography.

Linguistic. In linguistics, the term "Arawakan" has a technical usage of considerably broader scope. According to a current classification system of South American Indian language, Arawakan is one of 14 living language families in the Andean-Equatorial linguistic phylum. The Arawakan family at one time included perhaps as many as 100 separate languages, and these were unevenly distributed over the respectable portion of the hemisphere: from the peninsula of Florida in the north to Paraguay in the south, and from the Atlantic coast to the foothills of the Andes in eastern Bolivia. Following European contact, several major Arawakan speech communities disappeared, most notably the Taino dialect of the Greater Antilles. The process of linguistic extinction continues today, and many Arawakan dialects--mostly in Brazil--are kept alive by a few dozen individuals living in one or two villages. The largest speech community, about 45,000 persons, is the Goajiro of the Colombian-Venezuelan northern border. Because the Guianas Arawak of the ethnographic present are losing their indigenous language, Locono dialect speakers probably number fewer than 5,000 in the entire region.

There is a lack of fit between linguistic and ethnographic classification where the Arawak are concerned. This is exemplified in the curious fact that not all speakers of Arawakan languages are Arawak, and not all Arawak can speak an Arawakan language. There is simply no common cultural basis shared by Arawakan language speakers. While the traditional ethnographic portrait of the Arawak presents them as horticulturalists with matrilineal clans, the largest Arawakan speech community, the Goajiro, have subsisted for centuries by nomadic cattle pastoralism, a practice unique to South American Indians. Similarly, the Wapishana, an Arawakan language group of southern Guyana and northern Brazil, have a strong patrilineal, patrilocal bias. Conversely, the coastal Arawak of Guyana and Surinam, who do resemble the ethnographic portrait, are losing their facility in the Locono dialect, so that there are more Arawak than Locono speakers.

The Locono dialect has existed in written form since the 1850s, when missionaries in the Guianas began to produce biblical translations in the local tongue. These exercises, however, have not encouraged more than a handful of Arawak to use the written form, and then never in spontaneous communication. With the slow but steady decline in the number of Locano speech communities, even the future of the oral form is problematic.

The first people encountered by Christopher Columbus in the New World were the Taino-speaking Arawak inhabitants of the present-day Bahamas, Cuba, and Hispaniola (the Dominican Republic and Haiti). Believing that he had reached the outer islands of Japan and China, the explorer referred to them as "Indios." The term was accepted by contemporary voyagers and later chroniclers and eventually became a gloss for the indigenous peoples of the Americas. Because there were as yet not other known Indian societies with which to compare the islanders, these Arawak groups did not immediately receive a tribal name.

Type of canoe used by Taino in 16th century. Drawing from Oviedo y Valdés.

They were evidently sufficiently alike in dress, language, and custom for the Spanish adventurers to see no need to distinguish among them.

The Spaniards learned from some of the Bahama Arawak that their land was called Lucaya, and thereafter these groups were designated Lucayos. In literature, the Arawak of the Greater Antilles are often referred to as the Taino, a term that has passed into accepted archaeological and linguistic usage. Its derivation is probably from the Antillean Arawak term for a social class of nobles, the *ndaino*.

The etymology of the word "Arawak" itself is uncertain, and doubtless owes as much to European writers as to the Indian inhabitants of the Greater Antilles and northeastern South America. Older speakers of the Locono dialect in present-day Guyana will supply the curious ethnographer with etymologies, but these are of doubtful validity. There are at least two conflicting folk etymologies for "Arawak." The more popular theory claims that the word is derived from *aru,* the Locono generic term for cassava. The other version gives the source word as *arua,* Locono for jaguar. Borrowings from European and other Indian languages make it virtually impossible to determine the accuracy of either etymology.

History of the Arawak. The period preceeding European discovery was a tumultuous one for native populations in the Circum-Caribbean area, because Carib groups were everywhere engaging, conquering, and enslaving the Arawak. Before the Carib intrusion, Arawak populations had predominated in the area, stretching from a northernmost outpost on the peninsula of Florida through both the Greater and Lesser Antilles and over much of the Guianas and the Venezuela coastline. When Columbus arrived, the Carib had already swept through the Lesser Antilles chain--from the mainland to the Virgin Islands off Puerto Rico-- and driven out, killed, or enslaved the Arawak they found there.

From the first voyage of Columbus (1492-93), a distinction was made between the peaceful Indios the Spaniards met on the larger islands and a fierce people to the south whom the Antilleans described as "Caribs" or "cannibals." Columbus is responsible for insinuating this distinction between "good" Indians and "bad" Indians into the European consciousness. From the earliest days of Spanish exploration, therefore, the Arawak were considered by Europeans to be a civilized and benign people, in contrast with the virtually unknown Carib, whose supposedly evil intentions made them the objects of Spanish enslavement and hostility.

Although demographic features of late 15th- and early 16th- century Antillean societies are sparsely documented, these are nevertheless better known than the mainland tribal distribution for the same period and later. In the 16th and 17th centuries, the area between the Orinoco and Amazon deltas was an uncolonized region separating the Spanish in Venezuela from the Portuguese in Brazil. This, and the uninviting nature of the mangrove thickets that make up the Guianas coastline, led the early explorers to christen the area the "Wild Coast."

Along the Wild Coast, as in the islands, Arawak groups were in deadly conflict with Carib. While the available documentation is insufficient to determine the nature and extent of demographic change on the Guianas coast in the 16th and 17th centuries, it is clear that the Arawak there fared better than their counterparts in the Lesser Antilles. From the earliest records to contemporary

House styles of 16th-century Taino showing differences based on class. Circular house was for commoners; rectangular house for chiefs. Drawing from Oviedo y Valdés.

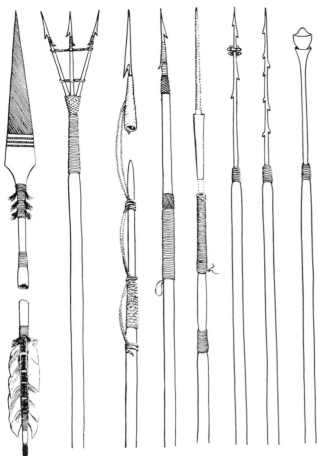

Arrowhead types used by the Central Arawak tribes of South America. Included are a three-pronged leister point and a detachable harpoon head tied to a shaft.

ethnographic accounts, Carib and Arawak settlements are found interspersed on the numerous rivers that break up the coastline, indicating that intertribal hostility never resulted in the mass exodus of Arawak from wide regions and their replacement by Carib. The introduction of Dutch and English trading outposts and plantations in the 16th and 17th centuries added a new element to the demographic equation, so that possible incipient displacement of Arawak by Carib instead became wholesale depopulation and dislocation of the entire indigenous population.

On the islands, the first European contacts with an indigenous American population resulted in catastrophic mortalities for the latter, often to the point of extinction. Population estimates for the Antillean Arawak at the time of the Discovery vary widely. For Hispaniola alone, they range from a low of 100,000 suggested by such scholars as Angel Rosenblat in 1954 and Julian H. Steward and Louis C. Faron in 1959, to a high of 3,000,000 suggested by the most authoritative Spanish chronicler of the period, Bartolome de Las casas.

In a recent evaluation of various Spanish sources, published and archival, Carl O. Sauer estimated the pre-contact population of Hispaniola to have been 1,000,000 to 1,100,000, with a like number from the combined populations of the remaining islands in the Greater Antilles. In any case, by 1519, the Arawak of Hispaniola and countless Arawak from the other islands brought to Hispaniola as Spanish slaves had been reduced to a few thousand survivors. The decimation was a combination of the shortsighted ruthlessness of fortune-seekers, Arawak susceptibility to alien diseases, and ecological imbalance produced by the introduction of new plant and animal species to the islands. Before the end of the 16th century, the Antillean Arawak had ceased to exist as a sociocultural entity. Those who did not die off were assimilated into the emergent Spanish-African-Creole slave society.

Excluding archaeological remains and historical references, one of the few indications of Arawak habitation in the Greater Antilles is the folk custom of attributing Indian ancestry to certain peasant families living in the mountainous interior of the larger islands.

Culture of the Arawak. Knowledge of aboriginal Arawak social organization in the islands and along the Guianas coast is extremely limited. Since the Arawak societies of the Greater Antilles had completely deteriorated within a few years of European discovery, all information about them is derived from a few Spanish chroniclers such as Las Casas, and from archaeological research. The Guianas did not attract thorough chroniclers until long after indigenous social conditions had vanished, and even today there are few monograph studies of Indians of the Guianas.

Since the appearance of the *Handbook of South American Indians* (1946-50), it has been an anthropological practice to make a major typological distinction between the "theocratic chiefdoms" of the Greater Antilles and the "tropical forest peoples," which include the Guiana Arawak as well as a great variety of cultures distributed throughout lowland South America. The distinction is based on the presence of complex sociocultural forms in Antillean socity and the absence of these among Arawak groups of the Guianas and other tropical forest peoples.

The island Arawak. The "theocratic chiefdoms" of the island Arawak were native aristocracies in which a class of hereditary rulers (*cacique* or *caciqua* in Taino) were the apex of a four-tiered class structure. The other three classes were the nobles (*naboria*). The *cacique* and *naboria* classes, and the others to some extent, were endogamous--i.e., there was no possibility of interclass social mobility through marriage. Kinship was

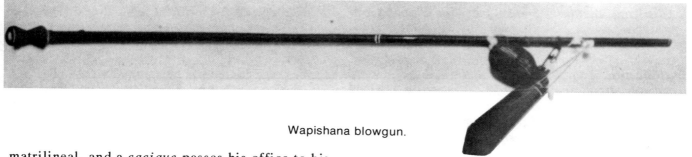

Wapishana blowgun.

matrilineal, and a *cacique* passes his office to his eldest sister's eldest son.

Parallel to the social hierachy, there was believed to exist a supernatural hierachy of nature spirits which affected the success of men and the reproductive powers of women and of the earth, and which were represented in religious figurines, or *cemi*. Powerful men--*cacique* or *ndaino*--owned *cemi* of powerful spirits, while commoners owned *cemi* of corresponding status. The *cemi* of the *cacique* were housed in separate buildings, actually incipient temples, where persons in the area under the *cacique's* administration (the *caciquazgo*) came to present offerings at harvest time. These parallel hierachies of men and spirits formed the basis of an aristocratic political order which was maintained apparently without a warrior class and without major internecine conflict.

Political and ceremonial elaboration in the large islands was made possible by the presence of large, compact populations supported by intensive horticulture and a bountiful harvest of fish and sea turtles. The staple crops were tuberous plants--principally bitter cassava or manioc--although corn (maize), beans, and squash were also known. The method of cultivation was not the shifting slash-and-burn horticulture of the mainland, but a more permanent system involving the construction of numerous earth mounds in garden plots (*conuco*) of varying sizes. Terracing was practiced on steep slopes and, in arid southwestern Haiti, the Arawak had built the only known irrigation system in the Circum-Caribbean area. There being no large land animals, hunting was of minor importance. The absence of such prey may also account for the Antillean Arawak use of the spear thrower instead of the mainland bow and arrow. Another peculiar feature of Antillean Arawak culture was the absence of alcoholic beverages, which were u-biquitous on the mainland.

Villages were formless collections of large houses, or *maloca,* each of which reportedly contained 10 to 15 individual families. On Hispaniola, with about 1,000,000 inhabitants, villages contained 200 to 500 families. The largest village population recorded was about 3,000. A varying number of neighboring villages formed a district,

with a minor *cacique* as its recognized head. These districts in turn were part of five great provinces of indigenous Hispaniola, each headed by a major *cacique*. The *cacique-cemi* complex operated within this organizational framework and involved all village residents in a set of political and ceremonial obligations.

The mainland Arawak. For the Guianas, much of what is known about the social organization of the indigenous coastal Arawak has been inferred from what was later learned about the Indian peoples of the remote interior. It is certain that the Locono populations were less dense and their social institutions less complex than those of the Taino, yet it is doubtful whether early coastal Arawak society entirely conformed to the ideal type of "tropical forest peoples."

Political organization was tied to kinship-based rights and privileges and probably did not extend beyond the village. The headman of the village was an elder kinsman and affine (relative by marriage) to most of the people living there; these ties were the basis of his authority. Shamanism was the predominant, probably exclusive, belief system, and the position of shaman often was held by the village headman. In this way, secular and supernatural powers were fused, though on a more elementary level than the *cacique-cemi* complex of the Antilles. Villages probably contained several hundred persons, and populations of more than 1,000 were rare. Except for temporary military alliances, each village was an autonomous political unit. A system of matrilineal non-localized clans cut across the atomistic political system, for a Locono could travel to another village and find members of his own clan there who were prepared to extend their hospitality.

The indigenous coastal Arawak economy was based on the exploitation of several environments. Slash-and-burn horticulture of bitter cassava was practiced on one- to two-acre plots and provided the staple of life. Palm nuts, honey, and other forest products were gathered in season. Fish from the rivers and forest animals provided protein. In addition, shellfish and crabs taken from the mangrove-choked ocean beaches must have figured prominently in the indigenous diet, as evidenced by large shell middens found on several rivers. The fact that these middens are found 40 to 50 miles upriver, near the topographical boundary of marsh forest and true tropical forest, supports the contention-- advanced by Peter Kloos in 1971-- that Indian villages of the Guianas are situated to exploit the most varied ecospheres possible. Most contemporary coastal Arawak villages are also located in this transitional zone. In order to utilize the resources available from their gardens, the forest, the river, and the sea, indigenous villages must have been more like way- stations than continuous, permanent abodes. Their inhabitants probably spend considerable portions of each year away from the village, either at forest camps or on the beach during carb season.

Effects of colonization. Undoubtedly, because the Locono lived on a continental land mass rather than on an island, and because they were organized in small, secluded and seminomadic groups rather than in large communities, they were able to survive the colonial era, while the Taino vanished from the Antilles. Except for sporadic slave raids, the Dutch and English who colonized the area between the Amazon and Orinoco deltas adopted a policy of treating the surrounding coastal tribes as trading partners. In this, they differed markedly from the Spanish, who were after gold. A trading outpost--such as the Dutch post of Kyk-over-al ("look over all") at the headwaters of the Essequibo--would be set up on one of the rivers of the Wild Coast, and local Indian groups would be encouraged to trade forest products for European goods. There is evidence to suggest that the Arawak were attracted to the posts because they provided a degree of protection from Carib raiding parties. The stereotypes Columbus established of the peaceful, tractable Arawak and the warlike, cannibalistic Carib were thus reinforced by the Dutch and English experiences in the Guianas, where the Arawak settled closer to the trading posts than did the Carib and, as a consequence, acquired more European ways.

The transition from trading outposts to plantation agriculture which took place in the 17th and 18th centuries had an important effect on the place of the Arawak in the colonial societies of the Guianas. The introduction of large numbers of African slaves permanently altered the demographic composition of the region and presented the local Arawak and Carib with new problems in intergroup relations. Particularly in the Dutch colonies of Demerara and Essequibo (now in Guyana), the Arawak and Carib were encouraged by the mercantile administrator, Storm van's Gravesande, to align themselves with the Dutch against the masses of black slaves. In a classic example of the policy of divide- and-rule, Gravesande created a kind of bush police force from coastal Arawak and carib groups, whose presence on the plantations intimidated the blacks and whose paid services were used to capture or execute escaped slaves. Elsewhere in the Guianas, the Indians were not employed in this manner, with the result that communities of escaped slaves (called maroons or Bush Negroes) were formed in the interior of Surinam.

In British Guiana, emancipation of the slaves in 1834 and the consequent decline of the sugar plantations resulted in an abrupt loss of status for the coastal Arawak. The planters and colonial officials no longer found the subsidies paid the Arawak and other Indians expedient, and they were left to shift for themselves. Since the intercultural relations between Arawak and European and Arawak and black which developed in the slave society had fundamentally altered indigenous Arawak life, there could be no return to the old ways. The following decades saw widespread demoralization and population decline among coastal Indian groups of the area, and particularly among the Arawak who were more committed to the old system than other Indians. The 1891 census of British Guiana reported a total of 7,463 coastal and near interior Indians, including the Carib, Warrau, and Arawak. These had survived primarily by placing themselves in the care of missions, which were increasingly active in the colony following emancipation.

Demography. In sharp contrast with Indian groups of interior South America, the Indians of the northeastern littoral have steadily increased in numbers since the 1950s. Locono populations have followed this trend, and today there are between 9,000 and 10,000 living in 35 to 40 villages located on the lower portions of coastal rivers in Guyana, Surinam, and French Guiana. Because of the advanced state of acculturation, or Creolization, of the Arawak in modern Guyana and Surinam, and the consequent difficulty of determining who is and who is not Arawak, exact population figures are difficult to determine. Figures given here are based on those Arawak residents in recognized Indian settlements, and they do not reflect the growing number of ethnically mixed Arawak who may return to their home villages on occasion to reactivate their Indian identity.

Of the three countries in the Guianas, Guyana has by far the largest Arawak and total Indian population. In 1970, there were approximately 40,000 Indians living in about 150 recognized Indian settlements. In the mid-1970s there were 23 such settlements in which coastal Arawak constituted the predominant tribal group(it should be noted that most of these contained at least a few

Carib, Warrau, or tribally mixed Indians as well). The coastal Arawak population of Guyana in 1970 numbered around 7,500, again depending on how criteria of Arawak identity are reckoned, so that about 19 percent of Guyanese Indians were Arawak.

In Surinam, there were in 1964 a total of about 7,300 Indians. Of these, only about 4,300 lived in recognized Indian settlements. The Arawak made up about 40 percent of this tribal population, or approximately 1,700. This population was distributed among ten villages. In French Guiana there were, in the mid-1970s, perhaps a few hundred Arawak, but most of the country's sparse Indian population consisted of non-Arawak interior groups.

Acculturation. The Arawak of modern Guyana and Surinam are being increasingly drawn into their national societies. They can no longer function as members of isolated tribal communities but, for better or for worse, must become citizens of a nation. Their traditional subsistence base of cassava horticulture, hunting, and fishing, is not adequate to sustain their growing populations, let alone provide them the opportunities that Western-style education has taught them to seek. In most Arawak communities, the practice of taking outside employment or securing money through timberwork or fishing has gone on for several generations, and it is now a traditional feature of their village and domestic life. In consequence of their participation in the cash economy, they have entered into the national political arena. National political parties in both Guyana and Surinam court Indian votes, and in the past two decades a number of Indian political spokesmen have emerged. A few of these new leaders have broken with the national parties to form Indian-based political parties and interest groups. A justifiable concern shared by all coastal Indian groups in the two countries is the status of Indian rights to their traditional farmlands and fishing and hunting grounds.

The governments of Guyana and Surinam have an official policy of Indian integration, which is an enlightened and humane alternative to policies pursued a century earlier in North America. It is not exactly clear, however, what "integration" can mean in the context of political factionalism and in view of the very serious economic problems that beset both countries. In the mid-1970s, it appeared that an increased awareness of tribal and racial identity was forming among the Arawak, even as they become more deeply involved in national life.

BIBLIOGRAPHY-

● FLORIDA, STATE OF. The Florida Historical Society Quarterly. FL: April, 1933.

ARAWAKAN FAMILY

(South America and West Indies;) is the name given to an extensive family of languages in South America and the West Indies. Such a group is composed of languages for which there is evidence of a common origin--one extinct tongue from which all the others in the family were derived through processes of language change.

Arawakan is of particular interest because some of its members were the first native tongues encountered by Christopher Columbus and the Spanish in the New World. Lucaya, spoken on the Bahamas, was a dialect of Taino, the language of the Greater Antilles generally. It was in this area that the Spanish established themselves and from which they launched the conquest of Mexico.

To the south, on the Lesser Antilles, before and during this period, was an Arawakan population being overrun by Carib Indian warriors who killed off the men. The newly captured wives continued to speak their native language, which they taught to their children. Farther to the south, along the north coast of South America, a number of other languages of the family were spoken, including Shebayo, Caquetio, and Arawak (from which the family gets its name).

With most of the natives of the Caribbean area speaking Arawakan languages, it is not surprising that the etymologies of many European words for distinctively Indian things, such as hammocks and canoes, go back to these languages and have cognates elsewhere in South America.

Arawakan has generally been considered to be an independent family, but one scholar, Joseph H. Greenberg, has indicated that it is only one part of an Equatorial branch of an Andean-Equatorial family. This branch is composed of Tupian (including Arikem), Timote, Cariri, Zamuco, Guahibo-Pimiqua Saliban, Totmaco-Taparita, Mocoa, Tuyuneri, yuracare, Trumai, Cayuvava, and Timucua as well as Arawakan. Its languages are scattered throughout South America north of the mouth of the Parana and Uruguay rivers, where Buenos Aires now is, and beyond into the West Indies and central Florida. In the Andean branch is the language of the Incas, Quechua, as well as many others on and near the Andes from Colombia to Tierra del Fuego.

Geographical distribution. Taino was spoken on Hispaniola (present-day Haiti and the Dominican Republic) and Cuba, and probably spoken throughout the Greater Antilles. The Arauan languages are spoken in the drainage of the Purus and Jurua rivers, tributaries which flow into the Amazon in central Brazil from the southwest. Amuesha, Apolista, and Chamicuro are, or were, spoken in the mountains of Peru. Uruan is found in the highlands of Bolivia, but at one time, it is believed, it was spoken over the greater part of Peru and Bolivia.

The Maipurean branch is found in the eastern foothills of the Andes and scattered throughout the northern half of the Andes and scattered throughout the northern half of the continent. Although many of these languages have disappeared, some are still in use. Recent research has been done in Bolivia on Moxo and Baure of the southern branch of Arawakan; in Peru on Piro, Ipurina, Campa, and Machiguenga of the pre-Andean group; on Goajiro, Piapoco, Cauyari, Yucuna, and Tariana of the northern branch; and on Wapishana.

Features of proto-Arawakan. Largely because scholars have lists of words from more of the Arawakan languages than they have grammars, reconstruction of the original language, proto-Arawakan, has been only of words and their parts. Among the languages of the family, and perhaps also of other Equatorial languages, there are certain features which must have been in proto-Arawakan. These include person-marking prefixes *nu-* (first person singular) and *p-* (second person singular), which occur on possessed nouns, on verbs to indicate the subject, and as initial elements of independent pronouns.

There were also other nominal prefixes which apparently set off several classes of nouns, rather like genders in European languages. There is evidence for such word parts beginning with *t-, k-, m-*, and *n-*.

As for the phonemes, or significant sounds of proto-Arawakan, evidence is found for *p, t, k, m, n, c* or *ch, x* or *kx, l, i,* and *a*. There were doubtlessly others, but the evidence for them is not at all clear.

Among the vocabularies, there is evidence of words peculiar to proto-Arawakan, setting it off from its contemporaries among the Equatorial languages. For example, there are reflexes of a word for "road" or "path" in the most divergent branches in Peru and in six diffeent subgroups of the Maipurean branch. Among divergent Arawakan languages, there are words for "cold" similar to Tupian words for "wind." Apparently, a change in meaning of this word made proto-Arawakan different from proto-Tupian.

Changes of this sort also set off subgroups of Arawakan from one another to result in the classification outlined in the table.

Cultural and historical implications. From the geographical distribution of, and the degree of affiliation among, the known languages of the family, it can be suggested that proto-Arawakan was spoken in, or near, the montana area of Peru and Ecuador. From there, an early form of Uruan spread out southwards in the highlands of the Andes. Apolista moved in the same direction.

Amuesha and Chamicuro stayed within the general area, while proto-Maipurean and early Taino probably went northwards down the Ucayali River and eastward along the Amazon. Because most of the subgroups of Maipurean are spoken north of the Amazon, it would seem that proto-Maipurean was spoken there, perhaps in the drainage of the Rio Negro from where its descendant spread throughout the Tropical Forest area and on to the Caribbean coast. By the time Island Carib of the northern subgroup made its way onto the Lesser Antilles, Taino had already made its way to to the Greater Antilles.

Some archaeologists have linked the development and spread of Tropical Forest culture with the history of Arawakan. Culture associated with proto-Arawakan may have been influenced by highland cultures. If so, the speakers of this language and its immediate descendants could have carried the cultural elements with them as they went down the rivers, as suggested by Betty Meggers of the Smithsonian Institution, Washington, D.C. If Tropical Forest culture developed midlength of the major rivers, then the speakers of early Maipurean may very well have developed and spread these cultural traits, as suggested by Donald Lathrop of the University of Illinois.

ARIKARA

(U.S.; Plains) are the northern-most group of a Caddoan linguistic family. Together with the Mandan and Hidatsa, they form the Three Affiliated Tribes, most of whom live on the Fort Berthold Reservation in North Dakota.

Culture. The Arikara were an agrarian people who established villages of earth lodges in convenient locations safe from enemy attack and close to streams.

The women raised corn, beans, and squash in their gardens and gathered berries from the hills, while the men hunted buffalo, deer, and other wild game. Game provided food, clothing, cooking utensils such as buffalo horn bowls and spoons, and decorative dress for religious ceremonies and entertainment.

The Arikara were generally a peace-loving tribe, but when driven to war, they were known to harass the enemy far into the night and into the next day. The ancient ones or the old people, say, however, that the Arikara were friendly by nature.

Archaeologists have discovered the remains of medicine lodges in the form of large circles in Arikara village ruins. In these lodges the sick were healed and medicine ceremonies performed. (Medicine refers not only to something that is used to heal, but also to anything unusual, holy, mysterious, or deeply respected.) Medicine men would periodically perform miracles in the presence of

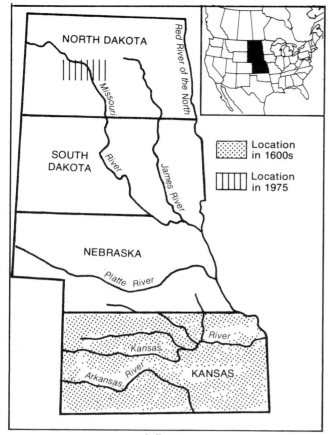

Arikara

spectators. For a person to become a medicine man, he would have to leave the safety of the village to fast for three or four days. During this time, he underwent extreme deprivation until he was "blessed" in a vision by some bird or other animal, which was then considered holy to that person. The animal in the vision was believed to give the medicine man powers for the remainder of his lifetime.

Central to Arikara social and religious life were the 12 sacred medicine bundles, which are believed to have contained items gathered during the tribe's migrations. Over the centuries several of the sacred bundles have been lost and others destroyed. Of the five bundles remaining in the mid 1970s, four were in the possession of tribal elders and one was on display at the Four Bears Museum near New Town, North Dakota. Another relic preserved by the Arikara was a sacred peace pipe of unknown age or origin.

In the early days of the tribe, there was an organization of men who wore their hair in a closely cropped style. They are believed to have been the fanciest warriors of the tribe, who danced in special ceremonies and created general merriment.

Tribal history. Because the Arikara had no written language, tribal history and culture were handed down by word of mouth in the form of storytelling from grandfather to grandson, father to son, uncle to nephew, or grandmother to granddaughter, mother to daughter, aunt to niece. According to this oral history, the tribe is a subdivision of the Pawnee, whom the Arikara called Skidii. Because many items included in the sacred bundles came from Southwest and deep South, the tribe places its origins in that region. They believe that they first migrated into the Great Plains after crossing deep canyons, fording deep streams, and fighting bears. The tribe, numbering between 3,000 and 4,000 in the late 18th century, moved from the region of present-day Kansas to Nebraska, South Dakota, and North Dakota, establishing villages along the Missouri River. Oral history includes stories of several bands that broke from the tribe during this period.

Conflict arose between the Arikara and white traders in the Missouri River Basin, resulting in the first battle of the U.S. Army with a Plains tribe in 1823. During the Plains Indian wars, the Arikara fought with the white man against their old enemy, the Dakota (Sioux). Many of the warriors enlisted in the U.S. Army as scouts, including Bloody Knife, scout to Gen. George Custer.

It is believed that the Arikara joined with the Mandan and Hidatsa in forming the Three Affiliated Tribes in the mid-19th century, after the Arikara had been greatly reduced in numbers due to war and smallpox epidemics. The alliance grew out of an earlier relationship in which first the mandan and then the Hidatsa traded and intermarried with the Arikara. After the Plains Indians wars, missionaries and educators contacted the tribe. The first teachers first set up a school in Like-A-Fish-Hook village for the young Arikara children. The Fort Berthold Reservation, with headquarters in New Town, North Dakota, was established for the Three Affiliate Tribes in 1871, and by 1885 they had founded scattered family farmsteads. Construction of the Garrison Dam and discovery of oil forced a removal to new homes on the reservation in the 1950s. In the 1970s, about 700 Arikara lived on the reservation.

Contemporary life. Most of the Arikara in the mid-1970s lived in the eastern segment of the Fort Berthold Reservation in the community of White Shield, named for one of their greatest chiefs. They retained their zest for fun and spirit of merriment. Although the Victory Dance Society and various medicine organizations are no longer in existence, the Warbonnet Dance and powwows are performed according to the old traditions.

The tribal members are active in community affairs, church organizations, and school activities. The young people are well educated; many attend college, some attend graduate school, and almost all graduate from high school.

Arikara men at a Grass Dance at Fort Berthold Agency, Dakota, in 1886.

The Arikara have adapted to the ways of the white man and live, by and large, like any other citizen. They raise livestock, operate farmland, and work for tribal programs. They have long since given up hoeing by hand to plant their traditional crops of corn and beans, and generally grow wheat, barley, and other cash crops instead. A few full-blooded Arakara remain, but most have intermarried with other tribes and non-Indians. The Arikara will take up arms only when the United States is at war with other nations, contributing soldiers to the U.S. armed forces during World Wars I and II, the Korean conflict, and the Vietnam War. Most of the Arikara speak English fluently, but few can speak their native tongue. Population figures for the Arikara were 928 in 1970.

Every once in a while, a deer or an antelope will stray into the eastern portion of the reservation and a lucky man might find himself enjoying a traditional Indian supper once again.

BIBLIOGRAPHY-

● CHRONICLES OF OKLAHOMA. 1924.
● DORSEY, GEORGE ADAMS. Traditions of the Arikara. Washington: The Carnegie Instution of Washington, (pub. no. 17) 1904.
● FEDERAL WRITERS PROJECT. Arikara Indians. Vermillion, SD: University Museum, 1941.
● HODGE, FREDERICK WEBB. Handbook of American Indians North of Mexico. Washington: Smithsonian Institution: BAE Bulletin No. 30: U.S. GPO, 1907.
● SWANTON, JOHN R. The Indian Tribes of North America. Smithsonian Institution: BAE Bulletin No. 145: U.S. GPO, 1952.
● TAYLOR, JOSEPH HENRY. A Romantic Encounter. North Dakota Historical Quarterly v. 4, 1929/30.
● WILL, GEORGE F. Magical and Slighthand Performances by the Arikara. ND: North Dakota Historical Quarterly.
-----Arikara Ceremonials. North Dakota Historical Quarterly, 1930.

ARIKEM

(South America; Brazil) are an extinct tribe of the Mato Grosso region, who formerly lived along the headwaters of the Jamari and Candeias rivers and along the Massanganga River, a tributary of the Jamari, all three being right-bank tributaries of the upper Madeira River. The name "Arikem" was given to these people by the neighboring Urupa Indians and adopted by the Brazilian *seringueiros*("rubber collectors"); it is also spelled "Ariken" and "Ariquewme." They were also known under the name "Uitate," but they called theymselves "Ahopovo." They lived in the Guapore cultura area of Brazil, and their language, which has been erroneously classified as Chapacuran, is actually a Tupi language with many foreign elements.

Culture. An Arikem village was comprised of two dwellings and an ossuary hut or temple. Huts took the form of low vaults; poles bent across a central rectangular framework provided the curve of the ridge people and the walls. Palm leaves covered the outside of the house. The Arikem cultivated cassava (manioc), which they prepared by grating on a piece of rough bark. To grind corn (maize), they used a semicircular wooden slab, which they rolled back and forth in an elonated wooden trough. They also spun cotton, manufactured hammocks, and made pottery, including large, truncated conical vesels, and baskets decorated at the grip with a cotton wrapping; arrows were made by attaching two halved feathers to the shafts by a cotton thread wrapped at regular intervals. Musical instruments included reed flutes. Male personal ornamentation consisted of feathers or wooden plugs inserted in the ear lobes, cotton bands worn around the ankles (these were also worn by women), and fibers tied around the end of their long hair. They also painted themselves with vegetable pigments. Necklaces were made from strung river shells and trimmed with feather tassels.

The Arikem dead were usually buried in the dwelling hut under their own hammocks. The remains of famous chiefs, however, were kept in the ossuary hut or temple; the skeleton was enclosed in a bark-cloth bag and the skull in a special three-legged, feather- trimmed basket. These relics were decorated with feathers and shells and were hung in a hammock below a jaguar skin. Near the roof of the hut were stored gourd dippers with trimmed handles, polished stones, stone axes with a hole through the butt, and labrets made of resin. The labrets were probably war trophies. Bundles of arrows captured from other Indian tribes were leaned against the walls. Other baskets contained charred human bones.

Tribal history. When Marshal Candido Mariano da Silva Rondon, a Brazilian explorer, first learned of the Arikem in 1909, they had already been displaced by earlier Bolivian invaders. The Bolivians were later replaced by Brazilian *seringueiros,* who continued to kill the Indians and expell the survivors from their villages. Rondon pursuaded the *seringueeiros* to halt these practices, and by 1911 the first peaceful relations between the Neo-Brazilians and the Arikem were established. Within a few months, the Arikem villages were open to outsiders, and the Arikem, even the women, soon learned Portuguese. This contact, however, also brought severe epidemics of diseases introduced by whites, and young women of the tribe were carried off to the cities. As a result, when Rondon himself first met the Arikem in 1913, he found the 60 surviving Indians living in four villages in a state of disorganization. In an attempt to remedy the situation, Rondon built a village for the dispersed members of the tribe near one of the telegraph stations he had established in what is now the Territory of Rondonia. He hoped

Arikêm

that the Indians would become telegraph workers, and for this reason he sent a young Arikem boy to Rio de Janeiro to learn to operate the telegraph line. Nevertheless, by the mid-20th century the tribe was extinct.

BIBLIOGRAPHY-

● STEWARD, JULIAN H. Handbook of South American Indians. 7 Vols., Washington, DC: U.S. Govt. Printing Office, 1946-59.

ARIVAIPA

(U.S.; Ariz.) An Apache tribe that formerly made its home in the canyon of Arivaipa Creek, a tributary of the Rio San Pedro, although like the Chiricahua and other Apache of Arizona, they raided far southward. They were reputed to have laid waste every town in North Mexico as far as the Gila prior to the Gadsden purchase in 1853, and with having exterminated the Sobaipuri, a Piman tribe, in the latter part of the 18th century. In 1863 a company of California volunteers, aided by some friendly Apache at Old Camp Grant on the San Pedro, attacked an Arivaipa rancheria at the head of the canyon, killing 58 of the 70 inhabitants, men, women, and children--the women and children being slain by the friendly Indians, the men by the Californians- -in revenge for their atrocities. After this loss they sued for peace, and their depredations practically ceased. About 1872, they were removed to San Carlos agency, where, with the Pinalenos, apparently their nearest kindred, they numbered 1,051 in 1874. Of this number, however, the Arivaipa formed a very small part.

BIBLIOGRAPHY-

● HODGE, FREDERICK WEBB. Handbook of American Indians North of Mexico. Washington: Smithsonian Institution: BAE Bulletin No. 30: U.S. GPO, 1907. Smithsonian Institution: BAE Bulletin No. 145: U.S. GPO, 1952.

ARKOKISA

(U.S.; Tex.) A people formerly living in villages chiefly along lower Trinity River. The Spanish presidio of San Agustin de Ahumada was founded among them in 1756, and 50 Tlascaltec families from South Mexico were settled there, but the post was abandoned in 1772. They were allied with the Aranama and the Attacapa, and were on friendly terms also with the bidai, but their linguistic affinity is not known. According to Sibley, they numbered about 80 men in 1760-70 and subsisted principally on shellfish and fruits, and in 1805 their principal town was on the West side of Colorado River of Texas, about 200 miles southwest of nacogdoches. They had another village north of this, between the Neches and the Sabine, nearer the coast than the villages of the Adai. Sibley speaks of the Arkokisa as migratory, but they could not always have been entitled to that characterization. It is probable that, owing to the conditions incident to the intrusion of the white race, the people became demoralized; their tribal relations were broken up, their numbers decimated by disease, and the remnant of them was finally scattered and disorganized. Of their habits, very little is known; their language seems to have been distinct from that of their neighbors, with whom they conversed by signs.

BIBLIOGRAPHY-

● BOLTON, HERBERT EUGENE. Athanase de Mezieres and the Louisiana-Texas Frontier, 1768-1780. Cleveland, OH: The Arthur H. Clark Co., 1914.

AROSAGUNTACOOK

(U.S.; Maine;Canada) was a tribe that after 1675 became prominent in wars with the English in present-day Maine.

According to ethnologist James Mooney, the Arosaguntacook were in the Abnaki Confederacy and spoke an Abnaki dialect. Their name has many variations which are often confused with the name of the Androscoggin River, on which they lived in the vicinity of present-day Lewiston.

The Arasaguntacook were involved in several wars with the English between 1675 and 1725. As a result, their town was burned in 1690, and the tribe merged with two other nearby tribes sometime during the period. After an Indian defeat in 1725, the combined tribe moved to St. Francis, Canada, where all three were often called Arosaguntacook.

BIBLIOGRAPHY-

● HODGE, FREDERICK WEBB. Handbook of American Indians North of Mexico. Washington: Smithsonian Institution: BAE Bulletin No. 30: U.S. GPO, 1907. Smithsonian Institution: BAE Bulletin No. 145: U.S. GPO, 1952.

ARROHATTOC

(U.S.; Va.) A tribe of the Powhatan confederacy, formerly living in Henrico county. They had 30 warriors in 1608. Their chief village, of the same name, was on James River, 12 miles below the falls at Richmond, on the spot where Henrico was built in 1611.

BIBLIOGRAPHY-

● HODGE, FREDERICK WEBB. Handbook of American Indians North of Mexico. Washington: Smithsonian Institution: BAE Bulletin No. 30: U.S. GPO, 1907.

ARROHATTOC

(U.S.; Va.) A tribe of the Powhatan confederacy, formerly living in Henrico county. They had 30 warriors in 1608. Their chief village, of the same name, was on James River, 12 miles below the falls at Richmond, on the spot where Henrico was built in 1611.

BIBLIOGRAPHY-

● HODGE, FREDERICK WEBB. Handbook of American Indians North of Mexico. Washington: Smithsonian Institution: BAE Bulletin No. 30: U.S. GPO, 1907.

ARUA

(South America; Brazil) is an extinct people of the area around the mouth of the Amazon River. When the first explorers arrived at the mouth of the Amazon early in the 16th century, they found several Indian tribes, one of which they called "Arua." This name has been applied to archaeological sites and pottery from the island of Mexicana, Caviana, and Marajoo, and the adjacent mainland. Some sites are associated with glass beads and other European items that establish their post-contact data. The sites are located on the banks of small streams near the coast. Pottery is sparse and limited to the surface, suggesting that the villages were small and frequently moved.

The Arua buried their dead in large urns set on the surface of the ground in cemeteries in the interior of the islands, remote from the villages. Among offerings placed in the urns were small bowls, stone axes, beads of pottery or green nephrite, and pottery figurines. Domestic pottery was generally undecorated, but burial urns often had a row of rings impressed onto the upper part of the neck.

The Arua differ from earlier groups that inhabited the mouth of the Amazon by making polished stone axes and using nephrite beads and pendants. Their possession of these and other cultural elements characteristic of the Antilles indicates they may have come from the north. This view is supported by the presence of the earliest sites on the mainland north of the Amazon; these include villages and ceremonial constructions in the forms of rows and cirles of erect stones. The Arua had a reputation for being outstanding warriors and offered such strong resistance to European conquest that a few survived until the beginning of the 19th century.

BIBLIOGRAPHY-

● STEWARD, JULIAN H. Handbook of South American Indians. 7 Vols., Washington, DC: U.S. Govt. Printing Office, 1946-59.

ASHLUSLAY

(South America; Gran Chaco) are a tribe which, together with the Mataco, Choroti, and Macca Indians, formed the Mataco-Macca linguistic family. They inhabited the plains north of the Pilcomayo River from Fortin Guachalla to the Esteros region and the upper Rio Confuso, reaching even the Rio Verde, but were concentrated near Fort Munoz. They were first mentioned in anthropological literature in 1883 and were visited by two ethnologists, Wilhelm Herrmann and Erland Nordenskiold in the early 1900s.

The Ashluslay were known to the white settlers of the Chaco region either as Chulupi, Chunupi, or as Tapiete. The name Ashluslay was first popularized by Nordenskiold.

The Ashluslay remained relatively isolated and underwent little cultural change until the beginning of the 20th century when they began to accumulate horses, cattle, and other European goods from Argentinian mestizos with whom they came in contact when they began to migrate south for seasonal work in the sugarcane plantations. During the Chaco War (1932-35) between Bolivia and Paraguay many of the Ashluslay migrated permanently to Argentina, where they had problems with the gendarmery and the army, and they formed strong contacts and relations with the Guaycuruan tribes of the Toba and Pilaga, their former enemies. Many Ashluslay settled in five religious missions; still others became laborers in Argentinean and Paraguayan *estancias* (cattle ranches) and plantations; still others developed small farms. Together with most of the Chaco Indians they were exploited as cheap labor after the Chaco area was opened to white colonization in the early 20th century, and most of the region was sold as private property. The Indians were discriminated against not only by the white colonizers and *estancia* and plantation owners but also by the mestizo laborers and farmers.

Location in 1800s
Location in 1975

Ashluslay

Tribal culture In prehistoric times, the Ashluslay, like most of the Chaco Indians, were nomadic bands of food collectors, fishermen, and hunters; they were made up of a few extended families practicing magic rites through shamanistic activities. In the remote past they had no agriculture or pottery, nor did they practice basketry. They used net bags, dressed in skin cloaks, and lived in simple communal houses. They settled later, like the majority of the Chaco Indians, after being influenced by agricultural tribes coming from both the Andean and the Amazonian areas. They learned the use of pottery, agriculture, and other important features, although they never ceased to be seminomadic peoples with a strong emphasis on wild food collecting and hunting, even after their contact with the European conquerors.

Subsistence activities. Although the main crops raised in the Chaco in historical times were corn (maize), sweet manioc, beans, pumpkins, anco, watermelons, gourds, sweet potatoes, tobacco, cotton, sorghum, and sugarcane, the Ashluslay had a strong preference for raising corn. Both men and women worked together using a digging stick or a wooden paddle-shaped spade as a basic agricultural implement. The Ashluslay sometimes traded corn for dried or smoked fish, but they themselves fished collectively for about two or three months yearly. They used conical wicker baskets in the lower waters, and set wickerwork fish traps in the larger streams; during the dry season they used nets.

The Ashluslay hunted on an individual basis, especially when a group moved or travelled to a new place. Most of the men scattered in search of game, while the women continued to advance slowly. They sometimes used the common Chaco device of burning grassland or bush. Generally, they ate everything they caught without any reluctance, although they did have some food taboos. Normally, they roasted or boiled their meat, but sometimes they baked it in an earthen oven. They made cakes of algarroba flour, ate the terminal shoots of palm, and concocted a mush from pods called *porotos del monte(Capparis retusa)*, which are similar to string beans. Other important wild foods were the algarrobe and chanar, which were ususaly stored in great quantities in the summer for use in the winter. The Ashluslay seasoned their food with the ashes of saladillo plants. They used a square, sharp- edged piece of wood to open and scale fish, and they used calabashes as plates, with shell or horn spoons. Mortars were dug out of palm tree stumps but, when they were travelling, the Ashluslay would improvise mortars by digging pits in the ground which they lined with skins or hard clay.

They had domesticated dogs, which probably were introduced into the Chaco area by the European conquerors. They also had large flocks of sheep, goats, and chickens. In general, they shunned the flesh of their domesticated animals. The Ashluslay also had cattle and horses, although they did not base their economy on them, as did most of the Guaycuruan tribes.

Dwellings and clothing. The Ashluslay lived in crude huts, usually resided in long communal houses which were merely a series of individual huts linked together. They were often built with an ellipsoidal ground plan with one slightly concave side and some times faced each other across a street or a plaza. Under mestizo influence, the houses became higher due to a rigid framework with poles and rafters covered by leaves or grass. Simple square sheds were usually erected in front of their houses for cooking or resting. Their villages were relatively larger than most of the Chaco Indians, sometimes numbering about 1,000 inhabitants. They also had a kind of men's club house, and occasionally a crude palisade was erected in front of the houses to protect the open sheds. Rough skin and rush mats were used for beds and seats.

Like most of the Chaco Indians, the Ashluslay men and women wore skin cloaks until sheep were introduced and they began making wool and woolen blankets. Contact with the mestizo population added the poncho. They also wore sleeveless shirts and woolen belts with geometric motifs, sandals similar to those of the Andean Indians, and fiber or woolen bags. Men sometimes wore headdresses — a red woolen band bedecked with shell disks or glass beads and fringed with natural or dyed feathers. Like most of the Chaco Indians, they wore wooden plugs or disks in their ear lobes but did not use labrets in their lips as did the Guaycuruan tribes. They used mussel shell necklaces and beadwork pendants. The Ashluslay were very proficient at beadwork, having learned the skill from missionaries. The shaman in their magic ceremonies used to have a skirt of rhea feathers. The Ashluslay used wooden or bamboo combs. Tattooing was quite common and and generally women were more profusely tattooed than men. Body painting was also quite common. For transportation they generally had donkeys. The weapons used were bows and arrows and sometimes spears, clubs, and bolas. The Ashluslay took sclaps as war trophies which they dried over smoke and mounted on a wooden hoop. They had a drill to build fires, but flint and steel were also used.

Social and political organization. The Ashluslay had a sense of a collective property for the tribe or the band; fishing and game hunting were usually shared by the extended family of the household. The fields belonged to those who cultivated them, and the crops were shared by all the household members. For personal possessions they had kinds of property masks, such as a special pattern woven in the corners of their blankets. Stealing was very rare. Trade with other tribes or bands was based principally on barter.

The Ashluslay's social organization was initially a composite band of extended families of relatively larger groups, reaching a few hundred persons; they were bound to their hunting, fishing, and agricultural territory, and because of that they sometimes lived in semipermanent villages. Residence rules were generally matrilocal, although descent rules were basically patrilineal. Their political system was based on a democratic chieftainship; the position of the chief ruled a group of related bands. Many times the chief was a shaman and often military leader; his position was dependent upon his wisdom, skill, and courage. Abortion and infanticide were relatively common, although they were very fond of their children. They celebrated girls' puberty rites, but there is no clear evidence for boys' initiation rites. After puberty, girls obtained almost complete sexual freedom, marriage being a few years later and with a minimum of ritual. There were no strict policies regarding exogamy. The monogramic marriage prevailed, although polygyny was not absent.

The belief system of the Ashluslay, as that of most of the Chaco Indians, was dominated by a magic and shamanistic character. Their supernatural world was full of impersonified spirits, such as goblins or ghosts. They also had a kind of demon, but they did not have deities nor a supreme being. At the most they only had mythic culture heroes.

Contemporary situation The traditional culture of the Ashluslay has changed a great deal since the Chaco War. Though they continue collecting wild food, hunting, and fishing, their economy has shifted strongly to farming, depending on the trade of their products—less on barter and more on the money market economy. Their agriculture is still on a semisubsistence basis. They have become more tied to the Paraguayan and, especially, the Argentinean capitalist economy, as wage laborers in tanning, wood or sugarcane cutting, and cattle industries. Consequently, they have adopted much of the mestizo culture, not only in their economic activities and the Spanish language but also in dressing, cooking and eating of food, religion, and medicine.

They have also been subjected to many of the mestizo diseases. On the other hand, they have managed to retain something of their cultural identity.

In 1946 the Ashluslay population of the Pilcomayo River was estimated to be about 6,000 (divided into 4 subtribes); it is likely, however, that their number was greater. At the beginning of the 20th century, they were estimated at about 10,000.

BIBLIOGRAPHY-

● STEWARD, JULIAN H. Handbook of South American Indians. 7 Vols., Washington, DC: U.S. Govt. Printing Office, 1946-59.

ASSEGUN

(U.S.; Mich.) A traditional tribe said to have occupied the region about Mackinaw and Sault Ste. Marie on the first coming of theOttawa and Chippewa, and to have been driven by them southward through lower Michigan. They are said, and apparently correctly, to have been either connected with the Mascoutin or identical with that tribe, and to have made the bone deposits in North Michigan.

BIBLIOGRAPHY-

● HODGE, FREDERICK WEBB. Handbook of American Indians North of Mexico. Washington: Smithsonian Institution: BAE Bulletin No. 30: U.S. GPO, 1907.
● MURDOCK, GEORGE P. Ethnographic Bibliography of North America. New Haven, CT: Human Relations Area Files Press, 1975.
● SWANTON, JOHN R. The Indian Tribes of North America. Smithsonian Institution: BAE Bulletin No. 145: U.S. GPO, 1952.

ASSINIBOINE

(U.S.; Great Plains) are a people who call themselves Nakoda ("the people") or Nakota ("the generous ones"). To the Chippewa they are known as As'see'nee pai-tuc ("those who cook with stone"). In Canada they are known as the Assiniboine. Through years of separation, differences in dialect and customs have developed, between their common origin and consider themselves a single people.

Origins, location, and language. Pierre Jean DeSmet, a French Jesuit missionary of the early 19th century, stated that the Assiniboine were once members of the Yanktonai band of the Dakota (Sioux). The oral tradition of the Assiniboine, however, refutes that claim. According to oral history in all Assiniboine tribal bands, their origins are Algonquian. Scholars of Assnninboine descent were involved in research in this area in mid-1970s.

Tribal history states that the Assiniboine originated in the Lake of the Woods and the Lake Winnepeg areas of Canada and became allied with the Cree. In 1744 a division was noted and "the people" divided again. Some bands moved west into the valleys of the Assiniboine and Saskatchewan rivers in Canada while others moved south into the Missouri Valley. The bands inhabited an area from the White Earth, Minnesota, region west to the Sweet Grass Hills of Montana. They also lived and roamed north of the U.S.-Canada border to a line running east and west from Hudson Bay to the Rocky Mountains. Thirty-three bands of Assiniboine have been identified. According to Edwin T. Denig, the Assiniboine returned to the Missouri Region between 1800 and 1837, numbering about 1,200.

The Assiniboine language is a dialect of Dakota, a subdivision of the Siouian family. In many respects, it would be considered a simple language. A mini-analysis was conducted by Ken Ryan, an Assiniboine from the Fort Peck Reservation, utilizing the International Phonetic Alphabet. He developed a phonetic Assiniboine alphabet and found that there are 26 consonants, and 6 vowels in the language.

Tribal culture. The Assiniboine were typically large- game hunters, dependent on the buffalo for considerable part of their diet. They used buffalo hides for clothing and receptacles and lived in hide tipis. By about 1750 the Assiniboine hunting grounds embraced all of the Canadian prairies. Both the Canadian and U.S. branches occasionally slaughtered entire herds by driving them into compounds. The meat was roasted on spits or boiled in hide bags by means of hot stones. The Assiniboine also made pemmican, which they traded or ate themselves. The dog was the only aboriginal

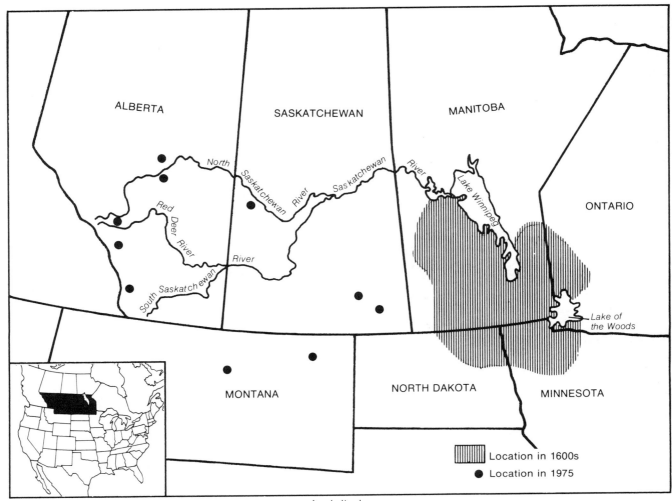

Assiniboine

domestic animal and was generally used to carry packs and pull travois, although the pups were sometimes eaten for religious purposes.

Most Assiniboine attached great importance to visions, and these took precedence in religious life. The elements of ceremonies and rites were performed individually or in groups. They included offerings, prayers, the solemn unfolding of a pack containing sacred objects, and the singing of sacred songs. Tremendous importance was attached to songs, which were repeated according to their mystic number. The Assiniboine considered sweating a necessary purification before participation in any major ceremony. Their favorite incense for major ceremonies was made from sweet grass. Tobacco was, as a rule, reserved for ceremonies and other solemn occasions. The pipes were handed and passed according to definite tribal traditions.

The Assiniboine believed in a great power—the Creator. They lived their religion every day. Therefore, they made sacrifices, fasts, and prayers to this unknown power, which they knew from ac-

tual phenomena had an existence. Mythological stories were told mainly for amusement. Most of them, however, contained a moral or ambiguous meaning and were interesting and imaginative.

The Sun Dance, an annual religious ceremony, was prohibited by the U.S. Department of the Interior in 1904, but the ban was removed in 1935. The Sun Dance has been extinct in Assiniboine culture since the late 1950s because the "keepers" died before handing down the rituals. Some Assiniboine participated in sun dances of other tribes in the late 20th century.

The Assiniboine were quite warlike. A periodically functioning police force was characteristic, and club-like organizations promoted the military spirit. A military society controlled every large camp, with the chief generally abiding by its decisions. The Assiniboine utilized the bow and arrow, a long-handled spear for close fighting, and three or four types of stone-headed clubs.

The Assiniboine have a peculiar style of decorative and pictographic art. Their sign language and decorative paintings on hides emphasized

Assiniboine camp scene showing decorated hide tipis and dogs fitted with travois.
Drawing by Carl Bodmer (1833) appeared in Maximilian's, *Travels* (1843).

straight-lined geometrical designs. The style of painted figures on rawhide illustrates a highly distinctive culture. The women made fine porcupine quill embroidery, and skill was displayed in the attachment of the feathers.

Feminine chastity was highly prized, but romance was by no means lacking in the sex life of the Assiniboine. The Assiniboine had a deep love for children. Discipline, although mild, was not entirely lacking.

Tribal history. The Assninboine and the Dakota were bitter enemies from early history. At one time the Assiniboine joined with the Chippewa and the Cree in fighting the Dakota for control of the buffalo country. With their Cree allies, the Assiniboine fought against the Blackfoot Confederacy for control of the Canadian prairies during the mid-18th century. Other enemies included the Blackfoot, Gros Ventre, and Flathead. By the late 18th and 19th centuries, however, some Blackfoot and Assiniboine were at peace.

The French explorer Duluth (Daniel Greysolon, Sieur du Luth) established relations with the Assiniboine in Canada in 1678 when he explored the Lake Superior region in search of a water route to the Pacific. The Assiniboine acquired horses and firearms, which altered their hunting and transportation methods, by intertribal trading in the mid-18th century.

Reliable estimates of the Assiniboine population prior to the 19th century are not available. Their population was estimated at about 8,000 to 10,000 in the early 19th century, although one source placed it as high as 25,000. About 4,000 Assiniboine died in the smallpox epidemic of 1836, and the population steadily declined until the late 19th century.

The Assiniboine in the United States accepted the 1851 treaty of Fort Laramie. They agreed to allow free access to wagon trains on the Oregon Trail, the building of roads, and the establishment of a chain of U.S. forts in their country. Soon afterward, they affiliated themselves with the Blackfoot and signed the treaty of 1855 at Fort Laramie, which set aside territory for Indian rights, but not a reservation. The Fort Belknap Reservation was established in 1870, and in 1888 it was moved to its present location in northcentral Montana. The Fort Peck Reservation was established in 1871; it was moved to its present location in northeastern Montana in 1877.

Hank Adams.

The policy of the U.S. government was to provide the Assiniboine with the necessities of life that they could no longer provide for themselves. Emphasis was placed on assimilation into the general society. Land was allotted in small tracts, children were sent to federal boarding schools, and Indian religious practices were repressed under the Religious Crimes Code. As a result, many individual Indians did become assimilated, but the Indian community as a whole suffered.

The Canadian Assiniboine signed three treaties with their government: Treaty No. 4 (September 15, 1974); Treaty No. 6 (August 23, 1876; September 9, 1876); and Treaty No. 7 (September 22, 1877). The Assiniboine ceded lands to Canada and in return received one square mile for each family of five, the right to hunt and fish in tracts surrendered to the government, schools, and some agricultural equipment.

Contemporary life. The Assiniboine were spread over a wide geographic area in the late 20th century. In the early 1970s, they numbered more than 1,500 in Canada and may have exceeded 4,500 in the United States. Their principal location in Canada was the Stony Reserve in Morey, Alberta; smaller bands were scattered over various other reserves in Alberta and Saskatchewan. Those who resided in the United States shared the two Montana reservations of Fort Belknap and Fort Peck with their traditional enemies, the Dakota and the Gros Ventre.

Although the Assiniboine had adopted some of the white man's ways, they retained many more of their own. Their family ties were strong and they practiced the Indian custom of sharing their possessions. They also continued to prepare foods that were enjoyed by their ancestors and participated in Indian celebrations, giveaways, and feasts.

(see map page XV)

BIBLIOGRAPHY-

● BLAIR, EMMA HELEN. The Indian Tribes of the Upper Mississippi Valley and Region of the Great Lakes... Cleveland, OH: The Arthur H. Clark Co.
● GABRIEL, RALPH HENRY. The Pageant of America: the Lure of the Frontier... New Haven, CT: Yale University Press, 1929.
● HABERLY, LOYD. Pursuit of the Horizon, A Life of George Catlin. New York, NY: The Macmillan Co., 1948.
● HARMON, GEORGE DEWEY. Sixty Years of Indian Affairs, Political, Economic, and Diplomatic, 1789- 1850. Chapel Hill, NC: University of North Carolina Press, 1941.
● HODGE, FREDERICK WEBB. Handbook of American Indians North of Mexico. Washington: Smithsonian Institution: BAE Bulletin No. 30: U.S. GPO, 1907.
● HUMFREVILLE, J. LEE. Twenty Years Among Our Hostile Indians. New York, NY: Hunter & Co.
● INDIAN OFFICE REPORT. 1856, 1869, 1870, 1876, 1883, 1887.
● LOWIE, ROBERT H. The Assiniboine. Anthropological Papers of the American Museum of Natural History, no. 4, 1910.
● MURDOCK, GEORGE P. Ethnographic Bibliography of North America. New Haven, CT: Human Relations Area Files Press, 1975.
● RICHARDSON, ALFRED TALBOT. Life, Letters and Travels of Father Pierre-Jean de Smet, S. J. 1801-1873. New York, NY: Francis P. Harper, 1905.
● SCHOOLCRAFT, HENRY R. History of the Indian Tribes of the U.S.; Their Present Condition and Prospects... Philadelphia, J. B. Lippincott & Co., 1857.
● SCHULENBERG, RAYMOND F. Indians of North Dakota. North Dakota History, v. 23, Oct., 1956.
● STANLEY, HENRY M. My Early Travels and Adventures in America and Asia. New York, NY: Charles Scribner's Sons, 1895.
● SWANTON, JOHN R. The Indian Tribes of North America. Smithsonian Institution: BAE Bulletin No. 145: U.S. GPO, 1952.
● WISSLER, CLARK. Indians of the U.S., Four Centuries of Their History and Culture. New York, NY: Doubleday, Doran & Co., 1940.

ASURINI

(South America; Brazil?) The Asurini are a native people inhabiting the left bank of the Tacantins River speaking a language belonging to the Tupian family. They are closely related linguistically and culturally with other Tupian speaking groups in the same region, including the Parakanan, the Surui and the Juruna. They should not be confused with the Asurini of the Pacaja River, a tributary of the Xingu.

Name and location. The Asurini (also spelled *Assurini*) inhabit an area of dense tropical forest rich in Brazil nut trees *(Bertholettia excelsia;* Portuguese, *castanha-do-para).* Their traditional territory lies along the Tocantins River within the Brazilian State of Para at about S3 - 40' latitude, W 50 longitude, bounded on the west by the Rio Jacunda and on the north by the Igarape Trocara.

Economy. Since outside observers have never visited an Asurini village, little is known about their subsistence economy. It is probable that they cultivated manioc, maize, pumpkins, tobacco and other crops, utilizing the slash-and-burn technique. The extent of reliance on hunting and fishing is unknown nor is it known whether they traditionally built or utilized watercraft. There is no accurate information regarding exchange of goods among the Asurini.

Social and political structure. Prior to pacification, the Asurini lived in small settlements, consisting of a single communal dwelling, all the male inhabitants of which belonged to a single patrilineage. The local group was exogamous, leading to the formation of alliances through marriage with other local groups. According to the ethnologist Roque Laraia, siblings maintained strong ties of loyalty and support even after marriage. Marital disputes, which were frequent, thus led to conflict between brothers-in-law as a man came to the defense of his sister in her quarrel with her husband. This conflict, in turn, tended to weaken alliances between lineages and even to generate violent disputes among them.

Polygyny was permitted, and considered prestigious. Marriage of a man to the daughter of his father's sister was preferred. Sister's daughter marriage is also a preferred form, according to Laraia. This is curious because it not only would put a man into potential competition with his own sons for the same women, but also sister's daughter becomes mother's brother's daughter marriage, a non-preferred type.

The system of kinship terms has some unusual features. While the terms on the first ascending generation are bifurcate merging, there is a distinction on ego's generation between children of father's sister and children of mother's brother. This is consistent with the preferential marriage stated above.

Each local group was led by a headman chosen on a basis of prestige, the size of his family, and his prowess as a warrior. While there was no institution of a "tribal" chief, certain local headmen did temporarily attain leadership over more than one local group, perhaps in time of warfare.

From the background just given, it may be assumed that the Asurini were given to a system of shifting alliances and to raids and counter raids between local groups.

Religion and cosmology. The Asurini apparently shared a number of customs and beliefs with other Tupian speaking societies of the region, but little of a specific nature is known. They share a belief in Mahira, a culture hero, with many other Tupian groups. Upon puberty, the lower lips of children were pierced. Ear lobes were also pierced to introduce ornaments. Nothing is known about their shamanistic practices.

History. The history of contact between the Asurini and the surrounding Brazilian society is particularly dramatic for the many episodes of violence which occurred. During the late 19th and early 20th centuries, the middle and lower Tocantins became a relatively important center of the extraction of latex and Brazil nuts from native trees. As early as 1849, the Asurini were blamed for the massacre of an entire Brazilian settlement at Alcobaca on the Tocantins River.

In 1927, construction began on the Tocantins Railroad, built to bypass a section of the river unnavigable because of rapids. In 1928, the Asurini began a series of attacks against various points along the railroad lying within their traditional territory, looting tools and other goods and causing several deaths. Over the next 25 years, a number of punitive expeditions were mounted by officials of the railway. In 1928, a party of 40 Brazilians surprised a group of Asurini at a hunting camp killing eight adults and capturing two children who, after a show of resistance, were also murdered. The heroic efforts of the old Indian Protection Service (SPI) to pacify the Asurini were undone several times by the hostility of the railroad workers to the Indians.

Finally, in 1953 the headman Koaci?nema* led two local groups into the SPI Post at Troaca, saying that they were under attack by another tribe. Of the 190 Asurini who came, 50 died within a year in an epidemic of influenza and dysentary. After the epidemic, Koaci?nem's rival, Sakawe?ia* led his group out of the Post into the forest. In 1956, Koaci?nema had a dispute with his followers only to be killed by his rival in the forest. Two years later remnants of this group straggled back into the Post, followed in 1962 by the 30 remaining followers of Sakawe?ia. As of 1967, only 58 Asurini were known to survive, most of them living as wards of the state at the Indian Post Troaca, now under the jurisdiction of the National Indian Foundation (FUNAI). The combined influence of the expanding Brazilian frontier, introduced diseases, and the very fractiousness of Asurini society were more than the society could resist.

_____
*Exact spelling of name is in doubt.

BIBLIOGRAPHY-

● STEWARD, JULIAN H. Handbook of South American Indians. 7 Vols., Washington, DC: U.S. Govt. Printing Office, 1946-59.

ATACAMA

(South America; Argentine, Chile) who spoke a dialect of the wide-spread Andean-Equatorial language family, occupied small oases in the Atacama Desert of northernmost Chile and the arid uplands

Atacama

of northwestern Argentina in the province of Jujuy. They became extinct as a cultural and social population during the colonial period. What we know of them is derived from archaeological studies. Because of the extreme aridity of the environment, many artifacts such as basketry, woven goods, leatherwork, woodwork, human mummies, and of course the more durable ceramic and stone manufacturers are extremely well- preserved and enable anthropologists to piece together something of the culture and social organization of these desert people. Today, archaeologists are still excavating this area because these people were an important link between ancient Peruvians and the Araucanian Indians of central Chile.

The population of the Atacama was small, scattered in accordance with the few water sources in their territory which was wedged between the Inca to the north (who later had settlements as far south as the modern city of Santiago, Chile) and the Diaguita who occupied a large area of transverse, east- west, valleys to the south. Place names in Atacameno which are still used by contemporary Chileans, Peruvians, and Argentineans serve as a guide to the extension of their territory in preconquest times, indicating that their very small settlements were extremely dispersed and attesting to the probability that they traded widely with the Diaguita and the Inca and were referred to as "the middlemen of the Andes." In the same manner as other coastal people in the Andean region from northern Peru to central Chile, the Atacama built

roads, unpaved but staked out, which were used by llama caravans. Judging from archaeological stratigraphy, it is possible that Atacameno culture lasted for two thousand or more years making it a contemporary of the Tiahuanaco civilization in Peru; however, archaeologists are not in full agreement on their chronology. Just before the Spanish conquest of Andean South America, the Diaguita penetrated Atacama territory and later on the Inca conquered both the Atacama and the Daiguita as well as the northernmost Araucanian-speaking people, the Picunche. The social organization of the Atacama was thoroughly disrupted during the early decades of the Spanish conquest of Chile. The few vestiges of their culture were destroyed in the nineteenth century during the exploitation of the nitrate fields and copper mines in this area.

The Atacama were small-scale irrigation, horticulturalists who had domesticated herds of llama and alpaca. They also had dogs which they sometimes mummified and placed in the graves of their masters. There is some question, however, as to whether this was accidental dessication or true mummification. Atacamenos used simple digging sticks and wooden shovels to plant and cultivate. The principal crop was maize, but beans, squash, quinoa, chili peppers, and gourds as well as potatoes, tobacco, and cotton were also grown. They irrigated their gardens by means of stonelined troughs which carried water for a considerable distance, characteristic of the basic Andean tradition. Hunting was not important but the Atacama who lived near the Pacific Ocean fished and collected shellfish.

Atacamenos lived in small, enclosed villages central to their fields. The basic building material was stone out of which the walls of the houses and the defensive enclosure wall surrounding the village were constructed. This last was built with slots large enough for the villagers to shoot arrows at attackers. Atacama houses were rectangular and very small, the largest measuring approximately ten by thirteen feet. They usually contained storage bins and sometimes served as burial crypts.

Atacameno clothing was in the Andean tradition with the men wearing slit-necked shirts, the women short-like dresses, and both sexes having ponchos. They manufactured blankets from llama wool, made shirt-type garments from guanaco or vicuna leather, and were famous, as are certain Peruvian peoples, for their birdskin capes. Pelican skins were also used for decorative purposes. Ornaments such as rings, pins, earrings, bracelets, breastplates, beads, and pendants were commonly found in archaeological sites along with numerous leather-covered paintboxes which suggest that bodypainting was a customary practice. The Atacamenos manufactured a great variety of wooden objects which were heavily influenced by the Peruvian-Bolivian Tiahuanaco culture. The ceramicware of the Atacama was diverse and also was the result of diffusion from the north of Andean South America; that is, at least from the Nazca, Tiahuanaco, and finally Inca. So too was their metalware, much of which was obtained through trade. The basic metal was copper but they also worked some gold and silver and finally discovered, again through diffusion from the north, how to make bronze. As revealed in archaeological sites, stone artifacts, mostly utilitarian, included several arrow styles, lances, pestles, and so forth.

Archaeologists such as Ricards Latcham, Max Uhle, and Junius Bird have concluded that "virtually nothing is known of the social and political organization of the Atacamenos." It is likely that Atacama villages were organized around concepts of patrilineality and that the men designated as chiefs were lineage elders, but this is very uncertain. These chiefs apparently did not exercise authority beyond their own community. There are no indications of high-level political organization comparable to developments in the Central Andes.

It is possible that the Atacamenos had a concept of a supreme deity. There is also evidence of the importance of shamanistic practices for the curing of illnesses. Burial practices among these people were varied and it is obvious that great care was taken of the dead. Graves were well-tended and everyday clothing, blankets, tunics, belts and the like were buried with the corpse. Multiple burials were common. Natural rock caves served as tombs, as did graneries, and burial under the floors of houses were frequent. Mummies have been found, most of which were infants, with the viscera removed and the cavity stuffed with straw. Wooden sticks had been inserted to make the body rigid and the entire body of the infant had been coated with clay and painted.

All of these indications might suggest that sometime in the pre-Spanish period, the Atacamenos had developed, largely through diffusion from the high culture of the Central Andes, a more sophisticated form of chiefdomship that is attested to by status burial, fortified villages, irrigation agriculture, the concept of a high god, and other cultural and social appurtenances shared by chiefdoms of eastern Bolivia, the sub-Andes, and the Circum- Caribbean.

BIBLIOGRAPHY-

● STEWARD, JULIAN H. Handbook of South American Indians. 7 Vols., Washington, DC: U.S. Govt. Printing Office, 1946-59.

ATACAMENO

See ATACAMA.

ATAKAPA

(U.S.; La., Tex.) is an extinct tribe which occasionally practiced cannibalism.

The word *Atakapa* comes from either the Choctaw or Mobile nation and means "Man-eater." French settlers in Louisiana called them *Atakpa,* but the Spanish called those living in Southeast Texas *Akokisa*. Except for the name there was no difference between the Texas and Louisiana bands. The Atakapa called themselves *Yukhitishak,* but the meaning of that word is lost. Their language comes from the Tunican stock, as does the Chitimacha who traded regularly with the Atakapa.

The Atakapa lived along the gulf coast of Louisiana and Texas from Vermillion Bayou to Trinity Bay, according to their legends and religion their people came from the sea after a great flood drowned the rest of the world.

In 1650 there were about 1,500 Atakapas.

Physically they were short and stout, wearing few clothes. They practiced head deformation and older Atakapas had facial tatoos.

Unlike most southeastern tribes they ate mostly fish, although they made periodic trips inland to hunt buffalo. They also grew maize. Occasionally they ate their enemies' flesh.

Cabeza De Vaca heard of the tribe in 1528, calling them the *Han*. Despite this early contact they remained relatively isolated from whites until the 1700s. In 1721 Bernard Dela Horpe, Captain Beranger and Sewars de Belle-Isle kidnapped some Atakapas, bringing them to New Orleans. But these escaped, returning home. In 1779 sixty Atakapas from Vermillion Bayou joined Gabeza in his expedition against British forts along the Mississippi. Later, Atakapas sold much of their land

The home of Armojean Roen, one of the last speakers of the Atakapa language.

to Creoles and moved West. But one village remained at Mermentou until 1836 when many went west to join other Atakapas in Oklahoma. There their numbers steadily declined until, by the early 20th century, there were only a few older tribe members who remembered their language.

(see map page XIV)

BIBLIOGRAPHY-

• DYER, V. O. The Lake Charles Atakapas. Galveston, TX: 1917.
• SWANTON, JOHN R. The Indian Tribes of North America. Smithsonian Institution: BAE Bulletin No. 145: U.S. GPO, 1952.

ATFALATI

(U.S.; Oreg.) A division of the Kalapooian family whose earliest seats, so far as can be ascertained, were the plains of the same name, the hills about Forest Grove, and the shores and vicinity of Wappato lake, Oreg.; and they are said to have entended as far as the site of Portland. They are now on grande Ronde reservation and number about 20. The Atfalati have long given up their native customs and little is known of their mode of life. Their language, however, has been studied by Gatschet, and our chief knowledge of the Kalapooian tongue is from this dialect.

BIBLIOGRAPHY-

• HODGE, FREDERICK WEBB. Handbook of American Indians North of Mexico. Washington: Smithsonian Institution: BAE Bulletin No. 30: U.S. GPO, 1907.
• MURDOCK, GEORGE P. Ethnographic Bibliography of North America. New Haven, CT: Human Relations Area Files Press, 1975.
• SWANTON, JOHN R. The Indian Tribes of North America. Smithsonian Institution: BAE Bulletin No. 145: U.S. GPO, 1952.

ATHABASCA

(Canada) A northern Athapascan tribe, from which the stock name is derived, residing around Athabasca lake, Northwest Territory. Ross regards them as a part of the Chipewyan proper. They do not differ essentially from neighboring Athapascan tribes.

BIBLIOGRAPHY-

• HODGE, FREDERICK WEBB. Handbook of American Indians North of Mexico. Washington: Smithsonian Institution: BAE Bulletin No. 30: U.S. GPO, 1907.
• MURDOCK, GEORGE P. Ethnographic Bibliography of North America. New Haven, CT: Human Relations Area Files Press, 1975.
• SWANTON, JOHN R. The Indian Tribes of North America. Smithsonian Institution: BAE Bulletin No. 145: U.S. GPO, 1952.

ATHAPASCAN

(U.S.; Alaska, Calif., Oreg.) is the name given to a language family, or a set of related dialects, spoken by a large number of North American Indian groups. Geographically, the language stock consists of three divisions: Northern, Pacific Coast, and Southern. More than 30 tribes speak a dialect of Athapascan in North America.

The Northern groups of Athapascan Indians occupy an area extending from the interior of Alaska to the western shores of Hudson Bay. They border on Inuit territory to the north, that of the Plains tribes to the south, and Northwest Coast Indians to the west. This area is sometimes referred to as the Western Sub-Arctic, and includes such Indian Tribes as Ingalik, Koyukon, Tanana, Kutchin, Tutchone, Hare, Dogrib, Yellow-knives, Slave, Beaver, Chipewyan, and Sarsi.

The Pacific Coast division consists of the Hupa and Mattole in southern Oregon and northern California. The Southern division occupies a very large area in the Southwest, including, Arizona, New Mexico, western Texas, and some portions of Mexico proper. The Navaho in eastern Arizona and western New Mexico; the Apache east and south of the Navaho; the Kiowa Apache of the Southern U.S. Plains; and the Toboso of Northern Mexico speak Athapascan.

As the most widely distributed of all the Indian linguistic families in North America, the languages which comprise the Athapascan family are related to each other and at times stand out from other native American languages with considerable distinctiveness. Phonetically, they contain frequent checks and aspirations, continuants, and gutteral sounds. Morphologically, they are marked by sentence verbs of considerable complexity, primarily because of many root changes indicating the number and character of the subject and object. Between the various languages there appears a great deal of regular phonetic change. While certain words are found to be common, each language, independently of the others, has formed many nouns by composition, and transformed the structure of its verbs. Thus the wide differences in culture among the various peoples of the Athapascan stock point to a long separation of the family. Archaeological investigations into the origin and forebearers of Athapascan Indians have revealed a long record of prehistoric settlement. Atahapascan culture appears to be at least 2000 years old.

The Northern division, also known as the Na-Dene can itself be broken down into three groups: eastern, northwestern, and southwestern. Dialects and cultures vary. In the Pacific division, the culture throughout the territory is also by no means uniform. For the most part, the language here met with a transition through intermediate dialects from one end of the region to the other. Known to have had at least five dialects in recent times, the Pacific coast Athapascans, most notably represented by the Hupa, exhibit the lnaguage with predominantly consonantal sounds. Rarely do words

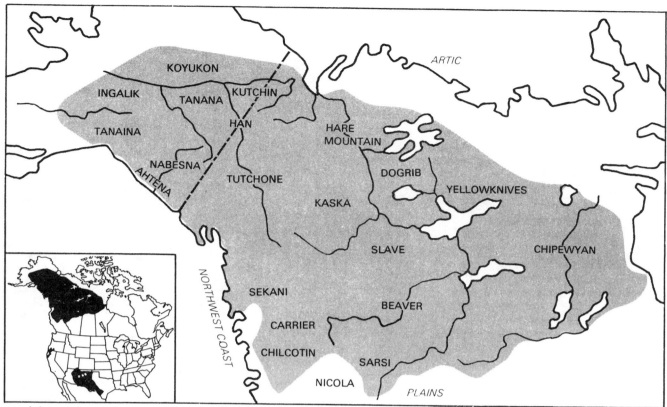

Athapascans (all tribes) Western Sub-Artic. Inset also shows Northern Pacific Coast, and Southern locations.

or syllables begin with a vowel. Verbs usually consist of two or more syllables, and rarely express ideas of equal rank. In the southern division, cultures and dialects also differ, and point up the general tendency of the Athapascans to have been influenced by their nieghbors. It is thus difficult to describe any distinctive Athapascan culture. It is only the language which unites these peoples.

The tribes of the north, especially in Alaska, have adopted customs of the Inuit; the Nahane have adopted the culture of the Tlingit; the Sarsi and the Beaver have been influenced by their Algonquin neighbors. The Pacific Athapascan exhibit little culture difference from their neighbors, the Salish, etc. And in the Southern area, the Navajo and even the Apache show social patterns and organization which can only be attributed to the Pueblo. The only tribes which may show any "Athapascan" culture are the eastern groups of the Northern division, such as the Chipewyan. They tend to exhibit similar social organization and hunting patterns.

The tribes of the Pacific and Southern division appear to have migrated to their present locations between 1000 and 1500. Descendants today of the bands which came from the area of Lake Athabasca, they little resemble their ancestors.

ATHAPASCAN SPEAKING FAMILY
Athapascan

—*Ahtena, Bear Lake, Beaver, Carrier, Chipewyan,*
Dogrib, Han, Hare, Ingalik, Kaska, Koyukon, Kutchin, Mountain, Nabesna, Sekani, Slave, Tanaina, Tanana, Tuchone, Yellowknife in the Subarctic area of northwestern Canada and Alaska.

—*Chiloctin, Nicola* on the Northwest Plateau, western Canada.

—*Hupa, Mattole* in southern Oregon and northern
California.

—*Sarci* on the northwestern Canadian plains.

—*Kiowa-Apache* on the southern U.S. Plains.

—*Apache, Navaho* in the U.S. Southwest.

Related

—*Haida, Tlingit* on the Northwest Pacific Coast.

—*Toboso* in northern Mexico.

(see map page XVI)

BIBLIOGRAPHY-

● HODGE, FREDERICK WEBB. Handbook of American Indians North of Mexico. Washington: Smithsonian Institution: BAE Bulletin No. 30: U.S. GPO, 1907.

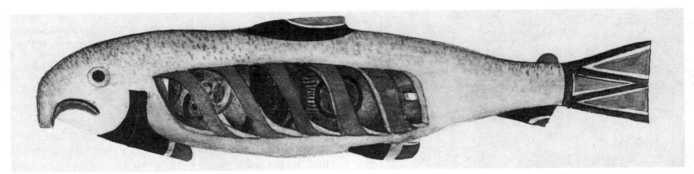

An Athapascan carved wooden salmon with the figure of a man inside, from Sitka, Alaska. The photograph is of an 1878 watercolor of the carving drawn by J. G. Swan.

● MURDOCK, GEORGE P. Ethnographic Bibliography of North America. New Haven, CT: Human Relations Area Files Press, 1975.
●PALMER, ROSE A. The North American Indians, An Account of the American Indians North of Mexico. New York, NY: Smithsonian Institution Series, Inc., 1929.
● SWANTON, JOHN R. The Indian Tribes of North America. Smithsonian Institution: BAE Bulletin No. 145: U.S. GPO, 1952.
● WISSLER, CLARK. The American Indian, An Introduction to the Anthropology of the New World. New York, NY: Douglas C. McMurtrie, 1917.
----- Indians of the U.S., Four Centuries of Their History and Culture. New York, NY: Doubleday, Doran & Co., 1940.

ATKA

(U.S.; Alaska?) The Atka were great hunters of the sea otter, and the furs they sold during the Russian occupancy made them wealthy. About half of them learned to read and write their own language, of which Russian missionaries made a grammar. With Christianity and civilization the Russians introduced alcohol, for which the natives developed an inordinate craving, making their own liquor, after the importation of spirits was forbidden, by fermenting sugar and flour. Their diet of fish and occasional water fowl is supplemented by bread, tea, and other imported articles that have become indispensable. The native dress, consisting of a long tight-sleeved coat of fur or bird skins, overlapping boots that reached above the knee, has been generally discarded for European clothing, though they still wear in wet weather a waterproof shirt of intestines obtained from the sea- lion. All are now Christianized, and nearly all live in houses furnished with ordinary things of civilization.

BIBLIOGRAPHY-
● HODGE, FREDERICK WEBB. Handbook of American Indians North of Mexico. Washington: Smithsonian Institution: BAE Bulletin No. 30: U.S. GPO, 1907.
● MURDOCK, GEORGE P. Ethnographic Bibliography of North America. New Haven, CT: Human Relations Area Files Press, 1975.
● SWANTON, JOHN R. The Indian Tribes of North America. Smithsonian Institution: BAE Bulletin No. 145: U.S. GPO, 1952.

ATSAHUACA

(South America; Peru, Bolivia) is the generic name for Indians including the Yamiaca, who inhabited the montana (tropical forest low highlands) of southern Peru and possibly northern Bolivia. The Atsahuaca and Yamiaca dialects are very similar indicating that these peoples must have separated during the colonial period. According to one of the most authorative South American linguists, J. Alden Mason, Panoan-speakers of the Atsahuaca dialect are made up of the Atsahuaca, Yamiaca and possibly the Araua. The montana region in which they lived is one of considerable cultural and linguistic diversity. There is no recent information about the Yamiaca branch of the Atsahuaca but at the beginning of the 20th century, Panoan-speaking peoples in this region were estimated to number between five and eight hundred. In 1904 the Atsahuaca proper were counted at 20 individuals living along the Atsahuaca and Malinowski Rivers, roughly latitude 13 S, longitude 70 W, north of Lake Titicaca.

Both the Atsahuaca and the Yamiaca lived along rivers and streams (mostly unnavigable for the Atsahuaca) where they cultivated the sandier and more productive soils in the typical widely-scattered pattern. They were slash-and-burn horticulturalists who grew maize, hot peppers, wett manioc, (*yuca*), gourds, native cotton, bananas, potatoes, sugar cane, papaya, and pineapples. The basic foods were bananas (probably plantians), maize, and manioc. They also made beer from bananas and manioc and mead from honey which they gathered.

In addition, these peoples fished and exploited river resources such as turtles and their abundant eggs whenever possible. Fishing was done with harpoon arrows and in still waters, the fish were drugged, possibly with *timbo,* a bark commonly used in the tropical forests of South America. The Atsahuaca have been described as good hunters and indications are that hunting was as important as horticulture and fishing in their economy. They used hunting dogs but it is not known whether this was an aboriginal practice or a result of contact with Spanish colonial society. The Yamiaca who lived near navigable streams used dugout canoes and rafts whereas the Atsahuaca who generally lived near small streams did not. The differences among these groups make an important suggestion about the influence of ecological adaption upon peoples who were otherwise culturally and linguistically isomorphic.

As did many other tropical forest peoples in South America, the Atsahuaca-Yamiaca cooked meat on a *babracot,* a wooden grate-like frame supported by four legs on which the meat is suspended over the fire. They also used clay pots of their own manufacture in which they prepared a common jungle dish—pepper hot. They also knew how to make simple wooden boxes, sew mats, and weave wicker baskets.

As an indication of the cultural and social diversity among groups in this corner of the world, the Atsahuaca-Yamiaca peoples, identical in so many respects, had very different domicilary arrangements which in the absence of detailed ethnography suggest different concepts of social organization. On the one hand, the Atsahuaca of the Malinowski and Atsahuaca Rivers lived in simple lean-tos covered by a brocade of palm leaves. In contrast, the Yamiaca of the Yaguarmayo River lived in large communal houses in extended family units. Their houses contained homemade fibre hammocks and platform beds, a scene very different from the elementary family lean-tos of the Atsahuaca.

Although very little is known about the sociopolitical organization of these people, it seems apparent that in the past when the society was more populous, chieftainship was important and households were integrated along political lines of authority. Social organization appears never to have been very complex, however. The chief was very likely a shaman with curative powers and the Atsahuaca are said to have shown great respect for him, "whispering in his presence." There is no adequate description of their supernatural beliefs and cosmology. It has been stated that the Yamiaca, upon the death of a man, buried his possessions with the body and destroyed part of the deceased's crops. This is a practice found frequently among tropical forest peoples.

What remains, then, are bits of exotica about an extinct society: men pierced the corners of their earlobes and noses with sticks or feathers; *urucu* and *genipa* were used as dyes for painting their bodies. Other types of ornamentation included necklaces, elaborate feather headdresses. The simple barkcloth clothing was often adorned with paint and with decorative edging, sometimes made of feathers.

The Atashuaca-Yamiaca were typical of many small Indian societies in existence at the time of the European conquest of South America. These societies were unable to maintain their cultural and social integrity under conditions of contact and dwindled in population to the point that they became totally absorbed into the prevailing culture. What we know of them suggests that they were rather similar to other tropical forest peoples and thus we may learn something about them from the ethnographies of nearby peoples who have been more adequately described.

(see map page XVIII)

ECUADOR

BRAZIL

PERU

Lake Titicaca

BOLIVIA

CHILE

Location early
20th century

Atsahuaca

BIBLIOGRAPHY-
● STEWARD, JULIAN H. Handbook of South American Indians. 7 Vols., Washington, DC: U.S. Govt. Printing Office, 1946-59.

ATSINA

See GROS VENTRE.

BIBLIOGRAPHY-
● COUEE, ELLIOTT. Forty Years a Fur Trader on the Upper Missouri, the Personal Narrative of Charlie Larpenteur, 1833-1872. New York, NY: Francie P. Harper, 1898.
● HODGE, FREDERICK WEBB. Handbook of American Indians North of Mexico. Washington: Smithsonian Institution: BAE Bulletin No. 30: U.S. GPO, 1907. America. New Haven, CT: Human Relations Area Files Press, 1975.
● SWANTON, JOHN R. The Indian Tribes of North America. Smithsonian Institution: BAE Bulletin No. 145: U.S. GPO, 1952.
● WISSLER, CLARK. Indians of the U.S., Four Centuries of Their History and Culture. New York, NY: Doubleday, Doran & Co., 1940.

ATSUGEWI

(U.S.; Calif.) A Shastan tribe formerly residing in Hat Creek, Burney, and Dixie valleys, California. Their language is quite divergent from that of the Achomawi, from whom they regard themselves as distinct. Very few of them survive. *(see map page XVII)*

BIBLIOGRAPHY-
● HODGE, FREDERICK WEBB. Handbook of American Indians North of Mexico. Washington: Smithsonian Institution: BAE Bulletin No. 30: U.S. GPO, 1907. America. New Haven, CT: Human Relations Area Files Press, 1975.
● SWANTON, JOHN R. The Indian Tribes of North America. Smithsonian Institution: BAE Bulletin No. 145: U.S. GPO, 1952.

ATTACAPA

(U.S.; La.) A tribe forming the Attacapan linguistic family, a remnant of which early in the 19th century occupied as its chief habitat the Middle or Prien lake in Calcasieu parish, La. It is learned from Hutchins that "the village de Skunnemoke or tuckapos" stood on Vermilion river and that their church was on the West side ofthetage (Bayon Teche). The Attacapa country extended formerly to the coast in S. W. Louisiana, and their primitive domain was outlined in the popular name of the Old Attacapa or Tuckapa country, still in use, which comprised St. Landry, St. Mary, Iberia, St. Martin, Fayette, Vermilion, and, later, calcasieu and Vernon parishes; in fact all the country between Red, Sabine, and Vermilion Rivers and the Gulf. Charlevoix states that in 1731 some Attacapa with some hasinai and Spaniards aided the French commander, Saint Denys, against the Natchez. Penicaut says that at the close of 1703 two of the three Frenchmen whom Bienville sent by way of the Madeline river to discover what nations dwelt in that region, returned and reported that they had been more than 100 leagues inland and had found 7 diffeent nations, and that among the last, one of their comrades had been killed and eaten by the savages,who were anthropophagous. This nation was called Attacapa. In notes accompanying his Attacapa vocabulary Duralde says that they speak of a deluge which engulfed men, animals, and the land, when only those who dwelt on a highland escaped; he also says that according to their law a man ceases to bear his own name as soon as his wife bears a child to him, after which he is called the father of such and such a child, but that if the child dies the father again assumes his own name. Duralde also asserts that the women alone were charged with the labors of the field and of the household, and that the mounds were erected by the women under the supervision of the chiefs for the purpose of giving their lodges a higher situation than those of other chiefs. Milfort who visited St. Bernard bay in 1784, believed that the tribe came originally from Mexico. He was hospitably received by a band which he found bucanning meat beside a lake, 4 days' march West of the bay; and from the chief, who was not an Attacapa, but a Jesuit, speaking French, he learned that 180, nearly half the Attacapa tribe, were there, thus indicating that at that time the bribe numbered more than 360 persons; that they had a custom of dividing themselves into two or three bodies for the purpose of hunting buffalo, which in the spring went to the West and in the autumn descended into these latitudes: that they killed them with bows and arrows, their youth being very skillful in this hunt: that these animals were in great numbers and as tame as domestic cattle, for "we have great care not to frighten them:" that when the buffaloes were on the prairie or in the forest the Attacapa camped near them "to accustom them to seeing us." Sibley described their village as situated "about 20 miles West of the Attakapa church, toward Quelqueshoe;" their men numbered about 50, but some Tonica and Huma who had intermarried with the Attacapa made them altogether about 80. Sibley adds: "They are peaceable and friendly to everybody; labor, occasionally for the white inhabitants; raise their own corn; have cattle and hogs. They were at or near where they now live, when that part of the country was first discovered by the French." In 1885 Gatschet visited the section formerly inhabited by the Attacapa, and after much search discovered one man and two women at Lake Charles, Calcasieu parish, La., and another woman living 10 miles to the South; he also heard of 5 other women scattered in West Texas; these are thought to be the only survivors of the tribe.

BIBLIOGRAPHY- (See Attacapan Family.)

ATTACAPAN FAMILY

(U.S.; La., Tex.) A linguistic family consisting solely of the Attacapa tribe, although there is linguistic evidence of at least two dialects. Under this name were formerly comprised several bands settled in South La. and N.E. Texas. Although this designation was given them by their Choctaw neighbors on the East, these bands, with one or two exceptions, do not appear in history under any other general name. Formerly the Karankawa and several other tribes were included with the Attacapa, but the vocabularies of Martin Duralde and of Gatschet show that the Attacapa language is distinct from all others. Investigations by Gatschet in Calcasieu parish, La., in 1885, show that there were at least two dialects of this family spoken at the beginning of the 19th century an eastern dialect, represented in the vocabularly of Duralde, recorded in 1802, and a western dialect, spoken on the 3 lakes forming the outlet of Calcasieu River.

BIBLIOGRAPHY-

● BOLTON, HERBERT EUGENE. Athanase de Mezieres and the Louisiana-Texas Frontier, 1768-1780. Cleveland, OH: The Arthur H. Clark Co., 1914.
● HODGE, FREDERICK WEBB. Handbook of American Indians North of Mexico. Washington: Smithsonian Institution: BAE Bulletin No. 30: U.S. GPO, 1907. limits of the U.S., 1513-1561. New York, NY: G. P. Putnam's Sons, 1901.
● MURDOCK, GEORGE P. Ethnographic Bibliography of North America. New Haven, CT: Human Relations Area Files Press, 1975.
● SWANTON, JOHN R. The Indian Tribes of North America. Smithsonian Institution: BAE Bulletin No. 145: U.S. GPO, 1952.
● WISSLER, CLARK. Indians of the U.S., Four Centuries of Their History and Culture. New York, NY: Doubleday, Doran & Co., 1940.

ATTIGNAWANTAN

(Canada; Ontario) One of the largest tribes of the Huron confederacy, comprising about half the Huron population, formerly living on Nottawasaga bay, Ontario. In 1638 they were settled in 14 towns and villages. The Jesuit missions of St. Joseph and La Conception were established among them.

BIBLIOGRAPHY-

● HODGE, FREDERICK WEBB. Handbook of American Indians North of Mexico. Washington: Smithsonian Institution: BAE Bulletin No. 30: U.S. GPO, 1907. America. New Haven, CT: Human Relations Area Files Press, 1975.
● SWANTON, JOHN R. The Indian Tribes of North America. Smithsonian Institution: BAE Bulletin No. 145: U.S. GPO, 1952.

AUAKE

(South America; Brazil-Ven.) is an almost extinct tropical rainforest tribe living on the Brazil-Venezuelan border, in the Northern Amazon culture area. As many other Amazonian tribes on the

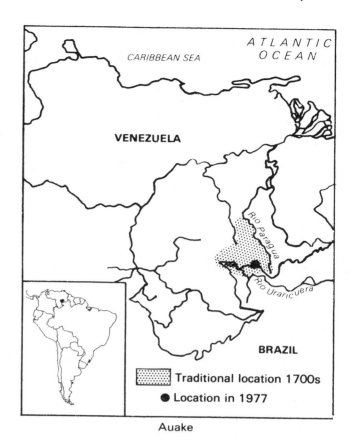

Auake

verge of extinction, very little has been published about their extinction about their culture and history.

Tribal name The current name *Auake* is not a self-designation. It was Lobo D'Almada who contacted them first in 1787 and referred to them as *Aoaquis*. In the literature, the name appeared as *Oewaku* and currently as *Awake, Auake,* or *Auaque*. Carib speaking people of the area call them *Arutani;* and the Yanomama, with whom they are intermarried, refer to them as (rak). They call themselves both *Urutani* or *Uruak*.

Territory The traditional area occupied by the Auake extended from the upper Paragua River (Venezuela) to the Uratani mountain, in the Pacaraima range dividing Venezuela from Brazil, and south to the Maraca Island of the Uraricuera River in Brazil. Today the Auake are confined to the headwaters of the Paragua and Uraricaa Rivers, where they are intermarried with the (Yanam) Yanomama. A few Auake individuals integrated with the Pemon (Carib) are also found in the mid Paragua region.

Language Their generic affiliation is still uncertain. Traditionally their language had been classified as the only member of an independent language family called *Awake*. In 1960 a new classification of South American languages has tentatively listed Auake as a member of the

Marco-Tucanoan family. Recent lexical comparison shows similarities between Auake and some Arawak languages. No linguistic study of Auake has ever been published.

Summary of tribal culture Today, most of the Auake cultural traits are similar to, but not as elaborate as that of their Pemon neighbors. The same can be said of the Yanam (Yanomama), the people they live with. Most probably the Yanam have borrowed many Carib cultural traits from the Auake.

Their subsistence economy is based on slash-and-burn horticulture in which manioc (sweet and bitter varieties), banana, yams, and sweet potatoes are the main products. Hunting, fishing, and gathering supplement their diet. Tobacco is planted and used to be smoked for shamanistic purposes. Now however it is not smoked but is held in their mouths between their lips and teeth like the Yanam. For witchcraft they sniff hallucinogenic powders. A few cotton trees are also planted near the house and the cotton is spun for making hammocks and for trade purposes. Fermented manioc drink, made with chewed cassava bread is their preferred beverage at their monthly parties. Their main weapons are still bow and arrows, but during the last ten years a few shotguns have been acquired from diamond miners. Their typical village is one colonial house which contains from four to fifteen nuclear families. They prefer patrilineal exogamous, cross cousin marriages with matrilocal residence. Cousin terminology is of the Iroquois type. Girls marry soon after puberty and have their children four to five years apart. Puberty rites for girls consist mainly of a month's diet. Both men and women wear a small cotton loin cloth and decorate their bodies with blue Jenipa and red pigments from Bixa Orellana seeds. Now, as the Yanam, they cremate their dead but probably in the past they buried them. They used to trade cotton balls, and other items they obtained in Brazil, with the Pemon and Mayongong (Carib).

Summary of tribal history There are very few historical references concerning the Auake, the first being that of the Portuguese Colonel Lobo D'Almada who in 1787 reported them at the headwaters of the Cauame River, just southeast of the Maraca Island on the Uraricuera River (territory of Roraima, Brazil). At that time their immediate neighbors were the Purukoto Pemon (Carib) located in the area of the Uraricaa River, and the Maracana just south of them. At the beginning of the last century the Yanam, arriving from the Southwest in little groups and at different times, penetrated the area and within a century caused a displacement of the Purukoto to the east and practically exterminated the Maracana. The Auake,

who were first reduced in number and then forced northward by the Maracana, tried to oppose the Yanomama expansion to the Uraricaa and Paragua Rivers but, being reduced to about seventy people, at the turn of the century, they began intermarrying with the Yanomama. Names of rivers and mountains in the area of the Uraricaa and upper Paragua River are in the Auake language, suggesting that they occupied the area before the Yanomama and ever the Carib.

Contemporary tribal situation and population figures

It is estimated at the beginning of the last century the Auake numbered at least three hundred. Their struggle against the Maracana, the Yanomama and later epidemics resulting from their intermittent contact with outsiders reduced their number in the early sixties to seventeen non-mixed Auake. There were also about 20 others who were of mised origin, Yanomama-Auake.

Today there are about ten non-mixed Auake of whom only five can speak their language. In the lower Paragua there are a few individual Auake who are intermarried with the Sape and the Pemon. Most of the Auake however, are mixed with the Yanomama in the upper Paragua and Uraricaa Rivers. They all speak the Yanam variety of Yanomama and culturally are the same as the Yanam. Until 1962 they were quite isolated from the non-Indian world having only sporadic contacts with either Venezuelan or Brazilian nationals, but since then they have entered into intermittent or seasonal contact with diamond miners with the unfortunate consequences of fights, epidemics, and a cultural change which was not slow enough to ensure their survival. Some Auake young males, instead of staying within their group to ensure cultural autonomy, tend to leave for "down river" to become cheap laborers in a "civilized economy." *(see map page XVIII)*

BIBLIOGRAPHY-

● STEWARD, JULIAN H. Handbook of South American Indians. 7 Vols., Washington, DC: U.S. Govt. Printing Office, 1946-59.

AUGUSTINE RESERVATION

is a small reservation of 502 acres in Riverside County, California. It was established in 1893 for the Augustine band of Mission Indians. Located in the desert of California, it has a tribal enrollment of 2 as of 1969, and no Indian residents.

The tribal headquarters are in Thermal, California. The nearest city to the reservation is Indio, 15 miles away. Augustine, situated on flat, desesrt land, has an average rainfall of under 4 inches per year, and temperatures reaching as high as 120 . Most services to the tribe are available in Indio.

AVOYEL

See NATCHEZ.

AWANI

(U.S.; California) A division of the Miwok living in Yosemite valley, Mariposa county. Powers states that the name Yosemite is a distorted form of the Miwok *uzumaiti,* 'grizzly bear,' a term never used by the Indians to designate the valley itself or any part of it. Awani, the name applied by the natives of the valley, was the principal village, which by extension was given to the whole valley and its inhabitants, who occupied it when snow permitted. The Awani had 9 villages, containing 450 people, when the whites first came, and they seem to have had a larger number than earlier period. At present the population is unknown, but small. The 9 villages were Awani, Hokokwito, Kumaini, Lesamaiti, Macheto, Notomidula, Sakaya, and Wahaka.

BIBLIOGRAPHY-

● HODGE, FREDERICK WEBB. Handbook of American Indians North of Mexico. Washington: Smithsonian Institution: BAE Bulletin No. 30: U.S. GPO, 1907.
● MURDOCK, GEORGE P. Ethnographic Bibliography of North America. New Haven, CT: Human Relations Area Files Press, 1975.
● SWANTON, JOHN R. The Indian Tribes of North America. Smithsonian Institution: BAE Bulletin No. 145: U.S. GPO, 1952.

AWEIKOMA

(South America; Brazil) is a name in use primarily among North American ethnologists. It designates a small but highly prominent tribe of southern Brazil, classified linguistically in the Ge family. Aweikoma are closes linguistic and culture relatives of the neighboring Caingang. Indeed, these latter speak an almost indistinguishable language.

Among Brazilian settlers the Aweikoma are known as *Botocudo.* This name derives from the Portuguese word for lip plug (*botoque*), such as Aweikoma men aboriginally wore. And in this they may be distinguished from Caingang. However, *Botocudo* is now used primarily for a macro-Ge tribe of eastern Brazil, from whom the Aweikoma are wholly distinct (*see* Boptocudo). Aweikoma are also known as *Caingang* (or *Kaingang*), owing to their linguistic- cultural similarity to that people. Among Brazilian ethnologists they are known as *Xokleng* (or *Shokleng, Xokreng, Xokre, etc.)* This word derives from the Caingang name for them. The designation *Aweikoma* sems itself to have been at one time the native term for one of a pair of moieties.

Aboriginally, Aweikoma occupied a vast tract of subtropical forest and savanna land. This territory encompassed most of what is now east-central Santa Catarina, a state in southern Brazil. Ethno-

Aweikoma

historical evidence indicates, however, that Aweikoma probably came to this territory from somewhere to the north and west. This migration occurred most likely sometime in the early 19th century.

There were in the 19th century three Aweikoma communities, each consisting of 200 to 600 individuals. Each of them was on hostile terms with the encroaching Brazilian settler society. One community established peaceful contact with members of the Indian Protection Service (SPI) in 1914. Its members were settled on a reserve near the town of Ibirama, where the survivors can be found today. According to a recent survey, there are some 303 Aweikoma at Ibirama. A second community was already severely decimated, when around 1918 peaceful relations were established with the SPI. A few survivors reside today without officially recognized reserve near Porto Uniao. A third community had its locus farther south, near the city of Lajes. They continued hostile until around 1940, when they abruptly vanished. Some evidence indicates that a few survivors may remain to this day isolated in the Serra do Taboleiro, near the Atlantic coast south of Florianopolis.

Aboriginally, Aweikoma subsisted primarily in the products of hunting and gathering. But their diets were often supplemented by corn, beans, squash, and other items obtained in raids on Brazilian settlements. Culturally, hunting was

Kamren, last of the great Aweikoma shamans, prior to 1932. Note the lip-plug, metal-tipped lance arrows, waist cords, all aspects of Aweikoma material culture.

into two or more trekking groups. These wandered over a specified area, systematically exploiting the available game and fruit. Politically, trekking groups were also the loci of factions. When a schism occurred, it usually involved a falling out between trekking groups.

Each community consisted of a number (probably 10-20) of household groups. Each household consisted of several nuclear families. The rule of residence was uxorilocality. The households of a village were arranged spatially in a semi-circle around a central plaza. Such semicircles opened to the west, where Aweikoma say is located the "land of the dead." Villages were organized internally as well according to age grades. There were no unilineal groupings. Recent research, however, suggests that there was a non-unilineal moiety system, intersecting with three non-unilineal classes. Moiety and class membership was transmitted "bilaterally" along with names, which passed from dead kinsmen to young children. The intersection of moieties and classes gave rise to six groupings, each associated with a distinctive body-paint design. The kin terminology had as well a markedly bilateral character.

Aweikoma had two principal kinds of collective ceremony. One (angyidn ceremonies) focussed on death as a life cyclic passage. For some two to four weeks following a death, the surviving spouse was secluded outside the village. The key ceremony focused on his or her subsequent reintegration into the community. A second principal type (angradin ceremonies focussed on very early childhood. These ceremonies were held in grandest form in conjunction with the giving of lip plugs to infant boys, and the thigh tattooing of girls.

Aweikoma have a large stock of myths and tales. One key cycle (the wainkredn) recounts the tribal origin, migration, and creation of animals (tapirs, jaguars, and snakes). It is told by two men sitting opposite one another. One recites one syllable, and it is immediately repeated by his partner. The myth is in this was told in duplicate, this dualism reflecting a general dualistic principle governing Aweikoma social life. Only the wainkredn is told in this way. All other myths are simply narrated. Among these myths, a key one focusses on the origin of death. It concerns the relationship between two brothers and a "giant falcon." Aweikoma have as well a host of other myths, and numerous political-historical narratives.

Aweikoma usually endeavor to cure minor illnesses by means of various plant infusions. They have special concoctions for such maladies as snakebite, headache, and wounds. It is only in serious cases that a shaman intervenes. His cure is effected by invoking animal "spirit masters." Most

considered most important. And Aweikoma actively hunted with bow and arrow many of the numerous game species, especially tapir and wild pigs, which abounded in the southern Brazilian forests and savannas. They engaged however in almost no fishing. From the point of view of collecting, emphasis was on the Araucaria collecting, emphasis was on the Araucaria pine nut, which was probably the king pin of their adaption. These nuts were present in great abundance on the campos. The Aweikoma had developed ways of storing them for periods of up to a year. Consequently, it was on Araucaria nuts they could rely when all else failed.

Semi-permanent villages formed the basic unit of social organization. Each village was both a politically and economically self-contained unit, under the leadership of a patrilineally recruited chief. However, villages remained co- residential units for only two or three months per year. This was during the summer ceremonial season (February-March), when game was especially abundant. For the remainder of each year, villages split up

Aweikoma "religious" conceptions concern these spirit masters.

Aweikoma history prior to the 19th century is largely terra incognita. Some have identified Aweikoma with the ancient Guayana Indians, who inhabited the region near Sao Paulo in the 16th century. But this connection requires more evidence. Most of what we know about early Aweikoma history comes from their own historical narratives. These convey a definite impression that their social organization underwent a revloutionary upheaval, sometime around 1800. Prior to this time, they seem to have had a system of exogamous patrimoieties, much like those of Caingang. However, the system collapsed during a political schism. This gave rise ot various changes in the social organization.

Probably around this time, Aweikoma migrated into Santa Catarina region, where they are located today. This area was at that time largely unpopulated. But by the mid-1800s Brazilian settlers were already penetrating these backlands. Inevitbly, conflicts arose. Aweikoma raided Brazilian homesteads, and the settlers retaliated. Organized expeditions of *bugreiros* or "Indian hunters" were sent out to subdue them. And some attempts were made at peaceful contact. Nevertheless, hostilities continued into the 20th century.

Today there is only one officially recognized reserve for Aweikoma. With an area of some 41 square kilometers, it is but a fraction of their aboriginal territory. Still, it is richly forested and contains some good agricultural land. The Brazilian government through FUNAI has focused its efforts on converting Aweikoma from hunter-gatherers into agriculturalists. Aweikoma however have thus far preferred other modes of subsistence, such as extraction of *palmito,* which more closely resemble aboriginal patterns. But reserve life has brought numerous changes. Aweikoma no longer regularly perform their collective ceremonies, and many beliefs and practices are disappearing. Indeed, some Aweikoma have been firm believers in "Brazilianization." It is in spite of this that Aweikoma society remains a cohesive entity, distinct from the encompassing settler society.

BIBLIOGRAPHY-

● STEWARD, JULIAN H. Handbook of South American Indians. 7 Vols., Washington, DC: U.S. Govt. Printing Office, 1946-59.

AWETI

(South America; Brazil) The Aweti speak a language of the Tupian Family. They inhabit the headwaters of the Xingu river in Mato Grosso State in Central Brazil where they comprise a single village, with a population of about 45 persons. The

Aweti

Aweti form a part of a larger multilingual society with close ties and relatively homogenous cultural practices, including the Kamaiura (also Tupian), the Mehinacu, Waura, and the Taualapiti (Arawakan), the Kuikuru, Kalapalo, Matipu and Nafuqua (Cariban) and the Trumai (language unclassified). (Entries under these societies should also be consulted).

Name and location.

The Aweti (also spelled *Aueti, Aweto, Auiti,* etc.) speak a language derived from a very widespread language family with speakers from the Amazon to Paraguay. They live within the Xingu National Indian Park created in 1961 and under the administration of the Brazilian National Indian Foundation. Their village is located near the Tueatuwari River, an affluent of the Culuene River, itself a headwater of the Xingu.

Economy. Slash-and-burn horticulture is the principal economic pursuit of the Aweti and by far the most important crop is bitter manioc which is processed into manioc flour and flat beiju cakes for storage and consumption. Other crops include maize, pumpkins, watermelon, and the pequi *(Caryocar brasilensis)* and mangaba *(Hancornia aoecuisa Gomes).* Fishing is the other important subsistence activity. It is practiced primarily by men who fish individually with hook and line, fish traps and bow and arrow, and communally using a native vine to stun the fish in sluggish streams.

Small animals such as birds and monkeys are hunted and eaten, but most large animals are tabooed and are hunted only for trade with non-Indians in the area.

Unlike many groups in South America, the contemporary Aweti have a developed sense of private property which may include gardens, tools, food stocks, as well as songs and a knowledge of myth and ritual. There is a vigorous trade, based on reciprocal exchange between individuals in the material goods mentioned above. There is also a ritual form of trade known among the Aweti by a Kamaiura term, *moitara,* which may occur within or between villages. In this ritual, an object is placed on the ground as an offering. A person interested in the object may bring another object and place it before the first one. If the owner of the first object feels the trade is fair one, he or she will pick up the proferred item and the transaction is consummated. Each trade is observed by the public at large and commented on at length.

Each group, in the upper Xingu, specializes in a particular manufacture, although not apparently because of any variation in the availability of raw materials to any group. The Aweti along with the black bow which they may exchange, for example, with the Waura who specialize in pottery. George Zarur and other authors suggest that the specialization is artificial and exists to strengthen the interdependency among the villages while maintaining their separate identities.

In spite of the isolation of their reserve, the Aweti and other Xinguanos are engaged in an increasing amount of trade with visiting Brazilians who bargain for native handicrafts in exchange for steel tools, firearms, ammunition, even transistor radios. Some of the goods are distributed gratis by FUNAI agents and the Aweti have come to depend on them very heavily. In some cases, conflicts have been generated over who shall receive certain goods, and the beginnings of conspicuous consumption can already be discerned even in this remote and protected society. In some instances, Xinguanos have even been known to ask for payment to pose for photographs for visitors.

Social and political structure. The major determinants of the division of labor are age and sex. Adult men are responsible for felling and burning new garden plots, for fishing and many ceremonial activities. Many objects are produced by men including ritual vestments and decorations, canoes, paddles, manioc graters, mortars, bows and arrows, small tools, etc. There are few exclusively female activities but women predominate in harvesting and processing manioc, child care, cooking and other domestic chores, fetching water and firewood, carrying loads, etc. There are few specialists but a few people are especially sought

after as shamans or in the manufacture or certain musical instruments or masks.

In 1971 there were five residential houses in the Aweti village plus a ceremonial flute house. Each contained from one to three nuclear families linked by consanguineal ties. The houses are arranged in a roughly circular pattern around the flute house which occupies the center. There is a preference for marriages between men and the daughter of their father's sister or mother's brother. Postmarital residence is matrilocal until the first child is born and then a couple is free to return to the husband's household. Marriages are usually arranged by the parents of the bride and groom and the groom pays a substantial bride price to his wife's parents as well as hunting for their household for a year or more. There are no descent groups, clans or moieties, but there appears to be a kind of reciprocity set up between men who exchange sisters or daughters as marriage partners. Marriage is rather fragile and many first marriages end in separation. A frequent cause of separation is unfaithfulness and indeed the Aweti are no exception to the very common practice in the Xingu of maintaining multiple liaisons at one time. Second marriages are evidently more lasting and involve a greater commitment by the spouses to each other. Poligyny, especially sororal poligyny, is permitted but rare, restricted generally to men of high rank.

The system of kinship terminology is basically bifurcate merging except that a suffix distinguishes ego's own father from ego's father's brother and other classificatory fathers. On ego's generation, malse distinguish between older and younger male siblings while females do not. The children of same sex siblings refer to each other by the same terms as brothers and sisters, while those of cross-sex siblings use a term which may be glossed as "affine" independently of the sex of the relative or that of ego.

Political leadership among the Aweti appears to be rather diffuse. Traditionally, there appears to have been no single chief of the village but rather a group of high status men known as *morekwat* who enjoyed prestige and influence due not only to their position in the kinship network in the village but also from being descended from another *morekwat.* Today, the *morekwat* status still exists but Brazilian administration has added the status of capitao (*"village chief"*) who answers to the administration, distributes trade goods and in general serves as liaison between Brazilian society and the Aweti.

There is little day-to-day aggression within the Aweti village, but conflicts and tensions do arise. They are expressed primarily through the attribution of witchcraft to persons to whom others feel animosity. Through a campaign of innuendo and insinuation, such accusations may reach a point where any misfortune will be blamed on the accused. A shaman may skillfully manipulate the situation so that accusations fall on persons with whom they have personal quarrels and especially those without much kinship or political support within the village. In some cases, the individual may be assassinated for his alleged witchcraft practices and in others he may be forced to flee the village. Thus shamanism and gossip may exercise powerful control over the behavior of persons.

Raiding and warfare between villages have now been suppressed by the FUNAI administration, but until recently, the Aweti were involved in the system of shifting alliances, raids and counter raids which were characteristic of a long period of upper Xingu history. Other villages may still be regarded with distrust but hostilities appear to have been minimized by FUNAI sanctions as well as the ceremonial exchanges which are quite frequent in the Xingu.

Religion and cosmology. As stated above, the Aweti participate in a social system which goes beyond the limits of their village and language group. One aspect of this social system is an integrated ceremonial structure which is justified and explained by a series of myths which belong to all the Xinguano societies enumerated above and which provide an account of the origins of the world and of the different societies within it. The Xinguanos believe that many natural objects such as plants, fish, furry animals and stars are connected with a kind of spirit called *mamae*. These *mamae* are propriated by the proper observance of custom and ritual. An omission or the act of a sorcerer can turn a *mamae* against a person making him sick or killing him.

Karytu is the name of the *mamae* of fish and also of the ritual flutes. These instruments are kept hidden in the flute house away from the eyes of women; if one should set eyes on the flutes, she would be gang raped by all the men of the village. At night the village plaza belongs to the men and the flutes who perform the *Karytu* ritual almost daily. George Zarur suggests that the *Karytu* symbolizes the corporate unity of men in the village and the inferiority of women. It mobilizes cooperative labor among the men who must fish, claear gardens, or build houses as a group. Among many other rituals, the Aweti also practice the well known *kwarip* in which logs are erected and decorated in memory of important persons who have died in the past year and at which girls in puberty seclusion are finally permitted to rejoin the village.

History. The Aweti appear to have changed remarkably little since 1892 when they were visited by von den Steinen who described certain aspects of the culture. The Villas Boas brothers who founded the Xingu Indian Park in 1961 and administered it until recently, suggest that the Aweti were among invaders from the West who made war on all the societies then living in the upper Xingu headwaters region, more than 150 years ago. Due to the isolation of the Xingu Park and to the political skill of the Villas Boas, the Aweti and other Xinguanos have been spared the brutal shocks that have accompanied pacification and contact over the rest of Brazil. But the expanding Brazilian frontier is already encroaching on the Aweti and soon there will be an opportunity to test whether the protective policy of the park will have been effective.

BIBLIOGRAPHY-
● STEWARD, JULIAN H. Handbook of South American Indians. 7 Vols., Washington, DC: U.S. Govt. Printing Office, 1946-59.

AXION

(U.S.; N.J.) A division of the New Jersey Delawares, formerly living on the East bank of Delaware River, between Rancocas Creek and the present Trenton. In 1648 they were one of the largest tribes on the river, being estimated at 200 warriors. Brinton thinks the name may be a corruption of Assiscunk, the name of a creek above Burlington.

BIBLIOGRAPHY-
● HODGE, FREDERICK WEBB. Handbook of American Indians North of Mexico. Washington: Smithsonian Institution: BAE Bulletin No. 30: U.S. GPO, 1907.
● SWANTON, JOHN R. The Indian Tribes of North America. Smithsonian Institution: BAE Bulletin No. 145: U.S. GPO, 1952.

AYLLU

(Mexico;??) In Inca and Aymara societies, a number of unrelated extended families, living together in a restricted area following certain common rules of crop rotation under more or less informal leaders is called an ayllu (aylyo) or community. There is no doubt that some sort of social group corresponding to the modern ayllu existed in ancient times also, but its nature is not easy to establish. Writers who dealt with *Inca* society assumed that the ayllu was a clan, and attributed to it all the classical clan characteristics: matrilineal descent, exogamy, totemism, etc. Their conclusions have never been seriously questioned, and the modern summaries repeat the old assumption without attempting to prove it. It is timely to reexamine the question in the light of the historical and ethnological evidence.

Any attempt to establish the nature of the ancient ayllu by study of the chroniclers faces a serious difficulty in the looseness of Inca terminology. The word *ayllu* is used in Spanish with several very different meanings: (1) the lineages of the *Inca* royal class, each composed of the direct descendants of an Emperor in the male line; (2) the social unit of several extended families with which we are now concerned; (3) occasionally, the moiety. The word *ayllu* seems to have been a general word for "kin-group," and its specific meaning was probably made clear by the context. It is quite important to sort out those references to the ayllu which specifically concern the social unit under consideration.

There is little doubt that the ayllu was, at least in theory, a kin group. Dictionary definitions and chroniclers' statements all indicate that, in all its uses, the word *ayllu* implied some sort of relationship which, though very remote or even mythical, must have been an important social bond. As to its functions in restricting marriage, the ayllu was theoretically endogamous. The only evidence cited to indicate ayllu exogamy is Viceroy Toledo's decree regulating the ayllu affiliation of children of inter-ayllu marriages. The decree states that disputes had arisen when the father's ayllu refused to let the children go back to the mother's ayllu after the death of the father, and orders that the mother be allowed to take her children with her. Far from demonstrating ayllu exogamy as the standard practice, this decree indicates that, as late as 1570, marriage outside the ayllu was still so rare that no tradition was recognized to govern the affiliation of the children, and that the resulting disputes had reached Spanish courts.

The evidence for descent in the male line is overwhelming. It refers to the inheritance of public office, for, if marriages were arranged within the ayllu, it would obviously make no difference in which line ayllu affiliation was traced, and no rule was necessary. Rulers, however, married women from other communities for political reasons, and, in such cases, the children belonged to the father's family.

In order to classify the ayllu as a totemic group, it would be necessary to show that the ayllus had animal (or plant) names, or that they traced their descent from these animals and had some sort of ceremonial attitude toward them, such as not eating them or performing certain rites for their increase; that the animal was used as a symbol of the ayllu; or some combination of a substantial number of such traits.

Ayllus were ordinarily named for a place or a person, judging from the small proportion of preserved ayllu names which are translatable; none seem to have been named after an animal. Individuals frequently bore animal names, but were just as often named for abstract qualities or given traditional names the meaning of which had been lost. Although there seems to have been some tendency to use names of prominent ancestors, the *Inca* had no system of family names, and no rigid rules for naming their children. Ayllus traced their origins to mythical ancestors—animals, persons, or natural objects—which were worshiped, but there identified with an animal species. For example, if an ayllu claimed descent from a parrot, it accorded parrots in general no special reverence. The meat of animals of the same species as the mythical ancestor was not taboo, and no rites were performed for its increase. That persons and natural objects as well as animals might be mythical ancestors suggests that animals played no predominant part in mythology. An interesting example of the use of animals as symbols is that the *Inca* Emperors kept a sacred white llama (napa), which was in a sense a dynastic symbol. Two explanations were given of its origin: first, that it represented the first llama seen on the earth after the flood, and second, that it was brought from the cave where the *Inca* originated by the mythical ancestor who was a person. Neither explanation identifies the llama with the ancestor, and the *Inca* had no taboo whatever against eating llama meat.

To summarize, the *Inca* ayllu was a kin group with theoretical endogamy, with descent in the male line, and without totemism. It was, therefore, not a clan in the classical sense at all. There is no historical or ethnological evidence to support the theory that the social group from which the ayllu developed was, in some prehistoric era, a true clan.

The ayllu owned a definite territory, and each married couple cultivated as much of it as they needed for their support. Under the *Inca,* the family lots were redistributed every year to ensure equality of opportunity and a proper rotation of the crops, but it is not certain whether this practice existed before the *Inca* conquest. Before the *Inca* conquest, the other ayllu members cultivated their chief's fields and probably also cultivated plots for the support of their local shrines. The *Inca* systematized this division of land by setting aside certain fields in each community for the support of the government and of the shrines. In modern Indian society, certain relatives regularly exchange labor on a man for man, day by day, basis, a custom called *Ayni.*

In pre-Hispanic times, the ayllu in Aymara culture seems to have been the largest political unit next to the state itself, and was probably utilized then as now chiefly for administrative purposes. In some outlying districts, remote from towns, the ayllu community for all practical purposes.

The ayllu is a social and geographical unit and usually bears a descriptive place name. An individual takes the ayllu of his birth, but if he moves permanently to another locality he may change it, or if a woman marries outside her ayllu, she usually joins that of her husband. Although an ayllu occasionally has a myth which claims a common place of origin for its inhabitants, the people do not claim descent from a common ancestor. The early writers are not entirely clear, however, as to whether these origin legends applied to ayllus as a whole or to lineages within them. The ayllu is composed of several unrelated extended families, each of which traces its descent from a separate tunu, the most remote ancestor in the male line whose name is remembered. Ayllu affiliation does not formally govern marriage, but ayllus tend to be endogamous.

The members of an ayllu have little group feeling, unless the ayllu is very small, and seldom operate as a unit. They tend, however, to resent an outsider who takes up permanent residence and may unite to oust him. Occasionally, they construct a road under the supervision of the headman as they formerly united to cultivate the lands dedicated to his support. Although many ayllus possess common grazing land and although all ayllu, there is no communal agriculture. The ayllu as a whole has few important ceremonial functions. The most important fiestas and rites are performed by one or more extended families, age groups, or friendship groups.

The headman of an ayllu is called *hilaqata*. As he holds office for a year, he is often metaphorically referred to as "year father." In Bolivia, in recent times, his term has been limited to 6 months. The *hilaqata* is distinguished by special dress or insignia, which varies regionally. Theoretically, the *hilaqata* is now chosen by the Governor of his district; actually, he is selected by the people of his ayllu, who discuss the matter informally, after which members of the ayllu council convey their wish to the former *hilaqata,* who in turn advises the Governor of the people's choice. He is selected from the age group designated as "mature men." The new leader is then introduced to the people by his predecessor and ceremonially takes a drink and a pinch of coca with each with each household head *(utani)* in his ayllu.

The ayllu leaders settle inter-ayllu land disputes and each informally arbitrates intra-ayllu quarrels, many of which never reach the local courts of law. Today, he apprehends criminals and keeps track of the school children and reserve soldiers for the Federal Government. He also takes charge of the systematic crop rotation on the land tracts *(ainoqa)* of his ayllu, for which he receives a share of the crops. Formerly, he was entitled to a quarter of the produce from the plots reserved for him (the *suwu* lands) in compensation for the time spent in the performance of his official duties, the rest of the produce being used to support the ruler of the *Aymara* state. In pre-Spanish times the most important function of the ayllu headman was to be executive of the communally owned ayllu land and supervisor of the division of the land tracts *(ainoqa)* of his ayllu into family plots *(sayana).* Although in Bolivia communal land ownership by the ayllu has been abolished in theory, redistribution of the family plots continues under the supervision of the aylly leader at the time of Carnival in February or March.

During crises, the ayllu leader sometimes calls a general meeting, which is usually attended by only mature and elderly men.

Each ayllu possesses an informal council composed of public- spirited men and natural leaders *(p'eqena),* wise and successful men *(amauta,* and old men respected for their age and knowledge. In Chucito (Peru), the council is informal to the extent that qualified adults frequently disagree in listing the individuals whom they consider to belong in these categories. The council merely is advisory to the headmen. It has no formal meetings, only informal discussions in the fields or in the house of one of the members.

BIBLIOGRAPHY-

● BOWDITCH, CHARLES. P. Mexican and Central American Antiquities, Calendar Systems and History. Washington, D. C.: Bureau of American Ethnology- Bulletin 28: GPO, 1904.
● SWANTON, JOHN R. The Indian Tribes of North America. Smithsonian Institution: BAE Bulletin No. 145: U.S. GPO, 1952.
● THOMAS, CYRUS. Indian Languages of Mexico and Central America and Their Geographical Distribution. Bureau of American Ethnology Bulletin 44: Washington, D. C.: GPO, 1911.

AYMARA

(South America; Bolivia, Peru) people are one of the largest and most important civilizations in South America, ranking second in number to the Quechua Indians. Approximately 600,000 Aymaras live above 12,500 feet in Bolivia and Peru. They have adapted genetically to the high altitude with an extra pint of blood and lung capacity; they are barrel chested, short of stature, and have sharp features, characteristic of the Mongoloid race from whom they descended in Paleolithic times. Aymara men are strong, capable of carrying several hundred pounds on their backs, and their wives are beautiful with oval dark eyes and long dark hair braided to their waists. The men wear red, orange, brown, and black ponchos, and the women dress in mantles of similar color. Their clothes are ornately woven into designs of animals and geometrical forms. Although Aymaras have

Aymara woman working in the field in Bolivia.

been characterized as "violent," they are sensitive, intelligent, and friendly people.

The language, known as Aymara, emphasizes guttural sounds. For example, they employ six phonemes for K, each distinguishing a meaning. Whereas English expresses concepts with word phrases, Aymaras add suffixes to word stems. *Warmi,* for example, is a Aymara root word for "woman" and sometimes has five suffixes. The word *warminakaraquiniwachejjaya* means "also for the women in the future!" Although Aymara has a phonetic system and grammar similar to Quechua, its roots and suffixes are independent, except for recent exchanges. Aymara and Quechua are classified in separate families, related remotely in the past. They probably descended from Hokan Siouan, a linguistic phylum originating thousands of years ago in North America. In pre-Hispanic times, the Incas tried to impose the language of Quechua on the Aymaras, but they were unsuccessful. Today, the language of Aymara is spoken by 231,935 Peruvians (4.4% of the population above 5 years of age) and by 1,368,990 Bolivians (25% of the population). However, the number of Indians who remain Aymara in culture and social organization is about 600,000.

The Aymaras constitute a complex agraria civilization because they exploit multiple resource from different ecological levels. They specialize in the extraction of the resources where they live and then exchange their produce with that of another level. Aymaras live in the lowlands, central, and highlands of the Andes. A minority of Aymara live in the Yungas, a subtropical rainfall forest of the eastern slopes of the Central Andes. The rich loamy soil of this heavily forested area produces fruit, vegetables, and coca on slopes from 4,000 to 9,000 feet. These Aymaras live on small farms surrounding colonial settlements of Sorata Chulumani, Coropata, Chuma, and Apolo. Coca is important to Aymaras for its slightly narcotic effect which alleviates the stresses of color hypoxia, and exhaustion. It is also used as currency and in ritual. The majority of Aymara inhabit the Altiplano, which is a plateau from 12,000 to 14,000 feet between the eastern and western ranges of Bolivia and Peru. These Aymaras live in nucleated settlements (50 to 150 families) spread throughout this vast plateau where they farm potatoes, oca, quinoa, and barley; wheat and corn in lower fields; and broadbeans and onions along the shores of Lake Titicaca, where they also fish. The average family cultivates three acres. Certain areas of the Altiplano support up to 135 people per square mile; as a result, the Altiplano is a major agricultural region for Bolivia, Peru, in terms of the number of people working the land and the total acreage under cultivation.

Aymaras employ farming techniques which are ecologically efficient. They fertilize with sheep dung, then flood the field with water, and finally-plow it with oxen. They plant by hand, cultivate, and harvest with a digging stick which has a metal blade. Because of frost and drought in these altitudes, farming is a gamble in the Andes; but they plant a variety of potatoes in different zones as a buffer in case one crop fails. These astute farmers have more than 100 species of potatoes and oca, from which they naturally select the variety that grows best in their area. They also dehydrate potatoes into *ch'uno,* and oca into *qhaya* to preserve and transport them. During the coldest month, they freeze the potatoes and oca at night, then stomp the moisture out with their feet when the sun thaws these crops in the morning. Reduced to the size of a marble, *ch'uno* is later steamed and eaten — a delicacy to all Andeans with its rubbery texture and nutty taste. Highland herders are unable to produce them with meat; this exchange results in a balance of proteins and carbohydrates for farmers and herders.

Aymara herders live on levels between 14,000 and 17,000 feet, where they graze alpacas, llamas and sheep on a vast, rolling highlands, *puna,* abundant with a tough bunchgrass (*fichu*). They follow their flocks and live apart in small settlements (about 10 families) dispersed across these tundra-like grasslands. The llamas and sheep supply Andeans with beasts of burden, cheese, fertilizer, leather, milk, meat, rope, and wool.

For more than one thousand years, the Aymara people have suffered conquest and oppression, yet they have kept many of their customs. Aymara civilization probably began during the Early Intermediate period (AD 150-800) of South American history and attained its apogee during the Middle Horizon (AD 800-1100). Tiahuanaco, a principal Middle Horizon site, is located in the center of the Altiplano; this site suggests a great ceremonial center to which came the Indians of the Altiplano on pilgrimages. The ritualists embued them with symbols and belief systems. Aymaras still practice rituals similar to those practiced at Tiahuanaco; they offer meals to the mountains and reverence earth-shrines. The Aymara religion is telluric in that these Indians look to the earth and its natural minifestations for identification of self and society.

After the decline of the Tiahuanaco around 1100, the Aymara nations arose as a loose federation of deverse groups throughout the Central Andes. They counted somewhere between several hundred thousand and a million. These tribes feuded with each other so that when the Incas began their conquest of the Andes, the Aymaras were divided and subsequently conquered by the Inca Emperor Pachacuti (1438-71), who extended Quechua rule into the Altiplano. Pachacuti divided the Aymara tribes and people by sending them to colonize distant zones of the Andes. The Aymara group of Lupaca, for example, were settled away from their home territory around Chucuito in faraway places along the Pacific Coast to plant corn and cotton. During Inca rule, the Aymaras increased their access to more ecological niches because of colonization.

Afer the Spanish conquest oᶠ the Altiplano in 1542, the Aymaras were virtually slaves under the encomiendas: they worked in the plantations and mines for their Spanish overlords. By the 17th century, 75% of the Aymaras had died because of epidemics and cruel conditions within the mines: according to a census in 1591, there were only 35,000 tributary Indians (not including women, children, and men over 50 years).

At first Dominican and later Jesuit missionaries tried to convert the Aymaras to Catholocism. The missionaries burned their idols and whipped those accused of heresy. Viceroy Toledo (1569- 1581) moved large populations of Aymaras into *Reducciones* where they could be converted. He prohibited them from painting their faces, and sleeping on the floor. Toledo also executed Tupac Amaru, an Indian leader who revolted against Spanish oppression.

An Aymara Indian on Lake Titicaca

Unrest, however, continued among the Aymaras until another valiant leader, Tupaj Katari, arose in 1781 to lead 10,000 Aymaras against the colonialists. His forces beseiged the city of La Puz for 183 days, until he was forced to retreat to Penas, where he was captured, drawn and quartered. Chopping off his head, they posted it in La Paz. Nonetheless, another leader, Pumacahua captured Puno and La Paz in 1814; the Aymaras had finally conquered their colonizers, but at the price of decimation.

After Independence, republican legislators endeavored to change Aymara economic and social organization by land laws, based on concepts of private property. Since 1954, Agrarian Reformists in Bolivia have legislated that the Aymara communities define their boundaries, elect leaders, and establish economic links with national centers. As a result, the communities are feuding over boundaries, exchanging fewer resources, and decreasing their ties through marriage. In other words, vertical exchange is being replaced by horizontal links (trucks and airplanes) to economic centers where goods are purchased at competitive prices and sold by middlemen at profitable gains.

Nevertheless, the ayllu continues to be an important basis of social-cultural organization for the Aymaras. The ayllu is associated with lineage, land, and metaphor. Aymaras descending from the same ancestor belong to the same kinship lineage; it may be a patrilineage or matrilineage. Aymaras living on the same territory belong to a territorial ayllu; they feed the earth- shrines of their territory. Moreover, territorial ayllus are often understood according to the metaphors of animals and people. The Qollahuaya Aymara, for example, understand the three levels of their mountain according to the anatomy of a human body.

Aymara religion is linked to the ayllu in that ritualists feed the earth-shrines of the ayllu. The ayllu of Kaata, for example, has 13 earth-shrines throughout its levels. Ritualists feed these shrines coca, blood, and llama fat. This ritual activity symbolizes to the communities on the three levels of Mount Kaata that they constitute on ayllu.

The Aymaras are famous for curanderos and diviners. The most famous are the Qollahuayas of the Province Bautista Saavedra in Bolivia. Qollahuaya herbalists have a pharmacology of over 1,000 medicinal remedies; they have a long tradition of bone setting and trephination. Qollahuaya deviners cure by rituals; they divine the courses of misfortune and perform elaborate rituals to the earth. Indians from all over the Andes call upon Qollahuayas for curing and rituals.

In sum, the Aymara represent a large group of native Americans who have maintained their culture and social organization throughout many invasions by foreigners. The Aymaras appear to be aggressive to foreigners, but this is because they mistrust white people. In reality, Aymaras are friendly, intelligent, and sensitive. They have passed along a vast tradition of divination, curing, farming, herding, and food processing. It is encouraging to the human race that the Aymaras are increasing.

BIBLIOGRAPHY-

● STEWARD, JULIAN H. Handbook of South American Indians. 7 Vols., Washington, DC: U.S. Govt. Printing Office, 1946-59.

AZTECS

(Mexico) More properly the Tenochca, or Mexica, since the nahua-speaking tribes of the Valley of Mexico are more correctly referred to Aztecs collectively, were late-comers to Mesoamerica. From the beginning of the Classic period onward, the instability of the northern cultural frontier of Mesoamerica was a reflection of the constant recruitment of "barbarian" tribes to the Mesoamerican way of life.

The boundaries of Mesoamerica shifted in accord with the movements of these "Barbarians" southward and the Mesoamericans northward. The Aztecs were one of the late barbarian groups, along wih other Nahua-speaking tribes, who acquired Mesoamerican culture. Temporally, the Aztecs fall entirely into the Post-Classic period. As a distinctive group they apparently never came in contact with the Classic cultures of Mesoamerica. The distinction of Classic Teotihuacan long preceded their advent. Other Nahua and non-Nahua-speaking groups were fully engaged in the development of the Post-Classic culture pattern when they appeared on the scene. The Post-Classic marks the appearance of true cities in Mesoamerica, and we have mentioned the various descriptive terms applied to the cultural reorientation of the Post-Classic, noting especially the increasing militarism, secularism, and urbanism.

For the Post-Classic in the Valley of Mexico there is a number of historical records written soon after the Conquest. From these arises an idea of the nature of the political organization and military history of the region. The term Chichimec plays an important role in the Post-Classic history of this region. In the native histories of the term Chichimec is nearly always used when referring to the wild tribes to the north or to late-comers or adherents to Mesoamerican culture. Generally, the term Toltec referred to the bearers of Mesoamerican culture. In this sense then the Toltecs long preceded the Aztecs, but one must remember that this apparently was a generic term, so that at the Conquest both the Toltecs of Tula and the Aztecs were called Toltec. This is important to note since it has long been maintained that the Toltecs were a completely separate group who reorganized Mesoamerican culture following the disintegration of the Classic. Toltec is a term best utilized for the Mexican Post-Classic Mesoamericans whatever their linguistic affiliations or origins were.

Physiography and climate The environment of the Aztecs stands in high contrast to that of the Classic Maya. The Valley of Mexico marks the southern limit of the *Mesa Central* of Mexico. It is a basin which was filled with lakes and marshy land, surrounded by high mountains at the time of the Aztecs. In the valley floor, the altitude runs between 7000 and 8000 feet while the high mountains rim most of the circumference of the valley. Standing with their crests high above the snow line are the volcanic peaks of popecatepetl and Ixtaccihuatl, Smoking Mountain and White Woman, respectively, in Nahua. The former rises to 17,343 feet. It is believed that during early clasic times the area was well forested with pine. However, as the population increased these trees were so decimated for firewood that most of the mountain slopes were denuded by the end of the Classic. Added to this, the rainfall is relatively low in this region, and the natural cover of the Valley of Mex-

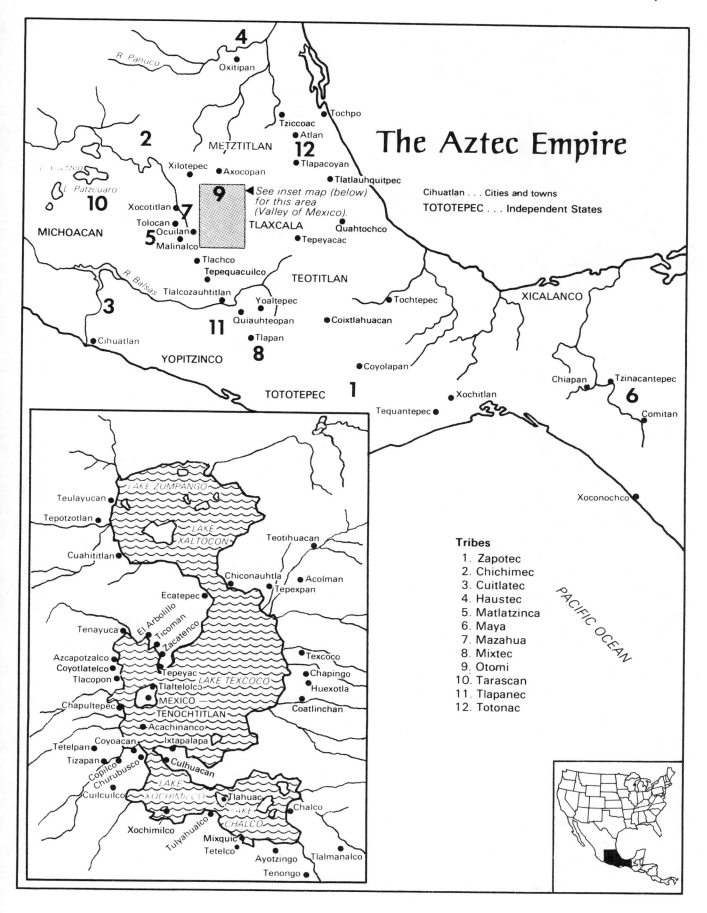

The Aztec Empire

Cihuatlan . . . Cities and towns
TOTOTEPEC . . . Independent States

See inset map (below) for this area (Valley of Mexico).

Tribes
1. Zapotec
2. Chichimec
3. Cuitlatec
4. Haustec
5. Matlatzinca
6. Maya
7. Mazahua
8. Mixtec
9. Otomi
10. Tarascan
11. Tlapanec
12. Totonac

PACIFIC OCEAN

The Aztec Sun Stone, found in 1790, represents the sun during the fifth era of the Aztec cosmovision, surrounded by the four previous cosmogonic eras.

ico at the advent of the Aztec was extremely sparse. In fact, the control of water resources became one of the major tasks of the tribes of the area.

Living in the region which presented the dual problems of a semiarid climate and a basin which collected the available water in lakes and marshes, measures were needed which would both kpreserve the water for use and control the accumulation in the lakes. During Classic times most of the settlement was confined to the slopes of the adjacent mountains and the level land away from the marshy regions. Thus, the Classic occupation of Teotihuacan resorted to irrigation in order to utilize the water for the production of food. It was not until Post-Classic times that the water resources of the lakes were fully exploited, although before this the natural lacustrine life which was edible was used. By the fourteenth century, population pressures in the region generated a group of warring towns in the valley. In fact, the Tenochca found little space in which to settle, and much of their history prior to the founding of Tenochtitlan was motivated by a search for cultivable land. The founding of Tenochtitlan on an island in Lake Texcoco brought into full use *chinampa* system of cultivation. Essentially this is a means of constructing fields which amount to floating islands, and was the answer to the land shortage of Post-Classic times. The floating fields, or gardens, consisted of a woven mat base covered with soil. As the plants grew on this raft plot, the roots sought out and achored the plot to the bottom of the shallow lake, and soon new static land had been created. The economic and population expansion of the Tenochca was made possible by the full expoitation of the chinampa method of cultivation.

It is not implied that the Tenochca were the only group who practised theis method for it was widely used in southern Mexico at the time of the Spanish Conquest. Today the kremnants of these chinampas can be seen in the still-cultivated floating gardens of Xochimilco.

Unlike the Classic Maya, the Post-Classic peoples of the Valley of Mexico, through the direction and organization of large pupulations paralleled other areas of the world in which the appearance of civilization has required kthe control of water resources through major public works. Not only were the water resources of the valley controlled through the irrigation systems of Classic times and the chinampas of Post-Classic but major efforts were exerted in changing the character of the lakes by means of dikes.

The Valley of Mexico presents what we would term temperate climate throughout the year. A rainy and a dry season indicate the more southerly latitude of the area. Moreover, while the nights are cool and sometimes cold, only rarely doses snow fall, but hail is not uncommon. In Mesoamerica the environmental contrast between the Aztec and the Classic Maya could not be greater.

History The traditional history of the Aztecs begins in AD 1168. Their origin was supposedly an island in the middle of a lake to the north or northwest of the Valley of Mexico. Here they began their wandering by building boats to take them ashore. On the shore they discovered a cave, or seven caves, in which a stone image of Huitzilopochtli, the humming bird god, spoke to them and advised them on their journey to the Valley of Mexico. At each stop his advice was heard and those who did not wish to follow it always met with dire results. The Tenochca tribe of the Aztecs claim to have come into the Valley of Mexico from the northwest viaTula and Zumpango, and settled first in the area known today as Chapultepec. Little attention was paid them upon arrival and they made their way to Chapultepec without any great interference on the part of other groups already occupying the region. However, they appeared at a time when the population was beginning to show signs of increase and settlements were expanding. The date was AD 1248. According to the traditional histories, the previously quiet and peaceful Tenochcas began to generate enmity among their neighbors because of their wife-stealing habits and their generally disgusting—to their neighbors at least—religious practices which emphasized human sacrifice. As a result, the towns of Tepanec, Xochimilco, and Culhua banded together and crushed the Tenochcas. The chief, Huitzihuitl, and most of the tribe became serfs of the town of Culhuacan. The date traditionally is *ca.* 1300. However, some escaped to a low-lying island in the lake and there founded Tenochtitlan. The date of the actual founding of Tenochtitlan is in some doubt. The two dates most often cited are 1325 and 1337. Between the founding of Tenochtitlan and 1375, when the Aztecs became a distinct, organized tribe again, they went through a period of better learning Mesoamerican culture and distinguishing themselves in battle.

Coxcox, the king of Culhuacan, found himself at war with Xochimilco and asked his captives for aid. During this war the Tencohcas distinguished themselves and asked for a daughter of Coxcox to help found a dynasty with their own chief. However, the Tenochcas sacrificed the girl, flayed her, and performed a ceremonial dance wearing her skin as a costume. Coxcox in his anger drove them all into the lake where some of the more acculturated are said to have intorduced stone architecture to Tenochtitlan. Before 1375, the Tenochcas gradually became more powerful. So much so that at the date they asked Culhuacan for a chief who then became Acamapichtle under whose rule the Tenochcas were tributaries and allies of the Tepenac of Azcapotzalco against Tenayuca and Culhuacan. His successor, Huitziluitl II, married the daughter of Tezozomoc of Texcoco, and thus insured the position of the Tenochca during the major struggle for power between Texcoco and Tepanecs. In the end, Texcoco was defeated. However, Maxtla, one of the sons of Tezozomoc, gained leadership of Texcoco through murder and intrigue, exiling Nezahualcoyotl the rightful heir. Maxtla attempted to gain control of the entire valley, and when he murdered Chimalpopoca, the Tenochca joined in alliance against him. Under Itzcoatl, the new Tenochca chief, and Nezahualcoyotl, Maxtla was overthrown. With this victory the Tenochcas won their freedom, and a military class came to the fore mainly through land division of the mainland. Itzcoatl (1428-1440) reorganized the Tenochcas. Temples were constructed, the city was planned, constructed, and connected with the mainland by causeways, and a religious hierarchy and civil government were founded. Also, Itzcoatl began a systematic conquest of tribes not subject to Tenochtitlan and Texcoco. In this way, Xochimilco and Chalco had acknowledged supremacy of the allies by the death of Itzcoatl. Moctezuma I succeeded Itzcoatl in 1440, and was in power until 1469. He had been the general during the preceding regime during the conquest of Chalco. He continued the alliance with Texcoco, and also extended the conquest of Chalco. He continued the alliance with Texcoco, and also extended the conquests to Puebla, Vera Cruz, Morelos, and Guerrero. The reign of Moctezuma I was marked by a number of important events. The conquest of Puebla introduced many new religious ideas and gods to the Tenochcas. Tenochtitlan grew mightily, creating the necessity of the construction of an aqueduct from Chapultepec bringing fresh water to the city. Also, the lake was diked for better control of the water resources. But more important was the overall incorporation of the Aztec into Mesoamerican culture, albeit they added their own interpretation. Azayacatl succeeded his father, Moctezuma I, in 1469 and continued conquests to the west to Matlatzinca, and southwards to Oaxaca, Tehuantepec, and possibly to the Guatemalen border. However, he was severely beaten by the Tarascans of Michoacan, and this remained the only defeat until that by the Spaniards. Tozco succeeded his brother in 1479 and, although not noted for his military successes, constructed the great temple to Huitzilopochtli the War God, and Tlaloc the rain god. It is said that the military success. Ahuitzotl succeeded his lack of military advisors poisoned Tizoc for his lack of military success. Ahuitzotl succeeded his brother in 1486 and immediately, through a continuance of the alliance with Texcoco, reconquered Oaxaca and returned with 20,000 sacrificial victims. He also conducted a campaign against the Huasteca in northern Vera Cruz, but it appears that most of his time was spent in maintianing control over tribute peoples who apparently were in continuous revolt. Tenochtitlan continued to grow, so much so that a second aqueduct had to be constructed to bring water from the mainland. Ahuitzotl was a lover of war, women,

A glyph of the Aztec emperor Ahuítzotl whose name translates as "water beast."

and generally, of lusty living. During the supervision of public works against serious flooding of the city he received a serious head injury and died. A nephew, Moctezuma II, succeeded to power and his reign was filled with increasing disaster, not only from the continued revolts among the conquered tribes and towns, but also through the breaking of the long alliance with Texcoco. But more ominous than all these, the omens for the 1507 New Fire (52-year cycle) ceremony were the worst possible, and news of Spanish probing on the east coasts created an air of impending doom. Moctezuma II died in 1519, whether by disease or at the hands of the Spaniards is not known. His successor, Cuitlahuac, died of smallpox within a month, and Cuahtemoc, who led the fight against the Spanisrds was the last free ruler of the Aztec. He met his death at the hands of the Spaniards in 1524 during Cortez' march to Honduras.

The History of the Tenochcas, who became the foremost Aztec group, is one of increasing use of the Post-Classic culture. They contributed little in the way of originality to Mesoamerican culture, kbut what they adopted they utilized and developed in an intensive manner. It was they who brought the trends of secularism and militarism to the greatest heights. It was gthe Tenochcas who brought the development of true urbsan centers to full completion. The contrast with the Classic Maya is one which at first glance would seem to indicate an insuperable gap between the two. However, it must be remembered that most of the cultural elements and even cultural patternings which the Tenochcas so fully expanded were present among the Classic Maya. The differences between the two appear gto be far greater than they really were. The Classic Maya and the other cultures of Classic times laid the bases of Mesoamerican culture and developed much of its potential, and while the Aztec immigrants displayed different emphases in the use of Mesoamerican culture, it should not be forgottn that Mesoamerican was an area unified by culture history.

At the end of the fifteenth century the Valley Mexico was typified by settlements of a size and complexity which could be termed urban. They were not the ceremonial centers of the Classic Maya, but were fully occupied, fully functioning cities in the sense in which we think of the term. The Tenochcas were the dominant Aztec group and their city, Tenochtitlan, was the largest and most powerful center in all of southern Mexico. However, the analogy to a modern city must not be carried too far, since much of the urban organization was still based on extended kinship groupings and, consequently, a fully developed clan system had not emerged although there was a complex system of social stratification.

It will be remembered that Tenochtitlan was built on a low- lying island in Lake Texcoco, and had expanded its land area by constructing chinampa plots. The general plan of the city was rectangular and this form appears to have been maintained throughout the expansion of the city. The entire city was termed the *altepe* Tenochtitlan. The city was divided into four major sections, the *campans,* or the *barrios grandes* early Spanish terminology. The altepetl and the campan appear to have been tirritorial divisions. However, each campan consisted of several *calpul barrios* which ere also kinship units. The exact number of calpulli is somewhat in doubt although the most commonly accepted number is 20, and the number in each campan apparently varied. Each calpulli in turn consisted of several smaller subdivisions with a kinship baase known as *tlaxilacal(calles or barrios chicos).* The number of tlaxilacalli in each calpulli is open to question, but it appears there were two and sometimes three. Each tlaxilacalli was made up of family plots known chinampa. The division and use of the land was more complex than the territorial arrangement of the city and will be discussed below.

One approached Tenochtitlan from the mainland over wide causeways running from the north, west, and south to the city. The edges of the city were a mass of greenery, the cultivated chinampa, and behind them could be seen the white masonry buildings with the pyramidal temples standing above all other structures. When the edge of the city was reached the broad causeways ended, and the main thoroughfares became canals with foot paths running along side crossed by bridges at intervals. The main canals led to a central plaza which was used for communal gatherings. Here also were the main temples (the *teocalli,*) a huge wooden rack for the skulls of sacrificial victims, the living quarters for the royalty, and the market. As well, each of the calpulli sections had its own ceremonial center. The city was served by two large aqueducts bringing fresh water from the mainland. The one entering from the west came from Chapultepec, and consisted of two channels which allowed for alternate cleaning of the conduits. The one entering from the south from Coyoacan was constructed later by Ahuitzotl. The problem of sanitation was solved by stationing canoes at specified locations. These were then taken to the chinampa as fertilizer while urine was collected in pottery vessels to be used as a mordant in dyeing cloth. The continued existence of Tenochtitlan required a well organized system because the city was estimated to have had a population of 300,000 at the time of Cortez. From the description given by the Spaniards it would appear that public sanitation and water distribution were better than any which the Spaniards were familiar.

Housing varied according to social status. The commoners occupied rectangular, one or two roomed houses with earthen floors, wattle-and-daub walls, and thatched roofs. Walthier individuals lived in houses constructed on a raised platform which was usually faced with stone. The walls possessed stone bases and the body of the wall was completed either in stone or adobe brick. Large crossbeams, covered by small poles, and then a lime plaster, formed the roof. Even for the wealthy the house was not spacious, but usually shallow with a depth of two rooms with the back room open only to the front and containing the earth. The other rooms were open, fronted by a columnade which formed a regular courtyard in the rear, but no room possessed a window. however, social, sleeping, cooking Storage, and slave quarters were distinct from one another.

The living quarters of the ruling family were in essence more extensive forms of the houses of the wealthy. There were many patios arranged at different levels, and the rooms were more spacious and open to the air. As would be expected in a household which required 3000 attendants, guards, and specialized workers to function, the size and purpose of the rooms and patios varied greatly. The descriptions left by the Spanish conquistadores, however exaggerated they might have been, leave one with an impression of sumptuousness and barbaric splendor which could only have made these men more determined to win Aztec territory for their own.

Tenochtitlan was a true city. Busy with trade, mass movement of people on the causeways, and the center of a complex netwoek of fiefs payoing tribute which demanded an intricate combination of secular and religious administrative machinery, it marked the peak of Post-Classic cultural complexity. However, all was not well with the Aztecs in 1519, and a major element in the spanish Conquest was the inability of Aztec cultural complexity to maintain itself as an integrated and cohesive unit.

Economy   As in the remainder of Mesoamerica, the economic base of the Aztec lay in the milpa production of food plants. The plant inventory, and the tools and techniques used, were very much the same as those of the Classic Maya and the people of Mesoamerica today. However, among the Aztec there seemed to habe been little of the goals and philosophy associated with the Mayan peasant and his desire to adjust to the universe. The Aztec dealt with the universe in other ways.

The full development of the potentialities of the chinampa distinguished the Aztecs from other parts of Mesoamerica, but the food plants would be familiar to every inhabitant of this region. Maize, as always, dominated, but beans, squash, gourds, sweet potatoes, green and red peppers, avocados, and tomatoes were all produced to diversify the diet. The maguey, or so-called century plant, was important in the manufacture of the fermented beverage *pulque*. Pulque was important in the diet greens. Maguey was also important in religious ceremonies, and from it was produced a fiber used in making twine, rope, and woven containers, thorn needles as well as leaves for roofing and walls. Cotton and tobacco were raised. Other vegetable products were imported from Vera Cruz: chocolate, vanilla, pineapple, copal, and rubber. The number and variety of domesticated animals were few among the Aztec. Dogs, turkeys, ducks, geese, and quail were domesticated, but only the forst two were important. One of the several types of dogs wa fattened for food. The cochineal bug was kept for the manufacture of crimson dye, and the maguey have been domesticated for food.

The Aztecs made full use of their lacustrine environment. The great abundance of water fowl during seasonal migrations made them important as a food. They were taken with nets and the thhrowing stick. Large quantities of small fish were taken each day and traded in the markets. In addition to these products, several edible invertebrates were taken from the lakes. The *axayacatl,* a corixid water bug, laid eggs in bundles of tule placed in the water by the fishermen. The pupal and larval stages of the salt fly, *cuclin,* and *izcauitli* respectively, were harvested. These were combined in various ways to make *ahuautli* cake sold in the markets. An algae, the purple Oscillatoria of Nostoc, was collected and made into *tecuitatl* — another cake form. Crustaceans were represented by crayfish.

It will be remembered that the total situation among the Aztecs was one differentiated from the Classic Maya by the presence of true urban centers. In terms of cultural generalization, there is thus a condition of food surplus which in turn implies the possibility of a more complex division of labor. This is seen in Tenochtitlan by the specialization of economic activities. Although much of the craft production was in the homes, there was craft specialization by some levels of kin group organization. Individual families were no longer completely independent in economic activity, as is seen by the expansion of markets and the existence of such distinct groups as traders and merchants.

Craft production was specialized in terms of calpulli and tlaxillacalli although not to the degree that there was a complete exclusion of some craft work in all households such as weaving by women. There was the beginning of a division of labor which has led many authorities to claim the

women. There was the beginning of a division of labor which has led many authorities to claim the existence of guilds among the Aztec, and to assign social status and rank to these. However, it may be seen that social status and rank was based on the principal of those who governed and those governed in each kin and sectional division of Tenochtitlan. There were specialized craftsmen who worked with stone. Some specialized in the flaking of flint and obsidian, making flaked sacrificial flint knives and the long slender blades of obsidian used as knives. Others pecked, ground, and polished stone into the form of manos and metates, stone boxes for burning and storing the hearts of sacrificial victims, and incense burners. Some specialized only in working obsidian, grinding and polishing mirrors and vessels from the extremely hard and difficult volcanic glass. Others specialized in stone work associated with the public buildings, dressing masses of stone for construction and sculpture. Closely associated with the last activities were the masons who worked in stone fitting and in the uses of mortar. Although weaving was done by most women, there were those who specialized in textiles for the ruling classes and for trade. Most of the weaving was done with the belt loom so common throughout Mesoamerica and the techniques were highly varied. The most common characteristics were the almost exclusive use of cotton fibers; there was also the development of rectangular patterning, along with the fine embroidery with curvilinear as well as naturalistic design, batik and tie-dyeing, and velvet and brocade weaving in addition to the usual muslin weaves. Closely related to the weaving textiles was feather mosaic work made into shields and cloaks which were used as ceremonial insignia.

Other mosaic work was done with shell and turquoise, the latter being the one most prized material of the Aztecs. Sacrificial knives, masks and shields were covered with intricately fitted pieces of shell and stone depicting gods and ceremonial scenes.

Woodworking was also done by specialists and consisted of two sorts, ceremonial and utilitarian. Masks, idols, drums, and ceremonial throwing sticks were all elaborately and tastefully carved with ceremonial designs and very often combined shell and turquoise mosaic with the woodcarver's art. The drums were of two sorts, a vertical cylindrical form with a skin head and the horizontal slit gong so typical of the Maya. Utilitarian aspects of woodworking were very important to the Aztecs. Wooden beams instead of planks were cut from pine, and since the Aztec did not employ the corbelled vault with any great frequency these were important in all construction. The lake environment made canoes extremely important, and some woodworkers devoted all their time to the making of dugout canoes, although plank canoes were known as well. Given the canals of Tenochtitlan, some means of travelling from one section of town to another was necessary. This was accomplished by portable bridges which were placed at specified crossings when needed.

One important craft distinguished the Aztec from the Classic Maya. This was metallurgy. It will be remembered that the Classic Maya knew little of metals, and what was known either came in by trade or the importation of craftsmen. The Aztecs, as was the case with most of Post-Classic Mesoamerica, knew metallurgical techniques and made use of metal tools and implements. However, these had not superseded stone tools and implements by the time of the Spanish Conquest. This craft was very late in Mesoamerica and was never as well developed as it was in the Circum-Caribbean and the Central Andes to the south from whence it presumably diffused. Mining techniques among the Aztecs were simple, and the smelting of ores was accomplished by a forced draft using blow tubes. Copper was worked in its native state as well as being gilded. They also alloyed copper and gold which was cast by the *cire perdu,* or lost wax, method into bells and ornaments.

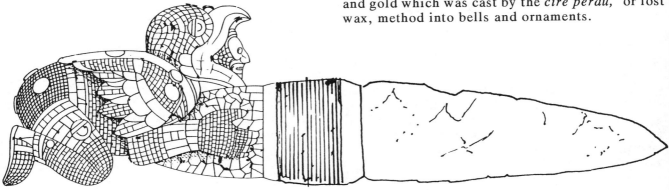

A Ceremonial flint knife was used to cut out the living heart of a sacrificial victim. The figure on the carved wooden handle, encrusted with turquoise mosaic, represents a warrior wearing an eagle headdress and a feathered cloak.

Ceramics were highly developed among the Aztecs and showed a much wider use than among the Maya. The techniques, however, were not as numerous as among the Classic Maya since the Aztecs used neither molds nor the primitive potter's wheel, the *kabal* (a rotating base moved by the foot without the benefit of the weighted wheel). All pottery was hand-made, and the vessels were decorated with polychrome designs emphasizing naturalism. There seeems to have been vessel forms for every conceivable use. The most common were goblets for pulque, graters for chili, an oval eating platter with a separate compartment for sauces, and *comales* for cooking tortillas. Decorated spindle wieghts, or whorls, were ceramic for the most part. Ceramics were used in construction to make large roof ornaments for temples, fired bricks for the back of fireplaces, and sometimes for building corners in the place of stone.

Merchants and traders did not work in the fields and were organized into groups similar to the calpaulli. This condition developed from the increased specialization in the handicrafts and the demand for raw materials ffrom outside the Valley of Mexico. Further, the traders performed a dual function by acting as spies. Trade was carried on over large distances with shells from the Caribbean, pottery from Salvador, and gold ornaments from Panama. The market system was well developed with each town of any size holding one at specified intervals. Some of these were very large, and were conducted daily, such as the one at Tlatelolco, a town adjacent to Tenochtitlan. The wealth and variety of this market astounded the Spaniards, some of whom estimated that 60,000 people occupied the marketplace on given days. Barter was the chief means of exchange, although cacao beans, gold quills, and crescent knives of copper served as a medium of exchange as did the more highly valued jade and turquoise on occasion.

Theoretically, the tribe of the Tenochca owned all of the land held. However, the immediate controlling unit was the calpulli. It has been maintained that the calpulli occupied the land they were originally assigned at the settlement of Tenochtitlan. According to the rules of land ownership, a calpulli could not take the land of another when their population expanded, although a family could gain the use of calpulli land other than its own. The chinampa system allowed for both the growth of arable land and the city. However, land use and ownership was closely tied to the social system which consisted of two main groupings: the *macehuales,* or common people and manual laborers, and the *pilli,* those who directed or coordinated work. These two social divisions cut across the tribe, the calpulli, and the tlaxilacalli, and were immediately associated with the division of what was produced on the land. In one sense, the calpulli was, then, a closed group of land owners. However, the land of the calpulli was divided into two classes, that cultivated for tribute and that cultivated for sustenance. The latter was divided into private land and the common land of the calpulli. The tribute land was worked by the macehuales under the direction of the pills, and the products were paid as tribute to the chiefs and the temples. This applied to both the tribal and calpulli categories. Private land was owned only in the sense that a given family had the right to work it. On the death of a man his sons inherited this right, but if there were no heirs, or it was nto worked within a two year period, the land reverted to the calpulli and could be reassigned.

Despite the expansion of the chinampas the Aztecs were suffering from a land shortage by the early sixteenth century, and conquest was being used as a technique for alleviating it. Those warriors who showed themselves valiant in battle were given grants in the conquered territory, and small Tenochca colonies were settled there to oversee the conquered peoples who worked the land.

However, conquest served for more than alleviating land shortage. Tribute became an important part of the economy of the Aztec, although it seems certain that tribute in the form of sacrificial victims was more important than other kinds.

Dress and ornament The Axtec strove to accentuate social status and rakn through dress and ornament. In general, four main groups could be distinguished in any social gathering. These groupings also showed internal differences in status and rank. The commoner men wore their hair long and uncovered as a sign of their status. The dress was simple, consisting of a loin cloth, a mantle knotted over one shoulder, and sandals of woven maguey fiber or leather worn only inl cold weather. the commoner women wore a two-piece outfit of a finely woven wrap-around blouse of *huipil*. Their hair was woven long and dressed in braids with interwoven ribbons of cotton or coarsely woven maguey. On occasion, the braids were twisted around the head.

The higher ranked pillis wore the same basic clothing, of similar materials but better made, usually decorated with elaborate embroidery. The chiefs and the wealthy wore feather cloaks, and the chiefs of all ranks wore a leather fillet from which hung two tassels. The highest ranking chiefs wore a diadem of gold or jade and turquoise as their badge of office.

Men in their role as warriors were distinguished by costumes modeled on the ocelot or the eagle,

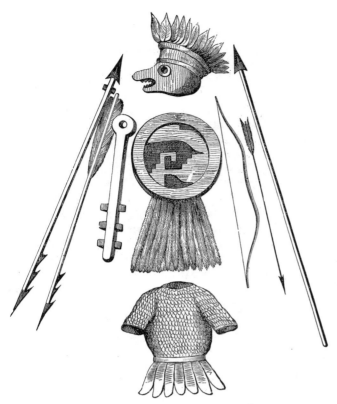

Aztec arms, shields, and war-dress

thus indicating their affiliation with one of the two important miliatary orders. Rich mantles and ornate feather headdresses, the latter consisting of a wicker harness held on the shoulders and covered with huge feather mosaics, further indicated the high social position of the military groups.

The priests and priestesses were as elaborately dressed as the warriors with their costume representing specific gods and goddesses. In addition, ornate ritualistic marks set this group apart.

Jewelry corresponded in complexity and richness to the social position of the wearer. Copper, gold, silver, jade, turquoise, emeralds, opals, moonstones, moxaics, and shells were all used, alone and in combination. Both men and women wore ear plugs, but men usually more elaborately ornamented than women. A well- dressed male displayed nose and lip plugs, other ornaments in these features, necklaces, pendants, armlets, and leglets.

As well, the Aztec utilized elaborate body painting as a means of designing social status and role. Red, blue, yellow, gray, and black were colors which indicated specific social and religious significance.

Aztec Art

As with the Classic Maya the major motivating force in Aztec art was religion. In all aspects of artistic expression the quality of monumentalism as its most prominent feature. Sculpture was the most highly developed form and its religion motovation made it an integral part of architecture or imparted architectural qualities to it. Painting and drawing were most weakly developed although even there monumentality and strict attention to detail are the clear characteristics. The Aztecs were stark realists in their approach to life and so is their religious art. It has severe realism and austerity which applies to both humans and animals. But this was not the whole of the art, for, while being realistic, the Aztec could express deeply religious esoteric ideas. This art has a ferocious quality, and the subject of death is so preponderant, that religious awe and respect for Aztec military power must have been inspred in most who viewed it.

Stone sculpture was essentially cubist in style. Huge blocks of stone were worked into figures of gods with only small openings in the stone to indicate arms and legs as separate from the great mass of the cube. Sculpture in the round emphasized form as volume, while low relief sculpture possessed a lightness and attention to detail. Coatlicue, the *Lady of the Serpent Skirt," mother of Huitzilopochtli, was a powerful and awesome goddess who embodied the ever-present frar for the the universe with which the Aztec were so preoccupied. The Aztec sculptor attempted to translate these qualities into stone. The head of Coatlicue is twin serpents, the hands and feet are armed with terrifying claws, the necklace is made of human hands and hearts, and the skirt is a writhing mass of serpents—all of this in monumental passivity combined with the dynamism of the horrors of a threatening universe. Low relief sculpture depicted young gods and goddesses of crops with a passive, calm demeanor, and usually showed some of the animal qualities of these gods. The Aztecs also molded lifesize figures and intricate, huge barziers in clay. The same qualities mentioned above were found in wood, bone, mosaic, semiprecious stone, and gold.

There was also a seacted as regents for sons and when they played a central role in the cementing of alliances with other tribes through marriage. In addition, some women reached high rank as priestesses although this was likewise exceptional.

The social organization of the Aztecs was based upon the calpulli with its ambilateral, endogamous character. Within the calpulli social stratification complex and aristocratically organized, but it was not independent of this kin organization. At the time of the Spanish Conquest class structure was oriented within the clan, but there was a developing social mobility made possible by the increase in trade and private ownership of land. While social mobility was possible, the higher ranks of Aztec society were inaccessible to one not born in

Aztec sepulchral vase

the ranking families. However, the fact that such uniformity of calss structure did extend throughout Aztec society may have foreshadowed the development of a true society-wide class system. The different rankings of the calpulli, the campans, and the increase in the number of private property owners, as well as the development of specialized economic groups, all pointed in the direction of a city-wide social stratification. The economic potential for the Aztecs to have developed a more complex class stystem was not available. Whatever may have been the outcome without European interference, the Spanish found a wonderfully rich and complex society when they entered the Valley of Mexico.

An Aztec entered the world with the aid fo a midwife who washed and swaddled the newborn infant. As soon as possible, a priest was called in to cast the horoscope of the child by consulting the *tonalamatl,* the book of the sacred almanac, to determine if the birthdate was lucky or unlucky. If the day was unlucky there were several ways of changing the true b theft of precious materials for religious purposes – a mortal crime; murder – death even if it was a slave; rebels and traitors – death; kidnapping – slavery; drunkenness and intemperate behavior of a high official – death; slander – the loss of lips and sometimes the ears; adultery – severe corporal punishment or death; incest – hanging. This brief inventory reveals that Aztec law was effacious if brutal. However, a strong sense of community solidarity supported the system.

In many ways, it is incorrect to speak of the Aztec empire, for the demand for city cultural autonomy among the Aztec tribes played down the

development of a true political empire. The Aztec made conquests, but these were mainly for the purpose of the tribute to be gained rather than new lands to be colonized and directly governed. Tribute was the chief political method of the Aztec, and the expansion of trading was not to gain economic control over other groups but knowledge of new lands, or old ones needing reconquering, from which to exact tribute in the form of human sacrificial victims and economic wealth. In this sense then, Tenochtitlan in company with other Aztec towns such as Texcoco were city states bolstered by military power rather than empires.

Warfare It will be remembered that the Post-Classic period was typified by war and warlike activities which, at least in degree, placed it in contrast with the Classic. In large part, this was a concomitant of a new religious orientation which demanded human sacrifice as the central feature of its ceremonies and dogma. As the city stated developed the organization and the motives behind warfare became more complex and demanded more efficient organization.

Warfare was important in Aztec economy and religion, but the major motivation was obscured by a number of secondary factors. In the main, the two important motives were economic tribute and sacrificial victims, and the latter by far overshadowed the former. However, many campaigns were fought for ostensible reasons of defense, revenge and purely economic motives. But throughout all Aztec warfare the central goal was to take captives for human sacrifice. The human sacrificial victim and war captive was held in such high esteem that a special heaven existed for them alone.

The Aztec army organization reflected the calpulli of Tencohtitlan. Thusm groups of 20 men were combined into larger units of 200 to 400 men. Each one of these larger units possessed a special flying squad of four to six men who acted as scouts and raiders. The units of the 200's to 400's wegre grouped together to form the calpulli unit under the command of the calpulli chief. These, in turn, were combined into four divisions under the four campan chiefs, although sometimes a campan's troops were divided into brigades made up of two or three calpulli, the high command of the army consisted of the tribal war chiefs.

The officers of the Aztec army were the executives of peacetime. Those who commanded the larger units of the army were the high tribal chiefs, the war chief, the campan chiefs, and the calpulli chiefs. The smaller units were directed by the ordinary chiefs – the tecuhtli, and the members of the warrior orders of the Knights of the Eagle and the Jaguar. The soldiers were all the able-bodied men of the tribe who had recieved their training in the telpuchcalli and in battle as squires to the knights.

The armament of the Aztec army was specialized into offensive and defensive forms. The most common offensive weapons were the wooden, obsidian-edged sword-club, the throwing stick and dart, and the thrusting spear. Also used, but less preferred, were slings and the throwing javelin. The Aztec warrior protected himself with a shield of wickerwork covered with hide, body armor of quilted cotton, and wooden helmets, although the last were more decorative than protective. As the Spaniards soon discovered, the quilted armor offered more protection against Aztec weapons that did the European metal form, and during the latter part of the Conquest a conquistador was more often seen wearing Aztec armor than his own. Although warriors used the same weapons,

Tezcatlipoca was the Aztec god of war, of providence, of night, of ubiquity, and of young warriors. Chief god of the city of Texcoco, this representation was discovered in Texcoco.

each one could elaborate his costume according to his social position. Thus, the amenities of social stratification were preserved even in war. Each campan possessed its arsenal (tlacochcalco) which was situated near the chief temple of the quarter, and its readiness was one of the chief duties of a campan chief or one of his deputies.

An offensive campaign was difficult to mount due to the nature of the territorial organization of political units which emphasized the city-state autonomy. Further, the lack of large domesticated animals made it difficult to provision a large army for an extended campaign, and the multitude of potential enemies made it extremely difficult to live off the country since a commander did not wish to emerge more than one army at a time. For all these reasons, seige operations were similarly difficult. Defense works became relatively unimportant, although every town and city took advantage of natural barriers and obstacles, and although defensive purposes were taken into account in town planning, purely defensive construction such as fortifications were rarely built. Strategical concepts were little planned movement of troops, and the main forms of battle tactics consisted of feigned retreat, ambush, and surprise. More common, as war strategy, were political manipulations through political alliance, and the spy systems of the merchants and traders.

The religious nature of Aztec warfare is seen in their conception of this activity as an earthly reenactment of the titanic battle of the opposing forces of nature, especially the Sacred War of the sun against evil forces each day. This was so important to the Aztecs that in times of relative peace the *War of the Flowers," a ceremonial contest between the warriors of two tribes or groups of tribes, was conducted, in order that prisoners might be taken for sacrifice without the costs of a formal war.

Writing Much more is known about Aztec writing than Maya hieroglyphics. This is due to the fact that the Aztec were a flourishing culture at the time of the Spanish Conquest, and because far more was preserved by the Spaniards than in Yucatan, partly through the interest of the Spanish themselves, and partly because the Aztec displayed greater resistance to European culture. In the main, Aztec writing can be termed a pictographic of rebus writing. There was little which could be called phonetic compared with maya hieroglyphics. In fact, much of the writing seems to have been an elaborate menemonic device, for according to Spanish records the writings were supplemented with complex oral traditions. But if the Aztec writing system lacked in versatility, it seems to have been put to far more varied uses than that of the Classic Maya. Of course, it is recognized that there is little knowledge of the uses to which Classic Maya was applied, but the extreme emphasis on sacred matters appears to have culturally limited its utilization. The Aztec, on the other hand, left behind annals of ancient times, records of contemporary events, year counts, yearly tribute accounts, specific records for each year, books concerning the events of each day, and even diaries. The Aztec tribes also attempted history. Events, the peoples or tribes involved, and places with name pictographs as well as year names were all carefully recorded. These histories were written in terms of a succession of years showing the whole time covered by the history and the important events recorded in their proper chronological possition. Tribal records were also kept showing names of towns and tribute paid, the lines of descent of the important families, the land occupied, land ownership, and so on.

Even though Aztec writing was a far less effecient device than that of the Maya, it may again be noted that the Aztecs had an urban culture with all its attendant complexity. The need for records, economic and otherwise, was much greater. Add to this the development of a true state with its need for records of places, population, tribute, etc., and the reason for the expanded use of writing by the Aztecs is not hard to understand.

Time measurement and calendar   Like the Maya, the Aztec measured time as a function of religion. However, the Aztec measurement of time, although they shared the same basic calendrical systems with other Mesoamericans, were not so accurate as those of the Classic Maya. Nor did they observe the number and length of time cycles which the Classic Maya so elaborately spun out. The Aztecs had two time counts, the tonalpohualli — the ritual year — and the solar year. These two were combined to give a 52-year cycle. However, the Aztec did not give numerical value to the 52-year cycles so Aztec history is still highly confused, for although the years in a given 52- year cycle are in sequence, the order of the cycles is mostly unknown. It is as if there were only the last digits of our time count to mark an event, let us say 76 to mark the American Revolution, but nothing to indicate whether it was 1776 or 1876.

The *tonalpolualli* was a sacred almanac of days written in a sacred book, the *tonalamatl*. This was a complex association of day names, day numbers, and gods similar to the tzolkin of the Classic Maya. The tonalpohualli consisted of 260 days divided into: (a) thirteen 20-day months consisting of the 20-day names of the Aztec solar month, and thirteen day numbers; the designation of these days was by name, then number; (b) twenty 13-day weeks, the number of the day preceded the day name here so that every week

An Aztec monument employed for astromonical observations. In the Nahuatl language, it depicts the year of the ruler Ahuitzotin.

began with number 1, and, thus, every week day could be distinguished from every other day. With these two systems every day could be distiguished in two days. There were gods asssociated with each of the 20 days and each of the 20 weeks. At times, 9 gods and goddesses were sequentially associated with the nights of the tonalpohualli. The same 9 gods were associated with the 13 stations of the day and the 9 stations of the night. It was by determining the justaposition of day names, numbers, and associated gods that an Aztec priest was able to cast a horoscope for any event. Like the Maya, the naturals appropriately before any event of importance, and the only way this could be done was through the consultation of the priest and his reading of the tonalpohyalli.

However, it was for the solar calendar that the Aztecs reserved their great ceremonies. Each solar year named for the day of the tonalpohualli on which it began. The 365 days were divided into eighteen 20-day months and an unlucky 5-day period at the end of each year. Each of these months was named for agricultural pursuits or products, indicating the origin of this calendar. Each of the 20 days of the month was numbered, this in addition to the tonalpohyalli numbers and names. Because of the limited combinations of day names and numbers, only 4 of the 20 day names could begin a year: House, Rabbit, Reed, and Flint Knife. Also, the relationship of the 13 day numbers to the 365- day year brought about a condition whereby the number of the day beginning the year increased by one each year: 1 Rabbit, 2 Reed, 3 House, 4 Flint Knife, 5 Rabbit, etc. In this way, every year of the 52-year cycle was distinguishable, since the 13 day numbers and the 4 day names could repeat themselves every 52 years.

Mention has been made of some of the shortcomings of the Aztec calendar when compared with the Maya. Added to the paucity of cyclical observance is the fact that there is no certain evidence that the Aztec reached a solution to time lag by the recognition of the leap year, nor did they make any of the complex calendric corrections achieved by the Classic Maya.

The Aztec numerical system was vigesimal although they had no way of marking place notation. Dots or circles were used up to 20. A flag indicated a value of 20 was used in repetition up to 400. A fir tree-like sign sidicating many hairs indicated 400 (20 x 20), and a bag signifying innumerable cacao beans equaled 8000 (20 x 20 x 20).

Religion   The Aztec approach to the universe and the supernatural reflected their urban life and the greater control of the universe which they possessed compared with the Classic Maya. Some authorities have contended that Aztec culture could only be understood if one assumed that basically all things revolved around religious affairs and concepts; but the Aztec was not as closely meshed with the total universe as the Maya. The greater control over human affairs, and nature, give one the impression that the Aztec stood apart from nature; and if he did not view himself as an individual so much as he viewed himself a member of of a human group apart from the universe and nature, this does not detract from the idea that he was interested in religious matters with a secular end in view. Here we are not attempting to ascribe modern western European secularism to the Aztec, but we are trying to place the Aztec and his religion in contrast to the Classic Maya. The Aztec was much concerned with nature, and thus with a series of observable cycles and rhythms of growth and the movements of heavenly bodies. The Aztec viewed the supernatural very much as if it were in great degree a counterpart of the human world, and because of this, supernatural beings were capable of good and evil in the way of man. The major importance of the religion was that it was concerned with determination of the cycles and rhythms of the universe in order to protect man. These rhythms and cyclical forms were the major source of ritual and daily life.

In the Aztec view, the world had undergone five creations and four destructions. Since these were all associated with cycles of nature and the affairs of gods, there was much concern over the portents

for the fifth destruction. These five ages of the world were termed Suns. The first age of the world was 4 Ocelot, during which time Texcatlipoca, the Smoking Mirror, presided, and became the sun at the end when jaguars devoured the men and giants occupying the earth. The second era, 4 Wind, presided over by Quetzalcoatl, the Feathered Serpent, was destroyed by hurricanes and all men became monkeys. The third age of the world, 4 Rain, presided over by Tlaloc, the Rain God, came to its end through the fall of fiery rain. During the fourth era, 4 Water, Chalchihuitlicue (Our Lady of the Turquoise Skirt), the water goddess, presided, destruction came in the form of a flood and all men were changed to fish. The fifth, and contemporary age of the world was 4 Earthquake, presided over by Tonatiuh, the Sun God, and was slated to be de-

In the foreground stands Coatlicue, the Aztec goddess of earth, the goddess of life and death, and the mother of gods. It represents the Aztec vision of the dual powers of the world and of life.

stroyed by eathquakes. This sequence can be viewed as a recapitulation of the disasters which beset the Mexican communities. Much of the Aztec religious life was an attempt to avert the fifth destruction of the world.

To the Aztecs the universe was a religious concept rather than a geographical one. This, at least, is the view of many Mexicanists. However, the Aztecs were excellent map makers, and grasped the extent of Mesoamerica through their conquests and the travels of their merchants and traders. Records were kept of the universe, and again there is the problem of deciding to what extent the Aztec were secular or sacred in their orientation. The religious universe was viewed in horizontal and vertical dimensions. Horizontally the universe consisted of the four cardinal directions and a center. The horizontal dimensions of the were associated with gods and their qualities which determined the portents for human affairs and destiny. The center direction was controlled by Xiuhtecuhtli, the Fire God, who apparently was one of the ancient gods of the Aztec. East was under the control of Tlaloc, the Rain God, and Mixcoatl, the Cloud God, and signified abundance. It has been suggested that this referred to Vera Cruz where the lower altitude and abundant rainfall resulted in a lush growth. South was dominated by Xipe, the Flayed One, and Macuilxochitl, Five Flower, both of whom were associated with spring, flowers, and growth, but at the same time this direction was considered evil. West was identified with Venus, and the god of knowledge and learning. Quetzalcoatl, presided over this favorable direction. Mictlantecuhtli, the Lord of Death, dominated the gloomy and awful northern dorection. Although the preceding is a simplified version of the horizontal universe, one might view this dimension as the association of the divine geography and climate.

The vertical dimensions of the universe consisted of 13 overworlds and 9 underworlds, heavens and Hells. These had no moral significance. The 13 heavens were occupied by gods in order dominated by the original creator, Tloque Nahuaque. One of these heavens was the home of Tlaloc, the Rain God, who received those dead by drowning, lightning, and other forms of water demise. Another heaven was divided into East and West sections, the East became the home of dead warriors and the West the home of women who died in childbirth. The remainder of the dead passed to the underworld, Mictlan. But this was no easy journey. These souls had to overcome many hazards on a four-day journey which took them between two mountains which threatened to crush them, past a giant snake and a monstrous alligator, across eight deserts and over eight hills, through a freezing wind filled with stone and obsidian blades, and finally across a broad river on the back of a small red dog. When the traveler reached the end of his journey he made offerings to the lord of the dead, and was then assigned to one or more of the nine hells for a probationary period of four years before admission to Mictlan was given. One can associate the vertical dimensions of the universe with social stratification and rank among the gods and men, and the exaltation of the warriors and those who produced warriors for Tenochtitlan would seem to bear this out.

The pantheon of Aztec gods is heavily populated, and in many ways it is contradictory, duplicative, and highly complicated. As an example, the writer Valliant lists 63 gods. These he categorizes as great gods (3), creative gods (4), fertility gods (15), rain and moisture gods (6), fire gods (3), pulque gods (4), planetary and stellar gods (12), death and earth gods (6), god variants (6), and a miscellaneous group (4). But the complicated association of aspects, directions, colors and the like, precludes any full treatment here. The following represents a small but distinctive sample of this godly world.

Three powerful and complex gods dominated the supernatural world of the Aztecs: Huitzilopochtli, Tezcatlipoca, and Quetzalcoatl. Huitzilopochtli, the Hummingbird Wizard, was the war and sun god, and the chief god of Tenochtitlan. Tezcatlicopa, Smoking Mirror, was the chief god of Texcoco, the main adversary of Tenochtitlan among the Aztec city states. Tezcatlicopa, sometimes the adversary of Quetzalcoatl, was widely worshiped throughout the Aztec world, and a complicated and powerful cult was associated with many gods, but the cult dogma depicts him presiding over the four directions identified in his four aspects by sacred colors. The Red Tezcatlipoca was identified with Xipe, or with Camaxtli the god of Tlaxcala, and dominated the west. The Blue Tezcatlipoca dominated the night and the north, acting as the most implacable adversary and opposite to the Blue Tezcatlipoca. The White Tezcatlipoca was identified with Quetzalcoatl, and while he dominated the east signifying morning, he often dominated the west signifying evening. From his shortened version, it is apparent that the cult of Tezcatlipoca was moving in the direction of a synthesis of Aztec religion, but it had not assumed the proportions of domination by the time of the Spaniards.

Quetzcoatl, the Feathered Serpent, was the god of learning, civilization, the priesthood, and the plant Venus. He was widely worshipped, and in divinities. In Tenochtitlan a feathered serpent cult called him Xiuhcoatl who assumed two guises, that of the fire snake and the standard feathered Wind God, and was shown as a bearded personage whose face was covered by a protecting mask. Quetzalcoatl was also viewed as a historical personage, a great king of the Toltecs who purportedly went to the east to Yucatan, and after founding Post-Classic cities returned to Mexico. The Catholic priests tried to identify him with the blond St. Thomas, but in Mexico he was always associated with color black.

There were four creator deities, less closely associated with the affairs of men than most of the pantheon. Tlique Nahuaque was supreme and ineffable, in one sense the creative spirit in the universe, and in distant to men and their affairs. Only in Texcoco was there an organized cult for his worship. Tonacetecuhtli and Tonacacihuatl, Lord and Lady of Our Subsistence, were the creators and the parents or originators of other deities, supposedly heading the pantheon. Ometecuhtli was equal to the two preceding deities and was lord of duality, a concept with which the Aztec were much concerned.

The gods associated with the earth, rain, and growth were very important to the Aztec, for they intervened in the every day affairs of the people. Tlaloc, the Rain God, was an ancient god usually represented by eye rings, fangs, and a volute over the lips. In Tenochtitlan he shared a temple with Huitzilopochtli. Tlaloc, in addition to his identification with rain, was joined with Chalchihuitlicue and associated with growth and fertility, growth and vegetation, lakes and rivers — a constant coupling of dualities. A highly important god in this category was Xipe, the Flayed One. His special association was with spring, and he was always represented wearing a distinctive costume of flayed human skin which symbolized the casting off of skin of the old year and the spring life-renewal. Many other gods were associated with growth, youth, and games in this category, but among the most important were a special group associated with pulque. Mayauel, goddess of the maguey plant, possessed a special cult and had 400 sons associated with pulque in one way or another.

The gods of the earth and death were very important to the Aztec, since all things could be associated with the earth — even death. Tlaltecuhtli, the Lord of the Earth, was a male monster who consumed the sun each day. However, two goddesses were more widely worshipped in this category. Coatlicue, Our Lady of the Serpent Skirt, was the mother of the stellar gods, the mother of Huitzilopochtli, and in one sense was conceived of as the mother principle in the universe. Tlazolteotl was the goddess of dirt, the eater of filth, a mother of many gods, and the Earth Mother. She was worshipped under many synonyms, but her importance lay in the fact that great moral significance was attached to her, for the filth she ate was all the sins of man, and a rite of confession was part of her worship.

Tonatiuh, the Sun God, was the heavenly overlord, and was very closely associated with all Aztec life and religious practice since he daily engaged in mortal struggle with Tlaltechutli, an event the Aztec were much exercised about since they wished to prevent filth destruction of the world. There were several other gods who intervened in human affairs and were, in one sense, venerated above all others. These were mostly sky gods.

We have previously noted the duplication of political and priestly roles in Aztec society. This was especially true in higher ranks of the priesthood. In the special cults and temples, and to a certain extent among the lower ranks, there seems to have been a clearer delineation between priestly and secular statuses and roles. At the head of the Aztec tribe and Aztec priesthood was the *tecuhtli*, the "chief of men," who was the active leader in all important religious ceremonies. On the same level of importance, or perhaps slightly below, was the Snake Woman who supervised the temples of Tenochtitlan, the form of rituals, and the internal affairs of priesthood. Very often the "chief of men" had occupied the role of Snake Woman before his election. Two high priests of equal rank directed the cult acitvities of huitzilopochtli and Tlaloc. Quetzalcoatl- Tlamacazqui. Quetzalcoatl was an honorific term because he was the god of learning and priestly lore. Mexicatl-Teohuatzin was the priest who supervised general religious business in Tenochtitlan and the conquered towns, while his two assistants directed the instruction in the lay and priestly schools. There were other assistants for the pulque ceremonies. Each temple erected for a specific god or goddess had its special priest whose main role was to impersonate the god in rituals. These foregoing priests were aided by a series of assistants who in turn were supplemented by priestly aspirants occupying the bottom of the hierarchy. A number of temples were directed by priestesses and some had schools attached. However, the rank of the priestesses is not clear. There were religious practitioners outside the priesthood. These were the male and female practitioners of magic, in many ways analogous to the shamans among the North American tribes.

The role of the priesthood was to direct intellectual life, to keep the calendars in harmony, and to supervise the religious dramas that were the major ceremonial acts of the Aztecs. Because of the great importance of the religion in Aztec life some Mexicanists have gone so far as to term the Aztec state a theocracy. However, the close interrelationship of priestly and political roles does not appear to justify this concept, and when one considers the complicated social stratification and its calpulli, kin group identification, a throcracy seems hardly the term to characterize Tenochtitlan or any other Aztec town.

Central to all Aztec ceremonies was the practice of sacrifice. Although the Aztecs carried this farthest of all Mesoamerican groups, the idea was not restricted to this area. Blood sacrifice, especially through blood-letting from the tongue, ears, and genitals, was widely practiced by the Classic Maya. Likewise, the development of human sacrifice by tearing out the beating heart was not unknown to the Maya. The full development of this form of sacrifice appears to have taken place in and around the Valley of Mexico, and the Mexican Invaders of the Maya area took this complex with them. Just how many new concepts the Aztecs as a whole, or the Tenochca specifically, originated, is difficult to say. Certainly many authorities believe the Aztecs contributed little new to the Mesoamerican culture pattern. It is known that the Aztec received much of their godly pantheon and religious concept from the Puebla- Mixteca area. Whatever may have been the case, the Aztecs elaborated and intensified the practice of human sacrifice to a very high degree.

War captives were considered the best candidates for sacrifice, but slaves could be used in minor ceremonies with impunity. Women and children were sacrificed in fertility ceremonies, and there was, on occasion, ceremonial cannibalism. Self-sacrifice through blood-letting was very common and accompanied almost every ceremony, no matter its relative importance. The higher the social position, the greater amount of blood. The number of sacrificial victims in a ceremony varied according to its importance, but the high point was reached when its 20,000 captives were disposed of by Ahuitzotl after a two- year campaign in northern Oaxaca. Human sacrifice was the means whereby the Aztecs attempted to balance the good and evil forces in the universe, or even tip the scales in favor of man. Consequently, human sacrifice was necessary for the well-being of the tribe. But this became a vicious circle, for only through war could victims be gained and only through sacrificial victims could war be waged successfully.

The New Fire Ceremony, marking the end of the 52-year cycle, was the most important of all religious events. At this time, the beginnings of the tonallpohualli and the solar calendar coincided, with all of the attendant gods and qualities. The Aztecs believed that great danger lurked, for at this point in time the gods and nature could not easily withhold existence for men. The old altar

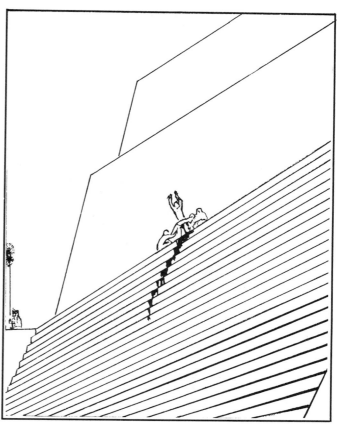

Human sacrifice on the steps of the Texcatlipoca pyramid

fires were extinguished and signs propitious for the kindling of new ones were anxiously watched for. The five unlucky, or useless days of the last year of the cycle saw all fires out, all furniture destroyed, much lamentation, fasting, and a general fear of catastrophe. At sunset of the last day the priests went to a volcanic crater in the floor of the Valley, the Hill of the Star, to await the passing at meridian of the Pleiades, a sign that the world would continue. When this occurred a new fire was kindled in the open breast of a freshly slain victim, and from this all the fires in the area were rekindled, first in the temples and then in the homes. The next day saw a hurricane of activity. Temples were renovated, houses were refurbished and refinished, there was fasting on special food, and much blood-letting and human sacrifice. The world was safe for 52 years more.

The fire sacrifice to the god Huehueteotl was one of the most brutal and terrifying of all Aztec ceremonies. The first day, prisoners of war and their captors danced together in honor of the god. The second day the captives were taken to the top of a ceremonial platform where they were stupified with the drug *yauhtli* (Indian hemp powder.) They were then bound hand and foot, hoisted on the backs of priests who danced around a huge fire. One by one the captives were dumped in the fire and allowed to roast. But before death they were hooked out and sacrificed while the heart still beat.

The cult of Texcatlipoca is possibly the begginning of an attempt in religious synthesis. Certainaly, the ceremony in honor of the Smoking Mirror was one of the most poignant of all Aztec religious rites. The handsomest and bravest prisoner of war became Tezcatlipoca, and was under the instruction of priests for a year. During the last month four handmaidens dressed as goddesses cared for his every want, and throughout Tenochtitlan he was the most honored of men. On the day of death he led a procession in his honor as the personified Tezcatlipoca through the city, showered with flowers, and amid much weeping. Upon his return to his living quarters he left for a small temple which he ascended, breaking a flute for each step, symbolizing the end of his happy incarnation. The victim was sacrificed in the usual manner by the wrenching out of the still-beating heart, but because of his great honor his body was carried down the steps by the priests rather than being cast down as was usual.

Aztec religion was devoid of moral and ethical purpose. The priesthood strove to keep man attuned to the rhythms of the universe and the gods, not by becoming a wholehearted part of it, but in order to avert the cyclical destruction of the world. There was a duality in Aztec religion in which good and evil forces, such as north and south, were constantly opposed. Certainly, there was an apprehension of impending doom and much uncertainty in Aztec religion. It was the task of the priesthood to alleviate this. But the Aztec ethos was not wholly centered on religion, for moral and ethical proscriptions were entirely within the social framework, and what the highly fluid social status might have developed is open to conjecture. The impression one receives is that the Aztec more easily separated the religious from the secular than did the Maya, that although religion through priestly geomancy entered all aspects of life, the Aztec in the Post-Classic world of a vastly expanded universe of knowledge and experience was either on the verge of becoming completely urboan or returning to the formative way of life much as the Classic Maya had done before him.

From The Native Americans: Prehistory and Ethnology of the North American Indians. Copyright 1965 by Robert F. Spencer and Jesse D. Jennings. Harper & Row, Publishers. Reprinted by permission.

BIBLIOGRAPHY-

● ADAMS, ENORY ADAMS. The Prehistoric World: or, Vanished Races. Cincinnati: Central Publishing House, 1885.

● MURDOCK, GEORGE P. Ethnographic Bibliography of North America. New Haven, CT: Human Relations Area Files Press, 1975.
● PRIESTLEY, HERBERT INGRAM. The Coming of the White Man, 1492-1848. New York, NY: The MacMillan Co., 1929.
● RISTER, CARL COKE. Border Captives, The Traffic in Prisioners by Southern Plains Indians, 1835-1875. Norman, OK: University of Oklahoma Press, 1940.
● SCHOOLCRAFT, HENRY R. History of the Indian Tribes of the U.S.; Their Present Condition and Prospects... Philadelphia, J. B. Lippincott & Co., 1857.
● STEWARD, JULIAN H. Handbook of South American Indians. 7 Vols., Washington, DC: U.S. Govt. Printing Office, 1946-59.
● SWANTON, JOHN R. The Indian Tribes of North America. Washington, DC: U.S. Government Printing Office, 1952.
● THOMAS, CYRUS. Indian Languages of Mexico and Central America and Their Geographical Distribution. Bureau of American Ethnology Bulletin 44: Washington, D. C.: GPO, 1911.

AZTEC-TANOAND

See KIOWA-TANOAN and UTO-AZTECAN.

BABINE

(Canada; British Columbia) A branch of the Takulll comprising, the Nataotin, the Babine proper, and the Hwotsotenne tribes living about Babine lake, British Columbia, with a total population in 1893 of 610 in 7 villages. The name was given to them by French Canadians from the custom of wearing labrets, copied from the Chimmesyan; and indeed their entire culture was greatly affected by that of the coast tribes.

BIBLIOGRAPHY —

● HODGE, FREDERICK WEBB. Handbook of American Indians North of Mexico. Washington: Government Printing Office, 1907.
● SWANTON, JOHN R. The Indian Tribes of North America. Washington, DC: U.S. Government Printing Office, 1952.

BAFFINLAND INUIT

(Canada; Northwest Territory) inhabit Baffin Island, the fifth largest island in the world, which is located in the Canadian Arctic Archipelago. Part of the Northwest Territories, and named after William Baffin, the Englishmen who visited the Island in 1616. Baffin Island is west of Baffin Bay and at the mouth of Hudson Bay. There are approxi-

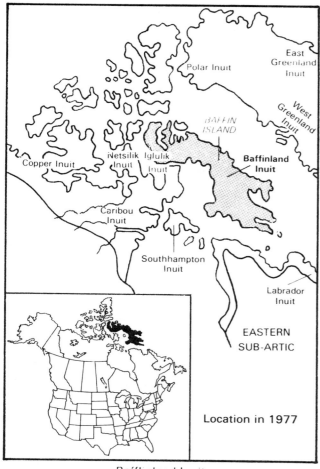

Location in 1977

Bafflinland Inuit

their clothing consists of a hooded jacket, knee-length pants, mittens, and boots. They travel over land with the aid of dogs and sleds, and over water with boats, including sails made from skins. Their tools include harpoons, bows and arrows (made from bones, horns, ivory and driftwood), needles, and goggles. Again depending upon the season, the Inuit live in several types of dwellings. In the summer, they use a tent made of skin made from animals or seals. In the winter, they live in their igloo, or snowhouse which is built of blocks of ice to form shelter. It is usually 12 feet high and 15 feet in diameter. The temperature inside is usually at the freezing point. The igloo is lined with skins to prevent the temperature from rising too much and melting the structure.

Social and political structure At the center of Baffinland Inuit life is the village or group. Each is independent socially and politically from the others, and warfare and disputes between them are unknown. The family kin each group at the same time is independent of the larger group; the male is the head of the family. The villges have no internal government, and there are no chiefs. Traditions or customs relate only to hunting, fishing, and family roles. Restraint is the guiding role in Inuit life, and cooperation is sought in all activities. When there are differences, and they are severe, they are settled by blood.

Beginning at the age of 10, children are instructed on the skills of Inuit life: hunting, building shelters, and surviving in the cold. Girls are taught the roles of adult females: food preparation, warming of clothes in the morning,, sexual restraint, and making and mending clothes.

Religion and philosophy Throughout their existence, the Baffinland Inuit, like other Inuit, have been superstitious in their daily living. They have charms to ward off evil. These charms consist of talismen, amulets, songs, and magic formulas designed to ward off ill health, trouble, or disaster. They believe in demonic spirits, spiirit-powers which control the universe (female in nature), such as the "Woman of the Sea"; "Mother of the Caribou," which, however, is mentioned in accordance with the walrus; and a spirit power of the land. Finally, the moon is seen as the guardian of the souls of man and animal.

In an climate as harsh and rigorous as Baffin Island, where the Inuit live, it is not hard to imagine the need for a religious order to guide and control nature.

20th century The Baffinland Inuit continue to survive in their habitat. Nature has not changed their ways, and even today, man has not. The Canadian Government has made efforts to preserve the ways and culture of one of the most remarkable peoples of all the tribes of the Americas.

mately 1,300 Baffinland Inuit inhabiting this island of 183,000 square miles.

Part of the Eastern Inuit culture, the Baffinland Inuit are hunters, fishermen, and traders. They speak Inupik, the language of the Inuit, and survive in an inhospitable environment.

Culture The staple of the Baffinland Inuit is the seal. Depending on the season, the seal is caught in the winter through a hole in the ice with a harpoon, and in the summer is harpooned from a boat called a kayak. Other foods of the Inuit are fish and walrus, most plentiful during the summer months. Whereas in the past the Baffinland Inuit used harpoons and the bow and arrow or lance exclusively to capture animals, today they are more often than not turning to the rifle for this purpose.

From the animals, the Baffinland Inuit produce skins for clothing, building materials, boat coverings, weapons and other tools. These skills date back to the 12th century AD, when the Baffinland Inuit came from the northwest. Though recent migrants to North America, they have adapted to the Arctic conditions with remarkable talents, and have stood the test of time. In this harsh climate,

BIBLIOGRAPHY –

● BOAS, FRANZ. "The Eskimos of Baffinland and Hudson Bay." Bulletin of the American Museum of Natural History. vol. 15, 1901.

BAGIOPA

(U.S.; Colo.) A tribe of whom Fray Francisco Garces heard in 1776, at which time they lived North of the Rio Colorado, where they are located on Font's map of 1777. The fact that Padre Eusebio Kino, while near the mouth of the Rio Colorado in 1701, heard of them from other Indians and placed them on the gulf coast of Lower California on his map of that date, has created the impression that the Bagiopa were one of the Lower Colorado Yuman tribes; but because they were never actually seen in this locality by the Jesuit and Franciscan missionaries of the period, they are regarded as probably having belonged to the Shoshonean family. The name is apparently of Piman origin.

BIBLIOGRAPHY –

● HODGE, FREDERICK WEBB. Handbook of American Indians North of Mexico. Washington: Government Printing Office, 1907.
● MURDOCK, GEORGE P. Ethnographic Bibliography of North America. New Haven, CT: Human Relations Area Files Press, 1975.
● SWANTON, JOHN R. The Indian Tribes of North America. Washington, DC: U.S. Government Printing Office, 1952.

BAHACECHA

(U.S.; Ariz.) A tribe visited by Onate in 1604, at which time it resided on the Rio Colorado in Arizona, between Bill Williams fork and the Gila. Their language was described as being almost the same as that of the Mohave, whose territory adjoined theirs on the North and with whom they were friendly. Their houses were low, of wood covered with earth. They are not identifiable with any present Yuman tribe, although they occupied in Onate's time that part of the Rio Colorado valley inhabited by the Alchedoma in 1776.

BIBLIOGRAPHY –

● HODGE, FREDERICK WEBB. Handbook of American Indians North of Mexico. Washington: Government Printing Office, 1907.
● MURDOCK, GEORGE P. Ethnographic Bibliography of North America. New Haven, CT: Human Relations Area Files Press, 1975.
● SWANTON, JOHN R. The Indian Tribes of North America. Washington, DC: U.S. Government Printing Office, 1952.

BAIMENA

(Mexico; Sinaloa) A former small tribe and pueblo, evidently Piman, 6 leagues S. E. of San Jose del Toro. The people spoke a dialect related to that of the Zoe, who lived next to them on the North in 1678. These two tribes traditionally came with the Ahome from the North. They are now extinct.

BIBLIOGRAPHY –

● BOWDITCH, CHARLES. P. Mexican and Central American Antiquities, Calendar Systems and History. Washington, D. C.: Bureau of American Ethnology - Bulletin 28: GPO, 1904.
● HODGE, FREDERICK WEBB. Handbook of American Indians North of Mexico. Washington: Government Printing Office, 2 vols., 1907-10.
● THOMAS, CYRUS. Indian Languages of Mexico and Central America and Their Geographical Distribution. Bureau of American Ethnology Bulletin 44: Washington, D. C.: GPO, 1911.

BAINOA.

(West Indies; Haiti) The Bainoa are known to have belonged to the Arawakan linguistic family. The tribe or "province" included all of the present Republic of Haiti south of the San Nicolas Mountains, except that portion west of the River Savane, and also southwestern Santo Domingo to the River Maguana or San Juan. A partial list of subdivisions, given by *Peter Martyr, 1912* , includes: Amaquei, Anninici, Bauruco, Camaie, Diaguo, Guarricco, Iacchi, Maccazina, and Xaragua. Specific population information for this tribe is not known.

BIBLIOGRAPHY –

● HODGE, FREDERICK WEBB. Handbook of American Indians North of Mexico. Washington: Smithsonian Institution: BAE Bulletin No. 30: U.S. GPO, 1907.
● SWANTON, JOHN R. The Indian Tribes of North America. Smithsonian Institution: BAE Bulletin No. 145: U.S. GPO, 1952.

BAKAIRI

(South America; Brazil) are a lowland South American Indian society speaking a language belonging to the Cariban family of languages. They are located in an upland region of Mato Grosso State near the headwaters of the Xingu autonomous villages and subsisted by hunting, fishing and slash-and-burn horticulture. Today, they are highly acculturated to the surrounding Brazilian society and are in danger of becoming entirely assimilated.

Name and location. The Bakairi are also known as the Cura. The term Bakairi has been in use since at least 1749 (Alternate spellings for Bakairi are Bacairi, Bacaeri, and Bakiri). J. Wheatley states that they refer to themselves as the "Cura" which he glosses as *we inclusive*. It seems plausible that proximate origins of the group are in the highland area which gives rise to the two great River systems, centered on about 14 S latitude, 53 W longitude. This is an area characterized by dense

Location in 1977

Bakairí

and knotted cotton hammocks. The principal weapons in von den Steinen's time was the bow and arrow. He also observed the use of the fire drill, stone axes hafted onto wooden handles, bark canoes with decorated paddles, etc. Fish weirs were made across streams but fish hooks and poisons were apparently not used.

Economy. Kalervo Oberg, who studied the Bakairi in 1947, reported tha Bakairi subsistence was based on horticulture, gathering, hunting and fishing in that order of importance. The principal cultivated crops were manioc (both bitter and sweet varieties), maize, sweet potatoes, and beans, ground nuts, potatoes, and pequi fruit trees. Other cultigens included urucu (Bixa orellana) for red body paint, cotton and tobacco. Steinen reported sugar cane among the acculturated Bakairi in 1884. Manioc was processed into Beiju cakes and flour and both maize and manioc were used to prepare a sweet, refreshing drink.

There is little data on what species were sought in gathering, hunting, and fishing expeditions. Fishing was carried our either by individuals using bow and arrow or by groups of men who constructed a weir to trap fish, or by fish traps individually manipulated. The extended family household was the principal unit of economic organization. Larger groups were sometimes assembled for the purpose of clearing gardens and erecting homes. Women formed a collective hammock-weaving group when a large cotton harvest permitted this.

Little is known about intervillage or intravillage trade. There are indications that the Bakairi participated in the ceremonial trading activities between villages of the upper Xingu basin. At these occasions, baskets, ornaments, hammocks and food were traded under supervision of the host and guest village chiefs. These were also the occasions for intervillage championship wrestling matches and, after the trading, a communal feast.

Social and political structure. As is typical in lowland South America, men are primarily responsible for the clearing of new gardens, building houses, hunting and fishing with bow and arrow. Bakairi men wove baskets but women were the weavers of straw mats. Women were primarily responsible for child care, cooking, and house keeping. Both sexes manufactured pottery.

In 1947, there were no preferential marriage rules but marriage was prohibited with a real or classifactory member of ego's nuclear family. Cousin marriage was common but not preferred. Marriages often took place within a household. Polygyny was permitted but rare. No specific rule for postmarital residence is recorded. Von den Steinen reports the presence of women and children from nearby societies in Bakairi villages,

evergreen forests along the rivers and a thinner, semi-deciduous forest in the uplands away from rivers. The villages were formerly located from 2-6km. away from the river banks and consisted traditionally from 2 to 6 communal dwellings built of thatch and poles, a guest house and a ceremonial house.

Bakairi material culture. Little is known about the Bakairi in early contact times, but von den Steinen's accounts are invaluable. In 1884, some Bakairi already wore western clothing and were able to speak Portuguese. They raised cattle in addition to more traditional subsistence pursuits and they lived under direct Government administration. The Bakairi in the Xingu drainage, however, built large communal houses with rounded corners and a central ridge pole. They closely resembled the house styles of the peoples of the upper Xingu basin.

The Bakairi once went completely naked except that women wore a tiny palm-leaf triangle as pubic covering. Persons of both sexes pierced the nasal septum to allow feathers to be introduced. Red and black body paint of highly individualized design was worn as well as feather headdresses, especially on festive occasions. Music was made with large bamboo flutes played in pairs by men. Other manufacturers included pottery, decorated gourd containers, rattles, masks, combs, and animal figures fashioned from corn straw and other materials. They also manufactured several kinds of baskets, decorated boards for the house posts

which suggests the possibility of inter-village marriage as is common in the nearby upper Xingu region. Some of these persons are known to have been war captives.

There is no evidence of unilineal descent groups, clans or moieties among the Bakairi. The kinship nomenclature in 1947 was of the bifurcate-merging type with father and father's brother called by the same term, and likewise mother and mother's sister. The cousin terminology reflected this distinction with parallel cousins distinguished from cross-cousins. An unusual feature of the terminological system is the distinction of elder brother from younger brother, a distinction apparently not used for sisters.

While the ceremonial house was not off limits to women, there appears to have been a men's cult in typical central brazilian style. Men had exclusive possession of a pair of sacred flutes and they performed rituals adorned in straw masks which obscured their identity.

The villages visited by von den Steinen in 1884 and again in 1892 averaged around 40 persons in size, the largest one having a population of about 100. The distance between Bakairi villages was about one or two days by canoe along the river, and they apparently enjoyed friendly relations with one another. There is no indication of any political organization above the level of the village. Each settlement had an identifiable chief identified by the term *pimato*. Both von den Steinen and Oberg report that the chief had a certain authority among the villagers, and that he would coordinate collective activities and mediate disputes. By the mid sixties, this authority had dwindled to almost nothing and the chief hesitated even to suggest a given course of action to his people. There are presently certain informal roles, such as the "respected elder" and the *sodo* or "sponsor of corporate activity" who may exercise influence or certain occasions but never coercive power. Parties to a dispute may accept the advice of an elder or not as they choose. The shaman may exercise social control by accusing antisocial persons of witchcraft. While Oberg refers to the potential sanction of exile in 1947, Wheatley in 1972 remarks tha Bakairi already regard life away from their people as an acceptable alternative, thereby reducing the force of the threat of exile.

There are indications that the Bakairi once fought wars with neighboring peoples. Claudio and Orlando Villas Boas suggest that they fought their way into the upper Xingu region in a series of bloody encounters. Little is known about the warfare practices of the Bakairi.

Life cycle. An expectant mother goes into seclusion just after giving birth and may come out of seclusion at a festival sponsored by the infant's father. Fathers also sponsor feasts at the onset of puberty of their children. Pubescent children of both sexes are kept in dark corners of their houses making baskets and pots for two months or longer. The Bakairi believe that the longer the seclusion the stronger the child will be when he or she emerges. Marriages are arranged by the parents or older sibling of the boy with the parents of the girl. The latter receive gifts from the former.

Religion and cosmology. Little is known about native Bakairi religion, except for the few comments made about ceremonies and the men's cult. In spite of their many resemblances and relations with the upper Xingu groups, they apparently do not participate in the *Kwarip* festival so characteristic of that region. The Bakairi have a creation myth which involves twin brothers; Keri, or "sun," and Kame, or "moon" who are derived, apparently, from Arawakan myths where their roles are reversed. Descending from the sky where they were born, the brothers bring them sleep, fire and the rivers. Subsuquently, they arrive at the waterfall on the Parantinga River where they give rise to Bakairi culture, including festivals, dances, crops, etc.

A man may become a shaman among the Bakairi if he has the ability to dream or otherwise to "see" into other worlds and learn the causes of illness. He undergoes a period of training under another shaman and from then on his reputation depends on repeated demonstrations of his ability to cure. This is done by going into a trance with the aid of tobacco smoke and then "sucking" an offending object, such as a small stick, from the body of the sick person. Or he may search for a departed spirit while in a trance to cure a person afflicted with soul loss. Shamans also have a role in the scheduling and performance of rituals. Von den Steinen makes several references to "witches" which suggest that there may have been female shamans during his visists to the Bakairi.

History. The Western Bakairis, living on headwaters of the Tapajos were already highly acculturated in 1884, while the Eastern contingent living on headwaters of the Xingu were virtually uncontacted by Brazilians. The Western group was first contacted directly after 1820 by gold prospectors. An official document estimates their numbers at 200 in 1848, but probably ignores the existence of the Bakairi of the upper Xingu. Von den Steinen enumerated only 72 Western Bakairi in 1884, but records that they had suffered great mortality from a measles epidemic some years earlier. In the same year, there were 165 Bakairi to be counted in four villages along the Batovi. Von den Steinen plausibly speculates the the Eastern Bakairi had migrated into the Xingu region to escape the depredations and epidemics brought by the invading *bandeirantes* and gold prospectors. He points to the very slight difference between Eastern and Western groups and suggests that the split occurred in the 18th century. It would appear that the Eastern group are now united in a single group under the jurisdiction of the Brazilian National Indian Foundation *(FUNAI)* at the Simoes Lopes Indian Post on the Teles Pires River. In 1972, the population at the Simoes Lopes was about 175. The Western group live at another FUNAI post called Santana on the Rio Novo with a population of about 75.

The Bakairi on these two posts are now largely assimilated into Brazilian cultures and most of them are fluent in Portuguese, wear Western dress and raise horses and cattle. Some aspects of their ceremonial life have remained alive. Wheatley's account of them describes them as now highly individualistic and unresponsive to leadership, suggesting that true political power does not exist among the Bakairi. It is possible that this situation is more a product of the conditions under which the Bakairi were brought into Brazilian society than an anacient feature fo native social organization. In the near future, the Bakairi may cease to exist as a distinct social entity.

BIBLIOGRAPHY —

● STEWARD, JULIAN H. Handbook of South American Indians. 7 Vols., Washington, DC: U.S. Govt. Printing Office, 1946-59.

BANKALACHI

(U.S.; Calif.) A small Shoshonean tribe on upper Deer Creek, which drains into Tulare lake. With the Tubatulabal they form one of the four major linguistic divisions of the family. Their own name is unknown.

BIBLIOGRAPHY —

● HODGE, FREDERICK WEBB. Handbook of American Indians North of Mexico. Washington: Government Printing Office, 1907.
● SWANTON, JOHN R. The Indian Tribes of North America. Washington, DC: U.S. Government Printing Office, 1952.

BANNOCK

(U.S.; Idaho, Oreg., Wash.) are a Shoshonean speaking people who were one of the may seminomadic Plateau Indian tribes which ranged over the dry uplands of Idaho, eastern Oregon, and eastern Washington. Traditionally fishermen and hunters who wandered over the country in small, loosely-organized bands searching for game, wild seeds, berries, and roots of camas, the Bannock lived in close association with the Shoshoni. They called themselves Bana'Kwiit. With basketry techniques that ranked among the best in North America, they wove the grasses and scrubby brush of the Plateau into almost anything they used, including portable summer shelter, clothing, and watertight cooking pots. Having no clans, they counted descent on both sides of the family. They had little formal organization, with the few tribal ceremonies centered around the food supply. Most Bannock today live on the Fort Hill Reservation in Idaho. They number around 3,000.

Cultural history. The Bannock were a horse-owning group who became highly skilled horsemen counting their wealth in terms of the animal, which was introduced in the early 1700s. The Bannock are said to have been located in several areas of the Plateau throughout their history. Today's Fort Hall Bannock were actually located in eastern Oregon in early historic times, and the area between western Wyoming and western Idaho contained ranging Bannock. At other times Shoshoni or Northern Paiute were identified as Bannock by travelers and writers.

The linguistic similarity of the Bannock and the Northern Paiute leaves little doubt that they once formed a single group, but there is no means of knowing when the two tribes separated. They are now separated by more than 200 miles. The horse revolutionized Bannock economy by making it possible to use new methods of hunting which yielded greater wealth in foods and hides and enabled people to live in comparatively permanent groups. Families which previously had to live near their cached foods could now transport foods to a central location. Large groups of people,

Bannock of Fort Hall.

moreover, could travel together in search of foods. Buffalo were taken to Idaho while they lasted from the buffalo country of the High Plains. The Bannock wealth in terms of horses made them prey to roving war parties from east of the Rocky Mountains. This hostility was another factor in producing solidarity among smaller groups, and led to the beginnings of the band organization. By 1840, the Bannock were comparatively well organized into bands, although some small groups of foot Indians still existed. Among remnants of this scattered population were, perhaps, a few Bannock who were later incorporated with the Lamhi.

Hunting and gathering In spring, groups of perhaps six related families, which had camped together, set out, under the leadership of an elderly man, in search of foods. Whether searching for buffalo, berries, salmon, camas, or trading, the circumstances of the hunt depended on the individual. Their joining other groups depended upon where and when they traveled and whether they had horses.

After the buffalo became extinct in Idaho in 1840, large parties of Indians would go to Butte, Montana, and Wyoming to hunt them, starting usually in the fall. Fear of the Blackfoot compelled the Bannock to travel as a unit, often joining Lehmi, Nez Perce, Flathead, and other Shoshoni. On their hunt they usually procured various seeds, roots, and berries in the mountains. Buffalo hunting was accomplished merely by running down the animals with horses. The herd was first located, usually by several young men. There were no formal hunting scouts; and men on horseback rode after the buffalo and each shot three or four. The older men butchered the buffalo. Carrying dried buffalo meat and hides on their horses, the party returned home in the late fall. The chiefs directed the entire operation, with a semiofficial police force maintaining order and safety, especially in dangerous territory.

Social organization The Bannock and Shoshoni were closely related, and wintered together. There was no segregation of Bannock or Shoshoni in winter encampments, nor any named subdivisions. Fort Hall was home to most of them. Arriving home, they made camp circles for six to seven days, and during four of them they held the grass

"Uprising among the Bannock Indians—A Hunting Party Fording the Snake River southwest of the Three Teatons (Mountains)." Frederick Remington, 1895.

dance and scalp dance. They then scattered to erect houses for the winter. Perhaps six related families built their houses in a cluster. To supplement food for the winter, small groups went hunting for antelope in the plains. In addition, they caught fish by means of hooks, baskets, and harpoons. As increased horses permitted the band to grow, Fort Hall became the main winter headquarters. However, there was never such centralized political control that all memebers of the band could be forced to act as a unit, as exemplified by the frequent hunting trips of small groups of Indians.

Warfare and politics. Warfare was of considerable importance in establishing band solidarity, for although the Bannock were never at war with their immediate neighbors, raids by Blackfoot were a constant danger. The Arapaho were also hostile to the Bannock, but their raiding parties rarely reached Idaho. There was intermittent strife with the Ute, but rarely in Bannock territory. While the Shoshoni considered the white man friendly, the Bannock found him fair game for raids. The Bannock- Paiute War of 1877-8 was the important outbreak in Bannock history. The Bannock and Shoshoni were politically distinct in that each had their own chiefs. The chief, particularly of the band, was unimportant until the extinction of the buffalo. Most activities were carried out by family members, led by the *dagwaniwap*. He had an announcer, who was also his messenger. Succession was patriarchal; otherwise an influential man was selected by interested people and household heads. Duties of the chief were mainly concerned with warfare and the supply of winter food and fuel. He was not concerned with camp activities or disputes, and did not entertain.

Only after the extinction of the buffalo in Idaho and the greater contact of the white man did the role of the chief change. Band chiefs became important, and the band council was organized as an advisory forum.

Ceremonies. Each kind of dance of the Bannock was led by a special man whose knowledge of the dance and competence as a director enabled him to achieve leadership through tacit concent. Dances were held usually only by small divisions of the band. Band chiefs directed the scalp an grass dances. Only around 1900 was the Sun Dance introduced to the Bannock in Fort Hall.

As for marriage ceremonies, it was prohibited between any blood relatives. Otherwise, marriage was either orthodox and prearranged, or from capture and abduction. In the ordinary fashion, the male, seeing a female, asked her to accompany him to his father's camp. Her family was not consulted, and if she went with him, the marriage was consummated and continued as long as she re-

mained. Marriage by inducement occurred when a female's family solicitated a mate for her. This happened for several reasons, including age, security of the female, or desirability. The female's uncle acted as the intermediary in the marriage process. Marriage by abduction occurreed when a Bannock male stole a female, married or not, and made her his bride. The marriages, ordinary or not, were often polygymous, and the marriage bonds were often loose.

20th century. In the 1820s, the Bannock numbered about 8,000 and could be found in several areas of the Plateau. By 1870, they numbered, because of disease and starvation and the loss of hunting lands, less than 1,000. Intermarriage with the Shoshoni has made it difficult to determine the exact number of Bannock, but by 1969 they were estimated to number around 3,000 on the Fort Hall Reservation.

Fort Hall became a reservation in 1868. Located in the southeastern segment of Idaho, it is now home to the Bannock, who by the 20th century resemble little the Plateau peoples they once were. While the reservation is more than 500,000 acres, there is little work for the Bannock.

BIBLIOGRAPHY —

● HEBARD, GRACE RAYMOND., E. A. BRININSTOOL. The Bozeman Trail; Historical Accounts of the Blazing of the Overland Routes into the Northwest, and the Fights with Red Cloud's Warriors. Cleveland, HO: The Arthur H. Clark Co.
● HODGE, FREDERICK WEBB. Handbook of American Indians North of Mexico. Washington: Government Printing Office, 2 vols., 1907-10.
● HOWARD, MAJ.-GEN., O.O. My Life and Experiences among our Hostile Indians A Record of Personal Observations, Adventures... Hartford, CT: A. D. Worthington & Co., 1907.
● HUMFREVILLE, J. LEE. Twenty Years Among Our Hostile Indians. New York, NY: Hunter & Co.
● INDIAN OFFICE REPORT 1869, 1875, 1878, 1879, 1880, 1889.
● MADSEN, BRIGHAM D. The Bannock of Idaho. Caldwell, ID: The Caxton Printers, 1958.
● MURDOCK, GEORGE P. Ethnographic Bibliography of North America. New Haven, CT: Human Relations Area Files Press, 1975.
● PHILLIPS, PAUL C. Forty Years on the Frontier, As Seen in the Journals and Reminiscences of Granville Stuart. Cleveland, OH: The Arthur H. Clark Co., 1925.
● RICHARDSON, ALFRED TALBOT. Life, Letters and Travels of Father Pierre-Jean de Smet, S. J. 1801-1873. New York, NY: Francis P. Harper, 1905.
● SWANTON, JOHN R. The Indian Tribes of North America. Washington, DC: U.S. Government Printing Office, 1952.
● WHEELER, COL. HOMER W. Buffalo Days: Forty Years in the Old West... Indianapolis: The Bobbs-Merrill Co.
● WISSLER, CLARK. Indians of the U.S., Four Centuries of Their History and Culture. New York, NY: Doubleday, Doran & Co., 1940.

BARA

(South America; Columbia) are a named exogamous patrilineal group of approximately 200 individuals in the Vaupes territory in southeastern Columbia. In 1970 there were ten Bara settlements in the headwaters of the Tuquie, Pira-parana, Inambu, and Papuri Rivers. Dur to settlement exogamy and the patrilocal rule of residence, all married women in these settlements are non-Bara, and all married Bara women are to be found in other settlements in the region. The culture area is known as the Central Northwest Amazon: approximately half is Columbian and half Brazilian. Its territory lies at roughly 1' north lat. and between 69' and 71' west long. Bara at present are limited to the Columbian sector, but it is possible that they lived in Brazilian territory previously.

Bara refers to the aromatic leaves worn by men in their loincloth strings during ceremonies. A variant of their name is 8Northern Barasano," *The Bara* refers to those people who have inherited the Bara name, language, and certain other rights and property from their Bara fathers. A self-name, not completely synonymous, *s wai maha*, "fish-people."

The Bara language belongs to the Eastern Tukanoan family; Arawak and Carib languages are also represented. All Bara are mulitlingual, and all speak Tukano as a lingua franca. No indigenous writing system exists. Very few Bara spoke either Spanish or Portuguese in 1970.

Bara culture is a variant of the basic tropical forest culture characteristic of lowland South America, with a stress on swidden horticulture (bitter manioc is the staple crop) carried out almost entirely by women. Men clear the fields, hunt and fish and everyone gathers. Men build the long-houses, make baskets and hunting equipment, and manufacture ceremonial artifacts. Women make netted items and pottery and process almost all of the food. All Vaupes Indians (also referred to as *Tukanoans*) traditionally live in multifamily long-houses, one per settlement, on or near rivers. At present four to eight nuclear families inhabit a longhouse, but the recent settlement pattern of nucleated villages of one to four small houses is far more common today.

Bara and other Tukanoans distinguish themselves from the *Maku,* small groups of Vaupes Indians who are more forest- than-river-oriented, who speak non-Tukanoan languages, and who exhibit certain crucial differences in their social structure. The difference in river orientation is important, as well as the elaborate longhouse complex found only among Tukanoans. A third is, according to the Bara, a lack of horticulture among the Maku, which is not in fact correct.

Bara political organization does not extend beyond the autonomous settlement. Exceptions in the past were during times of war. Decision-making is by concensus; the headman leads with authority, but little real power. Shamans are the other part-time specialists, curing and protecting the settlement with techniques such as throwing water, sucking out intrusive objects, massage, and the use of hallucinogens for divination, for communing with spirits, and for travelling to other levels of the universe. Some shamans are suspected of sorcery: this type of power, like others, can corrupt.

Much ritual is male-centered, although women certainly perform important ceremonial roles. The main Bara rituals invlove male inititation, harvesting wild fruits, and food-exchanges with other (usually affinal) longhouse groups. *Yurupari,* a men's cult involving sacred trumpets forbidden to women's sight, is an important theme in Bara ritual and symbolism. Ceremonies last at least a day and involve elaborate body paint and ornamentation, music and dancing, chicha (manioc beer), and (for initiated men) coca chewing and taking hallucinogenic drugs. The long-house and its inhabitants are temporally and spatially transformed at the most ssacred part of these ceremonies, becoming one with the universe and the ancestors.

Very little is known of the Bara prior to the mid-nineteenth century, when some of the explorers through the Vaupes mentioned the Bara in their accounts. Since then contact between Bara and whites has been sporadic and has mostly involved missionaries, with the great exception of the rubber boom in the beginning of the 20th century. This was a period of great upheval, not the least being the spread of virulent epidemics, resulting in population decline and migrations, then disruptions in all areas of native life. Since then missionaries, both Catholic and Protestant, have had the most impact, moving Tukanoans (although relatively few Bara) into nucleated villages and mission towns, and requiring that school-age children be interned at missions for most of the year. More recently the Colombian and Brazilian governments have begun to participate more directly, but the outcome of these policies, for example the recent declaration that sections of the Colombian Vaupes are a mineral reserve (to facilitate uranium exploration), is yet to be seen.

BIBLIOGRAPHY —

● STEWARD, JULIAN H. Handbook of South American Indians. 7 Vols., Washington, DC: U.S. Govt. Printing Office, 1946-59.
● SWANTON, JOHN R. The Indian Tribes of North America. Washington, DC: U.S. Government Printing Office, 1952.

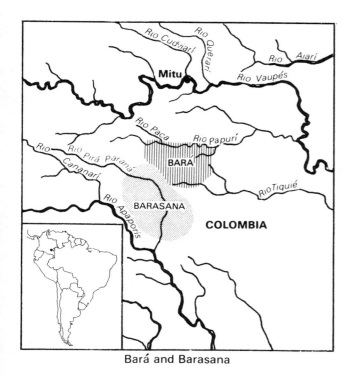

Bará and Barasana

BARASANA

(South America; Columbia) Indians of the south-west corner of the Vaupes culture area. They are a riverine people with highly elaborated mythological and cosmological systems. Most Barasana longhouses are on the mainstream and affluents of the river Pira- parana but a few are on the Apaporis near the Pira-parana's mouth. Alongside, and even interspersed with Barasana communities, are Tatuyo, Bara, Taiwano, Karapana and Makuna communities and there are representatives of yet more groups living in the longhouse groups dominated by these. This confusing situation is explained by the fact that the Barasana and equivalent units are not 'tribes'--they are patrilineal exogamous groups linkedby a network of marriage ties which extends over similar groups throughout the Vaupes region. Wives move into their husbands' longhouse communities on marriage but retain their own parrilineal group identity; thus a BArasana longhouse contains Barasana adult men and children together with in-married wives who may be Bara, Tatuyo, Makuna or of some other group.

Generally speaking each exogamous group has its own distinct language which members speak irrespective of languages spoken to them. Where this rule of linguistic exogamy applies, husband and wife speak separate languages, the children learning their father's language. Mutual comprehension is possible because the separate languages are closely related members of the Eastern Tukanoan family and because all children grow up

in multilingual situations. However, on the Pira-parana there are some exceptions to the rule: some of the southern kBarasana speak the Makuna language and the Taiwano speak Barasana.

Barasana is a word of unknown origin used only in dealing with whites. The Barasana loosely define themselves as *Yeba Masa,* people descended from *Yeba* a mythical hero associated with the earth,and they usually repudiate the name *Hanera/Panera* applied by other groups. Internally, they may be roughly divided into three blocks: one is on the central Pira- parana and its eastern affluents; another is on and around Cano Tatu, a western affluent and the third is on the lower Pira- parana, particularly Cano Comeyaka, and the Apaporis. Culturally the Barasana form a bridge between the cultures of the Apaporis to the South and those of the central Vaupes to the North and East. The sacred sites and myths of origin, which concern upstream journeys of anaconda-ancestors, suggest a possible migration into the Vaupes area from the lower Apaporis.

The Barasana divide onto numerous named sub-groups or 'sibs' which are arranged in hierarchical order from 'first born' to 'last born' like a set of full brothers. Within this hierarchy there are smaller sets of sibs whose members recognize specially close ties of descent with each other. Ideally those sets consist of five sibs, the 'elderbeing 'chiefs,' the second oldest 'dancers,' the next 'warriors', the next 'shamans' and the 'youngest',the servants'. In practice these sets are usually incomplete and there is little evidince of sib members practicing their correct grouprole. The sib gives rise to one or more longhouse communities each containing up to 30 members. Longhouses are usually at least two hours' journey apart. The house consists of an immense gabled roof, coming almost to the ground, with a main door for men and visitors in one end wall and a femake door in the opposite one. The nuclear families occupy separate compartments along the side walls toward the female end. The open part of the interior is used for coca preparation and male ritual at the male end, dancing and eating in the center and manioc preparation at the female end.

Cultivations are felled and burnt annually by men. The staple is bitter manioc, cultivated and processed by women, who also plant many subsidiary crops. Men cultivate and process coca, tobacco and yage--which yields a hallucinogenic drink used in ritual to experience the mythical, ancestral world. Men do all hunting fishing, combining blowpipes and traditional fishing methods with use of shotguns and nylon with metal hooks. Both sexes collect a wide variety of forest products including many fruits, caterpillars and frogs. Women make plain black pottery while men make an elaborate variety of basketry, wooden objects (including canoes) and ritual ornaments (made of feathers, bones, teeth, seeds, etc.). Most food is produced within the nuclear family and cooked by the wife but a large proportion is consumed at communal meals. In the evening men gather to chew coca and smoke cigars before retiring to their hammocks.

Every few weeks the subsistence routine is broken by a ritual gathering attended by several longhouse communities. Manioc beer prepared by the female hosts is drunk throughout. The men, transformed by their ornaments, consumed large quantities of coca, tobacco, and yage, while alternately chanting origin myths and dancing. The principle types of ritual gathering are *foodexchane cance,* at which affinal groups exchange smoked meat, fish or insects, *fruitharvest dance,* at which sacred musical instruments are played over seasonal fruits, and *male initiation,* at which the most sacred flutes and trumpets representing group ancestors are played and women and children are excluded. The post-initiation seclusion has much in common with the seclusion for parents and child after birth and that for menstruating women. In each case a restricted diet of manioc starch, ants, termites, and water is prescribed and reintegration is achieved by administering chili pepper and then the other foods in a carefully controlled series. All ritual events are supervised by shamans who are also believed to have powers of curing and bewitching. At death, burial is in the house, which is often abandoned.

There is no fixed political institutions despite the hierarchy apparent in the formal relations between sibs. Intergroup relations are dependent on the exchange of invitations to rituals, accusations of evil shamanism and, formerly, raiding and killing. Marriage should take the form of direct sister exchange between bilateral cross-cousins, although women frequently are raided from distant communities. Polygyny is restricted to a few ambitious longhouse leaders.

Little is known of the Barasana before this century although it is clear from their own accounts that killing was common and its cessation has had a far-reaching effect on interaction between groups. At the turn of the century, traditional patterns were already in decline as a result of the rubber industry. The brutal treatment Indians received as workers and during conscription drives caused many groups to abandon traditional house sites for the hidden headwaters. In spite of rubber exploitation, Barasana territory remained more isolated than surrounding areas owing to the treacherous rapids on the Pira- parana. It was not until the middle 1960s that the first mission posts were established. One Catholic post (Colombian

Javerians) and four Protestant posts (North Americans of Wycliffe Bible Translators/Summer Institute of Linguistics) were founded on the river each with an airstrip built by Indians, in quick succession. The industrial merchandise given in exchange for Indian labour consolidated the economic position of the missionaries and primpted a sharp decline in traditional values. Depradations from rubber gatherers, deaths from introduced diseases and migration to rubber-working frontier communities have undoubtedly led to a large decline in population over the last 100 years to an estimated figure of 300 to 400 Barasana in 1970. There is news of an uranium extraction project in the Colombian Vaupes but no further details are available.

The Barasana are still probably the least deculturated of the Eastern Tukanoan groups. Let us hope that their way of life will be respected.

BIBLIOGRAPHY —

● STEWARD, JULIAN H. Handbook of South American Indians. 7 Vols., Washington, DC: U.S. Govt. Printing Office, 1946-59.

BATACARI

(Mexico; Sinaloa) A subdivision of the Cahita, speaking the vacoregue dialect and formerly subsisting by hunting in the vicinity of a large lagoon 3 leagues from Ahome, N. Sinaloa. They afterward united with the Ahome people under the Jesuit missionaries and abandoned their wandering life.

BIBLIOGRAPHY —

● BOWDITCH, CHARLES. P. Mexican and Central American Antiquities, Calendar Systems and History. Washington, D. C.: Bureau of American Ethnology- Bulletin 28: GPO, 1904.
● HODGE, FREDERICK WEBB. Handbook of American Indians North of Mexico. Washington: Smithsonian Institution: BAE Bulletin No. 30: U.S. GPO, 1907.
● MURDOCK, GEORGE P. Ethnographic Bibliography of North America. New Haven, CT: Human Relations Area Files Press, 1975.

BATTLE MOUNTAIN COLONY

is an Indian reservation in Lander County, Nevada, on which about 160 Shoshone Indians reside.

Established in 1917 by executive order, the Battle Mountain Colony is 680 acres, all of which is tribally owned. While the tribe derives no income on the reservation, members do work outside the reservation. The tribe is informally organized, and is governed by the general council and a tribal council of six.

The Indians on the reservation are descendants of the Western Shoshone Indians, who in the years following the Civil War were on difficult terms with the United States Government because of a

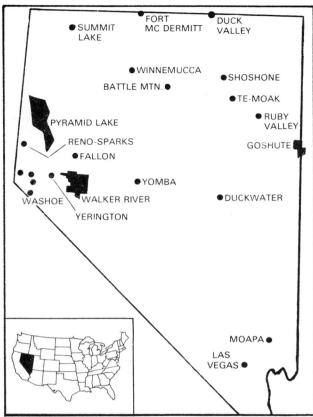

Battle Mountain Colony and other reservations in Nevada.

BAUMER CULTURE,

in Southern Illinois, is representative of the Early Woodland tradition that displaced the Archaic tradition in that area.

The basis of the economy emphasizes the transitional nature of this culture, that in some respects Baumer was an elaboration on the Archaic. Hunting and gathering seem equally important. These were a great number and variety of points, but there were also many pestles, bell-shaped and conical, and multiple-pitted lap mortars as well as chipped, polished digging hoes and fully grooved axes and hammers.

Homes were made of large square logs in separate holes rather than trenches. Refuse pits were circular with flat bottoms and bell-shaped apertures. Burials were placed at the back of irregular pits. Unlike later burials, associated goods and tools were not buried. Pottery was molded with fabric, tempered with clay or limestone, and fired by brush fires.

BAY MILLS RESERVATION

is an Ojibwa reservation of 2,189 acres in Chippewa County, Michigan. With a population of 300, the reservation Indians maintain their cultural ways in some respects.

The area which now is Bay Mills reservation was purchased by the Methodist Society for the Indian community. Acquired in accordance with the treaty of 1855, additional land was purchased under the Indian Reorganization act of 1934. The tribe is organized under a five member executive council elected by all eligible voters of the tribe, and hold office for 2-year terms. All eligible members of the tribe constitute the General Tribal Council.

The Ojibwa have a long history in the Great Lakes area. However, by 1855, the failure of the Great Lakes Tribes to band together against invading settlers meant the loss of their land and, finally, their way of life. On the reservation, the Ojibwa still ive in wigwams and tipis during the summer minths, and take sweat baths. They also hunt and fish, and conduct cultural ceremonies. In other ways, however, they are no longer the Ojibwa who sided with Pontiac against the British in 1773; Tecumseh in the early 1800s; defeated the SAc at Ox Bow in 1830 over hunting and fishing grounds; and revered Hiawatha as a warriior-god.

The reservation provides such services as gas, electricity, sewage disposal, and water. The nearest health facilities are in Sault Sainte Marie.

shortage of food. Differences were resolved by 1880, at which time the Indians were given land rights.

Today, the reservatioln Indians exhibit little of their former cultural ways. They practice little their arts and crafts, and while their native language is still spoken, their cultural traditions are disappearing.

BATUCARI

(Mexico; Sinaloa) A subdivision of the Cahita, speaking the vacoregue dialect and formerly subsisting by hunting in the vicinity of a large lagoon 3 leagues from Ahome, N. Sinaloa. They afterward united with the Ahome people under the Jesuit missionaries and abandoned their wandering life.

BIBLIOGRAPHY —

● BOWDITCH, CHARLES. P. Mexican and Central American Antiquities, Calendar Systems and History. Washington, D. C.: Bureau of American Ethnology- Bulletin 28: GPO, 1904.
● MURDOCK, GEORGE P. Ethnographic Bibliography of North America. New Haven, CT: Human Relations Area Files Press, 1975.
● THOMAS, CYRUS. Indian Languages of Mexico and Central America and Their Geographical Distribution. Bureau of American Ethnology Bulletin 44: Washington, D. C.: GPO, 1911.

Bay Mills Reservation

BAYOGOULA

(U.S.; Miss.) A Muskhogean tribe which in 1700 lived with the Mugulasha in a village on the West bank of the Mississippi, about 64 leagues above its mouth and 30 leagues below the Huma town. Lemoyne d'Iberville gives a brief description oftheir village, in 1880, which he says contained 2 temples and 107 cabins; that a fire was kept constantly burning in the temples, and near thedoor were keptmany figures of animals, as the bear, wolf, birds, and in particular the *choucouacha,* or opossum, which appeared to be a chief deity or image to which offerings were made. At this time they numbered 200 to 250 men, probably including the Mugulasha. Not long after the bayogoula almost exterminated the Mugulasha as the result of the dispute between the chiefs of the two tribes, but the former soon fell victims to a similar act of treachery, since having received the Tonica into their village in 1706, they were surprised and almost all massacred by their perfidious guests. Smallpox destroyed most of the remainder, so that by 1721 not a family was known to exist.

BIBLIOGRAPHY –

● HODGE, FREDERICK WEBB. Handbook of American Indians North of Mexico. Washington: Government Printing Office, 1907.
● MURDOCK, GEORGE P. Ethnographic Bibliography of North America. New Haven, CT: Human Relations Area Files Press, 1975.
● SWANTON, JOHN R. The Indian Tribes of North America. Washington, DC: U.S. Government Printing Office, 1952.

BEAR RIVER INDIANS.

(U.S.; North Carolina) Also called the Bay River Indians *Rights, 1947* . They were a tribe mentioned by Lawson, and were associated with the Algonquian tribes. They also may have been a part of the Machapunga. *Lawson, 1709* gives the name of their town as Raudauqua-quank and estimates the number of their fighting men at 50. *Mooney, 1928* places them with the Pamlico as of the year 1600 and gives the two a population of 1,000.

BIBLIOGRAPHY –

● HODGE, FREDERICK WEBB. Handbook of American Indians North of Mexico. Washington: Smithsonian Institution: BAE Bulletin No. 30: U.S. GPO, 1907.
● SWANTON, JOHN R. The Indian Tribes of North America. Washington, DC: U.S. Government Printing Office, 1952.

BEAR RIVER INDIANS.

(U.S.; California) Also called Ni ekeni, the name they applied to themselves and to the Mattole. They were a body of Indians living along Bear River in the present Humboldt County for whom no suitable native name has been preserved. The tribe belonged to the Athapascan linguistic family, and were most closely connected with the Mattole, Sinkyone and Nongatl tribes to the south and east. According to *Nomland, 1938* their villages included Chilsheck, on the site of the present Capetown; Chilenche, near the present Morrison Ranch; Sehtla, near Capetown; and Me'sseah, a name for a natural amphitheater, the training place for shamans, where a few families lived. The population, included with the Nongatl, was 1,129 in the census of 1930. The United States Office of Indian Affairs reported 23 "Bear River" Indians in 1937.

BIBLIOGRAPHY –

● SWANTON, JOHN R. The Indian Tribes of North America. Smithsonian Institution: BAE Bulletin No. 145: U.S. GPO, 1952.

BEAVER INDIANS

(Canada; British Columbia, Alberta) are Athapaskan speaking hunting people who live along the Peace River between the Rocky Mountains and Lake Athabasca. Their neighbors are Athapaskan speaking Slave adn Sekani to the North and West and Algonkian speaking Cree who moved into the Peace River area in historic times. In pre-historic times the Beavers may have been in contact with Athapaskan speaking Chipewyan and Sarsi at the eastern edge of their territory.

The Beavers have always been a nomadic hunting people whose way of life was closely linked to

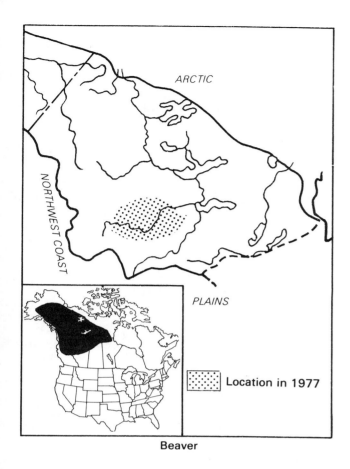

Beaver

The Beaver Indians called themselves *Dunneza*, "our people." They did not think of themselves as a single tribal unti but rather as a population sharing common territory, history, adaptation, traditions, dialect and kinship. During most of the year people lived in local bands of about 30 people. During the summer the bands that shared a common home range would come together for a short time for social and ceremonial activity. The nomadic movements of local bands throughout most of the year was controlled by the distributioin of fish and game resources. Bands moved regularly from one hunting area to another in order to manage their resources efficiently. Hunting territories were not owned exclusively by particular bands or individuals but were open to any of the bands that made up the larger summer group.

Kinship terms were used for reference and address among people who shared a common home range. Kinship was traced through both mother and father and terms of relationship were used to distinguish between people who could marry one another and those who could not marry. Categories and terms of relationship were extended out to include all people who had social contact with one another but kinship was not used for defining social groups cush as the clans and lineages found among people like the northwest coast Indians. Marriages could take place between people within the same local band as long as they were in the correct kinship relation to one another. Marriages could also take place between people from different bands. Often marriages were established between people of differnet ages and generations. The word *Dunne-za,* "our people," represented the strong feeling of interdependence the Beaver Indians felt for one another.

Before Europeans introduced guns, knives, and wire for snares the Dunne-za practised communal hunting techniques involving the coordinated efforts of a number of people. These included drives, surrounds and snaring of big game animals. These communal hunts were organized by people who were believed to have the power to see the pattern of the hunt in their dreams. They gave instructions for the placement of people in the hunt and they also organized communal singing and dancing. They were known as Swan People or "Dreamers." Their power to see a pattern of events that lay in the future was a particular application of the more general belief that every important activity should be foretold in the esperience of dreaming. All adult Dunne-za had powers were referred to in dreaming and they were first encountered in childhood vision quest experience.

The vision quest was a key instrument of Dunne-za adaptation. Through the experience of being sent out into the bush alone after being care-

the lives of animals. Their overall population size as well as the size and composition of groups depended on the natural resources of the 75,000 square miles of territory they occupied. The total native population within this vast area was probably never more than about 1000, giving an average overall population density of around one person per 75 square miles.

The life of these nomadic hunters was traditionally adapted to a variety of animal resources. Along the prairies and parkland flanking the Peace River there were wood bison in pre-contact and early historic times. To the North in the muskeg and forest country there are moose, deer, and caribou. In the Rocky Mountains at the western edge of Beaver Indian territory there are mountain sheep, mountain goats and marmots as well as black bear and grizzly bear. There are also beaver, fish, waterfowl and fur bearing animals throughout the territory. Because their territory was entirely within the arctic drainage the Beaver Indians did not have access to salmon like the Athapascan speaking Carrier to the southwest of them. Their principle adaptive strategy involved resource management through nomadic movement from one hunting area to another according to season.

fully instructed in traditional knowledge coded into their oral traditions and stories, the Dunne-za child learned to relate his or her life to the lives of animals. The vision quest was an educational as well as a religious experience. The competence and control gained through the vision quest was symbolized as a power derived from one of the "giant animals" that in mythic times lived by hunting people. The prototype of this experience of empowerment is stated in the myth of a culture hero who transforms all these giant animals into the forms known today. His pwer to transform human- like animals into food is the power of control over adaptive relationships to their natural resources that Dunne-za children gain in their own vision quest experiences.

The Dunne-za valued the ability to move easily more then the possession of bulky material artifacts. Their technology emphasized techniques over artifact. Many of their most sophisticated techniques such as snaring animals in communal hunts involved very little in the way of complex material objects. Their most elaborate technology had to do tiwh an understanding. Their most elabaorate art form was their oral tradition, a form of expression that is completely portable. Although utilitarian objects such as clothing, snowshoes and bark containers were artfully made and pleasingly decorated, the Dunne-za chose to make their most complex symbolic statements in the medium of oral imagery rather than through the creation of artistic images. Because their art and technology was inherent in their relationship to the natural environment rather than objectified in material art and artifact, many Western observers have viewed them as culturally impoverished. This perception is largely due to the bias of people whose own culture values material representation of its ideas. When Dunne-za culture is viewed from its own terms of reference it comes into focus as rich, complex and sophisticated in the elegance and

efficiency of its solutions to the basic problems of adaptation to the boreal forest and riverine environment.

The meaning of individual experience among the traditional Dunne-za was closely dependent on their relationship to the natural environment. The first appearance of Europeans and the fur trade altered that relationship as early as the beginning of the nineteenth century. In recent years the land itself has been taken from the Dunne-za in many areas and their relationship to ist natural resources profoundly altered. The meaning of their lives has undergone an equally profound alteration. They are currently attempting to redefine their traditions in realtion to contemporary conditions. The traditional dreamers have become prophets or religious leaders who seek to see ahead to a new pattern of relationship that will restore meaning to their lives.

BIBLIOGRAPHY —

● GODDARD, PLINY E. "The Beaver Indians." Anthropological Papers of the American Museum of Natural History. vol. 10, 1916.
● HODGE, FREDERICK WEBB. Handbook of American Indians North of Mexico. Washington: Government Printing Office, 1907-10.
● MURDOCK, GEORGE P. Ethnographic Bibliography of North America. New Haven, CT: Human Relations Area Files Press, 1975.
● SMITH, GEORGE MARTIN. History of Dakota Territory. Chicago, IL: The S. J. Clarke Publishing Co., 1915.
----- South Dakota, Its History and Its People. Chicago, IL: The S. J. Clarke Publishing Co., 1915.
● SWANTON, JOHN R. The Indian Tribes of North America. Washington, DC: U.S. Government Printing Office, 1952.
● WITHERS, ALEXANDER SCOTT. Chronicles of Border Warfare: or, A History of the Settlement by the Whites, of Northwestern Virginia. Cincinnati, OH: The Robert Clarke Co., 1895.

BELLABELLA

(Canada; British Columbia) are a confederation of Heiltsuk- speaking tribes living on Millbank Sound, B.C. In their language, a dialect of Kwakiutl, they are called the Heiltsuk. The name *Bellabella* is an Indian corruption of the word *Millban,* that was taken back into English.

Bellabella legends claim River's Inlet and the Burke and Dean channels as their place of origin. A confederation of Kokaitk, Oetlik, and Oeatlik, they were a particularly warlike nation, largely because they were flanked by the Tsimshian, and the Bella Coola (*qq.v.*) Haida war parties from Queen Charlotte Island also raided the Bellabella coasts.

Like most other Northwest Pacific tribes their social organization evolved clans and rank with nobles and lower class people. Unlike other tribes, such as the Bella Coola whose rank and property descended through males, such rank descended through females.

Beaver Indians singing and dancing.

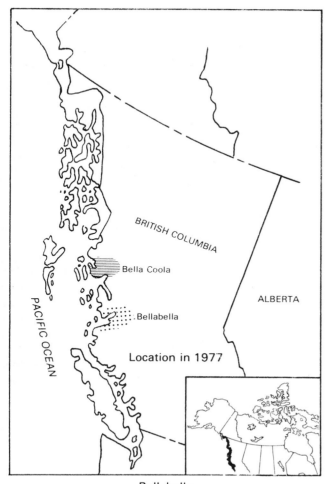

BRITISH COLUMBIA

Bella Coola

ALBERTA

Bellabella

PACIFIC OCEAN

Location in 1977

Bellabella

BIBLIOGRAPHY –

● HABERLY, LOYD. Pursuit of the Horizon, A Life of George Catlin. New York, NY: The Macmillan Co., 1948.
● SWANTON, JOHN R. The Indian Tribes of North America. Washington, DC: U.S. Government Printing Office, 1952.

BELLA COOLA

(Canada; British Columbia) live on the central Pacific coast. Although they speak a Salishan language, their present location isolates them from other Salishan-speaking peoples and places them among Wakashan (the Bellabella and River's Inlet Indians) and Athapaskan (the Carrier and Chilcotin) speaking groups. The term "Bella Coola" that labels them is derived from a Bella bella appellation *Bilxula or Blxwla*. Any meaning of this term other than the designation of the Bella Coola is unknown.

The Bella Coola presently occupy a site jusst above the mouth of the Bella Coola River, that flows westward into the North Bentinck Arm of the Burke Channel. Before the first quarter of this century additonal sites were regularly occupied. Within the Bella Coola Valley itself, there existed somewhat more than two dozen villages, and farther afield were two more clusters of villages, one of which lay at the Burke Channel. The other lay along the Dean and Kimsquit Rivers at the northern end of the Dean Channel. No term in the Bella Coola language denotes these three clusters as a whole. The area occupied by the villages in the Bella Coola Valley was known in Bella Coola as *nuxalk*. This term now designated the entire valley and appears in words for both the people *(nux-alk-mz* 'a Bella Coola') and the language *(?it-nuxalk* 'to speak Bella Coola').

The number of Bella Coola is now approximately 650. In the 1920s the population reached a low of 300-400, but before contact with Europeans, the population must have been in the thousands. Archaelogical evidence suggests the presence of human habitation in the region as long ago as AD 500. Linguistic evidence additionally suggests a relatively long separation of the Bella Coola language from the genetically related Salishan languages to the south. We may then suppose a Bella Coola presence on the Dean and Burke Channels for a similar length of time.

The native culture of the Bella Coola was consistent with that of the northwest coast societies that surrounded them. The economy was based primarily on the use of fish (especially salmon, abundant in the rivers of the area) and hunting. The wood and bark of the cedar tree supplied material for housing, canoes, clothing and utensils for hunting, fishing and cooking.

And, like the Kwakiutl, to whom they were related, the Bellabella had elaborate secret societies which handled the major religious functions.

Villages consisted of the wooden houses now famous among Pacific coast tribes. For food they relied mainly on seafood, both fish and mammals such as seals.

Bodiga and Maurelle were the first whited to establish contact with the Bellabella in 1775. Immediately afterwards they were visited by English and American traders and explorers. Mackenzie wrote not particularly welcome and he was always afraid of attack. Fort McLougulin was established in Bellabella Territory in 1833, but Victoria City's foundation in 1843 had a greater influence on their lives. By the 20th century they christianized and gave up all rituals.

In 1780 there were 2,700 Bellabella but a plague decimated their numbers. In 1900 there were 300; today there are about 900 living in the same area.

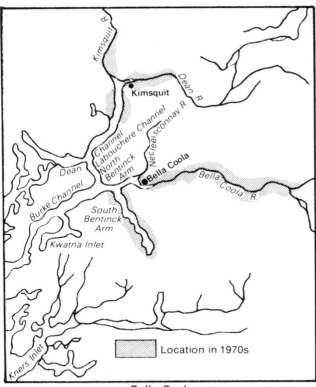

Bella Coola

A characteristic motif of Bella Coola social organization was village autonomy. Each of the separate villages possessed its influential members (recognized on the basis of wealth and potlatches), but no organized governing hierarchy, and corrdinated activity of the villages was rare. The organizing factor of Bella Coola life was membership in an "ancestral family" which passed to a person via patrilineal and matrilineal ancestry. An individual might be reckoned to belong to as many as eight ancestral families, descent being calculated for this purpose as far back as the great grandparents. It was through this membership that a person acquired his name(s), taken from the traditional oral accounts of the origin of each family. The motif of autonomy extended even to this aspect of a person's life. Marriage was generally endogamous to the ancestral family; this custom, was to preserve and reinforce the family. Independence is also reflected in accounts of Bella Coola cosmology that appear in the oral tradition, in accord with which each family was placed on earth in separate episodes and at separate locations.

Traditional life was organized about a yearly cycle that emphasized the gathering and storage of fish from early spring to late fall and the winter period of ceremonties centering on the societies called the *kusyut* and the *sisawk*. It is in the ceremonial performances that Bella Coola art is especialaly manifest in the carved and painted masks worn by the participants.

The relationship of the Bella Coola with other Indian groups in the area was generally amicable, but war was not unknown. In spite of gthe value placed on endogamous marriage, marriage occurred with non-Bella Coolas, especially between the Bella Coola and other the noethwestern coastal, mesoamerica, parts of Guatemala, and Venezuela, the parcelling out to specific bands within each tribe would be the work of securing fishing, hunting, and plant foods; each group would channel its take to each chief who would redistribute equitably the foods to all tribe members. Alaskan Tlingit Indians for generations sought out the nagoon berry, related to the raspberry of which one species was called the Arctic raspberry. They were known to mix the berries witha fish grease and fern leaves, which would be stored in in the earth.

Plains Indians women throughout the year would pick more than a dozen kinds of wild fruits and berries from persimmons to choke cherries, taking special pride in their task. Well known was the high-protein pemmican, made from pilverized strips of buffalo meat mixed with dried and ground berries and fat, yielding the long-keeping year-round food. Cultivated by the Blackfeet, tobacco was smoked in ritualistic prayers and dances. To counteract the strong taste, tobacco was modified with black berries, sumac leaves, and willow bark.

BIBLIOGRAPHY —

● BANCROFT, HUBERT HOWE. The Native Races of the Pacific States of the North America. San Francisco, CA: 1874.
● BOAZ, FRANZ, BILXULA. Annual Report of the U.S. National Museum. (pp. 646-51), 1895.
-----"The Mythology of the Bella Coola Indians." Memoirs of the American Museum of Natural History. , 1898.
● HODGE, FREDERICK WEBB. Handbook of American Indians North of Mexico. Washington: Government Printing Office, 1907.
● KOPOS, CLIFF. Bella Coola. Vancouver: Mitchell Press Limited, 1970.
● MCILWRAITH, T. F. Annual Archeological Report of the Minister of Education. Ontario, Canada: 1924-25.
● MURDOCK, GEORGE P. Ethnographic Bibliography of North America. New Haven, CT: Human Relations Area Files Press, 1975.
● SMITH, H. I. Ethnology Among the Bella Coola and Carrier Indians. American Anthropologist, (pp. 36- 40), 1925.
● SWANTON, JOHN R. The Indian Tribes of North America. Washington, DC: U.S. Government Printing Office, 1952.

BEOTHUKAN FAMILY

(Canada; Newfoundland) So far as known only a single tribe, called Beothuk, which inhabited the island of Newfoundland when first discovered, constituted this family, although existing vocabularies indicate marked dialectic differences. At first the Beothuk were classified either as Eskimauan or as Algonquian, but now, largely through the researches of Gatschet, it is deemed best to regard them as constituting a distinct linguistic stock. It is probable that in 1497 Beothukan people were met by Sebastian Cabot when he discovered Newfoundland, as he states that he met people "painted with red ocher," which is a marked characteristic of the Beothuk of later observers. Whitbourne, who visited Newfoundland in 1622, stated that the dwelling places of these Indians were in the North and West parts of the island, adding that "in war they use bows and arrows, spears, darts, clubs, and slings." The extinction of the Beothuk was due chiefly to the bitter hostility of the French and to Micmac invasion from Nova Scotia at the beginning of the 18th century, the Micmac settling in West Newfoundland as hunters and fishermen. For a time these dwelt in amity with the Beothuk, but in 1770, quarrels having arisen, a destructive battle was fought between the two peoples at the North end of Grand Pond. The Beothuk, however, lived on friendly terms with the Naskapi, or Labrador Montagnais, and the two peoples visited and traded with each other. Exasperated by the petty depredations of these tribes, the French, in the middle of the 18th century, offered a reward for every head of a Beothuk Indian. To gain this reward and to obtain the valuable furs they possessed, the more numerous Micmac hunted and gradually exterminated them as an independent people. The English treated the Beothuk with much less rigor; indeed, in 1810 Sir Thomas Duckworth issued a proclamation for their protection. The banks of the River of Exploits and its tributaries appear to have been their last inhabited territory.

De Laet describes these Newfoundland Indians as follows: "The height of the body is medium, the hair black, the face broad, the nose flat, and the eyes large; all the males are beardless, and both sexes tint not only their skin but also their garments with a kind of red color. And they dwell in certain conical lodges and low huts of sticks set in a circle and joined together in the roof. Being nomadic, they frequently change their habitations. They had a kind of cake made with eggs and baked in the sun, and a sort of pudding, stuffed in gut, and composed of seal's fat, livers, eggs, and other ingredients." He describes also their peculiar crescent-shaped birch-bark canoes, which had sharp keels, requiring much ballast to keep them from overturning: these were not more than 20 feet in length and they could bear at most 5 persons. Remains of their lodges, 30 to 40 feet in circumference and constructed by forming a slender frame of poles overspread with birch bark, are still traceable. They had both summer and winter dwellings, the latter often accommodating about 20 people

each. Jukes describes their deer fences or deer stockades of trees, which often extended for 30 miles along a river. They employed pits or caches for storing food, and used the steam bath in huts covered with skins and heated with hot stones. Some of the characteristics in which the Beothuk differed from most other Indians were a marked lightness of skin color, the use of trenches in their lodges for sleeping berths, the peculiar form of their canoes, the non-domestication of the dog, and the dearth of evidence of pottery making. Bonny-castle states that the Beothuk used the inner bark of *Pinus balsamifera* as food, while Lloyd mentions the fact that they obtained fire by igniting the down of the bluejay from sparks produced by striking together two pieces of iron pyrites. Peyton, cited by Lloyd, declares that the sun was the chief object of their worship. Carmack's expedition, donducted in behalf of the Beothic Society for the Civilization of the Native Savages, in 1827, failed to find a single individual of this once prominent tribe, although the island was crossed centrally in the search. As they were on good terms with the Naskapi of Labrador, they perhaps crossed the strait of Belle Isle and became incorporated with them.

BIBLIOGRAPHY —

● HODGE, FREDERICK WEBB. Handbook of American Indians North of Mexico. Washington: Government Printing Office, 1907.
● MURDOCK, GEORGE P. Ethnographic Bibliography of North America. New Haven, CT: Human Relations Area Files Press, 1975.
● SWANTON, JOHN R. The Indian Tribes of North America. Washington, DC: U.S. Government Printing Office, 1952.

BERSIAMITE

(Canada;) One of the small Algonquian tribes composing the eastern group of the Montagnais, inhabiting the banks of Bersimis River which enters St. Lawrence River near the gulf. These Natives became known to the French at an early date, and being of a peaceable and tractable disposition, were soon brought under the influence of the missionaries. They were accustomed to assemble once a year with cognate tribes at Tadoussac for the purpose of trade, but these have melted away under the influence of civilization. A trading post called Bersimis, at the mouth of Bersimis River had in 1902 some 465 Natives attached to it, but whether any of them were Bersiamite is not stated.

BIBLIOGRAPHY —

● HODGE, FREDERICK WEBB. Handbook of American Indians North of Mexico. Washington: Government Printing Office, 1907.
● MURDOCK, GEORGE P. Ethnographic Bibliography of North America. New Haven, CT: Human Relations Area Files Press, 1975.

BETOI

(South America; Columbia, Venezuela) (Betoy) spoke a dialect of the Tucano linguistic family. Now very likely extinct as a society, they were first described in the early 17th century by explorers and Jesuit missionaries who encountered these Indians in their native region of western Venezuela bordering on Colombia. along the Arauca River, a mountainous, humid, and naturalaly well-irrigated region. Betoi were culturally and linguistically related to neighboring peoples such as the Situfa, Ayrica, Ele, Arauca and several other societies. Very little is known about any of these people. The best information was gathered by three Jesuits, Gumilla (1745), Oveido y Banos (1824), and Rivero (1883) and in the first decades of the twentieth century by the anthropologist, Koch-Grunberg.

The Betoi were slash-and-burn horticulturalists who raised typical tropical forest crops, manioc and maize, assorted fruits such as pineapples and bananas (probably plantains). Hunting with bow and arrow was an important activity and among the game eated were puma, jaguar, tapir, peccary, and deer. They also ate snakes. Fishing was important and the Betoi made dugout canoes for travel along the many rivers. They made pottery cooking vessels, gourd containers, wove mats, and the Betoi proper made barkcloth clothing.

The Betoi were patrilineally organized under the leadership of an elder male, the chief, and lived in large extended-family households called *caney*. These communal dwellings were built in the usual tropical forest pole-and-thatch fashion, the thatch being either grass or palm leaves. Rivers (1883) noted that alaong the Girara River there were 18 such houses which had a total population of 450, an average of 25 persons in each house, some of which were as much as 200 feet long and 30 feet wide. These houses were customarily srtung aot along the river banks for the Betoi did not live in nucleated villages as did mant other propical forest peoples.

Marriage between household members or other close relatives was forbidden so that each extended family and probably nearby and closely-related families constituted an exogamic unit. Polygyny wa permitted, by there is no information about its importance or extent. The Betoi had the custom of arranging the marriages of their children within a year or so after their birth. When the children grew up and married, the event was celebrated by the two families at a drinking festival where *chicha* (manioc beer) was consumed. Prior to the ceremony, the male kinsmen of the betrothed couple hunted and fished in order to accumulate provisions for the wedding feast. Kinfolk throughout the area came to celebrate the

Betoi

wedding. The young man went to the bride's house in the company of an elder male relative to exchange gifts such as beads, *quirpas,* which were of economic and symbolic importance. These *quirpas,* made of shells gathered from the rivers, had monetary value, the longer the string of shells, the greater the value. *Quirpas* were used in trade with neighboring peoples and were also used to pay for labor within one's own group.

At the approaching birth of a child, the father took special precautions (the *couvade*). he spent a good deal of time lying down, mainly disengaged from norman activity, and refrained from hunting and doinfg such chores as cutting wood in the belief that these activities would be harmful to the newborn. The mother attended the father during this period and there were no special ceremonies for her benefit. Curiously, these people also practiced female infanticide.

At the death of an adult, the house was abandoned because it was considered to be contaminated by evil spirits. The family moved elsewhere and built another house. This custom has been described for the prople surrounding the Betoi and indeed it is widespread in tropical South America. Before leaving, the Betoi interred the dead man's body, his weapons, and ornaments under the house. Then the funeral ceremony, in which the closest relatives participated, took place. The ceremony was characterized by all adult relatives, male and female, playing musical instruments (gourd flutes). Flute-playing was especially important at funerals; however, the Betoi also used a hollow log drum which they hung over the ground and played with wooden clubs. The mourners painted themselves black with *genipa*. The widow, after participating in the ceremony, was supposed to spend a week or more wailing at the riverbank with her body painted black and her hair cut short. She was forbidden to remarry until a year had passed.

The Betoi believed in a sun god who was the creator and protector of mankind and in an evil spirit, *memelu,* which caused death. As with surrounding peoples such as the Jirara and Ayrica, there is a notable concept of complementary opposition between good and evil. The supernatural beings who caused flooding (possibly a Christian influence from missionaries), earthquakes, illness and death were forces of evil. A living force for good was the shaman who was able to cure illness by medicinal means but especially by grappling directly with the forces of evil against which he practiced his magical arts. When the shaman was engaged in curing, the patient and his relatives had to fast. The shaman was able to foresee the future after taking narcotic snuff. He also divined the meaning of bird and animal cries and made deductions appropriate to effecting cures of supernaturally-induced illnesses. He often interpreted his dreams.

Ordinary Betoi males could enhance their hunting and fishing ability and protect themselves against matural hazards in a number of ways, all of which were related to an overall struggle between good and evil forces and notions of homeopathic magic. For example, a man wounded his legs with a fish spine in order to catch fish; scratched his right arm with a peccary bone to insure hunting success; scarred his entire body to acquire bravery in inter-group hostilities; painted snakes on his legs to protect himself from snakebite. Sometimes houses as well were protected against human and supernatural enemies by building little huts in which benign and protecting spirits came to live.

BIBLIOGRAPHY —

● STEWARD, JULIAN H. Handbook of South American Indians. 7 Vols., Washington, DC: U.S. Govt. Printing Office, 1946-59.

BIDAI

(U.S.; Tex.) An extinct tribe, supposed to have belonged to the Caddoan stock, whose villages were scattered over a wide territory, but principally about Trintiy River, while some were as far North as the Neches or beyond. A creek emptying into Trinity River between Walker and Madison, bears the name of the tribe, as did also, according to La Harpe, a small bay on the coast North of Matagorda bay. A number of geographic names derived from this tribe survive in the region. The tribal tradition of the Bidai is that they were the oldest inhabitants of the country where they dwelt. This belief may have strengthened tribal pride, for although the Bidai were surrounded by tribes belonging to the Caddo confederacy, the people long kept their independence. They were neighbors of the Arkokisa, who lived on lower Trinity River and may have been their allies, for according to LaHarpe they were on friendly terms with that tribe while they were at war with the people dwelling on Matagorda bay. During the latter part of the 18th century the Bidai were reported to be the chief intermediaries between the French and the Apache in the trade in firearms; later they suffered from the political disturbances incident to the controversy between the Spaniards and the French, as well as from intertribal wars and the introduction of new diseases. As as result remnants of different villages combined, and the olden tribal organization was broken up. Little is known of their customs and beliefs, which were probably similar to those of the surrounding tribes of the Caddo confederacy. They lived in fixed habitations, cultivated the soil, hunted the buffalo, which ranged through their territory, and were said by Sibley in 1805 to have had "an excellent character for honesty and punctuality." At that time they numbered about 100, but in 1776-7 an epidemic carried off nearly half their number. About the middle of the 19th century a remnant of the Bidai were living in a small village 12 miles from Montgomery, Texas, cultivating maize, serving as cotton pickers, and bearing faithful allegiance to the Texans. The women were still skilled in basketry of "curious designs and great variety." The few survivors were probably incorporated by the Caddo.

BIBLIOGRAPHY —

● BOLTON, HERBERT EUGENE. Athanase de Mezieres and the Louisiana-Texas Frontier, 1768-1780. Cleveland, OH: The Arthur H. Clark Co., 1914.
● HODGE, FREDERICK WEBB. Handbook of American Indians North of Mexico. Washington: Government Printing Office, 1907.
● MURDOCK, GEORGE P. Ethnographic Bibliography of North America. New Haven, CT: Human Relations Area Files Press, 1975.
● SWANTON, JOHN R. The Indian Tribes of North America. Washington, DC: U.S. Government Printing Office, 1952.

BILOXI

(U.S.;La., Miss.) were first encountered by the French on the Gulf coast. That was in either 1688 or 1689. It was a peaceful encounter, and the first of a long series of Biloxi interactions with non-Indian groups.

The Biloxi called themselves the "First People." Europeans have called them *Annochy, Annochi, Biluxy, Bellochis,* and *Biluxi.* Today these "First People" have maintained their identity in central Louisiana where they have inter-married with Tunica and Choctaw. This tribal identity was strong enough to yield a unitary organization, the Tunica-Biloxi Tribe of Louisiana, in 1971. By 1975, the combined Tunica and Biloxi were recognized by the state of Louisiana, and the state government recommended Federal recognition.

Aboriginally, the Biloxi were typical of the settle horticultural pattern of the Southeastern United States, and among the first tribes on the Gulf Coastal Plain to feel the impact of the Europeans. Like others in the southeast, they soon found their fortunes tied to the politics of colonialism, and they began to suffer from the exigencies of disease and war. Never a large tribe, their population has declined steadily. There were a few hundred (420) at first contact. About a hundred thirty (70 in Texas and likely 60 in Louisiana) were counted in the 1850s; they now count about twenty-four in Louisiana with a few more in Oklahoma and Texas.

Tribal history, after initial white contact has involved a series of migrations inspired, in every case, by some European influence or another. As a result they are scattered across Louisiana, southeastern Oklahoma, and southwest into Texas and northern Mexico. The largest group remains in central Louisiana.

Their movements started in the 1720s when the French moved the tribe west to either Bayou St. John or Bayou Tchoupitoulas near New Orleans where they provided foodstuff for the fledgling French community. They had returned to their traditional village near Biloxi Bay by 1722, but their future was already linked to the French presence in the New World. Even today many of their descendants are French-speaking.

There are few other references to the Biloxi until after the French and Indian War. At that point the English allowed their Indian allies, the Creeks and Chickasaw, to pressure west a number of small tribes. Before European contact these small tribes, fearing the Creek and Chickasaw, had originally sought refuge on the coast.

The Biloxis and other associations with French and Spanish had merely antagonized old enemies. So they all began to shift west of the Mississippi River sometime after 1763. Groups that had closest French ties moved to the Spanish lands of central Louisiana, especially the Red River Valley. Not only the Biloxi, but also the Appalache, Alabama, Coushatta, Chatot, Pacana, Pasgcagoula, and Tohome or Mobilians all shifted to that area. The Biloxi settled on the west bank near

Biloxi

the junction of the Red with the Mississippi. This village was in Spanish territory across from the Tunica and Ofo villages. The Ofo were linguistaically similar people, logical neighbors. By 1780 this settlement was still occupied and contained Choctaw as well as Biloxi. By 1786, a Spanish grant of land was made to the Biloxi through their representative, a man named Borsa. It granted them land on the Avoyelles Prairie and was confirmed to Bosra in 1812 by the American government. According to both Biloxi and Tunica tradition, the Tunica and Ofo subsequently abandoned their villages in English territory and followed Biloxi across the river to the Avoyelles Prairie sometime araound 1786. Close interactions between these groups has been maintained and today, along with some Choctaw, they are all related. Before 1804, a Biloxi settlement had spring up adjacent to the Tunicana and Choctaw at Coulee des Grues near present-day Marksville, Louisiana. Conflicts arose over some game taken in a communal hunt, and the Biloxi sold their land to a Frenchman and moved again. Some likely went to Bosra's village, others went south to Bayou Rouge on the southern edge of the prairie--leaving three small villages (of 6 to 7 families each) in their wake. The Bayou Rouge settlement was composed of Alabama, Tunica, Ofo and Biloxi and had a Tunica chief, Panroy. However, most of the Biloxi had moved up Red River to a bluff at the Rigolet du Bon Dieu adjacent to their old friends, the Pascagoula, and across from two eastern groups, the Appalache and Tensas. This became their principal village, White Rock Village.

All these settlements continued well into the Americal Territorial Period. The Red River village was abandoned about 1825 when the chiefs took up lands further south on Bayou Boeuf. Two American traders claimed the village by right of a ratified sale in 1805, but archeological evidence suggests it was not totally abandoned until at least 1825.

Some of the residents of this village, White Rock Village, likely did leave it before 1805. Biloxi in East Texas, when encountered in 1830, stated they had left a village on the "Rigoles du Bon Dieu" in Louisiana prior to the Louisiana Purchase. Rather than to accede to Anglo-American domination they fled to the Nueces River in Spanish Texas, following their old Anglophobia. Biloxi descendants among the Black Seminole at Brackettsville, Texas, and Nacimiento, Mexico, also remembered this Red River village.

These Texas bands, dispersed from White Rock or Rigolets village, went firtst to Biloxi Bayou in Angelina County. They were in a village on the Nueces River in 1830. By the middle 1830s, some Biloxi had been drawn into the rebellion against the Americans led by the Mexican-Indian, Vicente Cordova, at Nacogdoches. In the years between 1838 and 1840, Biloxi accused of aiding Cordova were killed by Anglos. Some managed friendly terms with local whites, while other Biloxi left with Cordova's group in 1838. These were reported to have dispersed to the upper Sabine and Red River near Shreveport, Louisiana. A few of their descendants are still to be found there, in the Spanish-Apache- Choctaw communities on the Sabine River.

The other villages were gradually abandoned by the late 1820s. By then the Biloxi, Choctaw and some Pascagoula gathered on Bayou Boeuf with their chiefs; Mataha, the head Biloxi chief, Mingo, the Biloxi chief from Bayou Rouge and White Rock, and Big Head, a Pascagoula chief. Their settlement there encompassed some 60,200 acres and was again taken for debts by the American factors in the 19th century. Most of these Biloxi seem to have stayed in Louisiana, but joined their Choctaw neighbors on the marginal lands along Bayou Boeuf. It came to be called Pinewoods or Indian Creek. Biloxi and Choctaw lived in a dispersed settlement scattered along Bayous Robert, Clear and Indian Creek. Small splinter groups drifted into the Bayou Nez Pique drainage by the 1840s. Some with Pascagoula may have moved to the Alabama in Texas and a few Pascagoula were still there in the early 1900s. The 1900s saw the removal of some Biloxi and Choctaw from Louisiana to Oklahoma, and a few lived there on the Kiamichi River and among the Creeks on the Canadian.

Most Biloxi survived as a community in central Louisiana, and their descendants are still to be found near Lecompte an/or Marksville, Louisiana.

All the Biloxis spoke a Siouan language, its closest relative was Ofo, and after the Louisiana migrations the Biloxi were constantly associated with Tunica and ofo speakers. They also interacted with a number of Muskoghean speakers and used the Mobilian jargon, termed *Yama* by Louisiana Indians, almost as much as Biloxi. No longer used in conversation, the last Biloxi texts were recorded in the 1934 from Mrs. Emma Dorsey Jackson, the mother of Mrs. Rose Jckson Pierite, the widow of the last Tunica-Biloxi descendants near Marksville, Louisiana, have retained many words, and elderly people there can still sing many of the traditional songs.

The socio-political organization of the Biloxi has also undergone a number of changes. Apparently the Biloxi had some sort of clan system. Two clans could be recalled in the 19th century: *Ita anyadi* and *Onti anyadi,* Deer and Bear. These were retained at Bayou Boeuf where they may have been reinforced by interaction with the Alabama and Koasati who retained their totemic clan groups. By 1907 the clans had all but disappeared. However, the offspring of Biloxi women and Tunica fathers often used a separate Biloxi surname, the mother's family name. They used that name in the Biloxi community and another (patrinomial) in the Tunica village. Most Biloxi-Tunica unions resulted in the offspring living with the mother's family. In the 1920s the tribal interaction between the Bayou Boeuf Biloxi and Choctaw and the Tunixa intensified inter-tribal cances, stickball games drew the groups closer, and marriages between Biloxi, Tunica, and Koasati increased. Elderly people from Indian Creek village comment that they heard the Mobilian jargon more often after that. By the 1930s the Louisiana villages were breaking up; some men were following the sawmills to east Texas, others were moving their families into share-cropper cabins on plantations along Bayou Boeuf. The chiefs began losing much of their traditional authority, a process that seems to date back to the initial Texas migration from White Rock before 1805. The last traditional Biloxi-Choctaw chief at Indian Creek was a man named Obe Blue Eye. Later, in 1925, Elijah Barbry, an Tunica, was elected by both tribes. Since his time the Tunica-Biloxi have been united politically as well as by kinship. The last traditional chief, Joseph Pierite, Sr., died in 1975. He was of both Tunica and Biloxi descent. His son, Joseph Pierite, Jr., is present tribal chairman of the combined groups. Today an elected chairman echoes the political role of the chiefs, all of whom were also elected or appointed after the beginning of the nineteenth century.

Until the 1930s the chiefs also had certain religious functions, since they performed marriages. Gradually such traditional religion became a meld of Biloxi-Tunica-Choctaw-Ofo practices. Mourning ceremonies for the Choctaw and Biloxi became identical. A six months mourning period was broken by a final "cry" held by the women at the grave of the deceased, with a feast held that night. The sun and moon continued to be sacred, as were fire and cardinal directions. Certain were highly revered: the eagle, the rattlesnake, the owl, and the buzzard. These were all "medicine" animals and are still held in high regard by Biloxi and Tunica alike. Shamanism persisted and medicine people, both men and women, ere highly regarded. One was a specialist in curing respiratory deseases. During flu epidemics she walked from Indian Creek to both the Tunica and Coushatta communities to treat the sick, a distance of over fifty miles.

In the 1920s Jeff Abbey, a Koasati chief, introduced Christianity to the Biloxi and Choctaw. After his initial efforts the Methodists maintained a church on Indian Creek near Woodworth, Louisiana. Later, a Baptist church was established at the Tunica-Biloxi community near Marksville, Louisiana. Today others are Catholic or Pentecostal Christians. Certain practices, like grave offerings, placed in the coffins by family and friends, and special attention given cemeteries as sacred places continue. Myths are still recounted and the old religion honored if not commonly practiced.

Traditinal games, especially the men's and women's stickball play, *tolih*, continued well into the late 1930s. Missionaries discouraged it because of the drinking and gambling that accompanied it, but all older people still recall it wistfully. Ball sticks are still manufactured periodically, but no games have been played for nearly thirty years. A ball field, blessed by the eagle, was maintained about midway between the Tunica community at Marksville and the Choctaw-Biloxi community along Bayou Boeuf. Other fields and dance grounds were maintained at the villages.

The Biloxi-Choctaw were famous for their plaited cane baskets, a craft which has languished in the past two decades. However, Mrs. Rose Jackson Pierite and her daughters still weave traditional Biloxi coiled pinestraw basketry, which is distinct from that of their neighbors, the Koasati and Alabama.

In the 1840s the Biloxi preferred bright calico hunting shirts (collarless, long-sleeved, shirts worn outside and hanging below the hips), buckskin britches and brass or silver ornaments. A few at Marksville still do the fine tanning and smoking of deerskins for which the Tunica and Biloxi were famous. One man still makes fine brooches and rings from silver coins, another makes traditional horn spoons. Nineteenth century styles are still worn on ceremonial occasions. As late as the 1930s ball players had special dance costumes, adorned with silver and tiny bells or thimbles, and the chiefs still wore silver "crowns" or hatbands.

Cypress knees or iron kettle drums beat for the Horse Dance, Duck Dance, Chicken Dance, and Coon Dance. These dances lasted all night and sometimes a few, like the Choctaw "Changing Partners" Dance popular at Indian Creek, were danced to a fiddle tune. The Indian Creek Biloxi-Choctaw were famous for their fiddle players, and these men often played for whites as well as Indians. Today older men and women who still know the songs, keep the beat on the floor with a walking stick. Grandchildren *still* learn the old dance songs and steps. The children are beginning to listen again.

Construction is underway on a new tribal center at Marksville, Louisiana, and a new housing project is being planned. The Biloxi, along with their Tunica kinsmen, have refused to give up, to disappear or to assimilate. They are proud of their culture, and have no intention of giving up. They look forward to a new prosperity. *(see map page XIV)*

BIBLIOGRAPHY —

● BOLTON, HERBERT EUGENE. Athanase de Mezieres and the Louisiana-Texas Frontier, 1768-1780. Cleveland, OH: The Arthur H. Clark Co., 1914.
● DEBO, ANGIE. The Road to Disappearance. Norman, OK: University of Oklahoma Press, 1941.
● DORSEY, JAMES OWEN. The Biloxi Indians of Louisiana. Salem, MA: Salem Press, 1893.
● DORSEY, JAMES OWEN, AND JOHN R. SWANTON. A Dictionary of the Biloxi and Ofo Languages... Washington: Bureau of Ethnology, Bulletin 47, 1912.
● FOREMAN, GRANT. A Traveler in Indian Territory. The Journal of Ethan Allen Hitchcock... Cedar Rapids, IA: The Torch Press, 1930.
● HODGE, FREDERICK WEBB. Handbook of American Indians North of Mexico. Washington: Government Printing Office, 1907.
● MILLING, CHAPMAN J. Red Carolinians. Chapel Hill, NC: The University of North Carolina Press, 1940.
● MURDOCK, GEORGE P. Ethnographic Bibliography of North America. New Haven, CT: Human Relations Area Files Press, 1975.
● SWANTON, JOHN R. The Indian Tribes of the Lower Mississippi Valley and Adjacent Coast of the Gulf of Mexico. Washington: Bureau of Ethnology, 1911.
----- The Indian Tribes of North America. Washington, DC: U.S. Government Printing Office, 1952.
● WISSLER, CLARK. Indians of the U.S., Four Centuries of Their History and Culture. New York, NY: Doubleday, Doran & Co., 1940.

BLACKFEET RESERVATION

(U.S.; Mt.) is located in Glacier and Pondera Counties. It comprises an area of some 906,000 acres, of which 120,000 acres are tribal land, 775,000 acres are allotted land, 11,000 acres are government land, and the rest non-Indian land.

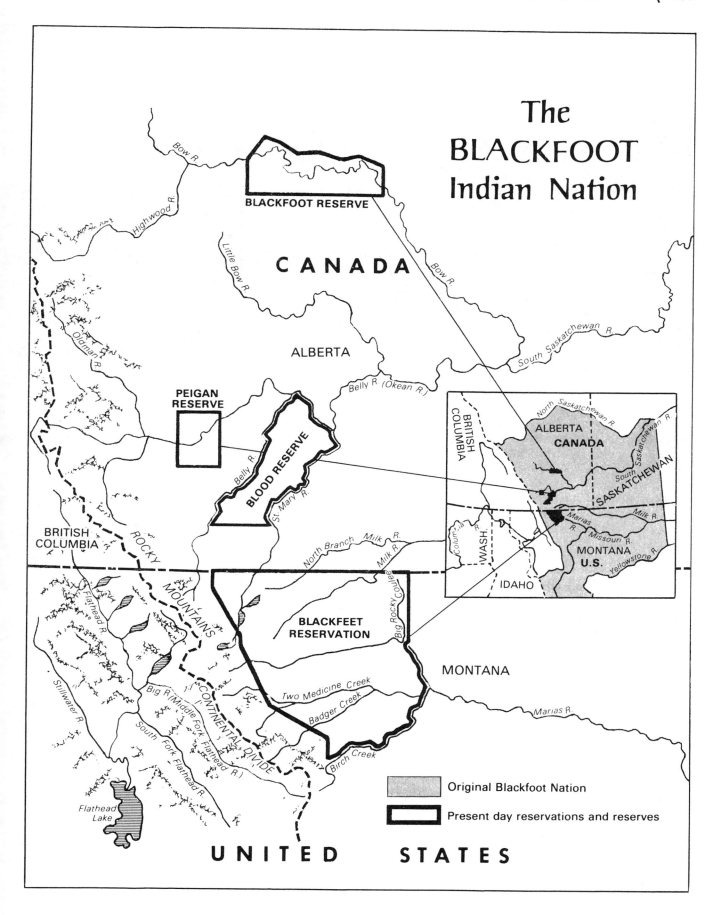

The
BLACKFOOT
Indian Nation

BLACKFOOT RESERVE

CANADA

Bow R.

Highwood R.

Little Bow R.

ALBERTA

Belly R. (Okean R.)

PEIGAN
RESERVE

Belly R.

BLOOD RESERVE

St. Mary R.

North Branch   Milk   R.

Milk R.

BRITISH
COLUMBIA

ROCKY

MOUNTAINS

Oldman R.

BRITISH
COLUMBIA

ALBERTA
CANADA

North Saskatchewan R

South Saskatchewan R.

SASKATCHEWAN

South Saskatchewan

Milk R.

Marias
R.

Missouri R.

Columbia R.

WASH.

IDAHO

MONTANA
U.S.

Yellowstone R.

South Saskatchewan R.

Big Rocky Coulee

BLACKFEET
RESERVATION

MONTANA

Flathead R.

CONTINENTAL DIVIDE

Big R. (Middle Fork Flathead R.)

South Fork Flathead R.

Stillwater R.

Two Medicine Creek

Badger Creek

Birch Creek

Marias R.

Flathead
Lake

Original Blackfoot Nation

Present day reservations and reserves

UNITED   STATES

Encampment of Blackfoot Indians

The residents of the reservation are Blackfoot Indians, descendants of the loose confederacy of Piegan, Blood, and the Blackfoot proper Indians which make up the Blackfoot peoples. They are of Algonquin stock. The Blackfoot were gathered onto the present reservation in 1888.

Of more than 6,000 Indian residents, more than 40 percent are unemployed. The median family income is $4,500 per year. The education level is 9th grade, and education grants are available to tribal members for up to $450 annually.

The Blackfoot tribe is organized under the Indian Reorganization act with a constitution and by-laws. The governing body is the popularly elected Blackfoot Tribal Business Council, which consists of nine members elected for 2-year terms. The average annual income for the entire Blackfoot tribe is estimated to be $500,000, most of it derived from minerals on the land, and some from other miscellaneous sources. The tribal headquarters are in Browning, Montana.

BIBLIOGRAPHY –

● INDIAN OFFICE REPORT. 1873, 1894.

BLACKFOOT

(Canada; Alberta) are an important Algonquin confederacy of the northern plains, consisting of the three tribes of Piegan, Blood, and Northern Blackfoot. Related to the Blackfoot are the Gros Ventre and the Sarsi.

The Blood, or *Kainah,* are an Algonquin tribe now living on the Blood Reserve in Alberta, Canada. The Blood are a division of the Blackfoot. The word *Kainah* maeans "many chiefs," but the term *Blood* probably oriiginated with the Cree, who applied it to the tribe's habitat of painting hands and bodies with red pigment for ceremony.

Until confined to their reservations in the late 19th century, the Blackfoot controlled most of the territory from the North Saskatchewan River in Canada to the southern headstreams of the Missouri River in Montana.

The origin of the name *Blackfoot* is dispute, but it is believed to have a relationship to the discoloring of the Indians' moccasins by the ashes of the prairie fires. It may, in addition, have reference to black-painted moccasins worn by several Indian tribes in the plains.

The seminomadic culture of the Blackfoot has been that of the plains tribes generally. They have been roving buffalo hunters, dwelling in tipis and shifting periodically from place to place, without permanent habitations, without pottery art or canoes, and without agricultural products except tobacco. By 1800, the Blackfoot had horses, and became noted for their many horse herds. Spreading over the plains region, they were constantly at war with their neighbors the Cree, Crow, Assiniboine, Flatheads, Dakota, and Kutenai. The Gros Ventre and Sarsi lived under their protection, however. While never regularly at war with the

United States, their general relationship with whites was one of distance at best.

Early estimates of the population of the Blackfoot gave the size of the tribe at 2,500 warriors, or 9,000 members in 1790. Becauseof disease and epidemics, the population of the Blackfoot is believed to have dropped considerably in the next 75 years. The official Indian report for 1858 estimated the population at a little over 7,000. By 1900 they were reported to number 4600. By the early 1970s, the population of the Blackfoot was at 12,000.

(see map page XV)

BIBLIOGRAPHY –

● MCFEE, MALCOLM. Modern Blackfeet. New York, NY: Holt, Rinehart, and Winston, Inc., 1972.
● MEANY, EDMOND S. History of the State of Washington. New York, NY: The Macmillan Co., 1909.
Indian Office Report. 1854, 1857, 1865, 1866, 1870.
● PHILLIPS, PAUL C. Forty Years on the Frontier, As Seen in the Journals and Reminiscences of Granville Stuart. Cleveland, OH: The Arthur H. Clart Co., 1925.
● QUAIFE, MILO M. The Journals of Captain Meriwether Lewis and Sergeant John Ordway... Madison, WI: State Historical Society of Wisconsin, 1916.
● WEBB, WALTER PRESCOTT. The Great Plains. Boston, MA: Ginn & Co., 1931.
● WILLARD-SCHULTZ, JAMES. Bird Woman (Sacajawea) the guide of Lewis and Clark. Boston, MA: New York, NY: Houghton Mifflin Co., 1918.
● WISSLER, CLARK. Indians of the U.S., Four Centuries of Their History and Culture. New York, NY: Doubleday, Doran & Co., 1940.
-----"Material Culture of the Blackfoot Indians." Anthropological Papers of the American Museum of Natural History. no. 5, 1910.

BORRADOS

(U.S.; N.Mex.) A tribe which, formerly resided in Tamaulipas, Nuevo Leon, and Coahuila. There is evidence that the tribe or a portion of it lived at one time in Texas, as the same authority says that the country of the lower Lipan Indians joined on the East that the Karankawa and Borrados in the province of Texas. The relationship of this tribe to the Coahuiltecan group is expressly affirmed by Bartolome Garcia.

BIBLIOGRAPHY –

● HODGE, FREDERICK WEBB. Handbook of American Indians North of Mexico. Washington: Government Printing Office, 2 vols., 1907-10.
● MURDOCK, GEORGE P. Ethnographic Bibliography of North America. New Haven, CT: Human Relations Area Files Press, 1975.
● SWANTON, JOHN R. The Indian Tribes of North America. Washington, DC: U.S. Government Printing Office, 1952.

BOTOCUDO

(South America; Brazil) is a name now used primarily for a tribe in eastern Brazil, classified linguistically as macro-Ge. Historically, the Botocudo occupied a considerable stretch of semi-mountainous forest. Their habitat was a region inland from the Atlantic coast between the Rio Pardo and Rio Doce, in what are now the Brazilian states of Esparito Santo and Minas Gerais. The Botocudo came into special prominence in Brazilian national affairs during the 19th century. They were engaged in a perpetual and often bloody conflict with the expanding frontier society. By the early 20th century, however, most of their once numerous bands had been subdued. Botocudo are now classified by ethnologists as "culturally extinct."

The name *Botocudo* derives from the Portuguese word *botoque*. This is used by Brazilians for the impressively large wooden lip and ear discs, which were the characteristic bodily ornament of Botocudo men and women. The name has also been used for two tribes of southern Brazil; the Ge-speaking Aweikoma and Tupi-speaking Xeta. Both of these groups used lip ornaments. Neither however is closely related to the Botocudo. In the historical literature, Botocudo have also been called *Aimore* (or *Aimbore, Ambure*), *Guerens, Borun,* and *Engerakmung.*

The Botocudo seem aboriginally to have been a nomadic hunting and gathering people. They roamed through the forests in bands of from 50 to 200 or more persons. In 1884 their total population was estimated to be 5,000. Just how many distinct bands there were remains an open question. One reliable account specifically enumerates ten. Judging from overall population figures, there may have been many more.

Botocudo

The aboriginal economy was based primarily upon hunting, fishing, and collecting. During the 19th century, foodstuffs were obtained as well in raids on Brazilian settlements. Along with other eastern Brazilian tribes, hunting technology focused upon use of the bow and arrow. These implements enabled Botocudo to make use of numerous species, especially tapir, wild pigs, monkeys, capibaras, and various large game birds. They used the bow and arrow as well in fishing.

In the Botocudo area, as in much of central Brazil, there is a marked seasonal variation in rainfall. During winter (May through September) it is dry, although not so dry as in some interior regions. And during summer (October through April) it is wet, with heavy rainfalls. This has affected the Botocudo adaptation. It was primarily during the dry season when collecting assumed special importance. For at that time certain key fruits ripened, especially sapaucaia (*Lecythis pisonis*) and coco imburu (*Coos, sp.*)

The highest-level unit of Botocudo social organization was the politically autonomous band. Bands were very often in conflict with one another. At the head of each band was a chief, whose influence seems to have depended primarily upon "supernatural power". Indeed, all chiefs were shamans (*yikegn*). They derived their power through interactions with benevolent spirits known as *maret*. But it is unclear just how much political power chiefs actually wielded. Some evidence suggests that their leadership was continually subject to challenge.

Each band was composed of a number of distinct household groups. The household in turn consisted usually of more than one nuclear family, occupying a single hut. Unfortunately, we do not know what rule of residence was operative. As regards to other aspects of the internal organization of bands as well, little is known. We cannot say whether there were clans, age groups, or other collective associations. Even the structure of their kinship terminology remains to be determined. On the basis of fragmentary data, it has been suggested that it may resemble a "generation system."

At age 7 or 8 boys and girls had their lips and ears pierced. No doubt this was a key life-cyclic event, as the large (7.6 to 10 cm. in diameter) lip and ear discs were probably emblematic of "Botocudo-ness." Yet there is no evidence of an associated collective ceremony. At some time (probably puberty) boys began wearing as well the characteristic penis sheath, with the penis sometimes tucked under a cord around the waist. While such sheaths were probably makers of manhood, however, there is again no evidence of an associated collective ceremony. The descriptions of ceremonial dances indicate only that these were performed in circular and semi-circular formations.

Botocudo are said to have believed in multiple souls, a given individual having as many as six. Sickness seems to have been related to soul loss. Most Botocudo medical beliefs concerned the efficacy of plant remedies. Botocudo had shamans, who learned of plant remedies from the *maret* spirits. But cures seem not to have been effected directly through supernatural agency.

Several Botocudo myths have been recorded. One concerns the origin of thunderstorms. Another relates how Hummingbird originally hoarded all of the water, which was finally liberated by Irara. Still another concerns the origin of cooking fire. This was originally in possession of Carrion Vulture, but it was stolen from him by Mutum. There are as well a number of other tales, including stories about the *maret* spirits.

Botocudo history goes back to the 16th century. Botocudo have been identified with the ancient Aimore, who at that early date harrassed the Portuguese colonists. The colonists responded with violence, and so began a bloody war that continued into the 19th century. Numerous atrocities have been alleged on both sides, the colonists even reportedly having poisoned the Indians and infected them with contagious diseases, transmitted through contaminated clothing left as gifts. Whatever the case, by the early 19th century many Botocudo bands had concluded peace. But a number of them continued on hostile terms.

Various heroic efforts were made by missionaries and others to protect these Indians. Around 1824 Guido Tomas Marliere, with help from the indigenous chief Pocrane, endeavored to settle the Botocudo in "colonies". This was followed by similar attempts. But even into the 20th century a few bands, especially those along the Rio Doce, remained openly hostile. They were finally settled around 1910 by the newly formed Indian Protection Service (SPI). In 1926 these Botocudo were reported to be localized at two posts situated on the Rio Doce, Pancas (in Espirito Santo) and Guido Marliere (in Minas Gerais). By 1939, the ethnologist Curt Nimuendaju found only 13 Botocudo at Pancas and 58 at Guido Marliere. Neither of these posts is in existence today. From all appearances, aboriginal Botocudo culture has vanished.

BIBLIOGRAPHY —

● STEWARD, JULIAN H. Handbook of South American Indians. 7 Vols., Washington, DC: U.S. Govt. Printing Office, 1946-59.

BRIGHTON RESERVATION

(U.S.; Fla.) located in Glade County, is home (as of 1969) to 272 members of the Seminole Indian tribe. Copmprising an area of 35,805 acres, the reservation is totally owned by the Seminole.

Following many years of conflict and disagreement between the United States Government and the Seminole, particularly under the leader Osceola, a truce between the Florida Seminoles and the United States was finally signed in 1934. Another such treaty was concluded in 1937. When troops were withdrawn, the Seminole continued to fear capture and exile. They lived in scattered locations, and pursued a nomadic existence, mostly by hunting and fishing. The development of the Brighton Reservation, along with the Big Cyprus and Hollywood Reservations, enabled the Seminole to ease their anxieites concerning the intentions of the whites.

Speaking a dialect of Crow-Creek, the Seminole live in small houses built with cyprus poles and thatched with palmetto leaves. Although the homes are still substandard, there have been recent attempts to improve conditions. On the land, the residents work in several trades. Some are cattlemen, some are cowboys, others are farm hands. Members make handicrafts for tourists, and run several shops, including a textile shop, trading center, and animal farm. Those that work off the reservation include technicians, heavy equipment operators, welders, construction workers, contrac-

tors, and orange-grove workers. Of the annual tribal income of several hundred thousand dollars, most of it comes from farming, business, and forestry.

The Seminole tribe has a constitution which was ratified in 1957. It has an elected five-member tribal council as its governing body, and problems of government, law, education, welfare, and recreation are handled through standing committees. The reservation has a housing authority to deal with the housing problem; a tribal development company; a village arts and crafts enterprise; and land development, recreation, and cattle raising enterprises. The reservation also raises mink and mines phosphates.

Services on the reservation include available water through electricity; sewer service for new housing; and a health clinic. There is also a theatre and community center on the reservation.

The temperature is always moderate. The nearby Florida State Indian Reservation, of 108,000 acres, which is administered by the Seminole and Miccosukee tribes, allows for hunting and fishing for all reservation members.

BRULE

(U.S.; S.Dak.) are a sub-band of the Teton division of the Dakota tribe. The Highland people, or Upper Brule, are on the Lower Brule Reservation, in Lower Brule.

The Brule were of woodland origin with a culture and economy based on hunting, gathering and fishing, and supplemented by limited horticulture. As they moved westward, they acquired horses and adopted the cultural pattern of equestrian nomads whose economic base was the buffalo, horse, and trade.

The Brule were habitually at war with other tribes, such as the Arikara and the Pawnee, as were all the divisions of the Dakotas, but they did not actively resist white immigration until the whites began to intrude in great numbers and decimate the buffalo herds. With the beginnings of the Plains Wars, the United States Government intervened. The Treaty of April 29, 1868 between the Dakota and United States Government was to a large degree brought about by the exertions of Swift Bear, a Brule chief. However, the treaty terms were subsequently broken by incoming whites, and further attempts to reach treaty agreements were to a great degree unsuccessful until the Dakota were relegated to their reservations by 1890.

Brule means "Burnt Thigh," the French translation of the Brule name *Sichangxu*. Mentioned by Lewis and Clark as early as 1804, they numbered

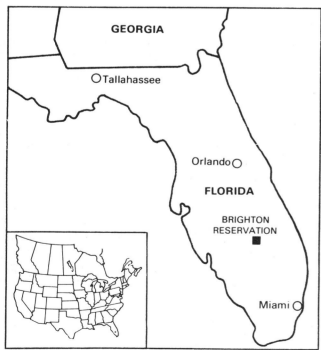

Brighton Reservation

Brule

several hundred at the beginning of the 19th century. They were then located on both sides of the Missouri, White, and Teton Rivers.

By the early 1970s, the Brule numbered over 10,000. There are approximately 7,000 Indian residents on the Rosebud Reservation, and several families on Pine Ridge Reservation, South Dakota. On the Lower Brule Reservation, there are approximately 600 Indian residents.

The Rosebud Reservation was organized under the Indian Reservation Reorganization Act of 1934 and operates under both a constitution and bylaws approved in the 1930s. The 22-member tribal council represents the 21 reservation districts. The Lower Brule reservation operates under a charter ratified in 1936 and a constitution and bylaws approved in 1960. It has seven member Tribal Council popularly elected. The Rosebud Reservation of nearly 1 million acres, is one of the larger reservations in South Dakota. The Lower Brule Reservation, however, is one of the smallest in both size (114,000 acres) and population.

BIBLIOGRAPHY —

● COUES, ELLIOTT. Forty Years a Fur Trader on the Upper Missouri... New York, NY: Francis P. Harper, 1898.
● GRINNELL, GEORGE BIRD. The Fighting Cheyennes. New York, NY: Charles Scribner's Sons, 1915.
● HEBARD, GRACE RAYMOND., E. A. BRININSTOOL. The Bozeman Trail; Historical Accounts of the Blazing of the Overland Routes into the Northwest, and the Fights with Red Cloud's Warriors. Cleveland, HO: The Arthur H. Clark Co.

● HYDE, GEORGE E. Spotted Tail's Folk. Norman, OK: University of Oklahoma Press, 1937.
● RICHARDSON, ALFRED TALBOT. Life, Letters and Travels of Father Pierre-Jean de Smet, S. J. 1801-1873. New York, NY: Francis P. Harper, 1905.
● WISSLER, CLARK. Indians of the U.S., Four Centuries of Their History and Culture. New York, NY: Doubleday, Doran & Co., 1940.

CABBASAGUNTI

(Canada; Quebec) A small body of Indians dwelling in 1807 in the village of "Saint Francais," on St. Francis River, Quebec, in which they wee named Cabbassaguntiac, i.ec., 'people of Cabbassaguntiquoke,' signifying 'the place where sturgeon abound.' The form Cobbisseconteag has been replaced by the modern Cobbosseecontee as the name of what formerly was Winthrop pond and outlet which flows into Kennebec River in Kennebec County, Maine. These Native Americans, it is reported by Kendall, regarded themselves not only as inhabitants of Cabbassaguntiquoke, but also as true *cabassas,* or sturgeons, because one of their ancestors, having declared that he was a sturgeon, leaped into this stream and never returned in human form. They related a tale that below the falls of Cobbosseecontee River the rock was hewn by the ax of a mighty manito.

BIBLIOGRAPHY —

● HODGE, FREDERICK WEBB. Handbook of American Indians North of Mexico. Washington: Smithsonian Institution: BAE Bulletin No. 30: U.S. GPO, 1907.
● SWANTON, JOHN R. The Indian Tribes of North America. Smithsonian Institution: BAE Bulletin No. 145: U.S. GPO, 1952.

CACAOPERA

(Central America; El Salvador) from *cacao-uara,* "river of cacao," is Matagalpa-speaking tribe of Indians living in the remote part of northeastern El Salvador, in the Department of Morazan; they inhabit two major villages, Cacaopera and Lislique. Little is known of their population or culture; they have been pushed back into the isolated backland by the more agressive Ladino culture of El Salvador, and are almost never brought into contact with the rest of the country.

BIBLIOGRAPHY —

● SWANTON, JOHN R. The Indian Tribes of North America. Washington, DC: U.S. Government Printing Office, 1952.
● CACHOPOSTALES (U.S.; Tex.) A tribe living near the Pampopa who resided on Nueces River, Texas. They were possibly Coahuiltecan.

CADECHA

(U.S.; Fla.) A former Timuquanan tribe in the Utina confederacy of middle Florida.

BIBLIOGRAPHY —

● HODGE, FREDERICK WEBB. Handbook of American Indians North of Mexico. Washington: Smithsonian Institution: BAE Bulletin No. 30: U.S. GPO, 1907.
● SWANTON, JOHN R. The Indian Tribes of North America. Smithsonian Institution: BAE Bulletin No. 145: U.S. GPO, 1952.

CADDO

(U.S.; La., Tex.) from their own name, *Kadohadacho,* "real Caddo," are a major Muskhogean-speaking tribe living in the southern Red River country of Louisiana and Texas; they are one of the least known major tribes of the United States. They were part of one of the three primary branches of the Caddoan Confederacy, the others being the Natchitoches and Hasinai.

When first met by Hernando de Soto in 1541, the Caddo occupied lands in Louisiana, and were the descendants of one of the great mound-building cultures of prehistoric North America. This location became the center of a contest for hegemony between France, Britain, Spain and the United States; tragically, the Caddo became inadvertently embroiled in these battles; and following the Louisiana Purchase, they were forced to cede their homelands in 1835 and migrated to Texas in the belief that they were escaping further conflict. There, they became the predominate tribe in that area, and ultimately gave the name *tejas* (tay-shas, meaning "friends, or allies") to the state. But with the settlement of the War with Mexico and the entry of Texas into the Union, they found that the formerly hospitable environment had radically changed, and in 1859 they Caddo were again forced to flee; this time they went into neighboring Oklahoma (then Indian Territory), where they were settled on lands located on the banks of the Washita River. Today, about 850 people, including remnants of the Anadarko, occupy a 63,608-acre reservation centering around Anadarko in Caddo, Canadian and Grady counties.

Early Caddoan dwellings were large dome-shaped, thatched structures, some measuring up to 60 feet in diameter and housing eight or ten families; these were supplemented by ceremionial houses of wood, which were built upon huge flat-topped man-made earthen mounds, hence the term "mound buildiers." Their culture was constructed around an intensive agricultural pattern, which they followed more actively than did their neighbors; it was based upon the cultivation of corn, beans, squash, seeds, nuts and tobacco. While they also did some hunting--chiefly for bear, deer, and small game--this became far more important after the acquisition of the horse, when they ranged out into the Southern Plains after the buffalo. The Caddo were one of the few Indian peoples who used the domesticated dog in hunting.

Caddoans were well-built, handsome people, with buckskin garments made from deerskin by the women; in summer time, they often went almost nude. They painted or tattooed their faces and bodies in elaborate patterns--the women were noted for this trait--and the men were famed for the elaborate hair decorations which often made use of colored dyes and feathers. The nobles of both sexes deformed the skull as a stauts symbol in a manner which elongated the top of the head to an extreme degree. An unusual custom was the practice of greeting strangers by weeping extravagantly when they came into the villages. Marriages were apparently very brittle, with divorces often and readily obtained by simple ritual separation. Matrilineal clans seem to have been customary; unwanted babies were killed off shortly after birth, but those children who were retained were nursed for years--often until puberty. The political structure had a highly-developed caste system in which nobels and persons with special skills held favored roles; there was an equally strong bureaucracy in the social life.

Shamans were the dominant religious leaders, and conducted elaborate ceremonies which persisted into historic times. Prisoners were tortured before being killed and eaten; this, including human sacrifice was not regarded as necessarily bad-- the act of sacrifice was necessary to feed the deities, and to keep the cycle of life-renewal unbroken. Belief in an after-life was customary, and the deceased were buried with their personal possesssions in an elaborate funerary observance. One interesting religious belief held that the First Person was a female, who gave birth to two daughters, one of whom eventually became the Mother of all the Caddo people.

Games were very popular among the Caddo, and they developed a wide variety of amusements; however, gambling was not as prevalent among them as with most Indian tribes. They have retained a remarkable proportion of the ancestral songs and dances which were once common, and the visitor to the Caddo region today will often be able to witness social affairs including the popular "Give-away Dance," which is perhaps the best-known.

Weaving was a well-known Caddo art, in which great use was made of nettle, bark and similar plant fibers. Pottery was an even greater art of these people--the incised blackware vessels which they made in great numbers have been familiar art objects to artchaeologists and art historians for many decades. Both of these arts, unfortunately, are no longer practised by contemporary Indians. A preeminent Caddo craft was the art of making bows from Osage orange wood; these were so well-made that Indians came from great distances to obtain them in trade. This, and other trade activities, took the Caddo on long-distance journeys whereby they not only extended their influence, but learned of other Indian tribes as well.

(see map page XIV)

BIBLIOGRAPHY —

● BOLTON, HERBERT EUGENE. Athanase de Mezieres and the Louisiana-Texas Frontier, 1768-1780. Cleveland, OH: The Arthur H. Clark Co., 1914.
● CHITTENDEN, HIRAM MARTIN. The American Fur Trade of the Far West: A History of the Pioneer Trading Posts and Early Fur Companies of the Missouri... New York, NY: Harper & Bros., 1902.
● CHRONICLES OF OKLAHOMA. Dec., 1924; Sept., 1929; Sept., 1934; Autumn. 1949; Summer. 1950.
● CURTIS, NATALIE. The Indians' Book: An offering by the American Indians of Indian Lore... New York, NY: Harper & Bros., 1907.
● DEBO, ANGIE. The Road to Disappearance. Norman, OK: University of Oklahoma Press, 1941.
● DORSEY, GEORGE A. Traditions of the Caddo. Washington, DC: Carnegie Institution of Washington, 1905.
● EASTMAN, ELAINE GOODALE. Pratt, The Red Man's Moses. Norman, OK: University of Oklahoma Press, 1935.
● FOREMAN, GRANT. Advancing the Frontier, 1830-1860. Norman, OK: University of Oklahoma Press, 1933.
----- Indian Removal. The Emigration of the Five Civilized Tribes of Indians. Norman, OK: University of Oklahoma Press, 1932.
----- Pioneer Days in the Early Southwest. Cleveland, OH, The Arthur H. Clark Co., 1926.
----- A Traveler in Indian Territory. The Journal of Ethan Allen Hitchcock... Cedar Rapids, IA: The Torch Press, 1930.
● GABRIEL, RALPH HENRY. The Pageant of America: the Lure of the Frontier... New Haven, CT: Yale University Press, 1929.
● HARMON, GEORGE DEWEY. Sixty Years of Indian Affairs, Political, Economic, and Diplomatic. 1789- 1850. Chapel Hill, NC: University of North Carolina Press, 1941.
● HUMFREVILLE, J. LEE. Twenty Years Among Our Hostile Indians. New York, NY: Hunter & Co.
Indian Office Report. 1849, 1859, 1864, 1874.
● KAPPLER, CHARLES J. Indian Affairs, Laws & Treaties. Washington, 1833.
● ROYCE, CHARLES C. Indian Land Cessions in the U.S. Washington: 18th Annual Report, Bureau of Ethnology, 1896-97.
● SEYMOUR, FLORA WARREN. Indian Agents of the Old Frontier. New York, NY: and London: D. Appleton- Century Co. Inc., 1941.
● SWANTON, JOHN R. The Indian Tribes of the Lower Mississippi Valley and Adjacent Coast of the Gulf of Mexico. Washington: Bureau of Ethnology, 1911.
----- The Indian Tribes of North America. Washington, DC: U.S. Government Printing Office, 1952.
----- "Source Material on the History and Ethnology of the Caddo Indians." Bureau of American Ethnology Bulletin. no. 132, 1942.

CADDOAN

(U.S.; Ark., La., Okla., Tex.) is one of the most important divisions of the large Muskhogean language family (see MUSKHOGEAN). It included three primary confederacies, each of which was composed of several sub-divisions, as well as a number of independent tribes. The largest confederated group was the *Hasinai,* inhabiting the region between the Neches and Sabine River, and including eight smaller tribes: Anadarko, Hainai, Nabedache, Nacogdoche, Nacono, Namidish, Neches, and some remnanat Nasoni. A smaller group was the *Kadohadacho,* the "heart" of the people, from whom the name Caddo (from *Kadohadacho* ,"real Caddo") is derived; they lived at the great bend of the Red River in northwestern Texas and southwestern Arkansas, and constituted the Kadohadacho, Nanatsoho, the Nasoni proper, and remnant Natchitoches people. Some scholars include the Cahinnio, but these were wanderers who apparently joined whoever was close at hand from time to time. The smallest was the *Natchitoches* proper, living around the present-day town by that name in Louisiana. There were three independent peripheral Caddoan tribes in this region: the Adai on the Red River; the Haish (also called Ayish, or Eyeish) living near San Augustine, Texas; and the Yatasi, who eventually split apart, with one section joining the Kadohadacho, and the other, the Natchitoches. Other groups of uncertain alliance, were the Doustioni, Guasco, Nacachau, Nacanish, Nacao, Ouachita, and Yscani. Major Caddoan-speaking segments who left the main confederation early and because individual tribes on their own included the Arikara, Kichai, Pawnee (also Pani, Tawakoni, and Wichita. (For more complete data refer to individual tribal entries.

CAGABA

(South America; Colombia) who speak a dielect of the farflung Chibchan language stock occupy an area in the extreme northern part of Columbia in the Sierra Nevada de Santa Marta close to the Caribbean Sea. Today, they number approximately 2,000 and their population seems to be stable. They constitute a very ionteresting example of deculturation, which means that they had a much more complex cultural and social organization before the Spanish Conquest. As a result of this upheaval, they retreated during the first quarter of the sixteenth century into the Sierra Nevada to high altitudes of 5,000 feet or more, where the environment could not support their former way of life. Because of this maneuver, however, they were able to survive, whereas the once-powerful coastal Tairona were overrun by the Spaniards and absorbed into colonial society, as were many other coastal peoples.

Village life was forced upon the Cagaba by the Spanish conquistadores for the purpose of facilitating taxation. Today, people live in settlements of the sort instituted during the early colonial period, but they leave them for part of the year during times when they cultivate land at different altitudes in the precipitous Sierra. Settlements now are formed around principal religious shrines or temples such as Mocotama, Taquima, Noavaka, and Nukangalahue, which are inhabited by priests, their wives, and their helpers. What has been described as secondary temples-- really men's houses--are also prominent in their settlements and are places where men sleep, work on tools and weapons, and discuss village affairs.

The Cagaba are horticultural people. The techniques they employ are basically the same as those used in pre-Spanish times. Nevertheless, nowadays they cultivate crops introduced by the Spaniards such as sugar cane, plantains, bananas, and their technology is improved by the use of the machete and the steel shovel. They also raise cotton and tobacco as cash crops to be sold to traders. Their subsistence crops consist of manioc, maize, potatoes, some pineapples and oranges, as well as onions, beans, and sweet potatoes. All of these crops are cultivated at the different altitudes most suitable to them. The Cagaba, therefore, make a vertical or altitudinal accomodation to their precipitous terrain, an ecological adjustment not uncommon throughout the highland areas of western South America.

Slash-and-burn horticulture is the standard technology and the hardest work is done by men. Trees are encircled so that they die, and in the following year, the smaller ones are cut down and the entire area burned over. In this fashion garden plots are cleared and the potash resulting from the burning helps to fertilize the soil. Women and children participate in all other phases of the horticultural cycle such as planting, weeding, and harvesting. The plots are usually small, less than an acre. Households have as many as five or six plots at different altitudes used for their various crops.

Hunting and fishing have always been relatively unimportant among the Cagaba. They now keep pigs and chickens as well as oxen, animals introduced by the Spaniards. Meat does not constitute a very important part of their diet. Owning an ox, however, is prestigious, and well-to-do men will kill an ox for food on a festive occasion. The internal organs of domesticated animals are highly prized. The Cagaba, however, are mainly vegetarians who eat a soupy mixture which sometimes contains fish or small pieces of meat. Men eat first, after which the women serve themselves and the children.

The Cagaba retain their traditional house types which are round and made of wattle and daub, having thatched, conical roofs which are made

Group of Charrua

separately, then hoisted on top of the walls of the house. Women manufacture the daub (adobe). Temples are built in the same manner as houses and are now called *casnamarias,* indicating Catholic influence on a basically aboriginal religion of great tenacity.

Congruent with important divisions of labor by sex, the Cagaba observe a sharply defined male-female dichotomy in living arrangements. Men have separate houses from their wives and neither husband or wife enters the other's house. Unfortunately, the symbolism of this residence pattern has not been analyzed by social anthropologists to date. Women are excluded from the temple, which in many villages serves also as the men's club and dormitory.

Cagaba have built remarkable wooden bridges across their rugged mountain landscape. The construction of these bridges is men's work and is done on an entirely voluntarily basis. There are archaeological relics from pre-conquest times of stone structures made of monolithic blocks--stairways, terraces--and the Cagaba still make stone terraces for their steeply-inclined garden plots. These serve to level the land and increase the cultivable area.

The elementary family is the basic economic unit among the Cagaba, but villages seem to be organized on a matrilocal residence pattern and are endogamous units. Descriptions of their social organizaiton are unclear. Women inherit land and other property, but only men inherit rights of possession to a temple. The time-honored classification of a priest-temple-idol complex seems to apply to the contemporary Cagaba, but lines of descent, inheritance, and succession to status are not clearly defined in the anthropological literature. There are exotic bits of information, the symbolism of which has not been analyzed, concerning marriage and sexual relationships. The Indian priest sanctifies marriage after discussion with the village elders. One year's bride service by the intended groom is made to the girl's father. During this period, the young man helps the girl's family with garden cultivation. There is no sexual intercourse between the young couple. When the term of service is completed satisfactorily, a hut is built on the periphery of the village for the newlywed couple. Consumation of the marriage is witnessed by the priest. Thereafter, copulation is never done in the house but occurs in the fields and is not supposed to be observed.

Puberty rites for boys and girls are important among the Cagaba and it is said that older women (widows) initiate boys into the sexual act in a ritual, stylized manner. Girls observe special food sanctions on their first menustration. Priests are in attendance at all of these rituals.

The Cagaba might be classified as a theocracy run by priests who instruct novices during a decade of training, guided by sacred songs, secret knowledge, and propitation of the "mother of all things" (Gauteovan). Priests cure the sick, temper the weather, and help souls to the afterworld. They are also shamanistically oriented to the cure of ailments through the uses of medicinal herbs and incantations.

BIBLIOGRAPHY —

● STEWARD, JULIAN H. Handbook of South American Indians. 7 Vols., Washington, DC: U.S. Govt. Printing Office, 1946-59.

CAHIBO

(West Indies; Haiti) Also called Cibao. The tribe, according to information given, belonged to the Arawakan linguistic family, except that a different language is said to have been spoken in the provinces of Cubana and Baiohaigua, but the difference may have been dialectic. *Peter Martyr's* words render it impossible to suppose the language of this entire tribe was distinct from the speech of the remaining Haitians. They were located in the northwestern mountain section of Santo Domingo, about the Desert Mountains or Cordilleras del Cibao. Some of their subdivisions include Cotoy, Dahaboon, Manabaho, and mountainous districts called Hazue, Mahaitin and Neibaymao. Specific population information for this tribe is not known.

BIBLIOGRAPHY —

● SWANTON, JOHN R. The Indian Tribes of North America. Washington, DC: U.S. Government Printing Office, 1952.

CAHINNIO

(U.S.; Tex.) A tribe visited by Cavelier de la Salle on his return from Texas in 1687, at which time they probably resided in S. W. Arkansas, near Red River. They were possibly more closely allied to the northern tribes of the Caddo confederacy than to the southern tribes, with whom, according to Joutel, they were at enmity. During the vicissitudes of the 18th century the tribe moved N. W., and in 1763 were on upper Arkansas River, near their old allies, the Mento. By the close of the 18th century they were extinct as a tribe.

BIBLIOGRAPHY —

● HODGE, FREDERICK WEBB. Handbook of American Indians North of Mexico. Washington: Smithsonian Institution: BAE Bulletin No. 30: U.S. GPO, 1907.
● SWANTON, JOHN R. The Indian Tribes of North America. Smithsonian Institution: BAE Bulletin No. 145: U.S. GPO, 1952.

CAHITANS

(Mexico; Sonora) a linguistic grouping, include the Yaquis, inhabiting the central coast of the state of Sonora in Northwest Mexico, the Mayos, living south of the Yaqui along the southern coast of Somora and the northern coast of Sinaloa, and several smaller groups. Many Yaquis inhabit special reservation areas whereas Mayos live interspersed with mestizos, non-Indian Mexicans. Working as small scale farmers, wage labor and fishermen, they borrow money from the bank, request irrigation water from the hydro commission, and plant the recommended commercial crops such as corn, sesame, cotton, soy beans, safflower, wheat, and cotton. With cash or credit from the sale of their crops or fish, Mayos and Yaquis purchase much of their food such as coffee, meat, sugar, bread, and even some tortillas in the local mestizo markets. Nearly all of their clothing and material culture is identical to that of rural mestizo peasant farmers. However, reflecting the fusion of indigenous and Christian patterns, the Mayo-Yaqui belief and ceremonial system is unique. The Yaqui pueblo political organization is highly developed nd tightly integrated with the ceremonial and mythical systems, whereas modern Mayos have developed and elaborated new religious movements and lost political autonomy. Among both groups, Saints' Day fiestas or ceremonies are celebrated with feasting, fireworks, and the entertainment of masked poskola and deer dancers and musicians. Especially elaborate are the Lenten and Holy Week ceremonies which are characterized by masked Pariseros who crucify Jesus and ultimately are destroyed by the power of God as Christ returns to the church from the land of the dead.

Tribal Name. The Linguistic term, Cahita, refers to Cahitan speakers, members of the three modern ethnic or "tribal" groups in southern Sonora and Northern Sinaloa, Mexico. The people themselves would not recognize the term, Cahita, and often use the names Mayo, Tehueco, and Yaqui to refer to themselves or their neighbors. More often, however, they use the term *yoreme* (yoeme, Yaqui) to designate themselves, indigenous peoples, and the term *yori* to mark non-Mayos or non-Yaquis (mestizos). Outsiders, especially non-Indians, refer to these peoples as Mayos, Teheucos or Yaquis depending upon the group in question or *indios* in opposition to themselves, *hente de razon* (people of reason). The terms Yaqui and mayo appear to have been drawn from the river valleys of the same names and further it has been suggested that the term Mayo signifies "boundary" and was applied to the people living along the Mayo or "Mayambo" river because they were "locked into" their boundaries or did not wish to communicate with outsiders. The Spanish mistakenly applied the native term, *kahita* (nothing) to the indigenous language. Apparently when the local people were asked the name of the language they spoke, the Spanish received the reply "kaita" meaning "nothing" or it has no name." Thus this response bacame the official name of the language of its speakers.

Social and cultural boundaries and subdivisions. Gaps in the information available and changes through time have produced shifting Cahitan natural, social, and cultural boudaries whose histories are not completely clear. Today Mayo-speaking peoples are concentrated along the lower Yaqui river area. Although the concentration increases in the lower river valleys towards the Gulf of California, Mayo peoples extend up the Mayo and Fuerte river valleys at least as far as the Alaqmos-Macusari area in the Mayo region. Although in the 1960s and 1970s some of the land between and beyond the river valleys had been opened to irrigation agriculture, much of these areas are sparsely populated desert regions covered with thorn forest of numerous varieties of large and small cactus and mesquite trees. Splitting the desert region between the Yaqui and Mayo valleys, the Arroyo de Cocoraqui provided the Mayo-Yaqui border, a region contested by both groups. On the other hand, the Arroyo de Masaica breaks the almost 100-mile stretch of coastal desert between the Mayo and Fuerte valleys. To the south of the Fuerte, groups of Mayos live in the Ocorini and Sinaloa river valleys. At the time of Spanish contact, this coastal area of Northern Sinaloa was occupied by a set to "dialect groups" belonging to the Guasave "family", although today we have essentially no information concern-

ing these groups, nor do we know much of anything regarding their languages. To the north of the Mayos, the Yaqui claim territory as far north as Guawyamas and many families live dispersed not only throughout Mexico but also in several small villages in the Tuscon and Phoenix areas of Arizona. However, the majority of modern Yaquis are concentrated on a special Yaqui reservation located in the northern sector of the Yaqui river area. Throughout this Cahitan area (chiefly the coastal plain of Southern Sonora and Northern Sinaloa embracing the three river valleys) Cahitan social and cultural boundaries are marked chiefly in terms of language and dialect spoken and social and ceremonial labor and exchange. Within this general area, considerable family movement exists with numbers of modern Mayo families living in Yaqui territory and vice versa, and Mayo river Mayos living in the Fuerte area and vice versa.

Territory. Lack of archaeological research in the area makes it difficult to delineate a precontact Cahitan territory, although since Spanish contact Mayo-Yaqui territory has remained stable with the exception of the gradual reduction in control over the territory. Modern Cahitan territory reflects a dramatic opposition between the fertile luxuriant Yaqui, Mayo, and Fuerte irrigation areas with fantastic agricultural production and high population density vs the thorn forest desert areas useful for wild fruits, woods, and animal products.

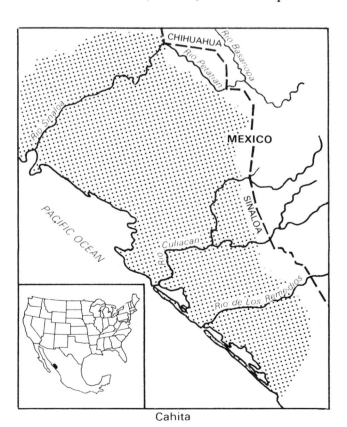

Cahita

The violent rivers dropping out of the rugged Sierra Madre Occidental Mountains and flowing across the coastal plain to the Gulf of California, have been tamed through the construction of huge irrigation dams. The hot coastal Cahitan territory is characterized by long periods of dry weather broken by heavy summer rains and slower winter ones producing between 40 to 80 cm. of rainfall per year. Precontact Cahitans relied upon river flooding to water crops of corn, beans, and squash while modern farmers irrigate their fields of cotton, wheat, and safflower. Even today Cahitans still use the remaining wild desert areas to supply some variety in their diet such as deer, small game, fish, shellfish, fruits of numerous cacti, beans of the mesquite, agave plants, and many other seed and fruit-producing plants. Although extreme and harsh in many ways, Cahitan territory is characterized by considerable ecological deversity, for example, the very rich marine resources of the beach and Gulf of California areas, the extremely fertile agricultural coastal plain, and the highly varied foothill region.

Language. As noted earlier, Cahita, actually refers to a language subfamily and not to a tribal unit. The Mayo, Tehueco, and Yaqui dialects constitute the Cahitan subfamily which is even closer to Mayo than is Yaqui. Today Mayos who have learned the Spanish alphabet in local schools write Mayo in terms of this alphabet, although in the pre-contact period, Cahitan does not seem to have been a written language.

Summary of tribal culture. Modern Cahitan culture is that of enclaved groups and involves the fusion of aboriginal beliefs, rituals, and symbols with 16th and 17th century Catholic beliefs and with more recent modern Mexican traditions. Thus modern Cahitan technology, subsistence, economics, and material culture are very much a part of modern Mexican national domination. However, Yaqui political organization and Mayo-Yaqui ritual symbolism and ceremonialism provide more unique aspects of the modern Cahitan way of life. Modern Cahitan technology and subsistence focus upon farming, fishing, and wage labor. Before conquest, Cahitans raised two food crops per year, relying upon river flooding, and fished and collected wild foods which constituted perhaps up to 40 percent of their diet. Jesuit missionaries introduced sheep, goats, and cattle as well as wheat and irrigation agriculture but did not basically change Cahitan economy. However, modern irrigation and farming technology has dramatically modified Cahitan subsitence. About three-fourths of the rural families hold some lands, either as private holdings or as ejido members (governmental granted and established farming societies). However more of families living in the larger villages and towns, someitmes as many as half the community, hold no land taxes, seed, fertilizer, inssecticide, etc., they are forced to plant cash crops such as wheat, safflower, alfalfa, and cotton, which are stipulated by governmental agencies. Besides farming, most households raise chickens while some keep pigs, turkeys, and cows. Modern Cahitans purchase prepared foods, sugar, coffee, lard and some wheat flour and corn meal, most clothing, and manufactured items, in the local store or area market. Most families own a jacal (mud thatch) or adobe house with separate cooking room, a table, chairs, folding cots or wooden beds, a set of enamel or glass bowls and cups and enamel spoons, and a wooden trunk for pictures, valuables, and documents. Meals always include corn or flour tortillas and very sweet strong coffee supplemented with a range of stews of beans, fish, or meat when it is available. Thus clothing, housing and furnishings, and foods tend to be typical of rural Mexican peasants and not uniquely Cahitan. The Cahitan economic system and the concept of wealth itself proves to be dual in nature: lands, productivity, and integration into the modern Mexican national economy ve respect and Holy Flowers. Ideally one should not hoard food or material goods but give freely of the productivity of one's fields in support of Cahitan ceremonialism and thus achieve respect in this world and heavenly rewards after death (Holy Flowers).

Traditional Cahitan social organization is based upon the nuclear family, the household, and the ceremonial center. The pre-contact social organization was charcterized by bilateral descent, bifurcate collateral kinship terminology, local group (rancheria) exogamy, suprarancheria political organization only during periods of warfare, and a council of rencheria elders in peacetime. Today many families utilize a modified Mexican kinship terminology, lineal and Eskimo, with Cahitan terms applied to parents, siblings, and children, and Spanish terms for aunts, uncles, cousins, and in-laws. In most households old people are still highly respected, although the tragedy of the infirmities of old age are clearly pointed out by younger family members. Ceremonial kinship is still extremely important with godparents selected at times of birth, marriage, and ceremonial participation. Cahitan terms are used for godparents and godchildren. Groups of coparents become crucial co-operative units especially in ceremonial contexts. In addition to godparenthood, the Jesuit missionaries emphasized membership in certain ceremonial sodalities and introduced a more complex pattern of village-government which had parallels to the older rancheria political organization. Valuing individuality and equality of adults, these political systems consisted of hierarchical ceremonial sodalities whose heads met in open town councils which included representation from each household of the community. Up to the present time, Yaquis have elaborated and conserved this political system whereas Mayos have lost political autonomy and have been incorporated into the modern Mexican political system. Their village-government has been absorbed by the modern Mayo church-ceremonial center organization.

The modern Yaqui town organization, a political system, is based upon five integrated realms of authority: the civil, the church, the military, the fiesta and the customs authorities. Each realm maintains its own net to officers who are ranked hierachically, in all over 60 distinct offices. In addition to political and juridicial powers, these sodalities are responsible not only for the regular round of Catholic calendrical ceremonies, but also for rites of passage such as baptisms, marriages, and funerals. Decisions resulting from open meetings of this town council are ideally based upon unanimous agreement reached after open discussion of the issues at hand. Less complex than the Yaqui, the modern Mayo church-pueblo organization consists of five helpers; the lay ministers; the Matichini dance sodality; the Parisero sodality (the Lenten masked male society) and the Paskome (fiesteros) who promise to serve the patron saint of the church through prayer, fireworks, food, and entertainment in the form of Paskola and deer dancers provided in honor of the saint. In general, the Mayo-Yaqui ceremonial cycle follows the life of Christ with an elaborate Easter Ceremonial in which the life, death, and resurrection of Christ is re-enacted. Village ceremonies for the Holy Cross, the Holy Spirit and Holy Trinity, Saint John and the Virgin of Guadalupe and the returning dead early in November are yearly highlights. The realms of nature and the supernatural also are organized as a family: with God, Our Father, identified as the sun; the Virgin, Our Mother, equated with the moon; and Jesus, the Child of Our Father and Our Mother. The animals of the forest are the Children of the Old Man of the Forest and the fish the Children of the Old Woman of the Sea. Rooted in this model, Mayos continue to experience visitations of Our Father and Our Mother and in order to avoid the wrath, punishment and destruction promised by Our Father who is angry with the secular state of the modern world, and continue to innovate ceremonies in honor of God and the Saints.

Summary of tribal history. As no archaelogical reports have been published describing the central Cahitan area, it is difficult to identify the pre-historic traditions. Early Spanish documents reveal a heavy population density and remarkable cultural complexity on the Sinaloa coastal plain just south of the major Mayo-Yaqui region. The earliest Spanish records describe sporadic contact with the Mayo and Yaqui such as a Spanish slave raid in 1533 and a prospecting expedition in 1564. By early 1600, Captain Hurdaide conquered the Indians south of the Mayo and Jesuit missionaries entered the area. In 1609 a huge force of some 7,000 Yaquis defeated Hurdaide and a group of Mayos with whom he had made a treaty. After this heavy battle and miraculous escape by Hurdaide, the Yaquis proposed peace and both Mayos and Yaquis requested missionaries, who were provided in 1614 to the Mayos and in 1617 to the Yaquis. A small group of Jesuits achieved broad changes in Mayo-Yaqui belief and technological systems through the following techniques: learning and teaching in the Cahitan language; working through Mayo-Yaqui native leaders; living directly with the people; and relying upon the army as little as possible. The mission villages, which were created by the Jesuits, became not only religious but also economic centers. Discovered in 1684 in the upper Mayo river valley, one of the richest silver mines of northwest Mexico attracted an increasing number of Spanish settlers to the area. Resentment grew until 1740, which marks the date of the first general Indian revolt. After the revolt the Jesuits returned until 1767 when they were expelled from the New World and within a few years secular clergy were assigned to the area. The eighteen hundreds were years of semi-autonomy with gradual mestizo land encroachment and Cahitan land loss which in part triggered a number of highly destructive local revolts, which ultimately resulted in Mayo pacification during the 1880s, and continued Yaqui guerilla warfare in the mountains above Yaqui territory and deportation of Yucatan. Since the 1890s, Mayos have produced prophets and revitalizaiton movements as mentioned in the preceding section, whereas Yaqui guerilla bands fought in the mountains until 1918. Mayos fought in the Mexican Revolution of 1910, after which lands were redistributed to many Mayos in the form of ejido memberships and to Yaquis as an autonomous reservation. Enforcing Mexican anit-church legislation, local mestizos burned Mayo churches and revived their ceremonialism while the Yaquis were re-establishing the mission towns located on the Yaqui reservation. In summary, the major processes of Cahitan culture change are: initial contact and missionization; slowly eroding socio-political autonomy and land loss; Mayo prophetic movements and Yaqui guerilla warfare; the Mexican Revolution of 1910; reconstruction and revival of a traditional way of life.

Contemporary tribal situation. Since modern Cahitans are enclaved groups, the contemporary situation depends a great deal upon the dominant Mexican nation and even international relations, although Yaquis are somewhat more isolated and independent than Mayos. These are probably appropriate concepts, as those unique social and cultural organizations which we have called Cahitan are not integrated into broader national systems but exist apart from them. Priests say mass no more than once or twice a year in the more progressive Mayo churches and never in the more isolated ones, while the Mexican government has been encouraging the Yaquis to vote out their village government and accept local Mexican governmental institutions which are integrated into the national level. As rural peasants, Mayos reside as neighbors with mestizos although reservation Yaquis tend to be more isolated. The settlement of Mayo house plot inheritance or land disputes has become an individual or nuclear family matter with mestizo lawyers and courts being called into the cases. Intermarriage and compadre ties with mestizos have tended to become individual concerns, although traditional Mayos dislike intermarriage and the selection of mestizo compadres. As low paid unskilled farm wage labor, Mayos are not distinguished from mestizos with regard to ethnic identity. Lower class social dances are produced and attended by both Mayo and mestizo individuals and families, although Mayo dances usually involve religious elements. Cahitan children attend the local Mexican schools as individuals and are not taught differently from the local mestizo children. As young men mature they have the option of joining the army. However, like the school situation they are not organized into Cahitan groups. Thus the Cahitan individuals participate in a range of Mexican national institutions. However, the participation is not in terms of Cahitan culture, and social units are not recognized by Mexican social and political structures. The interaction of individuals within these institutions takes place in terms of non-Cahitan aims, goals and values.

Population figures. The following population estimates must be recognized as extremely vague in nature and likely on the low side: at the time of the Spanish contact there were over 100,000 Cahitans with Yaqui and Mayos accounting for 60,000 of the total; one half the Mayos died of disease in the first 50 years of contact leaving around 13,000 to 15,000 Mayos in the late 1600s; the 1950 census lists slightly over 30,000 Mayo speakers and Yaquis numbered about 15,000 in the 1940s; and the 1970 census lists almost 28,000 Mayo speakers.

Conclusion Modern Cahitan culture represents a complex fusion of indigenous traditions combined with Jesuit teachings and 19th and 20th century modern Mexican culture. Isolated on a reservation many Yaquis still maintain autonomous town government, although politically Mayos have been incorporated into modern Mexico. Cahitan individuals participate in Mexican institutions such as schools, *ejidos,* markets, the army and the PRI political party, as peasant Mexican farmers and not in any special sense. Given this type of situation some Cahitan individuals assimilate, becoming mestizos and disappear as Mayos or Yaquis. On the other hand, in assimilating, very few real alternatives are open to the Cahitan individual who must enter at the bottom of the mestizo social stratification system with little hope of upward mobility. Thus many Cahitans prefer to seek prestige within their traditional culture and society, which they have reestablished in the case of the traditional "Eight Yaqui Pueblos" or which they adapted and revitalized in the case of the new Mayo religious movements, which continue to appear even up to the present time, January, 1979.

BIBLIOGRAPHY —

● BEALS, RALPH L. The Contemporary Culture of the Cahita Indians. Bureau of American Ethnology Bulletin 142, Washington, 1945.
● BOWDITCH, CHARLES. P. Mexican and Central American Antiquities, Calendar Systems and History. Washington, D. C.: Bureau of American Ethnology- Bulletin 28: GPO, 1904.
● EL PALACIO. pp. 55-57, March, 1945.
● SWANTON, JOHN R. The Indian Tribes of North America. Washington, DC: U.S. Government Printing Office, 1952.
● THOMAS, CYRUS. Indian Languages of Mexico and Central America and Their Geographical Distribution. Bureau of American Ethnology Bulletin 44: Washington, D. C.: GPO, 1911.

CAHUILLA

(U.S., Calif.) are a mountain, foothill and desert people of southern California, inhabiting in the old days much of western and central Riverside County and northeastern San Diego County. The usual Native American closeness to nature was enhanced among the Cahuilla by a deeper than usual and quite delightful acceptance of birds and mammals as cousin peoples. No one seems to know the exact derivation of the name Cahuilla, though the people say it was given to them by the Spanish. Their own name for themselves is the *Iviatim.*

Social and cultural boundaries and subdivisions The Cahuilla are included in the Southern California Culture Area, whose major creators were the populous Gabrielino and Chumash. The Cahuilla are divided culturally into the Pass

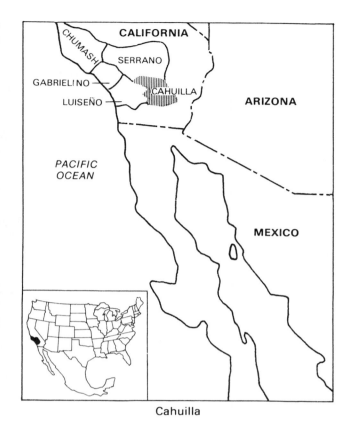

Cahuilla

Cahuilla of the San Gorgonia Pass area and the nearby area about Palm Springs, the Mountain Cahuilla of the San Jacinto and Santa Rosa Mountains and their foothills, and the Desert Cahuilla of the desert areas immediately east of these mountains. In the old days the Cahuilla as a whole were divided into two moieties for marriage purposes, the Coyote and the Wildcat, either side marring into the opposite moiety. Politically each clan or extended family was a unit in itself, occasionally working cooperatively with other clans for war, ceremonial occasions or large hunting round-ups.

Language The Cahuilla belonged to the Shoshonean Branch of the vast Uto-Aztecan language family, which extended from the hunting tribes of Shoshones in the northern Rockies to civilized Nahuan peoples of southern Mexico. They were a part of the wedge of Shoshonean-speakers who moved into southern California many years ago, and which included their Serrano and Luiseno neighbors to the north and west and the closely related Cupeno people on their southwest edge.

Summary of tribal culture Subsistence and economy. The wide-mesh hand seed-beater, rather than the digging stick, was the most common tool used by the Cahuilla for gathering plant food, as seeds, such as the acorns, chia and pine-nuts for the Mountain Cahuilla, and the seeds and pods of

the mesquite, agave and yucca for the Desert and Pass Cahuilla, were the main plant foods. Buds, fuits, flowers and leaves of about all varieties of cacti were also consumed.

The Cahuilla handling of mammal, bird and insect competition for plant food was very farsighted. At exactly the beginning time for gathering such foods the people came, the men also hunting the rodents, deer and rabbits, and the quail and other birds who competed with them, while the women and children hurriedly gathered seeds, flowers and fruit. All members of families joined together when there was an insect invasion, as when hordes of grasshoppers came. At such times fire lines were devised or firepits built into which grasshoppers could be driven in vast numbers to be roasted and then eaten. The bow and arrow, a deer disguise of head and antlers, and the curved rabbit stick were the principal tools used in hunting, though various traps and snares were also made. The thickly shaped bow, made of willow, mesquite or palm stem was of an inferior sort, but the hunters developed and taught their boys an extra-ordinary knowledge of the habits and ways of camouflage of their prey, great care being taken also to prepare oneself spiritually and by proper diet for the hunt.

Drought and disasters like earthquakes or floods, hit the people unevenly, but it is astounding how their social and religious systems, though with no political unity, helped their economy to stay in balance. Thus at the great social and religious gatherings, such as the one for the burning of effigies of the dead, clans came from all over to also trade and bargain with one another. Thus if the main food supply of one clan was wiped out by the roaring waters of a cloudburst in their canyon, they could still make basketry and pots or other useful articles and hunt meat, which they could then bring to such a social gathering to trade for the dried and preserved plant foods they needed.

Technology and arts. The rectangular and well-thatched houses were set on posts with forks at their tops, connected by cross-logs. In the mountains they had fairly steep roofs to keep off rain and snow, but the Desert Cahuilla usually had flat roofs and square houses.

Pottery was made by rolling, smoothing and baking clay, mixed with crush rock, to give it a deep red color. Linear designs made from a black mineral harmonized with yellowish-red wider areas. The tightly-coiled solid-cooking basketry included the basketry hats for women and the round, flat-bottomed carrying or storage baskets typical of Southern California. A carrying net was used sometimes also as a hammock for children. Rather unique for southern California and used mainly by the Desert Cahuilla was a very long and

Old Cahuilla woman grinding acorns.

pleasingly rounded stone pestle for grinding mesquite beans in a deeply-hallowed hard-wood mortar. Also unusually different was the use of the mescal agave leaf fibers and the bark of the common reed for making strings and ropes.

Social and religious culture. The Chungichnish cult or religion reached the Pass Cahuilla only very lightly, and the Desert Cahuilla not at all, hut was absorbed at least in outer form by the Mountain Cahuilla, who practiced the initiation ceremony where boys were given visions by a jimson weed potion, and sand paintings helped illustrate lectures on moral standards. Probably of more importance to the Cahuilla was the dramatic role played by their shamans. These men recieved their powers through dreams of spirit helpers, or with the help of an experienced medicine men. After a severe trial and initiation by older shamans, a youth could join a secret society of *puvalam*. The shaman (or *puul* usually had several powers, given him by different *teyewas* or spirit guardians. The major one was healing, mostly done by sucking disease ohjects out of the body. An important duty was to create food by performing magic, as when a shaman drew a miniature oak tree out of his hand to insure a good acorn crop. Some used powers to stop rain or bring rain as desired. Usually several *puvalam* helped at ceremonies by performing

magic dances to keep away evil spirits. However, sometimes a *puul* used his power for evil ends, such as killings, which usually ended his career as the people or other *puwalum* banded together to destroy him!

Brief history and present condition The Cahuilla were so isolated in deserts and mountains that the early Spanish and Mexicans did not conquer them, but when the white Americans came, the, Cahuilla temporarily joined with the Mexicans to fight against them. Soon diseases, such as smallpox, destroyed so many of them that their strength as a people ebbed from around 3000 in 1800 to 800 in 1910. Today their old population is coming back and they are beginning to feel as a united people, renewing past dances and ceremonies. Six fairly sizeable reservations and the wise use of water for fruit trees and other crops is helping their economy. (see map page XVII)

● STEWARD, JULIAN H. Handbook of South American Indians. 7 Vols., Washington, DC: U.S. Govt. Printing Office, 1946-59.

CAINGANG

(South America.; Brazil) The name Caingang was introduced in 1882 by Telemaco Morocines Borba to designate the non-Guarnai Indians of the States of Sao Paula, Parana, Santa Catarina, and Rio Grande do Sul, who previously were known as Guayana, Coroado, Bugre, Shokleng, Tupi, Botocudo, etc., but who were all linguistically and culturally related to one another and formed the southern branch of the Ge family.

The Guayana Indians appeared for the first time in the literature under the name of Guayana (Goyana, Goaianaz, Guayna, Wayannaz, etc.) *Staden (1925, part 2, chap. 3* (p. 445) mentioned them in the Capitania of Sao Vicente. Early documents assigned them to the plains of Piratininga and the region where Sao Paulo was founded. According to *Soares de Souza 1851, pp. 99-100* (p. 445), they were the dominant tribe of the entire coast of the State of Sao Paulo, from Angra dos Reis to Cananeia. Actually, they shared the seashore with the Guarani- speaking Tupinikin. The Portuguese chronicler described them as noncannibalistic people with softer dispositions than the Tupinamba, living in the open country, and shunning the forest where they were outnumbered by their Tupinamba neighbors. Tebyreca, who played such an important part in the early history of Sao Paulo, was a Guayana chief. The settlement of Pinheiros, near old Sao Paulo, was formed by Indians of that tribe. Since the toponymy of this region was Guarani, some authors considered the Guayana a Tupi-Guarani tribe. Although it is possible that the Guayana of Piratininga spoke Tupi, there was little doubt that the majority of Guayana belonged to a different family and were the ancestors of the modern Caingang. Early on, the name Guayana was still aplied in the State of Sao Paulo to a group of 200 Caingang who were settled in 1843 near Itapeva *Saint- Hilaire, 1830-51, 2: 439-461 Machado de Oliveira, 1846, pp. 248-254 (p. 455).*

The chronicler *Rui Diaz de Guzman 1914, p. 14* spoke of Guayana, Pattes (Basas?), Chouas, and Chouacas, who spoke related languages and had their habitat on the Piquiry River and the Rio Negro. *Lozano 1873-74, 1: 422 (p. 446)* called Guanana, Guayana, or Gualacho the non-Guarani "who lived on the Iguassu River and extended to the Atlantic." His description of the culture of the Guayana of the Iguassu River left little doubt that these Guayana were the modern Caingang, the more so that the only word of their language which he mentioned was the Caingang word (soul, "acupli"; modern, "vaicupli").

Azara 1904, pp. 404-407 (p. 446) divided the Guayana into two unrelated groups. The first ranged west of the Uruguay River from the region of La Guayra to an undetermined boundary in the north. These Guayana, who did not speak Guarani, practiced bloodletting, used long bows, and raised some crops, were certainly identical to the Caingang who later occupied the same territory and who shared the very culture traits enumerated by Azara.

The other Guayana Indians described by Azara spoke Guarani and lived on the right side of the Parana River from the Caraguarape River to the Monday River and on the left side from Corpus to the Iguassu River. The descendants of these Guarani-speaking Guayana resided, at the beginning of the 20th century, near Villa Azara, on a stream called Pira-pyta. They disclaimed any connection with the Caingang, although *Ramon Lista, 1883 (p. 446)* seems to have included them among the latter. *Vogt, 1904, pp. 216-218 (p. 446).*

North of these Guarani-speaking Guayana, on both sides of the Parana River, lived a Caingang subtribe called Ingain (Tain) or Ivotirocay, after the stream (a western tributary of the Parana River) on which they had their headquarters. Their bands were scattered from the stream of Ivotirocay to the vicinity of La Guayra falls. Their name, Tain, suggested closed affinities or identity with the Taven, who lived in the same region between the Parana, the Piquiry, and the Itatu Rivers. These Ingain or Taven were the Indians whom *Lista 1883 (p. 446)* and *Martinez 1904 (p. 446)* described as Guayana. (Also see *Ihering, 1904 a, pp. 23-44 (p. 446) Sampaio, 1897 (p. 446) Martinez, 1904 (p. 446)* and *Vogt, 1904, pp. 352-376 (p. 446).*

At the beginning of the century, Caingang groups could be found in the vast territory of the State of Parana between the Iguassu and the Paranapanema Rivers, but in later times, they had no settlements near either river, but were fairly numerous along the Tibagy and Piquiry Rivers. The Caingang who lived between the Rio das Cinzas and the Tibagy River called themselves Nyacfateitei, and they were separated by the Tibagy River from closely related Indians, who were their bitter enemies.

The names Votoro, Kame, and Cayurukre, given to Caingang groups of Guarapuava and Palmas, were simply appelations of moiety or class subdivisions and not, as it was long believed, of independent bands or subtribes. The Dorin, who lived on the river of the same name, and the Taven, whose habitat was bounded by the Parana, the Piquiry, and the Itatu Rivers, were true Caingang subgroups different from the subtribe of the Guarapuava region.

The first settlers of the Campos of Guarapuava found these plains in 1810 entirely occupied by Caingang. These Indians were placed in aldeas under the care of Father das Chagas Lima, who wrote the first eye-witness account of them. In order to prevent constant clashes between the Caingang and the first colonists, the Brazilian Government made various attempts to settle them

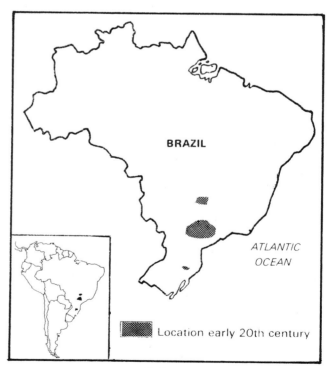

BRAZIL

ATLANTIC OCEAN

Location early 20th century

Caingang

in aldeamentos. In 1855-56, the settlements of Sao Pedro de Alcantara, San Jeronymo, and Jatahy were founded for them on the Tibagy River. However, many Caingang groups remained independent in the forests between the Piquiry, upper Ivahy, and the Iguassu Rivers. A census of the Caingang of the Guarapuava region taken in 1827 by *Father das Chagas Lima 1842, p. 62* (p. 447) reported the Kame, 152; Votoro, 120; Dorin, 400; Shocren, 60; and Taven, 240. In 1905, *Koenigswald 1908 a, p. 47* (p. 447) estimated the Caingang of the State of Parana at about 2,000.

Beginning in the 18th century, the Caingang of Sao Paulo, Parana, and Rio Grande do Sul were frequently designated as Coronado or Coroado (The Crowned Ones) because of their typical Franciscan-like tonsure, a hair style which they didn't abandon until years later. This unfortunate term was responsible for the confusion between the Caingang-Coroado and the Puri-Coroado, who seemed linguistically unrelated.

Lozano 1873, 1:69 (p. 447) applied the name "Coronados" to the Indians of the open plains or Campos de los Camperos, del guarayru, del Cayyu, de los Cabelludos, and de los Coronados between the Huibay (Ivahi) and Iguassu Rivers. These Coronado, who were certainly Caingang, were the same as the Gualacho (Gualachi), Chiqui, and Cabelludo, who lived in the same region. As a matter of fact, Lozano himself considered these names to be synonyms of Guanana (i.e., Guayana). In the Cartas Anuas of 1628 *Cartas Anuas, 1927-29, 20: 344* (p. 447), the Gualacho who did not speak Guarani lived 4 days' travel time from the mission of San Pablo, in the basin of the Tibagy River in the very heart of the Caingang region. Likewise, the Caagua (Caaigua, "Forest Dwellers") of the Jesuits who roved between the Parana and Uruguay Rivers, near Acaray in the region of La Guaira, were undoubtedly representatives of the Caingang subfamily. Jesuit maps indicated other Caagua in the region of Tape (State of Rio Grande do Sul), an area where Caingang groups lived until the 19th century.

The Indians whom *Azara 1809, 2: 70-75* called Tupy, and who fomed an enclave within the Guarani region, were also the ancestors of the modern Caingang of the upper Uruguay river. Their territory corresponded to the forested land east of the Uruguay River between the Jesuit missions of San Xavier and San Angel and between San Xavier and lat. 2723 S. Jesuit sources assigned to them the region extending between the headwaters of the Piratini (near San Miguel) and the Iguassu and Jacuhy (Igay) Rivers. There were no details in the short description of their culture given by Azara which did not fit modern Caingang: agriculture, tonsure, fiber cloth, shell necklaces, bow, etc. Moreover, modern Guarani still applied the name Tupi to the Caingang of San Pedro in the Argentine Territory of Misiones *Ambrosetti, 1895, p. 305* (p. 448).

The AweikomaCaingang groups of the State of Santa Catarina adopted the use of the labret and were therefore, often called Botocudo, a name which erroneously suggested a connection with the northern Botocudo of the State of Espirito Santa. The name Bugre, applied by the colonists to the Caingang had a pejorative meaning. It is a Portuguese word of the same root as the French "bougre." The Guarani also called the Caingang, Caauba, and Caahans *Serrano, 1939, p. 25* (p. 448).

At the beginning of the 20th century, there were five groups of wild Caingang, known as Coroado, between the Peixe, and the Aguapehy (Feio) Rivers. Formerly there were also Caingang groups on the lower Tiete River. They resisted the advance of the whites and continually assaulted the workers building the railroad from Sao Paulo to Corumba. In 1910, thanks to the efforts of General Rondon and of the Servico de Proteccao aos Indios, peace was established and many Caingang settled around the two government posts created for them near the Aguapehy (Feio) River. *Horta Barboza, 1913, p. 24* (p. 448) who was one of the inspectors of the Indian Service, estimated the number of Caingang in that region at 500. The Caingang of Sao Paulo were also known as Nyacfateltei (Nyakfa-d-ag-teie, "Those with the long frontal hair").

The Caingang who later established themselves around Palmas in the State of Parana came from the region between the Iguassu and Uruguay Rivers. In 1933, they lived in two villages near Palmas: Toldo las Longras, on the river of the same name, and Toldo de Chapeco, in the region of Xanxere. According to *Baldus 1935* (p. 449), the population of the first village was 108, that of the second was somewhat higher, but no exact figures were given. In earlier sources, the Caingang of the region of Palmas were often designated as Kame after one of their moiety subdivisions.

The nomadic or half-nomadic Caingang who ranged in the State of Santa Catarina from the Timbo River to the forests of the Serra do Mar, and from the Rio Negro to the Uruguay River, were better known as Bugre, a derogatory term given to them by their enemies, the white settlers, or as Shokleng, or Botocudo of Santa Catarina because of their wooden labrets. Nimuendaju called them Aweikoma, a word of their language meaning Indians. Although they differed culturally from the Parana, Caingang *Baldus, 1937 c* (p. 449), there is little doubt that they belonged to the same linguistic family, even if their dialect was not easily understood by the Caingang of Palmas.

During the whole 19th century, the Aweikoma-Caigang of Santa Catarina stubbornly opposed the encroachments of the Brazilian and German settlers. They were constantly pursued by professional Indian hunters, the famous "bugreiros," until the Servico de Proteccao aos Indios intervened on behalf of the remnants of the tribe. Most of them were settled on the Reservation Duque de Caixas (Municipality of Dalbergia), near the junction of the Plate River with the Rio Itajahi do Norte. In 1930, the reservation consisted of 106 persons. Another small group of Caingang were reported in 1935 at Sao Jao, south of Porto da Uniao.

The Caingang, who ranged north of the Uruguay River from the mouth of the Pepiri-guassu River to that of the Rio das Canoas and those who lived between the Rio das Canoas and the Rio Pelotas were distinct from the Aweikoma, though the demarcation between Caingang-Coroado and "Botocudo" cannot be exactly ascertained. The Caingang of the northern bank of the Uruguay River were the same as, or closely related to, the groups who had their villages between the Serra Geral, the upper Uruguay River, and the Sete Missoes.

In 1850, Jesuit missionaries founded three settlements for the Caingang of the upper Uruguay: Nonohay, Campo do Meio, and Guarita. The Indians of Nonohay numbered about 400; those of Campo do Meio, 90. The Jesuit missions were short-lived; Nonohay, however, was restored in 1872 with 300 Caingang, who at the end of the century, were almost entirely absorbed into the local rural population. According to *Von Ihering, 1895, p. 40* (p. 449), six "aldeamentos" of Caingang existed in 1864 in the State of Rio Grande do Sul, with a total population of about 2,000. In 1880, their number was already greatly reduced. In the same period "wild" Caingang were reported between the Taquari and Cahy Rivers. Later, their settlements were situated between Inhacora (Nucora, (long. 5415' W.) and Lagoa Vermelha (long. 5130' W.).

At the end of the 19th century, about 60 Caingang lived in the Argentine Territory of Misiones on the eastern slopes of the Sierra Central, 3 miles (5 km.) from the town of San Pedro, near the Yaboti River. According to *Ambrosetti 1895, p. 307* (p. 450), these Indians, who were known in the region as Tupi, had come from Palmas or Rio Grande by crossing the upper Uruguay River. A few years later (1902), some of them returned to Brazil.

Few data on the Caingang can be gleaned from the Colonial literature. Although the Caingang were often mentioned in the Jesuit texts on the Paraguayan missions, *Lozano 1873-74, 1:418-427* (p. 450) and *Azara 1904, pp. 402-407* (p. 450) were the only authors who gave short, but fairly accurate, descriptions of these Indians. The accounts of Father Luiz de Cemitille and of Telemaco Morocines Borba were, for many years, the best sources for information on these tribes. Later *L.B. Horta Barboza 1913* (p. 450) published very exact observations on their customs, which were supplemented by *Manizer 1930* (p. 450). *Ambrosetti 1895* (p. 450) wrote an article on the Caingang of San Pedro, in Misiones. The social organization and funerary rites of the Caingang were the subject of a special monograph by *Baldus 1937 c* (p. 450). *Henry 1941* (p. 450) studied the decadent remnants of the Aweikoma group and described their culture in psychological terms. Their language was known mainly through an excellent dictionary by *Father Mansueto Barcatta de Valfloriana 1918, 1920* (p. 450), and a linguistic analysis by *Jules Henry 1935* (p. 450). *Ploetz and Metraux 1930* (p. 450) attempted to bring together most of the data about the Caingang contained in the literature up to 1928.

The only Caingang who subsisted entirely by hunting and collecting were those of the State of Santa Catarina, the so-called Botocudo or Aweikoma. These Indians, however, remembered a time when they, like all other Caingang groups, practiced agriculture.

The ancient Guayana, ancestors of the modern Caingang, were described as relatively sedentary agriculturists, although the importance of hunting in their economy was noted by various writers. This was also true for the Caingang at the end of the 19th century. All their groups raised maize (red, white, and violet varieties), pumpkins, and beans (a white variety), but perhaps depended less than their Guarani neighbors on these crops. Like many Indians who had become acquainted with farming in recent times through the intermediary of some other tribe, the ancient Caingang were improvident and consumed their crops as they matured, storing none for the lean months ahead. On the other hand, *Horta Barboza, 1913, p. 34* (p. 451) stated that maize was as important to them as "wheat for the Europeans." The Caingang of the region of San Pedro (Misiones), observed by *Ambrosetti, 1895, p. 337* (p. 451), opened their clearings in tracts covered with bamboo or sparse bush. They broke the small trees with cudgels or by hand. When the dead trees were dry, they burned them and waited until the beginning of the rainy seasom for sowing. Women planted crops with digging sticks; they also harvested the crops and carried them home. Men did all the farming in the reservation of Palmas. In the more modern groups, the tiller of a field was recognized as its exclusive owner--if he died before harvest, the seedlings were destroyed.

When the Caingang were still living in their aboriginal condition, pine nuts of *Araucaria angustifolia* , a tree which had a distribution coinciding more or less with that of the tribe, was fundamental to the native diet. From April to June, the Indians gathered in the forests to climb the trees and knock down the ripened fruits, which the women helped to pick up. The climbing technique--also used in getting honey or in robbing birds' nests--was to pass one noose around the feet, another around the tree and the climber's back, and alternately move the two bands up the trunk. The Awekoma-Caingang used only a noose of bamboo strips.

The Caingang also collected wild tubers (*Dioscorea* sp.) and a great many wild fruits, such as jaboticaba (*Myrciaria* sp.), pitanga (Myrtaceae sp.), articu (*Annona montana*), pineapples, papaya (*Carica papaya*), caraguata (*Bromelia sp.*), etc. The starchy pith of the pindo palm (*Cocos romanzoffiana*) was formerly an important food item, but was later supplemented by manioc flour. Honey and the larvae of bees, and especially the larvae of the tambu beetle, which abounded in decayed palm and bamboo trunks, were prized delicacies. It was also reported in some sources that the ancient Caingang did not despise snakes or lizards.

The Caingang spent a large portion of their time hunting alone or in small parties. The dog, treated by some groups as an indispensable auxiliary, became a part of the tribe sometime after 1912. To develop the smelling powers of their dogs, the Indians exposed them to the smoke of the burnt skin of the game which they were to stalk. They never gave them the bones of game animals to gnaw, taking great precaution lest the game be offended.

An entire band participated in a peccary hunt, old and young. Preceded by dogs, they endeavored to drive the animals toward hunters, who shot them with arrows. The Aweikoma-Caingang followed droves of wild pigs for several days, killing all those which came within their reach. The Aweikoma-Caingang concentrated on hunting tapirs, which seemed to be abundant in their territory. They tracked them with dogs or followed the deep "runs" opened by the tapirs in the bush and pursued their prey until it was forced into a stream, where they could kill it with ease. Similarly, they drove deer into streams, where they shot or clubbed them.

In order to capture birds, hunters concealed themselves in a shelter built on a tree where the birds roosted, and snared them with a noose at the end of a long pole. To catch parrots, they used a tame parrot as a decoy; for pigeons, they put corn out as bait *Horta Barboza, 1913, p. 31* (p. 452).

The spring- pole traps were constructed like those of the Caingua or of the Chaco Indians. They consisted of a flexible sapling and a noose placed near a bait *Horta Barboza, 1913, p. 30* (p. 452).

As a rule, a hunter never ate the meat of the game he had slain, but gave it to some companion. He could not eat the flesh of a tapir he had killed before he had performed a rite in which he consumed premasticated tapir flesh and the charcoal of the burned tapir's windpipe wrapped in grass *Henry, 1941, p. 86* (p. 452). When the Aweikoma-Caingang killed a tapir, they stewed "tapir grass" on it and placated its soul with friendly words lest it prevent other tapirs from being caught. Monkeys were also asked to come and share the food of the hunter. Caingang of Sao Paulo considered jaguar and deer meat taboo *Horta Barboza, 1913, p. 32* (p. 452); others refrained on some occasions from eating paca, capybara, and armadillo flesh.

The Caingang, although fond of fish, were very poor fishermen. They shot fish with bows and arrows, impaled them with two- pronged spears, or caught them by hand in the falls when shoals of fish ascended the river to spawn. They also captured them by hand in small lagoons formed by floods, which they drained *Horta Barboza, 1913, pp. 32-33* (p. 452). The Caingang of Misiones blocked small streams with V-shaped stone dams. Against the openings, they built a platform on which they placed a large mat folded and tied up at one end like a huge bag.

After planting their fields, the Caingang of Misiones went fishing along the small tributaries of the Parana River. Later they moved to the Sierra Central to collect pine nuts, and afterward, returned to their fields for the harvest. During their wanderings, they hunted and gathered fruits and larvae in the forest. The women did most of the cooking, although men generally prepared the game they killed. The Caingang generally roasted the unskinned animal in ashes, on a spit, or on a rectangular babracot. The earth oven served for baking large slices of meat, such as tapir. A large pit was dug in the ground and lined with stones, and a fire was built within the hole until the stones were glowing. The ashes and embers were then removed, the stones covered with leaves, and the meat, carefully wrapped, was placed inside and buried under a thick layer of soil. Twelve hours later, the meat was taken out, perfectly cooked. Fish were broiled on a babracot, then stored on an indoor platform.

Women pounded maize with heavy wooden pestles in cylindrical wooden mortars, which were sometimes large enough to accommodate three workers at a time and too heavy to be moved. They also had smaller mortars with which they

Primitive Caingang wind shelter.

used stone pestles. Maize flour was prepared as mush or was kneaded into dough and baked in ashes. Maize kernals were often soaked in water to the point of rotting, mashed, kneaded into loaves with saliva added, and roasted in ashes. The pith of pindo palms was crushed in a mortar, sifted, and roasted in a pan, just as with manioc flour.

Soup was made from husked, chewed, soaked, and pounded pine nuts. They were also roasted in the shell on the embers; pine- nut dough might also be kneaded into small loaves and baked in the ashes. Pinons were preserved in tightly closed baskets soaked in water for a month and half. In the past, salt was unknown; tart malagueta berries (*Capsicum frutescens*) were used instead. To stir the fire or lift food to and from it, the Caingang used a curved withe *Manizer, 1930, pp. 772, 774* (p. 453) *Henry, 1941, pl. 2 f* (p. 453).

Lozano 1873, 1: 424 (p. 453) described the Caingang or Guayana hut as follows: "They stick in the ground a long forked pole against which they lean crosswise four other poles. In this way, they make four divisions covered with palm leaves. In each division lives a family with the children. Each compartment communicates with the other by small doors. In each community there are five or six such huts placed at convenient distance from each other so that everyone can hunt and fish."

This type of house eventually disappeared among the subsequent Caingang, but sometime in the 1930's, the Aweikoma remembered it as the house of the open savannas and were able to recon-

struct one *Henry, 1941, p. 166* (p. 453). The later Caingang dwelling was a lean-to, which was often made into a gable-roofed hut when two structures of this type were joined. The Aweikoma- Caingang lived either in an arched lean-to which was open on three sides or in a hut composed of two such units, the arches being made to descend to the ground at both ends *Henry, 1941, pp. 164-166* (pp. 453-54). Such dwellings were thatched with palm fronds or comparable materials. Most Caingang groups lived in houses identical to those of the Caingua. When on a journey, the Caingang slept in flimsy shelters or rested in a sort of nest which they built in the top of a tree *Horta Barboza, 1913, p. 35* (p. 454). Hammocks of cotton were a recent Caingang acquisition. The ancient Guayana slept, according to Portuguese chroniclers, on branches or skins. Their descendants, the Caingang, rested on large strips of bark or thick layers of palm fronds, but many groups later adopted platform beds.

The wild Caingang went naked except for a belt- -generally a skein of brilliant brown threads of the bark of the young *Philodendron* root or of palm twisted into a cord--and a square cloak (kuru) reserved for cold weather. This garment passed under the right arm and fastened on the left shoulder so as to leave both arms free. Women wore a short skirt made of caraguata fibers, secured around the waist by a wide belt of bark dyed a brilliant black. Both sexes wrapped strips or strings of peccary hair or of bark around their ankles. Some Caingang tied up the foreskin of the penis and tucked it under their belts. On solemn

Caingang houses.

occasions, Caingang women who were in contact with the Guarani missions wore a narrow sleeveless shirt (tipoy) made of caraguata fibers. *Koenigswald, 1908 b, p. 31* (p. 456), reproduced a feather apron which he described as a women's garment. Caingang women were also said to have used a bark band passed between the legs and fastened to the belt.

Some Aweikoma-Caingang of the State of Santa Catarina and of rio Grande do Sul wore long rosin labrets like those of their Guarani neighbors. Others had wooden lip sticks (generally made of pine knot) 2 inches (3/4 cm.) long "in the shape of a nail." This usage was responsible for the name Botocudo given to the Caingang in these States. Feather ornaments were common among the Caingang, but except for the small "visors" of short toucan feathers worn around the forehead, they were rarely described by observers. *Debret, 1941, pls, 11 and 12* endeavored to represent a "Coroado" (Caingang) chief displaying all his ornaments. The chief wore a fan-shaped feather headdress attached to his nape. Long feather tassels were tied to his upper arm and under his knees. The Caingang of the State of Parana donned, on festive occasions, a feather cape, that covered them from head to foot *Koenigswald, 1908 b, p. 27* (p. 456). If this ornament actually was used by these Indians, it may well represent a survival of the feather cloaks of the ancient Guarani.

During dances, men and women often strew down over their heads. Necklaces of seeds, animal teeth, bird bones, claws, and hoofs were generally slung around the shoulders; those composed entirely of monkey teeth were especially valued. The Caingang of Guarapuava and of Mi-

siones had necklaces of small shell disks (*Orthalicus phogera*). Some Caingang wore necklaces which weighed nearly 6 pounds! For many years, the Caingang wore a circular tonsure on top of the head; the fashion disappeared among adults after their contact with the whites, but was retained for small children. In later times, the Santa Catarina Aweikoma-Caingang of both sexes shaved the hair over the forehead and on top of the head *Paula Souza, 1924, p. 122* (p. 457).

The Caingang abhored body hair and always removed it. Combs consisted of small wooden splinters passed through a slit in a piece of reed. The Caingang seem to have used charcoal more than urucu for body painting. Among the Aweikoma-Caingang, certain body parts belonged to exogamic groups of people. The main motifs were dots, vertical lines, circles, and horizontal bars with vertical lines. The Caingang observed by *Manizer, 1930, p. 771* painted themselves only for funeral ceremonies. They regarded the black stripes on their chest as a protection against the ghosts. The pigment was charcoal mixed with honey and water or with the sticky sap of a creeper plant.

River navigation was not as important to the Caingang as to their Tupi-Guarani neighbors. To cross a river, the Aweikoma- Caingang chopped down a tree on each side of the river and connected the intervening space with a tree trunk braced with poles fixed on the river bed. Caingang women carried babies on their backs, often in a net, by means of bark tumplines. Among the Aweikoma-Caingang, these straps were 4 inches (10 cm.) wide, woven of embira fibers. Knapsacks were suspended by a tumpline.

According to *Koenigswald, 1908 b, p. 49* (p. 457) the Parana Caingang made net bags of caraguata fibers. The carrying baskets of the Caingang had a hexagonal weave, and, like those of the Tupi, were elongated and the rectangular knapsacks opened on top and on the outer side, so that only the bottom and sides supported the burden. Basketry containers woven from thin strips of split bamboo, frequently had stepped designs produced by alternating black and natural color strands. Some baskets, like those of the Guayana, were made in two parts that telescoped into each other. The Aweikoma had three main types of baskets: large baskets for transportation of goods; small, impervious water or honey containers of Taquara mansa strips coated with wax; and small receptacles, similarly waterproofed, used as cups and dishes.

Caingang textiles were made with the fibers of the ortiga brava, probably a Bromelia. Women seized the leaves with leather-covered hands, cut them at the base, and removed all the thorns, then macerated the leaves in water, dried, and finally crushed them. The fibers were then rolled into threads with the palm of the hand against the thigh. The threads, wound in a ball, were soaked in water mixed with ashes, then boiled, and again carefully washed; sometimes they were left in running water, so that they became white and flexible. Occasionally, part of the thread was dyed with catigua bark. Fabrics were woven by hand, sometimes on a simple loom, and always displayed a stepped, dark design which crossed the surface diagonally.

For pottery, the Caingang of Misiones used a blackish earth from nearby cliffs. For tempering material, they baked lumps of clay, then crushed and sifted them. The composition of the clay used by other groups is unknown. The potter first modeled the base of the pot by hand, then built up the walls by adding successive coils, smoothing the sides with her fingers or with pieces of wood or shell, a corn cob, a stone, or a metal spoon. To keep the clay soft, she sprinkled it with water or saliva. The following day, the pot was again smoothed, then left to dry in the shade and later in the sun. When thoroughly dry, the pot was covered with branches and fired in the open until red. Later, water mixed with ground maize was sprinkled on the pot "in order that it may be unbreakable." Cracks were filled with wax while the pot was still hot. The firing, however, was always imperfect; shards of the heaviest Caingang pots revealed a thick layer of unfired clay in the middle. The presence of a foreigner during firing endangered the process, and was said to possibly

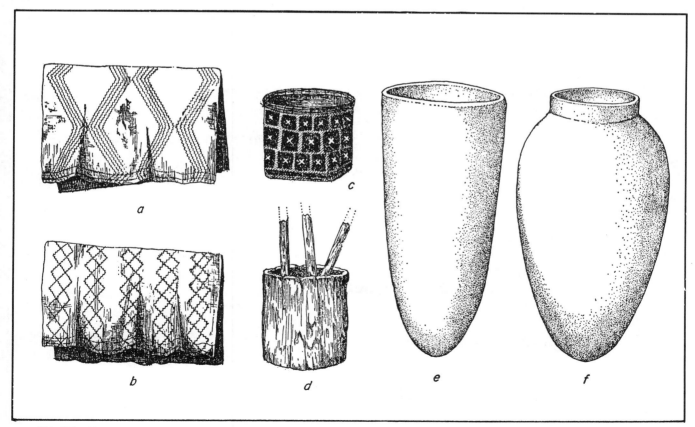

(A),(B), Kuras or nettle fiber cloaks (C), twilled basket, (D), wooden mortar, (E), (F), pottery jars

cause the pot to crack beyond repair. The Caing-ang of Misiones made their pots characteristically black by exposing them to smoke in a basket before they were fired.

Caingang ware had a conical base so that it could be set into the sand. The Caingang-Coroado made large beer jars, strikingly like Guarani jugs and funeral urns, with a conical body surmounted by a narrow edge. Besides large pots, the Caingang also manufactured flat roasting pans and conical drinking cups with thin walls.

The Caingang fire drill consisted of a stick of hard wood inserted into an arrow shaft and twirled between the palms of the hand. The hearth was a piece of soft wood. Dry palm shoots served as tinder. According to a single authority, the Caing-ang also produced fire by sawing one piece of wood with another, a procedure observed by Reng-ger among the Caingua, but otherwise not reported for South America. The fire was activated with a fan. To avoid having to make fire, the natives carried a glowing brand in a pot or in a section of bamboo coated with clay.

Bows were made of pao d'arco (*Tabebuia impetiginosa*) or of black ipe (*Tabebuia chrysantha*). Before the Caingang acquired iron, they wrought the bow stave into shape by rubbing it with sandstone and flint flakes, and smoothed it with the rough leaves of umbauba (*Cecropia* sp.). Finally, the stave was warmed against a fire and smeared with grease. At each end, a plaited bulge, or rarely, two right-angled notches prevented the caraguata or embira string from slipping. The stave was wrapped with strips of cipo embe (*Philodendron imbe*), which at both ends formed a bulge to prevent the string from slipping. Some Caingang bows were 9 feet long, but they generally averaged from 7 to 8 feet.

The arrow shaft, according to the locality, was made of taquara da frecha (*Gynerium sagittatum*), or of palo alecrim, a white wood that turned very light when dry. To straighten a reed, they lashed it against a horizontal piece of wood, fastening a weight at one end. Arrowheads were wide taquara splinters, barbed rods, wooden rods tipped with a sharp point of monkey or deer bones, and massive, blunt wooden knobs used for birds. Some bird arrows were also tipped with four slightly diverging sticks of thorns. In later years, the hunting and war arrows of the Santa Catarina Aweikoma-Caingang were tipped with duck-bill iron heads. Feathering was of the arched type (eastern Brazilian). Hunters always carried a ready supply of bone heads, shafts, and feathers to replace lost arrows. Spears were common among the Caingang, who tipped them with iron blades obtained from

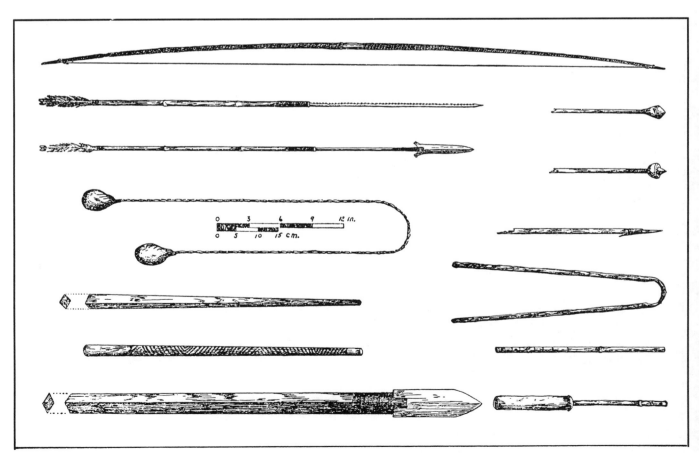

Caingang weapons and artifacts

the whites. The Aweikoma were extremely skillful in handling these weapons, which they decorated with fire-engraved designs and with basketry coverings.

The clubs of the Parana Caingang were short cylindrical cudgels covered with basketry; those of the so-called Botocudo were more or less tapering, with the cross section often prismatic, thus presenting sharp cutting edges. They were decorated with fire engravings and with a basketry sheath. The cudgels of the Sao Paulo Caingang had a bulging head and were from 5 to 6 feet long.

Countless stone rings were found on archeological sites of the State of Rio Grande do Sul. In the 17th century, some tribes of the upper Paraguay River used clubs with stone heads (itaiza), but there was no evidence that these Indians were Caingang, but more likely that they were Guarani.

To frustrate attack or pursuit by an enemy, the Caingang strewed the paths leading to their camps with caltrops made of sharp bone splinters bound in a bundle with cotton thread and wax. They also dug pitfalls in the bottom of which they placed sharp spears.

The Caingang of Palmas had two exogamous, patrilineal moieties, each split into two groups. *Baldus, 1935, pp. 44-47* (p. 461) did not give the names of the moieties, merely stating that they were called by the word for both "friend" and "two," and that fellow members considered one another cousins. On the other hand, he listed the four subgroups according to their prestige as follows: Votoro, Kadnyeru, (Kaneru), Aniky, and Kame. The reason for this preferential ranking could not be ascertained. Every individual was born into a moiety, but was assigned to one of the subgroups at a mortuary feast by a man or a woman of his own moiety.

Among the Caingang of Palmas, the father decided, when he painted a son or a daughter for the first time, to which of the two groups of his moiety he would forever belong *Baldus, 1937 c* (p. 462). The alleged purpose of this assignment was to equalize the groups numerically, so that they could be paired for dancing; but, as each group danced separately, the explanation was probably a rationalization. In fact, the two divisions were not even approximately equal. Members of each group could be recognized by their facial painting. The Kadnyeru displayed round patterns, the Kame stripes. *Horta Barboza, 1913, p. 39* (p. 462)

Nimuendaju's, 1914, pp. 373-375 (p. 462) earlier report concerning the Caingang between the Tiete and Ijuhi Rivers, spoke of two moieties associated with the ancestral twins Kaneru and Kame. The former was of fiery and resolute, but volatile, temperament, and of light, slim build. Kame, on the other hand, were mentally and physically slow, but persistent. Eacy moiety included three (formerly four) classes: Pai, Votoro, and Penye.

All natural phenomena were divided between these two moieties; the sun was Kame, the moon, Kaneru. In general, slender and spotted objects belonged to the Kaneru, clumsy and striped ones to the Kame. Their use in ritual was confined to the appropriate group.

The Aweikoma-Caingang lacked moieties, but had five groups with distinctive sets of personal names and body-paint designs. Although later genealogical inquiry failed to establish either strict inheritance of group membership or exogamy, the natives insisted that individuals bearing the same designs should not marry, so that a former patrilineal clan system was indicated *Henry, 1941, pp. 59, 88, 175 f.* (p. 462).

Concerning marriage rules between subgroups, *Horta Barboza, 1913, p. 26* (p. 462) gave the following information: "Marriages obey complicated rules depending on the groups (moieties) and sub-groups into which the Kaingang families are divided. The most important of these groups are the Camens and Canherucrens; marriages can take place only between the men of one groups and the women of the other. However, it must not be thought that it is licit for a Camen to marry any Canherucren for, in order to make things more complicated, there is a division into subgroups, fairly numerous. Individuals of a certain Kame subgroup can only marry a woman of a certain Canherucren (Kadnyeru) subgroup, save for a few exceptions which confuse a question which otherwise should be so simple."

The relationship system was based on relative age. A man called his father, his grandfather, and the men of their generations by the same term, and his mother and grandmother by another term. He used a single name for all male and female blood relatives, excepting real parents and grandparents and grandparents' siblings and own children. One word (child) served for all people much younger than ego and for the children of all people with whom he had sexual relations. There was a word for husband and another for wife. A single word applied to all relatives-in-law *Henry, 1941, pp. 177-178* (p. 462).

Chiefs wielded little authority. They worked in their fields and hunted like the rank and file of the group. Their position was conspicuous only when the community organized a big feast, which was always given in the chief's name. Chiefs also were the leaders of any collective undertaking. They maintained their hold on their people by distributing gifts and looking after their well-being *Koenigswald, 1908 b, p. 47* (p. 463). A chief who was overbearing or miserly was abandoned by his followers. The son of a chief succeeded his father if he was acceptable to the group *Horta Barboza, 1913, p. 25* (p. 463).

Formerly, a pregnant Caingang woman did not consort with her husband, and both observed food taboos. Women gave birth in the forest, sheltered from the supposedly maleficent moonbeams. A few days after delivery, the mother and child were fumigated, a rite accompanied by a drinking bout. Later, a Caingang woman bore her child wherever she happened to be, knowning how to take care of herself even if she was alone. Usually, she delivered squatting while a midwife embraced her from behind, raising her now and then until the travail was over. The navel cord was cut with a fingernail and tied with a caraguata string.

Among the Aweikoma, the placenta and umbelical cord, wrapped in medicinal herbs, were placed in a basket and sunk in the stream. The mother wound a long cord around the ankles of the baby and removed it 15 days later during a feast given by the father to a group of relatives. The umbilical cord was disposed of by the mother's brother or his wife or by the mother's sister, who later became ceremonial parents.

In other Caingang groups, the mother pulled open the infant's eyelids immediately after birth "in order that he might see," breathed into his eyes and ears, and pressed his temples and head from front to back. The father did not pay much attention to the baby until it was old enough to speak, and he then gave it 5 to 10 names. In the south, the names were bestowed without any rite after the above-mentioned ceremony.

The Caingang showed the greatest tenderness to their children, seldom punishing them or using harsh words. According to *Horta Barboza, 1913, p. 27* (p. 463), when a boy reached the age of 7, his mother rubbed his body with the leaves of a certain tree and poured water over his head to make him courageous and diligent. The child then received a new name. Later, he was allowed to adopt names that referred to notable incidents of his life.

In the Santa Catarina group, the perforation of the boys' lower lip at the age of 2 or 3 was marked by great celebrations. Women holding gourd rattles, danced with warriors, who beat the ground with their spears. The children were intoxicated with beer, and shaken until half unconscious, when their ceremonial fathers pierced their lips with a sharp stick *Henry, 1941, pp. 195-197* (p. 464).

According to *Baldus' census, 1937 c, p. 43* (p. 464), men were generally older than their wives, in some cases, as much as 15 to 20 years; among 37 percent of the couples, there was a difference of 10 years. A man married when he was 18 to 20 years of age. If his bride was not yet of age, he stayed with her parents, waiting for the first signs of puberty. In case of child betrothal, the lad's parents had to provide for the girl's subsistence.

Polygyny was mentioned in all the early sources, but the details vary. Some authors declared that it was an old man's privilege, otheres said that it was restricted to the chiefs, good hunters, or famous warriors. There were also indications of sororal polygyny and of marriage simultaneously to a woman and her daughter *Teschauer, 1929, p. 350* (p. 464). In Tupi-Guarani fashion, a girl often married her mother's brother. The Caingang of Palmas were, and always claimed to have been, monogamous.

Manizer, 1930 (p. 464) stated that although a man could not marry his cousin--he did not specify which--he usually took her as a concubine until her own marriage. If pregnancy occurred, meanwhile, the girl, as a rule, committed abortion. It often happened that a man grew fonder of his cousin than of his legal wife, and that he sometimes resolutely opposed her marriage. The continuation of such a relationship was bitterly resented by the legitimate wife.

For the Aweikoma, Henry inferred that 60 percent of all marriages were monogamous, a fair porportion of the remainder being polyandrous. A marriage ceremony witnessed by *Manizer, 1930, p. 776* (p. 464) took place during a drinking bout. Some old men seized the bridegroom and bride and pushed them toward each other in spite of the woman's resistance. Then they dragged them into the bridegroom's hut and left them there under a blanket. The following day, the woman ran away, but was brought back by force.

Matrilocal residence, formerly the Caingang rule, later became frequent, although many couples set up their own households. *Baldus, 1937 c, p. 43* (p. 464) heard "that only lazy men lived in their father-in-law's house and that, should the father-in-law die, the husband would have to 'govern' his mother- in-law."

Regarding the tribe's beliefs about death, they theorized that it might result from the abduction of the soul by some spirit or by the ghost of a relative. According to *Henry, 1941, p. 67* (p. 465), "The ghost-soul loves and pities the living whom it has deserted, but the latter fear and abhor the ghost- soul." At one point, the Aweikoma-Caingang cremated the dead and later collected and buried the bones, along with part of the deceased's property. After a cremation, they extinguished their fires and drilled fire anew. The soul of the deceased loomed as a peril, especially to the surviving spouse, who went into retreat, abstained from eating meat, and underwent lustration. To terminate mourning, the mourner's hair and fingernails were clipped, pounded up, and thrown into the water. Then followed a beer festival, accompanied by dances and songs, during which the widow drank beer from a bamboo tube. Keening was not confined to the period of death, but occurred throughout the following year whenever relatives recalled their bereavement.

The Caingang later interred their dead with knees drawn up. Chants were sung around the body during and after its transportation to the grave. One cemetery had two central tumuli, 10 to 20 feet by 18 to 25 feet (3 to 6 m. by 5.5 to 7.5 m.) surrounded by vertically walled ditches. The same tumuli were reported for the 18th century Guayana, ancestors of the Caingang. The corpse, with funeral deposit, was put in a deep chamber, roofed with palm fronds and earth. The villagers at once deserted the settlement and hastily constructed new dwellings in the woods. For 3 days they ate only palm shoots (palmitos) and maize boiled by throwing heated potshards in the water. They destroyed part of the deceased's property and imposed a strict taboo on his name.

The grave was periodically visited to renew the mound and to hold a memorial service with lamentations, dancing, chanting, and drinking. For several years, at dawn and dusk, the relatives of a dead person uttered funeral laments. In days of old, if a person died far away from his village, his companions interred his body on the spot but kept his head in a pot. On returning home, they celebrated a funeral ceremony and buried the head in the communal cemetery *Horta Barboza, 1913, p. 29-30* (p. 465).

Before the burial, the shaman, as he rattled his gourd by the corpse, warned the soul about the lurking dangers in the other world. He told it that it would arrive at two paths, one leading to the cobweb of a gigantic spider and the other to a trap which would precipitate it into a boiling pot. He also described the slippery path from which it might fall into a swamp, where a huge crab awaited it *Nimuendaju, 1914, p. 372* (p. 467)

But at last the soul arrived at an underworld in the west, where the forests teemed with tapirs, deer, and other game. The souls of the aged became young again and lived for the span of a human life. After a second death, the soul turned into a small insect, generally a mosquito or an ant, whose death ended everything, and it was for this reason that the Caingang never killed these insects *Baldus, 1937 c, p. 49* (p. 467).

A man who had been offended by some member of the community stood in front of his hut and in a loud voice, enumerated all his grievances, sometimes bursting into a chant. He ended with threats against his enemy who, in the meantime, behaved in the same manner on the other side of the camp.

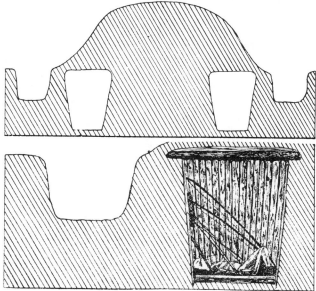

Caingang burial mound. Top: View of mound shortly after completion. Center: Cross section of mound showing location of burial chambers. Bottom: Cross section of burial chamber in mound with body and accompanying grave artifacts.

After reciprocal abuses that often lasted a whole night, the challenger, followed by a group of supporters, advanced toward the offender, who was immediately assisted by his own partisans. Both factions, armed with wooden clubs, fought a pitched battle, but were careful not to kill anybody. The sham battles of the Caingang were described by many observers and may well have been formalized brawls which were interpreted as sportive games.

Feuds between Caingang groups sometimes developed into regular warfare. When one group engaged another, the members of the Kadnyeru moiety subdivision always formed the first line. The Kame constituted the second line and entered the fight as a reserve to take the place of the exhausted Kadnyeru. Battles between related groups were always preceded by exchanges of insults and by other demonstrations of anger. Although no weapons but cudgels were used, blows were so lustily administered that many were seriously wounded or killed.

Wars against foreign tribes or the whites were less strictly patternized. The Caingang, like all Indians, relied mainly on surprise attacks carried on at dawn. After a general discharge of arrows, the warriors, armed with their clubs, rushed against the enemy *Horta Barboza, 1913, p. 42* (p. 467). Women and children were generally spared and were adopted by the victorious group. They cut off the heads of slain enemies but did not keep them as trophies.

When a Caingang visited another village, he hid in the vicinity until able to announce his presence to some relative. The host received him with his face covered with a cloth and did not look at his guest until food was served. If the visitor mentioned the death of some relative, the women started to wail *Ambrosetti, 1895, p. 321* (p. 468).

Most information on Caingang musical instruments came from *Manizer, 1934* (p. 468). The trumpets had a bell made of a thick section of bamboo and the blow hole on the side, a rare feature in South America. The bell of some trumpets was made of the involucres of the coqueiro or geriva palm (*Cocos botryophora*) *Teschauer, 1929, p. 348* (p. 468); *Debret, 1940, pl. 11* (p. 468). The clarinets were of the idioglotal type, that is, the tongue was split from the reed mouthpiece. The bell was either a gourd or a cowhorn. The Caingang also had an instrument which *Izikowitz, 1935, p. 254* (p. 468) called "slit-valve." According to *Manizer, 1934, p. 312* (p. 468), it consisted of a reed tube, closed at one end and crushed at the middle so that it bursted into longitudinal slits. He wrote: "In playing this instrument, an air current blown through the open end passes out through the slits thereby causing these to vibrate and produce a tone." Similar instruments were used by the Bororo and the Paressi-Cabishi.

The Caingang were among the few South American Indians who played the nose flute. This flute, about 3 feet (1 m.) long, had two stops at the distal end and one at the proximal end. The blow hole was in the septum of the reed, which had been left in place. Another flute, reproduced by *Izikowitc, 1935, p. 299, figs. a, g* (p. 468) had the same number of stops but was blown sidewise (transverse flute). It is possible that the latter type was also blown with the nose. The specimen was decorated with a basketry cover.

The Caingang also played the notched flute (quena) with four stops. They do not seem to have known the panpipes, although *Izikowitz, 1935, p. 408* (p. 468) attributed it to them on very flimsy evidence. This instrument did not turn up in the whole area, and its presence among the Caingang

would consitute an inexplicable anomaly.

The rhythms of dances and songs were beaten with the gourd rattle and the stamping tube. The handle of the rattle was often trimmed with bark strips and feather tufts; the gourd itself was covered with engraved designs.

The words of songs, generally improvised, referred to events taking place around the singers or alluded to past wars, hunting, and other economic activities. Sometimes a singer enumerated his grievances against a fellow tribesman, an action regarded as a challenge. The chants of the Aweikoma-Caingang were a succession of meaningless syllables, often sung on one note. These Indians seldom sang in unison.

The members of a Caingang subgroup danced together. The dancers, about 3 feet (1 m.) apart, formed two concentric circles around a line of fires, the men inside and the women inside. A singer in the center first shook his rattle, and placed each foot alternately before and behind, dancing sideways. At this signal, the other performers shoook their rattles, and both circles began to turn in one direction, following the rhythm of the song and rattle. Men without rattles hit the ground with stamping tubes. Behind them, women lifted their forearms and moved their empty hands slightly to each side in a kind of "blessing" gesture. When the leader was back to the starting point, he stopped and the others waited quietly until he was rested or was replaced by another leader.

While at play, Caingang children were very skillful at filliping sticks, maize kernels, and small arrows resting on the bent arm. Maize shuttlecocks were batted with the palm of the hand. Children spun tops made of a clay whorl or a lump of wax on a stick. The favorite Caingang adult sport was a mock battle between members of two communities, who hurled small clubs or, at night, firebrands at each other. Although these weapons might wound or even kill, casualties were not resented and did not call for blood revenge. This sport was played on open ground where heaps of clubs had previously been deposited. Women, protecting themselves with bark shields, ran among the players to pick up and hand the clubs to their men. The Aweikoma threw stones wrapped in small fiber bags, which were parried with short clubs. The Caingang were also fond of wrestling.

In regards to narcotics, a great many stone pipes were found in the Caingang area--a puzzling fact since smoking had not been observed among these Indians. However, drinking was a part of their lifestyle and the Caingang prepared intoxicants from maize, sweet pototoes, pine nuts, honey, and the fruit of several species of palm, especially buriti (*Mauritia vinifera*) and jussara (*Euterpe* sp.) Maize was slightly roasted over ashes, ground, and boiled in large pots for about a night. The next day, part of the mass was chewed, then boiled again with the remainder. Shortly before the feast, the liquid was transferred to a huge trough made of a tree trunk and half buried in the ground. The liquor was heated by a fire built around the trough or by red-hot stones or potshards which were thrown into it. During 2 or 3 days of fermentation, men danced around the beer, singing, shaking their rattles, and beating the ground with the stamping tubes. The beer was often mixed with honey.

The Aweikoma-Caingang started to prepare their mead a month before its consumption. A mixture of honey and water, to which they added the juice of a fern to "make the beer red" was fermented in wooden troughs from 5 to 6 feet (1.5 to 1.8 m) long made of tree stumps hollowed out by burning and chopping, then closed at both ends with wax. To accelerate fermentation, the beverage was heated every 3rd day with red-hot stones and then covered with pieces of bark.

The Caingang left messages in symbolic code for those who would be following the same path. A stick with honey indicated where a bees nest had been found; dolls and sticks represented a feast to which some group was being invited; an inclined stick showed the time of day at which some event took place; feathers scattered on the ground told of a successful hunting party, etc. *Manizer, 1930, p. 790* (p. 470). *Lozano, 1873, 1: 425* (p. 470) stated that to declare war, the Guayana (i.e., the Caingang) stuck an arrow into a tree near a path followed by their enemies. A circle of maize cobs on the ground or hanging from a tree was an invitiation to a drinking bout.

. As per their religious beliefs, the Aweikoma conceived the world to be strongly animistic, peopled with ghosts (kupleng) and spirits (nggiyudn) of all sorts who dwelled in trees, rocks mountains, stars, winds, and in large and small animals. To meet a spirit was, as a rule, an ominous event. But spirits might be friendly and appear to a man to offer their aid. Those who were assisted in hunting by a guardian spirit shared with it the game which they had killed. A man might even adopt a spirit child and place it in his wife's womb.

Aweikoma-Caingang shared the widespread belief that all animals had "masters," that is to say, spirits that controlled and protected them. Such spirits were willing to give up some of their kin to satisfy men's needs, but were angered if people destroyed them wantonly or if hunters refused an animal "offered" to them.

The Caingang shaman consulted spirits at night, puffing his pipe until he was surrounded by a cloud of smoke. The spirits talked to him in long whistles and told him where to find a favorable hunting ground or abundant honey. They might also reveal the outcome of an undertaking involving the band.

Shamans were also doctors, but this role was less conspicuous among the Caingang than elsewhere and was even absent among the Caingang of Palmas and of Sao Paulo. Among the decadent Aweikoma-Caingang, observed by *Henry, 1941, p. 76* (p. 470), shamans only treated members of their immediate family and did not receive a fee for their cures. The shaman knew many magic remedies, generally herbs, the virtues of which had been revealed to him by some spirit. A certain grass, said to be the favorite food of tapirs, was endowed with great medicinal virtues. It was used not only to cure, but also to prevent sickness *Henry, 1941, p. 83* (p. 471). Massages played a great part in therapeutics. Sometimes they were so violent that the practitioner stepped on the patient's stomach. The skin was frequently rubbed with pulverized barks or plants befor the treatment. Burning herbs were used therapeutically, particularly for wounds. A patient bitten by a snake was laid upon a slanting platform over a fire and given warm water to drink to make him vomit. *Manizer, 1930, p. 784* (p. 471) was impressed by the number of people whose heads, arms, or legs were swathed in *Philodendron* for therapeutic purposes. To lessen fatigue on a long walk, the Indians bandaged their legs up to the hip with tight braids. (Re: Caingang medicine, see *Paula Souza, 1918, pp. 750-753* (p. 471).

Bloodletting, which was practiced with a flint flake or a piece of glass, was a common cure for many ailments. Like many Indians, the Caingang treated fever with cold baths. Breathing on the affected spot was a common means of assisting a suffering person. Wounds were sprinkled with pulverized jaborandy powder.

When illness was caused by the loss of the soul, the patient might recover if appropriate words were spoken to induce the soul to return. It was often promised food. If the shaman's diagnosis revealed that the disease had been brought about by invisible missiles shot by a spirit, the cure consisted of extracting them with the mouth. This procedure, however, was observed only among the Aweikoma-Caingang of Santa Catarina.

To drive clouds away, old women blew against the right hand and waved it toward the clouds, spreading the fingers as if to disseminate their breath. When the Aweikoma-Caingang desired rain, they put their mouths to the water and blew. They took some in their hands and cried as they threw it upward, "Look here! Do like this." *Henry, 1941, p. 94* (p. 471) Ashes thrown into a river were expected to stop its rise.

According to *Lozano, 1873, 1: 427* (p. 471), Guayana shamans drank mate in order to consult spirits. Answering questions put to them by their clients, the shamans always said, "The grass (mate) told me this or that." Among modern Awiekoma, a man might be requested to drink mate and to belch while he is asked questions. A strong belch is interpreted as "No" and a weak one as "Yes" *Henry, 1941, p. 88* (p. 471).

In order to know which animals would be killed and where they would be found, the Aweikoma-Caingang set fire to a heap of pine- wood charcoal. The size of the spark corresponded to an animal species and the place where it twinkled indicated where the game would be slain. The Caingang of Sao Paulo believed that old women had the power of foretelling the future in dreams which they induced by taking the pulverized leaves of an unknown plant.

The "cult of the dead" was "the foundation and strongest expression of the spirtual culture of the Kaingang" *Baldus, 1935, p. 52* (p. 472), as the whole community took part in the ceremonies, and children were at this time assigned by their fathers or others to moeity subgroups. The aim of veingreinya, the main ritual, was to break the bonds uniting the living with the ghosts, who were driven to their last abode, where they remained harmless. It took place when the maize was green and pine nuts were ripe, that is, sometime between the middle of April and June. It was organized by mourners for a parent, a sister, or a son, but never for a wife or a daughter; according to Manizer, the initiative was taken by a distant relative.

The green bough placed above the tomb announced the coming performance; the news of which was carried to nearby settlements by messengers appointed by the "master of the dance." One of the heralds blew a horn; another informed the gathered listeners of the date.

In the meantime, the organizer piled up wood and gathered honey and maize, kept in pots in a special place, for liquor. For 3 days before the festival, men danced around these containers, crying and singing funeral songs. The fermented beverages, poured into large troughs dug out of bottle-tree trunks, were heated by throwing red-hot potshards into them. During the night before the feast, the organizer and his assistant went to the cemetery to cover the grave with earth. In the morning, the trough was dragged to the plaza and food was heaped around it. Men sang and beat the ground with a stamping tube.

On the day before veingreinya, the visitors, blowing horns and bamboo flutes, arrived and were met by their hosts and treated to beer. The following afternoon, the members of the moiety subgroups, adorned with their distinctive facial paintings, were led separately to the cemetery by relatives of the deceased. At the head of each moiety was a singer and three dancers, as well as the close relatives. On the way, the singer with his subgroups stopped by every tree at which the corpse bearers had rested en route and sang a song of meaningless syllables, shaking his rattle and kicking his feet back and forth. After this musical interlude, they resumed marching, but the other moiety had to go through the same ceremony. When the first moiety reached the cemetery, the same dance was performed over the grave, with the singer standing over the head of the deceased. The rest of the crowd remained outside the cemetery. then the other moiety danced over the grave. When the ghost was thought to have been expelled, everyone shouted for joy and ran in all directions. The moieties joined, and the mixed sounds of "flutes and laughter and cries were heard all over the place." The singers and dancers received liquor until completely drunk. Later the moieties danced in a double circle around bonfires lit on the plaza; finally, everyone drank to his heart's content.

A few variant details were given by *Manizer, 1930, p. 787* (p. 473). The relatives of the dead, who remained in their huts with their head covered with blankets, were forced to drink beer until they lost consciousness. Those who had gone to the cemetery painted black strokes over their bodies. Soon after, many pairs of participants, standing face to face, cried out in turn, "xogn, xogn," while the spectators sang lugubrious melodies. Then everyone danced counter-clockwise around the fire, keeping time with his bamboo tube.

The mythology of the Caingang is known mainly through a few myths collected by *Borba, 1904* (p. 473) and summarized here: Regarding their "origin of agriculture," the Indians suffered scarcity of food. A chief told them to cultivate a piece of land by fastening a creeper around his neck and trailing him on the ground. They did so, and 3 months later, his penis produced maize, his testicles beans, and his head gourds.

As per their "origin of fire," it came about when, according to Caingang mythology, Tejeto transformed himself into a white urraca (bird) and let himself be carried by a brook flowing by the house of the Master-of-fire, whose daughter picked up the bird and dried him by the fire. Tejeto stole an ember and was pursued, but hid in the crevice of a cliff. To strike him, the Master-of-fire thrust the end of his bow into the crevice. Tejeto made his nose bleed and smeared the bow with the blood. The Master-of-fire, convinced that he had killed the thief, went away. Tejeto kindled the dry branch of a palm. Since then, men have had fire.

Another myth concerned a great deluge that took

place in olden times. From the waters, there emerged only the summit of the mountain Crinji-jinbe, toward which the Kayurukre and the Kame swam, with firebrands in their mouths. The Kayurukre and the Kame were drowned, and their souls went to live in the center of the mountain. The Caingang and some Curuton or Are arrived at the summit of Crinjijinbe. They remained there several days crouched in the branches of a tree or reposing on the ground. The saracuras (a kind of bird), came with baskets full of dirt and began to fill the sea. They were aided in their work by the ducks. The Caingang who were on the ground could leave, but those who had climbed into the trees were turned into monkeys, and the Curuton were changed into owls. The Caingang established themselves in the vicinity of the Serra of Crinjijinbe. The Kayurukre and the Kame left the mountain, the former by a smooth and level path, and the latter by a rugged trail, due to the small feet of the Kayurukre and large ones of the Kame. Where the Kayurukre had been, a river gushed through the pass, but the place from which the Kame emerged remained just as it was. That is why they continued to go ask for water from the Kayurukre. The Caingang ordered the Curuton to seek the basket they had left at the foot of the mountain; the latter did not want to go back. Ever since then, they lived separated from the Caingang, who considered them fugitive slaves.

There was also the story of the creations of Kame and Kayurukre. Two brothers, Kame and Kayurukre, after having left the mountain, created jaguars from ashes and coals; then the antas or tapirs from ashes only. The tapir, who had a small ear, heard that he was ordered to eat herbs and branches, when the Creators had told him to subsist on meat. Kayurukre also made the great anteater, which he did not have time to finish, leaving it with a toothless jaw and tongue, which was only a little stick that Kayurukre in his haste, put in his mouth. Kayurukre made the useful animals, among them the bee; Kame, made the harmful creatures (pumas, serpents, wasps, etc.).

The brothers resolved to kill the jaguars. They made them get on a tree trunk thrown into a stream. Kame was to push the trunk and make it drift away. Some jaguars clung to the bank and Kame, frightened by their roaring, did not dare to push them into the water. It was on account of his faintheartedness that jaguars still exist.

The people of Kayurukre and those of Kame intermarried. As the men were more numerous than the woman, they allied themselves also with the Caingang. From that time on, Kayurukre, Kame, and Caingang considered themselves kinsmen and friends. In olden times, the Caingang did not chant or dance. One day Kayurukre, going to hunt, saw some branches dancing at the foot of a tree. One branch was crowned with a gourd, which tinkled and marked the rhythm of a melody chanted by an invisible being. Kayrukre's companions took the branches (stamping tubes), while he took the gourd (rattle). They danced with these instruments. A few days later, Kayurukre met the great anteater, who stood erect on his paws and began to chant. His song was identical with the one that Kayurukre had heard the day he saw the sticks dancing. Thus he learned that the mysterious chanter was the great anteater. The anteater demanded of him his sticks and then danced. He predicted that his wife would bear him a boy.

The Aweikoma-Caingang of Santa Catarina told only confused origin myths, but had stories about animals, among them, how Hummingbird hoarded water. Traditions of internecine feuds, however, loomed most prominently in their lore.

CAIZCIMU.

(West Indies; Haiti) According to information given, all the Indians in this province belonged to the Arawakan linguistic family. They were located in the eastern part of the present Dominican Republic, extending on the south side of the Bay of Samana to a point near the mouth of the Juna River and on the south coast of the whole island to the neighborhood of the mouth of the San Juan or Maguana. *Peter Martyr, 1912* defined it as reaching only to the coast just west of the present Ciudad Trujillo (formerly Santo Domingo City), but the subdivisions he named indicate the greater extension given above. Some of the subdivisions, described by Martyr as "districts or cantons," include Arabo, Baguanimabo, Guanama, Hazoa, Macorix, and Xagua. Specific population information for this tribe is not known.

CAJUENCHE

(U.S.; Calif.) A Yuman tribe speaking the Cocopa dialect and residing in 1775-76 on the East bank of the Rio Colorado below the mouth of the Gila, next to the Quigyuma, their rancherias extending South toabout lat. 32 degrees 33' and into central Southern California, about lat. 33 degrees 08', where they met the Comeya. At the date named the Cajuenche are said tohave numbered 3,000 and to have been enemies of the Cocopa. Of the disappearance of the tribe practically nothing is known, but if they are identical with the Cawina, or Quokim, as they seem to be, they had become reduced to a mere remnant by 1851, owing to constant wars with the Yuma. At this date Bartlett reported only 10 survivors living with the Pima and Maricopa, only one whom understood his native language, which was said to differ from the Pima and Maricopa.

BIBLIOGRAPHY —

● HODGE, FREDERICK WEBB. Handbook of American Indians North of Mexico. Washington: Government Printing Office, 2 vols., 1907-10.
● MURDOCK, GEORGE P. Ethnographic Bibliography of North America. New Haven, CT: Human Relations Area Files Press, 1975.
● SWANTON, JOHN R. The Indian Tribes of North America. Washington, DC: U.S. Government Printing Office, 1952.

CAKCHIQUEL

(Central America; Guatamela) are a Maya Indian group, most of whom live in the rugged midwestern highlands. Like the closely related Quiche and Tzutujil Maya, they retain many pre-Columbian cultural and subsistence practices. They were known to others and referred to themselves as the Cakchiquel long before the 16th century Spanish Conquest. The name may refer to "those of the red tree" (perhaps the breadnut of *ramon* tree, Brosimum alicastrum, Sw.).

Although they were politically united before the Conquest, today the Cakchiquel are divided into administrative-territorial townships *municipios*. The township is the center of their community life and identity, a distinct, almost tribal unit. the Cakchiquel occupy roughly the same area as they did prior to the Conquest: the present-day Guatemalan departments of Solola, Chimaltenago, Guatemala, Sacatepequez, and Esquintla. Most Cakchiquel towns are found north and east of Lake Atitlan.

Cakchiquel is a language of the Quichean group which belongs to the Macro-Mayan family. Quiche and Cakchiquel diverged early in the 15th century. Although many Cakchiquel speak Spanish, they also continue to use their native tongue.

The Indian ideal is the corn (maize) farmer, but each community also has craft and agricultural specializations which often are more important economically than the maize fields. The specialties sustain township differences in language, dress, and ritual; promote community solidarity; and help structure the native market system. The unit of production and consumption is the household, within which there is a strict division of labor based on age and sex. Many men also do seasonal work on Guatemala's Pacific Coast. Colorful markets bring together Indians from different towns, each with its traditional place in the market. The Cakchiquels, most very poor, work extremely hard all their lives, taking time off only during festival and market days.

Cakchiquel parents are relatively permissive with children. From late adolescence on, the male life-cycle is structured by the native religious-prestige system (*cofradia* or *cargo*). A man's wife and children support his participation in the system; hence it organizes their lives as well as his. Today, the monogamous Cakchiquel practice bilateral descent and neolocal residence. Relations with those outside the household are formal.

Cargo comprises a series of ranked, alternating civil and religious offices. The exclusively Indian *cofradias* care for the community saints and organize festivals. Elders, who have passed through all the posts, often control a community, although the theocratic aspect of *cargo* is no longer formally recognized by the Guatemalan government. The system stratifies and integrates the Indians. It also helps to maintain the corporate nature of Indian townships and limits their integration with the nation.

Cakchiquel religion is a fusion of missionary Catholicism and native tradition. For example, many Catholic-named saints retain the traits of ancient Maya gods. People, animals, and objects have guardian spirits. The Cakchiquel believe the universe is basically spiritual and moral; relationships with all spirits (human and otherwise) are prescribed; in an uncertain world one can but try to discern and obey the prescriptions; and there is ultimate justice in the universe.

Postclassic Quichean, including Cakchiquel, ruling elites claimed Toltec Mexican ancestry. They migrated from semilegendary Tollan (perhaps Tula in Hidalgo, Mexico) to the Gulf of Mexico, and finally entered Guatemala where, by the end of the 11th century, they subdued the native people. The elite soon became completely Mayanized. The Cakchiquel were allied or united with the Quiche until the 15th century when a deposed Quiche ruler, Quikab, advised them to establish their own "nation." The Cakchiquel founded their capital around 1450 at Iximche (corn plant) near present-day Tecpan. Like other such capitals, Iximche was a protected hilltop ceremonial-elite residence center ruling village-farming groups. The architecture of Iximche shows strong Mexican influence. The large residential kin groups (*chinamital*) may have had corporate functions, somewhat like the Aztec *calpul*. One of the two principal families was the Xahil (bat) clan. After the separation from the Quiche, the Cakchiquel continued warring against their neighbors until 1524, when the Spanish entered western Guatemala.

The Spanish ended the sociopolitical unity and independence of the various Maya groups and, at first, governed them through traditional local authorities. The Indians were congregated and segregated into corporate communities modeled after Spanish municipalities. The Cakchiquels were converted raapidly to 16th century Catholicism. While they suffered from new diseases, loss of unity and land, and political-economic exploitation under Spanish colonial and later Guatemalan national rule, they also worked out forms of accommodation with non Indians. The patterns laid down in the 16th century more or less endured into the 20th century.

BIBLIOGRAPHY —

● STEWARD, JULIAN H. Handbook of South American Indians. 7 Vols., Washington, DC: U.S. Govt. Printing Office, 1946-59.

CALAPOOYA

See KALAPUYA.

CALCHAQUI

(South America; Argentina) a subgroup of the Daiguita, *q.v.* inhabiting the Calchaqui, Quimivil and Santa Maria Valleys in Catamaraca and La Rioja provinces, Circa AD 900-1250. They were a widely feared and respected warlike people who developed a remarkably high level of civilization which demonstrates strong influences from the Tiahuanaco expansion into Argentina and neighboring Chile. Calchaqui architecture was primarily rectangular or circular houses of the *pirca* (dry masonry and stone) type of construction, located in informally- arranged cities. These houses, which are the earliest stone- walled structures in the Argentine region, made use of the *pucara* (fortified stone towers) built on hill-tops throughout the area, with walls up to five feet thick, and about ten feet in height; they were extremely effective until Spanish cannon was introduced into the region. The basis of everyday life was agricultural, supplementd by some hunting and food gathering. The Calchaqui are mentioned by chroniclers as being very well- dressed, wearing brightly-colored garments woven of alpaca, llama and vicuna wool; they paid great attention to head-dresses and coiffures, which may have been related to status or class differences--indeed, one of the most severe Spanish punishments inflicted on the people was to cut off their basketry and textiles, which have perished over the centuries; sufficient fragments have survived to indicate that these were familiar crafts at which the weavers excelled. Calchaqui rock artistry is found on the surfaces of caves and boulders throughout the northern area of the country, and is marked by the strong Diaguita fondness for strong, contrasting designs. Calchaqui and the related Aguada pottery is unique, with intricate designs incised, painted or modeled on the vessels; one unusual form is the large burial urns, particularly notable in Santa Maria, which were intende for children; these clay coffins were brilliantly decorated and interred in cemeteries reserved for juveniles, or occasionally included with adult burials. However, it is in metalworkk that the Calchaqui were particularly noteworthy; their beautiful copper and bronze axes, cast with elaborate desings, knives, plaques, "knuckle-dusters," and ceremonial shields have become famous throughout the pre-Columbian art world, and while less evident, the ability of the artisans to work gold and silver is equally impressive. Trophy heads were taken in battle to frighten enemies, as well as to strengthen the warrior's resolve; women even went into battle armed with torches, both for the purpose of setting fire to dwellings and for possessions of the enemy, as well as to force their menfolk to greater fury. Although contacted by the Spanish, invading the region form the north, the Diaguita were never entirely conquered, and caused the settlers continuous trouble with sporadic uprisings for many decades. They are entirely extinct today, although some of their descendants may have become assimilated into related Hokan-speaking tribes of Argentina and Chile.

BIBLIOGRAPHY —

● STEWARD, JULIAN H. Handbook of South American Indians. 7 Vols., Washington, DC: U.S. Govt. Printing Office, 1946-59.

CALIFORNIA

(U.S.; Calif.) At the time of their initial contact with Europeans in 1542 the California Indians had an estimated population of 275,000, one of the densest in North America. Many early explorers who visited the coastal and central tribes--the Chumash, Yokut, Pomo, Costanoan, Wintun, Maidu, and those later known by Mission names--described them as handsome, friendly and generous. They were evidently a gentle and peace-loving people, loosely aggregated in small bands, and lacking in tribal identity. The devastation of this great population was one of the most rapid and dramatic on record.

It can be said to have begun in 1769 when Father Junipero Serra came from Mexico and founded the first mission at San Diego, according to the Spanish policy of converting and pacifying the Indians in preparation for colonization. By 1823 twenty-one missions had been established along the Camino Real.

The Indians succumbed to conversion with little resistance. Many of them completely lost their tribal identity and were known only by mission names as Luisenos, Gabrielinos, or Dieguenos. They lived in pueblos near the missions and were trained in the mission schools and fields in agriculture, sheep raising, carpentry, weaving, leather work and other crafts. But forced labor did not agree with these simple, food-gathering people. They frequently attempted to run away and were punished by flogging or confinement.

In 1834 the newly formed Mexican republic secularized the missions and gave the Indian's lands to Mexican patriots who converted it into large stock ranches. The Indians who had developed a dependence on the missions and had lost their original culture were scattered to fend for themselves. They were no match for the influx of boisterous and pugnacious frontiersmen who swarmed to California in the Gold Rush of 1849. In the remainder of the century, forced labor, prostitution, alcohol, disease, and the ruthless extermination policies of vigilante committees took such a toll of the Indian population that by 1900 there were only 15,000 left.

There are few names of notable leaders among these people. But in 1872-73 the Modoc tribe of the Oregon border under Kintpuash, known to the whites as Captain Jack, resisted removal to a reservation and held out against the U.S. Army in the California Lava Beds for six months. They were defeated, and Captain Jack was hanged.

Today 12,500 California Indians live on 76 reservations or rancherias totalling 450,000 acres. But most reservations are small and offer no opportunity for development of industries. The Sacramento area office of the Bureau of Indian Affairs administers the Indian's trust lands. Other services are rendered by the state. Although the total population of California Indians is about 90,000 this does not represent native Californians so much as Plains or Southwestern Indians who have been attracted, like so many other Americans, to California life and live in the urban industrial areas.

CALIFORNIA CULTURE AREA

Since California lies along the path of a southern migration route for people crossing the Bering Strait from Siberia, it was settled at a very early date. In fact, the oldest human fossil found in North America is the "Laguna girl", skull a found at Laguna Beach, California, radio-carbon dated as about 17,000 years old.

Probably successive waves of newcomers passed through California continually. Some went on to make their homes in Mexico, South America, or the eastern U.S., but no doubt many small groups elected to stay there. As a result, California acquired a very large, but very diversified population before white immigration. The number of these people has been estimated at 275,000, but they lived in small, independent groups and spoke over 100 different languages or dialects. Every Indian language family was represented there. In one tribe, the now extinct Yahi, the men even spoke a different language from the women.

Nevertheless, the California people shared cultural traits in common. The climate and year-round abundance of food provided an easy life for them. Most of these Indians remained simple gatherers of wild food. They collected seeds and nuts of all kinds, but depended chiefly on the acorn from which, by elaborate processing, they removed bitter tasting and poisonous tannic acid. It was then ground and pounded into a flour or paste. Even among the tribes who hunted intensively, or among the coastal and riverine people who fished, acorn flour was a staple. Food was stored and surplus was traded, sometimes at considerable distances, for other goods.

The people lived in settled villages in permanent houses varying from plank houses in the north to thatched huts in the south. Chiefs and shamans were respected, but social organization does not seem to have been very formal.

The Californian's culture was simple and their arts undistinguished except for basketry, in which they excelled. Baskets were so finely woven they held water and could be used for boiling food with hot stones. They ranged in size from huge, durable storage containers to baskets so tiny that the weave was practically invisible. Today the art has been revived by Pomo, Yurok, Hupa, and Karok peoples.

Religions flourished in California. Among the secret societies was the Kuksu cult associated with the Pomo, Wintun, Maidu, and Costanoan tribes. Initiation into the cult was by stages. Each stage involved an elaborate rite performed by masked dancers, singers, and clowns whose roles were often hereditary. Dancers impersonated important animals or spirits such as coyote or thunder. The most important role was Kuksu, sometimes rgarded as a deity, otherwise as a first man or culture hero. His headdress was an enormous ball of feathered sticks.

Southern California had the *Toloache* cult, who celebrated the rites of *Chingichnich,* also regarded as a deity by some groups, but by others as a man who died but whose spirit resided in the jimsonweed. The hallucinogenic drug *datura,* obtained from this weed, was used in their rituals to obtain visions and guidance.

The general impression left by the Californians is that of an amiable but hapless people. However, their culture was so rapidly destroyed by white contact that there was very little of it left for sympathetic students of a later date to study. The discovery in 1911 of Ishi, a Yahi Indian who alone in the wilderness survived the annihilation of his tribe, suggests that the amiable Californians had important strengths and skills that enabled them to hold this desirable territory for several centuries.

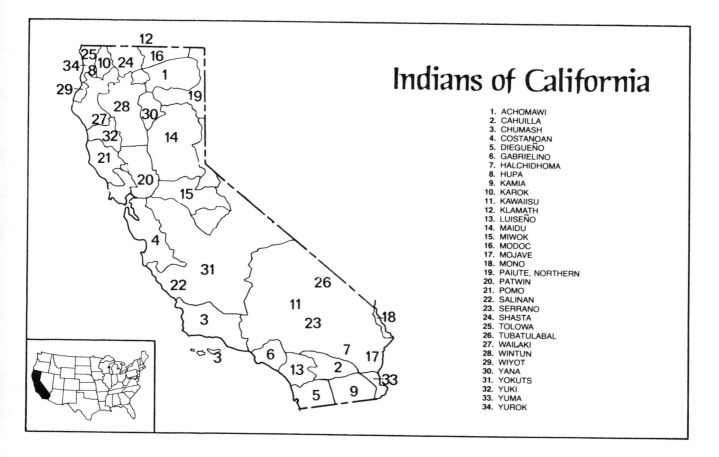

Indians of California

1. ACHOMAWI
2. CAHUILLA
3. CHUMASH
4. COSTANOAN
5. DIEGUEÑO
6. GABRIELINO
7. HALCHIDHOMA
8. HUPA
9. KAMIA
10. KAROK
11. KAWAIISU
12. KLAMATH
13. LUISEÑO
14. MAIDU
15. MIWOK
16. MODOC
17. MOJAVE
18. MONO
19. PAIUTE, NORTHERN
20. PATWIN
21. POMO
22. SALINAN
23. SERRANO
24. SHASTA
25. TOLOWA
26. TUBATULABAL
27. WAILAKI
28. WINTUN
29. WIYOT
30. YANA
31. YOKUTS
32. YUKI
33. YUMA
34. YUROK

BIBLIOGRAPHY —

● BANCROFT, HUBART HOWE. The Native Races of the Pacific States of North America. San Francisco, CA: 1874.
● BARROWS, DAVID P. Ethno-botany of the Coahuilla Indians of Southern California. Chicago, IL: The University of Chicago Press, 1900.
● DALE, EDWARD EVERETT. The Indians of the Southwest, A Century of Development under the U.S. Norman, OK: University of Oklahoma Press, 1949.
● DELLENBAUGH, FREDERICK S. Fremont and '49, The Story of a Remarkable Career and Its Relation to the Exploration and Development of our Western Territory, Especially of California. New York, and London: G. P. Putnam's Sons, 1914.
● DESERT MAGAZINE. Indian Cemetary Restored. Twenty-nine Palms, California. Chemehuevi Indian Cemetery, 60 Indians thought to be buried there... CA: vol. 21, no. 7, July 1958.
● DOOLITTLE, J. R. Condition of the Indian Tribes; Report of the Joint Special Committee... Washington, March 3, 1865, January 26, 1867.
● DUNN, J. P. Massacres of the Mountains, A History of the Indian Wars of the Far West. New York, NY: Harper & Bros, 1886.
● EASTMAN, ELAINE GOODALE. Pratt, The Red Man's Moses. Norman, OK: University of Oklahoma Press, 1935.
● GABRIEL, RALPH HENRY. The Pageant of America: the Lure of the Frontier... New Haven, CT: Yale University Press, 1929.
● GHENT, WILLIAM JAMES. The Road to Oregon, A Chronicle of the Great Emigrant Trail. New York, NY: Longmans, Green & Co., 1929.
● GREENHOW, ROBERT. The History of Oregon and California and the Other Territories on the North-West Coast of North America... Boston, MA: Little and J. Brown,1845.
● HALLENBECK, CLEVE. Spanish Missions of the Old Southwest. New York, NY: Doubleday, Page & Co., 1926.

● HEBARD, GRACE RAYMOND., E. A. BRININSTOOL. The Bozeman Trail; Historical Accounts of the Blazing of the Overland Routes into the Northwest, and the Fights with Red Cloud's Warriors. Cleveland, OH: The Arthur H. Clark Co.
● HOLMES. Anthropological Studies in California. National Museum, 1900.
● HUMFREVILLE, J. LEE. Twenty Years Among Our Hostile Indians. New York, NY: Hunter & Co.
● INDIAN OFFICE REPORT. Kidnapping of Indian Children and Selling them for Servants. pg. 10, 1857.
----- Five Reservations Have Been Established in California, 11,239 Indians Have Been Located. pg. 117, 1867.
● JACKSON, HELEN HUNT. A Century of Dishonor; A Sketch of the U.S. Gov't., Dealings with some of the Indian Tribes. New York, NY: Harper & Bros., 1881 reprinted Boston, MA: Little, Brown & Co., 1909.
● KELSEY, C. E. The Neglected Indians of Northern California. Contained in The American Indian and Missions; a reprint of articles in the Assembly Herald of Feb'y, 1915.
● MERRIAM, DR. C. HART. Has 20,000 card index regarding Indians of California, Nevada and Utah. Washington, DC.
----- Studies of California Indians. Berkeley, CA: Dept., of Anthropology of the University of California, 1955.
● PALMER, ROSE A. The North American Indians, An Account of the American Indians North of Mexico. New York, NY: Smithsonian Institution Series, Inc., 1929.
● PHILLIPS, PAUL C. Forty Years on the Frontier, As Seen in the Journals and Reminiscences of Granville Stuart. Cleveland, OH: The Arthur H. Clark Co., 1925.
● PORRERS, STEPHEN. Geological Survey-- Tribes of California. North American Ethnology, Vol. 3.
● PRIESTLY, HERBERT INGRAM. The Coming of the White Man, 1492-1848. (Vol. 1, A History of American Life.) New York, NY: The MacMillan Co., 1929.

• SCHOOLCRAFT, HENRY R. History of the Indian Tribes of the U.S.; Their Present Condition and Prospects... Philadelphia, J. B. Lippincott & Co., 1857.

• SHEA, JOHN G. Catholic Missions Among the Indian Tribes of the U.S. New York, NY: E. Dunigan & Bros., 1854.

• SMITHSONIAN REPORT. Ancient Graves and Shellheaps of California: Account of the Burial of Indian Squaw. San Bernardino CA: San Bernardino Co., 1874. Co.,

CALIMA

(South America; Colombia) are a prehistoric tribe and cultural period inhabiting the region of the Upper Cauca Valley near the present-day city of Medellin. Very little controlled archaeological work has been done in this region, and little is known of the life of the ancient Calima people; their designs on stone and pottery show some similarities to those found in San Augustin, although this relationship is uncertain. They were perhaps the earliest goldsmiths in Colombia, noted for their skill in fashioning large sheets of gold into breastplates and flat hammered gold ornaments; their later work is featured by exquisitely designed long slender cast gold pins with tiny human and animal figures on the top. Calima chronology has not been definitely established, but seems to have been at its height between AD 1-500, with every indication of at least 250-year extension earlier and later.

BIBLIOGRAPHY –

• STEWARD, JULIAN H. Handbook of South American Indians. 7 Vols., Washington, DC: U.S. Govt. Printing Office, 1946-59.

CALLAHUAYA

(South America; Bolivia) who live in the provinces of Munecas and Caupolican, La Paz Department, are historically a subtribe of the Aymara, but for centuries they have considered themselves to be ethnically distinct. They are supposed to have been court physicians to the Incas, and there is some conjecture that Callahuaya became the secret language of the royal Inca family. The Callahuaya were little affected by the Conquest. If anything, they seemed to profit by it, especially by the introduction of horses. Their survival rests on their position as famous traveling curers and charm sellers throughout the entire Andean region.

The Callahuaya continue to practice their aboriginal folk medicine and retain their customs, language, and prestigious position despite the advent of modern medicine. The continuance of pre-Incaic indigenous beliefs has helped to perpetuate their respected status and useful position within the Andean society. Their status and wealth are reflected in their expensive indigenous costume and the silver-worked saddles and stirrups of the Callahuaya horsemen. Members of this ethnic group may speak as many as four languages--Callahuaya, Queecha, Aymara, and Spanish. Except among themselves, they ordinarily speak one of the predominant languages. The herbal remedies known to the Callahuaya number in the thousands and are prepared from plants of both the highlands and the Oriente. Several historians credit the Callahuaya with having introduced quinine and ipecac to the Spaniards. In addition to their empirical remedies, they manufacture and dispense a large number of charms and amulets, designed not only as protectors against illness but also as bearers of good luck.

BIBLIOGRAPHY –

• STEWARD, JULIAN H. Handbook of South American Indians. 7 Vols., Washington, DC: U.S. Govt. Printing Office, 1946-59.

CALUSA

(U.S.; Fla.) were a tribe thought to belong to the Muskhogean division of American Indians. They occupied the southwest coast of Florida from Boca Grande Pass southward, an area called the Calusa sub-region of the Glades Culture area. The main town is thought to have been on Mound Key in Estero Bay.

Most of our knowledge of the Calusa comes from Spanish explorers, missionaries, and captives of the sixteenth century. Father Rogel, a missionary, and d'Escalante Fontaneda, a prisoner of the Calusa for many years, are primary sources. Father Rogel reports that the Calusa territory was called Escampaba in the Indian language, after the chief of a town thought to be the main town of the tribe. The early Spanish contacts called the chief of the tribe "Carlos" after the Spanish emperor, Charles V or derived from the Creek name for the tribe.

Although he does not tell us by what name the tribe called themselves, Fontaneda states that the tribal name meant "the fierce people." The name "Calusa" is probably derived from the Creek name for the people, *kalo salki* ('people'). Variants of this modern English form first appeared in the late eighteenth century.

The Calusa were a sedentary, non-agricultural people, dependent instead upon the rich marine resources of the surrounding waters. Unlike environments of most American Indians, the Calus area provides neither hard stone for traditional projectile points and tools nor good quality clay for pottery. There was some pottery, and some stone was brought in for tools, but the majority of the material culture was provided by shells from the sea, wood and fibers from the surrounding forests, and bones of land and sea creatures. This is probably the reason for continued use of archaic forms such as bone projectile points and spear throwers.

Calusa and other tribes of the Southeast.

The dependable food supply and the relative ease with which it was obtained made possible a centralization of authority, probably combining religious and secular powers, which made it possible to control enough manpower to construct the elaborate shell mounds, earthworks and canals typical of the Calusa area.

With less manpower devoted to food gathering, there was time for technological and artistic experimentation and development. Theirs was an extensive inventory of artifacts, all skillfully made, hammers, awls, chisels, knives, scrapers, gouges, dippers, spoons, gorgets, beads, pendants, picks, weights, and celt belts were made from shell. Some were crafted with wooden handles fastened in place with cord lashings.

A tool unique to this area is the shark's tooth knife with wooden handle with which they carved beautiful and sophisticated three-dimensional art forms. Wood was carved into tubs, bowls, mortars, pestles, amulets, tablets for religious use, decorative items, and float pegs for fishing nets, as well as ceremonial masks and figurines. Their art was some of the most highly developed and sophisticated of any primitive culture. There was also a great variety of excellent cordage, rope and netting made from local fibers.

With more available manpower, aggressive warfare became possible and by the time the Spanish arrived the Calusa controlled considerable territory. While boundaries of the territory controlled by the Calusa chief are imprecise, there is little doubt that much of South Florida, including at times the Keys, was under Calusa domination and influence. Contemporary estimates of the number of towns so dominated range from fifty to more than seventy, from which tribute was exacted in the form of feathers, food, fruits, roots, skins, and, in later times, Spanish captives as well as gold and silver from shipwrecks. As early as 1513 Ponce de Leon heard reports of the "Cacique Carlos and his gold."

Religious development accompanied the political expansion. Ceremonialism was highly developed and employed elaborate paraphernalia, including masks, large plaques and totemic objects, first made of wood, some later reproduced in gold, silver and copper.

Father Rogel reports that the Calusa pantheon included three principal deities with separate and distinct domains. Spirits of the dead were also important. At certain times (one source says "in the time of the harvest") human sacrifices were essential. In later years Spanish captives were the sacrificial victims. Heads of such victims were central elements in a dance. When a chief or his principal wife died, "servants" were sacrificed to accompany the dead. When a child of the chief died, sons and daughters of subjects were sacrificed.

At least the main Calusa town contained a temple on a mound in which the ceremonial masks and other paraphernalia were kept, and to which the chief retired at certain times, accompanied by a few close associates, to perform secret rituals. He was credited with bringing about the fruitfulness of land and sea. At times processions of masked figures moved down from the temple through the living areas, accompanied by singing of the women.

An exception to the tribe's incest rules required the chief to take his own full sister as his principal wife. Women related to chiefs of subject tribes were taken as additional wives of the chief in order to cement political alliances and to ensure the subjugation of these rites.

Society was stratified, with evidence of at least two classes, and probably some slaves. Persons of higher rank had access to some foods not available to lesser persons.

There is no definite information on the Calusa language. There was no writing system, and it seems the early Spanish contacts made no effort to record the language. It would likely have been of the Muskhogean linguistic family if, in fact, the Calusa were of such racial stock.

Feline carving from the Key Marco site.

The most reliable estimates place Calusa population in the sixteenth and seventeenth centuries between 4,000 and 7,000, with a probable 1,000 in the main village. Although their traditional hostility to all who entered their territory delayed their fate for an additional century, they were largely destroyed by Creek and English raids from the north during the first half of the eighteenth century. Any surviving remnants were probably either absorbed by the Seminoles or gradually forced down the Keys and eventually to Cuba where they were absorbed by the indigenous population.

(see map page XIV)

BIBLIOGRAPHY —

● THE FLORIDA HISTORICAL SOCIETY QUARTERLY. Vol. XI, No. 4, pg. 154, April, 1933.
● HODGE, FREDERICK WEBB. Handbook of American Indians North of Mexico. Washington: Government Printing Office, 2 vols., 1907-10.
● MURDOCK, GEORGE P. Ethnographic Bibliography of North America. New Haven, CT: Human Relations Area Files Press, 1975.
● SWANTON, JOHN R. The Indian Tribes of North America. Washington, DC: U.S. Government Printing Office, 1952.
● VOEGELIN, BYRON D. South Florida's Vanished People. Fort Myers Beach, FL: The Island Press, 1943.

CAMACAN

(South America; Brazil) (including the *Cutasho, Catathoy, Masascara, and Menian*) speak related dialects which belong to an isolated linguistic family in Brazil. They were once included in the *Ge* family, but they are now considered to be an independent linguistic family.

History   The *Camacan* remained for many years hostile to the Portuguese and fought against them until 1806. At the beginning of the last century, they lived in six or seven villages somewhat to the north of the Rio Pardo in Bahia province, Brazil.

In 1817 the *Camacan* who were settled at Jiboya, near Arrayal da Conquista in the State of Bahia, were visited by Maximiliam Wied-Neuwied. His short description of their culture is still one of the best sources of these Indians. At that time, *Camacan* lived in small "aldeas" under the rule of "directors" appointed by the government. They were mistreated and exploited by the colonists and their native culture was breaking down.

In 1819 Spix and Martius spent a few days with a group of *Camacan* settled at Villa de S. Pedro de Alcantara, under the care of a Capuchin missionary. They were told the *Camacan* had six villages in the forests along the Gravata River in the District of Minas Novas, but that the bulk of the tribe inhabited the region between the Rio da Cachoeira and the Grugunhy River, a territory of the Rio das Contas. They heard of the group established near Arrayal da Conquista in the Serra do Mundo Novo, and of another near Ferradas.

The French traveler Douville saw these Indians in 1833-34 on the Itahipe River and on Rio dos Ilheos.

In 1938 Nimuenfaju found 11 *Camacan* on a reservation shared with remnants of other tribes. The area aolloted to the several groups was at about longitude 40 W., between the Rio da Cachoeira and the Rio Pardo.

Culture   The *Camacan*, possibly numbering only a few dozen today, usually opened clearings on hilltops, where they cultivated sweet potatoes, beans, sweet manioc gourds, watermelons, yams, maize, cotton, cashews, papayas, bananas, oranges, and pineapples. They supplemented their diet by hunting, fishing, gathering considerable honey, and collecting wild fruits. A community in want would visit another village, where they helped exhaust the resources of the inhabitants. Crops belonged to the planters, but bananas, after a single harvest by the owner, could be plucked by anyone.

The dog was the only domesticated animal.

Houses were large communal houses accomodating as many as 20 families, each having its own sleeping platform, covered with fibers.

Dress   Originally, the men wore only a penis sheath of leaves. After European contact, women, formerly completely naked, adopted first a bark belt, later a string of fringes in front and behind, and, finally, a woven loincloth. Men wore neck-

laces of monkey teeth and tapir hoofs. The ony described specimens of feather ornaments were
showy: a feather headdress built on a net with a
crown of long tail feathers on the top. Men passed
feathers through the perforated lobes of their ears.

The *Camacan* tied a cotton string under the
knees and around the ankles of babies in order to
give an elegant shape to their legs.

The carefully depilated the face and body.
Chiefs wore a tonsure; most other men had their
hair clipped around the neck or let it fall over the
shoulder.

They painted themselves with urucu, genipa and
catua, a pigment extracted from the wood of
Broussonetia tinctoria and combined with castor
oil or grease. Men's favorite patterns were vertical and horizontal stripes on the body; women preferred half circles around their eyes and on their
breasts. Both sexes also smeared themsleves with
urucu leaving only the head, hands, and feet un-
painted.

Weaving Women were expert at spinning 4-ply
cotton strings, which they laced (meshed without
knots) or netted (meshed with knots) into beautiful nets with alternating yellow or red stripes. The
loom for the nets is described as an arched branch
stuck into the ground and crossed by a horizontal
stick corresponding to the lower edge of the fabric.

The *Camacan* wove on a vertical loom. The patterns on their cloth were obtained by dyeing the
threads with genipa, urucu, and with a yellow
wood (*Chlorophora tinctoria*).

Pottery Within the tribal territory, Nimuendaju
found sherds of some 20 large spherical vessels
without either a standing base or a special rim. At
least the lower half had been built up of a lump of
clay, the top being coiled, with rows of fingernail
impressions. Painting and plastic decoration were
lacking. The specimens depart from *Arawak* and
Tupi norms, but approximate in technique samples
from other tribes.

Weapons The bow, made of parauna wood, like
that of the *Patasho,* was characterized by a longitudinal groove along the outer side; it measured
from 7 to 8 feet (2.1 to 2.4 m.), but was shorter
than that of the *Patasho.*

Arrowheads fell into three usual classes, being
tipped with a bamboo knife, a sharpened brauna
rod, or--for hunting birds--with a bulbous root.
Feathering of the arched (eastern Brazilian) type,
was placed at some distance from the butt. War arrows are said to have been poisoned with the sap
of a creeper.

Childbirth customs At her first childbirth, a
woman was helped by an older woman, who placed
her in a hole in the ground. After the delivery, the
husband kept to his bed and refrained from eating

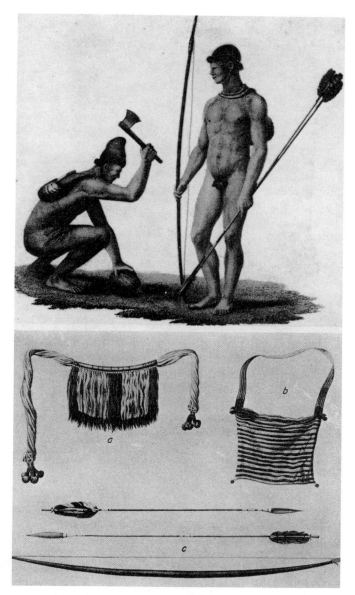

Patashó and Camacan weapons and artifacts.

tapir, peccary, and monkey flesh, subsisting on
bush yam and birds, while his wife carried on her
usual work. Children were nursed until the age of
3 or 4.

Parents never ordered their offspring about, but
consulted their wishes. As soon as possible, children made themselves independent of their families, planting crops and cooking for themselves at
an early age. After killing game, they shared it
with their parents as well as with the other members of the community.

Marriage customs Polygyny was tolerated by
the *Camacan,* but to avoid jealousy among the bachelors, men generally had only one wife.
However, couples separated very easily.

A young man wishing to marry had to ask the permission of the head of his group, who, on consenting, would "buy" the girl if she belonged to another community. A chief had to take as his wife another chief's daughter. The marriage ceremony was celebrated by a banquet and a drinking bout, during which the guests made presents to the newly wedded pair.

In case of divorce, the man had to provide food for his children even when his former wife remarried.

Death   A dead man, duly painted and with all his feather ornaments, was put, in a flexed position, in a grave 4 to 5 feet (1.2 to 1.5 m.) deep. His weapons and a jar full of beer were placed with him. When the grave was filled with earth, a fire was built on top of it, and the site then was covered with palm leaves and branches. A pot, the size of which indicated the age and sex of the deceased, was also placed on the grave. The relatives came now and then to leave an offering of meat. They interpreted the disappearance of the meat as a sign that the offering had been well received by the dead and henceforth tabooed the animal whose meat had been accepted by the soul. The sepulcher was later opened, and the bones were taken home and spread on a platform, painted, and placed in a funeral urn, which was buried in a shallow pit. The transfer of bones was celebrated by a great festival.

Funeral laments were uttered three times a day. A widower could remarry soon after the funeral, but a wodow had to wait for a longer period. The dead were worshipped at the beginning of the rainy season during a feast in their honor.

A dead man who had a grudge against the living, would return in the guise of a jaguar to take revenge. At a mother's request, the souls of good people were reincarnated in newly born babies. Otherwise, they went to a big hut in the sky, where they were assured of an abundant supply of food. The evil ones also flew to the sky, where their main pleasure was to cause storms.

Dances   Men danced in circles to the accompaniment of songs and gourd rattles. They were followed by pairs of women who held each other by the waist.

Drink   A drink was brewed of maize or of sweet potatoes, or occasionally, of papayas or honey. The maize or sweet potatoes were partly chewed and then sprinkled with hot water. The mass then was poured into a large trough dug into the bulky trunk of the bottle-tree *(barrigudo)*, which was half buried in the ground so that the liquid could be warmed without burning the bark.

Drinking sprees were sometimes combined with communal hunts to provide an ample supply of meat. On such occasions there might also be log races, run by two teams, *wadye* and *wana*, distinguished by their decorative paint. As a child grew up, its mother would assign it to one or the other team.

Mythology   One of the principal myths involves the Sun and Moon, the latter figuring as the fool-

Camacan dance.

ish, mischief-making brother, whom Sun several times restores to life. In one episode Sun assumes the shape of a capybara, thus getting the villagers to shoot at him, whereby he replenishes his depleted stock of arows. Cataclysmological ideas include a deluge, a conflagration, and a jaguar's attack on the moon during a lunar eclipse. The "Star Wife" story culminates in the husband's being carried back to earth by vultures. A remarkable parallel to the North American "bloodclot myth" is the story of the overpowering of a wrestling ogre by a hero who throws his opponent on the blade prepared for unsuspecting wayfarers; the conqueror destroys other fiends but anticlimatically dies at the hands of a brother of one of his adversaries. The folklore abounds in other fantastic elements, such as tribes of strong dwarfs, and lice-eaters. Animal characters are frequent, among them the jaguar, the tapir, and various birds.

BIBLIOGRAPHY —

● STEWARD, JULIAN H. Handbook of South American Indians. 7 Vols., Washington, DC: U.S. Govt. Printing Office, 1946-59.

CAMAYURA

(South America; Brazil) are a small tribe living in a single village by the lake *Ipavu,* at the Xingu National Park, Upper Xingu Basin, northeastern Mato Grosso.

Tribal name. Called *Camayura* by Indians and non- Indians, autodenomination is *Apiap.* Subject to doubts the proposed etymologies are *Cayamura: Cami* or *(Came,* sun in Arawak) *ivira* (tree in Camayura), meaning "people of the sun tree"; and *Apiap api* (to hear)- *ap,* meaning "those who hear completely."

Social and cultural boundaries. The Cayamura are one of the nine surviving tribes of the Upper Xingu Culture Area, sharing an almost homogenous culture with the Arawakan Waura, Mehinaku and Yawalapiti, the Cariban Cuikuro, Calapalo and Nahukwa-Matipuhy, the Tupian Aweti and the linguistically unaffiliated Trumai. At present the Camayura have no intertribal divisions, but it can be suspected that they existed and corresponded to the four villages existent in 1887.

Territory. Oral tradition recalls Camayura habitation sites near the confluence of Suya-Missu and Xingu rivers and at the eastern margin of *Ipavu.* Before 1887 they settled at the southern margin of the lake, where they lived at different spots from then to present. A short period was spent at the western bank of *Tiwatiwari* River (c. 1947-c. 1953). Historical territorial boundaries can be roughly traced: the Kuluene River to the north and east; the *Tiwatiwari* to the south and southeast; the Waura and Yawalapiti territories to the west and south (their exact limits are ethno-

graphically unknown). Agricultural activities were restricted in 1967 to the eastern and western margins of *Ipavu;* a small plot existed 3.6 km south of the village.

Lanaguage. Cayamura language *(Apaiwa ye'eng)* belongs to the Tupi stock, Tupi-Guarani family, a subfamily. (13 languages: Tupi-guarani, Tenetehara, Oyampi, Cawahib, Apiaka, Cayamura, Aweti, Tapirape, Xeta, Pauserna, Kayabi and maybe Canoeiro and Takunape.)

Summary of tribal culture. Cayamura ecology is typical of the Amazonian "tropical forest" terra firme adaptive pattern. Villages are on high ground safe from flooding, and must combine easy access to Ipavu lake (or to a small river: *Tiwatiwari,* c. 1947-c. 1953) and to semideciduous tropical forest where gardens are planted. Gardens being distributed around the lake, canoe transportation increases the geographic operational radius of the economic system. Around the village there is anthropogenic bush, savannalike vegetation and orchards of pequi *Caryocar butyrosum)* and mangaba (*Hancornia speciosa);* farther away is dry forest called "cerradao" and semideciduous tropical forest. To the north, across the lake, lays the wide, savanna and forest covered Kuluene floodplain with numerous ox-bow lakes. Those environmental sectors offer distinctive economic resources; most important are rivers and lakes for water and fish, the sole regular animal protein source, and semideciduous forest for slash-and-burn agriculture. The staple crop is bitter manioc, cultivated in association with many others food and non-food plants (maize, sweet potato, beans, squash, banana, sugarcane, uba cane, tobacco, cotton, urucu, etc.). On top of an almost continuous refuse heap which encircles the village, orange, lemon, mango and several of the above listed crops are found. Gathering brings in fruits, fibers, turtle eggs, honey, wood and straw. Hunting obtains feathers, jaguar claws, hides for commerce with non-Indians, and meat for a caged harpia eagle and for people observing food taboos.

Economic and other social activities are regualted by the alterance of a dry "cold" season from May to late September, and a rainy hot season from then to late April. Plots are cleared at the beginning of the dry season and burnt from July to late September; planting starts with the first rains. During the dry season, atmospheric conditions permit to process great quantities of manioc, stockpiled in part for the first rainy months, and fishing is very productive when the waters are at low-level. Food is abundant and travel conditions good during dry weather months, making them the choice period for intertribal ceremonialism, commerce, visiting and, in the past, warfare.

Agricultural implements were stone axes,

piranha teeth and digging sticks. Hunting, fishing and warfare employed bows, arrows and cylindrical wooden clubs (spear-throwers had only ceremonial usee). Traps, wooden fishhooks, poison, spears and cotton or vine nets were in use for fishing. Allt his is being combined with or replaced by steel implements, firearms, nylon dragging nets, etc. Stone axes were acquired from tribes to the north. They make no pottery; clay pots of different shapes and sizes are bartered from the Waura, but aluminum cauldrons are already present. Dugouts of Yuruna type are being substituted for the original bark canoe. Industrial implements increased productivity and reduced men's working time; fetching water with aluminum cauldrons reduced women's effort; canoe type substitution increased their working span and safeness. Elaborated basketry and painted gourds serve as containers.

Villages are round in plan, with several big, beehive-shaped houses surrounding a central plaza with a secret flute cult house, a *morerekwat* burial ground and a harpia eagle conical cage. Peripherical to the houses' circle is a working zone. Spatially, men tend to occupy central positions at the plaza and village, and women peripherical ones.

Domestic groups are bilateral extended families, normally a group of siblings, their wives, children and adherents. As marriage rules prescribe probatory uxorilocal followed by virilocal residence, sisters tend to leave the house. Domestic group leadership belongs to the house's owners, the father or senior brother of the group of siblings. Domentic groups are the major political, economic and cooperative units in the tribe. There is distinction between a *kamara* ("commoners") and a *morerekwat* (lit. "caretaker") category of people. Membership to the *morerekwat* "class" depends on inheritance, house building and ownership, and manipulation of other prestige factors. The most important *morerekwat* is the village leader (called *capitao* "captain," by non-Indians), who shares village leadership with house leaders and shamans. The last gather every night at the burial ground to smoke and discuss matters.

Descent is bilateral. First ascending generation terms are of *bifurcate merging* type, but cousin terminology is *hawaiian*. First descending generation terms are coherent with that combination. Second ascending and descending generation individuals are only distinguished by sex. Parallel cousin marriage is forbidden, cross cousin marriage is forbidden, cross cousin marriage preferential but not mandatory. Attenuated jocking relationships exists between cross cousins of opposite sex; attenuated avoidance occurs between ego and his or her spouse's father, mother and siblings of ego's sex.

Life cycle rituals are name-giving to infants one to three months old' ear piercing for boys at age 8 to 10; seclusion for both sexes at puberty; seclusion for adults at childbirth (with *couvade*), mouring and shamanistic initiation; four types ;of primary interment for the dead. Girls are liberated from seclusion at the *Kwarip* annual ceremonial. Shamanism is important; the tribe has numerous *paye*. Tobacco smoking induces trance for curative or divinatoy purposes. Fear of witchcraft is prevalent, neighboring domestic groups or friendly tribes being suspect; witch killing is relevant in intra-and intertribal political action as a social control mechanism. There is no witchcraft fear or attack directed against customary war enemies.

Mythology focuses on the *Mavutsini* "creation" cycle; what he really does is to transform preexistent things, bringing a new order into the cosmos. The twins *Kwat* and *Yai* (Sun and Moon, both male) completed their grandfather's work and then climbed to the sky thanks to an arrow chain. Other myths are, like this, tightly knit with complex ceremonialism, to which instrumental music, song feasts are *Kwarip* ("creation" reenactment honouring the dead), *Yawari* (spear-throwing contest), *Yamurikuma* (ritualized feminine cult), all with an intertribal climax. Ritualized sex antagonism is fundamental; women violating the flutes' secrecy are gang raped. Sportive hand-to-hand fighting and spear throwing at rituals are substitutes for war against friendly *Xinguan* tribes.

Pacific intertribal relations are intense through ceremonialism, marriage and commerce. Close social ties with other *Xinguan* tribes make the Camayura just one of the localized units of the culturally homogenous and linguistically diversified intertribal *Xinguan society*. Intertribal manufacturer specialization is one of the main supports of ritualized trade, contributing to integrate the area.

Contact with civilization introduced steel implements, weaponry and luxury items into the local commerce. Indian products were partially or totally displaced by them, and focus of commerce is changing from Indian/Indian to Indian/non-Indian trading. Increased technological effectiveness and productivity seems to have weakened extended family ties; a tendency to multiply domestic groups is noted. Artifacts are an emergent "surplus" to be bartered for industrial goods. Magazines, transistor radios, phonographs and tape recorders vehiculate a flow of information from outside which affects traditional worldview. National Park administration is representative of an exterior political power now taken into account at tribal decision making. Portuguese became spoken by most males, females using it poorly or not at all; it is the contact language with non-Indians and some neighboring tribes.

Summary of tribal history. Tribal history is almost unexplored. A habitation site near Suy-Missu Xingu confluence is the more distant evidence of early movements; a southward migration is suggested. Before 1887 they got permission to settle at *Ipavu* eastern margin, then Waura territory. Fear of Suya and Yuruna raids made them move to the southern margin of the lake, then south to *Tiwaitwari* (c. 1947), and back to *Ipavu* they often changed localization within a short radius; agricultural soil exhaustion seems not to be the cause. In 1887 they had 4 villages and were planning a fusion; by 1938 there was a single village. In 1965 the village was connected to *Ipavu* by a 720 m. earthen road; c. 1969 they began resettlement halfway to the lake along the same road, the process taking several years. At this locale they live in 1979. First kknown contact with non-Indians was that of Karl v.d. Steinen expedition in 1884, at the Ronuro Kuluene confluence; first civilized visit to the village was v.d. Steinen's in 1887. Inter-ethnic relations have been peaceful, except for the killings of the Camayura's *morerekwat* in 1884 and of an American journalist after 1926. In 1946 *Expedicao Roncador-Xingu* (leadered by the Villas Boas brothers) installed camp at *Yakare;* from then on interaction with non-Indians has been continuous. Now *Yakare* is a Brazilian Air Force outpost. Villas Boas' post was moved to *Tiwatiwari* and became headquarters of the Xingu National Park (1961). Ten kilometers away, for years the Camayura have been nearer than any *Xinguan* Indian to civilized influence. Culture change was accelerated with the Post's presence, the opening of DR-080 road through the Park (1971) and the approaching cattle ranches. Consequence of non-Indian contact was heavy depopulation brought by successive epidemics;and the most serious was the 1954 measles epidemic.

Contemporary tribal situation. Living at the Xingu National Park makes Camayura and other *Xinguan* tribes situation an exception among most Indian societies of Brazil. The boundaries of the Park keep away the economic pioneer fronts and the negative consequences of contact with them. Inter-ethnic relations are with Post's personnel, and with visitors originating in the upper strata of civilized society; authorities exert a strict control over contact. Tribal territory remains free from encroachment. Depopulation and disease are subdued and there is a definite trend towards demographic growth. Political dependence is concomitant with existence of the Park, a federal agency which provides territorial protection.

Gift-giving of industrial goods and medicines through *Posto Leonardo Villas Boas* creates an economic dependence which reinforces the political one. There is no direct interference on tribal

Four Camaiurá men at Xingu

affairs, but leaders take into consideration possible reactions of administrative authorities. That flow of nerchandise changes tribal technology; new information sources originate interest toward diversified aspects of civilized culture. Positive inter-ethnic experience and derived attitudes make the Cayamura vulnerable to other kinds of contact if the Park is for some reason exitinguished. Portuguese will soon be spoken by all non-infant males; as women have little interaction with Portuguese speakers, their use of the language is very poor. However, generalized bilingualism is a reality, with a diatopic dialect of Portuguese (due chiefly to interference) as a second language.

Population figures. Population was estimated from a minimum 216 to a maximum 264 individuals in 1887, and from 192 to 242 in 1938. In 1887 there were 4 villages, in 1938 just one. First census found 110 indians (1 village) in 1947-8. There were 112 in 1954 (reduced to 94 that same year by a measles epidemic), 115 in 1963, 118 in 1965, 119 in 1969, 118 in 1970, 131 in 1971 and 152 in 1974. Depopulation prevailed from 1887 to 1948, followed by a slight increase interrupted by the 1954 epidemic; population increased again till 1965, stabilized until 1970 and then started a rapid increase. There are no data after 1974.

BIBLIOGRAPHY —

● STEWARD, JULIAN H. Handbook of South American Indians. 7 Vols., Washington, DC: U.S. Govt. Printing Office, 1946-59.

CAMPA

(South America; Peru) is the name of a tribal group located in the tropical forest region, on the headwaters of the Amazon River in South America. The designation of "Campa" has long been applied to these people, but it is not a word in their language and is of uncertain derivation; they call themselves *ashaninka,* which means "our fellows."

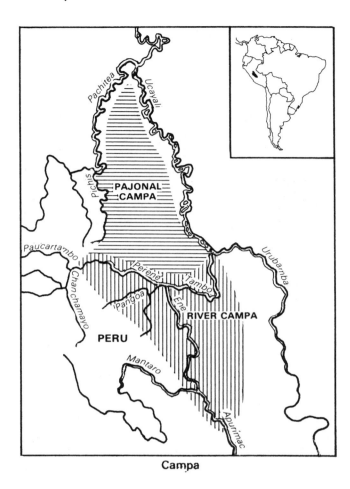

Campa

The Campa are in the western part of the Greater Amazonian culture area, forming the Anti culture cluster with their neighbors, the Amuesha and Machiguenga tribes. Two major Campa groups may be recognized: the Pajonal Campa of the Gran Pajonal region between the Pachitea and Ucayali rivers, extending to the banks of those rivers, and the River Campa, who live along the banks and tributaries of the lower Apurimac, Ene, Perene, and Tambo rivers. Although culturally very similar, these two groups have been traditional enemies and rarely inter-marry.

All Campa speak dialects of the same language, a pre-Andine Arawakan language in the Arawakan phylum. Estimates of the current Campa population size fall in the 20,000 to 30,000 range; reliable estimates of population size at any time in the past do not exist. Campa territory consists of some 30,000 square kilometers of rugged forest-covered land interspersed with small stretches of grassland, in the eastern foothills of the Andes just over the cordilleras from Lima. It extends roughly from latitude 9 S to latitude 12-45' S, and from longitude 73-20' W to longitude 75-20'W. Territorial boundaries have remained fairly constant in post-Contact times, except that the Campa relinquished in the Chanchamayo Valley in the west to colonists during the last century.

Campa culture The Campa subsist by hunting, fishing, and gardening. Using the bow and arrow, the Campa are expert in hunting game animals such as agouti, armadillo, deer, monkey, paca, peccary, and tapir, and game birds such as curassow, parrot, tinamou, and toucan. During the dry season the rivers and streams teem with fish, which are caught with the aid of such paraphernalia as the bow and arrow, fishweir, and fish poison. Most of their sustenance, however, comes from their gardens. They are slash-and-burn horticulturalists, growing manioc tubers, plantains, maize, and other cultivated plants. The men do the hunting and much of the fishing; they also clear and plant the gardens. The women do the harvesting and cooking, using a campfire, and make manioc beer in wooden troughs.

The Campa also cultivate cotton, and the women spin and weave garments from it--simple robes worn by both sexes. In addition, male costume commonly includes a ditty bag of the same cloth suspended by a strap from the shoulder, and perhaps a feather ornament hanging down the back and a wicker hat adorned with a couple of macaw tail feathers. Typically, female costume is completed with a baby-carrying sash of the same cotton cloth, with engraved bone pendants attached, and necklaces and chest bands of seeds. A family occupies its own house--a palm leaf roof set up on posts, usually open on the sides. Other Campa artifacts include utilitarian baskets, mats, and pottery; gourd containers and scoops; dugout canoes and balsa wood rafts; and some simple musical instruments and children's toys. These are all made from locally available materials. In recent times, however, the Campa have come to rely on some Western imports, particularly metal cutting tools, as well as shotguns, aluminum pots, tradecloth, and notions. A certain amount of trade occurs along set routes consisting of chains of trading partners.

The Campa commonly live in small hamlet communities scattered along the rivers and up in the hills. Each community consists of a few conjugal families living together congenially, perhaps with a dominant male acting as a headman. The hamlets are politically autonomous, except on occasion when an especially forceful man rises for a time to a position of leadership over a number of neighboring communities. Another high status is that of shaman, who leads in the periodic ceremony using the hallucinogen ayahuasca (*Banisteriopsis*) and diagnoses ilness by examining what allegedly emerges after sucking the affected part of a patient. On the basis of the diagnosis thus made, curing commonly involves the administration of herbal baths and drinks by whoever is tending the sick person.

The Campa life cycle involves a pregnancy diet adhered to by both parents, birth in a squatting position, restriction of both parents to the house for a few days afterwards, and dietary restrictions lasting until the child walks. Puberty passes unnoticed for a boy, but a girl is secluded in an enclosure in the house for a number of months, where she spins thread and is severely restricted in diet. Marriage usually occurs at a young age for both sexes, and although divorce is easy, many marriages are life-long. Nevertheless, given the relatively short life expectancy, those who live long enough may outlive several spouses. When death occurs, the corpse is thrown into the river or slung on a pole and carried some distance, to be buried or abandoned.

Campa cosmology conceptualizes of several strata, one of which--occupying an intermediate position--is our earth. This universe is understood to be populated by two great hosts of supernatural beings--good spirits *(maninkari)* and demons(*kamari).* In traditional Campa belief, good spirits populate the heavens, the clouds, the ends of the earth, and the high mountain ridges; they are human in form but may be seen as lightning flashes or as certain sacred species of birds and animals. Highest ranking of the good spirits are the gods *(tasorentsi),* including the Sun *(Pava),* his father the Moon *(Kashiri),* the god of rain *(Inkani-*

tari), and a transformer deity *(Avireri).* Demons abound in forest and river, and in an underworld, taking different forms: among these are jaguars, bats, certain demonic bird and insect species, dust devils, rainbow demons, and demons--human in form--dwellilng witbin the great cliffs of Campa territory. Essentially, the good spirits personify Campa concepts of excellence, goodness and comeliness, while the demons give form to all that is inimical and threatening in the Campa's world.

History of contact First European contact with the Campa occurred in the 16th century. It was not until the following century, however, that Franciscan missionaries entered Campa territory to establish missions there, and Spanish colonists followed in their wake. In 1742, a Highland Indian or mestizo calling himself Juan Santos Atahualpa with the title Apu Inca, and claiming to be the rightful heir to the Inca throne, made his appearance among the Campa. He called the Campa and neighboring tribes to rise and cast off the Spanish yoke, which they did under his leadership. It was another century before Europeans intruded upon Campa territory again, spearheaded by the Peruvian army in 1847. The South American rubber boom at the turn of the century caused great turmoil among the Campa, which culminated in a Campa uprising in 1914. By 1920, the Campa blockade of the Tambo River was broken, and since then there has been little resistance to travel by outsiders. Towns with surrounding plantations

Campa women and children relaxing.

Campa habitations.

had by then sprung up on the periphery of Campa territory, and Campa had begun working on the plantations in return for Western goods. In this century, Catholic missionary efforts among the Campa came to be rivaled by Protestant efforts, notably on the part of the Seventh-Day Adventists and the Summer Institute of Linguistics.

For the first four centuries of contact with Caucasians, Campa culture remained remarkably unaffected, except for a dependence on certain imports, and the general pacification of the area in recent decades under the influence of the Peruvian Guardia Civil. Since 1960, a new type of community has emerged and become common: a village built around a government-supported mission school. Even more recently, a new highway from the Chanchamayo Valley to the town of Satipo has opened the entire Perene Valley to settlement by Highland Indians, and the Campa there are under extreme assimilative pressure. The Western clothing now worn by most of the Perene Campa is a sign of the rapid erosion of the old culture. The extension of the Marginal Highway the length of the Tambo River can be expected to have similar results in that region. Proposals for Campa refuge area--a reservation in the Gran Pajonal and a national park on the east side of the Ene River-- have yet to be acted upon by the Peruvian government. It is doubtful that Campa culture as here described will long survive the implementation of the current Ley de Communidades Nativas (D.L. 20653), in effect since 1974, which refuses to recognize the existence of tribal entities in eastern Peru and throws open to colonization all lands apart from the small tracts for which the native communities can apply. Without a major change in government policy, the surviving tribal cultures of the Peruvian Montana are destined for speedy obliteration.

BIBLIOGRAPHY —

● STEWARD, JULIAN H. Handbook of South American Indians. 7 Vols., Washington, DC: U.S. Govt. Printing Office, 1946-59. *(see map page XVIII)*

CANARI

(South America; Ecuador) were absorbed into Spanish colonial society during the seventeenth century and since that time have been extinct as an independent culture. Prior to Spanish Conquest, they occupied the southern Ecuadorian highlands but were also represented on the coast where they bordered the Chimu kingdom. The pre-Spanish extension of their territory covered the provinces of Canari, Azuay, and part of El Oro. They spoke a Chimu dialect of the Chibchan language stock. Horticulturalists for a thousand or more years before the arrival of the Spaniards, they raised maize, beans, quinoa, potatoes, gourds, and cotton and also had herds of llama which they used for their wool and for meat. The meat was either freshly cooked or dried and preserved in the form of jerky. Women did most of the fieldwork such as preparing, sowing and harvesting. Irrigation systems were widespread in pre-Incaic times, attesting to the probability of abundant harvests and agricultural surpluses supporting a fairly complex social and political organization which was untimately brought into play in resisting Inca domination. Men were weavers, making clothing such as shirts ad blankets of cotton, and warriors. Both sexes wore leather sandals and women wore wrap around skirts down to their ankles. Men hunted deer, rabbit, birds and other small game. The principal weapons were palmwood spears and spearthrowers were used. Fishing varied in importance with locality.

The Canari had a rich culture and a complex social and political organization. They had peacetime chiefs and a fairly far-flung political federation. The high status of chiefs is indicated by the many ornaments of gold and silver and ornate shell jewelry which they wore. Spectacular archaelogical finds of gold and *tumbago* and ornate pottery are associated with status burial among the Canari and indicate the vast gap between commoner and politico-Spanish social organization. Chiefs also lived in rectangular stone houses with thatched roofs. These houses had patios where the chiefs conferred with their followers. This is in contrast to the houses of ordinary people which were oval and made of pole and thatch materials.

The Canari were famous for their craftsmanship in this region which stretched south as far as the northern reaches of the Chimu kingdom of north coastal Peru and to the Chibcha kingdom in central Ecuador. Gold and *tumbago* were used in the manufacture of crowns for the chiefs, masks, beads and other forms of jewelry, all of which have been uncovered in great abundance in their burial sites. The Canari also made excellent pottery which was widely traded in both pre and post-Spanish times.

From fragmentary historical sources we know that chiefs practiced polygyny and that chieftainship passed in a line of succession from fathers to sons who inherited their fathers' rank and wealth. The crystallized political hierarchy was rooted in concepts of patrilineality. The Canari had a complex political federation of which even the distant Jivaro who lived in the *montana* formed a part. Canari was a *lingua franca* over a very large region which was replaced by Quechua during the period of Inca expansion. The Canari maintained friendly relations with several of their neighbors with whom they traded cotton and salt and certain of their manufactures. Nevertheless, they fought with the Jivaro to gain control over them and to take Jivaro women as captives.

Communities were federated for defense. The

Canari

Canari painted thier bodies for warfare and decorated themselves with parrot feathers, the most important warriors also wearing silver chest pendants. A chief was supposed to be the bravest and most hard-working of all men and was buried with much ceremony and mourning. The chiefs received special flexed burial in very deep, circular graves. If the chief were a polygamist, his wives were killed and buried with him, as well as his servants. Various ornaments were also customarily placed in the grave upon which huge stones were piled.

The Canari resisted Inca conquest and made peace pacts with surrounding tribes to band together against Tupac Yupanqui, although they eventually succumbed to the Inca onslaught and were incorporated into the Inca empire shortly before the arrival of the Spaniards. The Inca established *mitamae,* colonies (i.e., outposts of other conquered peoples), in Canari territory to help put down rebellion. This was a technique used throughout their vast empire which sought to undermine the traditional social organization as it served to do among the Canari, especially at points such as Cojitambo and Chuquipata. Some Canari, in turn, were sent to Inca outposts throughout the southern reaches of the empire. However, according to Inca politics, the local Canari chief was supported and his authority enhanced. Although the Inca tried to supplant native religion, traditional Canari beliefs and religious organization, most especially their myths of origin involving mountains, rocks and trees, survived the short Inca domination, as did their myth that their ancestors emerged from a lagoon. Another element of belief which endured was the importance of a pre-Incaic sacred animal, the parrot (a woman diety of a parrot's face) which was also a major art motif among the Canari. More significant and long- lasting changes in values were introduced later by the Spaniards.

The Canari region was one of the northernmost provinces of the Inca empire, and one of the Canari chiefs conspired with and against the Inca at the same time (a double agent) resulting in Inca Atahuallpa ravishing the Canari territory in reprisal. All of this was brought to an end with the arrival of the Spaniards and the downfall of the Inca empire.

It was not long after the coming of the Spaniards that the Canari were put to work as sharecroppers and laborers on Spanish rural holdings and were also taxed under the *encomienda* system, both of which disrupted traditional community life and its economic basis. Although Ecuador was not as rich in gold as Bolivia and Peru, the wealthiest part of the province was in the south in Canari territory and thousands were put to work in goldmines in the second half of the sixteenth century. It was not long before only vestiges of Canari culture were seen in the growing mestizo population.

BIBLIOGRAPHY —

● STEWARD, JULIAN H. Handbook of South American Indians. 7 Vols., Washington, DC: U.S. Govt. Printing Office, 1946-59.
● SWANTON, JOHN R. The Indian Tribes of North America. Washington, DC: U.S. Government Printing Office, 1952.

CANARSEE

(U.S.; N.Y.) The fishing and farming native peoples formerly resident in the Borough of Brooklyn, New York and neighboring portions of Manhattan, Queens, and Staten Island have long been collectively known as the *Canarsee* Indians. The *Canarsee* were, however, only one of several *Munsee Delaware-* speaking groups that inhabited the southern parts of what is now New York City. Other native peoples usually identified as *Canarsee* have included the *Keshaechquereren* of central Brooklyn, the *Marechkawieck* of the downtown areas of Brooklyn and Manhattan, the *Nayack* of the Narrows between Brooklyn and Staten Island, and the *Canarsee* proper of the western Long Island were first mentioned indirectly in the November 5, 1626 sale of Manhattan Island to the Director-General of the Dutch West India Company colony of New Netherland, Peter Minuit. The Brooklyn affiliations of the grantors of Manhattan were indicated by the fact that settlements named *Werpoes* and *Sapohanikan* on lower Manhattan were relocated to the Red Hook section of downtown Brooklyn following the purchase of the island.

Isaak de Raisers noted in 1628 that the natives of Long Island planted corn, produced shell money called *sewan,* or *wampum,* and were subjected and forced to pay tribute to the *Pequot* of eastern Connecticut. Archaelogical excavations have further shown that fishing, shell fishing, hunting, and gathering were important western Long Island native subsistence stategies. The peoples of the area lived in villages containing one or more mat or grass covered longhouses, and periodically moved from coastal fishing camps to inland planting fields and hunting grounds.

The western Long Island groups made a number of land sales in Brooklyn to the Dutch between 1636 and 1639. The deeds were signed by the sachems *Penhawitz* and *Cakapeteyno* of *Keshaechequereren* and their followers. As *Keskachaue,* in the 1639 Manatus Map, *Keshaequereren* was located in the central interior of Brooklyn and identified as the principal native settlement on western Long Island. The 1639 Manatus Map further mentioned the settlements of *Techkonis,* just west of Prospect Park, *Wichquawanck,* at the later site of

Nayack, now Fort Hamilton on the Narrows, and *Marechkawieck,* across from lower Manhattan nearby the Brooklyn Navy Yard.

The land sales abruptly ended as Dutch attention was turned upon the *Raritan* when hostilities broke out between them in 1640. The Dutch enlisted the support of the lower Hudson River and Long Island native groups, and Western Long Island warriors participated in raids against the *Raritan* during 1641 and 1642. The *Marechkawieck* and their neighbors withdrew to the village of *Rechqua Akie,* at Far Rockaway, Queens County, following the Dutch attack against the *Wiechquaeskeck* on the night of February 25-26, 1643. The sachem *Penhawitz,* anxious to avoid war with the Dutch, concluded a hasty peace agreement with them on March 25, 1643. The *Marechkawieck* returned to their homes following the treaty, but relations with the Dutch remained strained, and many incidents occurred throughout 1643 and 1644. These did not, however, result in open warfare, and the *Massapequa* sachem *Mayauwetinnemin,* later known as *Tackapousha,* signed the August 30, 1645 peace treaty ending the Governor Kieft War "for those of Marechkaweick, Nayack, and their neighbors."

The *Marechkaweick* withdrew to the south following the end of the war and became known as the *Nayack* and *Canarsee.* Under their sachem *Matteno,* the *Nayack* remained at peace with the Dutch during the Peach War (1655-1656) and furnished warriors to fight against the *Espous* groups of the mid-Hudson valley during the latter part of the Esopus Wars (1659-1664). *Matteno* became deeply involved with the Hackensack of New Jersey during the 1650s, and both he and many of his people moved to Staten Island at that time. Most of these *Staten Isalnd Indians* joined the *Hackensack* on the New Jersey mainland following the English takeover of New Netherland on September 6, 1664. Those that did not incorporate into the Hackensack remained on Staten Island in increasingly smaller settlements well into the nineteenth century.

Other *Nayack* elected to remain in Brooklyn. The Labadist Jasper Dankaerts visited their village on the Narrows during September, 1679, and left a detailed description that included mention of the seven or eight families numbering some twenty-two persons that inhabited a lowslung longhouse approximately sixty feet long and fifteen or so feet wide. The *Nayack* do not reappear in the surviving documentation, and they probably either moved west to their Hackensack brethren or east to the *Canarsee, Rockaway,* or *Massapequa* soon after Dankaerts' visit.

The *Canarsee* were first mentioned as the grantors of land at Gravesend on November 3, 1650.

They were next noted as participants in the Esopus Wars along with the *Rockaway* under the leadership of *Tackapousha.* Last referred to in a document dated 1684, the *Canarsee* evidently united with either the *Rockaway* or the *Massapequa* during the latter 1680s.

The *Rockaway* and *Massapequa* became progressively connected with the *Setauket* and *Unchechange* of eastern Long Island. The sachem Tackapousha came to represent these groups to the English during conferences towards the end of the 1670s, and most of his followers moved among them after the evacuation of their last land holdings on western Long Island at *Cow Neck* during the 1680s. These groups became collectively known as the *Poosepatuck* during the eighteenth century, and their descendants continue to reside at the settlement near Patchogue, Long Island to the present day.

Not all of the western Long Island native groups elected to abandon their traditional homeland in Brooklyn. Their attachment to the soil and the graves of their ancestors was strong, and small family groups chose to remain in the back parts of the white settlements throughout the 1700s. Finally, in 1830, it was noted that *Jim de Wilt,* the last Canarsee Indian, died and was buried near his hut in the Canarsie section of Brooklyn.

BIBLIOGRAPHY —

● HODGE, FREDERICK WEBB. Handbook of American Indians North of Mexico. Washington: Government Printing Office, 2 vols., 1907-10.
● MURDOCK, GEORGE P. Ethnographic Bibliography of North America. New Haven, CT: Human Relations Area Files Press, 1975.
● SWANTON, JOHN R. The Indian Tribes of North America. Washington, DC: U.S. Government Printing Office, 1952.
● VALENTINE, DAVID T. History of the City of New York. New York, NY: G. P. Putnam & Co., 1853.

CANELO

(South America; Ecuador) lived in the rugged terrain of the *montana* region just north of the large area populated by the Jivaro. In 1581, the Spaniards settled them in a Dominican mission station where they were one of the first tribes in the area to be converted to Christianity. This is in distinction to their neighbors the Gae who rejected it to this day. The Canelo by 1581 had adopted Quechua as their language in response to conquest by the Inca in pre-Hispanic times. We have no knowledge of their aboriginal language and even their traditional cultural affiliations were obscure. They had much in common with the Zaparo and Jivaro and might possibly have been speakers of Zaparoan. However, upon being Christianized, they began to wear European clothing and learned to adjust to Spanish colonial society.

As early as 1560 small Spanish colonial towns were established in their territory and the Canelo and other Indians nearby were brought into the tribute-paying *encomienda* system which undermined the traditional tropical forest, horticultural way of life. Excessive labor in fields and mines and the ravages of European diseases wiped out most of these people. The Canelo and their neighbors rebelled and destroyed the Spanish towns and the turn of the century (1600), although the Dominicans retained their missions for many years thereafter.

The Canelo aboriginally were horticulturalists in the tradition of the *montana.* A native staple was sweet manioc. Other crops were sweet potatoes, peanuts, squash beans, papayas, pepinos, and several varieties of palm trees, especially the *chonta.* The introduction of the steel ax by the Spaniards made horticultural activities much easier than in traditional pre-Spanish times. New crops were also introduced such as the banana, yam, and sugar cane, but garden vegetables such as carrots, beets, lettuce, and so forth seem to have been rejected by the Canelo and other surrounding groups. The horticultural pattern among the Canelo involved single family cultivation of small plots. The men did the more onerous chores associated with killing and felling trees and burning over the area to be cultivated. Men, women, and children assisted one another in the round of horticultural activities from sowing through harvesting. The poor soil caused the Canelo to clear new fields every few years. Like most of the tribes in the *montana,* the Canelo made *chicha,* a native brew, from manioc for ceremonial use. They were outstanding among their neighbors, however, for their practice of distilling liquor, using large pots and bamboo tubes. This technology may well have been copied from the Spaniards.

Unlike many of the peoples of the *monata* who lived where streams were small and swift, the Canelo enjoyed an abundance of river resources. Shoals of fish swam up the rivers and their tributaries at certain times of year during which the Canelo and their neighbors engaged in intensive fishing activities. A river manatee could feed a large number of people and a sizable turtle could feed as many as 30. Turtle eggs were taken by the thousands during the hatching period. Turtle eggs were preserved in several ways, mainly by salting and soaking. Turtle egg oil was extracted and stored in jars to be used later for cooking as well as illumination. During the colonial period it was traded with the whites. Fishing was done in a number of ways which included use of the bow and arrow, spear, hooks, and drugs for fish in still waters. In all, the meat supply was abundant. Despite this, agriculture was the mainstay in Canelo subsistence activities.

The principal game animals hunted by the Canelo included several varieties of monkeys, armadillos, land turtles, peccary and birds of many kinds. The main hunting weapons were the bow and the spear but during the historic period, the Canelo and other tribes abandoned the bow in favor of the blowgun which was used for hunting small game. The shift from the bow and spear to the blowgun was facilitated by the fact that suitable poisons for the darts were readily available in the region. The Canelo grew *barbasco,* one of the fish poisons used in the *montana,* and even traded poison with the Colorado who crossed the Andes to obtain it. However, for the purpose of killing the river manatee and large turtles, the spear was still used. The Canelo made fishnets from a native fiber, *tucum.*

Much of their culture and social organization seems typical of the general type found in *montana* societies. However, the Canelo were the only tribe in their region who lived in palisaded villages for purposes of defense against their neighbors. Houses were of simple pole and thatch design, fairly common in the *montana.* Furniture consisted mainly of a platform bed, a wooden carved stool for men, and mats for women and children to sit on. Each community was composed of very few families and had populations ranging between fifteen and thirty. These settlements were strung out along the river systems. There is almost no evidence of the social organization of these communities, although it is likely that people who inhabited a single household were patrilineally related.

Religion may be described as animistic and involved a concept of nature spirits who operated both for good and evil. Shamans attempted to control these spirits and weere concerned with curing illnesses attributed to the forces of evil such as ghosts and other demons of the bush. The helper of a Canelo shaman was conceived to the the spirit of a python. *Huanto(Datura arborea)* was used aboriginally, especially by shamans, to bring on hallucinations which lasted for several days. During the historic period, the use of *huanto* and other hallucinogens spread to the general population and some people became addicts. Gambling was aboriginal and was a mortuary custom rather than one for gain. A dice game called *huairitu* was played at the wakes of close relatives to honor the dead, and the winner was considered to be the best friend of the deceased. Almost no information survives about Canelo mythology and folklore which was lost when they were so rapidly incorporated into Spanish colonial society and missionized by the Dominicans at a very early date.

BIBLIOGRAPHY —

● STEWARD, JULIAN H. Handbook of South American Indians. 7 Vols., Washington, DC: U.S. Govt. Printing Office, 1946-59.

CANICHANA

(South America; Bolivia) are an independent linguistic group. Before Jesuits invited them into the Mission of San Pedro on the upper Machup River in Bolivia, the *Canichana* had lived along the Mamore River and around the headwaters of the Machupo River.

History. The *Canichana* were visited in 1693 by Father Augustin Zapata, who estimated their number at 4,500 to 5,000. In 1695, they gathered in a mission, which was founded two years later with about 1,200 Indians. Even after 100 years of mission life, the *Canichana* retained their traditional disposition. They rose against the Spanish authorities in 1801 and 1820, and in the last rebellion burned the building containing the Jesuit archives.

A census taken in 1780 put the population of San Pedro at 1,860; another census of 1797, at 2,544. In 1831 there were still 1,939 *Canichana.* Their present number is unknown, but probably is no more than a few hundred.

Culture. Farming was less important in *Canichana* economy than hunting and fishing. The tribe caught caimans, which they relished.

Villages were protected by palisades.

When first visited by missionaries, both sexes went naked, but in the missionary era they were forced to wear cotton or barkcloth shirts. The *Canichana* were armed with bows and arrows and spears. In all probability, they were acquainted with the spear thrower.

Girls fasted 8 days upon reaching puberty, which was celebrated by a drinking bout. Polygamy was widely spread.

Drinking bouts were arranged as a reward for those who had helped a men clear a field. Fermented beverages were prepared with various fruits.

BIBLIOGRAPHY —

STEWARD, JULIAN H. Handbook of South American Indians. 7 Vols., Washington, DC: U.S. Govt. Printing Office, 1946-59.

CANONCITO

(U.S.; N.Mex.) is one of the three satellite Navajo communities that is separated by some 125 miles from the main Navajo Indian reservation. Despite the separation and isolation, the Navajos who live on Canoncito Reservation speak the Navajo language and retain the Navajo cultural values and have both economic and political ties to the main Navajo Reservation. Canoncito is located in

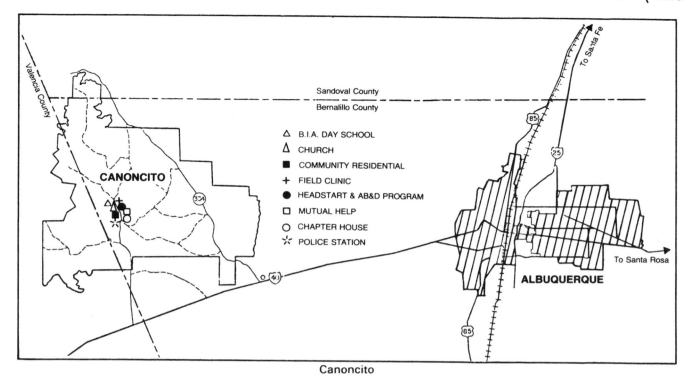

Canoncito

west central New Mexico, 35 miles west of Albuquerque, New Mexico and 150 miles from Window Rock, Arizona, the Navajo capital.

Population. The Navajo population of Canoncito in April 1974 was 1,242 of which 47195 were under the age of 16. The rate of population increase is about 2.5195 per year; 50195 of the population range in ages from 17 to 64 and 2195 are over 65 years of age.

History. Canoncito Navajos were those bands of Navajos who did not surrender to the U.S. Government in 1864 because of their isolation from the main Navajo tribe. Because of this they were treated more as Pueblo Indians than Navajos for many years by the federal government. The reservation was first surveyed by the government in 1910 and 1915 and last in 1954. The land base was created through a series of land exchanges and sale by the federal gervernment and the Navajo tribe. Congress in 1949 passed an Act which created a reservation out of these land holdings. All lands prior to this were acquired and held by individual allotments. The land is now held in trust by the federal government.

Geography and climate. The reservation consists of 77,899 acres. The land consists of flat features with wide canyons and low buttes and mesas. Mean elevation is around 5,500 ft. above sea level with temperatures ranging from a high of near 100 degrees in the summer to a low of 15 degrees in the winter. The average temperature is around 75 degrees. The climate is arid and winds are common with an annual rainfall of 8 to 12 inches.

Economy. The basic economy is livestocks, arts, crafts, farming, and government jobs. The community is rural with homes scattered all over the area. The main community consist of a store, a government school, government headquarters and a local community center, called Chapter. The population is underemployed, unskilled with a per capita income of around $800 per year and an average education level of five years of schooling.

Government. Three levels of governments have jurisdiction on the reservation; 1) The Bureau of Indian affairs (U.S. government); 2) The Navajo tribe; and 3) the local Chapter officers. The federal government provides school and social services programs. The Navajo tribal government provides public works, community services, livestock assistances and some social services. The local government provides individual assistances, livestock services, regulate community affairs and local leadership.

Resources and facilities. Income from the tribal government, $9,230 per year, Federal Trust Fund, $9-500, others $1,500 per year; 54 homes have utilities, there is a clinic and a community Chapter House. There is a kindergarten school and the BIA school is for grades 1 through 3. Grades 3 through 12 pupils are transported daily to Albuquerque public schools. The community has one full time police officer furnished by the Navajo tribe. The Community has no private sector other than the one store but a light industry would improve employment opportunities for the people. This will have to be achieved by the Navajo tribe.

There is presently an agreement with Exxon Corp. to explore for uranium deposits and if sufficient quantity is found, it could provide jobs and income for the community.

CAPE FEAR INDIANS

(U.S.; N.C.) were a tribe, possibly of Dakota descent, who lived near the mouth of the Cape Fear River, after which they have been designated. The actual name of the tribe is unknown, no words of their language have been preserved, and their disappearance in the early part of the 19th century has not been adequately explained. The Indians were first mentioned in 1661 by the English, who settled near Cape Fear River. By 1715, they were said to number 205 in several villages, one of which was called *Necoes*. They took part in the Yamasee War of 1716, and probably suffered losses as a result. They are mentioned in literature as late as 1751 (Albany Conference), although unoficially they were said to number about 30 in 1808.

BIBLIOGRAPHY —

● HODGE, FREDERICK WEBB. Handbook of American Indians North of Mexico. Washington: Government Printing Office, 2 vols., 1907-10.
● MILLING, CHAPMAN. Red Carolinians. Chapel Hill, NC: University of North Carolina Press, 1940.
● MURDOCK, GEORGE P. Ethnographic Bibliography of North America. New Haven, CT: Human Relations Area Files Press, 1975.
● RIGHTS, DOUGLAS L. The American Indian in North Carolina. Durham, NC: Duke University Press, 1947.
● SWANTON, JOHN R. The Indian Tribes of North America. Washington, DC: U.S. Government Printing Office, 1952.

CAPINANS

(U.S.; Miss.) A small tribe or band noted by Iberville, in 1699, together with the Biloxi and Pascagoula. The three tribes then numbered 100 families. Judging by the association of names, the Capinans may be identical with the Moctobi.

BIBLIOGRAPHY —

● HODGE, FREDERICK WEBB. Handbook of American Indians North of Mexico. Washington: Government Printing Office, 2 vols., 1907-10.
● MURDOCK, GEORGE P. Ethnographic Bibliography of North America. New Haven, CT: Human Relations Area Files Press, 1975.
● SWANTON, JOHN R. The Indian Tribes of North America. Washington, DC: U.S. Government Printing Office, 1952.

CAQUETIO

(South America; Venezuela) now nearly extinct, were an Arawakan- speaking people who once lived in the Peninsula of Baraguan and the offshore islands of Venezuela. With the coming of the Spanish who then sold them off as slaves, the Caquieto fled to take refuge in the jungles around Ele River in Venezuela. Although they lived in the coastal areas of the country, the Caquieto were traditionally farmers. They grew maize, manioc, and sweet potatoes. Their houses, each occupied by several families, were built around the fields to protect the crops.

Culture A man could take several wives. The tribe had a hereditary chief, under whose leadership they reigned over several other tribes; the chief was regarded as divine, said to have powers over nature. At the death of a nobleman, the body was burnt and the bones crushed into a powder which was added to a mixture of *masato* (a firewater made from *yucca* and then drunk.

(see map page XVIII)

BIBLIOGRAPHY —

● STEWARD, JULIAN H. Handbook of South American Indians. 7 Vols., Washington, DC: U.S. Govt. Printing Office, 1946-59.

CARA

(South America; Ecuador) Very little is known about the Cara. They were overrun in the early part of the Conquest Period and were quickly absorbed into Spanish colonial society. Even their aboriginal language affiliation remains unknown since they adopted Quechua as their language along with their incorporation in the Inca empire in pre-Spanish times. However, it is suspected that Cara is similar to the languages spoken by the Pasto, the Cayapa, and the Barbacoa who are affiliated with the Chibchan language family. For many years it was believed that the Cara had a widespread empire in pre-Incaic times, but there is no historical or archaelogical substantiation for this.

The Cara used to occupy one of the inter- *montana* valleys in highland Ecuador along with neighboring peoples such as the Pasto, the Panzaleo, the Puruha, Canari, and Palta, each of which constituted an independent tribal society. These peoples were almost completely destroyed by the Spaniards and their culture and social organization obliterated. Their different and mutually unintelligible languages which have been preserved. The last speakers of Cara presumably died in the 18th century.

The Cara occupied the province of Imbabura; their cultural affiliation to the Cayapa and Colorado seems very close and their one-time identity has been postulated on sketchy linguistic grounds. Some of their former settlements such as Otavalo, Cochasqui, Quilca and a number of others are presently recorded on Ecuadorian maps as highland Indian and mestizo communities.

During the Inca conquest of highland Ecuador, the Palta were quickly subdued. The Canari formed a federation with other tribes but eventually made peace with the Inca. The Cara put up the stiffest resistance and, overlooking old intra-ethnic rivalries, the Cara of the Otavalo and

Caranqui settlements banded together and held off Inca conquest for seventeen years. Eventually Huayana Capac defeated the Caranqui and according to tribal history killed thousands of Cara whom they then threw into Yaguar Cocha, afterwards called the Blood Lake. Following conquest, the Inca employed one of their administrative devices, the establishment of *mitimae,* colonies of Indians long since conquered in other parts of the empire who were now loyal subjects of the Inca. These settlers minimized the chances of revolt among the Cara and neighboring tribes. The traditional social and political organization of the Cara was further undermined by resettling some of the potentially fractious subjects as far away as Lake Titicaca in the Bolivian Andes.

Aboriginally, the Cara were intensive horticulturalists who grew maize, beans, potatoes, sweet potatoes and other crops. They had guinea pigs and engaged in hunting deer, rabbits and birds as the principal game animals. They used spears and spearthrowers in hunting and in warfare.

The Cara lived in fairly large settlements, particularly Otavalo, Cayambe, and Caranqui. Houses were thatched and had walls made of wooden posts and interwoven branches covered with daub both inside and out. The houses of the chiefs were larger then those of ordinary men and had a central post which distinguished them from the others.

In highland Ecuadorian fashion, both men and women wore large wraparound cotton blankets held together with copper and silver pins. They wore multi-colored belts around their waists. The form of dress was undoubtedly influenced by the Inca and was quite similar in nomenclature and appearance to clothing used elsewhere in the Inca empire.

The Cara had peacetime chiefs who enjoyed a great deal of prestige and who were supposed to be the strongest and bravest men of the communities. There is some indication that succession to chieftainship was along patrilineal lines. Anyone who cleared and cultivated farm land was considered its owner and could pass title to his sons. Chiefs had some communal land under control, the produce of which was used for the expenses of the community. Under Inca domination Cara chiefs were brought into the administrative hierarchy as *curaca,* a genreric term used by the Inca for local officials. It is also likely that the notion of communal lands controlled by the *curaca* was introduced by the Inca and that the idea of patrilineal inheritance of land was fostered by the Spaniards. The Cara maintained trade relations with peoples of the eastern lowlands with whom they traded for parrots and monkeys in exchange for blankets and salt. The Cara also imported cotton from the eastern lowlands.

The surrounding high, volcanic, snowcapped mountains were important in the religious life and beliefs of the Cara Indians. People thought of themselves as descendants from some of these more obvious landmarks which were personalized and imbued with sacred qualities. Shamans used to retire to the high mountains for meditation. Death was attended by an elaborate ritual ceremony. The deceased was mourned and wept over by his family and immediate neighbors. His body was taken to a burial ground where the grasses were burned off to scare away his lingering soul. Snakes played an important part in Cara mythology and were taken as both good and evil omens. The sight of a certain snake had a bad and even fatal influence on the people who, in order to prevent death, used to retreat to the hills to purify themselves through fasting for a week or more, eating only salt, coca and foods of ritual value. A person in such retreat was readmitted to his community by his relatives at the end of the period of fasting.

Since Inca control over Ecuador was short, it did not leave a deep impression on Cara religious life and mythology which survived into the colonial period. The greatest changes in supernatural attitudes were wrought by Christian missionaries bringing their grim, medieval Catholicism which spread as a thin layer over native beliefs and practices.

BIBLIOGRAPHY –

● STEWARD, JULIAN H. Handbook of South American Indians. 7 Vols., Washington, DC: U.S. Govt. Printing Office, 1946-59.

CARACA

(South America; Venezuela) are a Carib-speaking tribe of Indians; and (perhaps) also the name of the chief of that tribe; frequently the Spaniards attached the name of a chieftain to an entire tribe or village in error. In 1567 Diego de Losada conquered the area and founded the city of Santiago de Leon de Caracas, taking the name of the Indian inhabitants--by which the capital of Venezuela is known today. the Caracas people were so completely decimated by the Spaniards that we have almost no information concerning their culture or characteristics.

History   In Venezuela, there were various tribes now mostly extinct, known by the general name of *Caraca: Caràca, Tarma, Taramina, Chagaragoto, Teque, Meregoto, Mariche, Arvaco, Quiriquire, Tomuza, Mucaria, Aragua, Tacarigua, Naiguatae,* and *Guaraira.*

From the beginning of the conquest, the Indians resisted enslavement by the conquistadors. To this end, outstanding leaders, such as Guaicaipuro, chief of the *Teque,* united all the other chiefs and subtribes under their command. The principal confederated tribes were the *Teque, Taramaina, Arvaco,* and *Meregoto,* whose resistance to the conquistadors was well organized by 1561. By 1562, however, the first two Spanish colonies were established: Nuestra Senora de Coradalleda on the Atlantic coast, and San Francisco in the interior. The continued attacks of the Indians forced the Spaniards to abandon these settlements after a few years, but around 1565 Captain Diego de Lozada founded the cities of Santiago de Leon de Caracas in the Guairo Valley and Nuestra Senora de los Remedios. The Indians continued to resist the colonists, but in 1568 Guaicaipuro, chief of the federation died and soon the Spaniards executed 25 *Mariche* chiefs, thereby exterminating them.

Subsistence Activities. These tribes depended upon farming, hunting, fishing, and the gathering of wild fruits. *Caracas* crops included cacao, which was made into a hot drink, tobacco, cotton, agave(fique), sweet manioc, maize, and such fruits as genipa (mamon), cardones (datos), and cactus (tuna or comoho).

Animal foods included anteaters, deer, peccaries, hares, mute dogs, tapirs, such birds as partridges, parakeets, and pigeons, and lobsters, which were roasted. The Indians used snares and pitfalls; in open country they hunted with bows and arrows.

Domesticated bees, which were kept in calabash hives, were an unusual feature. Dried meat and other foods were kept in well- stocked storage places for use during wars and times of scarcity.

Clothing *Caracas* women wore a small cotton loincloth (bragas). "Virgins" (probably all unmarried women) also wore bragas but were distinguished by a cord worn around the neck. Men usually wore only a penis cover, perhaps a calabash. They cut their hair at ear level all the way around the head, wore gold ornaments, painted their bodies, and tattooed themselves by rubbing finely ground charcoal into scratches.

Technology Cord was made for women's belts and neck strings and for woven products. Weaving, though little developed, was practiced by the *Caracas,* who made women's loincloths and hammocks of cotton.

Social and political organization The *Caracas,* an essentially warlike tribe, had a graded military class with rank indicated by special tattooing. For one triumph in battle the right arm was tattooed; for another the breast received a design which was sometimes similar to that on the arm; and for the third a line was tattooed from each eye to the ear. Men of higher grades were priviledged to wear a jaguar-skin headgear or a necklace made of human bones or possibly of human teeth.

The tribes or subtribes were ruled by chiefs, or caciques, and in case of war they formed a confederacy under a single leader, like that under the *Teque* chief, Guaicaipuro. The chief of the *Maracapana* appointed a special war captain and designated men to guard the village palisades. If these men were lax, their commander was punished with death and his wives and children were made slaves of the chief. A similar punishment was imposed on people who used the hunting and fishing places reserved for the sovereign, and the culprits' goods were confiscated. It was the chief's prerogative to be guarded by four Indians, who always stayed in front of him in battle.

Children captured in war were spared and became a special class of slaves.

The *Maracapana* practiced polygyny. The principal wife governed the others, and her child inherited the father's goods and priviledges. If the principal wife had no children, the children of the wife who took her place when she died received the inheritance. It was the youngest of the sons to whom the inheritance passed; there was no primogeniture, though it is common elsewhere. A newlyweds' house was built by the bride's father, the groom furnishing the materials. After a ceremony in which the men of the tribe danced with the groom and the women with the bride, the latter was given to the shaman, who initiated her in the nutpials and turned her over to her husband.

(see map page XVIII)

BIBLIOGRAPHY —

● STEWARD, JULIAN H. Handbook of South American Indians. 7 Vols., Washington, DC: U.S. Govt. Printing Office, 1946-59.

CARAJA

(South America; Brazil) is the name given to three groups of Indians living along the Araguaya River: the Caraja proper, the Xambioa, and the Javahe. The cultural and social similarities among them are very great, and they recognize themselves as a single people ("we" in distinction to "outsiders"); and they speak the same language--Caraja, a branch of Macro-Ge, which is spoken widely in northeastern Brazil. In 1845, their total population was estimated at 100,000; in 1908, at 10,000; and during the 1940s was reduced to slightly more than 1,500. The Xambioa are probably extinct and the Caraja and Javahe very likely on the verge of extinction. Certainly their traditional life no longer exists and they may well have been culturally absorbed into the Luso-Brazilian backwoods population with whom they traded for more than two centuries. This article describes their way of life in the 1940s when they still constituted a viable society.

The Caraja proper lived in twenty villages on the main branch of the Araguaya River on the large island of Bananal; the Javahe had eight villages and the Xambioa, only two. All three groups of Caraja practiced slash-and-burn horticulture, hunted, gathered wild plants, and most importantly, depended quite heavily on fishing for their livelihood. Garden patches were cleared in the thick jungle along the rivers and tributaries in several steps. First, trees were encircled by cutting through their bark so that they would die the following year; smaller trees were felled. Then the entire area was burned over and cleared in readiness for planting. Men did almost all of this work, establishing the plots on ground high enough to prevent inundation during the rainy season. Since such favorable ground was scarce, some gardens were located several miles from a village and their owners travelled to and from them by canoe. The main crop was manioc, both bitter (i.e., poisonous) and sweet. Maize was second in importance, followed by potatoes, watermelons, squash, beans, bananas, peanuts, tobacco, cotton, yams, peppers, and several other tropical forest crops. A large number of wild plants were gathered, some for food and others for textile manufacturers and medicines. Turtle eggs were also collected and were important in the diet. Honey was obtained especially in preparation for village feasts.

Fish were the mainstay of the Caraja diet. People engaged in trapping and drugging in communal groups. Men also fished from the shore and from canoes with bow and arrow. Hook and line fishing was rare and very likely a recent borrowing from Brazilians. Hunting with bow and arrow and clubs was a very important male preoccupation but only a few animals were eaten, the main one being peccary which was hunted in a communal drive. The most important reason for hunting was to obtain feathers from parrots, herons, and flamingos which were used in decorations and even stored and used in exchange, much as currency.

Caraja villages were made up of one or two rows of houses occupied by women and young children and a communal house for married men and young bachelors. This arrangement was common to many tropical forest peoples in Brazil. There was also a special dry-season village arranged in the same manner but on the river's edge. The village was the basic unit of social organization and has been described as structured along lines of a kinship and lineage system known as one of "double descent." This implies that both patrilineal and matrilineal lineages exist and that each person has double lineage affiliation. One's patrilineage is

Caraja house.

important in certain aspects of living and one's matrilineage in others. Among the Caraja, the offices of chief, priest, and food-driver were patrilineally inherited as was moiety membership which governed marriage; however, village membership, adoption, and ties of affection were allegedly determined matrilineally. Further examination of this system might well have yielded a different interpretation. Marriages were usually monogamous but polygyny occurred. Villages were grouped into ceremonial units which appear to have lent mutual assistance in times of crop failure or poor fishing. Intervillage marriages took place as did intervillge feuds which seem to have been continual.

Besides feuding among themselves, the Caraja engaged in warlike hostilities, with their Ge-and-Tupian-speaking neighbors. Their principal tactic was a stealthy surprise attack by a raiding party. The bow and club were the main weapons. When possible, the Caraja would cut off a part of the foot of an enemy they killed. This was taken back to their own village where it was used to control the ghost of that enemy who then became the guardian of their village. Only women and children were taken captive to be incorporated as members of Caraja society.

A Caraja's progress through life was marked with certain ceremonies. Boys went through two initiation rites before attaining full status as young adults. Girls had their cheeks scarified upon reaching puberty. The next change in status occurred with marriage, at which time both sexes assumed full adult responsibilities. Around the age of forty-five years, a Caraja became an elder. All of these status changes in the life cycle involved changes in diet, dress, and behavior. When death came, corpses were handled in two ways according to how the person died. Those who had a viloent death were buried apart from those who

Caraja man.

their status patrilineally and were instructed in ritual by an elder. Shamans, on the other hand, were persons who exhibited special characteristics and were trained by older shamans to speak to supernatural beings. At death, the soul of the shaman was said to go the sky.

BIBLIOGRAPHY —

● STEWARD, JULIAN H. Handbook of South American Indians. 7 Vols., Washington, DC: U.S. Govt. Printing Office, 1946-59.

CARCARANA

This tribe, of whose name many variants can be found, presumably lived on the banks of the Rio Carcarana (lat. 32-33 S., long. 60-61 W.). According to *Del Techo, 1673* (p. 190), they numbered about 8,000. All the early writers link them with the Timbu, who dwelt in the Delta country across the Parana River, and it is evident that these two tribes were not only on friendly terms, but were practically identical in culture.

BIBLIOGRAPHY —

● STEWARD, JULIAN H. Handbook of South American Indians. 7 Vols., Washington, DC: U.S. Govt. Printing Office, 1946-59.

CARIB

(West Indies; Lesser Antilles) When Christopher Columbus arrived in the West Indies, he discovered that the islands of the Lesser Antilles were occupied by the tribes of war-like Carib Indians. Aboriginally, the island Carib linguistically and culturally resembled the tropical forest Indians living on the mainland of South America. In fact, according to one Carib legend, the Caribs set out from the mainland of Venezuela less than a hundred years prior to the visit of Columbus. Eventually they managed to occupy most of the Lesser Antilles, which was probably once inhabited by Arawak Indians. The Caribs were still expanding their territory at the time of European discovery, for they were conducting frequent raids against the Arawak of Jamaica.

Tribal name The Caribs used to designate themselves by the terms *callinago, kalina,* and *karina.* These names derived from the stem *kari* meaning "hurt" or "harm" and the suffix -*na* meaning "free from." The Caribs were referred to by other Indians by *calliponam, caripuna,* and *karifuna,* which means "people disposed to hurt." The names applied to the Caribs by early European colonists were generally thought to be corruptions of these names and included *calibi, canibi, caribe, carive, caribbe, charibbee, carib, charib, cariva, caribisce, callibishi, caribisi,* and *carabish.* The word "cannibal" is said to be a corruption of one of these terms. The modern-day Caribs are re-

died peacefully. However, in each case, the corpse was wrapped in a mat and placed in a shallow grave. Food and drink were provided until the next change in season, after which the bones were removed and re-buried in a second ceremony. It was believed that the souls of persons who died violently became wild bush spirits; those of persons who died quietly went to the village of the dead. At the time of the funeral, mourners cut themselves, destroyed the property of the deceased, and wept and wailed, continuing in such fashion for several days.

Caraja beliefs in the supernatrural were expressed in their cult of the dead and in a mask cult, each quite different from the other. The cult of the dead was concerned with pacifying ghosts and was led by a ceremonial priest. The mask cult was directed by a shaman and supernatural beings were impersonated by masked dancers. Both were men's cults and any woman who pried into their secrets was gang raped. The ceremonial priests inherited

ferred to in Dominica as *k'waib,* the French Creole term, and elsewhere by *Carib,* its English equivalent.

Social and cultural boundaries Traditionally the Caribs were organized on a tribal basis. Every island was comprised of a series of settlements, each of which had its headman. Each island also had one or more war chiefs, who led Carib warriors from different settlements to battle against neighboring Arawak Indians. Dominica had two major war chiefs the 17th century--one for the leeward side of the island and one for the windward side. Occasionally Caribs from different islands cooperated in raids against Arawaks and European colonists.

Territory at various historical periods The Spanish, who were the first European power to settle in the West Indies, made few attempts to subdue the Caribs, who at that time occupied most of the islands of the Lesser Antilles. During the 17th century, the English and French began to colonize these islands. As a result, during the next two centuries the territory occupied by the Caribs became drastically reduced. During the 17th century, the native populations of St. Kitts, Martinique, Guadeloupe, and Antigua began to dwindle rapidly. By the beginning of the 18th century, only two islands still had extensive populations of Carib--Dominica and St. Vincent. St. Vincent became a mecca for runaway black slaves, who interbred with the Caribs. The resulting mixture became known as the Black Caribs. In 1796 these Black Caribs were defeated by the English, who deported most of them to the island of Roatan off the coast of Trujillo, Honduras. From there they reached the coast of Central America. Today there are Black Caribs living in settlements from Stann Creek, Belize, in the north to Iriona, Honduras, in the south. In the west Indies today, only Dominica and St. Vincent still have recognizable populations of their original Carib Indian inhabitants.

Language Traditionally, two languages were spoken by the Carib people. The men spoke Cariban, a member of the South American Macro-Carib subfamily and the Ge-pano-Carib-stock. Carib women, many of whom were originally Arawak captives, spoke Arawak, which belongs to the Equatorial subfamily and the Andean-Equatorial stock. These languages, neither of which were written, are no longer spoken by the Island Carib today. Rather, the Indians of Dominica speak French Creole as their first language, while the Black Caribs of St. Vincent speak a form of English as their first language.

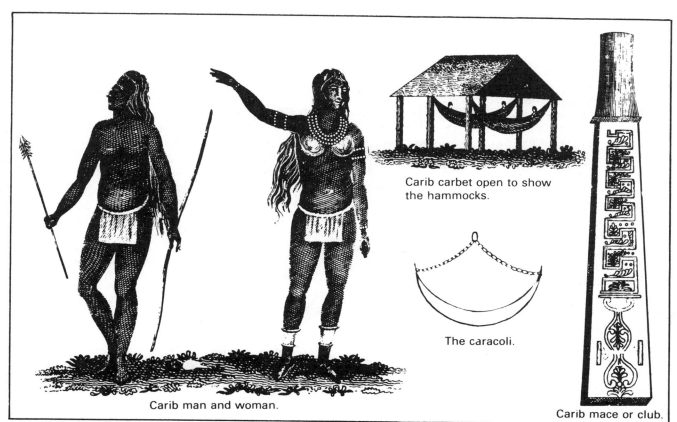

Carib carbet open to show the hammocks.

The caracoli.

Carib man and woman.

Carib mace or club.

Handbook of South American Indians.

Carib Indians and artifacts.

Summary of tribal culture Traditionally, the Carib Indians lived in a series of settlements, each of which was comprised of related family households. Although a few contained over 50 huts, many consisted of little more than an extended family. Each settlement was comprised of a group of small houses, where the women and children lived. The focal point of each settlement was the *carbet* or men's house, a long oval or rectangular structure made of poles and thatched with palm leaves. Men and boys ate, worked, visited, and slept in the men's house.

The basis of aboriginal subsistence was swidden horticulture. Land was held communally by each settlement and worked by individual families. Manioc, the Carib's staple food, was ground into flour to make cassava bread and fermented to make beer *(wiku)*. Manioc, yams, corn and other crops were cultivated in gardens *(maina)* by their homes and in provision grounds *(ishali)* in the mountains. Although the men cleared the land to make gardens, gardening was primarily women's work and was not considered as important as fishing.

Carib men viewed themselves primarily as fishermen and sailors. They were renowned throughout the Carribbean for their expertise not only in fishing but also in canoemaking. They constructed four different types of canoes, which ranged in size from small dugouts seating one person to large war vessels which held fifty passengers. Small nets and tortoise shell hooks and lines were used to catch fish. They also gathered shellfish by the shore and hunted crab along the river banks.

Warfare and communal ceremonies associated with it provided the cement that bound the different segments of Carib society together. Within the context of warfare village autonomy ceases, authoritarian leadership emerged, and a system of social stratification began to operate. When the Caribs decided to wage war against the Arawaks, men from various settlements assembled under the leadership of special war chiefs, who were chosen for life on the basis of their warfare prowess and ability to endure a series of painful tests. Warriors obtained prestige primarily by seizing jewelry from the enemy, killing a feared warrior, or by bringing home a live prisoner. Arawak women captives were usually bestowed by their captors on older Carib men and subsequently incorporated into the tribe as wives.

Most of the Caribs' communal ceremonies were connected with warfare. The decision to go to war was made at a meeting conducted in the chief's carbet. These ceremonies involved drinking, feasting and speechmaking in which the exploits of Carib heroes were recounted and the need to seek revenge, emphasized. Victory celebrations were also held in the carbet and involved ritual canabalism. Male captives were slain, cooked, and subsequently eaten by both men and women to increase the strength of the tribe.

In addition, the Caribs also performed various rites of passage. At the birth of a child, they practiced the couvade. The mother fasted briefly while the father lay in a hammock and observed food taboos for forty days. The father trained his sons to swim, fish, make baskets and canoes, and to hunt. Armed with bows and arrows, Carib men and boys hunted opossum, wild pig and agouti in the forests. The mother taught her daughters to cook, till the fields, weave cotton, and make hammocks.

Both sexes underwent a special ritual at puberty, which involved fasting and sacrification. In contrast to puberty rituals, the marriage ceremony was relatively simple. The young couple simply shared a ceremonial meal together for the first and last time. Post marital residence was usually uxorilocal, and polygyny was practiced. The death of a relative was the occasion of another ritual observance. The body was flexed and placed upon a stool in a grave located near the carbet. Every day for ten days relatives brought the deceased food and drink. Then friends filled in the grave and burned his possessions. Close relatives cut their hair and fasted. After the body rotted, they assembled again and drank *wiku*.

Caribs undergoing rites of passage were considered to be in a ritually dangerous state. If a Carib failed to take the precautions necessary to protect hinmself or his close relatives, sickness was said to result. In fact, the Caribs regarded taboo violation and sorcery as the two major causes of illness. When a person became seriously ill, he consulted a shaman, who performed a nightlong healing ceremony for the patient.

The Caribs viewed the universe as inhabited by a host of spiritual beings. Although some like the spirit helpers *(ioulouca)* were considered benevolent, most were either troublesome like the sea spirits *(oumecou)* or spirits of the dead *(oupoyem, acambouee),* or down right malevolent like the bush spirits *(mapoya).* To ward off bad spirits or to secure the support of benevolent ones, individuals or their families performed certain rituals.

Summary of tribal history Although the first Europeans encountered by the Caribs were the Spanish, it was the French and English who first posed a serious threat to Carib existence. During the 17th century these two powers established settlements on many of the islands in the Lesser Antilles. As a result, many Caribs were killed in battles with the settlers or fled to Dominica and St. Vincent.

The relationship between the Caribs and European colonists during the 17th century can be described as one of intermittent conflict punctuated by several short-lived peace agreements. In 1641 a peace treaty was negotiated between French colonists and Dominican Caribs planted their cotton. In 1654 a devastating war erupted between Carib and French settlers in Martinique. Several years later a second treaty, the Great Carib Peace of 1660, was signed in Guadeloupe by Caribs and English and French settlers. The two European powers agreed that "St. Vincent and Dominica shall remain property unto the Indian inhabitants thereof." Nevertheless, France and England made several attempts during the 17th century to colonize Dominica and St. Vincent. They were largely unsuccessful, for by the end of that century the Caribs were still in possession of these two islands, which were the last two remaining Carib strongholds. By this time St. Vincent

had become a haven for runaway slaves, who joined the Caribs to fight the Europeans.

During the next century the French and English continued to vie for possession of Dominica and St. Vincent. In 1748 Britain and France signed a peace treaty at Aix-la-Chapelle, France, in which Dominica and St. Vincent were left in undisturbed possession of the Caribs. Nevertheless, by this date French settlements were already firmly established on both islands.

In 1761 English forces landed on Dominica under the pretext of enforcing the Aix-la-Chapelle treaty and Carib rights. After burning their settlements, the English forced the French settlers to surrender. By this time the Caribs had withdrawn their settlements from the populated leeward coast and were living in the forests of the interior and on the remote windward coast. In 1763 a peace treaty was signed at Paris and Dominica was officially ceded to England. Peace was short-lived, however, for in 1778 French forces landed on Dominica and seized the island from the British.

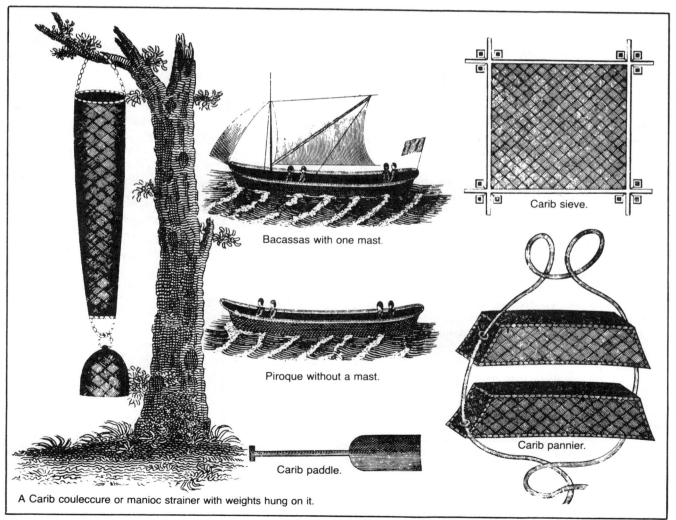

Bacassas with one mast.

Carib sieve.

Piroque without a mast.

Carib paddle.

A Carib couleccure or manioc strainer with weights hung on it.

Carib pannier.

Carib handicrafts.

French occupation was brief, for in 1783 Dominica was restored to England in the Peace of Versailles. Nevertheless, the French made two more attempts to recapture the island--one on 1795 and the other ten years later. Finally in 1805 the British assumed control of the island once and for all.

The 18th century was also a period of turmoil for the Caribs of St. Vincent. French settlements began appearing on the island during the mid 1770s. In 1776, however, the British captured the island. Seven years later the St. Vincent Caribs, who were referred to as "Black Chariabee" for the first time, were driven by the British onto a reservation in the northern half of the island. Though physically resembling the Negroes, these Black Caribs spoke South American Indian languages and were characterized by an Island Carib culture. In 1779 a small French force from Martinique once took the island, enlisting the help of the Black Caribs, but lost the island to the British in 1783 at the Treaty of Versailles.

In 1789 the Black Caribs, assisted by local Frenchmen, once more rebelled against the British. In 1796, however, the British brought in 4,000 troops to quell the rebels. A year later the British deported most of the Black Caribs to Roatan Island. Meanwhile the few remaining Black Caribs settled in villages in the northern tip of the island.

During the 19th century, the Caribs of Dominica and St. Vincent had dwindled to a few dozen families living in the most remote parts of the two islands. Although little is known about the St. Vincent Caribs during this period, the Caribs of Dominica apparently lost many aboriginal customs. They abandoned weaving, pottery making, the use of the bow and arrow, warfare, and many aboriginal religious ceremonies. It was during this time that the Caribs became Catholics. Nevertheless, they still had one practicing shaman, who they also regarded as chief. In 1903 the Dominican government created a 3,700-acre reserver for the Caribs on the windward coast, where they still reside today. Similarly, the Black Caribs of St. Vincent still live in villages located around the northern tip of the island.

Contemporaty tribal situation Since little published information is available on the Caribs of St. Vincent, this description will apply primarily to the Caribs of Dominica. Today 1,570 people, most of whom are of Carib descent, live on a reserve in Dominica. They have retained their aboriginal crafts of basketmaking and canoe making. The aboriginal-style house, however, has been replaced by rectangular frame houses with galvanized roofs. Separate buildings near the house serve as kitchens. Clothing is western and cloth is purchased in Roseau, the capital. Today's Caribs are primarily peasant farmers, practicing swidden horticulture. They still grow much of what they eat--yams, sweet potatoes, dashin, tannia, breadfruit, coconuts, and some manioc. However, both men and women devote considerable energy to planting bananas, their main cash crop. Fishing is still practiced by the men, but no to the extent it was aboriginally. Many Caribs are also engaged in wage work off the reserve.

The Caribs still pay allegiance to a Carib chief, who, along with four councilors, are elected every three years in government-supervised elections. This council represents the needs of the Caribs to the government and settles internal land disputes. Uxorilocal residence and matrilineal extended households were quite common during the first half of the century. Today the latter is being replaced by nuclear family households before they are legally married, most eventually get married in the Catholic Church.

Outside institutions have greatly affected Carib society. There are two primary schools on the reserve, a police station, numerous rum shops, and a Catholic Church. Today most ceremonies are Catholic, such as baptism, first communion, weddings, wakes, and St. Peter's Feast. In addition, Caribs, like other Dominicans, believe in witchcraft and *obeah,* the practice of black magic.

Population figures--past and present At one time both Dominican and St. Vincent were said to have Carib populations numbering between 4,000-5,000. In Dominica during the 1640s 5,000 Caribs were reported living there. During the next century the population dwindled rapidly. In 1730 Nicolas Le Grande, a French official who was visiting Dominica, claimed there were only 419 Caribs. By the end of the 19th century, there were only 20 or 30 families left. When the reserve was established for them in 1903, the Carib population was 400. Two-thirds of these Caribs were of mixed Indian-African descent. During the 20th century, however, the Carib population increased markedly. By 1946, 849 people lived on the reserve. By 1960 the population was 1,139, while by 1970 it totalled 1,570.

Similarly, the Carib popultion of St. Vincent decreased during the 18th and 19th centuries, while experiencing a regrowth during the 20th century. In 1789 the Black Caribs were said to number around 5,000. Of these, 4,000 were deported to the island of Roatan in 1797. In 1805, with the island firmly British, the census reports only a handful of Caribs. However, by 1960, 647 Caribs were reported living in Sandy Bay and 467 in Chateaubelair, two northern Vincentian villages.

Conclusions Although culturally and physically the Carib Indians of Dominica and St. Vincent resemble their Black neighbors, the Caribs seem to be in little danger of dying out. Despite their declining cultural distinctiveness, the Caribs of Dominica, for example, take great pains to stress their ethnic identity. They do this by emphasizing their Amerindian appearance, which is still possessed by some Caribs; the chieftancy; and historical legends. In fact, during the past few decades the Dominican Caribs have manipulated their Indian identity to protect their reserve from outside interference and to lobby for special treatment by the government. Also, non-Carib residents of both islands regard the Caribs as being members of an impoverished, yet distinct ethnic group.

BIBLIOGRAPHY —

● AMERICAN ANTHROPOLOGIST. pg. 343-349, July-Sept., 1950.
● STEWARD, JULIAN H. Handbook of South American Indians. 7 Vols., Washington, DC: U.S. Govt. Printing Office, 1946-59.
● SWANTON, JOHN R. The Indian Tribes of North America. Washington, DC: U.S. Government Printing Office, 1952.

CARIBOU INUIT

(U.S.; Alaska) are an Arctic people whose main food source is the caribou, which would also be used for other items such as skins for clothing. The Caribou Inuits also hunt moose, wolf, and fox, using bows and arrows, lances and traps. Some of these weapons had decorative carvings.

Their chief deity is the Mother of the Caribou, called *Pinga*. There are no actual legends involving her with creating the caribou or other animals. She is the guardian of both man and animal; although, unlike her aquatic counterpart, she does not interfere with the daily lives and activities of either man or animal. She has the power to reincarnate dead souls through the birth of children.

The Caribou Inuit believe in witchcraft and it was not unknown for them to kill man and women suspected of witchcraft. They also carry carved charams to ward off evil spirits.

The males are the dominant power both in family relationships and tribal business. Murder is fairly common amongst them. One anthropologist said every male he had talked to admitted killing at least one man.

The Caribou Inuit were a nomadic people following their main sources of food through the year. Their huts were simply constructed of wood and skin, easily transportable. Many of these Inuit continue their traditional lifestyle today.

BIBLIOGRAPHY —

● BIRKET-SMITH, KAJ. "The Caribou Eskimos." Report of the Fifth Thule Expedition 1921-24. vol. 5, 1929.

● WISSLER, CLARK. Indians of the U.S., Four Centuries of Their History and Culture. New York, NY: Doubleday, Doran & Co., 1940.

CARIJONA

(South America;) who speak a Carib dialect (*carihona* means "people" in the Carib language) are made up of a number of subgroups: the Hianacoto (eagle) with eight horses on the Cunary River; the Tsahatsaha (diving bird) with three houses on the Cunary and Mesay Rivers; the Mahotoyana (fire) on the Macaya River; and the Caikuchana (jaguar) with four houses on the Apaporis River--all in the northwestern part of Amazonia just north of the large block of Witoto peoples. Very little is known about the Carijona who are estimated to have numbered 25,000 in 1915 when they were studied by Whiffen. This is one of the last reports on them to be published. They traded with the Witoto and were famous for their poison which was used on blowgun darts. They were alleged to be "fierce, nomadic cannnbials," which is certainly not substantiated. the evidence for cannibalism in parts of South America is open to serious question and secondly, the Carijona obviously lived in settlements and were not nomadic. They resided in conical, multi-family houses. The chief's houses, at least, have been described as large, communal dwellings containing extended patri-families.

Like their neighbors, the Witoto, the Carijona peoples depended on bitter manioc for their basic subsistence crop. Along with other plants it was cultivated in gardens cleared by the slash-and-burn method. This typical tropical forest technique was initiated by encircling the bark of large trees in order to kill them. The next phases consisted of cutting down the smaller trees and burning over the brush after which the plot was cleaned out and planted. The heaviest work was done by the men and the planting, weeding, and harvesting was done by women and sometimes children. Most of the manioc was grown for home consumption but some flour was traded to Brazilians and some was used for the brewing of native *chicha* . Other crops were sweet potatoes, bananas, plantains, squash, pineapples, yams, mangoes, some maize, papaya, guayaba, and sugar cane. Chili peppers, tobacco, and coca were also grown. Fullest use was made of wild plants which were gathered mainly by women.

Hunting was most important among the Carijona peoples and the most common animals taken were peccaries, tapirs, paca, deer, cayman, monkeys, many birds, armadillos, and agoutis. The muzzle-loading shotgun was introduced and is the basic hunting weapon in recent times. Before that the blowgun and bow and arrow were the principal weapons. Snares and deadfall traps were also used in taking game. Hunting techniques differed according to the animal. The peccary was usually stalked by several hunters while most of the other game were hunted by individuals. Women sometimes accompanied men on the longer trips and were responsible for the upkeep of temporary sites, a fairly unusual practice among tropical forest people, the Jivaro being another noteworthy exception.

Fishing was always far more important than hunting, however, and was a man's principal economic activity. Fishing techniques have varied and included the use of metal hooks and lines, bow and long arrows, pronged spears, weirs, large basket traps, handnets, and fish poisons. All the Carijona had dogs, some of which were used for hunting and others kept as pets. Other household animals included monkeys, chickens, parrots, cats, pigs, and ducks, none of which were eaten. Chickens were sold to white traders.

A single, typical, large multi-family house, either rectangular or circular in form, often constituted the settlement or "village." The circular houses had conical roofs made of thatch. The population of a settlement ranged from about twenty to one hundred persons. Because the slash-and-burn form of horticulture results in leaching by the heavy tropical rains and soon leads to soil exhaustion, settlements were moved about every five years to a nearby area of virgin forest and located on a high bank of a stream to avoid inundation from flooding in rainy season. Household paraphernalia was simple and sparse. Each family owned its hammocks, a small collection of cooking pots, gourds for water, baskets, trays, presses and grating boards for manioc, and wooden stools for the men to sit on.

There is a general absence of information about social and political organization, either past or present. Archaeological studies are negligible, a typical failing in the tropical forest area and missionary and early travelers' reports are lacking for this society. Nowhere does it seem that political authority is or was very strong nor is there evidence of lineages and clans, as are found among the nearby Cubeo and Witoto. There is indication that descent is reckoned patrilineally.

When studied, the Carijona wore very little clothing; the women generally went naked and men wore a belt under which the penis was secured. Both men and women wore short hair. Although the Carijona lacked the custom of masks found elsewhere in this area, they had intricate headgear made of feathers which they wore during the ceremonial dances.

The details of their religious beliefs and activities are unknown. That they have a belief in nature spirits is indicated by the names of their settlements. Shamans play a part in effecting a healthy balance between malevolent forces and the Carijona and their major function is to cure supernaturally- caused illness.

BIBLIOGRAPHY —
● STEWARD, JULIAN H. Handbook of South American Indians. 7 Vols., Washington, DC: U.S. Govt. Printing Office, 1946-59.

CARINIACO

(South America; Venezuela) The only direct information on the Cariniaco was provided last century by the French M.D. and explorer J. Crevaux. During his third expedition to South America in the early 1880s, Crevaux had the opportunity to visit a series of Indian tribes in Venezuela, living between San Fernando de Atabapo (Upper Orinoco) and the Caura River (Lower Orinoco). He located the Cariniaco on the banks of the Orinoco, not far from the mouth of the Caura River. A slightly different location is given by L.R Oramas who, writing this century, relied on second- hand information and stated that the Cariniaco occupied in the past an area situated between the Caura and the Upper Cuchivero, i.e., their habitat was to be found to the south of the right bank of the Orinoco.

Without providing any additional information as to the circumstances of contact, Crevaux was able to collect a vocabulary of 206 Cariniaco words. Linguists working on Carib languages agree that Cariniaco, a member of the Carib family, should not be classified as a separate language. First of all, upon presenting his vocabulary, Crevaux refers to the Cariniaco *or Caribs*. The Caribs properly speaking call themselves *Cari'na* (or *Kari'na*). Hoff, on the other hand, upon comparing the vocabulary provided by Crevaux with other Kari'na vocabularies, concludes that the final syllable *co* of Cariniaco probably may be equated with the plural suffix - *kong* of *Kari'na* (*Kari'nakong*).

In view of the complete absence of historical and ethnological data, there exists no evidence which would allow us to even classify the Cariniaco as a distinct Kari'na cultural subgroup. In other words, the Cariniaco are to be treated as Kari'na, speakers of the Kari'na language and exponents of the Kari'na culture. *(see map page XVIII)*

BIBLIOGRAPHY —
● STEWARD, JULIAN H. Handbook of South American Indians. 7 Vols., Washington, DC: U.S. Govt. Printing Office, 1946-59.

CARIRI

(South America; Brazil) were on a higher level of culture than most eastern Brazilians. They grew manioc, maize, beans, and cotton; slept in hammocks; made pottery molded at the bases and coiled above, and had a simple loom. The houses were of the wattle-and-daub type, with roofing of palm fronds or other foliage. Their weapons included bows, arrows, and spears.

According to early historical sources, plurality of wives was permitted and divorce was easy. The chief exercised real authority only in warfare, but might derive power from the number of kinsmen supporting him. Except in cases of extreme old age, death was imputed to sorcery and the relatives would kill the evildoer. There were puberty rites for both sexes. Girls had their arms scarified in order to become good spinners, and boys correspondingly underwent mortification of the flesh in a ten-day festival. In order to make them good hunters and fishermen, their elders would burn fish and animal bones, drinking the ashes with the sap of some bitter herbs, scarifying the noves with teeth, and rubbing ashes into the skin. The boys were obliged to rise very early to hunt and had to present their game-bag to the older people, getting for their fare only a thin broth of maize or cassava.

After delivery a woman ate no meat, fish, eggs or meat broth, being restricted to a vegetable fare until teething set in, lest the child die or lack teeth. Doctors treated their patients with tobacco smoke or chants.

In 1938 the ethnologist Nimuendaju gleaned a few facts about the ancient Yurema cult. An old master of ceremonies, wielding a dance rattle decorated with a feather mosaic, would serve a bowlful of the infusion made from yurema roots to all celebrants, who would then see glorious visions of the spirit land, with flowers and birds. They might catch a glimpse of the clashing rocks that destroyed souls of the dead journeying to their goals, or see the Thunderbird shooting lightning from a huge tuft on his head and producing claps of thunder by running about.

Mythology Two myths are significant. In one of them Touppart, "God," sends an old friend to the earth to live with the Indians, who address him as "Grandfather." One day they go hunt, leaving their children with Grandfather, who transforms his wards into peccaries. After sending the parents on another hunt, he takes the transformed children to the sky up a tree, which he orders the ants to cut down. The *Cariri* vainly try to set the tree up again so they can climb down. Finally, they make a rope of their girdles, but it proves too short; they fall down to the ground and injure their bones. Nevertheless, they beg Grandfather to come back to earth, but instead he sends *badze* (tobacco), to which they thenceforth make offerings.

According to the other tale, the *Cariri* had but a single woman among them and begged Grandfather for more. He sent them hunting, made the woman delouse him, and caused her to die. He then cut her up into bits corresponding to the number of men. When they came back, he ordered them each to wrap his piece up in cotton and suspend it in his hut. He sent them hunting once more and, when they returned, the fragments had turned to women, who were already preparing food for the men.

BIBLIOGRAPHY –

● STEWARD, JULIAN H. Handbook of South American Indians. 7 Vols., Washington, DC: U.S. Govt. Printing Office, 1946-59.

CARISES

(U.S.; Calif.) One of a number of tribes formerly occupying the country from Buena Vista and Carises lakes and Kern River to the Sierra Nevada and Coast range, California. By treaty of June 10, 1851, they reserved a tract between Tejon pass and Kern River, and ceded the remainder of their lands to the U.S. Native name unknown. Judging by locality and associations they were probably Mariposan, though possibly Shoshonean.

BIBLIOGRAPHY –

● HODGE, FREDERICK WEBB. Handbook of American Indians North of Mexico. Washington: Government Printing Office, 2 vols., 1907-10.
● SWANTON, JOHN R. The Indian Tribes of North America. Washington, DC: U.S. Government Printing Office, 1952.

CARRIER

(Canada; British Columbia) are an Athapascan-speaking tribe living in the northern headwaters of the Fraser River. Called *Porteur* by the French, the name derives from the custom requiring the widow to carry the remains of her husband in a birchbark container on her back for some three years following cremation; eventually, these are buried as the culmination of a potlatch mourning festival. Their native name is *Takullui*, "the Water People," or more accurately, *Babine*, "Big Lips," referring to their fondness for elaborate labret ornaments. Numbering about 10,000 at the time of first white contact, they now total perhaps 1,000 people. Theirs is a semi-secondary culture in which hunting for game is a major occupation of the men, with salmon, plants and seeds provide secondary food supply. The Babine are divided into two major groups, living in two quite different types of dwellings: the northern people construct a below-ground-level home, whereas the southern Babine build large planked houses. Their social organization is a matriarchy divided into classes and castes, with religious beliefs devoted to spirits and a major sky god. The *potlatch* was the most important central ceremony, and functions essentially in the same manner as the related giveaway custom of the Coastal Indians of the Northwest although it is less elaborate than that of the Kwaki-

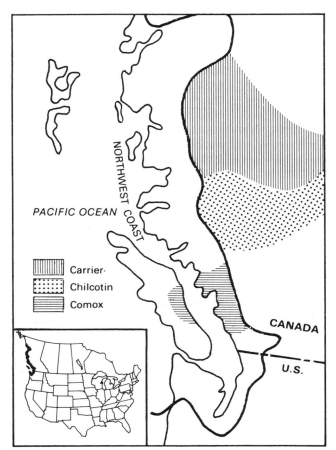

Carrier and other tribes of the Northwest Coast.

Carrier·
Chilcotin
Comox

utl. Woodcarving is one of several crafts practiced by the men, who formerly produced totem poles somewhat similar to those of the Northwest Coast people. While the concept of these poles probably originated with the latter, the Babine carving is less skillfully conceived and executed.

BIBLIOGRAPHY —

● JENNESS, DIAMOND. Indians of Canada. Bulletin of the Canadian National Museum., no. 65, 1960.
● MORICE, A. G. Carrier Sociology and Mythology. Transactions of the Royal Society. Ottawa, Canada, 1892.
● SWANTON, JOHN R. The Indian Tribes of North America. Washington, DC: U.S. Government Printing Office, 1952.

CARRIZO

(U.S.; Gulf Coast) now extinct, were an Indian tribe who spoke the language classified as Coahuiltecan. They lived along the Gulf Coast and inland on both sides of the Rio Grande River. A Southeastern tribe, the Carrizo called themselves "Commegrudo," and spoke the Coahuiltecan language called "Carrizo," language of the lower Rio Grande. Little data has been collected on the Carrizo, but they do not seem to have been attached to the land as agriculturalists, but rather followed the buffalo. They might have lived in tipis, and wore sandals instead of moccassins. According to recorded visits to the Carrizo in the 1880s, the tribe numbered about three-dozen at that time; it was said to have had a chief named Marcelino in the 1850s. The name Commegrudo means "eaters of raw meat."

BIBLIOGRAPHY —

● INDIAN OFFICE REPORT. pg. 209, 1892.

CASHINAWA

(South America; Brazil) are one of the many Panoan-speaking peoples of the Jurua-Purus Basin. They are located primarily on the Embira and Muru Rivers in the jungles of far western Brazil and also on the Curanja River in southeastern Peru. There are some cultural differences between these two segments of the population, although they visit one another and are related through intermarriage. Those in Peru originally fled Brazil at the beginning of the twentieth century to avoid the Brazilian rubber traders. Contact with the Peruvian Cashinawa was only made in 1946. In 1951, an epidemic greatly reduced their Brazilian kinsmen, returning somewhat later to Peru. By 1968, the population of the Peruvian Cashinawa had increased to 400 who lived in seven villages along the Curanja and Purus Rivers. The population of the Brazilian Cashinawa, although not easily estimated, seems to be considerably larger than that of Peru. Both groups are to a large extent still monolingual.

Culture The Cashinawa are horticulturalists who clear their garden plots by the standard slash-and-burn technique. Large trees are killed by encircling the bark of the trunk long before the planting season; smaller trees are cut down. Then the trees and brush of the entire area to be cultivated are burned over and cleared. This is the men's work. Men also do all the planting except for cotton which is done by women. Women do most of the harvesting. Cashinawa gardens are very large for the Purus region, measuring between 600 and 1,000 feet in length. The principal crop is sweet manioc, followed by a large number of others which include maize, beans, plantains, peanuts, sweet potatoes, various fruits, tobacco, and cotton.

Hunting is a very important communal activity of Brazilian Cashinawa men who absent themselves for a week or more at a time while the women, children and men who serve as their protectors remain in the village. Fishing expeditions are conducted in a similar manner. The main hunting weapon is the bow and arrow, and hunters prepare themselves by rubbing their bodies and weapons with magical plants. The most prized animals are monkey, peccary, tapir, and armadillo whose tail is made into a trumpet which is used by men on ritual occasions. While on the hunt, the men build temporary shelters to which they return nightly with their game which they preserve by roasting. After a sufficient meat supply has been acquired and prepared, the hunters return home, sending two men ahead to announce their success. Meanwhile, the women have been regularly engaged in dancing and singing songs which indicate their great need for meat. The hunters observe a special taboo upon their return, but the next day a great feast begins. From beginning to end, the hunting expedition is shot through with symbolic behavior. The Peruvian Cashinawa, however, regard hunting as a solitary activity, each man having his own hunting trails and returning to the village at night. Occasionally word comes of a large herd nearby and all the men of the village will set forth on a hunt. Shotguns are replacing the bow and arrow.

Fishing by drugging with *timbo* vines is the most common procedure, but shooting with arrows, harpooning, netting, and trapping are also done. Turtles and their eggs are eagerly sought and turtles are often penned up in pounds to be kept alive for future consumption.

As do most of the other peoples in the Jurua-Purus region, the Cashinawa live in large, extended-family households, each of which constitutes a separate "village." Among the Peruvian Cashinawa it is common for two extended families to form a village, one owning the territory upstream and the other downstream. These communal houses are surrounded by extensive gardens. Traditionally, the houses have no walls but are covered by a gabled, thatched roof which comes down very close to the ground. Inside are sparsely furnished compartments for the individual families. Each of these extended families is under the beneficient leadership of "an old man who owned many things and many crops," which he is expected to distribute among the members of the household. This *paterfamilias* organizes daily work groups, hunting and fishing parties, decides the agricultural cycle, and, as moral leader, arranges ceremonial drinking bouts and sees to the initiation of the young people at several stages in the life cycle.

By custom, when children are old enough to understand abstract ideas, they have their noses and lips perforated, put on decorative feather headdresses and capes, and listen to the household elder speak to them about food taboos. Cashinawa girls, upon reaching puberty, have their hymen cut in the presence of all the adult males of the house. When young adults are ready for marriage, they usually select a cross-cousin, i.e., a young man would marry his mother's brother's daughter (or a girl in this general kinship category) and go live with her in his uncle's house. Although it is not clear from the evidence, it is claimed that the Cashinawa were at one time matrilineal, and matrilocal marriage was practiced. Most marriages are monogamous, but household heads commonly have more than one wife.

The next and final stage of the cycle of life is, of course, death. But the interesting thing is the contrast between Cashinawa belief in a halcyon afterworld in which people live forever with the Great Ancestor in a land of milk and honey and their belief that the "shadow" of the deceased stays among the living as a ghost who frightens people and sometimes sucks their blood. The principal task of the Great Ancestor, or Old Father (whose wife is Old Mother), is to transport the souls of the dead to heaven and provide them with a good life. It is likely that Old Father is also a culture hero and the Creator of the Cashinawa.

Religious observances are not complex. Simple dances are held by adult members of each small community to propitate plant and animal spirits and others to insure abundant crops, good hunting, and so forth, but there seems to be no special ceremony devoted to the Great Ancestor. In addition to holding increase ceremonies, the people wear amulets in order to bring good luck and they may also take infusions of magically powerful herbs.

In Cashinawa society, shamans are distinguished from priests and deal with curing supernaturally-caused illness. Shamans are always males, and any man who feels a calling consults an older shaman who then instructs him in the art for a considerable period of time. The novice, who has to be able to talk with spirits in order to obtain power, must submit to cruel treatment which often involves castigation with thorny branches. After enduring this initiation, the novice is infused with magical objects such as small chips of wood, iron, beads, and others and has to observe food taboos. He is then ready to cure. The shaman calls up his familiar spirits to divine the cause of illness and uses magical knowledge to kill the person who is causing his client to be ill. The shaman is in constant danger in this world as he combats spirits who work for both good and evil.

BIBLIOGRAPHY –

● STEWARD, JULIAN H. Handbook of South American Indians. 7 Vols., Washington, DC: U.S. Govt. Printing Office, 1946-59.

CASTAKE

(U.S.; Calif.) One of several tribes formerly occupying "the country from Buena Vista and Carises lakes and Kern River to the Sierra Nevada and Coast range." By treaty of June 10, 1851, these tribes reserved a tract between Tejon pass and Kern River and ceded the remainder of their lands to the U.S. In 1862 they were reported to number 162 on Ft. Tejon res. Probably Shoshonean, though possibly Mariposan or Chumashan. Castac lake, in the Tejon pass region, derives its name from this tribe and affords a further clue to its former habitat.

BIBLIOGRAPHY –

● HODGE, FREDERICK WEBB. Handbook of American Indians North of Mexico. Washington: Government Printing Office, 2 vols., 1907-10.
● MESSAGE FROM PRESIDENT OF THE U.S. Communicating eighteen treaties made with Indians in California. June 10. 1851.
● MURDOCK, GEORGE P. Ethnographic Bibliography of North America. New Haven, CT: Human Relations Area Files Press, 1975.
● ROYCE, CHARLES C. Indian Land Cessions in the U.S. Washington: 18th Annual Report, Bureau of Ethnology, 1896-97.
● SWANTON, JOHN R. The Indian Tribes of North America. Washington, DC: U.S. Government Printing Office, 1952.

CATAWBA

(U.S.; N.C., S.C., Tenn.) during its height, was the most important Eastern Sioux tribe. The tribe's traditional home was in South Carolina, though some were in North Carolina and Tennessee. Today there are still about one hundred Catawba on a reservation in South Carolina. Originally, they may have migrated there from Canada.

Their language was the most aberrent of the Sioux linguistic family. They were also called the *Issa* which means river, and occasionally "flat heads" for they may have practiced head deformation.

According to myths the Catawba were descended from the one woman who inhabited the earth who married a descendant of the great spirit.

The Catawba were a sedentary people practicing agriculture. The women made some of the finest baskets and pottery of any tribe. They were ruled by a chief or a king who was selected by the tribe as a whole.

Throughout their history the Catawba were involved in wars which finally, along with a smallpox epidemic, decimated their population from 5,000 in 1600 to 1,400 in 1728 to just a few hundred in the 1800s.

Their first contact with whites was in 1566 by the Explorer Pardo; and from then on their relations with whites were generally good. In 1711-13 they joined the colonists in a war against the Tuscarora who had been denied certain trade priviledges and had gone on the rampage against the settlers. In 1715 the Catawba fought whites in the Yamasee war, but peace was quickly made. Later they fought a war with the Iroquois, but white intervention brought peace in 1754 so that both could battle the French. But then Catawba fought the Shawnee, who had killed their leader. Epidemics in 1738 and 1759 further reduced their numbers. During the Revolution they fought with the colonists. Much later, they sold all but one plot of land to whites. Then they were given a reservation, and because of their long cooperation with whites they were never removed from their land.

Catawba

(see map page XIV)

BIBLIOGRAPHY –

● BROWN, DOUGLAS SUMMERS. The Catawba Indians: The People of the River. Columbia, SC: University of South Carolina Press, 1966.
● DEBO, ANGIE. The Road to Disappearance. Norman, OK: University of Oklahoma Press, 1941.
● HODGE, FREDERICK WEBB. Handbook of American Indians North of Mexico. Washington: Government Printing Office, 2 vols., 1907-10.
● HOLMES, W. H. Aboriginal Pottery of the Eastern U.S. Washington: 20th Annual Report, Bureau of Ethnology, 1903.
● INDIAN TRUTH. The Catawabas of South Carolina. Vol. 21, no. 5, pg. 5, Dec., 1955.
● MILLING, CHAPMAN. Red Carolinians. Chapel Hill, NC: University of North Carolina Press, 1940.
● MITCHENER, CHARLES H. Ohio Annals: Historic Events in the Tuscarawas and Muskingum Valleys, and in other portions of the State of Ohio... Dayton, OH: Thomas W. Odell, 1876.
● MURDOCK, GEORGE P. Ethnographic Bibliography of North America. New Haven, CT: Human Relations Area Files Press, 1975.
● RIGHTS, DOUGLAS L. The American Indian in North Carolina. Durham, NC: Duke University Press, 1947.
● ROYCE, CHARLES C. Indian Land Cessions in the U.S. Washington: 18th Annual Report, Bureau of Ethnology, 1896-97.
● SCHOOLCRAFT, HENRY R. History of the Indian Tribes of the U.S.; Their Present Condition and Prospects... Philadelphia, J. B. Lippincott & Co., 1857.

- SIPE, C. HALE. The Indian Wars of Pennsylvania, An Account of the Indian Events, in Pennsylvania, of The French and Indiang War, Pontiac's War, Lord Dunmore's War... Harrisburg: The Telegraph Press, 1929.
- SWANTON, JOHN R. The Indian Tribes of North America. Washington, DC: U.S. Government Printing Office, 1952.
- WISSLER, CLARK. Indians of the U.S., Four Centuries of Their History and Culture. New York, NY: Doubleday, Doran & Co., 1940.

CATHLACOMATUP

(U.S.; Oreg.) A Chinookan tribe residing in 1806, according to Lewis and Clark, on the South side of Sauvies id., in the present Multnomah County, Oregon, on the slough of Willamette River. Their estimated number was 170.

BIBLIOGRAPHY —

- HODGE, FREDERICK WEBB. Handbook of American Indians North of Mexico. Washington: Smithsonian Institution: BAE Bulletin No. 30: U.S. GPO, 1907.

CATHLACUMUP

(U.S.; Oreg.) A Chinookan tribe formerly living on the West bank of the lower mouth of Williamette River near the Columbia, claiming as their territory the bank of the latter stream from this point to Deer id., Oregon. Lewis and Clark estimated their number at 450 in 1806. They are mentioned in 1850 by Lane as being associated with the Namoit and Katlaminimim.

BIBLIOGRAPHY —

- HODGE, FREDERICK WEBB. Handbook of American Indians North of Mexico. Washington: Smithsonian Institution: BAE Bulletin No. 30: U.S. GPO, 1907.
- SWANTON, JOHN R. The Indian Tribes of North America. Smithsonian Institution: BAE Bulletin No. 145: U.S. GPO, 1952.

CATHLAMET

(U.S.; Oreg.) A Chinookan tribe formerly residing on the South bank of Columbia River near its mouth, in Oregon. They adjoined the Clatsop and claimed the territory from Tongue point to the neighborhood of Puget id. In 1806 Lewis and Clark estimated their number at 300. In 1849 Lane reported 58 still living, but they are now extinct. They seem to have had but one village, also known as Cathlamet. As a dialect, Cathlamet was spoken by a number of Chinookan tribes on both sides of the Columbia, extending up the river as far as Rainier. It is regarded as belonging to the upper Chinook division of the family.

BIBLIOGRAPHY —

- HODGE, FREDERICK WEBB. Handbook of American Indians North of Mexico. Washington: Smithsonian Institution: BAE Bulletin No. 30: U.S. GPO, 1907.
- SWANTON, JOHN R. The Indian Tribes of North America. Smithsonian Institution: BAE Bulletin No. 145: U.S. GPO, 1952.

CATHLAPOTLE

(U.S.; Washington) The name meant "people of Lewis River." The tribe belonged to the Chinookan linguistic stock and were placed by *Spier, 1936* in the Clackamas division of Upper Chinook, but according to *Berreman 1937*, they were apparently with the Multnomah. They were located on the lower part of the Lewis River and the southeast side of the Columbia River, in Clarke County. The main village of the Cathlapotle was Nahpooitle, at the mouth of Lewis River, and the village of Wakanasisi was opposite the mouth of the Willamette River. *Mooney, 1928* estimated 1,300 Cathlapotle in 1780, and Lewis and Clark reported a total of 900 in 1806. At one time, the Lewis river was known by the name of Cathlapotle.

BIBLIOGRAPHY —

- HODGE, FREDERICK WEBB. Handbook of American Indians North of Mexico. Washington: Government Printing Office, 2 vols., 1907-10.
- MURDOCK, GEORGE P. Ethnographic Bibliography of North America. New Haven, CT: Human Relations Area Files Press, 1975.
- SWANTON, JOHN R. The Indian Tribes of North America. Washington, DC: U.S. Government Printing Office, 1952.

CATHLATHLALAS

(U.S.;) A Chinookan tribe living on both sides of Columbia River, just below the cascades, in 1812. Their number was placed at 500.

BIBLIOGRAPHY —

- BANCROFT, HUBART HOWE. The Native Races of the Pacific States of North America. San Francisco, CA: 1874.

CATUKINA

(South America; Brazil) In the Acre and Amazon regions of Brazil, along the Jeruna River and its tributaries, live the many Catukinian tribes. Numbering 1,000-2,000 in all, the people are agrarian, hunters and fishermen. Agricultural products include maize, manioc, and peanuts.

The scattered villages consist of a single, large, thatched bee-hive shaped house in which up to 250 people may live. These dwellings may be 150 feet round and 40 feet high.

The peoples belong to the Catukinian and Panoan linguistic family.

BIBLIOGRAPHY —

- STEWARD, JULIAN H. Handbook of South American Indians. 7 Vols., Washington, DC: U.S. Govt. Printing Office, 1946-59.

CAWAHIB

(South America; Brazil) known to Brazilian literature as "Parintintin," are a small, once warlike, Tupi-speaking tribe who, during the late 19th and early 20th centuries, terrorized rubber gatherers along 250 miles of the Madeira, driven there from the Tapajos in the mid 19th century. They have a patrilineal moiety ideology, although their actual social organization is more intricate.

The Cawahib speak a Tupi-Guarani language of the "h" variety, one of several closely related dialects spread along the Madeira and Machado rivers. They are one of the group of upper Tapajos tribes denoted as "Central Tupi," which include the Kayabi and Apiaca. Grammatical sketches and word lists may be found in Nimuendaju (1924) and Kracke (1978). Nimuendaju supposes the popular denomination "Parintintin" to be of Mundurucu derivation, although it does not fit Mundurucu phonological patterns. Their auto-denomination, Cawahib, simply means "people," or "friendly people" as opposed to *tapy'yn,* "enemy."

Pacified in 1923 by Kurt Nimuendaju (1924), they now live in clusters of small settlements scattered along tributaries through the territory they once dominated, which borders the east bank of the Madeira from the Marmelos (8 S) to the mouth of the Machado. To the west, they disputed with the Piraha and Diahoi for control over the Marmelos. The hostile groups with which they were surrounded, included the Brazilian rubber trappers along the Madeira, the indigenous tribes they found in the area when they arrived (of which the Mura Piraha) are the chief survivors), and a number of small, culturally and linguistically affiliated tribes--the Pai'i and Katupai'i, the Diahol, the Jupa (Bocas Pretas) and Apeiran'di to the south, the Juma west of the Madeira, and the Tenharem, who share the Kagwahiv moiety system. Only the last two survive as cultural enemies.

The Cawahib economy is based on hunting, fishing and shifting cultivation, principally of corn, manioc and varieties of potatoes. Fishing is done with bow and arrow from canoes in the dry season or platforms in the *igapo* in the rainy season, or by poisoning pools with *timbo.* Hunting, now done with shotguns, was done with feathered arrows of bamboo, with notched hardwood tip for large game and warfare. Shifting fields are cleared annually for gardening in jungle areas assigned by the headman. An individual might call a collective work party to help, feasting them in return. Women used to plant and harvest, although this is increasingly done in family groups. Canoes, once of bark, are the main transportation. Pottery has not been made in the memory of living informants. Hammocks are woven from cotton planted in the settlements.

Settlements now average three nuclear families or sixteen people, and Pyrehakatu's largest pre-pacification settlements seldom numbered more than thirty or forty in a single longhouse. They are always located on streams for access to canoe transportation and resources.

Nonlocalized exogamous patrimoieties are named after eponymous birds, the *kwandu* (harpie eagle) and *mytum* (curassow). The Kwandu moiety was also associated with the macaw, *tarave,* the name of the corresponding Tenharem moiety. The system is complicated by a Kwandu subgroup, the Gwyrai'gwara (associated with the *japu* bird) who intermarry with other Kwandu as well as with Mytum, constituting a third *de facto* patrisib. Marriage was in fact determined, however, by a complex cycle of exchanges, a brother giving his older sister away at marriage and later arranging marriages between his children and hers.

The kin terminology is a two-line system appropriate to moieties; sibling terms are extended to same-generation members of one's own moiety, cross cousins of the opposite moiety area designated *amotehe* (a term for "lover" in other Tupi languages), etc. Married *amotehe* of opposite sexes observe a formal avoidance of one another. The moieties are not, however, mentioned in the mythology, and the only ceremonial function seems to have been in the funeral rites: burial is carried out by male *amotehe.*

In rites of passage, an infant is given a "first name" or "play name" *mbotagwahav* by a mother's brother, establishing betrothal to one of his children. In later childhood a moiety-associated name is bestowed by a father's brother *ruvy.* Thereafter new names (selected from moiety sets of age-and-sex-appropriate names) were assumed on entering new stages of life, on major changes of status, or on certain special events. Boys received their first *ka'a,* penis sheath, from a father's brother. A woman, on her first menarche, was isolated for ten days in a hammock behind a partition, observing strict taboos, at the end of which she was carried to the river by her father and ritually bathed. Her first wedding followed the ceremony: the bride was placed by a father's brother in her husband's hammock, and they embraced and were lectured on the responsibilites of marriage. Marriage was concluded by a period of bride service, for the father-in-law *tuty* --five years for the first wife and less for later marriages--after which the son-in-law was theoretically free to leave, but usually remained in uxorilocal residence.

Polygyny was practiced, preferably sororal, but was never widely popular because of the complexity of familial relations involved: One man with five wives was scoffed at as imprudent. When a man took a second wife, his first might leave him if she so desired.

Warfare has been amply discussed by Nimuendaju (1924, 1948), although his position did not permit him an inside view of it. Raids were organized by any warrior moved to call one, and led by two *nhimboypara'ga,* "raid callers", whose position lasted only for the duration of the expedition. A principal object was to take an enemy head, which would be exhibited at an *akagwera toryva* ("head trophy fest"), a lavish ceremonial display celebrating the exploit, cosponsored by the head taker (who thus achieved the honored status of *okokwahav*) and another prominent warrior. There is some evidence for ritual consumption of parts of the slain enemy. The killer was obliged to undergo a period of ritual seclusion (like a new woman's menarche seclusion) and assumed a new name.

Curing, beyond the herbal level, was done by a shaman *(ipaji)* in a ceremony called *tokaia.* The *ipa*ji went into a trance (without drugs) in a small screen or shelter *(tokaia)* set up in the plaza, and made a spiritual journey through the various levels of the cosmos, asking help of each spirit he "met," concluding with Pindova'umi'ga, the powerful ancient chief who, ammoyed by quarreling among children, lifted his house and the best natural resources to the sky. He is to be distinguished from the trickster/culture hero Mbahira (Mair of other Tuoi mythologies) who originated many important cultural items and processes but has little to do in the current world. A third ancestor, the "Old Woman" (Gwaivi), was cremated by her sons and turned into the crops used today. These myths and a few others form the core of Cawahib mythology.

Dreaming is associated with shamanism. An *ipaji* or a layman may encounter spirits in dreams, or predict (and for a shaman, alter) the future through them. *Ipaji* were born via dreams; a shaman would dream of a particular Sky Person who announced that he would be born to a particular woman as a future *ipaji.* The chain has been broken by the death of the last Cawahib *ipaji* before he could pass on his knowledge to his "dreamed one."

Food taboos are an enduring, central part of ritual life. One set applies to all parents, from the birth of their first child to old age. Others are obtained during pregnancy, for the months following birth, and for sick individuals and their primary relatives. Agouti, which makes one lazy, is prohibited for young warriors. Handling manioc in any form is dangerous to a sick person. Sexual activity during a fish poisoning by timbo will interfere with the action of the poison, and between parallel cousins it will cause the death of parents and/or children of the offenders. Certain laws will make a hunter *panem*, unable to bag a particular species, or any species with a particular weapon.

Tupí-Cawahib Indians.

Tupí-Cawahib mother holding her child in a carrying band.

History. There is scant record of the Cawahib prior to their classic pacification by an expedition led by Kurt Nimuendaju in 1923, save for numerous melodramatic accounts of their raids on rubber tappers on the Madeira. Phonological affinities with the Uburu (Ka'apor) of Maranhao suggest an ultimate coastal origin, confirmed by legendary accounts of a journey upriver to their present location from a "land without water," crossing an expanse in which the shore was out of sight for two days (the lower Amazon above Marajo). In the first historical references to them, however, they were located at the confluence of the Arinos and Juruena rivers on the upper Tapajos. Nimuendaju (1924) has reconstructed the history of their ancestral tribe, denoted "Cabahyba" by Martius, from the first mention of them on the Tapajos in 1797, whence they were driven by the Portuguese-armed Mundurucu in the mid 19th century, scattering westward to end distributed in fragments along the Machado down to the present location of the Kagwahiv on the Madeira. Fission was a continuing process; a Pai'i chief described to one backwoodsman how the Kutipai'i split off from them over a leadership issue. In the late 19th century, Byahu (who met his end ambushed by a Piraha) may have been chief over all the group who called themselves Cawahib, but after his death they fell into subregional groups, with Diai'i holding sway in the upper Maici region, where Nimuendaju established his pacification post in 1923; and Byahu's son Pyrehakatu in the Ipixua region which he had opened up with a few of Byahu's sons-in-law.

After pacification, separate SPI posts were set up at Carnival on the Ipixuna and at the mouth of the Maici Mirim near Calamas. The SPI mandate was terminated in 1942 and the Carnival post turned over to the appointed chief Paulinho Neves (Ijet, Pyrehakatu's sons-in-law), but Garcia de Freitas stayed on as *pataro* at the Calamas post. The Cawahib were nominally converted by Salesians, and have abandoned traditional ritual, but maintain their beliefs, social patterns and food avoidances. A team of Summer Institute of Linguistics missionary linguists Helen Pease and LaVera Betts were at Carnival from after 1960 to 1976, and did linguistic research and medical treatment. Economically dependent on the gathering of *sorva* latex, a jungle product used in natural plastics, the Cawahib are hard pressed economically and diminishing in numbers. Groups near Humaita have been distrupted by the Trans-Amazon Highway. It is difficult for young people to find appropriate spouses of the opposite moiety, and the future for preservation of their social system is not bright. Many Cawahib retain, however, a strong pride in their history and values, and despite the universal disprisal of *indios* in Amazonas, they retain a certain local respect for their past valor and continuing determination.

BIBLIOGRAPHY —

● STEWARD, JULIAN H. Handbook of South American Indians. 7 Vols., Washington, DC: U.S. Govt. Printing Office, 1946-59.

CAYAPA

(South America; Ecuador) who number approximately 2,000 and speak a Chibchan dialect, are one of the last surviving Indian societies in the lush northwestern lowlands of Ecuador. They live in Esmereldas Province, a frontier region which is being settled by Spanish-speaking whites, mestizos, and blacks. The Cayapa are concentrated in four main groups, each with its own chief and other officials as well as a ceremonial center. The oldest of these units, Punta Venado, dates at least from the beginning of this century, indicating a remarkable degree of stability in a tropical forest habitat. The inaccessibility of their homeland has helped the Cayapa to withstand the incursions of Ecuadorian settlers.

The Cayapa are primarily horticulturalists who live along the Rio Cayapas and its tributaries. There are large, hilly sections and dense jungles within their territory which remain essentially unoccupied. Ecuadorian maps indicate the existence of Cayapa "villages" but these are little more than conglomerations of households and a church. During most of the year these villages are unoccupied and are used only periodically when a Catholic priest visits them to celebrate holidays. During the rest of the year the Cayapa live in widely-scattered, indipendent, extended-family households strung out along the river systems. The rectangular houses are of pole and thatch and are built on pilings as much as twelve feet off the ground, reached by removable ladders. This design is to compensate for occasional flooding from the river. Furniture is sparse and consists of hammocks used for both sleeping and sitting, and occasionally houses contain wooden seats for the male inhabitants. There are raised platforms along the sides of the buildings up to ten feet in length and seven feet in width and in the rafters there is another platform of bamboo where seldom-used articles and stored articles as well as food.

Near every household along the river banks there are groves of plantains, bananas, sugar cane, coca, and sweet manioc. Maize, beans, cotton, tobacco, and pineapples are frequently grown. Plantains are the staple crop of the Cayapa, each family having several acres of plantains which are used for home consumption and for a cash

foot transportation. They have large, dugout canoes, ranging from ten to twelve meters in length, which they use to convey their harvests of plantains to Ecuadorian river towns downstream. They also manufacture these canoes for sale in Ecuadorian towns.

Although Cayapa economy is largely subsistence-oriented, many of their crops and manufactures are sold to Ecuadorians. They now trade rubber, *tagua* nuts, and other forest products and grow cocoa especially for this trade. Some of their manufactures such as canoes, mats, fans, and other basketry are also sold. In exchange, the Cayapa buys metal goods such as axes, machetes, shotguns, fishhooks, fish spears, and copper tubing for their cane distilleries, as well as the women used for skirts and the men for tight breeches.

The principal Cayapa social unit is the extended-family household which consists of ten to twelve people as a rule. It is this unit which clears and works the horticultural land. There seems to be no formal interhousehold cooperation. The Cayapa have no suprafamilial corporate kinship groups such as lineages or clans. Their kinship system is of the bilateral type which gives approximately equal importance to both sides of a person's family. Within the family, men do all the hunting and fishing and the heaviest horticultural labor; women do all the foodgathering, cooking, and child-rearing as well as the weaving. All household members participate in clearing the land, sowing, and harvesting.

At the political level there is a chief for each of the four main tribal sections. The chief of Punta Venado, however, seems to be superior to the other three and represents the Cayapa before the provincial and national authorities of Ecuador. There are several other kinds of officials as well who have titles but whose duties overlap to a great extent. These officials help in marriage arrangements and in the settlement of disputes. They play an important part at the Christmas and Easter celebrations held at the ceremonial centers in keeping the peace and trying cases of a legal nature. It is on these occasions that young people are married by the chief and are subjected to a series of lectures and ceremonial whipping. These are also occasions of drunkenness.

The Cayapa have a syncretic form of religion, a blend of native beliefs and activities with those of Catholicism. Baptism, marriage, and succession to political office are sanctified by a visiting Catholic priest. Death is felt to be caused by evil spirits. These evil spirits hover over around the house of a dead person and the house is very often abandoned. Masses are held for the soul of the deceased.

Cayapa houses and village. *Top:* Typical dwelling along river. *Center:* Unfinished house showing roof structure. *Bottom:* Chief's house at Sapayo Grande.

crop. There are a number of pigs and chickens in most households. Pigs are fed on the bananas and the sugar cane is used to manufacture distilled liquor.

Even though horticulture is their mainstay, the Cayapa are skilled hunters, taking many varieties of rodents, deer, peccaries, armadillos, and birds. They exploit the plentiful river resources such as fish, shellfish, and crocodile eggs. Their diet, therefore, is both rich and varied. The rivers are also imdispensible to the Cayapa for travelling since the dense jungles are almost impenetrable to

Although the Cayapa are in no sense on the verge of extinction, they are being drawn more and more into the Ecuadorian regional economy and their culture and lifestyle have changed accordingly. Mestizos and blacks are buying or appropriating land from the Cayapa and competing with them in the cultivation and sale of plantains. Thus the Cayapa must be aware of the going price for plantains, the scheduled arrival of the banana boat, the price of rubber, and whether Ecuador of Colombia is paying the best price. It is said that the Cayapa is always at a disadvantage in his dealings with the outsider. It has become more and more important in their deaings with mestizos and *negros* for the Cayapa to learn to speak fluent Spanish. This is a prelude to rapidly changing values and mode of living.

BIBLIOGRAPHY —

● STEWARD, JULIAN H. Handbook of South American Indians. 7 Vols., Washington, DC: U.S. Govt. Printing Office, 1946-59.

CAYAPO

(South America; Brazil) refers to a Ge-speaking people whom westerners have seen fit to classify as Northern Cayapo and Southern Cayapo. The term was first used to designate the Southern Cayapo who have been extinct since the 19th century and who, although related to the Northern Cayapo will not be considered here since information about them warrants no more than this classifactory note.

The Northern Cayapo occupy a region in northeastern Brazil between the Xingu and Araguaya Rivers which, in the 19th century, was about 40,000 square miles with a population estimated at 5,000. Since that time, disease and contact with Brazilians in quest of rubber and Brazil nuts has brought about a severe decline in their overall population--even though as late as the 1950s a heretofore unknown village with 500 inhabitants was discovered. Population decline has made it almost impossible for traditional ways of social organization and lifestyle to be maintained.

Subsistence activities The contemporary as well as the historic Cayapo are slash-and-burn horticulturalists who also depend heavily on hunting, fishing, and gathering wild plants. The gardens are prepared by encircling the trunks of large trees so that they die in a few months; the smaller trees are felled. When all is dry, the entire plot is burned over and cleared for planting. The crops grown by the Cayapo range from the traditional maize, sweet potatoes, cotton, and tobacco to the more recently introduced plants such as rice, sugar cane, and bitter manioc. The village headman selects the fields for clearing and decides the agricultural cycle, usually after detailed discussion among household heads. Both men and boys do the clearing. There is a definite plan of crop and field rotation. The plots cleared are apportioned into nuclear faamily sections which are then cared for by a man, his wife, and children. Women do most of the harvesting.

Hunting constitutes an important subsistence activity. Men often hunt individually and may absent themselves from their villages for several days. Usually hunts are communal, especially in the quest of larger game such as peccary and tapir, when a very large amount of meat is needed to feed an entire village during a festival. A wooden club used either as a cudgel or thrown with great skill is the main weapon in hunting larger game. The bow and arrow is reserved for shooting birds, the feathers of which are used in ceremonial headdresses. Small game is usually eaten by the family of the hunter; the surplus is distributed among close relatives. Catches of large game are distributed on a village-wide basis by the headman. Tortoises are in great abundance and are even caught and kept alive for subsequent use.

Fishing is of less importance than hunting, although it still constitutes a major subsistence activity and its productivity is greatest during the dry season when fish are contained within the river banks. Groups of men engage in fishing. Determined by the headman and the council of elders, some men cut poisonous vines which, when beaten into the steam, drug the fish and make them easy to net or catch by hand; other men build weirs of branches or stones across the stream to slow the flow of water. The division of the catch is similar to that of large game. Individual fishing may take place at any time an is usually done with bow and arrow, although hook and line are sometimes used. Food gathering is of very great imnportance among the Cayapo as it is with many other tropical Indians. Men gather when returning from the hunt, especially if not much game was caught; but it is mainly women's work. The large variety of palms is exploited as well as the Brazil nut which occurs in abundance and may be easily stored. Considering their rather rudimentary technology and relatively small population, the Cayapo have a fairly complex social organization which not only centers around kinship and marriage institutions. There are, for example, two men's associations which function as work groups in village activities. Two village headmen are selected by these groups, each having complementary duties and obligations. They are chosen because of personal qualities of leadership and the experience which goes with age and a successful life, but they have no coercive authority. Every Cayapo goes through seven or eight age categories from infancy to old age, each of which entails different sets of rights and obligations. In early childhood a person becomes a member of one of four groups (two for boys and two for girls) which modify kinship relations with other members of that group. Boys eventually become members of the warrior set which is the most prestigious, carefree, and desirable period of their lives. When they pass from this status to that of husband and father, they take on the work-a-day duties of a full adult which they perform until they near the end of their active life when they pass into an old-age set.

The Cayapo are matrilineal and live in villages made up of several matrilocal, extended-family households which encircle a central plaza. There is a chief's house at one end and a men's house at the other end of the plaza. Well-worn paths led out in different directions to the river, the forest, the new gardens, the old gardens, and so forth. The head of each communal house is the oldest woman. She is instrumental in arranging marriages, an act which is done long before children reach puberty. The Cayapo are ideally monogamous, but adultery is widespread. Young men eventually leave their mother's house to live in the men's house. When a man marries and has children, he spends more time in his wife's house, his participation in domestic affairs reaching its highest point in old age.

Old men and women play important parts in ceremonial life and in curing minor illnesses, but the shamans are the curers *par excellence* and constitute the only specialized profession among the Cayapo. To combat sorcery they alone are able to obtain the help of the spirit world which is otherwise considered harmful to humans.

BIBLIOGRAPHY —

● STEWARD, JULIAN H. Handbook of South American Indians. 7 Vols., Washington, DC: U.S. Govt. Printing Office, 1946-59.

CAYUGA

(U.S.; N.Y.) an eastern tribe, were members in the great Iroquois Confederacy.

The Cayuga's traditional home is in the upper New York area, the Finger Lakes district. Today most of the Cayuga, about 100 live with the Mohawks on a reservation in Ontario, Canada; but 300 live still live in their traditional New York home.

Their language was Iroquoian and most of its cultural, religious, and political life followed forms of other Iroquoian nations.

For example, women held pre-eminent political power. Women would choose those chiefs, who were male, to attend the council of 50, the confederacy's council. Women would also a new chief when one died.

One of the Cayuga's family structures was the maternal family. This consisted of a female, her male and female descendents, and the female descendents of the first female descendents. Whichever women was at the head of this family kwielded great political power.

Another family structure was constructed simply of all the relatives of both a mother and father.

A mojor social unit with the Cayuga were their clans. These clans were under two divisions called phratries. Members of the clan engaged in social acitivities amongst themselves and with other clans, such as playing lacrosse. The Cayuga's villages were permanent. They lived in the famous longhouses. The women grew maize and collected squash. The men hunted deer for meat and skins for clothing.

The Cayuga had secret societies such as the Otter Society or the False Face Society. These had major medicinal value. One who was sick, and had a dream indicating which society to join, would join that society and be cured.

At one time, the Cayuga joined four other New York nations-- the Onondaga, the Oneida, the Mohawk, and the Seneca--forming the Iroquois confederation. These were known collectively as the Five Nations. In the early 1700s the Tuscarora joined the League which was then called the Six Nations.

Though the Cayuga was the smallest nation numerically--its three villages held a total population fo 1,000--it had great political clout. It sent ten chiefs to the council of 50, second only to the Onondaga's 14.

But the Cayuga's influence waned after its population was decimated from a series of battles between 1667-73 with the Susquehannah. In 1688 the Cayuga, Oneida, and Onondaga signed a neutrality pact with the British. Following the war America took revenge by drifing the Cayuga and others in the six nations to Canada, an action largely responsible for the League's breakup.

(see map page XIV)

BIBLIOGRAPHY —

● DE SCHWEINITZ, EDMUND. The Life and Times of David Zeisberger. The Western Pioneer and Apostle of the Indians. Philadelphia, PA: J. B. Lippincott & Co., 1870.
● DONALDSON, THOMAS. The Six Nations of New York. Washington: U.S. Census Printing Office, 1892.
● HARMON, GEORGE DEWEY. Sixty Years of Indian Affairs, Political, Economic, and Diplomatic, 1789- 1850. Chapel Hill, NC: University of North Carolina Press, 1941.
● HODGE, FREDERICK WEBB. Handbook of American Indians North of Mexico. Washington: Government Printing Office, 2 vols., 1907-10.
● MURDOCK, GEORGE P. Ethnographic Bibliography of North America. New Haven, CT: Human Relations Area Files Press, 1975.
● PALMER, ROSE A. The North American Indians, An Account of the American Indians North of Mexico. New York, NY: Smithsonian Institution Series, Inc., 1929.

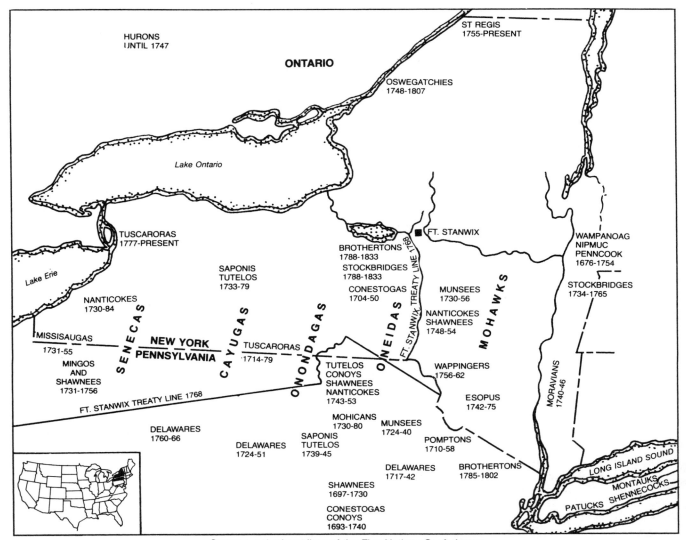

HURONS
UNTIL 1747

ONTARIO

ST REGIS
1755-PRESENT

OSWEGATCHIES
1748-1807

Lake Ontario

FT. STANWIX

TUSCARORAS
1777-PRESENT

Lake Erie

BROTHERTONS
1788-1833
STOCKBRIDGES
1788-1833
CONESTOGAS
1704-50

WAMPANOAG
NIPMUC
PENNCOOK
1676-1754

STOCKBRIDGES
1734-1765

SAPONIS
TUTELOS
1733-79

MUNSEES
1730-56

NANTICOKES
1730-84

NANTICOKES
SHAWNEES
1748-54

MOHAWKS

SENECAS

NEW YORK
PENNSYLVANIA

CAYUGAS

TUSCARORAS
1714-79

ONONDAGAS

ONEIDAS

FT. STANWIX TREATY LINE 1768

WAPPINGERS
1756-62

MISSISAUGAS
1731-55

MINGOS
AND
SHAWNEES
1731-1756

TUTELOS
CONOYS
SHAWNEES
NANTICOKES
1743-53

ESOPUS
1742-75

MORAVIANS
1740-46

FT. STANWIX TREATY LINE 1768

DELAWARES
1760-66

DELAWARES
1724-51

SAPONIS
TUTELOS
1739-45

MOHICANS
1730-80

MUNSEES
1724-40

POMPTONS
1710-58

LONG ISLAND SOUND

DELAWARES
1717-42

BROTHERTONS
1785-1802

MONTAUKS
SHENNECOCKS

SHAWNEES
1697-1730

PATUCKS

CONESTOGAS
CONOYS
1693-1740

Cayuga and other tribes of the Five Nations Confederacy.

● POWERS, MABEL. The Indian as Peacemaker. New York, NY: Fleming H. Revell Co., 1932.
● ROYCE, CHARLES C. Indian Land Cessions in the U.S. Washington: 18th Annual Report, Bureau of Ethnology, 1896-97.
● SCHOOLCRAFT, HENRY R. History of the Indian Tribes of the U.S.; Their Present Condition and Prospects... Philadelphia, J. B. Lippincott & Co., 1857.
● SHEA, JOHN G. Catholic Missions Among the Indian Tribes of the U.S. New York, NY: E. Dunigan & Bros., 1854.
● STONE, WILLIAM L. Life of Joseph Brant- Thayendanegea, including the Indian Wars of the American Revolution. New York, NY: George Dearborn & Co., 1838.
● SWANTON, JOHN R. The Indian Tribes of North America. Washington, DC: U.S. Government Printing Office, 1952.
● WAIT, MARY VAN SICKLE, AND WILL HEIDT JR. The Story of the Cayugas. Ithaca, NY: De Witt Historical Society of Tompkins County, Inc., 1966.
● WISSLER, CLARK. Indians of the U.S., Four Centuries of Their History and Culture. New York, NY: Doubleday, Doran & Co., 1940.

CAYUSE

(U.S.; Oreg., Wash.) are a Penutian-speaking people who live in Washington and Oregon.

They have been closely associated with the neighboring Nez Perces and Wallawalla, and regarded in early history as belonging to the same stock. However, they are linguistically independent. The Cayuse have been noted for their courage, largely because of their constant struggles with the Snake and other tribes who have been numerically superior. In 1855 the Cayuse joined in the treaty by which the Umatilla Reservation was formed, and since then have resided 1838 a mission was established among the Cayuse kby Marcus Whitman at the site of the present town of Whitman, Wallawalla Co., Wash. In 1847

Cayuse and their neighbors.

smallpox affected a large part of the tribe. The Cayuse, believing the missionaries to be the cause, attacked them, murdered Whitman and a number of others, and destroyed the mission. From early accounts it is difficult to differentiate the Cayuse from the Nez Perces and Wallawalla because in habits and customs they differed little from these peoples.

(see map page XVII)

BIBLIOGRAPHY –

● BANCROFT, HUBART HOWE. The Native Races of the Pacific States of North America. San Francisco, CA: 1874.
● EELS, MYRON, REV. History of Indian Missions on the Pacific Coast,--Oregon, Washington, Idaho. Philadelphia, PA: The American Sunday-School Union, 1882.
● GHENT, WILLIAM JAMES. The Road to Oregon, A Chronicle of the Great Emigrant Trail. New York, NY: Longmans, Green & Co., 1929.
● HODGE, FREDERICK WEBB. Handbook of American Indians North of Mexico. Washington: Government Printing Office, 2 vols., 1907-10.
● MURDOCK, GEORGE P. Ethnographic Bibliography of North America. New Haven, CT: Human Relations Area Files Press, 1975.
● RICHARDSON, ALFRED TALBOT. Life, Letters and Travels of Father Pierre-Jean de Smet, S. J. 1801-1873. New York, NY: Francis P. Harper, 1905.
● ROYCE, CHARLES C. Indian Land Cessions in the U.S. Washington: 18th Annual Report, Bureau of Ethnology, 1896-97.
● RUBY, ROBERT H., AND JOHN A. BROWN. The Cayuse Indians: Imperial Tribesmen of Old Oregon. Norman, OK: University of Oklahoma Press, 1972.
● SEYMOUR, FLORA WARREN. Indian Agents of the Old Frontier. New York, NY: and London: D. Appleton- Century Company, Inc., 1941.

● SHEA, JOHN G. Catholic Missions Among the Indian Tribes of the U.S. New York, NY: E. Dunigan & Bros., 1854.
● SWANTON, JOHN R. The Indian Tribes of North America. Washington, DC: U.S. Government Printing Office, 1952.
● WISSLER, CLARK. Indians of the U.S., Four Centuries of Their History and Culture. New York, NY: Doubleday, Doran & Co., 1940.

CAYUVAVA

(South America; Bolivia) resided on the westeren side of the Mamore River, 15 leagues above its junction with the Guapore River in eastern Bolivia. The Indians were scattered in small settlements along the main course of the Mamore River and along several of its small tributaries.

The *Cayuvava* were first encountered in 1693 by the Jesuit Missionary, Father Augustin Zapata. They then lived in large villages, each with a population which is said to have varied from 1,800 to 2,000 inhabitants. The *Cayuvava* were concentrated by the Jesuits in the Mission of Exaltacion, on the Mamore River, below its junction with the Yacuma River. In 1749, there were about 3,000 *Cayuvava,* in 1831, some 2,073; and in 1909, only 100. The population figure today is unknown, and the tribe may be extinct.

Culture The *Cayuvava* are described as good farmers who raised peanuts, sweet manioc, maize, and other plants. Their weapons were bows and arrows and chonta wood spears, the latter tipped with a sharp bone and trimmed with feathers. At the beginning of the present century, little of the original culture remained, but they still wore bark-cloth tunics and still fished with open-top conical baskets which were thrown over the fish in shallow places. *Cayuvava* men filled their incisor teeth, a custom rare in South America, and perhaps of African origin.

In the 17th century, the seven *Cayuvava* villages were apparently under the rule of a single chief. In the Mission of Exaltacion, the *Cayuvava* were divided into eight groups, corresponding perhaps to former tribes.

In 1695, Father Zapata found in the region occupied by the *Cayuvava* a large village with streets and a central plaza where the inhabitants, dressed in luxurious cloaks and covered with feathers, were gathered in front of a temple to make a sacrifice to the gods. The offerings consisted of rabbit, rhea, and deer meat placed on trays around a fire which was never extinguished.

Religion Only a few fragments of their religion are known. The *Cayuvava* called their good spirit or spirits Idaapa and the bad one Mainaje. They closed the mouth and nose of dying people to prevent the escape of death, that is to say, of the evil spirit which had attacked the patient. Men refrained from working when their wives menustrated.

BIBLIOGRAPHY —
● STEWARD, JULIAN H. Handbook of South American Indians. 7 Vols., Washington, DC: U.S. Govt. Printing Office, 1946-59.

CAZCAN

(Mexico; Zacatecas) Indians originally inhabited the Juchipila and Tlaltenago valleys. As a social and/or cultural entity, they no loner exist.

The name "Cazcan" is an hispanized version of "Cazcan" (pronounced: kashkan). The term "Teul-Chichimeca" was also used for a brief period by the Spanish, but the term was so generalized that it was soon dropped. "Mixton" is another generic term for the Caxcan. The name "Caxcan" appears to have unimportant among these Indians, as they identified themselves by hometown and province. Most suggested etymologies are too speculative and farfetched to merit repeating. The most likely suggestion is that the term connotes an ancestor complex.

The Cazcans were not organized into a tribe or tribes, but into highly competitive, pocket states with elite leaders. The major boundary was between the Cazcans of the Tlaltenango and Juchipila valleys, the former considered more conservative and the latter more warlike. Social and political boundaries also existed within each valley. Each unit was a polity which was headed by a town. The towns were ethnically diverse.

The Cazcans appear to have been expanding both towards the west and south, through raids and perhaps conquests, when they were first contacted by the Spanish. The Spanish soon encapsulated them in the Juchipila and Tlaltenango valleys, however. Very little is known about the area's archaeology, so nothing definite can be mentioned concering their territorial extension much prior to the Conquest. After the Conquest, they experienced a steady erosion of their territory.

As a language, Cazcan is dead. It is only known from a few brief vocabularies written down by Spanish in the 16th and 17th centuries. Disagreements in the methods of recording Cazcan phoentics makes using these lists difficult. It can be stated with cerainty that the language was part of the gereral western Uto-Aztecan branch, probably related to Huicholan or Southern Tepehuan. In addition, Cazcan appears to have had dialectical differences between the major valleys. Since the Cazcaan polities were ethnically diverse, it is most likely that several other languages were spoken within the zone.

The first Spanish mentioned extensive agricultural plots along the rivers (probably irrigated), in the upper terraces of the valleys, and in the hills. Maize, beans, and squash are most frequently mentioned. Some aboriginal terracing is still visible today. Hunting was of minor importance when compared to agriculture. The Cazcans had four types ;of settlements: a) Farmsteads, which were often seasonally occupied and consisted of permanent but simple platform/patio compounds of stacked rock structures with grass thatch roofs; b) Villages, which were numerous and often contained simple ceremonial architecture. Village platform/patio compounds were often coterminus and can cover over 20 hectares in extension; c)Ceremonial Centers, the most famous of which are San Andres de Teul in the Tlaltenango Valley, and Las Ventananas in the Juchilpa Valley, though many others existed. These centers had town residential areas, often sizable, as well as several complex courts where the elite elements of the polities lived. Pyramids, palaces, plazas, complex platforms, burial crypts, and hallways characterize these centers. Sime centers are fortified. All are monumental; d) Fortifications, calledpenoles, were improved positions located at the tops of high peaks within the valleys. The most famous is the Penol de Mixton, in the Juchilpa Valley. There is no ceremonial or residential architecure at the *penoles*.

Ceramics were an economic specialization. Copper was popular and fashioned into axes, adzes, projectile points, needles, awls, and knives as useful items that supplemented a well developed stone industry. Copper luxury items served as status markers. Bracelets, rings, ear plugs, sheets (possible mirrors), and bells were the most popular. It is known whether these items in copper were made locally or traded for. Complex work in shell is also evident. One type of ceramic, called Las Ventanas Negative Polychrome, was a high status marker and traded widely throughout the neighboring valleys. Technology and the arts were, in general, rather highly developed. Trade for obsidian, probably copper, turquoise, malachite, probably peyote, shell, salt, and feathers was highly developed. The area fully participated within a larger economic sphere along the northern frontier of Mesoamerica. Religious symbolism is poorly understand, but can be inferred from ceramic motifs. The coyote cycle, Quetzalcoatl, possibly Tlaloc, and possibly jaguars are the most frequent realistic motifs. This symbolism is fully Mesoamerican. Nothing is known about their folklore or details of their daily life.

The social organization was hieratic, culminating in patrilineally structured aristocratic families that ran the polities as minor kingdoms. The vcast percentage of people were commoners and farmers, but they were undoubtedly called upon for military service, builiding projects, and taxes. Military societies existed and caused the Spanish years of difficulty. They were aggressive, well organized, and innovative. A small percentage of people were palace retainers, mostly artisans. It is not known whether formalized slavery existed or not, but it is like. Human sacrifices occurred and were related to the agricultural cycle.

Cazcan history is, to this date, very poorly documented. It is clear that these valleys were Mesoamerican in traditioin from very early. The archaeology of the zone is in its infancy, so only a very vague chronology can be postulated. Around the time of Christ, formative influences of the Chupicauro style reached the Juchipila Valley. During the Classic Period of Central Mexico (AD 100-900), almost nothing is known from the zone except that complex burials were dedicated with elegant bichrome and negative bichrome ceramics. At times, polished black, engraved tripod vessels were also buried. It seems that during the late Classic and early Postclassic Periods (Postclassic--Ad 900 to Conquest) several sites began to become more elaborate. It is to this phase that the initial monumental constructions at San Andres de Teul, Las Ventanas, and El Chique belong. By the late Postclassic, at the dawn of the Conquest, many sites were extremely complex and monumental.

The polities at Conquest were militaristic and competitive both among themselves and with their non-Cazcan nighbors. The Spanish first contacted an important Cazcan settlement at Juchipila (probably then located at the ruin today called Las Ventanas). The first contacts in the 1520s were peaceful, but by 1540 the Cazcan had second

thoughts and the MixtonWar began. The Spanish were forced to move the new city of Guadalajara (then located at Nochistlan, Zacatecas) southwest to the Atemejac Valley by the violence of this war. Indeed, as Lopez-Portillo y Weber documented in his classic study of the war *La Rebellion de Nueva Galicia,* 1939, Mexico City), the Spanish lamost lost control over all of western Mexico. Within several years, however, the Spanish assumed the offensive and, with the capture of the Penol de Mixton, organized Cazcan resistance ended. The Spanish established new pueblos in both Cazcans valleys, forcing many Cazcans to relocate. The Spanish also brought in many Tlaxcaltecan Indians from Central Mexico to serve as pacifying coloninsts. Some Cazcans were organized into *communidades,* chartered land holding units. By the late 18th century, they had acculturated kwith their mestizo neighbors to form a regional, rural lifestyle that, while different, was no longer a distinct Indian ethnicity.

The descendents of the Cazcans today as town oriented farmers, town dwellers and merchants fully integrated into the national economy and culture. Only a few vague and confused legends, a few regional names for plants, many toponyms, and the stacked rock, grass roofed farmstead buildings are all that remain of the Indian past. Even the elegant ruins are being looted and vandalized for commercial purposes, though the most important are now protected.

Population figures are very hard to estimate. The Spanish at Conquest mention that the Cazcan were

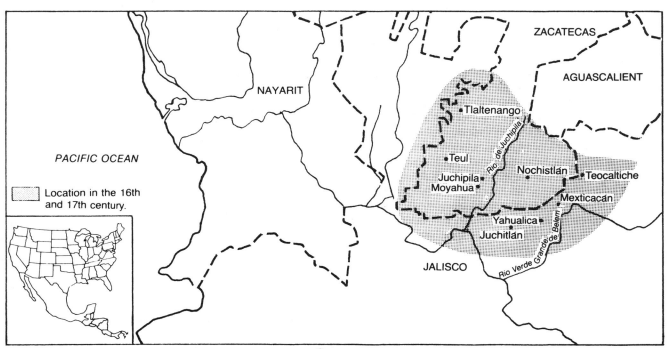

Cazcan

numerous, but gave no figures. No census from the early Colonial period has yet been found. Judging from the number and sizes of the late archaeological sites, though, population of the two valleys must have been considerable, probably in the tens of thousands.

The Cazcans no longer exist. Their history during the Colonial period and prehistory prior to the Conquest await exploration. These keys series of groups almost repulsed the Spanish from western Mexico. They were important as major polities along the northern frontier of ancient Mesoamerica. Their society and culture, while patrially marginal to the centers of high civilization, was highly developed and complex.

BIBLIOGRAPHY —

● BOWDITCH, CHARLES. P. Mexican and Central American Antiquities, Calendar Systems and History. Washington, D. C.: Bureau of American Ethnology- Bulletin 28: GPO, 1904.
● THOMAS, CYRUS. Indian Languages of Mexico and Central America and Their Geographical Distribution. Bureau of American Ethnology Bulletin 44: Washington, D. C.: GPO, 1911.

CHAKE

(South America; Venezuela) is a generic term used to designate a number of peoples who live in Venezuela west of Lake Maracaibo and who speak languages related to Cariban. Some of these people are also lumped under the mane, "Motilones," a term used since colonial times to indicate Indians with cut hair (and also "wild Indians.") This is an area known as the sub-Andes, throughout which in pre-Hispanic times there diffused cultural knowledge from the central Andes of Peru. People subsumed under the name Chake are the Aguas Blancas, Cuanguasata, Tucuco, Sicacao, Piriri, Chake proper and several others. So diminutive that they are almost pygmoid in stature, the Chake were missionized by the Capuchins in the late eighteenth and early nineteenth centuries. However, later in the nineteenth century, Indian-white relations were broken because of the protracted mistreatment of the Indians. From then on, the Chake attacked all who entered their territory, including explorers for oil. Since the second decade of this century there has been some lessening of hostilities by certain of the tribes. The Tucuco have for a long time been under the influence of Capuchin missionaries in the Los Angeles del Tucuco mission station which provides us with our most recent information. The total population of the modern Motilones, or Chake, is probably less than 2000.

The Chake are tropical forest cultivators who have a semi- migratory pattern of cultivation. Using the slash-and-burn technique, they clear large fields on wooded mountain slopes. They use steel axes to cut down the larger trees. The men do this laborious work as well as the planting while the women take care of the harvest. Among the crops grown by the Chake are manioc, sweet potatoes, yams, maize, beans, gourds, papayaa, pineapples, tobacco, cotton, and plantains. Maize and manioc are the staple crops. Hunting and fishing supplement agriculture. The Chake shoot animals and birds with bow and arrow, often from small blinds. They also fish with bow and arrow, use drugs, or seize fish by hand in small ponds which they make by damming rivers. They usually roast their meat on a *babracot*. Maize is eaten on the cob or it is ground with a *mano* and *metate* (slab stone) and wrapped in leaves and boiled. Manioc is pounded, mixed with water, and heated in a gourd until it coagulates. It is interesting that the Chake do not use salt and avoid all condiments. Today, they use a mixture of ashes and lemon to give zest to their food. The Chake drink *chica* made from maize. Chake villages are made up of a number of dwellings which are simple lean-tos or huts formed by double lean-tos with a small porch along the front. They have almost no furniture, lacking hammocks and evern wooden benches and sleep on the floor which is covered with mats or ferns.

The Chake manufacture textiles, basketry, ceramics, and their own weapons. Men build the lean-to huts, do the basketry work, knits bags, clear the forest, plant and sow, and make their own weapons and clay pipes; women spin, weave and make pots.

Little is known of the aboriginal social and political organization of the Chake people. In modern times they have become acculturated to a great extent by Capuchin missionaries who live in their area. In former times, the Chake seem to have been divided up into small political units headed by weak chiefs. Sometimes, several villages were consolidated under the leadership of a head man but in most cases, a chief seems to have been a patrilineal elder who had authority over his kinship group. Chake villages are related to one another through bonds of marriage. The principal rule governing marriage is that of patrilineal exogamy. It is common for marriages to be arranged by parents when their children are very young. Marriage, however, does not take place until after puberty. Among the Chake proper, monogamy prevails, although polygyny occurs kin some of the other generic Chake societies.

At birth, a Chake woman secrets herself in the forest and delivers without assistance. After birth, the infant is washed and women of all ages perform a dancing feast. The next rite of passage occurs at puberty and is most important in the celebration of a girl's first menses. A nubile girl runs away from her village and is ritually pursued and captured by old woman who shuts her up in a small shack where she remains for ten days. Marriage ceremonies involve the building of a house for the couple and celebrations with dancing, drinking, and singing. Adultery is avenged by a woman's brothers and closest patrilineal kinsmen who kill her lover as punishment for the crime. The Chake venerate the bones of the deceased. The body of a dead person is kept for two days in his hut and then is taken to an isolated shack where it is placed on the floor with the deceased's weapons near the body and all is covered with grass. After a month or so, the bones are collected and sewn into a piece of cloth after having been forced into a fetal position. All these operations are attended by dancing, drinking, shooting arrows into the air, and general cermonial festivities. The body is them hung from the hut froof for two or three years. Umtilmately, the bones of the deceased are carried to a mountain cave where they are deposited permanently.

Although the traditional religious system of the Chake is relatively unknown, there are a few practices which survive. There is belief in a supernatural being called *kioso,* and when it thunders, the Chake look up and say, "God *(kioso)* is angry." The discharge of arrows into the air occurs at the number of Chake ceremonies and is an important idea in their religious observaces. After the maize harvest, for example, men and women dance in separate groups and the men at a agiven moment shoot arrows up into the air. Sometimes the dancers are wounded by the failing arrows. As reflected in Chake mythology, there seem to have been four sky giants who were invincible. After they broke the rule of incest and their power, they could be slain by men. This accounts in part for the shooting of arrows into the sky. During a storm, Chake men threaten the clouds with their weapons and make great noises. They also practice some food taboos such as keeping fire and maize separated (maize is always boiled and never roasted and no man crosses a maize field while smoking) and a man avoids eating the game he himself has killed, for such action would spoil his prowess at hunting. Certain animals, the sun, moon, stars, fire, all have a place in traditional Chake mythology.

BIBLIOGRAPHY –

● STEWARD, JULIAN H. Handbook of South American Indians. 7 Vols., Washington, DC: U.S. Govt. Printing Office, 1946-59.

CHALCO

(Mexico) from *challi,* "mouth," *co,* "people;" hence "people from the mouth" is a term recalling the origin of the Chalca, and the circular carved stone upon which the mythological ideograph of

the name was preserved. This was the large band of settlers who arrived in the Valley of Mexico shortly after the Xochimilco, and the second group to separate peacefully from the Chicomoztoc in AD 1168 and seek their fortunes elsewhere. Their capital city, bearing the same name, was located southwest of Mexico City on the banks of old Lake Chalco. It was an important source of drinking water for Tenochtitlan, located as it was between Popocatepetl and Ixtaccihuatl. The name is also applied by modern archaeologists to a specific Archaic complex found in the region, dated *c.* 2000-1500 BC.

BIBLIOGRAPHY –

● BOWDITCH, CHARLES. P. Mexican and Central American Antiquities, Calendar Systems and History. Washington, D. C.: Bureau of American Ethnology- Bulletin 28: GPO, 1904.
● SWANTON, JOHN R. The Indian Tribes of North America. Washington, DC: U.S. Government Printing Office, 1952.
● THOMAS, CYRUS. Indian Languages of Mexico and Central America and Their Geographical Distribution. Bureau of American Ethnology Bulletin 44: Washington, D. C.: GPO, 1911.

CHAMA

(South America; Peru) (Tschama) are actually several tribes of the Panoan linguistic family who live in the Ucayali Valley. The tribes include the *Chamicura, Casibo, Capanawa, Pyymanawa, Remo, Mananava, Nianagua, Amahuaca, Maspo, Amenguaca, Ruanagua, Pichobo, Soboyo, Comobo, Mochobo, Nocoman, Mayoruna, Setebo, Shipibo,* and *Conibo.*

Population figures are not known, but the total is probably at least several hundred.

The river tribes, such as *Setebo, Shipibo* and *Conibo* used to raid and enslave their smaller linguistic kin. Today, the peoples are for the most

Chama walking aid for infants

part pacific, and cultivate food such as manioc, maize, and peppers, and tend cotton and tobacco. They also hunt and fish the rivers of the valley.

Traditional approaches to life allow the men several wives, including sisters and women slaves captured in war. Families, related through the famale line, live in villages which consist of a communal house. There are no social or political structures linking the settlements. In daily life, men clear land, after which women till the crops. The women also weave and make ceramics.

(see map page XVIII)

BIBLIOGRAPHY —

● STEWARD, JULIAN H. Handbook of South American Indians. 7 Vols., Washington, DC: U.S. Govt. Printing Office, 1946-59.

CHANA

(South America) In the 16th century there appears to have been two groups of Chana Indians, living respectively in the vicinity of Sancti Spirtitu and on the islands opposite the mouth of the Rio Negro (lat. 34 S., long. 58 W.). They maintained their separate identities during the Colonial epoch. The tongue of the Chana was described by *Oviedo y Valdes, 1851-55* , (p. 185) as gutteral, a statement born out by Larranaga, who compiled a vocabulary and grammar published by *Lafone Quevedo, 1922* (p. 185) and *Torres, 1911* (p. 185).

The Chana, like the neighboring Charrua, Yaro, Bohane, and Mocoreta, had no agriculture, but are said to have eaten algarroba beans, which grew wild in their vicinity. Their chief sustenance came from hunting and fishing. Their weapons are reputed to have been the bow and arrow and the spear and spear thrower. In the 18th century, they still made excellent pottery and used canoes.

Azara , 1809 (p. 186) wrote that, like the Guarani, they disinterred the bodies of their dead after the soft parts had perished in order to paint the bones with ocher and grease, and bury them anew with their accouterments. The children, he adds, were buried in great pottery urns, filled with ocher and earth, and covered with broad plates.

BIBLIOGRAPHY —

● STEWARD, JULIAN H. Handbook of South American Indians. 7 Vols., Washington, DC: U.S. Govt. Printing Office, 1946-59.

CHANA-MBEGUA

(South America) This tribe was mentioned by *Pero Lopes de Souza, 1861* (p. 186) and by *Oviedo y Valdes, 1851-55* (p. 186). The latter places them on the northern side of the Delta (lat. 35 S., long. 59 W.) opposite the Chana-Timbu, who, he said, spoke the same tongue. *Lopez, 1861* (p. 186) encountered them at the mouth of the Parana River, but the exact location was not known.

The woman and three men he saw were clad in skins. The woman wore her hair in a braid, and had lines painted or tattooed beneath her eyes. They all had caps made from the heads of jaguars, complete even to the teeth. They used small canoes, in contrast to the Charrua and Timbu, who had large ones.

BIBLIOGRAPHY —

● STEWARD, JULIAN H. Handbook of South American Indians. 7 Vols., Washington, DC: U.S. Govt. Printing Office, 1946-59.

CHANA-TIMBU

(South America) Very little is known about this tribe. *Ramirez, 1897* (p. 186) listed them among the "other nations" living near Sancti Spiritu at the mouth of the Rio Carcarana (lat. 35 S., long. 60 W.) and *Garcia de Moguer, 1908* (p. 186) stated that they lived on the other part of the river from the "Caracaraes." Both of these writers, however, distinguish them from the "Timbus" or "Atambies," and if they were not a distinct tribe, they were at least a subtribe of the Timbu or Chana. In addition, *Oviedo y Valdes, 1851-55* (p. 186) wrote that they occupied the south side of the Delta opposite the Chana-Mbegua and that both spoke the same tongue.

Oviedo y Valdes also wrote that the Chana Timbu were of greater stature than any other tribe of the Parana Delta, and that they normally went naked, although they had some skins of deer and otter. Their diet, in addition to the flesh of these animals, consisted of fish and maize. They also grew "calabashes," which possibly meant squashes.

BIBLIOGRAPHY —

● STEWARD, JULIAN H. Handbook of South American Indians. 7 Vols., Washington, DC: U.S. Govt. Printing Office, 1946-59.

CHANCAY

(South America; Peru) (*ca*. AD 1100-1470) were a prehistoric civilization in South America once inhabiting the Ancon, Chancay, Chillon and Huara Valleys of central Peru. Following the break-up of the Empire *ca*. 1150, the central coastal region fragmented into smaller individual units, with no great cities or monumental structures. Apparently the people had to entirely reorganize their political life, but lacked the leadership to do so quickly. There is little indication of an aristocracy or central religious strength, other than that observed by the individual, and there seems to have been none of the wide political organization for which ancient Peru is so famous. Artistically, the Chancay people were not distinguished; while pottery was commonly made,

it bears the signs of having been hastily constructed and carelessly finished. Most of it is a
redware with an over-all white wash upon which
designs are crudely painted in black or dark
brown; occasionally one finds an additional shade
of red or orange. The designs on the ceramics represent no observable oconography, but rather seem
to be random doodling. The first true bronze in
Peru comes from this period. Apparently the great
Chancay art was in weaving: the dry cemeteries
have preserved thousands of examples of color-
fully woven cotton and alpaca wool textiles which
reflect the superb artistry of the weavers. Most of
the weaving tools and "sewing kits" in museum
and private collections come from Chancay
sources, as do the magnificent woven feather
mosaic textiles, at which art they were unequalled.
Another popular Chancay art was the manufacture
of small textile dolls built upon reed bases, with
simulated costumes, and *genre* trees with birds and
flowers, all woven in colorful designs. Indeed,
Chancay art in general has much of the flavor of a
folk art, rather than the representation of professional, trained arts.

BIBLIOGRAPHY —

● STEWARD, JULIAN H. Handbook of South American Indians. 7 Vols., Washington, DC: U.S. Govt. Printing Office,
1946-59.

CHANE

(South America; Gran Chaco) the southmost representatives of Arawakan-speaking populations in
South America, occupied, in pre- Conquest times
the northeastern and northwestern edges of the
Gran Chico and the eastern foothills of the Andes,
an area where the tropical forests joined the
swamps and plains of the Gran Chaco. Originally
calling themselves Chana, a name which became
hispanicized as Chane, they are geographically
divided into two groups: those in the southeastern
portion of Bolivia north of the Pilcomayo River
along the Rio Grande, or Guapay, abutting the
Gran Chico and Argentina, are known as the
Chane; those living in eastern Paraguay along the
tributaries of the Paraguay River north of Asun-
cion are known as the Guana. Both groups were
peaceful, sedentary farmers and both were reduced
to vassalage by invading Tupian-speaking
peoples, the Chane by the Chiriguano and the
Guana by the Mbaya and Guarani, shortly before
and during the Spanish Conquest. Once one of the
more populous peoples of this region, both the
Chane and Guana were victims of frequent hostilities which continued into the twentieth century
when in the late 1930s, during the Chaco War, the
Paraguayan army uprooted Chane villages along
the lower Parapiti River and resettled the people
in the middle of the Gran Chaco, an area which had

never been their habitat. In the late 1940s it was
estimated that the Chane numbered about 600 and
the Guana, 1,200.

Even before the invasions of the Chiriguano, the
western Chane were adapting to the influence of
Andean culture and served not only as a buffer between the peoples of the Chaco and those of the
Andean foothills, but as a transmitter of Andean
culture to those groups living to the east of them.
There was active trading in pre-Conquest times
among the Andean, Tupian, and Arawakan peoples
and the Chaco Indians. The Chane retained many

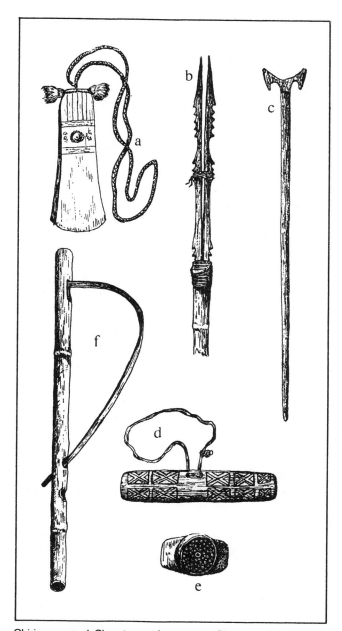

Chiriguano and Chané manufactures. *a*, Silver pincers used as
breast ornaments; *b*, bird arrow point; *c*, handle to wooden spade; *d*,
wooden whistle used as ornament; *e*, tin labret with mosaic inlay; *f*,
Chané pea-shooter.

of the tropical forest techniques of agriculture but were familiar with Andean methods as well, all of which the Chiriguano adopted when they overcame the Chane in the sixteenth and seventeenth centuries. The Chiriguano, in turn, influenced the Chane, so that what we know today of the Chane (cross reference Chiriguano). Thus the Chane have been modifying their lives in accordance with outside military, political and economic influences for hundreds of years and today are being rapidly assimilated into the prevailing Bolivian and Paraguayan societies.

The Chane are excellent farmers who practice a primarily tropical forest type of slash-and-burn the occasions that the Chane engaged in warfare with their neighbors, women played an important role in dancing and singing to encourage warriors to valorous exploits. These hostilities were small scale and were mainly raids to steal crops, cattle, and women. Nevertheless, the victorious party returned to their village with the heads of their vanquished enemies. The Chane are alleged to have been cannibals, as were their Chiriguano neighbors, and also to have been most often the victims of this practice. It has been reported that during the sixteenth century, the Chiriguano consumed 60,000 Chane in cannabilistic feasts. This is undoubtedly one of the many tall tales about South American Indians, for even the practice of cannibalism itself is not well documented.

Traditionally, the Chane marked the various stages in the life cycle and ceremonial activities. At the birth of a child, the father observed *couvade* for a few days, resting in bed and doing no work. The mother, immediately after birth, went to the river to wash and then smear her body with *urucu*. Both parents refrained from eating cerain foods for a specified period. All these observances were designed to protect and strengthen the newborn. At the onset of the first menses, Chane girls were confined for at least one month, and in aboriginal times, this seclusion was said to have lasted close to a year. Initiation rites for boys involved a group ceremony in which a shaman perforated their lower lips. This ceremony only took place when there was a large enough number of seven to twelve years old in the village. Bride service among the Chane of the Parapiti River was common at the beginning of this century, a system in which the groom moved in with his father-in-law to help with the crops, the arrangement usually ended with the birth of the first child. Death was greeted with loud wailings from the women of the village. The deceased was painted, dressed and placed in a large *chicha* jar. At graveside, the closest female relatives cut their hair and placed it on the grave. The widow observed a year's mourning period, wailing at specified hours every day. Chane believed that the soul encountered many hazards on its way to the "land of joy", open only to those who had never broken the traditions of Chane society.

Although Christian concepts have become part of the Chane religion, there is still a rich mythology and folklore which have their base in Arawakan tradition to which Tupian and Andean concepts have been added. Aboriginally, the Chane believed in nature spirits and ghosts, and the Chane masks now used at carnivals are a survival of this belief. Shamans played an important role in Chane society where their powers were required for rainmaking as well as curing. In villages they also served as counselors to the chief. The Chane did not tolerate failure by the shamans, putting them to death for not producing rain or stopping the ravages of diseasse in the village.

BIBLIOGRAPHY —

● STEWARD, JULIAN H. Handbook of South American Indians. 7 Vols., Washington, DC: U.S. Govt. Printing Office, 1946-59.

CHAOUACHA

(U.S.; Miss.) A small tribe living, when first known, on the East bank of the Mississippi, a short distance below the present New Orleans, La. Although they had aided the French in their Indian wars, they fell under suspicion after the Natchez war, and in consequence were attacked and a number of the people massacred, in 1730, by black slaves acting under orders from the French governor, who had in view the double purpose of weakening the power of the Natives and of overcoming any projected combination between them and the blacks. Subsequently they seem to have removed to the West side of the Mississippi, a little above their former position.

BIBLIOGRAPHY —

● HODGE, FREDERICK WEBB. Handbook of American Indians North of Mexico. Washington: Smithsonian Institution: BAE Bulletin No. 30: U.S. GPO, 1907.
● MURDOCK, GEORGE P. Ethnographic Bibliography of North America. New Haven, CT: Human Relations Area Files Press, 1975.
● SWANTON, JOHN R. The Indian Tribes of North America. Washington, DC: U.S. Government Printing Office, 1952.

CHAPACURA

(South America; Bolivia) whose population is now less than 1,000, included the following tribes: Chapacura proper, *Quitemoca, Rocorona, More (Itene), Huanyan, Matama (Mataua), Cujuna, Urunamacan, Cumana, Urupa, Jaru* and *Tora.*

Most of these Indians, now extinct, lived in Bolivia and Brazil. The culture of the various tribes of this family is little known.

In 1794, the Governor of the Province of Mojos,

Miguel Zamora, formed the new Mission of Nuestra Senora del Carmen with *Baure* Indians who had been taken from the forest of the upper Rio Blanco. The *Baure* converts, who actively helped to round up and transfer these Indians, called them to Guarayo, a general term given by Indians and mestizos to all independent and warlike Indians. These *Guarayo* (also called *Carmelitas* were later designated as *Chapacura* by the local authorities. A powerful *Tapacura* nation had existed in the 17th century in the region from which these Indians came. The name *Tapacura* occurs in most accounts of Gonzalo de Solis Holguin's journey. They were neighbors of the *Toro (Mojo),* and were friendly to the Spaniards. Some of them took part in the ill-horticulture. They have a large crop inventory which includes eleven varieties of maize and beans, pumpkins, gourds, melons, sweet potatoes, sweet manioc, peanuts, cotton and tobacco as well as some old world crops such as oranges, sugar cane and sorghum. Men clear the fields and till the soil, plant, but women and children help, especially at harvest time.

Chieftainship was patrilineally based, and according to information gathered in the early part of the twentieth century, power was inherited by the brothers of the deceased chief before it passed to his son. Sometimes a sister of the dead chief was able to assume political leadership of the village. The exact system of succession is, therefore, problematic. On fated *Mojos* expedition. When in 1630 Gonzalo de Solis Holguin entered the Province of the *Tapacura,* he was accompanied by a priest, who hoped to continue the missionary work among the *Tapacura* started by another priest. Some *Tapacura* were serfs of the Spaniards. It appears that European contacts with these Indians go back as far as the beginning of the 17th century. The *Tapacura* Indians of the Mission of Concepcion de Chiquitos, were Chapacuran.

Culture. Farming was practiced by all the members of the family and had greater importance than collecting or hunting, though wild Brazil nuts were almost a staple in certain periods of the year. Each family owned and tilled a field which nominally belonged to the family head. As fields continuously yielded one crop or another, there were only short periods of scarcity. The cultivated plants were maize, sweet potatoes, cara (yams), pineapples, gourds, bananas, papayas, cotton, and cayenne pepper. Peanuts were also grown by most of these Indians.

Wild plant foods included Brazil nuts, mangaba, wild cacao, and the fruits of various palms. Turtle eggs were also an important food item in September and October; eggs also were eaten. When on a collecting expedition, they lived in small triangular shelters.

The staple food was a sweet manioc. The tubers were peeled with a bamboo-splinter knife, washed, and grated on the thorny roots of the asahy palm. The pulp was boiled, carefully skimmed with a plaited spoon, strained through a mat made of thick sticks, and roasted on a fire pan. Manioc flour was either consumed at once or kept in a bark-cloth bag. Wafers of manioc were roasted in a pan; manioc buns were baked in ashes. The starchy manioc juice was boiled many times and drunk cold. Maize was ground on the flattened upper side of a horizontal log of about 16 feet (3 m.) long, with an oval, flat stone which, with one edge resting on the log, is rocked backward and forward among the grains. The flour was sifted through a special mat. It was baked into thin cakes on a fire pan.

The Indians kept many pets, especially birds, for which they made small cages.

Dwellings. Huts were generally located near the plantations. They were large lean-tos, 15 to 40 feet (about 5 to 14 m.) high supported by two rows of wooden posts. Mats of motacu palm fronds, which form the root itself, were lashed with liana on poles leaning against the rafters. The open side of the hut was closed in with upright palm leaves as the occasion required. Some huts were formed by placing two sloping shelters against each other. As many as eight families lived in one hut.

Dress. The dress of both sexes was a long bark-cloth shirt, which, however, was often discarded if it interfered with one's activities. The shirts were decorated with sewn or glued strips of bark cloth or were dyed with urucu. Outside their shirts, men used a belt of black or brown bark cloth sewn on it.

The complete festive attire of the Indians consisted of feather headdresses, monkey or sloth-skin caps, bark-cloth frontlets, feather bracelets, and ear sticks trimmed with feathers and *astrocaryum* or feather rings. Necklaces were strung with seeds or animal teeth.

Men and women parted their hair in the middle and clipped it at shoulder level. Some tied their hair up in a topknot with a bark-cloth band. Combs were made up of bamboo splinters (composite type). The Indians removed all body hair.

Transportation. Dugouts were about 33 feet (10 m.) long, and were propelled with narrow paddles which lacked a crutch or knob at the handle.

Babies were carried in a bark sling.

BIBLIOGRAPHY –

● STEWARD, JULIAN H. Handbook of South American Indians. 7 Vols., Washington, DC: U.S. Govt. Printing Office. 1946-59.

(U.S.; La.) A tribe, probably affiliated with the Caddo confederacy, living on a North branch of Red River of Louisiana in the 17th century. They were met by Bienville, in 1700 about 4 days' journey above the Kadohadacho, who dwelt on the main stream. The people were said to be at peace with the Hainai.

BIBLIOGRAPHY —

● HODGE, FREDERICK WEBB. Handbook of American Indians North of Mexico. Washington: Government Printing Office, 2 vols., 1907-10.
● MURDOCK, GEORGE P. Ethnographic Bibliography of North America. New Haven, CT: Human Relations Area Files Press, 1975.

CHARRUA

(South America; Uruguay) lived in the grassy plains north of the Rio de la Plata in what is now Uruguay, not far from the tropical rain forests. Charrua is a generic term imposed by sixteenth century European travelers to include a number of peoples in this area such as the Yaro, Guenoba, Bohane, Minuane, and the Charrua proper, who were culturally and linguistically related. Very little is known of their language which appears to be a dialect of Chane. Previously it was thought to be an unidentified linguistic isolate. The Charrua became extinct in the latter half of the nineteenth century after a series of wars with the Uruguayan troops.

In aboriginal times, the Charrua, like other peoples of the pampas and Patagonia to the south of them, were nomadic hunters and gatherers who practiced no horticulture. Fishing was of limited importance in their economy. There was sporadic use of canoes, a trait borrowed from their northern tropical forest neighbors. Fishing seems to have been of much greater importance before contact with the Spaniards than later on when Charrua had acquired European horses and their economy changed to a predatory one. This involved raiding Spanish settlements for horses and cattle. Although the Charrua maintained their independence from the Spaniards through centuries of incessant hostilities, their native culture began to disintegrate quickly after contact with Europeans. An indication of this is that by the eighteenth century, the Charrua are reported to have engaged in no fishing and had no canoes. Exact population figures for the Charrua at time of contact are not known, but they were more populous than many tribes in the region. However, the total population of the aborigianl Pampean-Patagonian Indians is estimated at only 36,000.

In pre-contact times, the Charrua lived in houses which were built of four stout poles set in the ground and covered with straw mats. After contact

Carrua stone plaques

with the Spaniards and the acquisition of horses, the Charrua gradually gave up their grass mat habitations in favor of *toldos* which were made up of horsehides sewn together and supported on fixed stakes. During this transitional period in their history, they also borrowed the idea and manufacturing techniques of netted hammocks from their northern tropical forest neighbors, the Guarani, who, in the seventeenth century and eithteenth centuries were sent by the Jesuits in futile attempts to subdue the Charrua.

It is known from archaelogical records that the Charrua knew how to make pottery long before their contact with Europeans. Although their utensils were crude black vessels which were sun dried, they served well to cook the rhea (*avestruz*) meat, their mainstay. They also manufactured a series of weapons which included bows and arrows, bolas, slings, and spears, all known from archaeological records as well. The Charrua were excellent archers and used the bow and arrow both in hunting larger animals such as deer and in warfare. They also used bolas with great skill. In aboriginal times they used the single-stone bola, but after conquest, adopted the two and three ball type from surrounding peoples with whom they had come into contact. When they adopted horse transportation, the Charrua, like other Indians of the southern plains and of the Chaco, also took on lances as principal hunting weapons which they used as well with great skill in warfare.

Warfare and lesser forms of hostility were relatively unimportant in pre-Spanish times. The Charrua, like their neighbors to the south, lived in small, autonomous bands, ecologically suited to their hunting and gathering exploitation of small territories. Families consisted of eight to ten persons who occupied a single mat dwelling. The bands consisted of about ten of these families under the weak authority of a lineage head. After contact with the Spaniards, the Charrua, like the other Indians of the pampas and the Chaco, became fierce warriors. Methods of warfare were quite simple. Women and children were hidden in some out of the way place while the warriors went ahead, advancing cautiously in order to surprise the enemy. The Charrua are reported to have skinned the heads of dead enemies, keeping the skulls as trophies which they used for ceremonial drinking cups. Chieftainship increased greatly in importance with the advent of raiding and guerilla warfare against the Spaniards.

Even after two centuries of attritional hostilities, the Charrua made great efforts to maintain as many aspects of their traditional culture as possible. These included tattooing the face with blue lines, using body paint in warfare, perforating the earlobes for pendants of shell, bone, and colored feathers, and the use of lip plugs, necklaces, and bracelets. Well into the nineteenth century, the Charrua continued to use traditional clothing such as deerskin belts and aprons and during winter, the fur robe of the type worn in Patagonia and the Chaco, made of skins of small animals which were sewn together and painted in geometric designs. Both men and women wore their hair long. Men made a knot at the back of their necks and inserted white feathers.

Litle is known of traditional social organization or phases in the life cycle of the individual. However, the Charrua were patrilineally organized and lived in extended families, each headed up by a kinship elder. Polygyny was practiced but to what extent is not clear. Puberty rites for girls and boys were celebrated with special ceremonies in which body painting and facial tattooing were prominent. Marriage took place shortly after puberty. It appears that patrilineal exogamy was the only strict rule regulating marriage; otherwise a woman was able to marry any man who asked her. If adultery was discovered, it was usually settled by a fistfight between the men involved but was not otherwise punished.

Death observances were important among the Charrua but all descriptions are post-contact and involve elements which are clearly the result of influence from the Spaniards. Burial of the corpse in

Group of Charrua

a communal cemetery was possibly one of these influences as is certainly the slaughtering of a horse on the grave of the deceased. The abondoning of personal property such as skin, cloaks, spears, and other weapons and utensils is very likely an aboriginal custom. After burial, close relatives underwent a long and painful period of mourning which included scarifying their arms, breasts, and sides with the knife or lance of the deceased and skewering the arms and legs. Both men and women cut off a finger joint during the mourning period which sometimes lasted as long as two months. It has been reported that old men and women had sacrificed all their fingers with the exception of thumbs during their lives.

Little is known of the aboriginal religion of the Charrua. It is clear that they believed in an evil spirit which caused death and disease and in witchcraft which was most often the cause of warfare. Shamans were used to control these forces of evil but there was emphasis upon individual action as well. Amputation of finger joints during the mourning period was thought to give protection from the disease or evil spirit which struck down the deceased. However, the most unusual aspect of Charrua belief was the emphasis on the individual's search for a "guardian spirit" through visions. This quest involved solitary fasting and the inflicting of wounds on the body until a living being appeared in the mind. This type of vision-seeking is not common to South American Indians and resembles more closely the ritual of the Plains Indians of North America.

BIBLIOGRAPHY —

• STEWARD, JULIAN H. Handbook of South American Indians. 7 Vols., Washington, DC: U.S. Govt. Printing Office, 1946-59.

CHASKPE

(U.S.; Ill.) A tribe or people mentioned by La Salle in 1683 as having come in company with the Shawnee and Ouabano at his solicitation to Ft. St. Louis, Illinois, his desire being to draw them away from trade with the Spaniards. It is not known to what Indians the name refers, but from the fact that La Salle speaks of them as allies of the Chickasaw, it is probable that their home was South of the present Illinois.

BIBLIOGRAPHY —

• HODGE, FREDERICK WEBB. Handbook of American Indians North of Mexico. Washington: Government Printing Office, 2 vols., 1907-10.
• MURDOCK, GEORGE P. Ethnographic Bibliography of North America. New Haven, CT: Human Relations Area Files Press, 1975.
• SWANTON, JOHN R. The Indian Tribes of North America. Washington, DC: U.S. Government Printing Office, 1952.

CHASTA

(U.S.; Oreg.) A tribe, probably Athapascan, residing on Siletz reservation, in 1867, with Skoton and Umpqua, of which latter they were then said to have formed a part. The Chasta, Skoton, and Umpqua were distinct tribes which concluded a treaty Nov. 18, 1854. The Chasta were divided into the Kwilsieton and Nahelta, both residing on Rogue River. J. O. Dorsey thought these may have been identical with Kushetunne and Nakatkhetunne of the Tututunne. Kane, in 1859, located them near Umpqua River. In 1867 the Chasta, the Scoton, and the Umpqua together, at Siletz agency, numbered 49 males and 74 females, total 123. They may be identical with the Chastacosta or form a part of the Takilma. They do not seem to have any connection with the Shasta, who did not extend down Rogue River below Table Rock, and who were generally bitterly at war with their Athapascan neighbors.

BIBLIOGRAPHY —

• HODGE, FREDERICK WEBB. Handbook of American Indians North of Mexico. Washington: Smithsonian Institution: BAE Bulletin No. 30: U.S. GPO, 1907.
• MURDOCK, GEORGE P. Ethnographic Bibliography of North America. New Haven, CT: Human Relations Area Files Press, 1975.
• SWANTON, JOHN R. The Indian Tribes of North America. Washington, DC: U.S. Government Printing Office, 1952.

CHASTA-SKOTON

(U.S.; Oreg.) A tribe or two tribes (Chasta and Skoton) formerly living on or near Rogue River, Oregon, perhaps the Chastocosta or (Dorsey in Journal American Folk-lore, III, 235, 1890) the Sestikustun. There were 36 on Grande Ronde reservation and 166 on Siletz reservation Oregon, in 1875.

At present, the Chastocosta, who speak the Athapashan language, number about 400.

BIBLIOGRAPHY —

• HODGE, FREDERICK WEBB. Handbook of American Indians North of Mexico. Washington: Government Printing Office, 2 vols., 1907-10.
• MURDOCK, GEORGE P. Ethnographic Bibliography of North America. New Haven, CT: Human Relations Area Files Press, 1975.

CHASTACOSTA

(U.S.; Oreg.) is an Athapascan tribe. The name comes from two words--Shista-Kwasta--the meanings of which are unknown. They lived along the lower course of the Illinois River and around the Rouge River in Oregon. Directly to the north of the Chastacosta were the Tututunne, or the Tutunni, who had exactly the same language and customs. Most of the tribes in that area shared similar customs and languages. Mooney estimated that at one time they and 100 other tribes numbered 5,000 people.

Unlike other Athapascan tribes they lived in permanent villages, which comprised a social unit. Males had dominant power both socially and governmentally, like other Athapascan males. Hunting and fishing comprised their main economy.

Little is known about their social customs or organizations. But they apparently did not have clans or designations of rank.

However, men were required to marry outside their villages, and their children belonged to their village. Women were socially inferior. Polygyny was common, and it was not uncommon for a wife to be buried alive in the same grave as her dead husband.

Despite this practice of men marrying outside the village, not all was peace and light between the different villages. Often they fought bloody and pitched battles. The Chastacosta also fought wars with the other nations.

Not much is known of their history or relations with whites. They were probably first contacted in the 18th century. It is known that in 1856 there was a summer of particularly severe fighting. Following that summer the Chastacosta were moved from their traditional home to Siletz Reservation in Oregon. Not long after they were moved they were joined by the Tututunne, the Coos and several other tribes.

When they were moved in 1856 there were some 153 Chastacosta; today there are only 30 to 40 still on the reservation.

BIBLIOGRAPHY —

● HODGE, FREDERICK WEBB. Handbook of American Indians North of Mexico. Washington: Government Printing Office, 2 vols., 1907-10.
● MURDOCK, GEORGE P. Ethnographic Bibliography of North America. New Haven, CT: Human Relations Area Files Press, 1975.
● SWANTON, JOHN R. The Indian Tribes of North America. Washington, DC: U.S. Government Printing Office, 1952.

CHATOT

(U.S.; Ala.) A tribe or band which the French settled South of Ft. St. Louis, on Mobile bay, in 1709. Bienville, wishing to change his settlement, "selected a place where the nation of the Chatots were residing, and gave them in exchange for it a piece of territory fronting on Dog river, 2 leagues farther down". According to baudry des Lozieres the Chatot and Tohome tribes were relatd to the Choctaw and spoke the French and Choctaw languages.

(see map page XIV)

BIBLIOGRAPHY —

● HODGE, FREDERICK WEBB. Handbook of American Indians North of Mexico. Washington: Government Printing Office, 1907.
● MURDOCK, GEORGE P. Ethnographic Bibliography of North America. New Haven, CT: Human Relations Area Files Press, 1975.
● SWANTON, JOHN R. The Indian Tribes of North America. Washington, DC: U.S. Government Printing Office, 1952.

CHAUI

(U.S.; NE.) A tribe of the Pawnee confederacy, spoken of by the French as Grand Pawnee. In the positions maintained by the 4 tribes of the Pawnee confederacy the villages of the Chaui were always between those of the Pitahauerat on the East and Kitkehahki on the West. In the council of the confederacy the Chaui held a prominent place, their head chiefs outranking all others, and being accepted as representative of the Pawnee, although without power to dominate all the tribes. Little that is distinctive isknown of this tribe. Little that is distinctive is known of this tribe. In 1833 they ceded to the U.S. their lands South of Platte River, Nebraska and in 1857 all lands on the North side of that stream, when the Pawnee when the Pawnee reservation on Loup River was established. This land was ceded in 1876 and their reservation in Oklahoma set apart. Here they now live. Having taken their lands in severalty, in 1892 they became citizens of the U.S. They were included in the missions established among the Pawnee. In customs and beliefs the Chaui did not differ from their congeners. They possessed many interesting ceremonies, of which that connected with the calumet *q.v.* has been preserved entirely and gives evidence of

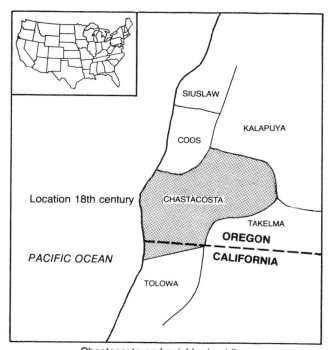

Chastacosta and neighboring tribes.

SIUSLAW

KALAPUYA

COOS

Location 18th century

CHASTACOSTA

TAKELMA

OREGON

PACIFIC OCEAN

CALIFORNIA

TOLOWA

their well-defined cosmogony and religious system. The divisions and totems are not known.

BIBLIOGRAPHY –

● HODGE, FREDERICK WEBB. Handbook of American Indians North of Mexico. Washington: Government Printing Office, 2 vols., 1907-10.
● MURDOCK, GEORGE P. Ethnographic Bibliography of North America.New Haven, CT: Human Relations Area Files Press, 1975.
● SWANTON, JOHN R. The Indian Tribes of North America. Washington, DC: U.S. Government Printing Office, 1952.
● WISSLER, CLARK. Indians of the U.S., Four Centuries of Their History and Culture. New York, NY: Doubleday, Doran & Co., 1940.

CHAUSHILA

(U.S.; Calif.) A Yokuts (Mariposan) tribe probably on lower Chowchilla River, in the plains and lowest foothills, their neighbors on the North being of Moquelumnan stock. As a tribe they are now extinct. They are confused with, but are distinct from, the Chowchilla, under which name the synonymy of both is given.

BIBLIOGRAPHY –

● HODGE, FREDERICK WEBB. Handbook of American Indians North of Mexico. Washington: Government Printing Office, 2 vols., 1907-10.
● MURDOCK, GEORGE P. Ethnographic Bibliography of North America.New Haven, CT: Human Relations Area Files Press, 1975.
● SWANTON, JOHN R. The Indian Tribes of North America. Washington, DC: U.S. Government Printing Office, 1952.

CHAVANTES

(South America; Brazil) are a Ge-speaking people, numbering 2,500-3,000 who live along the Xingu River.

They were first contacted by white men in the mid-1950s. Little is known of their history. Today they farm and eat roots, nuts, and fruits, although they greatly enjoy meats.

Their social and political structure is based on the clan. A man must marry outside his clan and is permitted to have several wives.

BIBLIOGRAPHY –

● STEWARD, JULIAN H. Handbook of South American Indians. 7 Vols., Washington, DC: U.S. Govt. Printing Office, 1946-59.

CHAWASHA.

(U.S.; Louisiana) The meaning of the name is unknown, although one interpretation was "raccoon place (people)." A reference to this tribe and the Washa by *Bienville* places them in the Chitimacha division of the Tunican linguistic stock. Earlier, John Swanton had erroneously concluded that they were Muskhogeans. The Chawasha were located on Bayou La Fourche and eastward to the Gulf of Mexico and across the Mississippi.

After the remaining members of De Soto's army had escaped to the mouth of the Mississippi River, they were attacked by Indians, some of whom had "staves, having very sharp heads of fish-bone." (See *Bourne, 1904, vol. 2, p. 202*) These may have belonged to the Chawasha and Washa tribes. The same two tribes were said to have attempted an attack on an English sea captain who ascended the Mississippi in 1699 (although that fact was never confirmed), but they were usually friendly to the French. In 1712, they moved to the Mississippi, according to *Bienville* , and established themselves on the west side, just below the English Turn. In 1713, (possibly 1715), they were attacked by a party of Chickasaw, Yazoo, and Natchez, who killed the head chief and many of his family, and carried off 11 people as prisoners. Before 1722, they had crossed to the east side of the river. In 1730, in order to allay the panic in New Orleans following the Natchez uprising of 1729, which resulted in the massacre of the whites at Natchez, Governor Perrier allowed a band of black slaves to attack the Chawasha, and it is commonly reported that they were then destroyed. The French writer, Dumont (1753), is probably right, however, when he states that only seven or eight adult males were killed. At any rate, they are mentioned as living with the Washa at Les Allemands on the west side of the Mississippi above New Orleans in 1739, and in 1758, they appear as constituting one village with the Washa. Except for one uncertain reference, this is the last we hear of them, but they may have continued for a considerable period longer before disappearing as a distinct body.

Mooney, 1928 gives an estimate of 1,400 for the Washa, Chawasha, and Opelousa together in the year 1650. Swanton's estimate for the first two and the Okelousa, as of 1698, was 700. This is based on *Beaurain's (La Harpe's)*estimate (1831) of 200 warriors for the three tribes. Around 1715, there were said to have been 40 Chawasha warriors; in 1739, 30 warriors of the Washa and Chawasha together; and in 1758, 10 to 12. The Chawasha attained temporary notoriety on account of the massacre perpetrated upon them by the black slaves, as mentioned above.

BIBLIOGRAPHY –

● Mooney, James. The Aboriginal Population of America North of Mexico. Wash., D.C.: Smithsonian Misc. Collection, Vol. 80, No. 7., 1928.
● SWANTON. JOHN R. The Indian Tribes of North America. Washington, DC: U.S. Government Printing Office, 1952.

CHAYOPIN

(U.S.; Tex.) One of the tribes named by Garcia as living at the missions about Rio San Antonio and Rio Grande in Texas, and identified by Mooney as a division of the Tonkawa. In 1785 there was a rancheria called Chayopin, with 8 inhabitants, near the presidio of La Bahia and the mission of Espiritu Santo de Zuniga, on the lower San Antonio.

BIBLIOGRAPHY —

● HODGE, FREDERICK WEBB. Handbook of American Indians North of Mexico. Washington: Government Printing Office, 2 vols., 1907-10.
● MURDOCK, GEORGE P. Ethnographic Bibliography of North America. New Haven, CT: Human Relations Area Files Press, 1975.
● SWANTON, JOHN R. The Indian Tribes of North America. Washington, DC: U.S. Government Printing Office, 1952.

CHEHALIS

(Canada; British Columbia) are a coastal Salishan nation, living in upper Washington state and part of British Columbia, Canada.

Chehalis was actually a collective name for several tribes that lived together and with the same social customs. Gibbs said the name belonged only to a village located at the entrance of Gray's Harbor. The name means "sand." The Chehalis are closely related to the Quinault.

Originally they came from the Chehalis River, but later they were located around Willapa Bay, on land formerly owned by the Chinook.

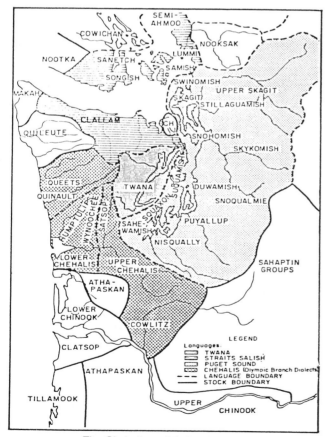

The Chehalis and their neighbors.

There were two classifications of Chehalis; the Upper Chehalis, living above the Chehalis River, and the Lower Chehalis, living below the river.

The lived in lodges like many other Salishan tribes. Fishing was their main source of food, as well as their major economic activity. They also collected berries.

There does not seem to be any governmental concentration. Apparently each village had its own government, probably consisting of a male chief. It is not known to what extent women were involved in government or what their general social status was.

They were first met by whites, it appears, in the late 18th century. The first definite white contact was with Lewis and Clark who estimated there were some 700 Chehalis. Apparently they did not get actively involved in trade.

While many nations suffered from epidemics the Chehalis were spared its greater ravages. By the mid 1800s the Chinook, their own nation decimated by disease, joined the Chehalis, dropping their native language.

Towards the mid and latter 1800s the Chehalis began to settle on reservations, later joined by other tribes. Today there are some 200 living with a few Chinook and Quinault on Washington reservations. *(see map page XVI)*

BIBLIOGRAPHY —

● BANCROFT, HUBART HOWE. The Native Races of the Pacific States of North America. San Francisco, CA: 1874.
● HODGE, FREDERICK WEBB. Handbook of American Indians North of Mexico. Washington: Government Printing Office, 2 vols., 1907-10.
● INDIAN OFFICE REPORT. 1860, 1876, 1877, 1879, 1880, 1881, 1892, 1893.
● MURDOCK, GEORGE P. Ethnographic Bibliography of North America. New Haven, CT: Human Relations Area Files Press, 1975.
● ROYCE, CHARLES C. Indian Land Cessions in the U.S. Washington: 18th Annual Report, Bureau of Ethnology, 1896-97.
● STANLEY, HENRY M. My Early Travels and Adventures in America and Asia. New York, NY: Charles Scribner's Sons, 1895.
● SWANTON, JOHN R. The Indian Tribes of North America. Washington, DC: U.S. Government Printing Office, 1952.

CHELAMELA.

(U.S.; Oregon) Also called Long Tom Creek Indians. The significance of the name Chelamela is unknown. The tribe belonged to the Calapooya dialectic division of the Kalapooian linguistic stock. They resided on Long Tom Creek, a western tributary of the Willamette River. *Mooney, 1928* estimated that the population of the entire Kalapooian stock was 3,000 in 1780. By 1910, that number had decreased to 106, and in 1930, it was 45.

BIBLIOGRAPHY —

● HODGE, FREDERICK WEBB. Handbook of American Indians North of Mexico. Washington: Smithsonian Institution:

BAE Bulletin No. 30: U.S. GPO, 1907.
● Mooney, James. The Aboriginal Population of America North of Mexico. Wash., D.C.: Smithsonian Misc. Collection, Vol. 80, No. 7., 1928.
● SWANTON, JOHN R. The Indian Tribes of North America. Washington, DC: U.S. Government Printing Office, 1952.

CHEMEHUEVI

(U.S.; Calif., Colo.) are a group of southern Paiutes in southeastern California and along the lower Colorado River. The nomenclature is Yuman for Paiute and distinguishes the Chemehuevi from their relatives of Nevada, Arizona and Utah. They have shifted their location frequently in historic times. Their old territory was on the lower Colorado River west-westward near the Kingston Range; south of Death Valley, near the Coso; and stretched southward through Providence Mountain to about the boundary of Riverside and Imperial Counties; the eastern half of the Mohave Desert, bordered on the west by the Serrano. In later years some Chemehuevis moved to Twenty-nine Palms, Torres Martinez Reservation. A new Chemehuevi reservation has been established in the eastern Colorado Desert, and they have reestablished themselves as a specific, territorially political, ethnic group. Some are involved in the Colorado River Indian Reservation. Some who came to the Colorado River settled on Cottonwood Island where the Mojave and Chemehuevi lived side by side. As a result of a war in 1867 between the Chemehuevi and the Mojave, many of the Chemehuevi fled to the desert, cocupying a very poor environment. There were over 1,000 inhabitants in their territory; there are 200 to 300 Chemehuevi today. Their name for themselves was Nuwo; they are part of the Numish speaking family. Their territory was crossed by the Mojave Trail, which many tribes used.

The Chemehuevi were hunters and gatherers, although some farmed small patches of land. They lived on wild game (antelope, deer, Chuckwalla mountain sheep, rabbits, desert chipmunks, various squirrels, wood rats, quail, etc.), reptiles, e.g. lizards, rattlesnakes, land turtles or tortoises, insects, seeds, mescal and yucca, mesquite, screwbean, sage, arrow weed, tule, pine nuts and wild grapes. The creosote bush was used for medicine, jimson weed for medicine and hallucination. Bears and foxes were sacred, as were eagles, bluejays, crows, owls, as well as buzzards, which were important in sacred stories and songs. Feathers of these birds were used in sacred context.

The Chemehuevi developed basketry to a high artistic form, and they made pottery like that of the Colorado River People. Basketry was coiled, closely woven, and elaborately designed with diagonal twining. The bow and arrow were used: a self bow with re-curved ends, painted, middle-wrapped; arrows were of cane shaft with flint tips. They wore feathered caps; hides for moccasins, rabbit skins for blankets, tanned shirts of antelope and mountain sheep. Hair style was peculiar to the Chemehuevi; tattooing was fashionable. Games included the women's dice with gum-filled shell-inlaid nut shells similar to the Western Yokuts.

Chemehuevi kinship is characterized by bilateral structure, close attention to large extended kinship relations, and marrying outside the immediate kin group. Mythography and story-telling were highly developed art forms, stories and songs being owned by separate, exogamous divisions. Significant song titles included deer, mountain sheep, salt, quail, and jay-owl songs. Each major group had a chief, each with a spokesman, two or three families under the leadership of a lesser chief. Several bands had a high chief. Chiefly families were prestigious; the chieftainship was political as well as sacred office, with regional jurisdiction.

Chemehuevi rituals were influenced by the Mohave and other people of the region. Funeral ceremonies were significant, the dead, along with their property, were cremated, and many people came together for these occasions. There were long series of mourning songs, hand game songs (known as bird songs), and doctoring (shaman) songs, each referring to a story of dreamed narratives. Other ceremonies were held for installation of chiefs, births, marriages, first food harvests. Culture heroes were coyote and his elder brother, puma. Concepts of a great, sacred mountain, an all powerful old woman were widely shared, including death of older brother and mourning for him. Coyote and puma were personifications of food. Shamans acquired song powers from other mythical beings and from "Numbuat." Dreaming was important. Sacred caves were important for storing sacred paraphernalia and visiting supernatural beings. Jimson weed was used in many ceremonies. Spirits of the dead were active; rites of death were sacred and of immense importance, elaborate preparations taking months and lasting several days to complete. In recent years the scalp dance and ghost dance have been used; the bear cult is present.

Personal names were used for all persons. In Chemehuevi cosmology water, earth, and sky comprised the world, numerous myths about the creation of the world and the beings personified within it. Times and seasons correlated with astronomical phenomena and with seasonal changes. Spring begins the year, winter is recognized in name, and the solstices are significant. Directions are mentioned in pairs: north, south, east, west. Close track was kept of meteorological phenomena. Runners or messengers held prestigious social positions. Irrigation was a learned art, with agriculture used along the Colorado River, where corn, beans, mellons, and pumpkins constituted an agriculture complex. Brush houses lasting for weeks or months were constructed--usually of willow, sometimes of wild grape--to a height of six feet.

BIBLIOGRAPHY --

● BANCROFT, HUBART HOWE. The Native Races of the Pacific States of North America.San Francisco, CA: 1874.
● CHEMEHUEVI TODAY. 1975-76 Annual Report of the Chemehuevi Program, 2 vols.
● HODGE, FREDERICK WEBB. Handbook of American Indians North of Mexico. Washington: Government Printing Office, 2 vols., 1907-10.
● INDIAN OFFICE REPORT. 1865.
● MURDOCK, GEORGE P. Ethnographic Bibliography of North America.New Haven, CT: Human Relations Area Files Press, 1975.
● STANLEY, HENRY M. My Early Travels and Adventures in America and Asia.New York, NY: Charles Scribner's Sons, 1895.
● SWANTON, JOHN R. The Indian Tribes of North America. Washington, DC: U.S. Government Printing Office, 1952.
● WISSLER, CLARK. Indians of the U.S., Four Centuries of Their History and Culture. New York, NY: Doubleday, Doran & Co., 1940.

CHEPENAFA.

(U.S.; Oregon) Also called Api'nefu, or Pineifu, by the other Kalapuya, as well as the Mary's River Indians, which was the offical and more popular name. The tribe belonged to the Calapooya dialectic division of the Kalapooian linguistic stock, and were sometimes regarded as a subdivision of the Luckamiut. They resided at the forks of St. Mary's Creek, near Corvallis. *Mooney, 1928* estimated that the population of the entire Kalapooian stock was 3,000 in 1780. In 1910, the census reported that there were 24 Chepenafa.

BIBLIOGRAPHY --

● HODGE, FREDERICK WEBB. Handbook of American Indians North of Mexico. Washington: Smithsonian Institution: BAE Bulletin No. 30: U.S. GPO, 1907.
● Mooney, James. The Aboriginal Population of America North of Mexico. Wash., D.C.: Smithsonian Misc. Collection, Vol. 80, No. 7., 1928.
● SWANTON, JOHN R. The Indian Tribes of North America. Washington, DC: U.S. Government Printing Office, 1952.

CHERAW

(U.S.;Southeast) An important tribe, very probably of Siouan stock, formerly ranging east of the Blue ridge, from about the present Danville, Virginia, southward to the neighborhood of Cheraw, South Carolina, which takes its name from them. In numbers they may have stood next to the Tuscarora among the North Carolina tribes, but are less prominent in history by reason of their almost complete destruction before the white settlements had reached their territory They are mentioned first in the De Soto narrative for 1540, under the name Xuala, a corruption of Suali, the name by which they are traditionally known to the Cherokee, who remember them as having anciently lived beyond the Blue ridge from Asheville. In the earlier Carolina and Virginia records they are commonly known as Saraw, and at a later period as Cheraw. We first hear of "Xuala province" in 1540, apparently in the mountain country southward from Asheville. In 1672, Lederer, from Indian information, located them in the same general region, or possibly somewhat farther north east, "where the mountains bend to the west," and says that this portion of the main ridge was called "Sualymountain" from the tribe. This agrees with Cherokee tradition. Some years later, but previous to 1700, they settled on Dan river near the south line of Virginia, where the marks of their fields were found extending for several miles along the river by Byrd, in 1728, when running the dividing line between the two colonies. There seem to have been two villages, as on a map of 1760 we find this place designated as "Lower Saura Town," while 30 miles above, on the south side of the Dan and between it and Town fork, is another place marked "Upper Saura Town." They are also alluded to by J. F. D. Smyth (Tour in U.S., 1784), who says the upper town was insignificant. About the year 1710, being harassed by the Iroquois, they abandoned their home on the Dan and moving south east joined the Keyauwee. The colonists of North Carolina being dissatisfied at the proximity of these and other tribes, Governor Eden declared war against the Cheraw, and applied to Virginia for assistance. This Governor Spotswood refused, as he believed the people of Carolina were the aggressors; nevertheless the war was carried on against them and their allies by the Carolinas until the defeat and expulsion of the Yamasi in 1716. During this period complaint was made against the Cheraw, who were declared to be responsible for most of the mischief done north of Santee river, and of endeavoring to draw into their alliance the smaller coast tribes. It was asserted by the Carolinians that arms were supplied them from Virginia. At the close of the Yamasi war the Cheraw were dwelling on the upper Pedee near the line between the Carolinas, where their name is perpetuated in the towm on Cheraw, South Carolina. Their number in 1715, according to Rivers, was 510, but this estimate probably included the Keyauwee. Being still subject to attack by the Iroquois, they finally-between 1726 and 1739-became incorporated with the Catawba, with whom at an earlier date they had been at enmity. Tbey are mentioned as with the Catawba but speaking their own distinct dialect as late as 1743. In 1759 a party of 45 "Charraws" some of whom were under their cheif, "King Johnny," joined the English in the expedition against Fort Du Quesne. The last notice of them is in 1768, when their remnant, reduced by war and disease to 50 or 60, were still living with the Catawba.

BIBLIOGRAPHY —

● HODGE, FREDERICK WEBB. Handbook of American Indians North of Mexico. Washington: Government Printing Office, 2 vols., 1907-10.
● MILLING, CHAPMAN. Red Carolinians. Chapel Hill, NC: University of North Carolina Press, 1940.
● MURDOCK, GEORGE P. Ethnographic Bibliography of North America. New Haven, CT: Human Relations Area Files Press, 1975.
● SWANTON, JOHN R. The Indian Tribes of North America. Washington, DC: U.S. Government Printing Office, 1952.

CHEROKEE

(U.S.; Southeast; Okla.) A powerful detached tribe of the Iroquoian family, formerly holding the whole mountain region of the South Alleghenies, in south west Virginia, west North Carolina and South Carolina, north Georgia, east Tennesses, and north east Alabama, and claiming even to the Ohio River. The tribal name is a corruption of Tsalagi or Tsaragi, the name by which they commonly called themselves, and which may be derived from the Choctaw, "cave people", in allusion to the numerous caves in their mountain country. They sometimes also call themselves Ani-Yun-wiya, "real people" or Ani- Kituhwagi "people of Kituhwa, one of their most important ancient settlements. Their northern kinsmen, the Iroquios, called them Oyatageronon "inhabitants of the cave country" (Hewitt), and the Delawares and connected tribes called them Kituwa, from the settlement aleady noted. They seem to be identical with the Rickohockans, who invaded central Virginia in 1658, and with the ancient Talligewi, of Delaware tradition, who were represented to have been driven southward from the upper Ohio River region by the combined forces of the Iroquois and Delawares.

The language has three principal dialects: (1) Elati, or Lower, spoken on the heads of Savannah River, in South Carolina and Georgia; (2) Middle, spoken chiefly on the waters of Tuckasegee River in west North Carolina, and now the prevailing dialect on the East Cherokee reservation; (3) Atali, Mountain or Upper, spoken throughout most of upper Georgia, east Tennessee, and extreme west North Carolina. The lower dialect was the only one which had the r sound, and is now extinct, The upper dialect is that which has been exclusively used in the native literature of the tribe.

History There seems to have been a Cherokee migration legend something like that of the Creeks according to which the tribe entered their historic seats from some region toward the northeast.

In 1540 De Soto seems to have passed through only one town that has a Cherokee name, but Pardo in 1566 learned of another, Tanasqui, which has a Cherokee appearance and may have given its name to Tennessee River. Continous contact between the Cherokee and the Whites began after Virginia was settled, when traders from that colony commenced to work their way into the Appalachian Mountains. Contact became more intimate with the founding of the Carolina colonies, and a contingent of 310 Cherokee joined Moore in his attack on the Tuscarora in 1713. In 1730 Sir Alexander Cuming staged a personal embassy to the Cherokee and afterward took seven of the Indians to England with him. In 1738 an enemy more serius even than White men made its first appearance in this tribe, namely smallpox, which cut down their numbers by nearly 50 percent. In 1755 the Cherokee won a great victory over the Abihka Creeks, who forthwith withdrew from the Tennessee River. Relations with the Whites were upon the whole friendly until 1759 when the Indians refused to accede to the demand of the Governor of South Carolina that a number of Indians including two leading chiefs be turned over to him for execution under the charge that they had killed a White man. He had asked also to have 24 other chiefs sent to him mearly on suspicion that they entertained hostile intentions. War followed, and the Indians captured Fort Loudon, a post in the heart of their country, August 8, 1760, after having defeated an army which came to relieve it. The year following, howevr, the Indians were defeated on June 10, by a larger force under Col. James Grant, who laid the greater number of the Middle Cherokee settlements in ashes, and compelled the tribe to make peace. In 1769 they are said to have suffered a severe defeat at the hands of the Chickasaw at the Chickasaw Oldfields. On the outbreak of the American Revolution they sided with the British and continued hostilities after its close down to 1794. Meanwhile parties of Cherokee had pushed down Tennessee River and formed new settlements near the present Tennessee- Alabama boundary. Shortly after 1800 missionay work was begun among them, and in 1820 they adopted a regular form of government modeled on that of the United States. In the meantime large numbers of them, wearied of the encroachments of the Whites, had crossed the Mississippi and settled in the territory now included in the State of Arkansas. In 1821 Sequoya, son of a mixed-blood Cherokee woman by a White man, submitted a syllabary of his own devising to the chief men of the nation, and, on their approval, the Cherokee of all ages set about learning it with such zeal that in a few months numbers of them were able to read and write by means of it. In 1822 Sequoya went west to teach his alphabet to the Indians of the western

Sequoya

division, and he remaided among them permanently. The pressure of the Whites upon the frontiers of the Eastern Cherokee was soon increased by the discovery of gold near the present Dahlonega, Georgia, and after a few years of fruitless struggle the nation bowed to the inevitable and by the treaty of New Echota, December 29, 1835, sold all of their territories not peviously given up and agreed to remove to the other side of the Mississippi to lands to be set apart for them. Traditional, linguistic, and archeologic evidence shows that the Cherokee originated in the north, but they were found in possession of the south Allegheny region when first encountered by De Soto. Their relations with the Carolina colonies began 150 years later. In 1730 the Jesuit (?) Priber started the first mission among them, and attempted to organize their government on a civiliozed basis. In 1759, under the leadership of Aganstata (Oconostota), they began war with the English of Carolina. In the Revolution they took sides against the Americans, and continued the struggle almost without interval until 1794. During this period paties of the Cherokee pushed down Tennessee River and formed new settlements at Chickamauga and other points about the Tennesse-Alabama line. Shortly after 1800, missionary and educational work was established among them, and in 1820 they adopted a regular form of government modeled on that of the United States. In the meantime large numbers of the more conservative Cherokee, wearied by the encoachments of

the whites, had crossed the Mississippi and made new homes in the wilderness in what is now Arkansas. A year or two later Sequoya, a mixed-blood, invented the alphabet, which at once raised them to the rank of a literary people.

At the height of their prosperity gold was discovered near the present Dahlonega, Georgia, within the linits of the Cherokee Nation, and at once a powerful agitation was begun for the removal of the Indians. After years of hopeless struggle under the leadership of thier great cheif, John Ross, they were compelled to submit to the inevitable and by the treaty of New Echota, December 29, 1835, the Cherokee sold their entire remaining territory and agreed to remove beynd the Mississippi to a country there to be set apart for them-the present Cherokee Nation in Indian Territory. The removal was accomplished in the winter of 1838-39, after considerable hardship and the loss of nearly one-fourth of their number, the unwilling Indians being driven out by military force and makeing the long journey of foot.

The Trail of Tears. The history of this Cherokee removal of 1838, as gleaned by the author from the lips of actors in the tragedy, may well exceed in weight of grief and pathos any other passage in American history. Even the much-sung exile of the Acadians falls far behind it in its sum of death and misery. Under Scotts orders the troops were disposed at various points throughout the Cherokee country, where stockade forts were erected for gathering in and holding the Indians preparatory to removal. From these, squads of troops were sent to search out with rifle and bayonet every small cabin hidden away in the coves or by the sides of mountain streams, to sieze and bring in as prisoners all the occupants, however or wherever they might be found. Families at dinner were startled by the sudden gleam of bayonets in the doorway and rose up to be driven with blows and oaths along the weary miles of trail that led to the stockade. Men were siezed in their fields or going along the road, women were taken from their wheels and children from their play. In many cases, on turning for one last look as they crossed the ridge, they saw their homes in flames, fired by the lawless rabble that followed on the heels of the soldiers to loot and pillage. So keen were these outlaws on the scent that in some instances they were driving off the cattle and other stock of the Indians almost before the soldiers had fairly started their owners in the other direction. Systematic hunts were made by the same men for Indian graves, to rob them of the silver pendants and other valuables deposited with the dead. A Georgia volunteer, afterward a colonel in the Confederate service, said: "I fought through the civil war and have seen men shot to pieces and slaughtered by thousands, but the Cherokee removal was the cruelest work I ever knew." To prevent escape the soldiers had been ordered to approach and suround each house, so far as possible, so as to come upon the occupents without warning. One old patriach, when thus surprised calmly called his children and grandchildren around him, and, kneeling down, bid them pray with him in their own langage, while the astonished onlookers looked on in silence. Then rising he led the way into exile. A woman, on finding the house surrounded, went to the door and called up the chickens to be fed for the last time, after which, taking her infant on her back and her two other children by the hand, she followed her husband with the soldiers. On reaching their destination they reorganized their national government, with their capital at Tahlequah, admitting to equal privilges the ealier emigrants, known as "old settlers." A part of the Arkansas Cherokee had previously gone down into Texas, where they had obtained a grant of land in the east part of the state from the Mexican government. The later Texan revolutionists refused to recongnize their rights, and in spite of the efforts of General Sam Houston, who defended the Indian claim, a conflict was precipitated, resulting, in 1839, in the killing of the Cherokee chief, Bowl, with a large number of his men, by the Texan troops, and the expulsion of the Cherokee from Texas.

When the main body of the tribe was removed to the West, several hundred fugitives escaped to the mountains, where they lived as refugees for a time, until, in 1842, through the efforts of William H. Thomas, an influential trader, they received permission to remain on lands set apart for their use in west North Carolina. They constitute the present eastern band of Cherokee, residing chiefly on the Qualla reservation in Swain and Jackson counties, with several outlying settlements.

The Three Cherokees came over from the head of the River Savanna to London 1762.
& their Interpreter that was Poisoned.

Copperplate engraving of the Cherokees

The Cherokee on the Cherokee Nation were for years divided into two hostile factions, those who had favored and those who had opposed the treaty of removel. Hardly had these differences been adjusted when the civil war burst upon them. Being slave owners and surrounded by southern influences, a large part of each of the Five Civilized Tribes of the territory enlisted in the service of the Confederacy, while others adhered to the National Government. The territory of the Cherokee was overrun in turn by both armies, and the close of the war found them prostated. By treaty in 1866 they were readmitted to the protection of the United States, but obliged to liberate their black slaves and admit them to equal citizenship. In 1867 and 1870 the Delawares and Shawnee, respectively, numbering together about 1,750 were admitted from Kansas and incorporated with the Nation. In 1889 the Cherokee Commission was created for the purpose of abolishing the tribal governments and opening the territories to white settlement, with the result that after 15 years of negotiating an agreement was made by which the governmeng of the Cherokee Nation came to a final end March 3, 1906; the Indian lands were divided, and the Cherokee Indians, native and adopted, became citizens of the United States.

The Cherokee have seven clans: Wolf, Deer, Bird, Paint. The names of the last three can not be translated with certainty. There is evidence that there were anciently 14, which by extinction or absorption have been reduced to their present number. The Wolf clan is the largest and most improtant. The "seven clans" are frequently mentioned in the ritual prayers and even in the printed laws of the tribe. They seem to have had a connection with the "seven mother towns" of the Cherokee, described by Cuning in 1730 as having each a chief, whose office was hereditary in the female line.

Population The Cherokee are probably about as numerous now as at any period in their history. With the exception of an estimate in 1730, which placed them at about 20,000, most of those up to a recent period gave them 12,000 or 14,000, and in 1758 they were computed at only 7,500. The majority of the earlier estimates are probably too low, as the Cherokee occupied so extensive a terrotory that only a part of them came in contact with the whites. In 1708 Governor Johnson estimated them at 60 villages and "at least 500 men" (Rivers, South Carolina, 238,1856). In 1715 they were offically reported to number 11,210 (Upper, 2,760; Middle, 6,350; Lower, 2,100), including 4,000 warriors, and living in 60 villages (Upper, 19; Middle, 30; Lower, 11). In 1720 they were estimated to have been reduced to about 10,000, and again, in the same year reported at about

1964 painting by Paul Pahsetopah

11,500, including about 3,800 warriors. In 1729 they were estimated at 20,000, with at least 6,000 warriors and 64 towns and villages (Stevens, Hist. Ga., 1, 48, 1847). They are said to have lost 1,000 warriors in 1739 from smallpox and rum, and they suffered a steady decrease during their wars with the whites, extending from 1760 until after the close of the Revolution. Those in their original homes had again increased to 16,542 at the time of their forced removal to the west in 1838, but lost nearly one-fourth on the journey, 311 perishing in a steamboat accident on the Mississippi. Those already in the west, before the removal, were estimated at about 6,000. The civil war in 1861-65 again checked their progress, but they recovered from its effects in a remarkably short time, and in 1885 numbered about 19,000, of whom about 17,000 were in Indian Territory, together with about 6,000 adopted whites, blacks, Delaware, and Shawnee, while the remainng 2,000 were still in their ancient homes in the east. Of this eastern band, 1,376 were on Qualla reservation, in Swain and Jackson counties, North Carolina; about 300 are on Cheowah River, in Graham County, North Carolina, while the remainder all of mixed blood, are scattered over east Tennessee, north Georgia, and Alabama. The eastern band lost about 300 by smallpox at the close of the civil war, In 1902 there were offically reported 28,016 persons of Cherokee blood, including all degrees of admixture, in the Cherokee Nation in the Territory, but this includes several thousand individuals formerly repudiated by the tribal courts. There were also living in the nation about 3,000 adopted black freedmen, more that 2,000 adopted whites, and about 1,700 adopted Delaware, Shawnee, and other Indians. The tribe has a larger proportion of white admixure than any other of the Five Civilized Tribes.

In 1934 The Tribal Reorganization program initiated by President Franklin D. Roosevelt and Commissioner of Indian Affairs John Collier enabled Cherokees and other Native Americans to reorganize their tribal institutions, fostering some rediscovery of their cultural heritage.

Tribal headquarters for Cherokee of the west is in Tahlequa, Oklahoma. Eastern Cherokee are located mainly in western North Carolina.

Total population, at present, is estimated at anywhere from 65,000 to over 100,000.

(see map page XIV)

BIBLIOGRAPHY –

● ARKANSAS LANDS. 48th Congress, 1st Session, Sen. Rept. 287, Report of Committee on Public Lands to Accompany S. 1574. March 10, 1884.
● BRONSON, RUTH MUSKRAT. Indians Are People, Too.New York, NY: Friendship Press, 1944.
● CHRONICLES OF OKLAHOMA. Boundary Survey, 1850.OK: pg. 268, Autumn, 1949; Summer, 1950, Spring, 1950: 1923, 1924, 1926, 1927, 1928, 1930, 1934.
● CUNNINGHAM, HUGH T. A History of the Cherokee Indians. OK: Chronicles of Oklahoma, 1930.
● DRAKE, SAMUEL. Biography and History of the Indians of North America.Boston, MA: J. Drake, 1835.
● EASTMAN, ELAINE GOODALE. Pratt, The Red Man's Moses. Norman, OK: University of Oklahoma Press, 1935.
● FOREMAN, CAROLYN. Cherokee Weaving and Basketry. Muskogee, OK: Star Printery, 1948.
● FOREMAN, GRANT. Indian Removal. The Emigration of the Five Civilized Tribes of Indians.Norman, OK: University of Oklahoma Press, 1932.
● HODGE, FREDERICK, W. Handbook of American Indians North of Mexico. Washington, DC: Government Printing Office, 2 vols., 1907-1910.
● INDIAN OFFICE REPORT. 1874, 1877, 1882, 1883, 1888, 1891, 1892.
● JACKSON, HELEN HUNT. A Century of Dishonor; A Sketch of the U.S. Gov'ts Dealings with some of the Indian Tribes.New York, NY: Harper & Bros., 1881 reprinted Little, Brown & Co. 1909.
● KNIGHT, OLIVER. History of the Cherokees.OK: Chronicles of Oklahoma, 1956.
● LA FARGE, OLIVER. The Changing Indian.Norman, OK: University of Oklahoma Press, 1942.
● MALONE, JAMES H. The Chickasaw Nation, A Short Sketch of a Noble People.Louisville, KY: John P. Morton & Co., 1922.
● MILLING, CHAPMAN. Red Carolinians. Chapel Hill, NC: University of North Carolina Press, 1940.
● MOONEY, JAMES. Historical Sketch of the Cherokee.Washington: Smithsonian Instution Press, 1975.
----- Myths of the Cherokee.Washington: 1900.
● MURDOCK, GEORGE P. Ethnographic Bibliography of North America.New Haven, CT: Human Relations Area Files Press, 1975.
● NILES REGISTER. Vol. 49, pg. 362, Jan. 24, 1835.
● O'BEIRNE, EDWARD S. The Indian Territory, Its Chiefs, Legislators and Leading Men.St. Louis, MO: C. B. Woodward Co., 1892.
● PEITHMANN, IRVIN M. Red Men of Fire.Springfield, IL: Charles C. Thomas, 1964.
● POWERS, MABEL. The Indian as Peacemaker. New York, NY: Fleming H. Revell Co., 1932.
● ROYCE, CHARLES C. Indian Land Cessions in the U.S. Washington: 18th Annual Report, Bureau of Ethnology, 1896-97.
● SCHOOLCRAFT, HENRY R. History of the Indian Tribes of the U.S.; Their Present Condition and Prospects.Philadelphia, J. B. Lippincott & Co., 1857.
● SCHWARZ, REV. EDMUND. History of the Moravian Missions Among Southern Indian Tribes of the U.S. Bethlehem, PA: Times Publishing Co., 1923.
● SHEA, JOHN G. Catholic Missions Among the Indian Tribes of the U.S.New York, NY: E. Dunigan & Bros., 1854.
● SIPE, C. HALE. The Indian Wars of Pennsylvania, An Account of the Indian Events, in Pennsylvania, of The French and Indiang War, Pontiac's War, Lord Dunmore's War. Harrisburg: The Telegraph Press, 1929.
● SWANTON, JOHN R. The Indian Tribes of North America. Washington, DC: U.S. Government Printing Office, 1952.
● THATHER, B. B. Indian Biography, or, An Historical Account of Those Individuals Who Have Been Distinguished.New York, NY: Harper & Bros., 1840.
● WISSLER, CLARK. Indians of the U.S., Four Centuries of Their History and Culture. New York, NY: Doubleday, Doran & Co., 1940.

CHESAPEAKE

(U.S.; Va.) were an Algonquin-speaking people who lived in Virginia at the time of the Discovery and were extinct as a tribe by 1669. Little more is known about them conclusively. They are estimated to have numbered about 100 in 1607, and possibly have been called "Ethesepiooc." The name Chesapeake means "country on a great river," and may have designated a small Powhatan tribe which resided near Norfolk, Virginia, in the 1600s. *(see map page XIV)*

BIBLIOGRAPHY –

● HODGE, FREDERICK WEBB. Handbook of American Indians North of Mexico. Washington: Government Printing Office, 2 vols., 1907-10.
● MURDOCK, GEORGE P. Ethnographic Bibliography of North America.New Haven, CT: Human Relations Area Files Press, 1975.
● SWANTON, JOHN R. The Indian Tribes of North America. Washington, DC: U.S. Government Printing Office, 1952.

CHETCO.

(U.S.; Oregon) The name, the tribe's own, meant "close to the mouth of the stream." The Chetco belonged to the Athapascan linguistic stock and differed little in culture from the other Athapascan groups immediately north of them and the Tolowa to the south. The tribe extended slightly across into northern California from their home in Oregon. They resided on each side of the mouth of the Chetco River, as well as on the Winchuck River. *Dorsey, in Hodge, 1907* recorded several villages, including Chettanne, Setthatun, Chettannene, and Nakwutthume, among others. *Drucker, in 1937* reported other villages including Hosa'tun, Natltene'tun, Tcet, and Tume'stun, among others. *Mooney, 1928* estimated that the population of 11 Athapascan tribes, including the Chetco was in the vicinity of 5,600. In 1854, a year after the Chetco had been moved to the Siletz Reservation, they numbered 241, and in 1861, they numbered 262. In 1877, there were only 63 of them residing on the reservation, and in 1910, the census reported 9 members. A river and a post hamlet in Curry County, Oregon were named after the tribe.

BIBLIOGRAPHY —

● HODGE, FREDERICK WEBB. Handbook of American Indians North of Mexico. Washington: Smithsonian Institution: BAE Bulletin No. 30: U.S. GPO, 1907.
● SWANTON, JOHN R. The Indian Tribes of North America. Washington, DC: U.S. Government Printing Office, 1952.

CHEYENNE

(U.S.; Minn., Great Plains) lived in the woodlands of Minnesota until near the beginning of the eighteenth century when they began moving into the Great Plains, first as semi-sedentary plant growers associated with the upper Missouri Mandan, Arikara and Hidatsa, later moving farther west developing horsemen and buffalo hunters. Finally they settled in the western part of the plains near the edge of the Rocky Mountains.

As first seen by explorers the Cheyenne appeared as an unusually shy woods people, fleeing from their better-armed enemies, the Assiniboine and the Ojibwa. Later they were driven west by the Dakota Sioux, with whom they eventually became allied. As horse-riding hunters of the buffalo their character changed dramatically, becoming for awhile a great warrior nation. They apparently were both very adaptable and very inventive for the developed some unusually distinctive traits, such as nearly complete chastitiy for their girls and women and a fluid yet remarkably strong legal system able to almost entirely eliminate inter-family and clan feuds.

The name *Cheyenne* is believed to be derived from the Sioux name for them, *Shi-hi-e-la* or *Sha-hi-e-na.* But the tribe called themselves the *Tsis tsis-tas,* meaning "the people" or "the cut or gashed people", because of their frequent use of self-torture. In the early nineteenth century the *Tsis-tsis- tas* joined with the *Suhtai,* a people talking a very similar language, to form one tribe now called the *Cheyenne.*

Social and cultural boundaries and subdivisions. By the early nineteenth century there were ten main Cheyenne bands: (1) The *Eaters,* probably the largest band and living mainly in the north; (2) the *Burnt Aorta,* a band whose women commonly sat with their feet turned to the left, directly opposite of all other Cheyenne women; (3) the *Hair Rope Men,* who alone among the Cheyenne, used rope of twisted hair; (4) the *Scabby,* called this because of an infection of scabs that once spread among them; (5) the *Ridge Men;* (6) the *Prognathous Jaws,* who did a distinctive Deer Dance; (7) the *Poor Men;* (8) the *Dog Men,* a large military society that also became a band; (9) the Suhtai, a band made of the people who once lived as a separate tribe under this name; and (10) the *Sioux-eaters,* meaning actually people who ate with the Sioux, since Sioux joined this band.

Gradually, in the middle of the nineteenth century, the Cheyennes broke up into two major divisions, those who stayed in the north around Southeast Montana and Northeast Wyoming, and those who moved south to Eastern Colorado and Western Oklahoma.

Language. The Cheyenne belonged to the immense Algonquian language family, which included most of the tribes of the northeast, such as the Abnaki of Maine and Ojibwa of the Great Lakes; also the Powhatan of Virginia, the Creek of central Canada, and the Blackfoot and Arapaho farther west.

Summary of tribal culture. — Subsistence of economy. For many centuries the Cheyenne were sedentary partially agricultural people, living in more or less permanent villages along lakes and rivers in Minnesota, then along the Red and Cheyenne rivers in North Dakota, next along the Missouri in North Dakota, in mud-walled semi-fortified villages, where they raised corn, beans adn squash like their neighbors, the Mandan, Arikara, and Hidsata. This progressive movement westward changed them from original gatherers of wild rice in the lake country and hunters of the deer as their primary game animal, to beginning hunters of the buffalo, at least in summer. Their evolution in this direction moved rather quickly soon after their discovery of the horse around 1760, since the horse gave them the means to exploit for food the great herds of buffalo and smaller herds of antelope that covered parts of the Plains, as well as herds of elk found in the hills and more wooded areas. Indians afoot had found these herds difficult to approach because of their speed, and, besides this, the herds wandered over vast areas, leaving some sections uninhabited for many weeks so that the Indians had to travel far to find them again. For Indians mounted on horses it was now much easier to follow the herds swiftly and come close enough to shoot arrows into their hearts or kidneys. A hunter had to be careful, however, as both buffalo and elk could turn swiftly and gore either an attacker or his horse before they could swerve away.

Like most Plains tribes, the Cheyenne, had very definite rules as to how the hunting could be done, and special soldier societies who took turns or were appointed as police to enforce the rules during hunts. These rules applied mainly during the late spring and summer when the herds gathered in large masses at places where the grass grew thick. At such times scouts were sent out in front of the band of hunters to search for the herds. When found they would use puffs of smoke as signals or send back a courier to notify the hunters they had found game. Immediately the police lined up the hunters in such a way that they advanced as a unit with no one allowed to get ahead to where they would alarm the herd before the organized attack could begin. Amy man caught sneaking off to hunt separately was chased down by police and not only severely beaten with whips but his weapons destroyed and even his horse killed. Sometimes such a hunter might ameliorate such punishment, when noticing his pursuers approaching, by making no attempt to escape, but getting off his horse, spreading his blanket on the ground, and standing behind this with his head down in

complete admission of his guilt. Then they would only cut his blanket into strips.

In properly disciplined hunts, the hunters would usually draw near a ridge top or high swale of the Great Plains, forming a line just out of sight of the herd, and springing forward to attack only when the soldier society chief gave the command. Then a wave of horsemen would sweep forward, each rider selecting the part of the herd wished to attack and all staying apart enough not to come into collision. Not unitl the herd started to move in alarm would they begin to yell, each hunter closing in on one buffalo, with older boys who had been allowed to come usually seeking out easier to kill calves. As each hunter had his specially marked arrows, once he had killed a buffalo it was marked as his, and he could ride on again to kill another until at last the herd had escaped into the distance. The excitement and the challenge and the rewards of this kind of chase were so great that it is no wonder that the Cheyenne were drawn away from the much tamer life of the sedentary agricultural villages of

Meat drying on rack at a Cheyenne summer camp in 1895

their past into the adventure offered by the seemingly unlimited game of the Great Plains.

While the hunters would often cut out a tongue or some other part of their prey to be eaten raw if they were hungry enough, messengers were quickly sent back to the camp to bring up the other people to help with the butchering, the women arriving with thrilling cries of praise for the brave hunters. Such a killing of buffalo in particular, was a time of great prosperity for the tribe, as the meat could not only be cooked and eaten on the spot or nearby, but it was also dried in the sun or smoked and kept as jerky for times when food was more scarce. Also the hides were stripped from the bodies, and the horns, sinew and other parts gathered to be used for clothing, decoration and other ways by much feasting and laughing, followed by dances in celebration, and deep sleep except for the guards watching for enemies.

Hunting elk was done more often by small parties or single hunters, perhaps by trying to corner the animals in canyons, or sneaking up on them in wooden areas. But antelopes were the most difficult to hunt because of their great speed, far swifter than horses. Their tremendous curiosity, however, often got them into trouble, as a hunter would dress up in a wolf skin and act crazily or wave a flag until a herd approached closely, while other hunters crept up to form a half circle and drive them to where still other hunters were waiting to shoot them. Another common way was to have a medicine man prepare an elaborate ceremonial hunt in which the herd was somehow lured into a trap by two virgins who carried special medicine arrows and ran a V- shaped course towards where the medicine man had magically located the herd. Indeed, magic and dependence on spiritual powers seemed often as important a part of the hunt to the Cheyennes as weapons and horses.

In drier and colder times of the year the herds, especially the buffalo, broke up into small bands and dispersed in many directions so the tribe could then allow a lone hunter or small group to seek what he or they could find.

In winter and during the times of the great later summer thunder and lightning storms or the fierce dust storms driven by the winds across the Plains, hunting was sometimes quite dangerous. Hunters could become lost, blinded by dust and sand, struck by lightning, or frozen to death in blizzards. In blizzards hunters sometimes saved themselves by cutting open the body of an animal they had just killed, especially a buffalo, taking out the hot and steaming entrails, and crawling inside the body or wrapping themselves in its fresh skin. It is considered amazing how these people, with their primitive tools, weapons and skin tents, lived through some of the terrible winters. When blizzards raged and snow was deep it was vital to have a reserve food supply on hand, and men had to break their way through the snow to open up ways for the horses to get to the bark of cottonwood or willow trees by the rivers or streams. Crude snowshoes were worn to hunt over the snow when food got desperately low. It is no wonder the people turned to spiritual powers for help in time for need and why they considered their ceremonies so important.

Women were nearly as active as the men in gathering food, especially in the warmer times of the year when they could take the children with them to help. A digging stick, often with a knob at one end to allow the body to press against it and drive the pointed end into the ground, was used to dig up such tubers as the Indian turnip (*Psoralea lanciolate*), or the red turnip (*P. hypogeae*). They could be eaten raw, but usually were boiled after being cut into slices. They were also dried in the sun to be preserved for winter, the dried parts being smashed up and then being used as thickening for soup. The fruit of the prickly pear cactus had to be handled with great care with twig brooms and "thumb gloves" or thimbles, with the fruit split and the seeds taken out, while the rest was dried in the sun to be used later in soups. Dozens of plants were used for food, including milkweed buds, thistles, chocke cherries, and many kinds of berries, making many tasty dishes, especially when mixed with pounded dried meat to make the famous pemmican, carried in bags on long marches for quick nourishment.

Parties of women and girls made a happy adventure out of their hunt for these foods, even though the work was often arduous, scattering over the prairies in chattering groups and coming together again as evening broke the monotony by gambling for what they had collected, throwing dice of buffalo bones or seeing who could throw their digging sticks the farthest. Sometimes the men played games with them, pretending to attack such parties or be attacked, and being "defeated" by the women calling them names and hurling sticks and dung at them (a man falling "wounded" when hit), or sometimes allowing men to win who had counted coup on an enemy and so merited respect. Besides fun, such games were probably a way to overcome sexual antagonism.

Other women's work of importance included gathering fquantities of wood for the fires, and taking down and putting up the tipis or tents whenever moves were made. Women worked in teams of two, practicing speed, as it was sometimes vital to move a camp away quickly to protect women and children from an approaching enemy. Downed tipis, other baggage and children were carried on travois dragged by horses.

"Cheyenne Way" by Joseph Kabance (Potawatomi) 1971.

Technology and arts. An oval-shaped river stone, lashed to a green willow stick with rawhide, and personally fashioned for most effective use, was the universal owman's tool for work around camp, pounding tent stakes, breaking up wood, crushing bones for soup and so forth. Skinning and tanning was a basic technical skill that each woman was obliged to have so she could make clothes and produce efffective tipis. After the skin was taken off with a sharp knife, made of obsidian usually in the old days (more recently of steel derived from the white man), the process of tanning began. Four tools, a scraper, draw-blade, flesher and a buffalo shoulder blade or softening rope were used. The scraper was a flat stone of circular shape with one sharp edge used to scrape off meat and fat. The adze-shaped flesher had a sharp flint lashed to one end of a piece of elk horn and was used for more delicate work to get the skin just the right thinness needed, this requiring great skill. The drawblade was made of a willow stick to whose inner side was glued a sharp bone splinter. This was used to shave off the hair while the hide was held over a sloped pole. The softening rope or buffalo shoulder blade with a large hole in it were each used either alone or in conjunction to laboriously often the chemically tanned skin by working it back and forth over a pole or pulling it through the hole of the shoulder blade, fastened to a tree. The chemical tanning was done with soapweed, brains and liver, all mixed with buffalo grease to make a paste that could be rubbed into both sides of the hide, which was then soaked over night before the softening process (described above) could be used.

A small tipi used eleven or more buffalo cow-hides, a big lodge 16 to 21. The women making a tipi usually called on her friends for help with the final softening of skins, giving a big feast when finished. Large amounts of thread were made out of buffalo sinew and then came a second feat to encourage all to help her cut and sew the lodge together in an all-day party. An expert lodge-maker, supplied with paint and a cutting knife, marked all the skins for proper cutting. A new tipi was a great event, especially when embellished with paint and numerous attractively designed rows of porcupine quills, and was dedicated with an elaborate ritual.

Robes of buffalo skin or elk were used for outer clothing in winter. The sewing of clothing was rather crude, the woman wearing a sack-like dress that hung well below the knees, the men wearing only breech clouts in good weather, a soft square of skin hung about the waist. In cold weather, the men wore leggings, which extended from the moccasins' tops to the crotch, some having long fringes or flaps of deer skin for decoration. Men's shirts were like the women's dresses, but reached not more than half-way to the knees from the crotch. Shirts and sometimes dresses might be highly decorated with quill embroidery or later with traders' beads. As beads became commoner, necklaces and bracelets were worn and made for decoration. Moccasins usually had a thick separate sole to give protection from cactus spines and sharp rocks.

Men made their own weapons, finely-fahioning bows and arrows by scraping to the right thickness, sinew-backing the bows and making arrowheads out of flint and obsidian until iron was introduced from the whites. Much work and craftsmanship was spent on making fine pipes, the wood of the stem and the soft sandstone of the head finely-carved and decorated.

A special profession and technique in itself was the capture of eagle feathers and their use in many decorations, especially for headdresses and pipes. A man prayed and fasted and then went to pit on a hill or mountain top where he lay under a covering of brush on which was layed a recently-killed animal. When the eagle came, the legs were seized and the bird pulled into the pit and strangled, a dangerous job! A sacred sweat bath and other rituals were done afterward to neutralize the eagle power.

(Note: the circle of life: birth, puberty, marriage and death, were very similar among all the Plains tribes. Since the Cheyenne were especially like the Sioux in this respect, these are described fully in the article on the Dakota Sioux.)

Cheyenne village

Social and religious culture. Cheyenne society was better integrated and organized than most Plains tribes, in fact coming very close to making the whole tribe into a unified nation. The basis of the society was, of course, the extended family, which developed with other related families into the band. But the Cheyenne belonged as much to his mother's side as to his father's, with all the kindred functioning on an equal basis. This helped prevent clan friction and allowed the development of a strong seniority system in which the peace chiefs, as wise and good leaders, formed the famous Council of Forty-four for the whole tribe, unique to the Cheyennes, and forming both a legislative and executive body in an oral and traditional sense. Another unique feature was that each of these chiefs was molded by social pressure and tradition into a man of great self-control, kindly, wise and pure of heart, and a giver of gifts and advice to the poor and needy. Each was elected for ten years, but, at the end of this period, if he did not show these qualities, he usually lost his job.

This pressure for courtesy among the Cheyenne was so strong that it extended to the bulk of the population of the tribe, showing itself in the respect given elders and women, the courteous ways of eating and in entering a tent as a guest, etc. The Cheyenne was astonished at the discourteous ways

Little Chief

of most whites they met and considered them "savages."

The military societies were a balance to the Council of Forty- four, though sometimes a goad or counter. At time of war especially the council asked the chiefs of the military clubs for advice and leadership; and sometimes a military club or its leaders might establish a new mode of conduct, as when Elk Soldier Society chiefs declared that there had been too much borrowing of horses in the tribe without asking permission of the owners first, and that hereafter such permissions of must be granted or no horses could be borrowed. There were five original military or soldier societies, but seven by the mid-nineteenth century. Each was led by two head chiefs and two assistant chiefs. Each society was marked by its special rituals, costumes, dances, etc., and five of the clubs had each four virgin daughters of tribal chiefs as women members, forming standards of purity and chastity to give the clubs good luck.

It was the military societies that not only acted in turn as police for the great buffalo hunts, but also policed the camps and acted as large war parties against other tribes. War parties, however, were more often organized by a single warrior who had enough prestige from previous parties to gather around him a group for an attack. Rather rarely, for great revenge trips against tribes that had severely hurt the Cheyennes, as against the Crow in 1820 and against the Pawnees in 1853, the tribe as a whole united under a war chief to go against the enemy. Individual warriors earned war honors (coups) by not only killing enemies, but striking them with coup sticks, stealing a horse, saving a comrade, or other deeds of bravery.

Justice and law in the tribe was unique. So strong was the law of chastity for girls and women, with chastity belts as a sign of their sacredness, that rape was almost unknown. Feuds between families or clans were extremely rare because of the Cheyenne abhorence of murder of tribal members. The law had great flexibility. It was developed both by the Council of Forty-four, by the warrior societies and sometimes by outstanding individuals, and meshed with the needs and desires of the people for justice.

The religion of the Cheyenne was based on three great ceremonies, all of which reinforced the teachings and rules of life given to the tribe by three culture heroes. These heroes were Sweet Medicine, who brought the *Four Sacred Arrows*, Erect Horn (of the Suhtai) who brought the *Sacred Buffalo Hat,* and a woman who long ago was captured by the Assiniboine, but escaped to come back to their tribe and teach them to have the *Council of Forty-four* and other methods of good government and justice. Sweet Medicine taught them the great *Arrow Renewal Ceremony,* which was used not only to renew the spiritual power of the tribe and bring them all into harmony, but also whenever the tribe had to be cleansed of a murder or other horrendous deed that brought "the smell of death." This ceremony was held at mid-summer, but only in those years when needed, and was a ceremony unique to the Cheyenne. The *Sun Dance* was brought to the people by Erect Horn of the Suhtai (modified later by the influence of the Dakota Sioux), and was held more often. It lasted eight days and was characterized by the leadership of a pledger and a priest, who used it not only to renew the religion of the tribe, but for individual acts of self-sacrifice and torture by men who wished to win success in war or to repay the Spirit Powers for help they had received (see the *Sun Dance* of the Dakota Sioux for more complete details). The third great ceremony was the *Massaum* (Crazy), a *Contrary* or *Animal Dance*. It was a hunting ritual, brought by Sweet Medicine to gain success in hunting, but had a good deal more humor and fun than the other ceremonies. Contraries, brave warriors, dedicated to do everything backward, delighted the people with their comic contrariness, while men dressed as animals danced and acted out the different kinds of hunts.

More than in other tribes, the medicine men of the Cheyenne were either distinctively priests, such as the priest who guarded the *Four Sacred Arrows,* or shamans who did healing. There were many powerful spirit beings whom the medicine man called upon to help the people, but one Great Being *(Heammawihio).* Often it seemed that the Cheyenne simply asked help of "the Powers" and were satisfied with whomever they thought had given them assistance. They believed also that when they themselves failed to live lives of goodness and harmony, it hurt the whole tribe, and this caused great disasters, such as the *Four Sacred Arrows* which were lost to the Pawnee in 1830, or the mutilation of the *Sacred Buffalo Hat* in 1865.

(see map page XV)

BIBLIOGRAPHY —

● ALLEN, PAUL. History of the Expedition under the Command of Captains Lewis and Clark, to the Sources of the Missouri. Philadelphia, PA: Bradford & Inskeep, 1814.
● CHRONICLES OF OKLAHOMA. pg. 90-97, 1921; pg. 350 1924; pp. 260-270 1928; pg. 11 1934.
● COUES, ELLIOTT. Forty Years a Fur Trader on the Upper Missouri.New York, NY: Francis P. Harper, 1898.
● COVINGTON, JAMES W. Causes of the Dull Knife Raid. OK: Chronicles of Oklahoma, vol. 26, 1948.
● CURTIS, NATALIE. The Indians' Book: An offering by the American Indians of Indian Lore.New York, NY: Harper & Bros., 1907.
● DEBO, ANGIE. The Road to Disappearance. Norman, OK: University of Oklahoma Press, 1941.
● DOWNEY, FAIRFAX. Indian-Fighting Army.New York, NY: Charles Scribner's Sons, 1941.
● DUNN, J. P. Massacres of the Mountains, A History of the Indian Wars of the Far West.New York, NY: Harper & Bros, 1886.
● EASTMAN, ELAINE GOODALE. Pratt, The Red Man's Moses. Norman, OK: University of Oklahoma Press, 1935.
● FOREMAN, GRANT. Pioneer Days in the Early Southwest. Cleveland, OH, The Arthur H. Clark Co., 1926.
● GABRIEL, RALPH HENRY. The Pageant of America: the Lure of the Frontier.New Haven, CT: Yale University Press, 1929.
● GHENT, WILLIAM JAMES. The Road to Oregon, A Chronicle of the Great Emigrant Trail. New York, NY: Longmans, Green & Co., 1929.
● GRAHAM, W. A. The Story of the Little Big Horn, Custer's Last Fight.New York, NY: and London: The Century Co., 1926.

● GRINNELL, GEORGE BIRD. A Buffalo Sweatlodge.reprinted from the American Anthropologist, Vol. 21, No. 4, Oct.-Dec., pp. 361-375, 1919.
----- By Cheyenne Campfires.New Haven, CT: Yale University Press; London: Humphrey Milford, Oxford University Press, 1926.
----- The Cheyenne Indians. 2 vols. New Haven, CT: Yale University Press, 1923.
----- The Fighting Cheyennes.New York, NY: Charles Scribner's Sons, 1915.
----- Some Cheyenne Plant Medicines. American Anthropologist, n.s. VII, pp. 37-43, 1905.
● HARMON, GEORGE DEWEY. Sixty Years of Indian Affairs, Political, Economic, and Diplomatic, 1789-1850.Chapel Hill, NC: University of North Carolina Press, 1941.
● HODGE, FREDERICK WEBB. Handbook of American Indians North of Mexico. Washington: Government Printing Office, 2 vols., 1907-10.
● HOEBEL, E. ADAMSON. The Cheyennes: Indians of the Great Plains.New York, NY: Henry Holt and Co., 1960.
● HOWARD, MAJ.-GEN., O.O. My Life and Experiences Among Our Hostile Indians A Record of Personal Observations, Adventures. Hartford, CT: A. D. Worthington & Co., 1907.
● HUMFREVILLE, J. LEE. Twenty Years Among Our Hostile Indians. New York, NY: Hunter & Co.
● INDIAN OFFICE REPORT. 1857, 1864, 1865, 1866, 1868, 1871, 1872, 1874, 1875, 1877, 1878, 1879, 1881, 1882, 1883, 1884, 1889, 1891, 1892.
● THE KANSAS HISTORICAL QUARTERLY. Nov. 1932; Aug. 193; 4Nov. 1948.
● KEELING, HENRY C. My Experience with the Cheyenne Indians. Topeka, KS: Kansas State Historical Society, 1909-1910.
● KELSEY, RAYNER WICKERSHAM PH.D. Friends and the Indians, 1655-1917. Philadelphia: The Associated Executive Committee of Friends on Indian Affairs, 1917.
● LLEWELLYN, K. N. AND E. ADAMSON HOEBEL. Cheyenne Way, Conflict and Case Law in Primitive Jurisprudence, The. Norman, OK: University of Oklahoma Press, 1941 (article appears in Indian Office Report, pg. 669-670, 1892.).
● MURDOCK, GEORGE P. Ethnographic Bibliography of North America.New Haven, CT: Human Relations Area Files Press, 1975.
● PALLADINO, S. J. Indian and White in the Northwest, A History of Catholicity in Montana, 1831- 1891.Lancaster, PA: Wickersham Publishing Co., 1922.
● PHILLIPS, PAUL C. Forty Years on the Frontier, As Seen in the Journals and Reminiscences of Granville Stuart.Cleveland, OH: The Arthur H. Clart Co., 1925.
● RISTER, CARL COKE. The Southwestern Frontier - 1865-1881. Cleveland, OH: The Arthur H. Clark Co., 1928.
● ROYCE, CHARLES C. Indian Land Cessions in the U.S. Washington: 18th Annual Report, Bureau of Ethnology, 1896-97.
● SCHOOLCRAFT, HENRY R. History of the Indian Tribes of the U.S.; Their Present Condition and Prospects.Philadelphia, J. B. Lippincott & Co., 1857.
● SCHULENBERG, RAYMOND F. Indians of North Dakota. ND: North Dakota History, vol. 23, 1957.
● SEYMOUR, FLORA WARREN. Indian Agents of the Old Frontier.New York, NY: and London: D. Appleton-Century Co., Inc., 1941.
● SWANTON, JOHN R. The Indian Tribes of North America. Washington, DC: U.S. Government Printing Office, 1952.
----- Some Neglected Data Bearing on the Cheyenne, Chippewa and Dakota History.American Anthropologist n.s., 32, pp. 156-60, 1930.
● UNDERHILL, RUTH M. First Penthouse Dwellers of America. New York, NY: J. J. Augustin Publisher, 1938.
● VESTAL, STANLEY. Dobe Walls, A Story of Kit Carson's Southwest.Boston, MA: and NY: Houghton Mifflin Co., 1929.
● WELLMAN, PAUL I. Death on the Prairie, The Thirty Years' Struggle for the Western Plains.New York, NY: The Macmillan Co., 1934.
● WHEELER, COL. HOMER W. Buffalo Days: Forty Years in the Old West.Indianapolis: The Bobbs-Merrill Co.
● WISSLER, CLARK. Indians of the U.S., Four Centuries of Their History and Culture.New York, NY: Doubleday, Doran & Co., 1940.

CHEYENNE, NORTHERN

(U.S.; Mont.) The popular designation for the part of the Cheyenne which continued to range along the upper Platte after the rest of the tribe (Southern Cheyenne) had permanently moved down to Arkansas reservation, about 1835. They are now settled on a reservation in Montana. From the fact that the Omisis division is most numerous among them, the term is frequently used by the Southern Cheyenne as synonymous.

(see map page XV)

CHEYENE, SOUTHERN

(U.S.; Okla.) That part of the Cheyenne which ranged in the south portion of the tribal territory after 1835, now permanently settled in a Federal Trust Area in western Oklahoma. They are commonly known as Sowania, "southerners" by the Northern Cheyenne, and sometimes as Hevhaitanio, from their most numerous division.

CHIAHA.

(U.S.; Georgia) Also called Tolameco or Solameco, which was said to signify "big town," a name reported by the Spaniards. The meaning of Chiaha is unknown, although it may contain a reference to mountains or highlands. (Cf. Choctaw and Alabama tcaha, Hitchiti tcaihi, "high.") The Chiaha belonged to the Muskhogean linguistic stock and in later times, spoke the Muskogee tongue, but they were also classed in the Hitchiti group. In later historic times, the Chiaha resided near the Chattahoochee River, but at the earliest period at which we have any knowledge of them, they seem to have been divided into two bands, one on Burns Island, in the present State of Tennessee, the other in eastern Georgia near the coast. One subdivision, the Mikasuki of northern Florida, are said to have separated from these people. Some of their villages, according to *Hawkins, 1948*, included Aumucculle, Chiahutci, and Hotalgihuyana.

Some confusion regarding this tribe as been attributed to the fact that in the sixteenth century, there appear to have been two divisions. The name first appears in the De Soto narratives applied to a "province" on an island at the Tennessee River, which J. Y. Brame identified as Burns Island, near the Tennessee- Alabama line. They were said to be "subject to a chief of Coca," from which it may perhaps be inferred that the Creek Confederacy was already in existence. Early in 1567, Boyano, Juan Pardo's lieutenant, reached this town with a small body of soldiers and constructed a fort, with Pardo joining him in September. When Pardo returned to Santa Elena shortly afterward, he left a small garrison there which was later destroyed by the Indians. Chehawhaw Creek, an eastern affluent of the Coosa, possibly indicates a later location of this band. The only remaining reference which might apply to them occurs in the names of two bodies of Creeks called "Chehaw" and "Chearhaw," which appear in the census rolls of 1832-33, but they may have also gotten their designations from the creeks they resided at. In 1727, there was a tradition among the Cherokee that the Yamasee Indians were formerly Cherokees who were driven out by the Tomahitans, i.e., the Yuchi, and in this there may be some reminiscence of the fate of the Chiaha.

In the Pardo narratives, the name "Lameco or Solameco" is given as a synonym for the northern Chiaha, and this may have been intended for Tolameco, which would be a Creek term meaning "Chief Town." This was also the name of a large abandoned settlement near Cofitachequi near the Savannah River, visited by De Soto in 1540, and since it was reported that the Chiaha were also in this region, it was suggested that they resided there as well. There is a Chehaw River on the South Carolina coast between the Edisto and Combahee, and as "Chiaha" was used once as an equivalent for Kiawa, possibly the Cusabo tribe of that name may have been related. It was also reported that the Chiaha had their homes formerly among the Yamasee. In 1715 they withdrew to the Chattahoochee with other upper Creek towns, probably from a temporary abode on Ocmulgee River. After the Creeks moved to Oklahoma, the Chiaha settled in the northeastern corner of the Creek Reservation and maintained a square ground there until after the Civil War, but eventually, they lost almost all of their identity. Some of them went to Florida and the Mikasuki are said by some Indians to have branched off from them. In the country of the western Seminole, there was a square ground, as late as 1929, which bore their name.

There are no figures for the northern band of Chiaha unless they could have been represented in the two towns of the 1832-33 census given above, which had total populations of 126 and 306 respectively. A southern division of a Spanish census of 1738 gives 120 warriors, but this included the Osochi and Okmulgee as well. In 1750, only 20 were reported, but in 1760 that figure increased to 160, although an estimate the following year showed 120. In 1792, *Marbury* reported 100 Chiaha and Apalachicola, and the census of 1832-33 showed 381 of the former. In 1799, *Hawkins* stated that there were 20 Indian families in Hotalgi- huyana, a town occupied jointly by this tribe and the Osochi, but in 1821, *Young* raised this figure to 210. He also reported 670 for the Chiaha proper.

The Chiaha tribe is of some note on account of the prominence given to one branch of it in the De Soto narratives. As mentioned above, its name, spelled Chehawhaw, is applied to a stream in the northern part of Talladega County, Alabama. It was given in the form Chehaw to a post hamlet of Macon County, Alabama; to a stream in Colleton County, South Carolina; and also to a small place in Seminole County, Oklahoma.

BIBLIOGRAPHY –

● HODGE, FREDERICK WEBB. Handbook of American Indians North of Mexico. Washington: Smithsonian Institution: BAE Bulletin No. 30: U.S. GPO, 1907.
● SWANTON, JOHN R. The Indian Tribes of North America. Washington, DC: U.S. Government Printing Office, 1952.

CHIAKANESSOU

(U.S.;) Mentioned by a French trader as a tribe of 350 warriors, associated with the Alibamu, Caouikas (Kawita), Machecous (Creeks), and Souikilas (Sawokli). Possibly the Creeks of Chiaha, the ending being the misspelt Creek *isti*, 'people'; or, less likely, the Chickasaw. On the De l'Isle map of 1707 "Chiacantesou," which is probably the same, is located much farther N. W., within the Caddoan country.

BIBLIOGRAPHY —

● HODGE, FREDERICK WEBB. Handbook of American Indians North of Mexico. Washington: Government Printing Office, 2 vols., 1907-10.
● MURDOCK, GEORGE P. Ethnographic Bibliography of North America.New Haven, CT: Human Relations Area Files Press, 1975.
● SWANTON, JOHN R. The Indian Tribes of North America. Washington, DC: U.S. Government Printing Office, 1952.

CHIAPANEC

(Mexico) controlled the Rio Grijalva and Rio Santo Domingo lowlands according to the Spaniards, who entered the central Chiapa depression in 1554. These people had their capital near the present Chiapa de Corzo. By 1959, the Chiapanec were reported to have been completely assimilated.

The Chiapanec were relative newcomers to Chiapas, entering the zone about AD 500. They are related linguistically to the Chorotega-Mangue of Nicargua, and it is assumed that they either travelled into Chiapas from the south or are of Mexican origin to the north, and the Chorotega-mangue migrated out of Chiapas to their present location to the south.

The Chiapa Depression, the traditional lands of the Chiapanec, is basin-like in form, with the watercourses of the Grijalva River and its tributaries as the principal natural feature. The depression is irregular, extending 250 kilometers in a southeasterly direction from Cintalapa to the Guatamalan border. The basin ranges in width from about 25 to 70 kilometers.

The prehistoric history of the Chiapa Depression holds significance, as the area lies in a strategic position midway between the Zapotec, Totonac and Olmec cultures to the west and that of the Maya to the east. The area does not exhibit carved stone stelae, and altars so common to the cultural tradition of their neighbors. The failure of the area to exhibit the widespread Mesoamerican stelae cult may represent the isolated and remote nature of the zone. Possibly trade routes passed to the north and south of the basin.

Over 70 sites have been located in the area of the upper Grijalva River alone, many of which are large and all prehistoric periods are represented. The Grijalva River basin is apparently well suited to human occupation, exhibiting fertile soils, timber resources, stone for construction materials, as well as clay for ceramic production. However, the area also represents one of the drier regions of tropical America, with a long dry season, irregualr rainfall and frequent droughts in particular areas of the valley. Some years exhibit flooding and erosion of the adjacent hills is common. The tributaries that feed into the Grijalva River flow throughout the year, and settlement in the prehistoric as well as historic times has clustered on the adjacent valley lands.

Prehistoric people farmed the choice agricultural lands located on the alluvial terraces along the Grijalava and its tributaries. Villages and ceremonial centers were initially built close to these lands. Later occupants and higher population densities necessitated settlement in the less desirable dry and hilly sites away from the rivers. These later settlements were in some cases large and complex, and mark the complex and well- organized nature of a society able to support populations distant from major water sources.

There exist no known native chronicles for Central Chiapas, and early historical reports are not extensive. Chiapas was subjugated by the Spaniards in 1524. However, the only eyewitness account of the conquest of Chiapa Indian populations was written by Bernal Diaz in 1568. The central Depression was occupied in the western section of the Zoque, the Chiapanec occupied the central area, and Maya groups were found to the east. Complicating this pattern was the influence of Mexican Aztecs, who had established political control over most of Chiapas to exact tribute as early as 1482. Bernal Diaz states that only the Chiapanec remained independent of the Aztecs.

The first Spanish intrusion into the Chiapas highlands occurred in 1523, ordered by Gonzolo de Sandoval, leader of the Spaniards stationed in Coatzalcoalcos. The conquered lands and peoples were divided by Sandoval among his men. However, these men chose to return to Coatzalcoalcos, rather than settle in Chiapas, and their subsequent attempts to exact tribute from their nominal tributaries were unsuccessful. Cortes sent men to aid in the pacification of Chiapas in 1523. Word was sent to towns to come and surrender to the Spanish. The representatives of Zincantan, Copanaguastla, Pinola, Gueyguistlan and Chamula all came, all of whom had been enemies of the Chiapanecs. Thus here, as in the Valley of Mexico, local hostilities played into the Spaniards' hands and gave them an early victory.

The 1523-24 foray into Chiapas ended, and

again, this time against the express orders of Cortes, no Spanish settlement was left in Chiapas from which to maintain the peace. Again the Indians resisted control. In late 1526, Cortes commissioned Diego de Mazariegos to reconquer the Indians of Chiapas. Mazariegos' mission (1527-28) put an end to massive armed resistance to Spanish rule in Chiapas for nearly two centuries. In March of 1528, Mazariegos founded Villa Real at Chiapa de Corzo, and the conquest of Chiapas was essentially complete.

The Spanish settlement of Chiapas centered at Chiapa de los Indios (the present Chiapa de Corzo) and at Ciudad Real or Chiapa de los Espanoles (presently San Cristobal de Las Casas), became the center of political control and the first center for ecclesiastic power. The Spanish conquest in the 16th century and subsequent developments in the 17th, 18th, and 19th centuries have had important impact on the Indian culture of the region.

The first bishop, Bartolome de las Casas, arrived in Chiapas in about 1545 with a group of 17 Dominican friars. Resentment against his liberal views on the treatment of Indians made it difficult for the Dominicans to carry on their work in San Cristobal de las Casas, and consequently they soon moved their headquarters to Chiapa de Corzo and established other convents in adjacent areas.

The earliest complete census with a breakdown by ethnic identity seems to be that of 1778. In that year there were 7,499 blancos and *mestizos* in Chiapas and 51,279 *indios*. Ladinos were spread far and wide across the state, with the result that few Indian communities were far from a settlement of Spaniards, but there were still no resident Latinos at all in nearly half of all Chiapas towns, and in all but four towns the Indian population was substantially larger than the non-Indian. Ladino settlements were proportionately more frequent at lower than at higher latitudes, suggesting that the interests of the Spaniards were better served, except for the political control points of Ciudad Real and Comitan, at lower altitudes where they could engage in raising sugar cane and cattle and in trading these items in Mexico and Guatemala.

Historic accounts of the Central Basin have stressed its isolated and provincial nature. However, as a result of the completion of the Pan American Highway, the area has experienced incorporation into the mainstream of Mexican national life. Zoque is still spoken in smaller villages, and traditional costumes are worn. Tzotzil and Tzetzal Mayan villages are found in the San Cristobal-Comitan altiplano, but no native-speaking "Indian" groups are found anywhere along the margins of the Grijalva, the lands traditionally occupied by the Chiapanec.

The acculturation of the Indian populations has consisted of the varied efforts to convert the Indians to Catholicism, to enforce political control and to educate the population. The conversion and control over the Indians has historically been most focused in the lowland areas of Chiapas, and this may account for the complete acculturation of the Chiapanec groups in the Central Depression.

BIBLIOGRAPHY –

● BOWDITCH, CHARLES. P. Mexican and Central American Antiquities, Calendar Systems and History. Washington, D. C.: Bureau of American Ethnology - Bulletin 28: GPO, 1904.
● SWANTON, JOHN R. The Indian Tribes of North America. Washington, DC: U.S. Government Printing Office, 1952.
● THOMAS, CYRUS. Indian Languages of Mexico and Central America and Their Geographical Distribution. Bureau of American Ethnology Bulletin 44: Washington, D. C.: GPO, 1911.

CHIBCHA

(South America; Colombia) culture of Colombia achieved an intensity comparable to that of the Central Andean Indians. The *Chibcha* are frequently compared to the *Inca*. However, the *Inca* empire represents the ultimate expression of a pattern whose roots lie deep in the archaeological past. The *Chibcha* culture has no such demonstrable antiquity. Nonetheless, the *Chibcha* culture had advanced so far that it is frequently classed as the third highest civilization of the Americas.

Chibcha culture whose population is difficult to estimate, was based on intensive sedentary agriculture, and as such is unique in Colombia. The cultivated crops were the same as those in the Central Andean region with the exception of a few of the root plants. The principal agricultural implements were a digging stick and a wooden spade. It is doubtful if irrigation was known in pre-Spanish times, and probably the *Chibcha* were less versed than the *Inca* in the use of fertilizers and in soil conservation. This region is beyond the natural range of llamas and alpacas, so that the dog and the guinea pig were the only domesticated animals. The absence of suitable domesticated animals made the high *paramos* virtually worthless to the *Chibcha*.

The common weapons were the spear and spear thrower, darts, slings and shields. The bow and arrow was known, but was not of great importance. A unique weapon was a two-bladed wooden sword. Transportation was limited to foot travel because of the lack of animals and streams suitable for navigation.

Stones, set up at intervals in circles, mark some of the house sites, but in general, building walls were of poles, in some cases coated with clay plaster. Stone masonry and construction with adobe brick were unknown. The chiefs lived in large compounds surrounded by pole palisades.

However, there were no large public works, such as large religious constructions, pyramids, mounds or fortified sites, which would have required the organization of mass labor. The houses were arranged in villages which never grew to the size of true cities.

The craftsmanship was in many senses inferior in quality to other areas of Colombia. Ceramics were completely made, but there was no great variety of forms nor outstanding artistry in decoration. Weaving fibers were limited to the domesticated cotton. The most elaborate decoration of cloth was in painting, either with roller stamps or freehand. Copper was rare and bronze was unknown. Most metallurgy was in gold or in a combination of gold, silver and copper, called *tumbaga*. Although goldworking techniques were numerous, workmanship was less competent than that of the *Quimbaya*. There was no stone carving, although wooden statues have been reported.

The clothing followed the Andean pattern: breechclout, shirt and shawl. Footgear was not worn. Noseplugs and earplugs were common, and the body was painted with roller stamps.

The hair-cutting, naming ceremony for children, practiced in Northwest Argentina, the Central Andes, and Ecuador, was also practiced by the *Chibcha*. Puberty ceremonies for both sexes were of considerable importance. Burial was elaborate, especially for chiefs, although the pattern of ancestor worship was not overemphasized.

Positions of chiefs and priests descended through the matrilineal line, and there is some evidence for matrilineal descent in other aspects of the culture. Clans, however, were not very important, and property was owned individually rather than collectively. The three major classes in *Chabcha* society were the nobles, the commoners and the slaves, that is prisoners of war. This class system was gradually assuming caste proportions. At least, the chief or ruler was of almost divine importance; his whole life was surrounded by complex protocol. There was also a specially trained and priviledged class of warriors with their respective war chiefs.

At the time of the Spanish Conquest, the *Chibcha* had begun the organization of states and were on their way to unite the whole territory under one leader. Two loosely organized states, ruled by the Zipa and the Zaque, were prominent at the time of the Conquest, and both were expanding. The conquered peoples were not incorporated with the thoroughness of the *Inca* political machine, but rather subjected to the payment of tribute.

Nemequene was a powerful *Chibcha* Indian ruler of the Zipa kingdom, which had its center at the site of Colombia's modern capital, Bogota. Nemequene is one of the few *Chibcha* kings for

Chibcha pottery and artifacts.

whom any detailed information (whether mythological or factual) exists, and he was the last Zipa ruler to live out his reign before the Spanish arrived.

The histories and legends agree that Nemequene succeeded Saguanmachica as Zipa ruler around the year 1490. Like his father, Nemequene had a single, burning ambition: to conquer the neighboring kingdom of Tunja (or Hunza), ruled by the Zaques; his Zaque opposite was called Quemuenchatecha, who lost his father in the same battle in which King Saguanmachica had died. From his capital of Bacata (the Indian equivalent of Bogota), Nemequene's brother, was to die in the protracted war against Ubaque. After victories over the rulers of Ebate, Simijaca, and Susa, Nemequene had an army of 60,000 to attack Tunja.

In the 24th year of his reign, according to the legends, Nemequene died at Choconta, having failed to defeat Tunja. He was succeeded by Tisquesusa, who was ruling at the time of the Spanish arrival in 1536.

Certain events of Nemequene's story (particularly in the war on Tunja) so closely parallel those of his predecessor's and successor's lives, they cannot be considered "facts" of historical reliability, for it seems the same story is being retold. The accounts of Nemequene's reforms of *Chibcha* law, and his expansion of the Zipa empire, may have more validity. Like the biographies of early European kings, his life must be considered as a blend of fact and legend.

The religious practices and beliefs were complex, but formalized religious organization was weak. A special group of priests participated in the ceremonies, but their principal function was that of intermediary between the people and the gods. Although a long period of training was necessary in order to become a priest and although the position was inherited, the priests themselves were not formally organized. Ceremonial centers, or temples, were but little different from the common dwellings. They did contain idols, and sacrifices, including human, were performed at them. The gods followed the Central American pattern of being departmentalized, that is, having specific functions, such as commerce or weaving, assigned to them.

Chibcha culture offered little resistance to the Spanish invaders, and since the conquest, the language and much of the culture have disappeared. This can be explained in part by the new introductions from the Old World which made radical changes in the economy. In comparison, it is difficult to explain why the *Aymara* held on to their language and customs with such tenacity while the *Chibcha* let both slip away. An important contributing factor to the elimination of the *Chibcha* culture is the fact that the Colonial Spaniards found the *Chibcha* territory ideal for their own settlements. It was the only region in Colombia where agricultural labor was both abundant and tractable. Spanish cattle could utilize the paramo country: Spanish oats and barley grew well in the high plateau region. Unfortunately, there was no place for the *Chibcha* to retire.

BIBLIOGRAPHY –

● STEWARD, JULIAN H. Handbook of South American Indians. 7 Vols., Washington, DC: U.S. Govt. Printing Office, 1946-59.

CHICKAHOMINY

(U.S.; Va.) was a tribe belonging to the Powhatan Confederacy.

The Chickahominy were located in Virginia, and, despite their small number, were one of the area's more important tribes.

The name means "related to the Powhatans," and part of their confederacy, the Chickahominy were never under the confederacy's complete power, as

were other tribes. This independence gave them a significant degree of political power.

Their political and religious leaders were the same. They seemed to have worshipped Oke, the God of Evil. Priests warned they could summon Oke at any time. It was the most effective threat and accounted for their power. There was also Ahone, the God of Good. The great religious ceremonies took place in large, wooden temples, sometimes 60 feet long.

The Chickahominy lived in wooden houses that were smaller versions of the temples. Though their name indicated they crushed corn they seem to have put less emphasis on agriculture than other Southeastern tribes. They relied mainly on meat and fish which they usually baked.

There is little data on their social structure.

The Chickahominy first gained notoriety as an English ally. Because of their cooperation with the English they were one of the few Powhatan tribes remaining after the American Revolution.

But there weren't many. In the mid-1660s there were probably some 900 Chickahominy. But repeated attacks by the Iroquois and other tribes reduced their population significantly. In 1722 the Albany Conference ordered the Iroquois and other tribes to stop molesting the Chickahominy. But by this time there were only 80 remaining.

By the 19th century the Chickahominy had ceased to exist as a separate unit. All Chickahominy since have been mixed-bloods.

BIBLIOGRAPHY –

● HODGE, FREDERICK WEBB. Handbook of American Indians North of Mexico. Washington: Government Printing Office, 2 vols., 1907-10.
● MURDOCK, GEORGE P. Ethnographic Bibliography of North America. New Haven, CT: Human Relations Area Files Press, 1975.
● SWANTON, JOHN R. The Indian Tribes of North America. Washington, DC: U.S. Government Printing Office, 1952.

CHICKASAW

(U.S.; Southeast) was an important tribe. Closely related to the Choctaw, they were a far more warlike group. One explorer wrote that no tribe was ever quicker to "go into the shedding of blood."

Linguistically the Chickasaw were Muskhogean. Their language served as a medium between whites and Indians along the lower Mississippi, just as the Chinook Jargon had served the same purpose in the Pacific Northwest.

They lived in the upper Mississippi State area, which was their traditional home. Their legends are the same as the Greek emigration legends, which say they came to Mississippi from the north. Here they remained until they were removed by the U.S. government to Indian Territory, now Oklahoma.

Their religious life was one of the preeminent

The last Chickasaw Council House, at Tishomingo, OK.

features of their culture. There was nothing under the Chickasaw universe which did not have a religious purpose or significance. This was demonstrated largely in their feeling for nature. They kept a lunar calendar and held celebrations at the beginning of each new full moon. They had a stringent set of taboos; possibly the most interesting dealt with a woman's menstrual period. During this time women had to go into a menstrual hut, and they were not allowed to have any contact with others in the tribe until the period was over. Regarding their dead the Chickasaws had a concept of heaven and hell. Those that lived a good life would spend a life of joy in the sky, but those that did not would suffer torture in hell. Religion, too, had medicinal purposes.

Their social structure, consisting of clans and totemic divisions, was also divinely ordinated. The tribe was divided into great divisions-- *Imosaktca* and *Intcukwalipa.* The Imosaktca had precedence over the Intcukwalipa and the *High Minko,* or chief, always came from the *Imosaktca.* There were a number of clans and members had to marry outside their clan. A child's clan membership came through the mother.

Each band had an autonomous government and together they confederated into a tribe. The government was patrilineal and all chiefs arrived at the position through clan and totemic rank.

Though monogamy was the rule the Chickasaws did allow polygamy. One writer noted they liked variety and mocked Europeans for their strict monogamous ways. Separation and divorce were permitted. Adultery was a serious crime. And any woman who was widowed had to spend a four year period of widowhood which could only be broken if her late husband's brother married her. A widower had to go through a simialr type of period, but only for four months.

Women performed the more menial tasks. It has been suggested the Chickasaws went to war, often at their wives' urging to gain slaves, which relieved them of the menial tasks.

In child rearing, women were completely responsible for raising girls, but men retained that responsibility for boys.

In the Chickasaw bands, life was organized on a household level. Each household had a winter and summer house, a menstrual hut and a corn storage bin. The winter house was in design and the summer house rectangular. Deer was the main form of meat, and was used for other items such as arrowheads and tools. Bears were also hunted and their claws and teeth used for jewelry. Fishing was important and there were some seasons when Chickasaws plainly preferred fish. Agriculture was also an important activity and the Indians grew corn, melons and pumpkins after they cleared the land. Women and children also collected wild berries. To cook their food the Chickasaws made simple clay pottery.

The Chickasaws also had a thriving trade with

other tribes, exchanging bear oil, deerskins and slaves for tools, pearls and copper sheets.

Their first white contact seems to have been with De Soto in 1540, who called them "Chicaza." They were lifelong enemies of the French, fighting several wars with them. Their first war with the French was in 1720. In 1736 they defeated the French at Amalahta, at the Long House, and at other places. They completely baffled the French, who tried to conquer them in 1739. The Chickasaws also fought other tribes. Along with the Choctaw they fought the Illinois, Mobilians, Osage and others. In 1715 they allied with the Cherokees to fight the Shawnee and in 1769 routed their former allies at Chickasaw Old Fields.

In 1786 a U.S. treaty set their northern boundary at the Ohio River. They began emigrating west of the Mississippi as early as 1822. In 1832-34 treaties were made that removed them to Oklahoma where their way of life began to disintegrate.

The nation remains today. During the 18th century there were between 2,000 and 6,000. Today there are roughly the same number, though many are no longer purebloods. *(see map page XIV)*

BIBLIOGRAPHY —

● BAIRD, W. DAVID. The Chickasaw People. Phoenix, AZ: Indian Tribal Series, 1974.
● CHRONICLES OF OKLAHOMA. 1925, 1927, 1929, 1930, 1933, 1949-50.
● DEBO, ANGIE. And Still the Waters Run. Princeton, NJ: Princeton University Press, 1940.
● GIBSON, ARRELL M. The Chickasaws. Norman, OK: University of Oklahoma Press, 1971.
● HODGE, FREDERICK WEBB. Handbook of American Indians North of Mexico. Washington: Government Printing Office, 2 vols., 1907-10.
● INDIAN OFFICE REPORT. 1828, 1839, 1845, 1857, 1870; 1872, 1873, 1875, 1880, 1881, 1883, 1890, 1891, 1893, 1894
● MALONE, JAMES H. The Chickasaw Nation, A Short Sketch of a Noble People. Louisville, KY: John P. Morton & Co., 1922.
● MURDOCK, GEORGE P. Ethnographic Bibliography of North America. New Haven, CT: Human Relations Area Files Press, 1975.
● NILES REGISTER. Vol. 37, pp. 364-7. (An address to Congress, asking that the Cherokee, Creek, Chickasaw and Choctaw be "sustained in the undisturbed enjoyment of their national and social rights."), Jan. 23, 1830.
● SWANTON, JOHN R. The Indian Tribes of North America. Washington, DC: U.S. Government Printing Office, 1952.
● YARROW, DR., H. C. A Further Contribution to the Study of Mortuary Customs of the North American Indians. Washington: 1st Annual Report, Bureau of Ethnology, pp. 87-203, 1881.

CHILCOTIN

(Canada; British Columbia) are an Athapascan tribe, living chiefly in the valley of the Chilcotin River. Their nearest relatives are the Carrier, who live to the north and who were the Athapascan people with whom they most frequently had contact.

In the past there was also some communication with the Kwakiutl to the southwest. On the east, the Chilcotin were separated from the Shuswap by Frasser River and did not hold very intimate relations with them. In earlier times the two tribes were constantly at war. Toward the south their nearest neighbors were the Lillooet, but contact between the two tribes was slight. In 1900, the center of territory and population of the Chicotin was Ansheim Lake; and from there they covered a considerable extent of country, the principal points of gathering being Tatlah, Puntze, and Chizaikut lakes. They ranged as far south as Chilco Lake, and at the time of salmon fishing were accustomed to move in large numbers down to the Chilcotin River; and always returned to their homes as soon as the season was past. More recently they have been moved east. Today there are a number of families leading the traditional life in the old tribal territory, in the woods and mountains to the west. These peoples are less influenced by civilization than their reservation relatives. For the most part, however, despite contact with the whites for a comparatively short period, the Chilcotin have assimilated the customs and ideas of their neighbors to such an extent that their own have largely disappeared. The sedentary Chilcotin have abandoned semi-subterranean huts, live like their white neighbors, and are a agrarian people who cultivate cereals, peas, and potatoes. Their population was estimated at 450 in 1900, and is nearly 1,000 today.

BIBLIOGRAPHY —

● JENNESS, DIAMOND. Indians of Canada. National Museum of Canada Bulletin, no. 69, 1960.
● SWANTON, JOHN R. The Indian Tribes of North America. Washington, DC: U.S. Government Printing Office, 1952.

CHILKAT

(U.S.; Ark.) from *tcil-kat,* "salmon storehouse" is the major subdivision of the Tlingit, *q.v.,* and a village by that name on Controller Bay, Alaska. Their homeland is at the head of Lynn Canal, where the important towns of Chilkoot, Klukwan, and Skagway are situated. This location at the mouth of several waterways leading to the ocean allowed them to control of the interior trade of the region. As a result, they became powerful traders, carrying products from the coast into the interior, and returning with manufactured and raw materials which they in turn distributed along the Pacific Coast. They were an extremely aggressive people, and were some of the most effective opponents of the Russians when the latter entered Alaska-- fiercely resisting all challengers to protect their hard-won territory, which had made them among the wealthiest North West Coast tribes. The contemporary Chilkat population is approximately 1,200 people. While they were skilled carvers, producing totem poles, ivory, bone and wood sculptures, undoubtedly the product for which they are best known, and to which their name has become inseparably attached was the famous "Chilkat Blanket" (more accurately, a robe or shawl; these were never used as blankets). However, that textile was actually apparently originally a Tshimshian product, who called it a "dancing blanket;" it was subsequently adopted by the Chilkat, perhaps due to the prevalence of mountain goats in their region, as well as the skill of women weavers. Eventually the wide-ranging trading activities of the men made them identified with the Chilkat people.

Among Indians, Klukwan women were regarded the finest weavers of these magnificent robes, which customary rectangular designs, and she actually works her patterns into circular forms. The designs themselves represent animals and humans in very abstract forms; identification of these is not always possible, since they are conventionalized to a point where realism is no longer visible. The basic subjects are usually totemic animals common to the region, such as raven, bear, whale, eagle, killer whale, etc., and unless one is initiated into the intricate symbolism, it is often impossible to identify the creature depicted in the essentially x-ray form of the design. These are originally painted on wooden "pattern boards" by the men, and then given to the women, who copy the designs onto their weaving. When the weaving is complete, the long fringe sections left at the bottom of the textile are filled out with extra lengths of mountain goat wool to provide the graceful, swaying fringe which is such an important part of the overall appearance. These are made in many sizes, from large robes about 72 x 38 inches to small aprons measuring 18 x 38 inches. The weave is also used for hats, shirts, leggings, and other smaller products, sometimes trimmed with otter or seal fur. They were only worn on ceremonial occasions, and even when they were commonly made, were regarded as extremely valuable, and carefully stored away when not in use. They were, along with the famous "coppers," the most valuable trade items of the Northwest coast Indian people, and had a particularly important role in the *potlatch* ceremonies.

Chilkat goat hair blanket, with design of a killer whale

BIBLIOGRAPHY —

● HODGE, FREDERICK WEBB. Handbook of American Indians North of Mexico. Washington: Government Printing Office, 2 vols., 1907-10.
● MURDOCK, GEORGE P. Ethnographic Bibliography of North America.New Haven, CT: Human Relations Area Files Press, 1975.
● SWANTON, JOHN R. The Indian Tribes of North America. Washington, DC: U.S. Government Printing Office, 1952.

CHILLIWACK

(Canada; British Columbia) A Salish tribe on a river of the same name, who spoke the Cowichan dialect, though anciently Nooksak according to Boas. Their population in 1902 was 313. Their villages, mainly on the authority of Hill-Tout, are Atselits, Chiaktei, Kokaia, Shlalki, Skaialo, Skaukel, Skway, Skwealets, Stlep, Thaltelich.

BIBLIOGRAPHY —

● HODGE, FREDERICK WEBB. Handbook of American Indians North of Mexico. Washington: Government Printing Office, 2 vols., 1907-10.
● MURDOCK, GEORGE P. Ethnographic Bibliography of North America.New Haven, CT: Human Relations Area Files Press, 1975.
● SWANTON, JOHN R. The Indian Tribes of North America. Washington, DC: U.S. Government Printing Office, 1952.

CHILLUCKITTEQUAW

(U.S.; Wash.) A Chinookan tribe formerly living on the North side of Columbia River in Klickitat and Skamania counties, from about 10 miles below the Dalles to the neighborhood of the Cascades. In 1806 Lewis and Clark estimated their number at 2,400. According to Mooney a remnant of the tribe lived near the mouth of White Salmon River until 1880, when they removed to the Cascades, where a few still resided in 1895. The Smackshop were a subtribe.

BIBLIOGRAPHY —

● HODGE, FREDERICK WEBB. Handbook of American Indians North of Mexico. Washington: Government Printing Office, 2 vols., 1907-10.
● MURDOCK, GEORGE P. Ethnographic Bibliography of North America.New Haven, CT: Human Relations Area Files Press, 1975.
● SWANTON, JOHN R. The Indian Tribes of North America. Washington, DC: U.S. Government Printing Office, 1952.

CHILULA

(U.S.; California) Also called Yurok Tsulu-la, or "people of Tsulu," the Bald Hills. Chilula is an Americanized version of that name. With the Hupa and Whilkut, the Chilula formed one group of the Athapascan linguistic stock. They were located on or near lower Redwood Creek from near the inland edge of the heavy redwood belt to a few miles above Minor Creek. Some of their villages included Noleding, Kingkyolai, Tsinsilading, Tlocheke, and Kinahontahding, among others. *Kroe*

ber, 1925 estimated that there were 500 to 600 Chilula before contact with incoming white settlers. They were later reduced to two or three families and a few persons that were incorporated with the Hupa.

BIBLIOGRAPHY —

● HODGE, FREDERICK WEBB. Handbook of American Indians North of Mexico. Washington: Government Printing Office, 2 vols., 1907-10.
● MURDOCK, GEORGE P. Ethnographic Bibliography of North America.New Haven, CT: Human Relations Area Files Press, 1975.
● SWANTON, JOHN R. The Indian Tribes of North America. Washington, DC: U.S. Government Printing Office, 1952.

CHIMAKUAN FAMILY

(U.S.; Wash.) A linguistic family of the N.W. coast, represented by one small tribe, the Quileute, on the coast of Washington. There was formerly an eastern division of the family, the Chimakum, occupying the territory between Hood's canal and Port Townsend, which is now probably extinct. The situation of these two tribes, as well as certain traditions, indicate that in former times the family may have been more powerful and occupied the entire region to the South of the strait of Juan de Fuca from which they were driven out by the Clallam and Makah. This, however, is uncertain. Within historic times the stock has consisted solely of the two small branches mentioned above. They have borne a high reputation among their Indian neighbors for warlike qualities, but for the greater part have always been on friendly terms with the whites. In customs the Quileute, or eastern Chimakuan, resembled the Makah and Nootka; all were whalers. The Chimakuan dialects have not been thoroughly studied, but the material collected shows the language to be quite independent, thoroughly studied, but the material collected shows the language to be quite independent, though with certain phonetic and morphologic relations to the Salish and Wakashan.

BIBLIOGRAPHY —

● HODGE, FREDERICK WEBB. Handbook of American Indians North of Mexico. Washington: Government Printing Office, 2 vols., 1907-10.
● MURDOCK, GEORGE P. Ethnographic Bibliography of North America.New Haven, CT: Human Relations Area Files Press, 1975.
● SWANTON, JOHN R. The Indian Tribes of North America. Washington, DC: U.S. Government Printing Office, 1952.

CHIMARIKO.

(U.S.; California) Also called Kwoshonipu, a name probably given to them by the Shasta of Salmon River, and Meyemma, given to them by *Gibbs, 1853* . Chimariko is from the native word, chimar, or "person." Originally considered a distinct stock, the Chimariko are now classed in the

Hokan linguistic family. They were located on the canyon of Trinity River from around the mouth of New River to Canyon Creek. Some of their villages included Chichanma, at Taylor Flat; Maidjasore, at Thomas; and Tsudamdadji, at Burnt Ranch. The Chimariko were estimated to have 250 members in 1849, by *Kroeber, 1925*; only a few mixed bloods are now living.

BIBLIOGRAPHY —

● HODGE, FREDERICK WEBB. Handbook of American Indians North of Mexico. Washington: Smithsonian Institution: BAE Bulletin No. 30: U.S. GPO, 1907.
● SWANTON, JOHN R. The Indian Tribes of North America. Washington, DC: U.S. Government Printing Office, 1952.

CHIMU

(South America; Peru) (AD 1000-1470), a great empire located in northern coastal Peru, rivaled

Chimu mantle

the Inca until it was finally conquered by Tupac Ypanqui in 1470. In many early accounts it is known as Chimor. Growing out of the earlier Mochica civilization, the Chimu people occupied the Chicama, Chimu, Lambayeque, Moche and Piura Valleys, starting in approximately AD 900, and bursting into full flower a century later. Much of their culture reflects a revival of Mochica civilization, albeit in a somewhat less sophisticated and less finished manner. At its height, the Chimu empire covered a region extending about 600 miles along the coast, and sent trading parties as far distant as Ecuador and Bolivia. The first true cities appeared at this time, united by a system of highways, and the state itself was the Tlingit called *maxin,* "body fringe," a tribute to the long, graceful fringe of the textile. They are woven on a suspension (or drop) loom, consisting of two uprights and a horizontal bar, over which the warp strings are loosely strung and allowed to hang. Since it often requires more than six months to complete a robe, the weaver must protect her yarn; the warp, therefore, is wrapped in small pouches to keep it clean. Colors are usually black, white, yellow and blue-green; originally obtained from native plant and mineral pigments these later became supplanted by aniline dyes. The warp threads are two-strand twisted and shredded cedar bark, wrapped with mountain goat wool. The tapestry weaving is connected with a raised-outline weave of three-strand twining, which allows a unique "round weave" giving the weaver a departure from the more highly-developed agricultural civilization in which corn was the most important crop, supported by an extensive irrigation system. The capital was Chan Chan, near Trujillo; this great site--probably more of a ceremonial center than a true political capital--covers approximately ten

▲ ANCIENT SITES
● MODERN CITIES
---- INCA EMPIRE

CULTURE AREAS

CHIMÚ

VICUS

MOCHE

NAZCA

CHANCAY

Pre-Columbian Peruvian culture areas.

Chimu pottery

square miles, and is composed of ten huge rectangular walled inner sections. The scope of the archetectural skills of these people in working adobe can be realized by the fact that the surviving walls even yet rise to a height of 40 feet in some sections; the torrential rains which assail northern Peru about twice every century have gradually eroded the walls away. However, some of the better-preserved walls still show carvings and painted mural decorations. That this was a vast, bustling civilization is reflected in the tremendous quantities of Chimu art in wood, metal, clay, and textiles to be seen in private and museum collections throughout the world; they far outnumber the examples from any other Peruvian civilization. Chimu ceramics are usually monochromatic, characterized by a monotonous blackware made in press-molds with stirrup spouts, often including small monkeys and humans modeled on the bridge of the spout. Some are erotic, many are scenes of daily life, but all have a somewhat lifeless quality in contrast to the lively art of the earlier Mochica people, even though this is a continuum of that esthetic. Most of the silver which has survived from ancient Peru is of the Chimu period, as well as the great sheet-gold mummy masks, wooden mummy faces, and

cast copper knives and pins. Some of the latter are marvelous examples of intricate casting, with small bells, and other ornaments all included in the separate-yet-attached single casting. Chimu weaving is well known, usually in cotton, llama, alpaca, and vicuna wool, but it is usually less common than that from Chancay; it is the one major flash of color which has survived from this period which tends othwise to express itself in rather drab terms.

BIBLIOGRAPHY –

● STEWARD, JULIAN H. Handbook of South American Indians. 7 Vols.. Washington, DC: U.S. Govt. Printing Office. 1946-59.

CHINANTEC

(Mexico) live in relative isolation in the region known as the Chinanti, northwestern Oaxaca, Mexico. This tribe is divided into approxiamately fourteen municipios, each with several dependent communities and isolated from each other by mountains. The ecological setting is primarily tropical rainforest and is watered by several main rivers, all of which lie within the Papaloapan River Basin.

The tribe is divided into four groups by the mountains, but none of the mountains is so high nor so difficult as are the barriers between the Chinantec and other, distinct tribes. The four Chinantec groups are: 1. those living in the Valle Nacional area (linguistically defined as the *He-me;* 2. those living in the District of Choapam (linguistically defined as the *Wah- Mi;* 3. those in the northern and western area, with the exception of, 4. those in a few villages near and including Yolox. Many of the settlements date from precontact days.

The tribal name, *Chinantec,* and the regional name, *Chinantla,* derive from the Aztec word "chinamitl" meaning "an enclosed space"--a word signifying anything from a corral to a mountain-girt valley. It is thought that the term originally referred to an ancient capital now gone; possibly once found in the Valle Nacional and possibly close to the present town of that name. But in the valley there are several archaeological sites that are isolated and enclosed, and it is impossible at present to state if any of these is the original Chinantla.

Chinantecan is a language affiliated with Otomian, Topolocan, Manguean and others, all classified as Otomanguean. Chinantec, with its different dialects, constitutes the Chinantec language family. Divergences between local forms of Chinantec, which is apparently a close complex of several languages, have been measured up to 15 minimal centuries apart by glottochronology.

Very little archaeology has been accomplished in the region. The earliest historical mention of the Chinantec is by Bernal Diaz, who stated that the people were a vigorous nation, expert warriors and enemies of the Aztec, to whom, according to Bernal Diaz, they were not subject. The Spanish made their first expedition into the Chinantla to search for gold. Cortes sent a small party to pan the rivers in the neighborhood of Tuxtepec. Large quantities of gold were said to have been recovered. No mention of other treasures in the area is made. It is possible that there was nothing to plunder, knowing the character of the Spaniards and their actions elsewhere in Mexico. It is probable that by 1520 there were no Chinantec kings and that the civilization of the Chinantec was already at a low ebb. Answers to the questionnaire sent by order of Charles V of 1579, indicated that, contrary to the statements of Bernal Diaz, the Chinantec were subject to Moctezuma and that they paid heavy tribute to the Aztec leader. In addition to tribute, the Chinantec were obliged to make special prayers to their gods on behalf of Moctezuma, and to observe certain ceremonies--supporting the fact that Moctezuma and his governor were influential in the area.

It appears that just after the Conquest two pestilances befell the region, and the population in the area was reduced to a twentieth of its former size. For example, in Usila, there existed in 1579, 400 subject Indians, where prior to the Conquest there had been 16,000.

In the early 17th century, Chinantec were contacted by missionaries. The conversion of the tribe to Christianity was effected by Villa-Alta, which then, as now, lay within Zapotec territory. Villa-Alta had been founded by order of Cortes in 1527 as a small Spanish garrison. In 1548, a Dominican monastery was founded at Villa-Alta. Chiefly due to the extreme difficulty of communication with the Chinantec, not only because of their language but also because they lived scattered in *rancherias,* the obstruction to their conversion appeared almost insurmountable. In 1581, the Chinantec received their greatest apostle. The Dominican, Fr. Francisco de Sarvia, was to devote nearly 50 years to their conversion. He was the first to teach the Chinantec to write their language, and many of the religious customs which he initiated are still practiced by them at present.

There were changes in the lifeways of the Chinantec as a result of the influences of the Dominicans and their successors, the secular clergy. The Chinantec were made to wear clothes and to live in villages instead of in *rancherias* or isolated farms. They occasionally cultivated crops for Spanish landlords and learned to grow coffee and later bananas and tobacco. Horses, donkeys and cows were imported, but did not survive. A few of the Chinantec learned to read and write in their own language, but not necessarily in Spanish. The friars taught them passion plays and gave them new dances in place of their own, or found for their old dances a Christian moral. The conversion was slow, but the old customs were entangled in the new Christian dogma. But the tribe has retained its language, the calendar, certain customs in their communal life, their costume, the manner in which the women dress, their hair, their food, and certain traits in their character.

The most important of the survivals is the calendar, preserved solely because it is of agricultural, not mythological significance, and the month names were constantly in use for decisions as to when to sow or reap the crops.

The organization of the Chinantec is much the same today as it was after the evangelization by the friars in the late 16th century.

The Chinantec are subsistence agriculturalists, relying primarily on maize and beans. They supplement their diet with fowl and pigs, some yucca and yams, and fish from the numerous rivers. Fish is not consumed by groups who live in the mountains, but those close to rivers use nets, lines, and harpoons with detachable points. Fish are cooked directly over the fire, and a form of stone boiling is also known. Dairy products are not part of the diet, and meat is uncommon. Wild fruits are gathered, and some communities also cultivate bananas and coconuts. Alcoholic drinks are used to excess, and tobacco is commonly smoked by males. Narcotic seeds and mushrooms may exist in the eastern area, but are not generally used elsewhere in the territory.

The variety of terrain among and within subregions, plus historic factors, have influenced settlement patterns. There are congregated, semicongregated and dispersed communities. Settlements generally occur on promontories or terraced

The dress of the Chinantec women is characteristically pre-Hispanic. It consists of a cotton huipil, woven in red and white bands on a waist-loom (later embroidered in animal motifs, flowers and geometric designs) and a wrap-around skirt. A ruffle of ribbon and lace sewn on to the sleeves was later introduced. Strips of ribbon in alternate colored rectangles are applied over the woven fabric and embroidery in two bands going from back to front over the shoulders.

mountainsides. Only in areas that were the ancient seats of power, Usila and Valle Nacional, are the settlements on valley bottoms, surrounded by hamlets on the adjacent slopes. In general, the town plans are variations of the standard pattern which Spanish administrators imposed contact in 1805.

The center of social organization is the family. It is monogamous, patrilineal, with tendencies toward the extended family through campadrazgo, or godfather relationships. The political hierarchy of local and territorial units from the municipo to small places is regulated by the Mexican Constitution, the state constitution, and related legislation. The municipal government is responsible for the administration of lesser hamlets. The Chinatec have added or adapted certain ritual behavior to the assumption of office. Furthermore, offices are rotated among the members of the towns, as well as among bario units if necessary. The village also sets its own local requirements for officers. The officers are also committed to the advisory committee, and is made up of the senior members of the settlement, who qualify for the position by age or service, or both. The organization of the Chinatec is tied to the immediate neighborhoods, and only limited identification with the larger state or nation is known.

The lowland Chinantec, retain no traditional major arts, crafts, dances, drama, or other outlets. Humor is generally unsophicticated, and relationships tend to be relatively formal. The highland Chinantec, on the other hand, have retained a few crafts. Quiotepec produces tiles and some pottery; pita weaving is remembered, but weaving baskets of cloth and a number of other crafts have disappeared within recent times.

Although immediately after the Conquest, the population of the Chinantec was devastated, the population has recovered from at least the 1870s to the present day. The population of the tribe was estimated to have been 40,000 in 1960. Yet there seems to be a notable variation among the subregions, the western and central areas showing rather larger growth, the northern and northwestern, significantly less.

National programs in the area have had an impact on the population, especially in the manner in which monolingualism has dropped. Since 1947, the Mexican government program to develop the Papaloapan Basin has resulted in rapid changes. The marginal and isolated areas have been provided with modern facilities for communication and transportation, education, sanitation, and other features.

The Chinantec remain a relatively isolated tribe of subsistence agriculturalists and removed from the mainstream of Mexican culture. Even in the present day, they live a lifestyle that was developed in the 16th century as a result of their contact with the missionaries. *(see map page XIX)*

BIBLIOGRAPHY –

● BOWDITCH, CHARLES. P. Mexican and Central American Antiquities, Calendar Systems and History. Washington, D. C.: Bureau of American Ethnology- Bulletin 28: GPO, 1904.
● STEWARD, JULIAN H. Handbook of South American Indians. 7 Vols., Washington, DC: U.S. Govt. Printing Office, 1946-59.
● SWANTON, JOHN R. The Indian Tribes of North America. Washington, DC: U.S. Government Printing Office, 1952.
● THOMAS, CYRUS. Indian Languages of Mexico and Central America and Their Geographical Distribution. Bureau of American Ethnology Bulletin 44: Washington, D. C.: GPO, 1911.

CHINOOK

(U.S.; Wash.: Canada; B.C.) was the most important tribe of the Chinookian linguistic family located in the Pacific Northwest. The Chinook was famous as a trading nation before a plague wiped it out.

The tribe was located in upper Washington state and Lower British Columbia. the Chinookian language stock is radically different from other language stocks.

The village was the chief village social institution of the Chinooks. Villages were fairly fermanent structures but the people moved around following their main food supplies which were salmon and berries. Their houses were wooden and long, holding three or four families, sometimes as many as 20 people.

There was a headman or chief in each Chinook village. Depending on a chief's qualities, he could be the major influence in several adjoining tribes.

Head deformation was a common trait among the Chinook. Anyone without a deformed head was considered a social disgrace. Heads were deformed by flattening infants' heads with boards. Only slaves, which the Chinook got through barter with other tribes, had normally shaped heads.

Though the Chinook were probably met earlier, Lewis and Clark established the first definite white winter. The caribou were the center of a large complex of beliefs and practices that were intended to show respect for the caribou by preventing abuses in the killing, processing, and use of caribou. Men provided caribou to the women who processed them for foodstuffs and other things. the men that disposed of the remains by either burning them in the camp or in the bush. Special attention was paid to remove caribou bone debris and keeping it away from the dogs.

They estimated then that there were approximately 16,000 Chinooks. Soon after, Chinooks became great middlemen in a thriving trade between whites, themselves and other tribes. This business

Chinook Burial

gave rise to the "Chinook jargon" a combination of English, Indian, French and Russian languages used by traders all along the North Pacific coast until the 20th century. Despite their native trade whites considered Chinooks deceitful and sometimes dangerous.

In 1829 a form of ague fever killed more than four-fifths of the Chinook. Subsequently united with the Chehalis Indians, a few hundred remained until about the 20th century. (see map page XVII)

BIBLIOGRAPHY —

● HODGE, FREDERICK WEBB. Handbook of American Indians North of Mexico. Washington: Government Printing Office, 2 vols., 1907-10.
● MURDOCK, GEORGE P. Ethnographic Bibliography of North America.New Haven, CT: Human Relations Area Files Press, 1975.
● SWANTON, JOHN R. The Indian Tribes of North America. Washington, DC: U.S. Government Printing Office, 1952.

CHIPAYA

(South America; Bolivia) of the Charangas area of Bolivia are still in existence. They make their living largely from trading llamas, sheep milk, and cheese to neighboring Aymara farmers for quinoa and potatoes. They practice some agriculture, but the terrain in which they live is the driest and least hospitable portion of the Altiplano, and their crop production consequently satisfies only a small part of their need. This group still uses a mode of dress imposed on them by the Spaniards four centuries ago.

Chipaya women.

Although they have not suffered as intensely at the hands of the Aymara as have the Uru, the Chipaya are also a dwindling population. Various estimates would suggest that there are no more than 300 of them. Surrounded by a large and probably growing population of Aymara, the Chipaya have increasingly intermarried with their neighbors. Aymara influence has been so strong that members of the group have been adopting the language for everyday use. Most Chipaya are bilingual in Puquina and Aymara, and recent reports indicate thatmany of the younger members of the group have never learned their ancestral tongue. Between the acculturation of the Chipaya and the drastic disappearance of the Uru, their common language, Puquina, will probably be extinct within a very few years.

BIBLIOGRAPHY —

● STEWARD, JULIAN H. Handbook of South American Indians. 7 Vols., Washington, DC: U.S. Govt. Printing Office, 1946-59.

CHIPEWYAN

(Canada) are the most easterly of the Canadian Athapaskan speaking tribes, a language family which includes the Apache and Navaho of the American southwest and a few small groups along the Pacific Coast of the United States. They refer to themselves as *dene,* but the word Chipewyan is reportedly derived from a Cree term referring to "pointed skins", a reference either to the hats the Chipewyan wore or their way of drying beaver hides during the early fur trade. They were called "Northern" Indians in the early accounts of the fur trade.

The Chipewyan were in contact with European fur traders on a sustained basis by 1715 but they may have had occasional contact with explorers and traders as early as 1640. At the time of contact the Chipewyan were centered on tree line in the Northwest Territories of Canada. Their early cycle took many of them far out into the barren grounds in summer and into the boreal forest in winter. The Chipewyan ranged beyond their home areas to engage in warfare, more properly raids, with their neighbors and particularly with the Cree and the Eskimo. They were an aggressive people who raided their neighbors but warfare, in a European sense, was unknown. The Chipewyan are great travellers and it is probable that they also engaged in wide ranging but sporadic trade. Their population roamed over an acre some 200,000 square miles though they did not have exclusive control of all of it.

By the 18th century the Chipewyan had begun a massive territorial expansion. This was brought about by increased involvement in fur trapping, a negotiated peace with the Cree, and depopulation of the Northern Prairie provinces by disease. The Chipewyan expanded westward between Great Slave Lake and Lake Athabasca, southwards to the Churchill River and eastward to Hudson's Bay at the present site of Churchill, Manitoba. At the present time the Chipewyan are found in Manitoba, Saskatchewan, Alberta, and the Northwest Territories and their population is some fifteen thousand, of which about half are recognized by the Canadian government as treaty Indians.

From the earliest accounts the Chipewyan appear to have been primarily concerned with the hunting of caribou. The barren ground caribou could supply most of the Chipewyan material needs and all of their dietary requirements. Caribou hides were used for clothing, storage vessels, mats, blankets, footgear, and teepee covers. They were processed into leather, worked with the hair on, used as rawhide and served many other purposes. The bone and antler of the caribou were used for tools, and the flesh provided food. Meat and fat were used fresh or dried to provide the reservoir of food necessary to survive the winter and the stomach contents of caribou were made into a soup which provided a basic source of plant food.

Caribou were crucial to the subsistence system and movement patterns of the Chipewyan but they were not the only food resource the Chipewyan had. Musk ox provided a critical alternate resource for life on the barren grounds and moose were a major food source in the forest. Many small animals and birds were used regularly as food sources with the most important being snowshoe hare, waterfowl, spruce grouse, and ptarmigan. Virtually all non- predatory mammals and nearly all birds were eaten; the most important ones were lynx, black bear, and grizzly bear. Beaver seems to have been particularly important as food animals during travels.

The role of fish in the Chipewyan diet is somewhat uncertain. They were used extensively as a food source during travel and are the largest single food source in the region but the extensive utilization of fish for food and the movement of families to fishing spots in the spring and fall may be characteristic of the 20th century with its larger dog teams.

The Chipewyan were only slowly drawn into the fur trade when compared to other Northern Athapascan tribes. At first they assumed a role as middle-men between other Athapaskan groups to the Northwest and the fur traders. The Chipewyan then began their expansion to the southwest. The transition zone of the boreal forest that was so rich in caribou was poor in fur-bearing animals. In order to gain the now desired western goods the Chipewyan were forced to trap their own furs. To do this they had to enter the boreal forest proper.

This expansion required major adjustments on the part of the Chipewyan as it meant exploiting an environment that lacked the barren ground caribou. Many Chipewyan returned to the transition zone frequently and most never left the transition zone but those that remained in the boreal forest, and their descendents, became quite different from the northern Chipewyan who are referred to as "caribou-eater." These differences are today marked by differences in dialect, kinship usage, social practice, and custom as well as different ecological adjustments.

By the beginning of the 19th century the Chipewyan were settled into a basic social pattern in which the bulk of the year was spent in the bush hunting and fishing. They lived in clusters of a few families or small villages. Occasional trips were made into trading posts but their basic life was one with little contact with outsiders. There were considerable variations in the degree of contact of non-Chipewyan with the more northern groups often a century behind southern groups in the degree of contact. This pattern remained relatively constant throughout the 19th century. It appears that the Chipewyan continued to use the traditional subsistence methods, the caribou pound, the fence, the spearing of swimming caribou, throughout the 19th century. Western technological items were added as the became available, particularly fishnets, but they were conservative and even the gun did not become the major subsistence tool until well after the appearance of the repeating rifle.

The slow process of adjustment to Canadian society in the 19th century, which was most noticeably marked by the withdrawal from the barren grounds in the North and increasing conformation of Chipewyan beliefs to Christian ones, was shattered by the influx of white fur trappers around the time of World War I. The intensity of contact increased greatly and the nature of the contact changed as different types of Europeans entered the North. Towns sprang up in great numbers, (e.g. Goldgfields and Stony Rapids) and a great many temporary alliances were formed between Indian women and white trappers. Treaty status, which meant little before this time, became important as Indians sold their treaty status to the government in order to obtain the right to purchase alcoholic beverages and have better access to the few jobs in the area.

The depression of the 1930s produced disruptions in the Chipewyan social system as small farmers (and small store owners) in the south lost their land and more whites entered the North in search of fur. As fur prices were relatively high during the depression many of the Chipewyan were in a period of relative affluence. Unfortunately the increased human predation upon the caribou combined with the very extensive use of poison by white trappers disrupted the ecological balance of most of the North and resulted in a drastic drop in the size of the caribou herds by the mid-1940s.

Even though most white trappers withdrew from the North with the beginning of the World War Ii boom, the post-war North was a bleak place for the Chipewyan. The severity of conditions was partly offest by the extraordinary high prices paid for a few fur species after World War II but by 1950 it was not possible for the Chipewyan in the North to sustain their basic subsistence economy. In response to the spectre of starving Indians, and the potential value of the region's massive uranium depostits, the various levels of Canadian government began to take an active interest in the north. The 1950s and 1960s were periods in which the Chipewyan were forced away from bush life and into permanent villages. Health care, schooling, welfare and other government services were increased greatly, an increase that has accelerated throughout the 1970s. By the late 1960s all the Chipewyan had become village dwellers, at enormous social and emotional cost, who exploited the bush on a limited and seasonal basis.

Technology and social life. At the time of contact the Chipewyan dressed largely in caribou hide clothing in the form of open crotched leggings and a lengthy shirt. Stone, bone, and wood were the primary naterials used for tools but some use was made of native copper. The dwelling was a tipi covered with caribou hides and seems to have averaged between seven and eight persons. The Chipewyan were highly mobile, moving several times a year at the minimum, and occasionally concentrations of Indians in excess of 200 people are reported but they were temporary.

Religion was based upon magical power obtained in dreams and this was most fully developed by the shamans. A great deal of concern was paid to ritual treatment of prey animals and the division of labor between the sexes was strictly enforced. Women, especially during menustration and pregnancy, were sources of pollution to the magical power of males. Women were strictly regulated in their conduct, particularly when it came to dealing with caribou and male hunting or magical implements.

Social organization was based upon extended families allied by ties of descent and marriage into small groups. Kinship was bilateral. Membership in groups was very fluid. There was no political organization that was formalized with offices or chiefs. Leadership was a function of influence derived from demonstrated magical power. Magical power was demonstrated through success at hunting, sorcery, or other competitive activities.

The Chipewyan were subject to the ill effects of a number of epidemics with the smallpox epidemic of 1781 and the Asian flu epidemic of 1918 being particularly disrupting. Recurring epidemics of measles, mumps, and other diseases as well as tuberculosis all resulted in a great many deaths. The population of the Chipewyan has risen more or less steadily since 1900 and has often increased dramatically in local areas after the arrival of effective methods of western medicine.

BIBLIOGRAPHY –

● BIRKET-SMITH, KAJ. Contributions to Chipewyan Ethnology. Fifth Thule Expedition Report, no. 5, 1930.
● JENNESS, D. Indians of Canada.Bulletin of the Canadian National Museum, no. 65, 1960.
● SWANTON, JOHN R. The Indian Tribes of North America. Washington, DC: U.S. Government Printing Office, 1952.
● WISSLER, CLARK. Indians of the U.S., Four Centuries of Their History and Culture. New York, NY: Doubleday, Doran & Co.. 1940.

CHIPPEWA

(U.S.; Midwest; Northwest; Canada)-popular adaptation of Ojibway "to roast till puckered up," referring to the puckered seam on their moccasins; from ojib "to pucker up" ub-way "to roast". One of the largest tribes north of Mexico, whose range was formerly along both shores of Lake Huron and Lake Superior, extending across Minnesota to Turtle Mountains, North Dakota. Although strong in numbers and occupying an extensive territory, the Chippewa were never prominent in history, owing to their remoteness from the frontier during the period of the colonial wars. According to tradition they are part of an Algonquian body, including the Ottawa and Potawatomi, which separated into divisions when it reached Mackinaw in its westward movement, having come from some point north or north east of Mackinaw. According to some reports they were settled in a large village at La Pointe, Wisconsin, about the time of the discovery of America. About 1612 they suddenly abandoned this locality, many of them going back to the Sault, while others settled at the west end of Lake Superior, where Father Allouez found them in 1665-67.

They were first noticed in the Jesuit Relation of 1640 ("people of the Sault"), as residing at the Sault, and it is possible that Nicollet met them in 1634 or 1639. In 1642 they were visited by Raymbaut and Jogues, who found them at the Sault and at war with a people to the west, doubtless the Sioux. A remnant or offshoot of the trie resided north of Lake Superior after the main body moved south to Sault Ste Marie, or when it had reached the vicinity of the Sault. The Marameg, a tribe closely related to if not a actual division of the Chippewa, who dwelt along the north shore of the lake, were apparently incorporated with the latter while they were at the Sault, or at any rate prior to 1670. On the north the Chippewa are so closely connected with the Cree and Maskegon that the three can be distinguished only by those intimately acquainted with their dialects and customs, while on the south the Chippewa, Ottawa, and Potawatomi have always formed a sort of loose confederacy, frequently disignated in the last century the Three Fires. It seems to be well established that some of the Chippewa have resided north of Lake Superior from time immemorial. These and the Marameg claimed the north side of the lake as their country. According to Perrot some of the Chippewa living south of Lake Superior in 1670-99, although relying chiefly on the chase, cultivated some maize, and were then at peace with the neighboring Sioux. It is singular that this author omits to mention wild rice (Zizania aquatica) among their food supplies, since the possession of wild-rice fields was one o the chief causes of thier wars with the Dakota, Foxes, and other nations. About this period they first came into possession of firearms, and were pushing their way westward, alternately at peace and at war with the Sioux and in almost constant conflict with the Foxes. The French, in 1692, reestablished a trading post at Shaugawaumikong, now La Pointe, Ashland county, Wisconsin, which became an important Chippewa settlememt. In the beginning of the 18th century the Chippewa succeeded in driving the Foxes, already reduced by a war with the French, from northern Wisconsin, compelling them to take refuge with the Sauk. They then turned against the Sioux, driving them across the Mississippi and south to Minnesota river, and continued their westward march across Minnesota and North Dakota until they occupied the headwaters of Red River and established their westernmost bank in the Turtle Mountains. It was not until after 1736 that they obtained a foothold west of Lake Superior. While the main divisions of the tribe were thus extending their possessions in the west, others overran the peninsula between Lake Huron and Lake Erie, which had long been claimed by the Iroquois through conquest. The Iroquois were forced to withdraw, and the whole region was occupied by the Chippewa bands, most of whom are now known as Missisauga, alhough they still call themselves Ojibaw. The Chippewa took part

Chippewa women harvesting wild rice

Chippewa women in costume

with the other tribes of the north west in all the wars against the frontier settlements to the close of the war of 1812. Those living within the United States made a treaty with the government in 1815, and have since remained peaceful, all residing on reservations or allotted lands within their original territory in Michigan, Wisconsin, Minnesota, amd North Dakota, with the exception of the small band of Swan Creek and Black River Chippewa, who sold thier lands in south Mighigan in 1836 and are now with the Munsee in Franklin county, Kansas.

Schoolcraft, who was personally acquainted with the Chippewa and married a woman of the tribe, describes the Chippewa warriors as equaling in pysical appearance the best formed of the north west Indians, with the possible exception of the Foxes. Their long and successful contest with the Sioux and Foxes exhibited their bravery and determination, yet they were uniformaly friendly in their relations with the French. The Chippewa are a timber people. Although they have long been in friendly relations with the whites, Christianity has had but little effect on them, owing largly to the conservatism of the native medicine- men. It is affirmed by Warren, who is not disposed to accept any statement that tends to disparage the character of his people, that, accoridng to tradition, the division of the tribe residing at La Pointe practised

cannibalism, while Father Belcout affirms that, although the Chippewa of Canada treated the vanquished with most horrible barbarity and at these times ate human flesh, they looked upon cannibalism, except under such conditions, with horror. It was the custom of the Pillager band to allow a warrior who scalped an enemy to wear on his head two eagle feathers, and the act of capturing a wounded prisoner on the battlefield earned the distiction of wearing five. Like the Ottawa, they were expert in the use of the canoe, and in their early history depended largely on fish for food. There is abundant evidence that polygamy was common, and indeed it still occurs among the more wandering band. Their wigwams were made of birch bark or of grass mats; poles were first planted in the ground in a circle, the tops bent together and tied, and the bark or mats thrown over them, leaving a smoke hole at the top. They imagined that the shade, after the death of the body, followed a wide beaten path, leading toward the west, finally arriving in a country abounding in everything the Indian desires. It is a general belief among the northern Chippewa that the Spirit often returns to visit the grave, so long as the body is not reduced to dust. Their creation myth is that common among the northern Algonquians. Like most other tribes they believe that a mysterious power dwells in all objects, animate and inanimate. Such objects are manitus, which are ever wakeful and quick to hear everything in the summer, but in winter, after snow falls, are in a torpid state. The Chippewa regard dreams as revelations, and some object which appears therein is often chosen as a tutelary diety. The Medewiwin, or grand medicine soceity, was formerly a powerful organization of the Chippewa, which controlled the movements of the tribe and was a formidable obstacle to the introduction of Christianity. When a Chippewa died it was customary to place the body in a grave, sometimes in a sitting posture, or to scoop a shallow cavity in the earth and deposit the body therein on its back or side, covering it with earth so as to form a small mound, over which boards, poles, or birch bark were placed. According to McKenney (Tour to the Lakes, 1827), the Chippewa of Fond du Lac, Wisconsin, practised scaffold burial in winter, the corpse being wrapped in birchbark. Mourning for a lost relative continued for a year, unless shortened by the meda or by certain exploits in war.

It is impossible to determine precisely the past or present numbers of the Chippewa, as in former times only a small part of the tribe came in contact with the whites at any period, and they are now so mixed with other tribes in many quarters that no separate returns are given. The principal estimates are as follow: In 1764, about 25,000; 1783 and 1794, about 15,000; 1843, about 30,000; 1851, about 28,000. It is probable that most of these estimates take no account of more remote bands. In 1884 there were in Dakota 914; in Minnesota, 5,885; in Wisconsin, 3,656; in Michigan 3,500 returned separately, and 6,000 Chippewa and Ottawa, of whom perhaps one-third are Chippewa; in Kansas, 76 Chippewa and Munsee. The entire number in the United States at this time was therefore about 16,000. In British America those of Ontario, including the Nipissing, numbered at the same time about 9,000, while in Manitoba and the Northwest Territories there were 17,129 Chippewa and Cree on reservations under the same agencies. At the turn of the century the Chippewa probably numbered 30,000 to 32,000-15,000 in British America and 14,144 in the United States, exclusive of about 3,000 in Michigan.

As the Chippewa were scattered over a region extending 1,000 miles from east to west, they had a large number of villages, bans and local divisions. Some of the bands bore the name of the village, lake, or river near which they resided, but these were grouped under larger divisions or subtribes which occupied certain fixed limits and were distinguished by marked differences. According to Warren there were ten of these principal divisions: Kechegummewininewug, on the south shore of Lake Superior; Betonukeengainubejig, in north Wisconsin; Munominikasbeenhug, on the headwaters of St Croix river in Wisconsin and Minnesota; Wahsuahgunewininewug, at the head of Wisconsin river; Ottawa Lake Men, on Lac Court Oreilles, Wisconsin; Kitchisibiwininiwug, on the upper Mississippi in Minnesota; Mukmeduawininewug, or Pillagers, on Leech lake, Minnesota; Sugwaundugahwininewug, north of Lake Superior; Kojejewininewug, on Rainy lake and right about the north boundary of Minnesota; and Wazhush, on the north west side of Lake Superior at the Canadian border.

In recent times, the Chippewa population has totaled approx. 65,000, divided about equally between the U.S. and Canada.

BIBLIOGRAPHY —

● BARNOUW. VICTOR. Chippewa Social Atomism. American Anthropologist, vol. 63, no. 5, pt. 1, Oct. 1961.
● CONGRESS. 43rd, 1st Session, H. Misc. Doc. 149, (Resolution of the Legislature of Minnesota Relative to Sale of School, Timber, and Swamp Lands.), Feb. 24, 1874.
-----46th, 2d Session, H. Rept. 1576. (Lands in Severalty to Indians...re: Bill to Authorize Sec'y of Interior to Allot Lands in Severalty to Indians), May 28, 1880.

Lodge of the Chippewa

● GILFILLAN, REV. JOSEPH A. The Ojibways in Minnesota. MN: Minnesota Historical Society Collections IX, 1898-1900.
● HARMON, GEORGE DEWEY. Sixty Years of Indian Affairs, Political, Economic, and Diplomatic, 1789-1850. Chapel Hill, NC: University of North Carolina Press, 1941.
● HODGE, FREDERICK WEBB. Handbook of American Indians North of Mexico. Washington: Government Printing Office, 1907.
● INDIANS AT WORK. vol. VII, no. 6, Feb., 1940.
● THE INDIAN IN MINNESOTA. A Report to Governor Luther W. Youngdahl. MN: By The Governor's Interracial Commission of Minnesota, 1947.
● INDIAN OFFICE REPORT. 1839, 1843, 1847, 1849, 1850, 1869, 1872, 1874, 1876, 1877, 1880, 1881, 1882, 1883, 1884, 1885, 1887, 1888, 1889, 1890, 1892, 1893, 1894.
● KAPPLER, CHARLES J. Indian Affairs, Laws & Treaties. Washington, 1833.
● KEISE, REV. ALBERT. Lutheran Mission Work Among the American Indians. Minneapolis, MN: Augsburg Pub., House, 1922.
● LEVI, CAROLLISSA. Chippewa Indians of Yesterday and Today. New York, NY: Pageant Press, 1956.
● LYFORD, CARRIE A. The Crafts of the Ojibwa (Chippewa). Phoenix, AZ Phoenix Indian School, 1943.
● MINNESOTA HISTORICAL SOCIETY. Collections of. vol. 5, St. Paul, MN: 1885.
● MURDOCK, GEORGE P. Ethnographic Bibliography of North America. New Haven, CT: Human Relations Area Files Press, 1975.
● NORTON, SISTER MARY AQUINAS. Catholic Missionary Activities in the Northwest, 1818-1864. Washington: The Catholic University of America, 1930.
● PRUITT, O. J. A Tribe of Chippewa Indians. Annals of Iowa, vol. 33, no. 4, 3d series, April, 1956.
● SWANTON, JOHN R. The Indian Tribes of North America. Washington, DC: U.S. Government Printing Office, 1952.

CHIQUITO

(South America; Bolivia) The province of Chiquitos of Eastern Bolivia, bounded on the south by the Chaco, on the west by the Guapay River, the north by latitude 15 W, and on the east by the Paraguay River, was home to a number of tribes and sub-tribes of Indians whose exact locations and linguistic affiliations at the time of European contact have been lost, if, indeed, they were ever known. Since the time of the Conquest, the Indians in this province have been lumped together as "Chiquitos", the "little ones," regardless of apparent cultural and linguistic differences. A linguistic isolate, Chiquitoan, is spoken in the region but since the time of the Conquest, it has been developed with some of deliberation into a *lingua franca* of the area and thus there is no way of determining its original distribution.

Spanish awareness of the Province of Chiquitos came early when in 1542, a party of Spaniards sailed up the Paraguay River and trekked westward on a four days' journey. In 1543, Cabeza de Vaca sent an expedition westward which encountered Chiquito Indians. Final conquest of the province occurred between 1557-1560, and the city of Santa Cruz was founded as a way to control the newly- subjugated Indians. However, after forty years, the settlement was moved and the Chiquitos reverted to their former way of life.

Late in the seventeenth century, a major threat to the Chiquitos arrived in the persons of Brazilian slavers who wiped out entire tribes and destroyed others by taking them to the coast of Brazil and selling them. The Jesuits, who were in the process of establishing missions in the province prevented the complete extermination of the Chiquito Indians be defeating the slave traders with the help of a small group of Spanish soldiers. In the ensuing sixty years, the Jesuits concentrated the Indians into the eight missions which they established. Starting as early as 1716, the Jesuits began using the Chiquitos to bring about the missionization of other tribes in the area by sending them and their greatly feared poisoned arrows against such people as the Carera, Mbaya, and Zamuco. Captives were brought back to the missions and the process of assimilation began. In modern times, descendents of these missionized tribes cannot be distinguished from the Chiquitos. In 1766, the year before the Jesuits were expelled from South America, a census of the missions showed a total population of 23,788 Indians. After the Jesuits left, life on the missions deteriorated; much of the native culture had been lost, and the Indians remained only partially assilimated--the Jesuits' goal never reached. Epidemics occurred and the population decliced quickly.

Precise information about the Chiquito proper is difficult to obtain, but it is known that they were horticulturalists of the tropical forest variety, cultivating sweet and bitter manioc, maize, peanuts, pumpkins, gourds, tobacco and pineapples. After the arrival of the Spaniards, they also grew rice and cacao trees. Their principal crop was sweet manioc. Men used hardwood digging sticks to till the fields. Although horticulture was the main subsistence activity, the Chiquito also depended upon hunting and fishing which they did on a seasonal basis, departing for the bush in small groups after the harvest. Bow and arrow were used, and fish were taken by trapping, shooting with bow and arrow, and drugging. Game was preserved during the hunt by broiling it on a *babracot*. In August, the men returned to the villages to begin work in the fields. In some areas of the province, wells were dug during the dry season.

Chiquito houses were small thatched huts, shaped like beehives, with doors close to the ground, presumably to keep out insects. In addition to several of these small huts, each village contained a men's house where young men and adolescent boys slept. These men's houses have been described as large, open sheds where visitors were received and feasts celebrated. Each Chiquito village was protected by formidable palisades of thorny hedges and by poisoned caltrops, causing the Spanish soldiers much difficulty in conquering

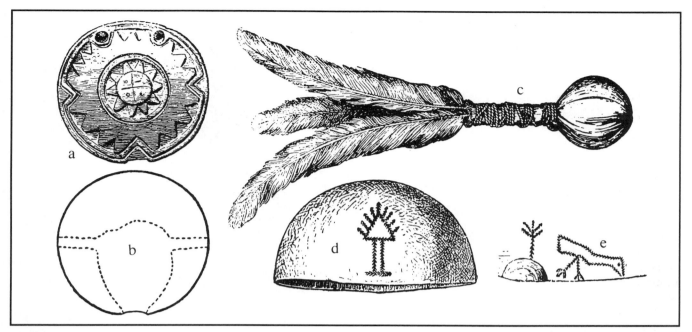

Artifacts from Chiquitos, *Churapa* Indians. *a*, wooden whistle; *b*, cross section of whistle; *c*, ball of cornhusks and feather for "shuttlecock" game; *d*, incised gourd; *e*, design from other side of *d*.

the Chiquito. Houses were simply furnished with hammocks and mats. Platform beds were a post-contact addition.

Little is known of the social and political organization of the Chiquito apart from the fact that they appear to have been patrilineally organized. Rank distinctions based on wealth, prowess in battle, and chieftainship existed. Chiefs were selected from a group of the best warriors and conducted village affairs with the aid of a council of old men. Polygyny existed, probably sororal, only among the chiefs, who, it was said, needed several wives to help organize the village feasts which were part of the chief's duties. Drinking bouts were arranged on a village-wide basis and neighboring communities were invited to spend several days drinking *chicha* made of manioc, maize, and fruits. During this time, old quarrels were adjudicated.

Rituals connected with the life cycle were reported for the Chiquito. The *couvade* was practiced after the birth of a child, and even before childbirth, the husband observed certain hunting taboos. No initiation rites were observed, but young men wishing to marry had to prove their hunting skills. This, of course, indicates the importance of hunting in the Chiquito lifestyle. Death was marked with a simple ceremony; the deceased was buried with his favorite weapon and food. The widow remarried after a short period of mourning.

More complex ceremonialism was seen in the Chiquito recreational activities, particularly in the dances and in their favorite ball game, played with a rubber ball for point score. Dancing and taunting preceded the game and to the victors belonged all the beer which was specially brewed for the occasion.

In addition to his social and military duties, the village chief was also a shaman who used his special powers to cure and to discover sorcerers. Disease was thought to be caused by one of four methods: an object entering the body, a spirit, sorcery, or breaking one of the traditional taboos. The shaman treated object intrusion by sucking and spirit entry by vomiting a blackish substance and beating on the ground around the patient to cause the spirit to flee. In cases of sorcery, the shaman was supposed to reveal the name so that the patient's family might take revenge. Women were often suspected of witchcraft, particularly any women of whom the patient might have dreamed. In the case of taboo transgression, the shaman treated the patient by encouraging him to make a full confession, a practice fairly rare in South America. The shamans rekindled their powers each new moon by going into seclusion and talking at length with their special spirits. Among the Chiquitoan tribes such as the Manasi, there was a distinction made between priests and curers, indicating Andean influence and the beginnings of a more complex social and political organization. The Chiquito proper believed in nature spirits and recognized the moon as a female deity but made no special worship of her. The forces of nature such as thunder and lightning showed that the spirits were angry. The Chiquito, however, gave great import to the omens and divinations which were derived from observing plants, animals, and birds.

BIBLIOGRAPHY –

● STEWARD, JULIAN H. Handbook of South American Indians. 7 Vols., Washington, DC: U.S. Govt. Printing Office, 1946-59.

CHIRICAHUA APACHE

(U.S.; Ariz., N.Mex.) (enemy) of the Southwest call themselves *dine,inde,tinde,*words that in various dialects signify "the people." Until they were subdued by the white man they were the most warlike tribe in the Southwest United States. Their fighting spirit was especially evident in the period 1870-1900, when the encroachments of white settlers roused them to fierce resentment. They are named for the Chiricahua Mountains of the Southwest.

History. When in 1879 the Chiricahua were placed on the Ojo Caliente reserve in New Mexico, the leader, Cochise made raids that caused the authorities to move them to Tularosa. Cochise escaped with a group of followers, but returned to his band when it was established on the Chiricahua Reservation in 1872.

The Chiricahua Reservation was abolished in 1876, and the Apache were moved once more, in accordance with the policy of concentration. In 1877 Geronimo, together with other chiefs, joined by members of the tribe from Mexico, began a series of raids in southern Arizona and New Mexico. In 1882 he surrendered to General George Crook, but three years later assembled another band and once more terrorized the settlers of southern Arizona. He and his band finally surrendered in 1886 and were imprisoned at Fort Pickens, Florida. Geronimo died in the military prison at Fort Sill, Oklahoma in 1909.

Another group of Chiricahua, under the leadership of Victorio, resented their transfer from the Mescalero Reserve in New Mexico and twice escaped from Carlos, only to be returned. When they had gone back to Mescalero for a third time, arrangements were made for them to be permitted to remain there. Indictments against Victorio and some followers, however, led him to flee and take to raiding again. Often opposed by troops outnumbering them four to one, Victorio's band of three hundred warriors inflicted more damage than received. When, in 1880, he was killed in a fight with Mexican troops, the rest of the group surrendered. In 1990 the Apache's last foray took place, when a group in Chiricahua raided a Mormon settlement.

Even after the Apache were at last restricted to their settlements, the white man persisted in his encroachments. Early in the 1890s a cattle com-

Victorio

pany was allowed to graze a herd of 2,000 cattle on the Apache reserve. Several years later, an Indian complained that the company's cattle were trespassing on his land. Investigation revealed that the company was pasturing 12,000 instead of 2,000 on the reserve, and was paying no grazing charges. The company agreed to a lease, and other big cow outfits moved in later. The income from grazing rights was an easy solution to an Apache's living problem, although it amounted to no more than $40 yearly for each Indian at the time.

Culture. The Indians' employment by the ranchers made them expert cowhands, and they decided that what they had to do for the white men they could do for themselves. They applied to Washington for the recovery of their lands, and in 1923 a sympathetic Indian commissioiner ordered the cattle companies off the reserve. The Indians were the final victors in the long struggle for possession; the last company left their land in 1936.

Originally a nomadic people, the Apache, whose numbers in the Southwest are several thousand, were little given to agriculture. But today they grow garden vegetables and are supplied with meat from their fine herds of cattle. These are a highly important factor in Apache company. On the San Carlos and Fort Apache Reservations are cattle. These reservations occupy a mountainous area of a hundred miles square in eastcentral Arizona.

The religion of the Apache is noteworthy for its great number of rituals. There is a ceremony for almost every event life may afford, and dances or songs are a part of certain ceremonies. The Apache conception of the deity is *Usen,* a being without sex or place, that cannot be approached directly, but whose influence must flow through such an object or phenomenon in nature as the sun, lightning, the owl, or the snake.

(see map page XVII)

BIBLIOGRAPHY —

● HODGE, FREDERICK WEBB. Handbook of American Indians North of Mexico. Washington: Government Printing Office, 2 vols., 1907-10.
● MURDOCK, GEORGE P. Ethnographic Bibliography of North America.New Haven, CT: Human Relations Area Files Press, 1975.
● OPLER, MORRIS EDWARD. An Apache Life- Way. New York, NY: Cooper Square Publishers, Inc., 1965.
● SWANTON, JOHN R. The Indian Tribes of North America. Washington, DC: U.S. Government Printing Office, 1952.

CHIRIGUANO

(South America; Bolivia) The Tupian-speaking Chiriguano are relative latecomers to the Andean foothills of eastern Bolivia, where they settled immediately south of the Llanos de Chiquitos at the northern end of the Gran Chaco from the upper Pilcomayo River to the upper Guapay River. Escaping from the Portuguese invasion of Brazil, the Chiriguano moved westward across the Gran Chaco in successive migrations from the last quarter of the fifteenth century through the sixteenth century in search of the "Land of the Grandfather," a search which ended at the very borders of the Inca empire. The warlike Chiriguano challenged the power of the Inca, raiding their settlements as well as those of other tribes in the area. One such party carried with it Alajo Garcia, the first white to visit the empire. Subsequent Inca reprisals did little to stop the Chiriguano who strengthened their hold on the area. The Chiriguano continued raiding throughout the seventeenth century, destroying settlements and harassing Spanish troops. Attempts to missionize the Chiriguano were quite useless and all the missions in the region were sacked by the Indians in the early eighteenth and early nineteenth centuries were the most successful. Pacified under the protection of the Franciscan missions until 1929, the Chiriguano prospered. Having an aboriginal population of only a few thousand, according to sixteenth and seventeenth century recorders, the Chiriguano in 1928 were censussed at some 20,000. But where Inca and Spaniard failed, the Chaco War succeeded in breaking up Chiriguano culture. Many of the Indians migrated to Argentina to work in the sugar factories; others slipped away and became assimilated into mestizo society.

When the Chiriguano arrived in eastern Bolivia, they found a large and economically advanced population of sedentary farmers known as the Chane. The Chiriguano quickly asserted control over these rather peaceful people, subjecting them to vassalage and establishing a relationship which resulted in the development of a common culture for both the Chiriguano and Chane (See CHANE). The Chiriguano retained their "lord-servant" relationship with surrounding tribes into modern times and even in the 1940s, the Tapiete of the Gran Chaco who speak Chiriguano as a result of long years of contact, still hired themselves to Chiriguano farmers on a seasonal basis for supplies of maize.

The Chiriguano adopted techniques of agriculture which they found among the Chane and since their new home did not abound in hunting and fishing resources, they came to depend upon agriculture far more than any other Tupian group. They raised eleven types of maize, pumpkins, several varieties of beans, sweet potatoes, sweet manioc, peanuts, cotton, tobacco, *urucu (achiote),* and adopted from the Europeans the growing of water-

Chiriguano women spinning

melons, oranges, melons, sorghum, and sugar cane. Men clear the fields and build tall fences around them to keep out animals, both wild and domestic. They till and sow the fields as well. At harvest, women and children help with the crops. Both hunting and fishing are very secondary activities, the latter only for those living along the Pilcomayo and Bermejo Rivers. The Chiriguano now raise sheep, cattle, horses, chickens, and sheep replacing the precontact llama.

Aboriginally, the Chiriguano built large, communal houses in which several families resided, each village being made up of three to five such houses grouped around a central plaza. Villages were palisaded. By the eighteenth century, houses were small and gabled, containing one or perhaps two closely-related nuclear families. Modern villages retain the aboriginal plan and have many houses grouped around a plaza. Each village contains a storehouse which is built on piles, possibly a carryover from their tropical forest days in the distant past. Furniture is simple, a platform bed, wooden benches, large storage vessels and shelves. Hammocks are used only during the day or as baby cradles.

The Chiriguano manufactures are numerous and their decorated pottery is especially noteworthy. They use both the band loom and the Arawak loom for weaving cotton and wool. They also make nets for catching birds and fish and for carrying objects as well as wickerwork baskets. Weaponry includes the bow and three different types of arrows, cudgels, and woolen slings, the use of wool being a result of Quechua influence.

The patrilineal villages of aboriginal times have given way to the modern Chiriguano village composed of a number of nuclear families with kinship ties to one another or to a common chief. In precontact times, Chiriguano chiefs were chosen for their abilities as warriors and orators and quite possibly were shamans as well. They had considerable influence over their own villages and an occasional chief was able to extend his power over other villages and become known as a paramount chief. The main functions of the chief were to act as administrator of village affairs and as leader of his people in battle. Raids were often planned by paramount chiefs who called together the village chiefs to receive their counsel and to encourage them to set forth. Chieftainship has carried into modern times with succession being patrilineally inherited, usually going to the chief's son unless he was considered unworthy. However, as with the Chane, there are instances of brothers of chiefs succeeding before the sons and a suggestion that women occasionally became leaders. Chiefs in recent years had servants but formerly they did all their own work. Symbols of their office were earrings, large ornaments, the *yanduwa*, a befeathered pole, and a carved stick.

The Chiriguano shared the same life cycle ceremonies with the Chane and the *couvade* has survived into contemporary Chiriguano society, although not in its original form. Today, Chiriguano men simply fast for a short period after the birth of a child. Both the Chiriguano and the Chane have many of the same religious beliefs which have altered by the Christian concept of the "true god" whom the Chiriguano call, "Our Creator." Certain Tupian elements have survived in Chiriguano mythology, such as the myth of the Twins who climb up to the sky on a chain of arrows and become the Sun and the Moon. Versions of Andean myths may be found as well. As in Chane society, shamans held an important place and were treated with great respect until such time as their magical powers failed, after which they were often put to death. Shamans cured by traditional methods of blowing and sucking and were aided in the ministrations by old women who were called upon for diseases whose cure required drugs. The Chiriguano used enemas and body painting as precautions against disease and tried to stop epidemics by erecting poles on which magical signs were carved around the village.

BIBLIOGRAPHY —

● STEWARD, JULIAN H. Handbook of South American Indians. 7 Vols., Washington, DC: U.S. Govt. Printing Office, 1946-59.

CHITIMACHA

(U.S.; La.) is a tribe which still inhabits their traditional Louisiana homeland.

Chitimacha is a Choctaw word meaning "they have cooking vessels." The name they had for

Black Yellow Red

Chiriguano pottery

themselves *Panteh Pimpkansh* meaning "men altogether red," a designation adopted to distinguish themselves from white settlers. Their language stemmed from the Tunica linguistic family. Some scholars believe there may have been a connection between the Iroquois, Lakota and Chitimachan languages.

One of the most noteworthy things about the Chitimacha culture was their caste system. The chief and his descendents were nobility and treated with great respect. However if a nobleman married a common woman he lived in her quarters. This does not mean he lost his position; he simply went and lived with commoners. But many noblemen would not marry a commoner if there were no noblewomen to marry. As this happened often enough, the governmental line was occasionally threatened with extinction. In other marital aspects Chitimachas were strict monogamists and women seem to have had significant influence in government.

Apparently the noon-day sun was their chief deity.

In their economy the Chitimachas were like the Atakapa, who made greater use of fish and other aquatic foods than did most southeastern tribes. The Chitimacha also did a lively business trading flint with the Atakapa. Their basketry was superb and many examples are in art museums today.

Their first encounter with whites was during the explorations of Iberaide and Bienvide. At that time, around 1650, there were 3,000 Chitimacha. The French quickly took serious note of the Chitimacha when they murdered a Frenchman. This started a fierce war, and the Indians were finally forced to sue for peace.

Culture. The Chitimacha Indians lived by fishing and agriculture and were the most advanced of the Louisiana Indians in the arts of basket-making and metal-work. They raised beans, pumpkins, melons, maize and constructed houses of wooden frames with roofs of mud and palmetto leaves. Community graneries protected the grain from mice. Chitimacha baskets, particularly the "double" basket where both the inside and the outside are intricately woven, are considered to be the finest ever produced. Unfortunately the art was both time-consuming and difficult and is no longer practiced. The early Indians buried their dead in large mounds, some in the shape of flying birds and placed food beside the graves for the ancestors to use. They have legends of men hunting with dogs and of a young man who was lost in the sky while hunting an still wanders there. Their women had a strong voice in tribal affairs and were even elevated to the status of Chief, an honor rare among American Indians.

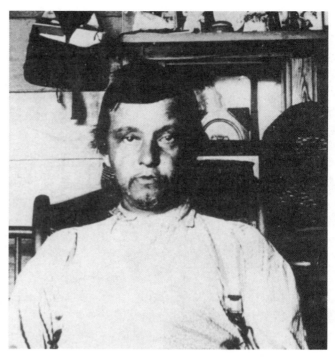

Benjamin Paul, last chief of the Chitimacha Indians, and one of the last speakers of their language

Today there are Chitimachas living on a reservation in Louisiana. Their main employment is work in the oil fields.

BIBLIOGRAPHY —
● HODGE, FREDERICK WEBB. Handbook of American Indians North of Mexico. Washington: Government Printing Office, 2 vols., 1907-10.
● HOOVER, HERBERT T. The Chitimacha People. Phoenix, AZ Indian Tribal Series, 1975.
● MURDOCK, GEORGE P. Ethnographic Bibliography of North America. New Haven, CT: Human Relations Area Files Press, 1975.
● SWANTON, JOHN R. The Indian Tribes of North America. Washington, DC: U.S. Government Printing Office, 1952.

CHOCO

(Central America; Panama and South America; Bolivia) number about 20,000 living in the area along the Pacific coast of Panama and northern Colombia, one of the densest tropical forests in South America. Small groups of Choco have been reported as far away as the Cayapas River in Ecuador. Although the Choco have been drawn more and more into the banana economy of Colombia and Panama, they retain a majority of aboriginal customs and their social organization remains traditional.

The Choco are a riverine people who live in small settlements strung out along the intricate network of waterways in Colombia and Panama. Little is known of Choco history but it seems that they have been migrating northward from Colom-

Chocó

These settlements develop along sandy, arable sections of the rivers on which they live and where they cultivate their principal crop, plantains, which constitute their basic means of subsistence and their main cash crop. Houses are built on stilts and are of pole and thatch construction, usually without walls. They are set well back from the river's edge in order to guard against seasonal flooding. Plantain groves lie between the river and the houses. The Choco also raise maize, manioc, rice, lemons, oranges, cacao, coffee and sugar cane, all in small amounts and for household consumption only, in the jungle behind their houses well away from the river. Their vegetable diet is supplemented by game animals and fish. In areas where fish are abundant, they provide a daily supplement. The Choco also hunt many kinds of birds, monkeys, peccaries, agoutis, and other small animals.

The Choco sell most of their harvest of plantains which they ferry downriver in large (ten to twelve meters) dugout canoes to Panamanian and Colombian river towns where they are sold for cash. They buy canned foods, lamps, kerosene, matches, cloth, hardware such as machetes, kitchen utensils, adornments for personal use, as well as some alcoholic beverages and tobacco.

The Choco manufacture all their household furniture and equipment with the noted exception of some metal pots and pans, machetes, and muzzleloading shotguns which have replaced some of the traditional tools and weapons. They make fiber hammocks which are used principally for children. Adults and grown children sleep on platform beds, sometimes enclosed by mosquito nets. In general, furniture is sparse and consists of wooden, carved seats and an assortment of storage boxes. Before their involvement in cashcropping and the wide-

bia into Panama for centuries, according to demographic studies and oral histories. This migration has increased in tempo in recent decades, stimulated by the northward movement of the Colombiano *negro* population of Colombia. The Choco do not compete with the Colombians and Panamanos for land but adjust to pressure from outsiders by retreating into the unpopulated frontier regions. They express a restless dissatisfaction with "too many Colombianos and Panamanos" whom they simply try to avoid.

The Choco do not live in villages but form loose clusters of closely-related households on river banks. These settlements range from a scant 20 or so individuals to upwards of 200. When the population increases beyond the point of available horticultural land, young married couples move away to begin new settlements in virgin territory. The Choco have no strong allegiance to their settlements. People do not engage in communal activities of an economic, political, or ritual nature. They are simple members of a sector along a river which has certain definable physical boundaries and provide land. The are no chiefs or other administrative leaders.

The Choco practice slash-and-burn horticulture.

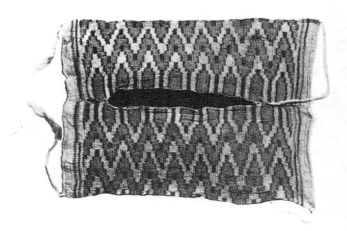

Mataco looped carrying bag

Mataco hockey game

spread use of calico cloth, the Choco made clothing from barkcloth, a technique still practiced but dying out. They continue to make basketry of the twill, wicker and coiled varieties. Gourds are still used for storing water, as dishes, and as spoons. They manufacture coiled pottery mainly for magical purposes, although some utilitarian ware is made.

Choco kinship is reckoned bilaterally which means that relatively equal importance is given to members on both sides of one's family. The bilateral extension of the kinship ties through one's first cousins on both sides of the family constitutes one's *imberana*. This is the most closely-related unit among the Choco and generally encompasses the members of several households in the settlement. It also constitutes the largest exogamous group, the members of which are forbidden to marry one another. Preferential marriage among the Choco occurs between persons who stand in the ralationship of second cousin to one another. Aside from these restrictions and preferences, a Choco is free to marry any other Choco. An important constraint on the willy-nilly contacting of marriage however, is the widespread Choco fear of strangers as possible agents of evil. Therefore, people tend to marry people they have known for many years. The Choco are ethno- endogamous and to not marry non-Choco which indludes Cuna, Colombianos, Panamanos.

The Choco have a deity who is considered to be a culture hero who brought basic knowledge to the people. He is an otiose deity who is not supplicated. More important in the everyday life of the Choco are the very many bush spirits who operate for both good and evil. Some of these dead spirits are considered to be the souls of the dead. Shamans are an essential part of the religious life. They undergo years of training and many of them travel great distances to become students of well-known shamans. Illness is believed to be caused by possession of evil spirits. A sick person seeks out a shaman who exorcises the evil spirits by using chants, invoking and depending upon the strength of his spirit helpers, and holding poisonous snakes near the person's body. Many shamans keep the extremely lethal fer-de-lance in wicker baskets in their houses. Copious drinking of *chicha* is part of the curing ceremony and a drug, *datura sanguinea* is used to induce dreams.

The Choco indicate a great reluctance to be incorporated into western society. Since they live in a region which is unattractive to whites and have an open frontier to the north of them, it might be supposed that they can maintain their traditional culture for some time to come. However, the last link in the Pan-American Highway is scheduled to be constructed through their territory. Once this occurs and the Choco are exposed to western, industrialized society, there is no telling what effect it may have on their survival.

(see map page XIX)

BIBLIOGRAPHY —

● STEWARD, JULIAN H. Handbook of South American Indians. 7 Vols., Washington, DC: U.S. Govt. Printing Office, 1946-59.

CHOCTAW

(U.S.; Southeast) are the largest Mushogean tribe in North America. Along with the Cherokees, Chickasaws, Creeks and Seminoles, they were one of the "Five Civilized Tribes," for they adopted white culture more rapidly than other tribes.

The Choctaws were closely related to the Chickasaws and orginally they may have been one tribe. Many of their customs are similar, but the Chickasaws were far more warlike.

Their legends state, and recent scholarships has confirmed that they emigrated to their territory in south Mississippi from areas northeast. They probably arrived sometime around the eighth or ninth century AD.

What has especially intrigued many theological scholars is the comparisons between this "exodus" and the Biblical one. According to legend the Choctaws followed a great pole that led them southwest. When they arrived at the chosen spot the great pole stood completely upright. This compares to the pillar of cloud and fire Moses and the Hebrews followed to Canaan.

Governmentally they operated under a system of dual governments, one for peace and one for war, like the Cherokees. However, not much is known about the actual details of this government.

Socially they were organized into two phratries under which were several clans. Marriages had to occur outside the clan and apparently membership in a clan descended maternally. A father had no control over0 his children. Children obeyed their oldest maternal uncle. Although morality was not strict, moral deviates were not tolerated. A husband had the right to expell his adulterous wife.

The most interesting aspect of their religious life, which was generally similar to the Chickasaws, was their burial customs. The dead body was set on a scaffold where it stayed for several days until the flesh had decomposed. Then the family gathered around where a bone-picker, a special old man or woman, tattooed to designate position, and who grew long fingernails for this purpose, would mount the scaffold and clean the bones of flesh. The skull was then painted vermillion and the bones placed in a bone house. Poles decorated with wreaths were placed around the grave to aid the soul in its ascent.

In their village life each household had two houses-one for winter and the other for summer-like the Chickasaws. The winter house was circular shaped to conduct a moist heat. The summer house was rectangular. Agriculture was the main business to which men attended. Corn was the principle crop. The also hunted and fished.

Though they were generally peaceful it was conceded everywhere that they were skillful warriors, an ability they had to develop to survive constant attcks by the Chickasaw. Most wars fought were defensive rather than offensive.

Their first white contact was with De Soto in the 1500s. They always had very close relations with the French. Red Shoes, an important Choctaw, tried to start an English party among the Indians, but failed. Later, in the early 19th century Tecumseh tried to get them to join his revolution but out of thousands of warriors, only thirty joined him.

Several Choctaws were noted for their outstanding statesmanship, among them Pushmataha who

Choctaw handicrafts

is buried in the Congressional Cemetery in Washington.

In 1830 the Choctaws, under Chief Dancing Rabbit, were forced to accept a sham treaty, similar to the Cherokee Treaty of New Echota, ceding their lands to the U.S. It was only ratified by a minority of the Choctaws, and when the rest tried to protest, President Jackson refused to recognize them. They were removed to Indian Territory, now Oklahoma.

There they established a constitutional form of government, similar to the U.S. structure, which they refused to abandon until Oklahoma joined the Union in 1912.

History. The Choctaw were one of the most powerful tribes in what is now the Southeastern United States. The first white man to encounter them, Hernando de Soto, fought a fierce battle with the Choctaw in 1540. The Indians, although defeated, terrorized the Spanish. After 1700, the Choctaw tribe was caught between and cleverly divided by the French and English. After 1780, the tribe was caught in a similar situation between United States and Spanish interests. Between 1783

Choctaw ball players with lacrosse sticks

and 1830, the Choctaw signed a series of eight treaties which gave away most of their land. The Treaty of Dancing Rabbit Creek, in 1830, which provided for the removal of the tribe to Oklahoma, included a provision allowing those so choosing to remain in Mississippi. The last group to move left Mississippi in 1903, and from then until 1916, the remaining Choctaw were largely forgotten. A series of epidemics brought the tribe to the attention of the Senate which prompted an investigation. In response to the dreadful conditions revealed, federal money was appropriated for schools and services to the tribe.

Culture. The tribe is and has been predominantly agricultural, raising crops typical of the area-squashes, beans, corn. The Choctaw dislike war and prefer to settle disputes over the table. Their game of stickball, an often deadly sport, was used to settle differences between tribes. The tribe is democratic and places women in a prominent, rather powerful position. A part of the Mound Builders' culture, the Choctaw are the builders of the Nanih Waiya, or Mother Mound from which the first Choctaw are said to have been born. Choctaw all learn their own language first and English in school so that most of the tribe is at least bilingual.

(see map page XIV)

BIBLIOGRAPHY —
● ABEL, ANNIE HELOISE. History of Events Resulting in Indian Consolidation West of the Mississippi. American Historical Association, 1906.
● ALLEN, REV. L. L. Thrilling Sketch of Life of Distinguished Chief Okah Tubbee, alias William Chubbee, son of head chief, Mosholeh Tubbee, of Choctaw Nation. New York, NY: 1848.
● BENSON, HENRY C. Life Among the Choctaw Indians, and Sketches of the South-West. Cincinnati, OH: L. Swormstedt & A. Poe, 1860.
● BOLTON, HERBERT EUGENE. Athanase de Mezieres and the Louisiana-Texas Frontier, 1768-1780. Cleveland, OH: The Arthur H. Clark Co., 1914.
● BUSHNELL, DAVID L. JR. The Choctaw of Bayou Lacomb Street--Tammany Parish. Washington: (Published as Bulletin 48, Bureau of Ethnology, 1909.
● CHRONICLES OF OKLAHOMA. 1926, 1927, 1928, 1929, 1932, 1934, 1948, 1949, 1950.
● CONGRESS. 44th Congress, 1st Session, H. Rept. 499; 66th Congress, 2nd Session, H. Rept. 573.
● DEBO, ANGIE. The Rise and Fall of the Choctaw Republic. Norman, OK: University of Oklahoma Press, 1934, 1961.
----- The Road to Disappearance. Norman, OK: University of Oklahoma Press, 1941.
● EASTMAN, ELAINE GOODALE. Pratt, The Red Man's Moses. Norman, OK: University of Oklahoma Press, 1935.
● ELDER, S. B. Life of Roquette--Work on Choctaw Indians, valuable to ethnologist of the South. New Orleans, LA: The William Harvey Miner Co., St. Louis, 1913.
● FOREMAN, GRANT. Advancing the Frontier, 1830- 1860. Norman, OK: University of Oklahoma Press, 1933.
----- Indian Removal. The Emigration of the Five Civilized Tribes of Indians. Norman, OK: University of Oklahoma Press, 1932.

----- Pioneer Days in the Early Southwest.Cleveland, OH, The Arthur H. Clark Co., 1926.

● GABRIEL, RALPH HENRY. The Pageant of America: the Lure of the Frontier.New Haven, CT: Yale University Press, 1929.

● HARMON, GEORGE DEWEY. Sixty Years of Indian Affairs, Political, Economic, and Diplomatic, 1789-1850.Chapel Hill, NC: University of North Carolina Press, 1941.

● HODGE, FREDERICK WEBB. Handbook of American Indians North of Mexico. Washington: Government Printing Office, 2 vols., 1907-10.

● INDIAN OFFICE REPORT. 1839, 1858, 1864, 1865, 1870, 1872, 1891.

● KAPPLER, CHARLES J. Indian Affairs, Laws & Treaties. Washington, 1833.

● LANE, JOHN W. The Five Civilized Tribes in Indian Territory; Extra Census Bulletin.Washington: Department of the Interior, U.S. Census Printing Office, 1894.

● LOWERY, WOODBURY. The Spanish Settlements within the Present Limits of the U.S., 1513-1561.New York, NY: G. P. Putnam's Sons, 1901.

● MALONE, JAMES H. The Chickasaw Nation, A Short Sketch of a Noble People.Louisville, KY: John P. Morton & Co., 1922.

● MILLING, CHAPMAN. Red Carolinians. Chapel Hill, NC: University of North Carolina Press, 1940.

● MURDOCK, GEORGE P. Ethnographic Bibliography of North America.New Haven, CT: Human Relations Area Files Press, 1975.

● O'BEIRNE, EDWARD S. AND HARRY F. The Indian Territory: Its Chiefs, Legislators and Leading Men.St. Louis, MO: C. B. Woodward Co., 1892.

● POUND, ARTHUR. Johnson of the Mohawks, A Biography of Sir William Johnson, Irish Immigrant, Mohawk War Chief.New York, NY: The Macmillan Co., 1930.

● ROYCE, CHARLES C. Indian Land Cessions in the U.S. Washington: 18th Annual Report, Bureau of Ethnology, 1896-97.

● SCHOOLCRAFT, HENRY R. History of the Indian Tribes of the U.S.; Their Present Condition and Prospects.Philadelphia, J. B. Lippincott & Co., 1857.

● SEYMOUR, FLORA WARREN. Indian Agents of the Old Frontier.New York, NY: and London: D. Appleton-Century Co., Inc., 1941.

● STANLEY, HENRY M. My Early Travels and Adventures in America and Asia.New York, NY: Charles Scribner's Sons, 1895.

● SWANTON, JOHN R. The Indian Tribes of the Lower Mississippi Valley and Adjacent Coast of the Gulf of Mexico. Washington: Bureau of Ethnology, 1911.

----- The Indian Tribes of North America.Washington, DC: U.S. Government Printing Office, 1952.

----- Source Material for the Social and Ceremonial Life of the Choctaw Indians. Washington: Bureau of American Ethnology Bulletin, no. 103, 1931.

● SWANTON, JOHN R., AND HENRY S. HALBERT. A Dictionary of the Choctaw Language.Washington: (Published as Bulletin 46, Bureau of Ethnology, 1915.

● WEBB, WALTER PRESCOTT. The Great Plains.Boston, MA: Ginn & Co., 1931.

● WILLIAMS, SAMUEL COLE. Adair's History of the American Indians.Johnson City, TN: The Watauga Press, 1930.

● WISSLER, CLARK. Indians of the U.S., Four Centuries of Their History and Culture. New York, NY: Doubleday, Doran & Co., 1940.

CHOLON

(South America; Peru) are part of the Laman linguistic family and live in the Huallaga Valley in Peru.

History and culture. During the 17th century, Indians east of Cajamarquilla, probably including Cholon, had often raided the Highlands and even destroyed the villages of Condurmarca and Collay. But in 1670, they sought peace. Beginning in 1676, the Franciscans undertook to Christianize the Cholon. The Mission of Buenaventura de Apisonchuc was built by Father Francisco Gutierrez de Porres, who wrote a grammar, a dictionary and several religious books in the Cholon Hibito together numbered 4,800 persons. In the missions, the Indians were divided into bands and companies and had regular hours of labor. The Cholon numbered about 900-1,000 in 1829. In 1925, they occupied the area south of Pacisa between the Huallaga River and the Rio del Valle. Their language still survives, and although the population number is unknown, it is estimated at several hundred. The Indians grow sweet manloc, maize, peanuts and cotton. To supplement their diet they also hunt and fish. Their culture includes weaving and ceramics.

BIBLIOGRAPHY –

● STEWARD, JULIAN H. Handbook of South American Indians. 7 Vols., Washington, DC: U.S. Govt. Printing Office, 1946-59.

CHONO

(South America; Chile) The circa 300-mile strip of the southern Chilean archipelago, from about 4330' to 48 S. lat., which constituted the habitat of the Chono, is a region of hilly islands, deep fiords, and tortuous channels, in which travel was, of necessity, mostly by water. The Chono were, like the Alacaluf and Yahgan, a distinctly canoe people. The climate is marked by a predominance of damp, cloudy days, by very high rainfall in all seasons, well over the 80 inch (100 cm.) per year mean, by strong-to-violent prevalent westerly winds, and by temperatures cool without being severe. The islands and mainland coast are mostly covered with dense, extremely wet, temperate rain forest.

The northern limit of Chono territory--the dividing line between the southernmost Araucanians of southern Chiloe and the northernmost Chono of the Guaitecas Islands region--was Corcovado Gulf, as is clear from the 16th-, 17th-, and early 18th-century first-hand sources, Goicueta, Ferrufino, Venegas, Pietas, and Olivares. That the early Chono lived or wandered as far south as the Taitao Peninsula is reasonably clear from Garcia. They probably extended a little farther south, to the Gulf of Penas and the Guaianeco Islands, at least in the middle or later 18th century, but the point is open to some question, as the Chono ethnic identity with or relation to the "Huilli," "Caucahue," and "Guaiguen" of this region just south of Taitao Peninsula is not clear.

The Chono were in contact from very early times with the Araucanians of Chiloe. They raided the

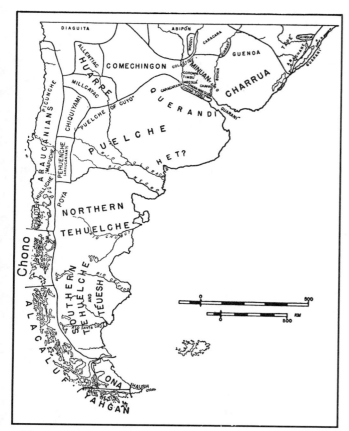

Chono, and other tribes of southern South America, at the first European contact period.

thropology was gotten with the advent of the Jesuit missionaries, Fathers Estevan, Ferrufino, and Venegas, to Chiloe and the Guaitecas Islands in 1609-13--data recorded in the *Cartas Anuas, 1927* (p. 48) and cited or drawn upon in the writings of Fathers del Techo, Rosales, Olivares, and Lozano. Around the middle of the 18th century, some further light was shed on Chono anthropology by Byron, Campbell, Bulkeley and Cummins, and the anonymous author of the Affecting Narrative, all of whom were members of the crew of the Wager, which was shipwrecked on the Guaitecas Islands in May of 1741, and by Father Garcia in his account of his missionary expedition of 1766-67 to the Guaianeco Islands. Since then, additional knowledge of Chono culture has been negligible.

Not a single word of the Chonoan language has been identified except, perhaps, the word Chono itself. From historical sources on the Chono, however, certain general conclusions regarding their language can be formulated. That the Chono spoke a tongue distinct from the Araucanian of southern Chile and of Chiloe has been abundantly recorded and there is no ground for assuming that Chono may have been a highly divergent dialect or language of the Araucanian family. That they spoke a Tehuelchean-Onan (Chon) dialect is extremely unlikely. That their language was distinct from that of the Alacaluf or of the archipelagic canoe-using natives immediately south of them, beyond about 48 S. lat., is slightly more probable than not, but such difference, if it existed, may have been merely dialectic. In any case, there is a lack of even near-solid scientific ground for classifying Chono as a distinct, isolated linguistic family.

Various first-hand accounts of Chono territory indicated that it was thinly populated, but exact data on the total population is not available, as there are only a few figures, from missionary records. The Jesuit missionaries baptized 220 Chono of the Guaitecas Islands region and estimated that there were not more than 50 other Chono at the time, 1612-13, in the region. A century later, in 1710, hard pressed by raids of both the Chilotans and the more southern Indians, 30 Chono families, and shortly after, 200 families, or more than 500 natives, were settled under the Jesuit missionaries on Huar and two other islands in the Gulf of Reloncavi. They, or some of them, were still there in 1736, but in 1795, Moraleda found no Indians on Huar.

In 1745, some Guaineco Islands Indians were brought back and established on Chonchi Island under mission auspices. In 1765 the Island of Cailin, just off the southeastern coast of Chiloe, was set aside as a mission for the Chono, and later

Chilotans to secure iron and other plunder. The Chilotans raided the Chono and took women and children as captives. The Chono of the Guaitecas Islands used to capture "Huillis" farther south, to keep them in a sort of drudgery servitude and to sell them to the Chilotans.

The name Chono (etymology unknown), probably the name which the people called themselves, was first recorded in Ferrufino's letter of 1610. Other tribal denominations used by early Spanish writers for natives living in the region between Chiloe and the Guaianeco Islands are: Huilli (Huille; from Araucanian willi, "south"), Caucahue (Caucau; Araucanian kaukau, "gull"), and Guaiguen (Araucanian waiwen, "south" (wind)). Some of these "Huilli," "Caucau," and "Guaiguen" were probably Chono. In this region there may possibly have been more distinct tribes than one, or two or more well-constituted subdivisions of one tribe, although there is no clear evidence of such.

Contact was first made by whites with the Chono on the Ulloa expedition in 1533. The first description of them was given by Goicueta, the chronicler of the Cortes Hojea expedition of 1557-58. A half-century later, some further data on Chono an-

came many Caucahue and Calen. In 1779, 11 Guaineco were persuaded by Fathers Marin and Real to return with them to Chiloe coast, but left about a year afterward. In 1780-81 the Chono established on Cailin moved to Chaulinec Island, east of Lemui. In 1788, Moraleda reported 21 or 22 families of Chono on Apiao Island, east of Chaulinec. In 1790, the surviving 22 Chono on Chaulinec returned to Cailin.

After this date, the Chono's trail is lost almost completely until 1875, when Captain E. Simpson came across a sole family of "Chono" in Puquitin Channel between Ascension Island and the Guaitecas Islands. There are no later reports of surviving Chono. All later observers since 1875 declared that the islands north of Taitao Peninsula were uninhabited except by a few whites or Chilotan Indians. The Chono appear to have become completely extinct, unless they were from the beginning, as is not improbable, only a branch of the Alacaluf, and later merged with their Alacaluf counterparts south of the Taitao Peninsula.

Knowledge of the Chono culture is exceedingly meager. No single survey covers even material culture in any detail, while social and religious culture is almost a complete blank. First- hand sources included: *Goicueta, (1557-58) 1879* (p. 50); *Ferrufino, 1927*(p. 50); *Venegas, 1927*(p. 50); *Campbell, 1747* (p. 50); *Byron, 1768*(p. 50); and *Garcia, J. (1766-67), 1889* (p. 50). The data given by *Del Techo, 1673* (p. 50), *Rosales, 1877-78*(p. 50), *Olivares, 1874*(p. 50), and *Lozano, 1754-55*(p. 50) were largely derived from Ferrufino and Venegas. Data on the canoe-using Indians from J. Garcia and Byron are cited as Chonoan. Inasmuch, however, as their "Caucahue" and "Chono" respectively cannot be shown beyond all doubts to have been true Chono, the citations were made with some reservation.

In most respects, Chono culture was identical with, or similar to, that of the Alacaluf. Certain elements of Araucanian culture had spread down the coast as far at least as the Guaitecas Islands. Such were: sporadic gardening and herding, the polished stone ax, and the plank boat. Such diffusion was readily understandable in view of the known raiding and trading contacts of the Guaitecas islanders with the Chilotans.

There is no evidence of Tehuelche influence upon Chono culture, although the Chono may possibly have been in sporadic contact with the Tehuelche along the mainland coast. The "gigantic" Caucahue described by some sources, as distinct perhaps from the smaller-statured Caucahue described by others, who were observed at various times in or near Chono territory, may possibly have been of Tehuelche stock, but it was not confirmed.

Fish, shellfish, and seals constituted the basic diet. Birds, eggs, and stranded whales were also eaten. Water and seal oil were the customary beverages. No systematic agriculture was carried on, but there was some evidence of sporadic cultivation, even in pre-Contact times, of the potato in the Guaitecas Islands region, and, in the post-Contact period, of maize and barley.

Before the influx of the whites, the only domesticated animal was the dog. Some of the Chono north of Taitao Peninsula bred small, long-haired, shaggy-maned dogs, and from their hair made short mantles. In later times, the Chono kept a few sheep and goats. Cormorants were captured at night with torches and clubs. In seal hunting, a "lazo" (not a lasso) and a long heavy club were used by the Caucahue. "Canquen" (Chloephaga, a goose), when molting and unable to fly, were rounded up and driven to land by throwing pebbles at them from canoes, and were then slaughtered with clubs.

The women were accustomed to diving for shellfish. According to *Goicueta, 1879, p. 518*(p. 51), the Chono used a wooden fishhook, but that was not confirmed. Fish nets were made of bark fiber, and seal nets, of rawhide. The dogs were trained to help in the fishing. Hot stones were employed for boiling fish in bark buckets. Seal meat was sometimes eaten raw, a piece being put in the mouth and cut off close to the lips with a shell.

Huts were of sticks covered with boughs, bark, or skin. Those observed by *Byron, 1768, p. 123*(p. 51) were of beehive or domed construction, the framework consisting of branches stuck in the ground in a circle and bent over at the top, where they were bound with a kind of woodbine, split by holding in the teeth. Those described by *Venegas, 1927, p. 381*(p. 51) were, inside, barely the length of a man's body and so low that one had to kneel in order to keep from touching the top. In some cases, only the bark or skin cover was carried around in the canoe from camp to camp, in other cases, the pole framework was carried as well. The hearth was in the center of the hut.

Clothing, including short mantles covering the shoulders only, and longer ones reaching to a little below the waist, was of skin, woven dog's hair, bark, and woven down or feathers. A pubic covering, made of large, hard leaves (kelp?) cast up by the sea, was also used *Ferrufino, 1927, p. 111*(p. 51). No head or hand covering or footwear was reported.

Red, white, and black face and body painting was in use, and the tonsure was sometimes worn. Scarification was practiced, but no tattooing was recorded, nor was any form of bodily mutilation, or of finger, ear or nose ornament. Necklaces of shell and bone, and feather diadems were in vogue. *Garcia, J. 1889, p. 28*(p. 51) observed one man around the north end of Fallos Channel with two bird wings on his head.

Travel was almost entirely by water. No rafts, balsas, skin boats, or dugouts were reported. As early as first European contact, in 1553, the plank boat, similar to the one used by the Araucanians of Corcovado Gulf, was employed by the Chono between Corcovado Gulf and Cape Tres Montes. It was originally of three planks, caulked with bark, and made, without axes or adzes, with use of fire, flints, and shells. Usually it leaked a good deal and required much bailing. There was a portage route from the Chonos Archipelago across the Isthmus of Ofqui to the Gulf of Penas. The plank boat was taken apart for portaging and put together again at the end of the portage. In later times, from about 1767, a sail was sometimes used. In the middle 16th century, south of the Gulf of Penas, only bark canoes were used, made of thick slabs of bark, which were crescent-shaped. In the course of time, the plank boat largely replaced the bark canoe, gradually spreading down the coast from the Gulf of Penas and being first reported in the Strait of Magellan, near the western end, in 1765 *Cooper, 1917, pp. 195-204 passim*(p. 52)

Pottery was absent from this tribe's culture. The Chono "wove" mantles or blankets of dog's hair, of bark fiber (presumably woven), and of bird down, but no details on technique are available, nor is there information on basket-making skin dressing, or stoneworking. Buckets were made of bark. The flint axes and adzes attributed to the Chono by *Pietas, 1846, p. 503* (p. 52) were not unlikely of Chilotan origin, as were the stone axes that have been occasionally found in Chono territory. Some kind of stone and shell tool was used in making plank boats.

The usual weapons of the tribe were the spear and club, the former with a head of bone, probably single-barbed. *Byron, 1768, p. 129*(p. 52) stated that the natives, most likely Chono, but not certainly so, with whom he was in contact, used "bows and arrows sometimes, but always the lance." All other first-hand observers did not offer further information, and no arrowheads appear to have been found archeologically in Chono territory. Neither slings nor spear throwers were reported. Torches were made of bark. There is no information on fire-making methods.

There is only a small amount of information on the nonmaterial aspects of Chono culture. The tribe was reported to be monogamous. The "Chono" cacique who guided Byron from Wager Island to Chiloe apparently had two wives, an older and a much younger one, perhaps a mother and her daughter by a previous marriage. It is very doubtful, however, whether he was a real

Chono or was representative of Chono culture.

The Chono had some kind of headmen or chiefs, but what authority they had, if any, is uncertain. Delco, the "cacique principal" of the Guaitecas Islands, was at the same time, an appointee of the Spanish authorities of Chiloe. The Chono raiding expeditions among their neighbors to the south and north have been previously noted. Chono weapons were spears, clubs and stones. There was no report of shields or armor, and cannibalism was not recorded. Gathering fuel, diving for sea urchins, and searching among the rocks for shellfish were tasks of the women; cutting poles for the hut, sealing, and apparently cormorant hunting, were tasks of the men.

The Chono were in trading relations with the Chilotans. Besides serving as middlemen in taking captives among their southern neighbors and selling them to the Chilotans as "slaves," the Chono themselves kept some of these captives in a kind of drudgery slavery.

In one case reported, a father cut his hair to celebrate the birth of a child.

Burial in caves was common. One instance of platform burial was recorded. Burial in embryonic posture or with knees flexed to shoulders occurred.

There was no mention of musical instruments by any sources, and there were no details on dancing (cf. infra) and singing. *Garcia, J., 1889, p. 29*(p. 53) was welcomed by the men and women dancing and singing most of the night; the singing reminded him of a lullaby crooned to put an infant to sleep. There was apparently no native Chono intoxicant.

There is only scattered data on certain rites and observances concerning religion. *Byron, 1768, pp. 145-146*(p. 53) and *Campbell, 1747, pp. 61-62*(p. 53) gave short descriptions of a rite, apparently religious, performed by men and women. Vocalizations began by deep groans and gradually rose to "a hideous kind of singing." The participants, in frenzy, snatched firebrands from the fire, put them in their mouths, and ran about burning everyone they came near. At other times, they would cut one another with mussel shells until smeared with blood. And so the ceremony went on until exhaustion ensued. When the men stopped, the women began. Byron's Chrisitan cacique kept aloof, and stated that "the devil" was the chief actor among the Chono on these occasions.

A person could harm another if he possessed a bit of the latter's hair. *Garcia, J. 1889, p. 29*(p. 54) reported a case (probably but not certainly Chono, as in much of the information from Garcia) of death from black magic wrought by obtaining hair from the top of the victim's head. Garcia was told that only hair from the top of the head would serve; that all the natives of the vicinity cut the hair from the crown of the head for fear of sorcery; that the possessor of such hair, if he wished to harm the person from whom it was stolen in sleep, would place it between two stones, dance around it all night invoking the "demon," and from time to time, pound, strike, and pierce it; that, if he wished to cause the victim's death, he would take it to sea and tie it to some kelp, or would go to the mountains and throw it down trees. The purloined bit of hair was kept tied with whalebone.

Garcia's Caucahue (probably Chono) blacked their faces with charcoal on entering a lagoon in which icebergs were floating and on the banks of which snow lay, "to salute the snow, lest they die," and on another occasion, one of them painted his face to bring good weather. The Caucahue with Garcia were much incensed at a Spaniard who threw his poncho in the sea water to wash it; the Moon, they said, would be angry and send them bad weather.

It was taboo to look at a flock of parrots passing overhead, lest bad weather follow; to throw kelp or shellfish on the fire, lest the sea become rough; to throw shells in the water, with Byron being severely rebuked for throwing limpet shells from the canoe into the water.

In curing her husband, who was suffering from some malady of the back, a woman massaged his back and chest, spurted water on him from her mouth, cried, wept, and moaned, and applied her mouth to his back. Then another woman came and anointed him and smeared him with "colo" on the arms, chest, and back. He himself dived into the water many times daily. The rite was a magical one, Garcia was told.

Regarding the tribe's mythology, lore and learning, as well as etiquette, no information was available.

BIBLIOGRAPHY —

● STEWARD, JULIAN H. Handbook of South American Indians. 7 Vols., Washington, DC: U.S. Govt. Printing Office, 1946-59.

CHONTAL

(Mexico) from Nahuatl *chontalli* , "foreigner" (*chonta* , "a field;" an ancient name for a savage), is a reference to several Indian groups living mainly in Oaxaca and neighboring Tabasco, Mexico. The 7,500 Chontal are divided into two major peoples living in nineteen villages: the Highland Chontal, whose largest center is Ecatepec, with about 200 houses settled at a 5,000-8,000 foot altitude, and the more numerous Lowland people, whose 5,000 inhabitants live in Huamelula, Astata and neighboring villages. Chontal, a Hokan tongue, is closely related to the Chol and Chorti, with whome they share a common culture. They regard Chontalpa (Nonoalco) as their ancient homeland, in which region they were living when they were conquered by the invading Aztec tribes. The Chontal are primarily an agricultural people who have developed a smoothly functioning mutual relationship over the years in direct proportion to the ecology and environment of their region, trading back and forty such resources or products lacking in the other. The basic foodstuffs are corn, bens, squash, chili pepper, and sugar cane; mescal is produced as a cash crop. Chontal dwellings are primarily of bamboo and adobe, although some wealthier people enjoy thatched or tile roofs and solid adobe walls. The social patterns are essentially rural Mexican in nature, with *fiesta* days which follow the Spanish calendar, and a political structure which, while imposed by the national government, allows for an elected *presidente* and *alcalde* who govern the village. The religion is basically Catholic, but strong elements of ancient native patterns are still observed throughout the year. The village is the core of Chontal life, and as in most Indian cultures, the individual is subservient to the needs of the group. The Chontal homeland is isolated to an extreme degree, and the people have experienced very little outside contact. While by no means ignorant of the world around them, they do represent some of the most isolated of Mexican Indians. A considerable confusion has been recently introduced by art historians who have unfortunately applied the term *Chontal* in reference to a specialized pre-Columbian art style found in Guerrero. Apparently one varient of the Mezcala art form, but not identical to it, this has no relationship to the contemporary people by that name. *(see map page XIX)*

● BOWDITCH, CHARLES. P. Mexican and Central American Antiquities, Calendar Systems and History. Washington, D. C.: Bureau of American Ethnology - Bulletin 28: GPO, 1904.
● STEWARD, JULIAN H. Handbook of South American Indians. 7 Vols., Washington, DC: U.S. Govt. Printing Office, 1946-59.
● SWANTON, JOHN R. The Indian Tribes of North America. Washington, DC: U.S. Government Printing Office, 1952.
● THOMAS, CYRUS. Indian Languages of Mexico and Central America and Their Geographical Distribution. Bureau of American Ethnology Bulletin 44: Washington, D. C.: GPO, 1911.

CHOPTANK

(U.S.; MD) Apparently at tribe consisting of three subtribes--the Ababco, Hutsawap, and Tequassimo--formerly living on Choptank River. In 1741 they were given a reserve near Secretary Creek on the South side of Choptank River in Dorchester county on the Eastern shore, where a few of mixed Native American and black blood still remained in 1837.

BIBLIOGRAPHY —

● HODGE, FREDERICK WEBB. Handbook of American Indians North of Mexico. Washington: Government Printing Office, 2 vols., 1907-10.
● MURDOCK, GEORGE P. Ethnographic Bibliography of North America.New Haven, CT: Human Relations Area Files Press, 1975.
● SWANTON, JOHN R. The Indian Tribes of North America. Washington, DC: U.S. Government Printing Office, 1952.

CHOROTEGA

(Central America; Costa Rice and Nicaragua) were readily accessible from the coast and were quickly overrun by the Spanish conquerers. The great majority of the Indian groups of this area have long been extinct culturally if not racially. Practically all that survive today were dislocated from their aboriginal habitats to new and often drastically different regions and for 400 years they have been subject to influence not only from the Spaniards but from the descendants of Negro slaves who penetrated most of the Caribbean islands and coast.

The area occupied by the Chorotega extended principally along the Pacific coast of Nicaragua and Costa Rica in Central America. These people are thought to have migrated to this zone from Mexico from two to four centuries before the conquest of the area by the Spaniards.

Northern Honduras and central Nicaragua is characterized by crustal folds giving rise to the present configuration of river valleys and ridges. Vulcanism of Pleistocene and recent times has modified the land in many ways including the formation of Lake Managua and Lake Nicaragua. The Pacific lowlands, less extensive than those found adjacent to the Caribbean, are formed largely of volcnaic material and recent alluvium. The Pacific coast is characterized by winter winds and summer monsoons.

The Chorotega were the descendants of the first definintely identifiable migration of peoples from the north. The affiliation between spoken languages in southern Mexico and in the zone known to be occupied by the Chorotega lend credance to the assumption that the group migrated into Central America. The language dialects belong to the family Oto-Mangue. Otomi, Popoloca, Mazateca and Chiapanec, languages spoken in southern Mexico, belong to the same family. In the area occupied by the Chorotega, Choloteca was spoken along the northern shores of the Gulfo de Fonseca, Mangue was spoken in the area between Lake Managua and the Pacific and Mangue was also reported to have been spoken near Quepos in Costa Rica.

The Chorotega have been known by various local names: the Choloteca, the Mangue and the Oritina or Gurutina. Although these groups may have spoken local dialects and possibly had minor cultural differences, the Chorotega were basically a homogeneous culture.

The Pacific west coast of Costa Rica and Nicaragua, including the important Nicoya peninsula, is known to be archaeologically rich, but with a few exceptions has not been systematically studied. The prehistoric structures of Costa Rica and Nicaragua in the Pacific region include flat-topped mounds of earth and stone often surmounted or surrounded by stone statues representing human beings, animals or both.

Burial methods include the use of urns, cremation, and inhumation. Both articulated and disarticulated bodies occur in urns as well as the ashes of cremated bodies. Urn burials are reported from many coastal sites. Inhumation, often in mounds, was practiced in all parts of the Nicaragua region and was almost universal in Nicoya.

The prehistoric ceramics of Nicaragua and Costa Rica, despie borrowing and blending on the borders of the zone, form a discrete unit. The two main ceramic divisions in the Pacific region comprise the Polychrome adn Monochrome Wares. Ceramic figurines and whistles are also represented. Work in metal does not seem to be abundant in the Pacific region. Stone artifacts include elaborately carved metates, maces or club heads (very tropical in Nicoya graves). Stone bark beaters are also found. Jade amulets, particularly celt-shaped pendants, are very characteristic of the Nicoya region.

The most striking correlation between the archaeological record and ethnic groups is between the distribution of Nicoya Polychrome and the Chorotegan and Nahuatl-speakers. This correlation between the ceramic wares and carved stone of the archaeological period and the ethnic group remains problematic until more extensive archaeological work is carried out.

There have been at least four migrations from the north into Central America of peoples from Mesoamerica. The consequences of the migrations were that when one group replaced another in a restricted area repercussions were felt over the length and breadth of the land. As the Mesoamerican migrations occurred, the territory of indigenous groups as well as the lands of the new migrants changed with the fortunes of conflicting groups for the lands.

The Chorotega and other Mesoamerica groups that migrated into Central America brought certain polychrome ceramic wares but also other traits including the game of *voladores* , the custom of tongue piercing and certain religious practices that are definitely Mesoamerican, not Circum-Caribbean.

The tribes carried on intensive farming, which

out-ranked hunting, gathering and fishing in its productiveness and which supported a dense population and large villages. The typical community was a larger, compact, planned village of several hundred to several thousands persons. It consisted of pole-and-thatch houses arranged in streets and around plazas. The settlements were surrounded by palisades. In the villages were temples, special high-status households and storehouses.

The political organization of the Chorotega seemed to be characterized by a democratic form. A council of old men was selected by popular vote. It chose for its supreme head a "captain general," who acted as chief, particularly in war. If he died in battle another chief was chosen. Apparently the council had considerable power; it could kill the chief it had elected and chose another. The system was so strong that the Spaniards had to abolish it. They dissolved the councils and established divisions governed by appointed caciques, thus creating a sort of feudalism which they could control.

Religion centered around the temple cult. The temple was a special structure which sheltered idols to which offerings were made. Rituals are not clearly described but those mentioned in myths and occasionally in ritual are usually celestial, the sun and moon being especially prominent and the stars frequently named. Ceremonies were performed in honor of various gods on holy days, at the cacao harvest and on occasions of birth and death. There is occasional evidence of a jaguar cult both in religious practices and in art motifs.

Commerce centered in the markets. Each town had one in which all commodities, even slaves, were traded. A special official enforced all regulations. Cacao, maize and cotton were bases of exchange. Men were forbidden to enter the market of their native towns for these were run by the women and the boys. Strangers, however, could enter them to trade.

The Chorotega men wore sleeveless tunics of woven cotton cloth and breechclouts made of a long strip of cloth wound about the body and passed between the legs. The Orotina men also tied a thread to the prepuce. The Orotina women were said to wear an elaborately decorated breechclout, the ends of which passed over a narrow belt and hung down to form small aprons front and back.

According to the accounts from the 16th century of Oviedo y Valdes, the Chorotega took great care of their hair. The decoration and ornaments, including the way in which a man shaved his head, all indicated his social status and his success in battle. Men were said to pierce their tongues and ears and some were said to scarify their penis. Women also pierced their ears and wore quantities of necklaces, some of gold beads and medallions.

Body painting and tattooing were common. The followers of the caciques bore identifying marks. Elaborate body painting was used on ceremonial occasions. Cranial deformation was common.

The Chorotega customs of marriage have not been described specifically but the common people were apparently monogymous while the upper classes might be polygynous.

The young men were carefully trained and organized in companies which stood regular watch and were constantly ready for battle. Cannibalism was widespread.

A comparison of data from the modern tribes with those from the earlier chroniclers and from archaeology shows that all but the very backward and isolated tribes have suffered drastic changes. Gone are the intensive horticulture, the dense population, the large villages, the class-structured society, the mounds, temples, idols, and priests, the warfard, cannibalism, and human trophies, the elaborate death rites, and even the weaving, ceramics and stone sculpture. The modern tribes who retain a predominantly aboriginal culture carry on small-scale slash-and-burn farming, and many of trhem now hunt and fish more than they till the soil. They live in small villages, weave simple cloth, and make only plain pots. Their society is unstratified, their religious cults are scarcely remembered, and the principal survival of former days is the shaman.

BIBLIOGRAPHY –

● STEWARD, JULIAN H. Handbook of South American Indians. 7 Vols., Washington, DC: U.S. Govt. Printing Office, 1946-59.

CHORTI

(South America; Guatemala), from *tcor* , "cornfield," *ti* , "mouth; language;" i.e., "cornfield speakers," or "corn-grower's language" (a term of identity within the community), are an isolated group of Hokan-speaking Indians living in the Department of Chiquimula, Guatemala, and neighboring Copan, Honduras who separated from the Chol and the Chontal. They speak a dialect which differs from Chol in the substitution of R for L; the two are otherwise mutually intelligible. The Chorti live in two major divisions: the Highland people who inhabit small *aldeas* around Olopa; and the Lowland folk, in a like number of rural settlements whose main center is Jocotan. They are a self-sufficient agricultural people whose crops are the result of time-tested, strict ecological practices which take advantage of the particular environment of thie homeland. The Lowland people, who can raise two crops of corn a year, live on an abundance of that food, supplemented by beans, vegetables, some chickens and turkeys. The Highland Corti, on the other hand, can raise only a single harvest of corn a year, and therefore must supplement their diet with beans, squash, deer meat obtained by hunting in the mountains; plus some fishing, and modest crops of melons, squash, bananas and vegetables. Sugar cane, tobacco, and some domestic animals are raised primarily as cash crops which are sold in the markets, and some copal is raised for religious use and trade to other Indians. Mules, horse and cattle-raising are a very limited activity, and usually sold. The Chorti practice a variety of handcrafts, each of which is traditional within that area, and identified with it. Pottery is made in the Highland, where better clay is found, while basketry is a Lowland occupation, as is hat-weaving. Even here, the village limit is noticeable: one makes only loop-handled vessels, while another produces pottery without handles-wooden tables are made in a single village, and wooden dugouts come from a quite separate community. Although weaving was more widespread in earlier times, today it is much more limited, and is intended primarily for garments and for sale in the market; most clothing is commerically woven material purchased in the market. The people depend upon the outside world primarily for hardware and some special manufactured items; beyond this, they rarely venture into the Latino world. Socially, the people follow ancient Mayan patterns; politically, their world centers around the village, with annual election of officials and priests, who govern in a combined federal government-cumnative tradition fashion. The Catholic religion is universal, but ancient customs are so deeply imbedded into the religious framework that it is not possible to clearly delineate the two, and the Chorti make no effort to do so; very few have joined the Protestant faiths who have made sporadic efforts to proselytize with limited success.

BIBLIOGRAPHY —

● STEWARD, JULIAN H. Handbook of South American Indians. 7 Vols., Washington, DC: U.S. Govt. Printing Office, 1946-59.

CHRISTANNA INDIANS

(U.S.; Va.) A group of Siouan tribes, which were collected for a time in the early years of the 18th century at Ft. Christanna, on Meherrin River, near the present Gholsonville, Virginia. Governor Spotswood settled these tribes there about 1700 in the belief that they would form a barrier on that side against hostile Indians.

BIBLIOGRAPHY —

● HODGE, FREDERICK WEBB. Handbook of American Indians North of Mexico. Washington: Government Printing Office, 2 vols., 1907-10.

● MURDOCK, GEORGE P. Ethnographic Bibliography of North America. New Haven, CT: Human Relations Area Files Press, 1975.

CHUGACHIGMIUT

(U.S.; Alaska) An Inuit tribe occupying the territory extending from the West extremity of Kenai peninsula to the delta of Copper River, Alaska, and lying between the Kaniagmiut and Ugalakmiut. The Ugalakmiut have been almost absorbed by the Tlingit, who are encroaching on the chugachigmiut also, who are now poor, although blubber, salmon, cod, halibut, ptarmigan, marmot, and bear are obtained in abundance, and occasionally a mountain sheep. The sea otter has become scarce, but silver fox and other fur-bearing animals are hunted and trapped, and the fish canneries afford employment. The hair seal is abundant, furnishing covers for the kaiaks as well as meat blubber, and oil. The tribe numbered 433 in 1890.

BIBLIOGRAPHY —

● HODGE, FREDERICK WEBB. Handbook of American Indians North of Mexico. Washington: Government Printing Office, 2 vols., 1907-10.

● MURDOCK, GEORGE P. Ethnographic Bibliography of North America. New Haven, CT: Human Relations Area Files Press, 1975.

● SWANTON, JOHN R. The Indian Tribes of North America. Washington, DC: U.S. Government Printing Office, 1952.

CHUKCHANSI

(U.S.; Calif.) A Mariposan tribe, forming one of the northern divisions of the family, the remnants of which now occupy the foothill country between Fresno Creek on the North and San Joaquin River on the South, from a little above Fresno Flat down to the site of old Millerton, California. In 1861 they were on Fresno reserve and numbered 240. Naiakawe, a noted prophet about 1854, was a member of this tribe, and Sloknich was chief about the same time.

BIBLIOGRAPHY —

● HODGE, FREDERICK WEBB. Handbook of American Indians North of Mexico. Washington: Government Printing Office, 2 vols., 1907-10.

● MURDOCK, GEORGE P. Ethnographic Bibliography of North America. New Haven, CT: Human Relations Area Files Press, 1975.

● SWANTON, JOHN R. The Indian Tribes of North America. Washington, DC: U.S. Government Printing Office, 1952.

CHUMASH

(U.S.; Calif.) were a clever and artistic people, not a true tribe, but a linguistic group of similarly-speaking tribes, though with some dialects as different as Spanish is from Italian. In pre-white days they inhabited almost all what is now Santa Barbara County, the southern part of San Luis Obispo County, the western part of Ventura County, and small parts of southwestern Kern County and northwestern Los Angeles County, much of it facing the Pacific Ocean and including the three large islands in the Santa Barbara Channel. The land they inhabited had a generally mild climate of low rainfall and much sunlight, and was comparatively rugged, with the west to south easterly ranges of mountains rising from 2,000 to 4,000 feet high, except where Mt. Pinos reaches over 8,000 feet altitude in northern Ventura County.

Since the Chumash were divided into many small and independent tribes they did not, so far as we know, give themselves any national name. The name Chumash was given to them by the Spanish, probably from the Indian name for Santa Cruz Island *Mi'Chumash* . The Yokuts of the San Joaquin Valley region called the Chumash the *Tokya* .

Social and cultural boundaries and subdivisions. On the basis of food supplies and also cultural diversity the Chumash can be divided into two major subdivisions, the interior and northwest coastal, and the southern coastal and island. Both belonged to the Southern California Culture Area, noted for its steatite soft stone eating vessels, fast-paddled board canoes, roofless ceremonial enclosures and elements of the Chingichnish religions which used the *Datura* plant in concoctions to give visions. This was perhaps a subdivision of the larger Southwestern culture region because of the use of sandpaintings. Island was much the richer in food supplies and in complexity of culture because of the vast quantities of fish that could be gathered in the Santa Barbara Channel, the populous villages and the maritime trading.

History of territory and language. Some archaeologists divided ancient human occupancy of this territory in California into three divisions, the Oak Grove People of far back BC times (long headed people with sloping brows and protruding teeth), The Hunting People of recent BC centuries and the first Millenium AD (round-headed with Mongolian features), and the modern Chumash of the last thousand years of more (medium-headed and with softer features). Other archaeologists feel they have evidence these three types of human beings graded into each other gradually. The Chumash were succeeded by the Caucasians who practically destoyed them as people in the nineteenth century.

Linguistically the Chumash were a branch of the large Hokan language family that included the Pomo, Karok, Shasta and Yana in northern California, and, in southern California, included the Salinan and Esselen neighbors of the Chumash to their immediate north, while the more highly organized and warlike Yuman peoples inhabited what is now San Diego and Imperial Counties to the south. The Stishini dialect of the Chumash of southwestern San Luis Obispo County is so different from the other dialects that some anthropologists consider it is the language of a distinct people.

Summary of tribal culture. Food gathering. In the northwest coastal and interior subdivision of the Chumash the people subsisted mainly on acorns, with game animals, such as the deer, elk and rabbits, second as a food supply. Third in the interior area were seeds and berries, while sea shell life was third along the northern coast. Fish in this whole subdivision was a poor fourth. In the southern coastal and island subdivision, on the other hand, the Chumash subsisted first on the large fish population that found good shelter in the great kelp beds of the Santa Barbar Channel, while lush crops of the acorns of the valley and lie oaks were second, shellfish third, and game animals fourth. Along the coast large kitchen middens or refuse piles of shellfish, bones, etc. can still be found.

Acorns were gathered in the fall, with men and boys using long poles or climbing up to knock them from the trees. Women and children picked them up to place in large carrying baskets of twine weave. The acorn meat had to be broken out of the shells, then pounded with stone or wood pestles in basket mortars attached at the bottom with asphaltum to hollowed rocks. This coarse flour was leached in pits in the sand lined with leaves, warm water being poured over the flour to take out the poison. Molded into coarse cakes, the acorn meal was later either baked into bread in earth ovens or boiled in steatite stone pans to produce mush. Other food plants that were commonly eaten either raw or cooked were the cattail, carizo grass (for sugar), laurel, mushrooms, pinon nuts, soap plant, sugar brush, watercress and wild cherry.

Hunting was done mainly by the bow and arrow, though traps and snares were made, and spears used against larger game, such as elk and bear. Deer were often stalked by using a stuffed deer's head as a disguise, the hunter moving on all fours and acting like the deer. Deer and antelope were sometimes rounded up and driven into barricaded compounds to be killed. Sea mammals, such as seals, sea otters and sea lions, were clubbed on islands and beaches or harpooned in the sea.

The coastal Chumash became extraordinarily adept at fishing and their biggest asset was the unique *tomol* or plank canoe. The canoes were made by cutting down trees in the interior mountains and splitting the trunks into planks with whale-bone wedges. The planks were carried down to the beach where they were cleverly sewn together with strong twine. All seams were hevily caulked with black asphaltum, sometimes inlaid with sea shells. A double paddle was usually used and Chumash canoemen completely amazed the Spanish sailors with their speed. Large fish, such as tuna or swordfish, were harpooned while smaller fish were caught in long dip nets or seine nets, using floats, or with hook and line. The fish were most plentiful from March to early November, so that the people had to do much drying of fish in the sun to preserve some for use in winter. Shellfish were pried off the rocks, and the shells carved or ground into such things as fishhooks, dishes and shell money.

Arts, crafts and money. Shell money, formed fromparts of large clam shells and ground into circular beads were made into necklaces of various lengths, the length determining value. The Chumash were the chief traders and producers of shell money in southern California. The Chumash were a cut above surrounding tribes in arts and crafts, especially in their fine canoes and beautiful carved steatite (soap-stone) figurines and dishes. Recent discoveries of exquisitely beautiful and elaborate religious paintings in a hidden cave in the interior demonstrate a high talent and spiritual feelings.

Social and religious qualities. Our knowledge in this field is extremely limited because the Chumash culture died so swiftly under the cruel impact of the white conquest. We know they had a fairly elaborate social system, especially in the large villages.

(see map page XVII)

BIBLIOGRAPHY –

● LANDBERG, LEIF C.W. The Chumash Indians of Southern California.Los Angeles, CA: Southwest Museum, 1965.
● SWANTON, JOHN R. The Indian Tribes of North America. Washington, DC: U.S. Government Printing Office, 1952.

CHUNUT

(U.S.; Calif.) A former important Yokuts tribe in the plains East of Tulare Lake, California. They were enemies of the Tadji at the North end of the lake, but on friendly terms with the hill tribes. They lived in long communal houses of tule. Their dialect formed a group with the Tadji and Choinok.

BIBLIOGRAPHY –

● HODGE, FREDERICK WEBB. Handbook of American Indians North of Mexico. Washington: Government Printing Office, 2 vols., 1907-10.
● MURDOCK, GEORGE P. Ethnographic Bibliography of North America.New Haven, CT: Human Relations Area Files Press, 1975.
● SWANTON, JOHN R. The Indian Tribes of North America. Washington, DC: U.S. Government Printing Office, 1952.

CIBONEY

(West Indies) now extinct, were the original inhabitants of the Antilles. This is indicated by archaeological traces of a pre- agricultural hunting and fishing population have been found throughout Cuba and in many parts of Haiti, apparently at an earlier date that the Arawak population wherever the two happen to overlap. There is little doubt that the Ciboney were widely distributed during prehistoric times and that they were pushed back into their historic position as a result of the advent of the more advanced Arawak and Carib.

History. When the Spaniards first arrived in Cuba, they were told that the Arawak had taken away the most of the island from the Ciboney, enslaving them or driving them into isolated sections of the central and western parts of the island. The Spaniards mention five "provinces," or chieftainships, in the west, named (from west to east) Guanahacabibes, Guaniguanico, Marien, Habana, and Hanabana. It is not clear whether any or all of these were Ciboney at the time of the conquest; the names are Arawak but only Ciboney sites have been found in these provinces.

In Haiti the bulk of the population was also Arawak, but there were said to be isolated groups of Ciboney-like Indians living on the long narrow Peninsula of Guaicayarima in the southwestern part of the island. As in Cuba, these Indians are supposed to have been driven into this peripheral position as a result of the Arawak migration from South America.

With the exception of the province of Habana in Cuba (which may not have been Ciboney), the Spaniards rarely visited the inaccessible regions occupied by the Ciboney. The fate of those Indians is, consequently, unknown, except in the extreme western part of Cuba, where some are said to have survived until the Spaniards colonized that part of the island at the beginning of the 17th century. At that time, the Indians attacked the cattle of the settlers with bows and arrows, and rewards had to be offered for their extermination. There are legends that some of them survived until the middle of the 19th century.

Language. Nothing is known of the Ciboney language beyond the fact that it was probably different from both the Arawakan and the Cariban. The work "Ciboney" seems to be derived from the Arawak "siba," which signifies rock, and eyeri, man; it may have been given by Arawak who say Ciboney people living in caves. The size of the Ciboney population is unknown, but it must have been small, since the people lived in isolated groups in inaccessible places.

Culture. The Ciboney were fish eaters. Their sites contain the bones of fish and great quantities of shells, including clam, conch, mussel, oyster

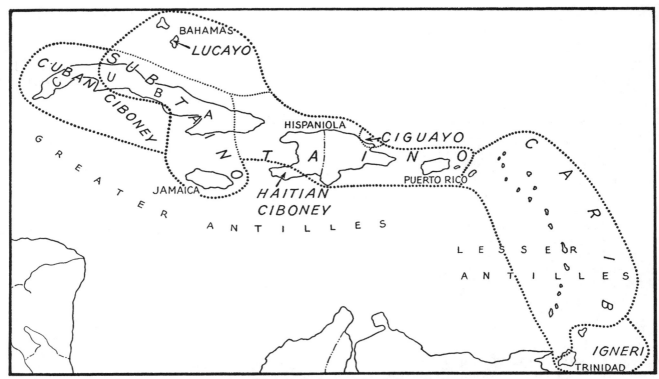

Tribes and cultures of the Antilles.

and snail, many of which have been perforated to extract the meat. Land and sea crabs, the manatee or sea-cow, ant the turtle were also eaten. The hutia, a rodent, and the almiqui, a small insectivorous mammal which formerly existed in great abundance in Cuba, the iguana or giant lizard, snakes, and birds were all probably hunted with special techniques. The people also nourished themselves with a number of native fruits, including the caimito, the corojo, the guanabana, the guayaba, the mamey, the manon or chirimolla, and the roots of various plants. According to the explorers, there were no cultivated crops.

The vegetable foods may have been prepared in mortars and on milling stones, of which a number have been found. The could then have been mixed in bowls of wood and stone, which are also known from the archaeological remains. Food may often not have been cooked, although fish and shell food were probably roasted over fires.

Dwellings. The evidences from both the archaeological remains and the historical sources is that the Ciboney lived in rock shelters and caves. They probably dwelt also in the open, where it is doubtful that they constructed more than the simplest windbreaks of brush or palm thatch. Their villages were probably small and semipermanent; one might be justified in calling them camps.

Dress. According to the conquistadors, the Ciboney wore little clothing, perhaps only girdles or breechcloths made from vegatable and stone, with which the Indians must have adorned themselves. The presence of red and yellow ocher suggests that the Ciboney colored their bodies or faces, possibly during ceremonies or ritual periods. They did not deform their foreheads, as did the Arawak.

Transportation. As an island people who placed great emphasis upon fishing, the Ciboney had boars, possibly the dugout canoe. On land it is likely that they traveled only on foot. Although they may have moved from place to place when the wildlife became exhausted, it is doubtful that they undertook long journeys.

Technology. The technology of the Ciboney was primitive, as indicated by specimens of limited workmanship, including objects of stone, shell, bone and wood. These indicate that the principal technological processes were battering with stone hammers, chopping with the shell gouges and (in Haiti) with stone axes, and cutting by means of flint chips. A few areas in both Haiti and Cuba have yielded traces of the grinding and polishing of stones with combination hammer grinders of the same material. Haiti reveals a knowledge of the flaking and rechipping of flint blades. Bark cloth, basketry, and gourd containers may have been present.

Social and political organization. To judge from the nature of their sites and the utensils they have left us, the Ciboney had a primitive social organization. Each local group, consisting of several families living together, may have constituted an independent band. At Cayo Redondo, one of the larger sites in Cuba, it has been estimated that the total population of such a band was 100. Each group of Ciboney in Haiti held all its property in common. In any case, trade must have been rare, sa few indications of it have been found in the sites.

Nothing is known of the life cycle of the Ciboney beyond the traces of their burials. When the Spaniards first encountered the Indians of western Cuba, they uttered war cries and fought with stones and wooden clubs. In Haiti, the flint daggers which are common in archeological collections may have been used for warfare. The presence of stone balls and disks in many of the Cuban and Haitian sites suggests some sort of game, which may have had a ritual function, as indicated by the deposition of balls in some of the graves.

Religion. Perhaps the most significant statement that can be made concerning the Ciboney religion is that it was unlike theat of the Arawak. There are none of the typically Arawak *zemis* in Ciboney sites. The *gladiolitos* , or ceremonial stones, however, may have a religious function. The presence of stone balls in the burials, finally, are considered an indication of a belief in life after death.

BIBLIOGRAPHY –

● SWANTON, JOHN R. The Indian Tribes of North America. Washington, DC: U.S. Government Printing Office, 1952.

CITIZEN POTAWATOMI

(U.S.; Kans.) A part of the Potawatomi who, while living in Kansas, withdrew from the rest of the tribe about 1861, took lands in severalty and became citizens, but afterward removed to Indian Territory (Oklahoma). They numbered 1,036 in 1890, but by 1900 had increased to 1,722, and in 1904 the number was given as 1,686.

BIBLIOGRAPHY –

● HODGE, FREDERICK WEBB. Handbook of American Indians North of Mexico. Washington: Government Printing Office, 2 vols., 1907-10.
● MURDOCK, GEORGE P. Ethnographic Bibliography of North America.New Haven, CT: Human Relations Area Files Press, 1975.
● SWANTON, JOHN R. The Indian Tribes of North America. Washington, DC: U.S. Government Printing Office, 1952.

CLACKAMAS

(U.S.; Oreg.) are small Indian tribe of the Chinook linguistic stock. At the time of the discovery of America they numbered several thousand; in 1806 they were counted at 1,800; by 1900 at less than 500; and today (1970s) they numbered a few. By the Dayton Treaty of 1855, the Clackamas ceded their lands to the United States, and were removed to Oregon reservations. Today few tribal members practice traditional methods.

BIBLIOGRAPHY –

● HODGE, FREDERICK WEBB. Handbook of American Indians North of Mexico. Washington: Government Printing Office, 2 vols., 1907-10.
● MURDOCK, GEORGE P. Ethnographic Bibliography of North America.New Haven, CT: Human Relations Area Files Press, 1975.
● SWANTON, JOHN R. The Indian Tribes of North America. Washington, DC: U.S. Government Printing Office, 1952.

CLALLMAN

(U.S.; Wash.) are a Coast Salish group in the Northwest Coast culture area. The Clallam have been referred to as *Sklallam, Noosdalum and Nusdalum.* The Clallman people were distributed aboriginally over a wide are on the Olympic Peninsula, State of Washington, ranging from Port Gamble, Washington to the east, to the Hoko River, at the western extreme of the northern Olympic Peninsula.

The Clallam's closest cultural and linguistic relatives are the *Sooke, Songish, Saanich, Lummi, Samish and Semiahmoo* . Together with Clallam, these tribes as a group are referred to as Straits Salish. The language spoken within the Straits Salish cultural group is also referred to as Straits Salish.

Clallam as a dialect of Straits Salish is considered to be the most divergent speech form. Most recently, Clallam has been re- examined and considered to be an independent language and separate from the Straits Salish dialects. In 1962 there were fewer than 100 speakers of Clallam remaining. In 1974 there were fewer than 10 fluent speakers of Clallam on the Lower Elwha Reservation, near Port Angeles, Washington.

The Clallam refer to themselves with several different names, as, for example, Nu-sklaim, meaning "strong people", nexws'a?em, meaning "Clallam people", and nexws'a?ucen, meaning "language of the Clallam people".

Skokomish (Twana) borders Clallam territory to the east. The Twana and Clallam languages are mutally unintelligible. Swinomish is a Puget Salish are also mutually unintelligible. This speech situation illustrates that there were wide areas of social and linguistic contact between speakers of different Salish languages and that multilingualism for the Clallam, as for many other Northwest Coast tribes, was the rule rather than the exception.

The Clallam, as did other Northwest Coast peoples, depended principally on sea foods in

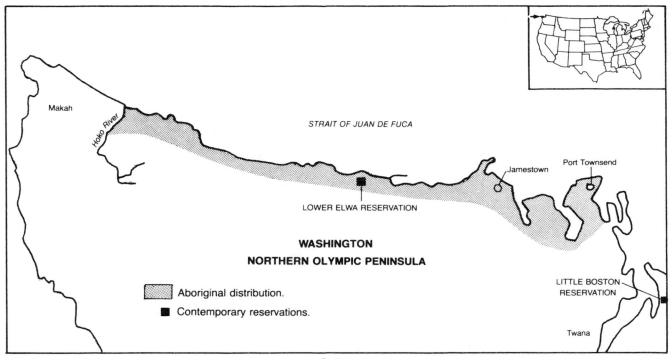

Clallam

their diet. Fishing wsa the most significant subsistence activity with the highest percentage of food being obtained in this fashion. Villages were located near fishing grounds, e.g., mouths of rivers, to facilitate this activity. A wide variety of fish were obtained during various times of the year, e.g., spring salmon from mid-April to July, humpback salmon from August to the end of October, silver salmon from October through December.

In order to maximize the availability of fish, temporary migrations were undertaken. Migrating in this way took Clallam families into the traditional territories occupied by their neighbors. This economic situation was interesting since it demands a prior foundation of amiable social relationships and multilingualism.

The Clallam women played an active role in subsistence activities. Women, with the help of children and slaves, were responsible for gathering roots, berries, sprouts, and sea food. The women gathered sea food which did not require fishing. Gathering plant foods was an intensive activity during certain times of the year and less intensive at other times. Gathering activities continued throughout the year. Plants were uses for a wide variety of purposes.

Clallam society was divided into autonomous political and economic social groups, e.g., villages. Each permanent village was composed of a number of houses. Relatives occupying the same house were called by the Clallam equivalent of "house- relatives".

Marriages to close relatives, e.g., cousins, was prohibited. Optimally, especially for higher class men, brides were to be selected from outside of their own village. Marriages outside of Clallam culture also occurred. This type of marriage system functioned to unite people within the Clallam tribe and also between the Clallam tribe and other tribes in the area.

There were no formal political institutions in Clallam society. Clallam political behavior remained within the boundaries of influence of one person over another. It was frequent for political influence to follow the lines of kinship and age, e.g., the oldest family member is most influential.

Supernaturalism, e.g., religion, magic, ritual, myth, played a large and significant role in Clallam society. The strong belief in influential supernatural agents affected all aspects of everyday life. Skills in fishing and hunting were associated with the power of acquired supernatural agents. This power was acquired through a long and arduous period of isolation and deprivation away from one's family and village. This period of purification which included daily bathing in cold water and fasing was necessary to encounter supernatural agents.

There was no strong distinction made between shamanistic spirit power and spirits of the layman. Individuals who were able to sustain a period of long and intensive spirit acquisition were often rewarded wigh shamanistic power. A shaman, Indian doctor, did not practice until several shamanistic spirits were obtained.

Layman's spirits were achieved through a period of less intensive spirit seeking. For a layman, the acquisition of a single spirit was often satisfactory.

Life in the Clallam afterworld was similar to life on earth; however, natural events in the afterworld were ordered oppositely to corresponding natural events on earth, e.g., summer on earth was winter in the afterworld. The afterworld was located physically beneath the living world and upside down.

Dreams played a significant role in the lives of Clallam individuals. Dreams foretold events and were often the stage for the return of deceased relatives. The Clallam terms for "dream" and "gaining spirit power" are linguistically related. Individuals clearly understood that "dreaming" and "gaining spirit power" were different events; however, the processes were considered quite similar.

The first recorded contact withthe Coast Salish and Clallam tribe occurred in 1790. The Spanish explorer, Lieutenant Quimper, sailing the Princess Royal, ventured as far east into the Strait of Juan de Fuca, as Dungeness. In 1792, the explorer Vancouver contacted the Clallam.

Quimper, in 1790, noted that the Clallam at Dungeness were using pieces of copper and beads as ear ornaments and English, Portuguese and Chinese coins for the same purpose.

The Clallam signed a treaty ceding their lands, except for a reservation area and subsistence areas, e.g., hunting, fishing grounds. This treaty was negotiated by Governor Stevens of the Washington Territory and is named the Treaty of Point-No-Point. The Clallam were assigned to the Skokomish (Twana) Reservation on the Hood Canal.

Disease played an important role in the history of the Clallam people. A severe smallpox epidemic entered the northern Olympic Peninsula area from the Lower Chehalis via the Satsop. The disease first struck the Twana, along the Hood Canal, to the east of the Clallam tribe. It spread into Clallam territory and moved northward on to the tip of Vancouver Island, British Columbia. The epidemic left a gap on the southern shore between Sooke and Songish which was later filled by Clallams migrating to Vancouver Island.

The disease had an important effect on social structure and organization. Within the native interpretative system a member of the upper class of society if the offspring of an upper class family. claiming membership in the upper class is a de-

monstration of ancestry and heritage. Even contemporary Clallam people refer to low class individuals as having "no family." This is a cultural way of saying that a person who is without ancestry is also without heritage.

Today, there are two Clallam reservations: 1) the Lower Elwha Reservation, located along the banks of the Lower Elwha River, just west of Port Angeles, Washington, and 2) the Little Boston Reservation, near Port Gamble, Washington. The Little Boston Reservation was established by Clallams from Clallam Bay and from the Elwha River area who migrated east to Port Gamble for employment in the saw mill. The Lower Elwha Reservation was established late in the 1940s and is the home of relatively few Clallam families.

BIBLIOGRAPHY –

● HODGE, FREDERICK WEBB. Handbook of American Indians North of Mexico. Washington: Government Printing Office, 2 vols., 1907-10.
● MURDOCK, GEORGE P. Ethnographic Bibliography of North America.New Haven, CT: Human Relations Area Files Press, 1975.
● SWANTON, JOHN R. The Indian Tribes of North America. Washington, DC: U.S. Government Printing Office, 1952.

CLATSOP

(U.S.; Oreg.) A Chinookan tribe formerly about C. Adams on the South side of the Columbia River and extending up the river as far as Tongue Point and South along the coast to Tillamook Head, Oregon. In 1806 their number, according to Lewis and Clark, was 200, in 14 houses. In 1875 a few Clatsop were found living near Salmon River and were removed to Grande Ronde reserve in Oregon. The language is now pracically extinct, and the remnant of the tribe has been almost wholly absorbed by neighboring groups.

BIBLIOGRAPHY –

● HODGE, FREDERICK WEBB. Handbook of American Indians North of Mexico. Washington: Government Printing Office, 2 vols., 1907-10.
● MURDOCK, GEORGE P. Ethnographic Bibliography of North America.New Haven, CT: Human Relations Area Files Press, 1975.
● SWANTON, JOHN R. The Indian Tribes of North America. Washington, DC: U.S. Government Printing Office, 1952.

CLOWWEWALLA.

(U.S.; Oregon) Also called Fall Indians, Tumwater Indians, Willamette Indians, and Willamette Falls Indians, all popular names for the tribe. The significance for the name Clowwewalla is unknown; phonetically it is pronounced Gila'wewalamt. The Clowwewalla belonged to the Clackamas division of the Chinookan linguistic stock, and they resided at the falls of the Willamette River. Some of their subdivisions were said to include the Cushooks, the Chahcowahs, and the Nemalquinner mentioned by Lewis and

Clark. The tribe, or part of them, were called Cushook by Lewis and Clark, who estimated that they numbered 650 in 1805-6. On this basis, *Mooney, 1928* estimated there might have been 900 in 1780. They were greatly reduced by the epidemic of 1829 and in 1851, numbered 13. They are now apparently extinct.

BIBLIOGRAPHY —

● HODGE, FREDERICK WEBB. Handbook of American Indians North of Mexico. Washington: Smithsonian Institution: BAE Bulletin No. 30: U.S. GPO, 1907.
● SWANTON, JOHN R. The Indian Tribes of North America.Washington, DC: U.S. Government Printing Office, 1952.

COANO

(Mexico; Jalisco) Indians are poorly understood groups that originally inhabited a section of the highland lake zone of Jalisco, Mexico, and part of the adjoining Rio Grande de Santiago Canyon. As sociocultural entities, they no longer exist.

The term *Coano*(pronounced *koano*) apprently meant "hill- dweller," with a strongly-implied connotation of "barbarian." It was more a term of social designation that one of ethnic content. It seems obvious that the Coano were from various ethnic backgrounds and probably spoke many dialects. What the Coano called themselves is unknown.

The Coano were not tribally organized, but rather were frontier and marginal groups within and between the various well developed Indian states of the highland lake zone. The states of Etzatlan, Tlala, Xochitepec, and Ameca controlled most of the area in which the Coano lived. It is very possible that some of the Coano were a population substratum within these complex states.

With the chaos that followed the Spanish conquest of western Mexico, the Coano began to raid their neighbors, Spanish and Indian alike. Whether or not this was an older practice cannot be stated with certainty. The Spanish regarded them as "Chichimeca," i.e. barbarians, quite distinct from the townsmen of the Indian states that they had so easily conquered. The Coano were especially expansive and disruptive during the period of generalized Indian uprisings of the early 1540s. Since the term Coano is most probably a class designation rather than an ethnic term, the territory that they occupied at any one time depended upon the social and political extensions of their well-organized neighbors.

No vocabularies are preserved that are specifically identified as Coano. Although pockets of Otomi speakers existed in this section of western Mexico, most spoke dialects of the Western Nahuatl languages. It is assumed that the Coano did also. Their language(s) or dialect(s) are dead.

As groups on the frontiers of powerful and competitive Indian states, the Coano probably participated within a larger economic structure over which they had little or no control. Archaeological surveys in their heartlands, the Volcan de Tequila and Sierra de Ameca, indicate that the Coano lived in small, dispersed agricultural villages with few ceremonial buildings. The ceremonial buildings were simple, small platforms that served as bases for modest temples. Ancestor worship appears to have been the central theme of Coano religion. Simple Tlaloc-like figurines indicate that this rain god also was venerated. No village yet surveyed appears more complex than any other. The rectangular houses were often large and well made. They are roughly arranged around patios in compounds of 3 to 5 structures. The compounds probably represent an extended family social organization. Burials are in the compound areas in simple pits that are occasionally slab-lined. Offerings in graves are usually simple bowls and solid figurines, though green stone beads and pendants are infrequently found. The Coano were prolific workers in obsidian, and produced many types of projectile points and scrapers. The frequency of these artifacts indicates a dependence on hunting not seen among the lake-oriented townsmen. It is possible that the Coano, as hill-and-mountain-dwellers, exchanged their produce (hides, meat, potatoes) for the items common among the lake-dwellers (textiles, fish, ceramics, mold-made figurines, etc.). Because of the violent character of Coano Spanish contacts, very little concerning their culture was written down.

The time depth of the Coano can only be inferred from the archaeology of the surrounding areas. By c. AD 350, complex societies had evolved in the highland lake zone. The Teuchitlan Tradition was characterized by monumental circular pyramids, surrounded by circular patios which in turn were surrounded by circular banquettes. Atop these circular banquettes were 8 to 12 rectangular platform pyramids. Ball courts and palaces also are associated with these circular ceremonial structures. At Teuchitlan, a primitive, semi-nucleated city of perhaps 25,000 inhabitants was in full flower by around AD 700. The Coano, as specialized hill-and-mountain-dwellers, undoubtedly had their roots in this time period. With the Postclassic Period (c. AD 900/1,000 to the Spanish Conquest), Coano culture took its final form. The Coano house type of rubble filled, stone walls; the Tlaloc figurines; the mold-made items; and the distinctive black and white on red polychrome ceramics had their roots in the Post- classic, lake-oriented towns. One town, Etzatlan was a nucleated town with a population at Conquest of around 17,000 inhabitants. When Etzatlan's control over the area was ended by the Spanish in the late 1520s, many of that town's warriors left to join the still independent Indian state located at the mouth of the Rio Amea in the Banderas Valley, near present-day Puerto Vallarta. Some Coano warriors may have accompanied them. Also, some Etzatlan warriors took refuge in the nearby mountains and deep canyons. A long and violent epoch of resistance to the Spanish ensued. The several Spanish priests who attempted to convert the Coano were killed. By the early 1540s, the Coano were in full revolution and only a concerted effort by the Spanish averted the loss of the province. The Coano again revolted in the 1560s and 1580s. The Spanish respected their fierce warlike character and ability to accomplish well-executed ambushes. During the 1600s, the Coano apparently were completely subdued and are not heard of again. Many were enslaved and relocated. The rest presumably were acculturated.

As mentioned, the Coano no longer exist. The only trace of them that is preserved is in the local accounts of the martyrization of the early Franciscan priests who attempted to convert them and the legends of their presumed barbarous behavior. Contemporary mountain farmers on occasions still use localities that the Coano originally improved. As a culture, they have been completely forgotten.

Aboriginal population estimates for the Coano are not given in the Spanish accounts. If the Coano were indeed a population substratum, their numbers must have been considerable. Archaeological surveys in the mountains of the lake zone indicate that they must have numbered at least several thousand.

The Coano await further study in archaeology and the archives. They were an important and specialized group along and within the frontiers of the Indian states of the highland lake zone of Jalisco, and they may have been a population substratum within these states. Their revolutions almost cost the Spanish control over the rich lakeside provinces.

BIBLIOGRAPHY —

● BOWDITCH, CHARLES. P. Mexican and Central American Antiquities, Calendar Systems and History. Washington, D. C.: Bureau of American Ethnology - Bulletin 28: GPO, 1904.
● SWANTON, JOHN R. The Indian Tribes of North America. Washington, DC: U.S. Government Printing Office, 1952.
● THOMAS, CYRUS. Indian Languages of Mexico and Central America and Their Geographical Distribution. Bureau of American Ethnology Bulletin 44: Washington, D. C.: GPO, 1911.

COCHITI

(U.S.; Southwest) A Keresan tribe and its pueblo on the west bank of the Rio Grande, 27 miles south west of Santa Fe, New Mexico. Before moving to their present locatiom the inhabitants occupied the Tuuonyi, or Rito de los Frijoles, the Potrero de las Vacas, the pueblo of Haatze on Potrero San Miguel or Potrero del Capulin, and the pueblo of Kuapa in the Canada de Cochiti. Up to this time, which was still before the earliest Spanish explorations, the ancestors of the present San Felipe inhabitants and those of Cochiti formed one tribe speaking a single dialect, but on account of the persistent hostility of thier northern neighbors, the Twea (to whom is attribute this gradual southerly movement and through whom they were compelled to abandon Kuapa), the tribe was divided, one branch going southward, where they built the pueblo of Katishtya (later called San Felipe), while the other took refuge on the Potrero Viejo, where they established at least a temporary pueblo known as Hanut Cochiti. On the abandonment of this village they retired six or seven miles south east to the site of the present Cochiti, on the Rio Grande, where they were found by Onate in 1598. The Cochiti took an active part in the Pueblo revolt of 1680, but remained in their pueblo for 15 months after the outbreak, when, learning of the return of Governor Otermin to reconquer New Mexico, they retreated with the Keresan tribes of San Felipe and Santo Domingo, reenforced by some Tewa from San Marcos and by Tigua from Toas and Picuris, to the Potrero Viejo, where they remained until about 1683, when it was reported that all the villages from San Felipe northward were inhabited. Between 1683 and 1692 the Cochiti, with their San

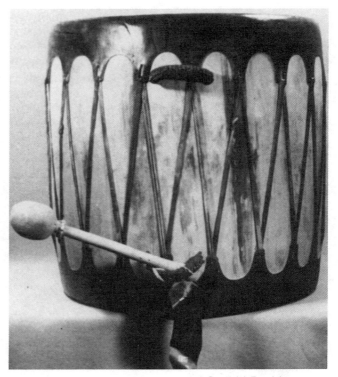

Drum made by Jim Herrera of Cochiti Pueblo.

Felipe and San Maracos allies, again took refuge on the Potrero Viejo. In the fall of the latter year they were visited in their fortified abode (known to the Spaniards as Cieneguilla) by Vargas, the reconqueror of New Mexico, who induced them to promise to return to their permanent villages on the Rio Grande. But only San Felipe proved sincere, for in 1692 the Cochiti returned to the Potrero, where they remainded until early in the following year, when Vargas, with 70 soldiers, 20 colonists, and 100 warriors from the friendly villagers of San Felipe, Santa Ana, and Sia, assaulted the pueblo at midnight and forced the Cochiti to flee, the Indian allies leaving for the protection of thier own homes. The force of Vargas being thus weakened, the Cochiti returned, surprised the Spaniards, and succeeded in liberating most of the Indian captives. Vargas remained a short time, then burned the pueblo and evacuated the Potrero, taking with him to Santa Fe a large quantity of corn and other booty and nearly 200 captive women. Cochiti was the seat of the Spanish mission of San Buenaventura, with 300 inhabitants in 1680, but it was reduced to a visita of Santo Donimgo after 1782. These villagers recognize the following clans, those marked with a asterisk being extinct: Oshach (Sun), Tsits (Water), Itra (Cottonwood), Shuwhami (Turquoise), Mohkach (Mountain Lion), Kuhaia (Bear), Tanyi (Calabash), Shrutsuna (Coyote), Hapanyi (Oak), Yaka (Corn), Hakanyi (Fire), Dyami (Eagle), Tsin (Turkey), Kuts (Antelope), Shruhwi (Rattlesnake), Washpa (Dance-kilt), Kisqra (Reindeer?). In addition, Bandelier notes an Ivy and a Mexican Sage clan. Present population is about 300. The Cochiti people occupy a grant of 24,256 acres, allotted to them by the Spanish government and confirmed by United States patent in 1864.

BIBLIOGRAPHY –

● DUMAREST, NOEL. Notes on Cochiti, New Mexico.Memoirs of the American Anthropological Association, no. 6, 1919.
● GOLDFRANK, ESTHER SCHIFF. The Social and Ceremonial Organization of Cochiti. Memoirs of the American Anthropological Association, no. 33, 1927.
● HODGE, FREDERICK WEBB. Handbook of American Indians North of Mexico.Washington: Government Printing Office, 2 vols., 1907-10.
● LANGE, CHARLES H. Cochiti: A New Mexico Pueblo, Past and Present. Austin, TX: University of Texas Press, 1959.
● MURDOCK, GEORGE P. Ethnographic Bibliography of North America.New Haven, CT: Human Relations Area Files Press, 1975.
● SWANTON, JOHN R. The Indian Tribes of North America. Washington, DC: U.S. Government Printing Office, 1952.

COCONOON

(U.S.; Calif.) A Yocuts tribe, said by Johnston in 1851 to "live on the Merced River, with other bands, under their chief Nuella. There are the remnants of three distinct bands residing together, each originally speaking a different language. The aged of the people have difficulty in understanding each other." The vocabulary given by Johnston is Yokuts. Merced River is, however, otherwise known to have been inhabited only by Moquelumnan tribes. The Coconoon are also mentioned by Royce together with 5 other tribes from Tuolumne and Merced rivers, as ceding all their lands, by treaty of March 19, 1851, excepting a tract between the Tuolumne and the Merced. If these statements about the Coconoon are correct, they constituted as small detached division of the Mariposan family situated among Moquelumnan groups midway between the main body of the stock to the South and the Cholovone to the N.W.

BIBLIOGRAPHY –

● HODGE, FREDERICK WEBB. Handbook of American Indians North of Mexico.Washington: Government Printing Office, 2 vols., 1907-10.
● MURDOCK, GEORGE P. Ethnographic Bibliography of North America.New Haven, CT: Human Relations Area Files Press, 1975.
● SWANTON, JOHN R. The Indian Tribes of North America. Washington, DC: U.S. Government Printing Office, 1952.

COCOPA

(U.S.; Ariz., Mexico; Baja California) from their Mojave name *Kwikapah* , of unknown meaning, are a Yuman-speaking tribe living in the delta of the Colorado River adjacent to San Luis, Sonora, and El Mayor, in Baja California, Mexico; a small number live in Yuma County, Arizona. They are most closely related to the Kohuana, Kalyikwamai, Dieguerio and Kamia peoples of southern California, and due to their living conditions, in time divided into the Mountain Cocopa and the River Cocopa. They were visited by the Europeans in 1540 when Hernando de Alarcon sailed up the Gulf of California to the dealt; their name first appears in the literature in the records of Juan de Oriate, who visited them in 1604, reporting that they inhabited 9 *rancherias* . Francisco Garces spent some time among them in 1776, commenting that they numbered some 3,000 persons occupying the northern section of the delta area; subsequently most of the trive moved south closer to the mouth of the Gulf, in effect becoming a wholly Mexican tribe. The boundary line of the Gadsden Purchase was drawn through their territory in 1854, which caused some Cocopa to become American residents, with the balance-about one-half-remaining in Mexico. This proportionate division continues to the present day.

The Cocopa particpated in the unsuccessful 1851 revolt on the Cupeno leader Antonio Garra, but most of their warfard was directed towards their hereditary enemies, the Yuma, Kamia and

Mohave, in which they were usually aided by the Maricopa, Pima, and on occasion, the Papago. In 1907 a 340-acre tract was set aside which they shared with the Yuma, and in 1917 an Executive Order established the Cocopah Reservation around Somerton, Arizona, consisting of 528 acres; a further 62-acre lease was granted in 1956. In 1934 the Cocopa accepted the precepts of the Indian Reorganized Act, thereby setting up a new political structure for the tribe; their new Constitution was formally adopted in 1964, and the tribe is presently governed by a 5-man Tribal Council. The population is approximately 441 persons in the United States, plus an additional 350 in Mexico.

The Cocopa are a well-formed and physically attractive people, above average stature, whose basic culture is the usual hunting- fishing-gathering economy common to most Yuman peoples of the Southwest. The availability of water from the delta provides a fertile soil for growing crops, and a few individuals maintain small plots, raising corn, squash, and beans; some other small crop farming, including cotton, is cultivated. Salinity reaches far enough into the mouth of the delta region to cause occasional difficulties, and flood or drought is a regular danger. The Cocopa do not live in villages or compact settlements; rather, the standard living pattern is a loose family cluster of the half-dozen or so families occupying scattered wattle-and-daub dwelllings, isolated from other similar clusters by as many as five or ten miles.

The traditional political system did not include "chiefs" in the usual sense of the term, although recognized "wise elders" or more expressive persons were listened to in daily activity. When warfare or serious crisis called for concentrated leadership, one individual would usually temporarily take on the burden; if his assertion of leadership was accepted by the group, he was followed for the duration of the effort; after which time he usually retired tohis everyday role. The basis of such a position seems largely to be the willingness of someone to step forward and assume the unwanted responsibility.

The Cocopa were not a particularly warlike people, although they have always given a good account of themselves when challenged. The bow and arrow, sturdy carved wooden "potato masher" club and hide shield common to the Southwestern desert people were the usual weapons. Although living near a large body of water, they apparently never developed sailing craft to any extent; such water travel as became necessary was by means of tule or balsa rafts. Clothing was made from the inner bark of the willow; men went nude or wore a barck breechout, while women usually wore a similar garment or added a bark apron or skirt. Hide sandals were worn to protect the feet; shell ornaments and jewelry were popular, nad tattooing of the face and body completed the personal decoration. Cotton was woven by the women on a horizontal loom similar to the type used by the Pima; men wove rabbit-skin blankets used for body covering or as sleeping robes, and on occasion, willow bark blankets. Women also made pottery, which was of good quality; it is less commonly seen today, having been supplanted by metal containers-most of the black-on-redware vessels of this style is made by the Maricopa or Pima potters. Basketry is no longer made, with a few single exceptions; it was never of high quality, and did not become a widely-manufactured product.

Cocopa religious concepts are not highly organized, nor are they well understood. The known deities live in and around the land-all mountains have resident gods, some also live in trees and brush, and there are no guardian spirits, magical charms, or sacred paraphernalia of the type so commonly found among most other North American tribes. There is a single Great Creator, *Makwayak* , who made all things; other supernaturals are the Sun, a male; the Moon, female; as well as the Coyote, Turtle, Owl, Eagle, Spider, Serpent, and similar creatures. The social control which derived from this system was effected by the shamans, who listened to the directions of the gods, who came to them in dreams to reveal their guidance.

The major social concern of the tribe was death. Shamans officiated at all mourning rites, which culminated in the great 6-day *Karuk* festival which overshadowed all other activities. When a person died, the person was prepared for the funeral; everyone gathered for the cremation services, at which time all personal property was burned, accompanied by excessive mourning and crying-an emotional expression which exceeded by far the displays of grief manifested by almost any other North American tribe. This demonstration of pent-up emotion apparently provided an emotional release, as well as an assurance that the body had been properly sent into the next world, thereby satisfying the ghost of the dead. The Cocopa believed that the ghosts were reluctant to leave the area of the living and would stay near the dwelling place unless they were properly dispatched to the other world. It was to this end that much of the seemingly excessive emotional display was addressed-for if the ghosts did not leave, misfortune would inevitably result. Yet for all of this preoccupation with death, there was no fear of dying. And, since the name of the deceased was never mentioned again, and an elaborate procedure existed to wipe out the memory of departed ancestors, no Cocopa genealogy existed; it is impossible to trace past relationships beyond those of the immediate living generations.

BIBLIOGRAPHY —

● BOWDITCH, CHARLES. P. Mexican and Central American Antiquities, Calendar Systems and History. Washington, D. C.: Bureau of American Ethnology - Bulletin 28: GPO, 1904.
● GIFFORD, E. W. The Cocopa. CA: University of California Publications in American Anthropology and Ethnology, vol. 31, 1933.
● HODGE, FREDERICK WEBB. Handbook of American Indians North of Mexico. Washington: Government Printing Office, 2 vols., 1907-10.
● MURDOCK, GEORGE P. Ethnographic Bibliography of North America. New Haven, CT: Human Relations Area Files Press, 1975.
● SWANTON, JOHN R. The Indian Tribes of North America. Washington, DC: U.S. Government Printing Office, 1952.
● THOMAS, CYRUS. Indian Languages of Mexico and Central America and Their Geographical Distribution. Bureau of American Ethnology Bulletin 44: Washington, D. C.: GPO, 1911.
● WILLIAMS ANITA ALVAREZ DE. The Cocopah People. Phoenix, AZ: Indian Tribal Series, 1974.

COEUR D' ALENE

(U.S.; Id.) presently live on a reservation in Northern Idaho. It generally encompasses the western two thirds of Benewah County and the southern one third of Kootenai County. It took thirty years of Indian diplomacy to get Congress in 1891 to officially set this land aside for the Coeurd' Alene. Throughout their history, the Coeurd' Alene have shown remarkable judgement in dealing with whites. Known by the name the early French-Canadian trappers gave them, Coeurd' Alene, which translates into pointed heart, they consistently refused to trade with the trappers or anyone else for low prices. Unlike their neighbors, they remained sharp and careful bargainers.

The Coeur d' Alene call themselves Skitswish and their language closely resembles that of the Flathead Indians in Montana. These languages belong to the Salishan language family, a large group of languages distributed over Montana, Idaho and into Washington and British Columbia. Salishan is thought, by some linguists, to be an offshoot of the great Algonquian stock.

Another characteristic besides language most often recognized among Salishan groups was their desire to settle near water. The Coeur d' Alene settlements began with the Pelouze River and then extend to the Pend d' Oreille Lake, then eastward to the Coeur d' Alene Lake and the Saint Joseph River, then westward along the southern rim of the water of Pelouze River back to the beginning. This fertile land, abounding in edible roots, fruit, fish berries, sheep, elk, deer, and beaver provided a rich and secure food supply. The Coeur d' Alene did not farm nor domesticate animals during the early period of their history in this region. Hunting and gathering with the help of their domesticated dog was all they needed for subsistance.

The Coeur d' Alene nation was politically divided into three primary bands each with its own charismatic and changing chief. Friendship and intermarriage united the small groups and during the winter months the three major bands split into smaller autonomous sections numbering thirty or more. Individual territorial rights of both the smaller and larger bands were respected. Polygyny, patrilineal descent, patrilocal residence rules and shifting local headmanship formed the political social structure of the small groups. Manufacturing consisted mainly of basketry, some crude pottery, and woven rabbit skin clothing. The people were generally poorly equipped for warfare, the bow they had was used for hunting and was made from the horns of mountain sheep.

Religious practices. Religious practices centered around the individual rather than the group. Belief in the supernatural derived its content from dreams and visions. Personal revelation, sought by everyone, was the major focus of the religious system. Large group gatherings and dances of ritual character were held only on a limited scale at the beginning of the food gathering season. Otherwise the small groups remained separated.

Somewhere around 1760 and before any substantial relations were developed with the whites, the Coeur d' Alene acquired the horse. This acquisition dramatically changed their lives. They gave up the semi-sedentary, hunting and gathering pursuits of their earlier days and assumed many of the traits of the Plains Indians. They made buffalo hunting a major tribal endeavor. Securing food was no longer a family or small band project but now required the cooperative help of large members of tribal peoples. More people were needed to insure both the success of the hunt and protection from the Plains Indians. With the introcution of the buffalo economy, many Coeur d' Alene left their rivers and lakes and migrated to the high mountains to protect their horses from the neighboring tribes. Once they began to travel east in search of the buffalo, they found that they were on territory claimed by other Indians. They were on the land of the Sioux, the Crow and the Blackfoot. Even though the Coeur d' Alene allied with neighboring groups in their area, the Nez Perce, Flathead and Koutenai, they never emerged victorious from any encounters with the Plains Indians. Even their alliances with the surrounding Idahoan tribes were tenuous due to their long history of separation, isolation and border disputes. It became more and more difficult for them to form alliances against the Plains Indians. During the Indian War of 1858, their neighbors the Nez Perce became a major factor in the defeat of the Coeur d' Alene and this led to a sharp decrease in their population.

While their antipathy towards outsiders contributed to their population reduction, because of their many border wars, it also served as a barrier against the invasion by the whites. The fur traders, who had established posts throughtout most of the west by the beginning of the 19th century, had a difficult time entering Coeur d' Alene Territory.

While the Coeur d' Alene successfully forestalled trappers, they were less successful in discouraging the Jesuits. In 1842 the Jesuit missionaries established a permanent mission on the Coeur d' Alene River. The priests had great success in their efforts to teach the Indians the fundamentals of farming and they got them to settle into the broad fertile valley and drastically reduce their buffalo hunting ways. By 1880 very few Coeur d' Alene went into the plains to hunt and by 1885 the buffalo were practically extinct. By 1890 the last of the Coeur d' Alene settled permanently, with the help of the Jesuit Mission, onto the reserve. They became the Catholic Indians of the North.

The church helped build roads and began to teach the Coeur d' Alene how to clear the land for the crops of corn and wheat. While there was strong conflict between the authority of the chief and the authority of the church the manner in which these disagreements were settled began to lay the foundation for church supremacy over the Coeur d' Alene which was to continue for many generations. The priests were successful. Much of the Jesuit success in missionizing the Coeur d' Alene, however, must be credited to the Coeur d' Alene themselves. They had shown a great interest in learning about Catholicism. In view of all that the Jesuits were able to accomplish in cooperation with the Coeur d' Alene, from settling down on the reservation to successful farming, it must be acknowledged that the Jesuits were a potent force in the lives of the Coeur d' Alene.

The Coeur d' Alene experienced, in a relatively short period of time, the transition from small, autonomous bands, living hunting and gathering lives, to horse involved buffalo hunters, who required the help of all the members of the tribe. The change from small bands consisting of semi-sedentary groups to large single nomadic communities with a center and a central authority was profound. Swiftly upon that change came the next. First the introduction of the mission, then the fighting among the neighboring Plains tribes, and finally the decimation of the buffalo. This led to a more rapid life change.

The Coeur d' Alene settled down, became farmers and stock breeders on their reservation. Their current economic situation includes farming, ranching and the leasing of their land to non-Indians. In a very short period of time they went from small bands to large political hunting units to sedentary farmers and land holders. Part of their economic and social success stems from their ability to change, the fertility of their land and their willingness to farm it. *(see map page XVII)*

BIBLIOGRAPHY –

● HODGE, FREDERICK WEBB. Handbook of American Indians North of Mexico.Washington: Government Printing Office, 2 vols., 1907-10.
● MURDOCK, GEORGE P. Ethnographic Bibliography of North America.New Haven, CT: Human Relations Area Files Press, 1975.
● SWANTON, JOHN R. The Indian Tribes of North America. Washington, DC: U.S. Government Printing Office, 1952.
● TEIT, JAMES A. The Salishan Tribes of the Western Plateaus.Washington: Bureau of American Ethnology Annual Report, no. 45, 1927-28.

COEUR D' ALENE RESERVATION

(U.S.; Id.) is home to nearly 525 Coeur d' Alene Indians. The reservation is in Benewah and Koutenai counties, Idaho, and is 69,299 acres, about one quarter of which is tribally owned. The rest is alloted land.

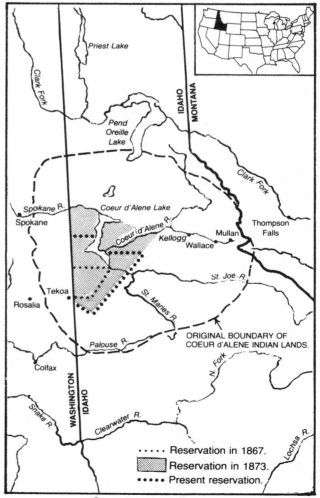

Coeur d'Alene Reservation.

The Coeur d' Alene were once one of 25 semi-nomadic Plateau Indian tribes. They were peaceful but dissatisfied with land treaties being negotiated in the mid-1800s. In 1858 the Coeur d' Alene united with the Spokane, Palouse and Yakima Indians to defeat federal forces in Rosalia, Washington. The following year, as a result, they were overwhelmed by United States forces, and placed on reservations, including this one. Their lands were ceded to the United States.

Today, no longer fisherman and hunters like their ancestors, the tribe resides placidly on the reservation. Their few ceremonies center around the gathering and growing of food supplies. They are organized under a constitution approved in 1949, and amended in 1961. The constitution provides for a general council form of government. The seven members are elected for a 3-year term to administer tribal business activities. Unemployment on the reservation is high, with nearly 50 of the people out of work. Tribal income annually is $30,000; a scholarship fund is available for students to continue their education beyond high school.

COLORADO

(South America; Ecuador) Before the arrival of the Spaniards in South America, the Colorado Indians lived in the lush Pacific lowlands between the mountains and the coast of western Ecuador. There they cultivated maize, chili peppers, cotton, and guavas, caught fish and extracted salt, all of which they traded with the highland peoples of Ecuador, even crossing the Andes to obtain fish poisons for the Canelo. The Colorado, whose name came from their liberal use of red body paint (achiote), are the southernmost extension of peoples speaking dialects of the Barbacoan division of the Chibchan language family. As such, they belong to a group of scattered Pacific lowland tribes ranging from the Choco in northern Colombia and Panama to the Cayapa and Colorado in the south whose tropical forest culture was far more consistent with the Indians of the Amazon than with those of the Andes.

Known also as the Campaz, and preferring to call themselves Tsatchela, the Colorado did not feel the impact of the Spanish conquest immediately for the climate of the wet lowlands did not attract the Europeans in the early part of the colonial period. Nonetheless, by the end of the colonial period, nearly every tribe west of the Andes was destroyed as the area was settled, as it is now, by montuvios, peoples of mixed white, Indian, and black ancestry who consider themselves Ecuadorians, not Indians. The only surviving aboriginal groups are the Cayapa and the Colorado who fled from their lowland home to the forested western slopes of the Andean cordillera, the Cayapa to the north and the Colorado just south of them. It is interesting to note that both the Cayapa and the Colorado by tradition believe that they originated in the highlands, moving from there to the lowlands sometime in the distant past. It is possible that this tradition made the adjustment from lowland to mountain slope more successful. Yet, they have been followed by the inexorable process of settlement. The Colorado occupy the upper reaches of the tributaries of the Emeraldas and Daules rivers; and this area in the western part of Pichincha Province has been heavily colonized

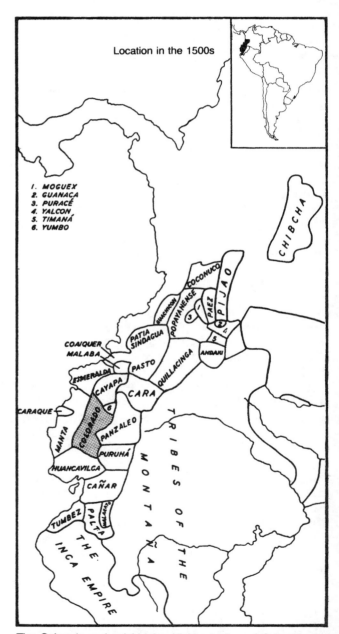

The Colorado and neighboring Highland tribes of Colombia and Ecuador.

by Ecuadorians since the 1930s. During World War II, an all-weather road was opened and the end of Colorado cultural and social institutions was in sight. More and more Ecuadorians have since settled in this region and most of the Colorado have been incorporated into the highland plantation economy. By 1950 there were approximately 300 Colorado left in two centers, Santa Domingo de los Colorados and San Miguel.

The Colorado are known as excellent cultivators, growing plantations, sweet manioc, yams, peppers, and cacao in fields near their houses. They also clear fields in the forests and plant such crops as maize, rice, pineapples, and citrus fruits. They also raise their own medicinal plants and *barbasco* , a drug used in fishing. Men clear the fields, fish, hunt and make nets while the women cook, weave and tend their children and domesticated animals which include guinea pigs, pigs, chickens and dogs. Both men and women cooperate in cultivating and harvesting the fields and in taking the produce to Ecuadorian market towns. The Colorado fish in the tributaries of the rivers, using nets, traps, and hooks as well as *barbasco* . Hunting is not very productive in this region, but the men shoot monkeys, agoitis, and an occasional deer with muzzle-loading shotguns. Before the turn of the century, blowguns with clay pellets were the main hunting weapons for birds.

Like th Cayapa, to the north, the Colorado have no nucleated villages but live dispersed in the forest near their fields. There is a church which marks the center of a settlement and to which the Colorado come for Catholic ceremonies, baptism, marriage, masses for the dead; and so forth, which occur at infrequent intervals when the circuit-riding Dominican priest visits the region. Houses are large frame buildings without walls, the palm-thatched roofs supported by posts. There is often a separate sleeping section within the house. Platform beds are used for sleeping. Each household is economically self-sufficient in terms of the traditional system.

No real information is available about the traditional social and political organization nor is the exact composition of the multi-family household known. What might have existed as political leadership has long since disappeared. However, some descriptions of the rituals connected with life cycle events have been written. At birth, there is no specific ceremony save the parents observing certain food taboos until the infant's navel was healed. The influence of the church may be seen in the appointing of godparents for each child. A puberty ritual is noted for boys only in which the shaman conducts a nose-piercing ceremony for those ten to twelve years old. After this event, the boy may begin painting his body and drinking

Colorado Indians, early 20th century

nepe . Girls are married soon after puberty but boys wait somewhat longer. Marriages are performed by the shaman and are occasions for great feasting with music, dancing, and drinking. Marriages are considered final when blessed by the priest.

Colorado funeral rites are a mixture of traditional beliefs and highland influence. The deceased is dressed in his best clothes and is guarded by relatives for one day during which time they weep loudly, drink, and sometimes dance. Special games of the types seen among the highland Indians are played with rubber balls or burning wood. These games serve a dual purpose: to keep mourners awake and more importantly to prevent the spirits which caused the death from attacking the survivors. The body is then placed in a shroud and suspended above the ground under the floor of the deceased's house. A platform is placed over the body and a string connected to the roof is tied around his neck. The string helps the soul to depart quickly from the body. After leaving some food and a candle, the relatives abandon the house. At each full moon, the oldest member of the family comes back and touches the string gently. When it breaks at the touch, the soul has left the body.

Colorado religious life shows the effects of the long period in the eighteenth and nineteenth centuries when they had resident Catholic priests among them. All formal ceremonies and rites of passage, with the possible exception of the funeral rite, show Colorado attachment to the Cathoic ritual. However, in the process of day-to-day activities, the aboriginal Chilbcha concepts as well as those of other highland Indians are evident. The traditional creation story gives an important plact to the two major Andean volcanoes, Cotopaxi and Chimborazo. There is a strong belief in good and evil spirits as causes of good fortune and of disease. Shamans play a large role in Colorado society, especially in recent times as the Catholic priest has all but disappeared from the community and what political leadership there had been in the past is no longer evident. The shamans are held in such high regard that they are often called upon to journey up into the highlands to practice their curing prowess. It has been said that Colorado shamans treat not only Indians but mestizos as well. Disease was believed to be caused by sorcery and by evil spirits. Colorado share the montana belief that diseases is caused by the intrusion of sharp spikes which must be sucked out by the shaman. The Colorado practice therapeutic diet also to cure disease in which the patient, his relatives, and the shaman observe certain food regulations in order to facilitate the cure. During the actual ritual, *nepe* , a narcotic, mildly hallucinogenic drink, is taken by both the shaman and his patient. Brandy is also consumed, drums and rattles are beaten, trance dancing takes place, and finally the sharp spine is sucked out and displayed for all to pay witness to the shaman's great power.

BIBLIOGRAPHY —

● THE COLORADO MAGAZINE. Vol. XIX, No. 5, September, 1942; Vol. XX, No. 2; March, 1943.
● CONGRESS. 43rd Congress, 2nd Session, H. Ex. Doc. 88; 44th Congress, 2nd Session, S. Ex. Doc. 42.
● DUNN, J. P. Massacres of the Mountains, A History of the Indian Wars of the Far West.New York, NY: Harper & Bros, 1886.
● HEBARD, GRACE RAYMOND., E. A. BRININSTOOL. The Bozeman Trail; Historical Accounts of the Blazing of the Overland Routes into the Northwest, and the Fights with Red Cloud's Warriors.Cleveland, OH: The Arthur H. Clark Co.
● INDIAN AFFAIRS, LAWS AND TREATIES. 1871, 1873, 1879, 1881.
● RISTER, CARL COKE. Border Captives, The Traffic in Prisioners by Southern Plains Indians, 1835- 1875.Norman, OK: University of Oklahoma Press, 1940.
● STANLEY, HENRY M. My Early Travels and Adventures in America and Asia. New York, NY: Charles Scribner's Sons, 1895.
● STEWARD, JULIAN H. Handbook of South American Indians. 7 Vols., Washington, DC: U.S. Govt. Printing Office, 1946-59.
● SWANTON, JOHN R. The Indian Tribes of North America. Washington, DC: U.S. Government Printing Office, 1952.

COMANCHE

(U.S.; Plains) a Ute word meaning enemy, is the name generally applied to a group of "nomadic" southern Plains Indians of Shoshonean linguistic stock and Rocky Mountain orgin, who first appeared in the Spanish documents of New Mexico a little after 1700. In the eighteenth century they were also known to the French and later to the Americans as Padouca or Pado, a name probably originally applied by the French to various Plains Apaches, whose country to the northeast and east of Santa Fe was taken over by the Comanches in the course of the eighteenth century. Early nineteenth American documents also referred to the Comanches as Ietans. The Comanches' name for themselves is *Nemena* or "The True People" ("Human Beings"). The signs for Comanche in Plains sign language refer both to the Comanches' Shoshonean origin and to their separateness from other Shoshoneans, some of whom were called "Snakes." On the north Plains the sign for Comanche was indicated by a snake crawling forward or, after this sign was made, by flipping the hand over and again indicating a snake, signifying "another snake." On the south Plains the sign for Comanche was a snake crawling backwards.

Horses and plunder drew the Comanches from the mountains into raiding the Indian pueblos and Spanish rancherias of New Mexico, and the military and organizational advantages inherent in large horse herds permitted the Comanches to take possession of the south Plains and there establish the first "typical" Plains adaptation. Little is known of Comanche culture until about 1830, while most of the ethnographic descriptions of this group apply to the period of about 1850-1874, by which time the Comanches were a typical Plains tribe, little resembling their Shoshonean forebearers, contrary to statements by those who stress the "Shoshonean orientations" of the Comanches. On the south Plains, in the early nineteenth century, the Comanche homeland extended from the Arkansas River to the Nueces and from about the Pecos to the middle Brazos. Although various semi-sedentary tribes also hunted in part of this country, the Comanches and their Kiowa allies (with whom the Kiowa-Apaches were associated) regarded this land as theirs. Later the southern Arapahoes and southern Cheyennes peaceably shared in the Comanche and Kiowa range. The Comanche language became the lingua franca or "court language" for the southern Plains.

Ecology. Horse nomadism on the Plains involved a number of complex ecological "trade offs," so that more than one set of choices could be found amongst a given Plains group at any given time. The increase in horse herds not only made pursuit of the buffalo more efficient, but also meant that more meat could be dried and carried to offset food scarcities engendered by the erratic movement of the buffalo, and especially to meet the common food scarcity in very late winter or early spring. But the increased size of horse herds also meant that a group would have to move more frequently through the exhaustion of forage for horses. Put simply, without considering numerous complications, the basic choice was between small groups with relatively long term residential stability and large groups that had to move frequently to secure horse forage. It is well known

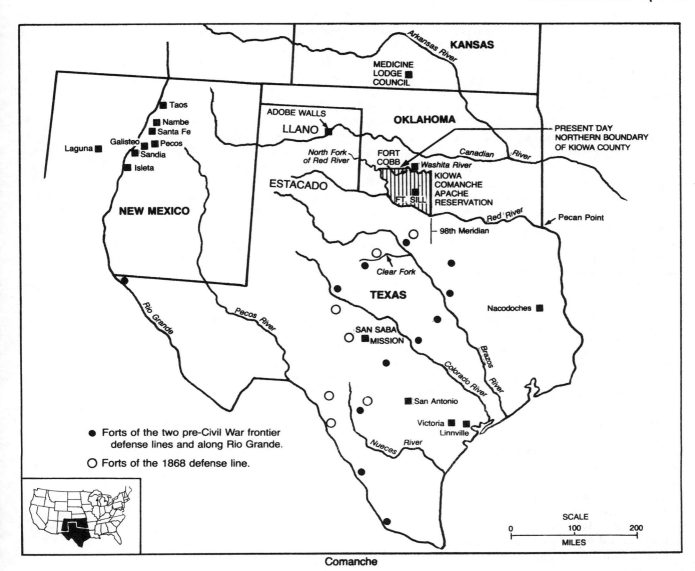

Comanche

that large groups of Comanches aggregated in the summer, examples being Thomas James' estimate of 1,000 lodges and Catlin's of 600-800 lodges. Although there was a tendency to disperse into wooded bottomlands in the winter, it is sometimes forgotten that large aggregations did occur in the winter months, such as Jacob Fowler's (1821-2) report of Comanches in a multi-tribal camp of 700 lodges with a herd of 20,000 horses.

The Comanches were not merely passive participants in the Plain's ecosystem, but had developed techniques to help shape their environment. Although fire cycles are common in any grassland, the Comanches set fires in favored areas to insure more succulent grass next year. In addition, the Comanches were competent horse breeders who practiced gelding to build up their horse herd and select for the brave, fast and agile horses needed for buffalo hunting, an activity with a high horse mortality rate.

The frequent early references indicating that the Comanches ate only buffalo meat are assuredly wrong; ethnobotanists have identified more than twenty wild plants eaten by Comanches, but the early references do show how preponderant buffalo meat was in their diet. The techniques used by the Comanches in buffalo hunting were the surround, in which a mounted party caused a small herd or portion of a herd to move in a circle while the hunters on the edge of the circle shot the animals, and "running," where hunters chased individual animals. The Comanches, unlike most Plains Indians, frequently used a spear against buffalo. Only when the buffalo failed and famine threatened did a band resort to the magical communal antelope hunt. Horses were another emergency food.

Social and political organization. The extended family was the basic building block of Comanche society and, as a band chief's family was the core around which his band formed, largfe and powerful families often played important political roles. It was not by accident that there was a marked tendency for band chiefs to be sons of band chiefs. A band chief had to have a good war record and see that his followers were not lacking in the necessities of life, food and horses primarily. By producing wealth and giving it away, a band leader maintained his following and validated his own status. Hence, a large family which contributed wealth was a great asset to a social climbing Comanche. The principal familial prop to the chief was his "brother," which in the Comanche kinship system included not only a man's own siblings, but his male cousins as well. Comanche families created alliances with other families by marriage. As a man grew in importance he would attract followers from these allied families.

Bands composed of an extended family core and often a varying number of allied families were the basic subsistence units of Comanche society. In 1878, shortly after going onto the reservation, the subsistence band (which became the reservation "beef band" drawing rations together) averaged forty-seven people.

An important chief was the leader of his own subsistence band, but was also followed by a number of other chiefs, often unrelated to him, and their subsistence bands, who looked to the great chief for guidance and support. Hence the number of people following a particular chief might range from a single subsistence band of no more than twenty people to a collection of subsistence bands of a thousand or considerable more people.

Confusion has surrounded the Comanche "divisions" because of substantial variations in their reported numbers. Late eighteenth century Spanish sources reported three divisions, "Cuchanecs" or "Cuchanticas" ("Buffalo Eaters"), "Yamparicas" ("Yap Eaters"), and "Yupes" ("Timber" or "Stick People"), as did David Burnet in 1819 (Comanches, "Yamparacks", and "Tenawas" or "Liver Eaters") and some American Indian agents in the 1860s and 1870s ("Quahadas", "It-chit-a-bundah" or "Cold Weather People," and "Penatekas"). Spanish and Mexican sources of the early nineteenth century (Padilla 1820, Berlandier 1829), as well as De Cessac in 1882, reported only two divisions. Late American sources, on the other hand, claimed a considerable larger number of divisions. In 1847 Butler and Lewis claimed six divisions, while agent Neighbors in the 1850s reported eight, and in 1861 Pike, the Confederate agent, mentioned five, as did W. P. Clark in 1885. In 1885, Ten Kate, who obtained information through a U.S. military interpreter, stated there were seven divisions. In late American documents

"Nokoni" was a frequently mentioned division name, but other division names were sometimes given only once or twice by one or two writers ("Pohonim," "No- na-um" or "Noonah" which is reminiscent of the Comanche name for themselves, "Hai-ne-na-une," and "Par-kee-na-um").

There is reason to believe that the Comanche divisions corresponded to meaningful Comanche political groupings. The late increase in names does not indicate an increased knowledge of the Comanches, but rather a confusion of synonymous terms. For example, Neighbors recognized that "Hois" and "Penateka" were synonyms, but "Yupe" was also a synonym, as was probably "Tenawa." "Yamparica" can be equated with "Cold Weather People," and "Cuchantica" with "Nokoni" and "Quahada." At least from the late eighteenth century, the Comanches seem to have been organized into three divisions, each of which had a generally recognized pre-eminent chief. That one division sometimes made war while the other divisions were at peace with their enemy shows that the divisions were the highest level of effective political organization among the Comanches, although joint councils of divisions and, at least occasionally, a head chief of all divisions was sometimes recognized.

The conculsion that the divisions were important political groupings is supported by the meager data on Comanche soldier and medicine societies, which suggest that each Comanche division had its own societies. Table 1 collates the probable synonyms for the Comanche soldier societies with Lowie's information on the divisions inwhich the societies were found. The officers of each soldier society had various kinds of special paraphernalia such as lances and sashes, and each society appears to have owned the rights to a particular dance. The earliest (1820s) account of a Comanche soldier society reported that members of the Wolf society wore an untanned wolfskin strap and were pledged not to flee in desperate struggles. In addition to the lodges of the soldiers, there was a lodge for the old men.

Recognition of a head chief for all Comanches was the policty of the Spanish and American governments, a policy which before about 1840 seems to have received some Comanche support, but by the middle of the nineteenth century there was such a multiplicity of interests among the Comanches that no chief ever again attained enough prestige to be recognized by all Comanches. In 1786 the Spanish claimed that the leading Cuchantica chief had been elected head of all Comanches. Burnet stated that in 1819 "the three divisions collectively acknowledge one head or grand chief, the extent of his authority...depending more on the force of his personal character

Comanche Division:	Lowie (1915):	Lowie (1915):	Clark (1885):	Ten Kate (1885):	Berlandier (1829):
Yamparica	Crow	Crow	Raven	Crow	
Quahada	Little Horse	Colt		Little Horse	
Quahada	Big Horse	Horse		Big Horse	
Nokoni and Penateka	Fox	Swift Fox	Swift Fox	Fox	
All Divisions	Buffalo	Buffalo	Buffalo Bull	Buffalo Bull	
				Turkey Cock	
	Drum		Gourd	Gourd	
			Afraid of Nothing		Wolf

Table I
Comanche Soldier Societies

than on the investments of office." Burnet reported that Parrow-a-Kifty, a Tenawa, was head chief. And in 1835 the United States Commissioners heard the Comanche Ichacoly (Catlin's Ee-Shah-ko-nee) say: "I will tell you the same thing I told you before. I am the only head chief of my nation."

Culture and life cycle. Comanches were very concerned with personal cleanliness and adornment. Adults bathed every morning, to the point of breaking ice on streams, and washed before eating. Young children of both sexes went nude, but older girls wore smaller versions of women's tow piece (by mid-nineteenth century spliced together) leather dresses. Although men usually wore only a cloth breechclout in summer, they sometimes wore leather or cloth leggings and hide skirts. All ages and sexes wore hard-soled moccasins, and in winter wore buffalo robes, often decorated with beads and paint. After contact, silver an cooper ornaments, especially brooches, were popular. From the middle nineteenth century, American manufactured clothes began to supersede native dress. Men wore their best clothes to war, often including spectacular headdresses, and frequently made tatoos around wounds as well as painting themselves. While women wore hair cropped at the neck, men wore long queues, often with horsehair spliced in to make them several feet long.

Transportation equipment was developed, although the travois, among most Plains Indians the most important accessory to the horse, may have been only an imporvised affair (baggage packs tied to tent poles drug by horses). In addition to the horse travois, a few poor Comanches followed at the tail of a moving camp with dog travois. The lack of travois elaboration may have been due to Comanche horse wealth; a horse can pull more than it can carry. The horse rich Comanches were one of the few Plaines tribes to use pack horses and pack saddles (made of rawhide pads). Riding saddles were of the Spanish type, with stirrups and a high pommel and cantel (less deep on women's saddles) made of rawhide-covered wood, cinched with a hide strap. Women seem to have used cruppers. Bridles were plaited hide or hair. Babies were carried in a fur lined pocket attached to a board equipped with straps for placement on the mother's back, the pommel of a saddle, or a tree or lodgepole in camp.

Comanche camps (and camp-life) were pretty much the same whether composed of only a few or five hundred lodges. There is no authenticated reference to orderly arrangement of lodges or the camp circle of the northern Plains. The only pre-reservation dwelling was the conical buffalo-skin (later canvas) tipi, using a "four pole foundation," which vaired in size according to the number of inhabitants and wealth of the owner. Heating and ventilation was achieved by combination of a central fire pit, eared flaps around the vent, and a tipi liner. Tipis were often elaborately decorated with designs and drawings. Brush shelters were sometimes made by travelers and brush arbors were sometimes erected in camp. Comanche men might have more than one wife (often sisters) and impor-

Comanche Indian Village, in the Valley of the Washita, 1871

tant men had separate tipis for each wife (as many as ten) and her children, clustered around his principal lodge. It seems probable that such groups shared in food preparation.

Food preparation and untensils were simple. Fire was made by fire-drill. Meat was roasted on sticks or boiled. (Before traders introduced kettles this was accomplished by dropping hot stones into an animal skin or buffalo pouch). Bear oil was used like lard. Corn was obtained through trade and used to make gruel, which was eaten with wooden spoons from bark bowls or, following European contact, tin or sometimes ceramic dishes. A kind of bread was made from locust pods. Pemmican, pounded dried meat and berries, stored in rawhide containers (parfleches), was eaten without further preparation. Solid food was eaten off a board or piece of leather. There is some evidence that hte Comanches made a few baskets.

Activites were determined by sex and age. Women's work included: firewood and plant gathering; food, hide and container preparation; manufacturer of clothes and tipis; erection of the lodge; packing of camp equipment. Men were primarily concerned with the procurement of meat; the manufacture of weapons, hunting and horse equipment; warfare. Children had a happy existence. There was a richly developed, formalized

vocabulary, heavy in redundant syllables, used for talking to babies, which was gradually replaced as children learned adult speech patterns. The threat of supernatural (owlghost) sanctions was used to discipline, rather than corporal punishment. Children's play was mostly imitations of adult activities; girls, for example, played house and had dolls. Older boys, however, attended the horse herds.

Games, often involving adult gambling, were of considerable importance to adults as well as children. Individual competitive sports included archery and arrow throwing, and foot and horce racing. The hand game ("bullets" or "buttons", played by two parties, was a leading gambling game, as were several forms of dice. Betting occurred on other games as well, such as the shinny and double ball games played by women. Other social gatherings included story and myth telling, and dances. Some games and all dances involved music by drums, rattles, whistles, and singing. (Flutes and the single-string violin, an example preserved in the Field Museum, were also apparently used.) Until late pre- reservation times these gatherings were never marred by drunkenness; the Comanches were noted for their sobriety.

Very little is known about Comanche communal dances (during which there were aggregations of subsistence bands). Lowie, in 1912, found that the Comanches were "...in part very unwilling." informants. He thought the Comanches had a festival of several weeks duration in which all the soldier societies performed their dances. This would be reminiscent of the Cheyenne Massaum ceremony in which individual medicine societies participated. Only in the 1930s and in 1945, when few pre-reservation Comanches were alive, were further data obtained. One informant thought the Buffalo Hunting Dance (apparently Lowie's "festival") had been the most important ceremony, but no details were known. (The buffalo "society" of Table 1 may refer to this dance rather than to a particular society.) The report of a Green Corn Dance is based on a fraudulent source (Nelson Lee) and the misinterpretation of another (the novel *Matouchon*, in which "Melville," based on the real missionary Methvin, saw a dance at an unidentified, but apparently Caddoan, not Commanche, village.) It is often stated that the Sun Dance, generally the most important High Plains ceremony, appeared among the Comanches in 1874, but some anthropologists, notable Shimkin, have suggested a much earlier appearance. Be that as it may, at least by the mid-nineteenth century, many Comanches attended the annual Kiowa Sun Dance.

Other dances and ceremonies appear to have belonged to particular medicine societies. According to Hoebel, the "medicine" or "power" was obtained through a vision and then shared with less than a dozen others. The members of such societies had similar talismen and ritual paraphernalia. It is not known if the medicine men supervising the three most important rituals found in subsistence bands were members of specific societies. The three rituals were the Owls Spirit Seance, called to obtain information on lost objects or absent people, the Beaver Ceremony, a cure for illness from sorcery, and the Eagle Dance.

Public pipe smoking was the most common ritual among the Comanches. Sometimes this was a component of other ceremonies, sometimes it occurred by itself to mark solemn events.

Most Comanche religious practices were concerned with personal "medicine," but some things, such as the sun, had much more power than others. Any man could obtain "medicine" by presentation, through the "sharing" mentioned by Hoebel, or through a vision, usually during adolescence. At the time of a successful vision quest, a guardian spirit outlined the often onerous ceremonial requirements for maintaining the power given, and presented a talisman (or several objects) which was placed in a "medicine bag," and a power song (the so called "death songs" sung before battle). Shields, lances, and war bonnets almost all had ritual obligations attached to them. "Power" was

manifest in its ability to protect its owner and entail his success. If a man was killed or unsuccessful in life, it was a sign that his "power" was false or that he had not carried out his ceremonial obligations.

The concern with "medicine" was exemplified at many life cycle crises. At birth a midwife attended, but if delivery was difficult, a man of special "power" was called in. While the camp was moving a woman might halt and give birth, then rejoin the band, but in camp a special lodge might be set up for delivery. There the mother stood upright, with legs apart, grasping a stake which had been driven in the ground near the edge of the lodge. In early days the baby was washed and painted in red ochre, then wrapped in furs. If twins were born, one was sometimes killed, as was the case if the child was born deformed. (Occasionally abortions were induced by the mother beating her stomach with stones.) Naming might occur any time after birth, but always by the time the individual had emerged from babyhood, and was im-

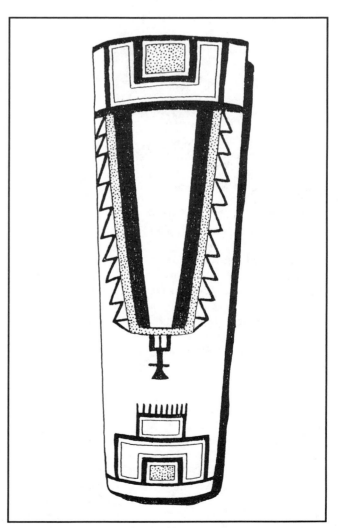

Comanche medicine case.

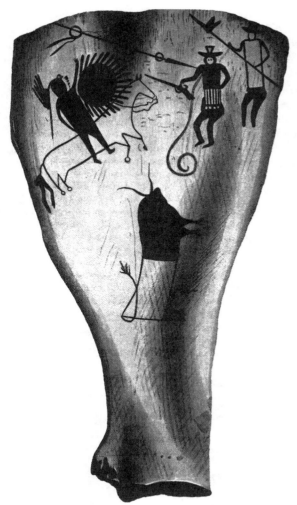

Comanche Inscription on the shoulder blade of a buffalo

portant as names had the power to affect life success. Hence a medicine man or warrior, men of proven "power, bestowed the name at a public ceremony. The next important life passage was adolescence, marked for girls by menstruation and the vision quest for boys. At first menstruation, and monthly thereafter, a woman had to live in a separate hut, as the blood nullified all "medicine." Some boys obtained visions unsought, but others sought out lonely spots and fasted (but did not engage in the self-torture of some Plains tribes).

Marriages marked adulthood for young men and women, although pre-pubescent girls seem to have occasionally been reared in the lodges of their husbands. Men generally did not marry until they were established warriors, at age twenty-five or more. Premarital sex was not uncommon. Girls, not boys, could make sexual advances and some early reports called the unmarried women "very dissolute" to the point of some having intercourse with dogs, which Berlandier said was common among Comanche men, although homosexuality

was rare. This Comanche "dissoluteness," however, was contradicted by Lehmann, a Comanche captive in the 1870s. Marriages were arranged in that horses and other gifts were sent by a suitor, through an intermediary, to the father of the woman, who could decide to accept or reject the gifts (and the marriage) without consulting the woman. Sometimes, however, lovers eloped. A man could have as many wives as he could support, but most men had only one. Women could not engage in extramarital sex, although a man might permit his classificatory brothers, especially when he was absent on the warpath, as well as trading partners visiting camp, to sleep with his wife. A woman's adultery was punished by beatings or cutting off her nasal septum, or sometimes by death, although a woman might escape punishment if her paramour was stripped of his property by her husband, who might whip the paramour in lieu of taking his goods.

War was viewed as a man's pre-eminent occupation; much care was lavished on war equipment and there were many social occasions where a man recounted his coups (war honors), the greatest being touching a live enemy. Scalps were taken primarily for the victory celebration at camp, which could only be held if no Comanches were lost. Most war parties were rather small and were organized to avenge the death of a Comanche or to take horses, but in summer very large expeditions of several were organized. The actual attack on the enemy was often at night, when, according to Dodge, the Comanche was "the most dangerous of all Indians." Adult captives were usually killed or taken back to the village for torture, especially by the women, although captive women were sometimes taken for sexual service. Captive children were often adopted, but young children were usually tortured to death. Special war equipment included poison made from rattlesnake venom for application to arrows (later to bullets), buffalo hide shields and shield covers, and warclubs (which had generally ceased to be used about 1860). Most war techniques (smoke signals, for example) and equipment (such as quivers for bows and arrows-weapons later replaced by guns, lances, and knives) had uses other than in war.

War losses were largely responsible for the disproportionate ratio of woman to men, but, if not killed by enemies, a Comanche, before the spread of European diseases, could generally look forward to a long life. The Comanches were expert in treating arrow and gunshot wounds and in setting fractures with bandages, as well as having an extensive knowledge of medicinal plants. Sweat lodges-closed domed structures in which water was sprinkled on stones heated outside-were also used in medicinal treatment. But medicines and magic could not prevent aging, and when the aged could no longer take care of themselves, they were abandoned.

Like Plains Apaches had also suffered at the hands of the Comanches; by 1739 the Farones had been driven from the Canadian, and in the 1750s the Paloma and Cuartelejo Apaches finally established near Pecos.

Guns permitted the Comanches to take the central and southern High Plains from the Apaches, but changed intertribal relations in other ways as well. Most guns they obtained (along with corn) from the horticultural Caddoan villagers of the eastern Plains (who got them from Mississippi Valley French traders); horses, buffalo meat and robes were given in exchange. In the 1740s, although the Comanches were still trading with the village tribes, they began to have direct access to French traders. By 1748 the Comanches, who wished to restrict others' direct access to French traders, were at war with their former Ute friends. This marks the beginning of the classic Plains warfare pattern- the northern tribes raiding the horse rich tribes of the south. Soon the horticultural Pawnees and Osages, two tribes which continued to war with the Comanches until almost reservation days, were raiding southward.

With a ready supply of guns the Comanches attacked New Mexico mercilessly and began penetrating deep into Texas as well. The New Mexican Spanish launched an unsuccessful expedition in 1742; Comanche plundering continued. Between 1744 and 1749 Comanche raids had caused the death of 150 at Pecos Pueblo alone. In 1748 the Spanish managed to halt a raid on Pecos and in 1751 they killed almost a hundred Comanches returning home from attacking Pecos and Galisteo Pueblos. Although this may have given New Mexico a short breathing space, the Comanches began appearing in the vicinity of the San Saba River mission and San Antonio. In 1758 they attacked the Lipan Apaches, their perennial enemies until the reservation period, at the San Saba mission, and next year chased a Spanish punitive expedition all the way from Red River back to south Texas. Within ten years the Lipans were driven from the San Saba country and the mission was eventually abandoned, as the Comanche threat grew in New Mexico as well.

The establishment of small Spanish garrisons at Pecos and Galisteo Pueblos and attempts to make peace did little to halt Comanche raiding; the Comanches penetrated even further into the pueblo country. In 1762 peace was established in New Mexico for a few years and reestablished for less than a year in 1771. The Comanche attacks were often only small raids but sometimes, as in 1772 when 500 Comanches attacked Pecos, were at-

tempts to sack a pueblo. Galisteo, Taos, Nambe, Sandia, Laguna and Isleta Pueblos were raided through the next five years.

The Spanish introduced a peace policy in Texas in the early 1770s, making peace with all the raiding northern tribes except the Comanches. In 1777 an attempt was made to extend the peace to the Comanches, but serious steps were taken only in 1783, and it was 1786-7 before peace was attained. At the peace negotiations a head chief was recognized by most of the Comanches and his task was to deal with the Spanish. The Spanish goal was peace between the Comanches and Utes, both of whom they hoped to use in their war with the western Apaches and Navajos.

With the Comanches pacific, the Spanish undertook making them sedentary. It was reported in 1787 that a Comanche chief had asked Spanish help in establishing a pueblo. Soon Spanish women built a number of houses on the Arkansas, but the pueblo was abandoned a few months later.

The 1787 peace was more enduring than Comanche occupation of the Arkansas pueblo, lasting until the unrest engendered by the 1810 Mexican revolution and penetration of the southwest Plains by Anglo-Mexican traders. The early nineteenth century raids on the Texas frontier were primarily to obtain horses for the American trade, a new source (or a replacement of the extinct French source) of manufactured goods in addition to the long established indirect trade through the eastern Plains horticultural villages. By the 1820s the Comanches had traded thousands of horses and mules to Anglo-Americans through three main channels: Nacodoches, Pecan Point, and the Kansas River.

The wave of eastern tribes which swept the Plains from the 1820s to about 1840 as a result of the federal relocation policy resulted in another realignment of Plains tribes. The Kiowas, who had come from the north, became allies and associates of the Comanches about 1790, but a portion of the Arapahos and especially their Cheyenne allies,

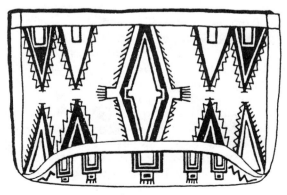

Comanche painted rawhide bag.

who soon followed the Kiowas, fought the allied Comanches and Kiowas (with the Kiowa-Apaches). In the face of the emigrant threat, about 1840 or a little earlier, the Cheyennes and Comanches and their allies made peace, which strengthened the military position of all of them and assured the Cheyennes access to Comanche horses. And in the late 1830s and 1840s, the Comanches now free of a northern threat, tremendously expanded their raids on the northern Mexican states.

Even before the 1836 battle of the Alamo, the Republic of Texas sought to achieve peace with the Comanches, a task later hampered by the short tenures of Texas presidents and resulting fluctuations in national Indian policy. Throughout the period of the republic, most Indian battles were fourght by companies of Texas Rangers. Serious wars began in 1840, after Houston's 1838 peace, when more that thirty of the Comanches who came to negoiate at San Antonio were killed at the Council House. In retaliation about 500 warriors destroyed the town of Linnville and attacked Victoria. When Houston again became president (December, 1841) he sought to reestablish peace, but was unsuccessful, although a treaty was made in 1844.

During the 1840s the Comanches were again ravaged by diseases. In 1848 smallpox struck, followed by the 1849 cholera epidemic. The 1816 smallpox epidemic was also severe, but it was not known if the 1833 cholera epidemic made headway among them.

Soon after the United States annexed Texas, plans were made to make the Texas frontier secure. In 1848 the federal government began a chain of forts from Red River to the Rio Grande: Forts Worth, Graham, Gates, Croghan, Martin Scott, and Inge. Settlement had passes this line in less than two years and a second line of forts were built beginning in 1851: Forts Belknap, Phantom Hill, Chadbourne, McKavett, Terrett, and Clark.

With the annexation of Texas the Anglo-Americans of the east ceased to be a ready market for Comanche plunder and there was a great increase in the "Comanchero" trade (primarily thousands of stolen cattle) with the Mexican traders of New Mexico (even though New Mexico had also been annexed to the United States). The Comanchero trade persisted into the 1870s after reaching its height immediately after the Civil War (while the frontier was still ungarrisoned) with the establishment of the Loving-Goodnight cattle trail to New Mexico. As Comanches increasingly again frequented the approaches to Santa Fe, the federal government sought by the 1853 Fort Atkinson treaty, to end the threat to the caravan trade. This treaty called for annuity of $18,000 for ten years

in exchange for promises of halting raids in the United States and Mexico.

The next year the Texas legislature, which controlled the public domain in Texas, provided minute reserves for the Comanches and other tribes, but few Comanches ever resided on them. These reserves were the Brazos Agency (4 leagues, later doubled) and the Clear Fork Comanche Reserve (4 leagues). Only a portion (about 400) of the Penatekas went to their reservation. In 1847 large numbers of non-reserve Comanches moved into the country between the Canadian adn Arkansas, from which they launched unprecedented attacks on Texas, which were answered by state punitive expeditions. Meanwhile Texas citizens demanded removal of the reservations, which resulted in the relocation of the reserves to Indian Territory (Wichita Agency north of the 1868 Comanche Reservation) where Fort Cobb was built for their protection. The Penatekas stayed on their reservation even after the Comanche Reservation was established.

With the Civil War, federal troops were withdrawn from Texas, and although the Confederates

Quanah Parker was chief of the fierce Kwahadi band of Comanche. They were defeated in their attempt to quell buffalo hunting by whites in the Texas panhandle. He thereafter encouraged his followers to not only retain their old customs, but also to learn the white man's ways.

made a treaty in 1861 and established an agent at Wichita Agency, the Comanches soon ignored the peace. Even the Penatekas took to raiding after Wichita Agency was destroyed by federal affiliated Delawares and Shawnees in 1862. Texas suffered greatly from the Comanches during the war and some counties on the northwest Texas frontier were depopulated to the point that county organization was abandoned.

In October, 1865, in attempting to reassert federal Indian control, the United States, in exchange for Comanche, Kiowa, and Kiowa-Apache assent to federation with the Cheyennes and Arapahos, offered the "federated" tribes most of the Llano Estacado (Staked Plains) and all the Indian Territory west of the 98th meridian as a reservation. The agreement floundered by the refusal of the Texas legislature to grant Texas land.

It was some time before effective control of the frontier was gained by the United States. By 1867 Texas was aflame from extremely heavy raids, while the northern and central Plains tribes were also at war. That year Hancock and Custer's central Plains campaign proved a fiasco for the army.

A new federal policy was introduced after the January, 1867, report on the "Conditions of the Indian Tribes," and in October, 1867, a peace commission met with the five "federated" tribes at Medicine Lodge Creek. This last treaty signed by the Comanches gave them a reservation in the southwest corner of the Indian Territory and annuity goods for thirty years, in exchange for their other land claims. The new direction in Indian policy became Grant's "Peace Policy" with the appointment of Quakers to positions of authority in the Indian Office.

The army did not rely only on the Quakers; by 1868 some of the old posts of the Texas defense line had been regarrisoned and new posts built, although active campaigning was necessary to enforce the reservation policy. A campaign with converging columns from Kansas, Colorado, and New Mexico, to drive in all absentee Indians ended with the Battle of the Washita (November, 1868) and the apparent acceptance of reservations by the south Plains tribes. In late December, 1868, the Comanches received their first annuity, and a few days later Fort Sill was begun to watch them, but within a year a large number of Comanches (including all the Quahadas) was absent. Mackenzie's fall, 1871, campaign against the recalcitrant Comanches was unsuccessful, but his destruction of their village in the summer of 1872 brought the Quahadas to the reservation.

The final extermination of the great southern buffalo herd was a time of social turmoil for the Comanches. From 1872 through 1874 almost four million buffalo were killed. Isatai, a prophet who claimed his medicine would drive out the Americans and restore the herds, led the Comanches in a Sun Dance, preparatory to the last great Comanche "uprising," but he was discredited when the first major attack (Adobe Walls, June, 1874) failed. Nevertheless, numerous raiders swarmed into Texas while the army campaigned on the Staked Plain. Quahada resistence became futile when Mackenzie, at the September battle of Palo Duro Canyon captured their horse herd and killed over a thousand ponies, although the Quahadas, the last "wild" Comanches, did not surrender until June,

Young girls in decorated buckskin dresses. Wanada Parker, daughter of Quanah Parker, is on the left.

1875. To prevent a future outbreak, the Comanche horses (over 6,000) were sold or killed on their return to the reservation and there were nine Comanches among the south Plains Indian "ringleaders" sent to prison in Florida. In addition, the agents prohibited dancing and set to work to break the authority of the chiefs. Though there were no more general outbreaks, there were occassional raids into the 1880s.

On the reservation, peyote use, which had been known among the Comanches since the 1860s or earlier, quickly became a focus of "nativism" and the Comanches (with the Kiowas) were the principal agents of peyote diffusion, but the Comanches, except for the Penatekas, had little to do with the 1890 Ghost Dance fervour. Through the 1880s and 1890s the Comanches leased large portions of their reserve for grazing (in 1893 almost a million and a third acres for over $200,000). A strange blend of idealism and land hunger brought about the General Allotment Act, which by 1901 led to the division of communal lands and the allocation of one hundred-sixty acres to each Comanche. The remainder (the largest part) of the reservation was then sold to non-Indians.

Population. Early nineteenth century population estimates run from Catlin's grossly inflated 40,000 to Burnet's commonly quoted 10 to 12,000. There are no compelling reasons, however, to believe that the Comanches ever numbered more than 6 to 8,000. by the 1860s they had been reduced to less than 2,000.

(see map page XV)

BIBLIOGRAPHY —

● BOLTON, HERBERT EUGENE. Athanase de Mezieres and the Louisiana-Texas Frontier, 1768-1780. Cleveland, OH: The Arthur H. Clark Co., 1914.
● BRININSTOOL, E. A. Fighting Red Cloud's Warriors, True Tales of Indian Days When the West Was Young. Columbus OH: The Hunter-Trader-Trapper Co., 1926.
● CHRONICLES OF OKLAHOMA. 1923, 1924, 1925, 1926, 1928, 1931, 1934, 1941, 1942, 1949, 1950.
● CONGRESS. 40th Congress, 2nd Session, S. Ex. Doc. 60.
● DE SHIELDS, JAMES T. Cynthia Ann Parker; The Story of Her Capture. St. Louis, MO: William Harvey Miner Co., 1886.

● DEBO, ANGIE. Quannah Parker. American Heritage, 4, no. 4, June 1953.
----- The Road to Disappearance. Norman, OK: University of Oklahoma Press, 1941.
● DODGE, RICHARD I. Our Wild Indians, 33 years' Experience Among the Red Man of the Great West.
● DOWNEY, FAIRFAX. Indian-Fighting Army. New York, NY: Charles Scribner's Sons, 1941.
● EASTMAN, EDWIN. Seven and Nine Years Among the Comanches and Apaches. Jersey City: Clark Johnson, 1874.
● EASTMAN, ELAINE GOODALE. Pratt, The Red Man's Moses. Norman, OK: University of Oklahoma Press, 1935.
● FOREMAN, GRANT. Advancing the Frontier, 1830- 1860. Norman, OK: University of Oklahoma Press, 1933.
----- Indian Removal. The Emigration of the Five Civilized Tribes of Indians. Norman, OK: University of Oklahoma Press, 1932.

----- Pioneer Days in the Early Southwest. Cleveland, OH, The Arthur H. Clark Co., 1926.
----- A Traveler in Indian Territory. The Journal of Ethan Allen Hitchcock. Cedar Rapids, IA: The Torch Press, 1930.
● GABRIEL, RALPH HENRY. The Pageant of America: the Lure of the Frontier. New Haven, CT: Yale University Press, 1929.
● GHENT, WILLIAM JAMES. The Road to Oregon, A Chronicle of the Great Emigrant Trail. New York, NY: Longmans, Green & Co., 1929.
● GRINNELL, GEORGE BIRD. The Fighting Cheyennes. New York, NY: Charles Scribner's Sons, 1915.
● GRISWALD, GILLETT. Old Fort Still, The First Seven Years. Chronicles of Oklahoma, vol. 36, 1958.
● HARMON, GEORGE DEWEY. Sixty Years of Indian Affairs, Political, Economic, and Diplomatic, 1789-1850. Chapel Hill, NC: University of North Carolina Press, 1941.
● HEBARD, GRACE RAYMOND., E. A. BRININSTOOL. The Bozeman Trail; Historical Accounts of the Blazing of the Overland Routes into the Northwest, and the Fights with Red Cloud's Warriors. Cleveland, OH: The Arthur H. Clark Co.
● HODGE, FREDERICK WEBB. Handbook of American Indians North of Mexico. Washington: Government Printing Office, 2 vols., 1907-10.
● HUMFREVILLE, J. LEE. Twenty Years Among Our Hostile Indians. New York, NY: Hunter & Co.
● INDIAN OFFICE REPORT. 1837, 1845, 1847, 1854, 1855, 1868, 1869, 1870, 1871, 1872, 1874, 1880, 1882.
● JAMES, GEN. THOMAS. Three Years Among the Indians and Mexicans. (with notes and biographical sketches) St. Louis, MO: Missouri Historical Society, 1916.
● MURDOCK, GEORGE P. Ethnographic Bibliography of North America. New Haven, CT: Human Relations Area Files Press, 1975.
● NILES REGISTER. Vol. 50, April 16, 1836.
● POWERS, MABEL. The Indian as Peacemaker. New York, NY: Fleming H. Revell Co., 1932.
● RICHARDSON, ALFRED TALBOT. Life, Letters and Travels of Father Pierre-Jean de Smet, S. J. 1801-1873. New York, NY: Francis P. Harper, 1905.
● RICHARDSON, RUPERT NORVAL. The Comanche Barrier to South Plains Settlement. Glendale, CA: The A. H. Clark Co., 1933.
● RISTER, CARL COKE. Border Captives, The Traffic in Prisoners by Southern Plains Indians, 1835- 1875. Norman, OK: University of Oklahoma Press, 1940.
----- The Southwestern Frontier - 1865-1881. Cleveland, OH: The Arthur H. Clark Co., 1928.
● ROYCE, CHARLES C. Indian Land Cessions in the U.S. Washington: 18th Annual Report, Bureau of Ethnology, 1896-97.
● SEYMOUR, FLORA WARREN. Indian Agents of the Old Frontier. New York, NY: and London: D. Appleton-Century Co., Inc., 1941.
● SWANTON, JOHN R. The Indian Tribes of North America. Washington, DC: U.S. Government Printing Office, 1952.
● UNDERHILL, RUTH M. First Penthouse Dwellers of America. New York, NY: J. J. Augustin Publisher, 1938.
● VESTAL, STANLEY. Kit Carson, The Happy Warrior of the Old West, a Biography. Cambridge, MA: Houghton Mifflin Co., 1928.
● WALLACE, ERNEST AND HOEBEL, E. ADAMSON. The Comanches: Lords of the Southern Plains. Norman, OK: University of Oklahoma Press, 1952.
● WELLMAN, PAUL I. Death in the Desert. The Fifty Years' War for the Great Southwest. New York, NY: Macmillan Co., 1935.
----- Death on the Prairie, The Thirty Years' Sturggle for the Western Plains. New York, NY: The Macmillan Co., 1934.
● WHEELER, COL. HOMER W. Buffalo Days: Forty Years in the Old West. Indianapolis: The Bobbs-Merrill Co.
● WISSLER, CLARK. Indians of the U.S., Four Centuries of Their History and Culture. New York, NY: Doubleday, Doran & Co., 1940.

COMECHINGON

(South America; Argentina) lived alongside their neighbors, the Sanaviron and others, in the Sierras de Cordoba in northwestern Argentina just south of the Gran Chaco. The Sierras de Cordoba are the most southeastern extension of the Pampean Sierras and are composed of three cordillera running north to south from latitude 29S to 33S near longitude 64W. The Comechingon inhabited the fertile valleys and quebradas found between the cordillera where there were numerous streams which provided water for horticulture. Indeed, the Comechingon represented the southeastern limit of the Andean agriculture pattern into land of the southern hunting peoples. Spanish explorers gave name, "Provincia de los Comechingones," to this territory which today in included in the provinces of Cordoba and San Luis in modern Argentina. The Comechingon spoke a dialect of the Huarpe-Comechingon linguistic family, a classification covering many of the peoples in the northern part of Argentina.

Long extinct, the Comechingon in pre-Conquest times were fairly numerous, a reasonable estimate being some 30,000 with a density of 15 per km. As so often happened in the days of exploration, the Indians were identified by their outstanding physical characteristics rather than by the names which they called themselves, and thus the Comechingon became known as "the bearded ones."

Information about the first Spanish contacts with the Comechingon is sketchy and what exists is found in the old chronicles which were written after the first expedition in 1546 and were based on testimony of the survivors. More details about Comechingon life is found in government reports issued after the actual conquest and occupation of the territory late in the sixteenth century, but these, too, leave much unsaid. Archaeological work in the area has revealed surprisingly little about this once sizable population which was able to withstand the Inca onslaught but eventually succumbed to Spanish power and was assimilated into colonial society leaving little evidence of a former way of life.

The Comechingon were sedentary agriculturalists, growing the typical Andean crops of maize, beans, and quinoa on irrigated terraces. They tended large llama herds and raised barnyard fowl. Hunting guanaco, deer and rabbits was an important but secondary subsistence activity and fishing played no role in their economic life. Horses were not known to the Comechingon.

Many of these Indians lived in "stone houses," natural shelters of rock outcroppings which were modified by masonry work, a technique diffused from the Andes. Many such shelters are still used, at least on a temporary basis. There are also references in the chronicles to the fact that some Comechingon lived in partly subterranean dwellings which they dug themselves and which were said to be so constructed to protect themselves from the cold. A village was composed of several houses and was administered by a chief, possibly an inherited position. Each chief was independent of all others, a fact which caused the Spaniards no end of difficulty as they sought to place these Indians under the *ecomienda* system. However, there was cooperation among villages in forming raiding parties. There is no concrete evidence on the nature of Comechingon social organization, but some scholars have assumed that they were partilineally organized because they were hunters and warriors.

On the subject of warfare the Spanish chroniclers were more verbose and described in detail the fierce and effective attacks by the Comechingon and the unusual timing of their raids. Warriors, sometimes numbering in the hundreds with their faces painted black and red, attacked by night, "carrying fire." In close formation, the archers in one position, the spearthrowers in another, they went forth against either the Spaniards or neighboring peoples. It was written that they killed an armored horse with only five arrows.

There is no information about any live cycle observances by the Comechingon. Graves have been located which contain bodies placed on their sides in flexed position. There were no signs of grave offerings. Some variation in the positioning of the body has been reported. There were no true cemeteries as never more than five bodies in one group have discovered and graves were unmarked. All this indicates little emphasis on funeral ceremonies.

Archaeological remains of pottery fragments reveal coiled pottery with two types of decoration: incised or punctuated and net or textile impressed. Weaving was known and the early Spanish documents speak of both men and women wearing woolen tunics worked with beads to which long capes were added in winter. Some skins were worn also. But the most noteworthy legacy from the Comechingon are the remarkable rock paintings which exist on the walls and roofs of shelters as well as on appropriate rocks. These are varied and complex pictures, utilizing many colors but with red, white, and black predominent. They are of great artistic value and provide the only lasting ethnographic record of the Comechingon, depicting scens of daily life, local animals, and battles between themselves and the Spaniards with realistic precision.

Again, the historical record reveals nothing about religious life of the Comechingon apart from a vague statement that they worshipped the Sun and the Moon, the former because it helped to grow their food andthe latter because it aided them in their nighttime raids. This and a few grumbling and highly unreliable references by priests to devil worship, sorcery, and idols leaves us with no real information about Comechingon concepts of religion and morality.

BIBLIOGRAPHY —

● STEWARD, JULIAN H. Handbook of South American Indians. 7 Vols., Washington, DC: U.S. Govt. Printing Office, 1946-59.

COMECRUDO

(U.S.; Southwest) One of the few tribes of the Coahuiltecan family that have been identified. The surviving remnant was visited in 1886 by Gatschet, who found only 8 or 10 old persons who could speak the dialect, living on the South side of the Rio Grande, 2 of them at Las Prietas, Coahuila. Crozco y Berra placed them in Tamaulipas, Mexico, in the vicinity of the Tedexenos. They appear to have been known in the later times as Carrizos.

BIBLIOGRAPHY —

● HODGE, FREDERICK WEBB. Handbook of American Indians North of Mexico.Washington: Government Printing Office, 2 vols., 1907-10.
● MURDOCK, GEORGE P. Ethnographic Bibliography of North America.New Haven, CT: Human Relations Area Files Press, 1975.
● SWANTON, JOHN R. The Indian Tribes of North America. Washington, DC: U.S. Government Printing Office, 1952.

COMOX

(Canada; British Columbia) is a tribe located on Vancouver Island in the Pacific Northwest with a similar history as the Cowichan.

They were part of the Salishan linguistic family. The Comox tribe was the most abberant of the Salishan tribes. Culturally the Comox resembled the Kwakiutl.

Their houses were different from Salishan houses, being long, planked houses, with a sloping roof, the high side facing toward water. Inside there were fully enclosed family quarters. Their doors were carved to look like animals' heads. Their food, largely fish and other seafood, was roasted in spits, baked in earthen ovens, or stone boiled in wooden vessels. One thing they did that was traditionally Salishan was salt their seaweed cakes.

Their social structure was based on status. Nobles were highest and commoners lowest, but all considered themselves free men. Nobles treated commoners with courtesy and encouragement, for commoners could advance up the social system. Only lazy people were truly despised.

Primogeniture was the rule, but females could inherit property. Inheritance didn't necessarily go to the oldest son; it was allocated according to a parents' favorite children.

The marriage ceremonies of the Comox were some of the most elaborate of any tribe. Taking up to weeks at a time, weddings were also extremely expensive, fo gifts had to be exchanged with each of the guests and participants. Marriages were usually contracted between equals. But aristocrats occassionally went through a farce of marriage with no bride simply to gain property. For this reason marriages were often unstable.

The Comox's history was virtually the same as the Cowichan except they were first met by whites (1592) later than when Juan de Fuca met the Cowichan. At one time they were moved from their home at Cape Mudge by the *Lekwiltok* to Vancouver Island. Comox became an important group in trading with the whites, and for that reason they were never moved from Vancouver Island. Today there are several hundred still there.

BIBLIOGRAPHY —

● HODGE, FREDERICK WEBB. Handbook of American Indians North of Mexico.Washington: Government Printing Office, 2 vols., 190710.
● MURDOCK, GEORGE P. Ethnographic Bibliography of North America.New Haven, CT: Human Relations Area Files Press, 1975.
● SWANTON, JOHN R. The Indian Tribes of North America. Washington, DC: U.S. Government Printing Office, 1952.

CONESTOGA

(U.S.; Northeast) Kanastoge, "at the place of the immersed pole". An important Iroquoian tribe that formerly lived on Susquehanna river and its branches. When first met by Captain John Smith, in 1608, and until their conquest by the Iroquois confederation in 1675, they were in alliance with the Algonquian tribes of the east shore of Chesapeake bay and at war with those on the west shore. They were described as warlike and as possessed of a physique far superior to that of all the other neighboring tribes. By conquest they claimed the lands on both sides of Chesapeake bay, from the Choptank and Patuxent north to the territory of the Iroquois. In 1675, after their defeat, they established themselves on the east bank of the Potomac, in Maryland, immediately north of Piscataway creek, below which the Doag (Nanticoke) were then living. They formed a close alliance with the Dutch and Swedes, and with the English of Maryland. The Iroquois had carried on relentless war against them, with varying success, which finally reduced them from about 3,000 in 1608 to about 550 in 1648, while their allies brought the aggregate to about 1,250.

Champlain says that in 1615 they had more than 20 villages, of which only three were at that time engged in war with the Iroquois, and that their town of Carantouan alone could muster more than 800 warriors. The Iroquois of the north drove the Conestoga down on the tribes to the south and west, who were allies of the English, a movement involving the Conestoga in a war with Maryland and Virginia in 1675. Finding themselves surrounded by enemies on all sides, a portion of them abandoned their country and took refuge with the Occaneechi on Roanoke river, while the rest remained in Pennsylvania. A quarrel occurred soon with the Occaneechi, who made common cause with the white against the fugitive Conestoga, who were compelled to return to Susquehanna river and submit to the Iroquois. According to Colden they were all finally removed to the country of the Oneida, where they remained until they lost their language, when they were allowed to return to Conestoga, their ancient town. Here they rapidly wasted, until, at the close of the year 1763, the remnent, numbering only 20, were massacred by a party of rioters inflamed by the accounts of the Indian war then raging along the Pennsylvania frontier. About 1675 their stockade, where they were defeated by the Maryland forces, was on the east side of Susquehanna river, three miles below Columbia, Pennsylvania. Hermans map of 1676 located it at nearly the same point on the river, but on the west bank, The Swedes and Dutch called them Minqua, from the Delaware name applied to all tribes of Iroquoian stock; the Powhatan tribes called them Susquehannock0, a name signifying "roily river," which was adopted by the English of Virginia and Maryland. The names of their villages are Attock, Carantouan, Cepowig, Oscalui, Quadroque, Sasquesahanough, Testhigh, and Utchowig. The Meherrin on the river of that name in south east Virginia, were officially reported to be a band of the Conestoga driven south by the Virginians during Bacons rebellion in 1675-76.

BIBLIOGRAPHY —

● HODGE, FREDERICK WEBB. Handbook of American Indians North of Mexico.Washington: Government Printing Office, 2 vols., 1907-10.
● MURDOCK, GEORGE P. Ethnographic Bibliography of North America.New Haven, CT: Human Relations Area Files Press, 1975.
● SWANTON, JOHN R. The Indian Tribes of North America. Washington, DC: U.S. Government Printing Office, 1952.

CONGAREE

(U.S.; S.C.) A small tribe, supposed to be Siouan, formerly living in South Carolina. The grounds for including this tribe in the Siouan family are its location and its intimate relation with known Siouan tribes, especially the Catawba, with which it was ultimately incorporated; but according to Adair

Antiquities from the Congaree Indians

and Lawson the Congaree spoke a dialect different from that of the Catawba, which they preserved even after their incorporation. In 1693 the Cherokee complained that the Shawnee, Catawba, and Congaree took prisoners from among them and sold them as slaves in Charleston. They were visited in 1701 by Lawson, who found them on the N.E. bank of Santee River below the junction of the Wateree. Their town consisted of not more than 12 houses, with plantations up and down the country. On a map of 1715 the village of the Congaree is placed on the South bank of Congaree River about opposite the site of Columbia. A fort bearing the tribal name was established near the village in 1718. They were a small tribe, having lost many by tribal feuds but more by smallpox. Lawson states that, although the several tribes visited by him were generally small and lived closely adjoining one another, they differed in features, disposition, and language, a fact which renders the assignment of these small tribes to the Siouan family conjectural. The Congaree, like their neighbors, took part in the Yamasi war in 1715, as a result of which they were so reduced that they were compelled to move up the country and join the Catawba, with whom they were still living in 1743. Moll's map of 1730 places their town or station on the North bank of Congaree River opposite which ran the trail to the Cherokee country. It was South of lat. 34 degrees, probably in Richland county. They were a friendly people, handsome and well built, the women being especially beautiful compared with those of other tribes.

BIBLIOGRAPHY —

● HODGE, FREDERICK WEBB. Handbook of American Indians North of Mexico.Washington: Government Printing Office, 2 vols., 1907-10.

● MURDOCK, GEORGE P. Ethnographic Bibliography of North America. New Haven, CT: Human Relations Area Files Press, 1975.
● SWANTON, JOHN R. The Indian Tribes of North America. Washington, DC: U.S. Government Printing Office, 1952.

CONOY

(U.S.; Northeast) An Algonquian tribe, related to the Delawares, from whose ancestral stem they apparently sprang, but their closest relations were with the Nanticoke, with whom it is probable they were in late prehistoric times united, the two forming a single tribe, while their language is supposed to have been somewhat closely allied to that spoken in Virginia by the Powhatan. Heckewelder believed them to be identical with the Kanawha, who gave the name to the chief river of West Virginia. Although Brinton calls this "a loose guess," the names Conoy, Ganawese, etc., seem to be forms of Kanawha. The application of the same name to the Piscataway tribe of Maryland, and to the river, is difficult to explain by any other theory than that the former once lived on the banks of the Kanawha. In 1660 the Piscataway applied to the governor of the colony to confirm their choice of an "emperor," and to his inquiry in regard to their custom in this respect, replied:

"Long a goe there came a King from the Easterne Shoare who Comanded over all the Jndians now inhabiting within the bounds of this Province (nameing every towne severally) and also over the Patowmecks and Sasquehannoughs, whome for that he Did as it were imbrace and cover them all they called Vrrapoingassinem this man dyeing without issue made his brother Quokomassaum King after him, after whome Succeeded his other brothers, after whose death they tooke a Sisters Sonn, and soe from Brother to Brother, and for want of such to a Sisters Sonne, the Governm descended for thirteene Generacons without Jnterrupcon vntill Kittamaquunds tyme who dyed without brother or Sister and apoynted his daughter to be Queene but that the Jndians withstood itt as being Contrary to their Custome, wherevpon they chose Weghucasso for their King who was descended from one of Vttapoingassinem brothers (But which of them they knowe not) and Weghucasso at his death apoynted this other Vttapoingassinem to be King being decended from one of the first Kings this man they sayd was Jan Jan Wizous which in their language signifyes a true King. And would not suffer vs to call him Tawzin which is the Style they give to the sons of their Kings, who by their Custome are not to succeede in Rule, but his Brothers, or the Sons of his Sisters."

The order of descent in this extrat gives it an impress of truth. It indicates close relation between the Nanticoke and the Conoy, though the inclusion of the Susquehana (Conestoga) among the emperors subjects must be rejected. One of the tribes of the east shore from which this chief could have come was the Nanticole. Thirteen generations would carry back the date of this first emperor to the beginning of the 16th century. Lord Baltimores colonists in 1634 established a mission amongst them, and the "emperor" Chitomachen, otherwise known as Tayac, said to be ruler over a dominion extending 130 miles east and west, was converted, with his family. They were, however, so harassed by the Conestoga that a few years later they abandoned their country and moved farther up the Potomac. They, then rapidly decreasing, were in 1673 assigned a tract on that stream, which may have been near the site of Washington, D. C. The Conestoga, when driven from their own country by the Iroquois in 1675, again invaded the territory of the Conoy and forced that tribe to retire up the Potomac and into Pennsylvania. This was a gradual migration, unless it took place at a much later period, for Baron Graffenried, while searaching for a reported silver mine in 1711, found them on the Maryland side of the Potomac about 50 miles above Washington, and made a treaty of friendship with them. He calls them Canawest. About this time the Iroquois assigned them lands at Conejoholo on the Susquehanna, near the present Bainbridge, Pa., in the vicinity of the Nanticoke and Conestoga. Here they first began to be known as Conoy. Some of them were living with these tribes at Conestoga in 1742. They gradually made their way up the Susquehanna, stopping at Harrisburg, Shamokin, Catawissa, and Wyoming, and in 1765 were living in south New York, at Owego, Chugnut, and Chenang, on the east branch of the Susquehanna. At that time they numbered only about 150, and, with their associates, the Nanticoke and Mahican, were dependent on the Iroquois. They moved west with the Mahican and Delawares, and soon became known only as a part of those tribes. In 1793 they attended a council near Detroit and used the turkey as their signature.

The customs and beliefs of the Conoy may best be given by the following quotation from Whites Relatio Itineris, ca. 1635, although the authors interpretations of customs often go far astray:

"The natives are very tall and well proportioned; their skin is naturally rather dark, and they make it uglier by staining it, generally with red paint mixed with oil, to keep off the mosquitoes, thinking more of their own comfort than of appearances. They disfigure their countenances with other colors, too, painting them in various and truly hideous and frightful ways, either a dark blue above the nose and red below, or the reverse. And as they live almost to extreme old age without having beards, they conterfeit them with paint, by drawing lines of various colors from the extremities of the lips to the ears. They generally have black hair, which they carry round in a knot to the left ear, and fasten with a band, adding some ornament which is in estimation among them. Some of them wear on their foreheads the figure of a fish made of copper. They adorn their necks with glass beads strung on a thread like necklaces, though these beads are getting to be less valued among them and less useful for trade. They are clothed for the most part in deerskins or some similar kind of covering, which hangs down behind like a cloak. They wear aprons round the middle, and leave the rest of the body naked. The young boys and girls go about with nothing on them. The soles of their feet are as hard a horn, and they tread on thorns and briers without being hurt. Their arms are bows, and arrows three feet long, tipped with stags horn, or a white flint sharpened at the end. They shoot these with such skill that they can stand off and hit a sparrow in the middle; and, in order to become expert by practice, they throw a spear up in the air and then send an arrow from the bow string and drive it into the spear before it falls. But since they do not sting the bow very tight, they can not hit a mark at a great distance. They live by means of these weapons, and go out every day through the fields and woods to hunt squirrels, partridges, turkeys, and wild animals. For there is an abundance of all these, though we ourselves do not yet venture to procure food by hunting, for fear of ambushes. They live in houses built in an oblong, oval shape. Light is admitted into these through the roof, by a window a foot and a half long; this also serves to carry off the smoke, for they kindle the fire in the middle of the floor, and sleep around the fire. Their kings, however, and chief men have private apartments, as it were, of their own and beds, made by driving four posts into the ground, and arranging poles above they horizontally."

According to the same authority they acknowledged one god of heaven, yet paid him no outward worship, but strove in every way to appease a certain imaginary spirit, which they called Ochre, that he might not hurt them. They also worshiped corn and fire. The missionary probably here alludes to the use of corn and fire in certain religious ceremonies. The Conoy villages were Catawissa, Conedogwinit, Conejoholo, Conoytown, Kittamaquindi, Onuatuc, Opamemt, Peixtan.

Their decendants now live in the Nanicoke Community in Sussex County, Delaware and number about 400. *(see map page XIV)*

BIBLIOGRAPHY —

● HODGE, FREDERICK WEBB. Handbook of American Indians North of Mexico. Washington: Government Printing Office, 2 vols., 1907-10.
● MURDOCK, GEORGE P. Ethnographic Bibliography of North America. New Haven, CT: Human Relations Area Files Press, 1975.
● SWANTON, JOHN R. The Indian Tribes of North America. Washington, DC: U.S. Government Printing Office, 1952.

COOS

(U.S.; Oreg.) The name is an adaptation from the Kusan family. They spoke a Penutian-based language.

Now nearly extinct, the Coos lived along the central coast of Oregon, along Alsea, the Siuslaw, and the Umpqua, all of which are nearly extinct.

Scholars know virtually nothing about these tribes' social organization. What they do know comes from the few survivors who were moved from their traditional home in the 1850s.

It is known that their cultural and economic life was probably a cross between the Salish and Chinookian cultures, probably closer to the Salish.

If this is so, then the Coos probably lived in wooded lodges and depended on seafood and fishing as their major economic activity. Their government may have consisted of a male chief.

It is known that the Coos did not have clans, and allowed natural relationships to develop in the confined areas of the villages. We also know they did not practice head deformation.

Living along the coast in an area around the Coos River, the tribe probably extended much further down the river originally but was pushed into the more constrained area by their Athapascan neighbors.

When they were visited by Lewis and Clark in 1805, it was estimated there were some 1,500 Coos. In the 1850s they were moved to the Siletz Reservation in Oregon. Today there are possibly no pure-bloods left. *(see map page XVI)*

COOSA

(U.S.; S.C.), now extinct, were at one time a small but important Muskhogean people related in all probability to the Creeks, and living in South Carolina. At one time or another they were called "Couexi" (1562), "Cocao" (1569), "Kussoes" (1707), and lastly "Coosah" in 1743, after which there is no record of them. They opposed the colonist in the 17th century, but in 1675 ceded land to the English. By the middle of the 18th cen tury they appear to have been incorporated into the Catawba tribe, and some others may have joined the Creeks. They have also been referred to as the Cusabo. (See Cusabo).

BIBLIOGRAPHY —

● HODGE, FREDERICK WEBB. Handbook of American Indians North of Mexico.Washington: Government Printing Office, 2 vols., 1907-10.
● MURDOCK, GEORGE P. Ethnographic Bibliography of North America.New Haven, CT: Human Relations Area Files Press, 1975.
● SWANTON, JOHN R. The Indian Tribes of North America. Washington, DC: U.S. Government Printing Office, 1952.

COPALIS.

(U.S.; Washington) The significance of the name is unknown. The tribe belonged to the coastal division of the Salishan linguistic family. They were located at the Copalis River and the Pacific Coast between the mouth of Joe Creek and Grays Harbor. Lewis and Clark, in 1805, estimated a population of 200 Copalis's in 10 houses. The 5 individuals assigned to a "Chepalis" tribe in an enumeration given by *Olson*of the year 1888 probably refers to them. The name Copalis is perpetuated in that of the Copalis River, and in the post villages of Copalis Beach and Copalis Crossing, in Grays Harbor County, Washington.

BIBLIOGRAPHY —

● HODGE, FREDERICK WEBB. Handbook of American Indians North of Mexico. Washington: Smithsonian Institution: BAE Bulletin No. 30: U.S. GPO, 1907.
● SWANTON, JOHN R. The Indian Tribes of North America. Washington, DC: U.S. Government Printing Office, 1952.

COPEHAN FAMILY

(U.S.; Calif.) A linguistic stock formerly occupying a large territory, from Suisun and san Pablo bays on the South to Mt. Shasta and the country of the Shastan family on the North. Starting from the North, the East boundary ran a few miles East of McCloud River to its junction with the Sacramento and thence to Redding, a large triangle East of Sacramento River belonging to the Copehan; and from Redding, a large triangle East of Sacramento River belonging to the Copehan; and from Redding down the boundary was about 10 miles East of Sacramento River, but South of Chico it was confined to the West bank. On the West the summit of the Coast range formed the boundary, but from the headwaters of Cottonwood Creek northward it nearly reached the South fork of the upper Trinity. The people of this family were among the most interesting of the California Indians, with a harmonious language and an interesting mythology. Their social and political system was like that of all California tribes: their largest unit was the village, more extensive combinations being for temporary purposes only. The people compris-ing this family have been divided by Powers into two branches, the Patwin and the Wintun, differing considerably in language and customs.

BIBLIOGRAPHY —

● HODGE, FREDERICK WEBB. Handbook of American Indians North of Mexico. Washington: Smithsonian Institution: BAE Bulletin No. 30: U.S. GPO, 1907.
● SWANTON, JOHN R. The Indian Tribes of North America. Washington, DC: U.S. Government Printing Office, 1952.

COOPER INUIT

(Canada) are so named for their extensive use of cooper. Cooper was used for both weapons and tools. In addition, the Cooper Inuit also had a huge storage of soapstone, a valuable commodity. Some Inuit tribes were known to travel hundreds of miles to mine soapstone. The Copper Inuit also traveled south to harvest wood, which was scarce in the north.

The general location of the Copper Inuit seems to vary, but they are most associated with the Coppermine River in Canada.

They were the last tribe of Inuit to have contact with whites; hence there is still much material regarding their life patterns which is unknown.

It is known their chief deity is female. She is the Mother of Sea Mammals, called the "terrible one down there below." Legend says sea mammals were created when the joints of her fingers were cut off and fell into the sea. She ensures the food supply, and provides protection while gathering food. She has rules concerning unclean women, products of sea and land and dietary rituals. Curiously, rituals of the dead do not seem to involve her.

As legends indicate, sea mammals were an essential part of their diet although they also hunted caribou and moose inland, particularly on their wood gathering expeditions. During those expeditions they were sometimes forced to fight inland Indians for rights to hunt. Their dwellings were portable huts of wood and skin.

It is believed they would trade with other Inuits as far east as Baffinland for such valuable commodities as soapstone and wood.

BIBLIOGRAPHY —

●JENNESS, DIAMOND. The Life of the Copper Eskimos. Report of the Canadian Arctic Expedition, vol. 12, 1922.
● MCGHEE, ROBERT. Copper Eskimo Prehistory. National Museums of Canada Publications in Archaeology, no. 2, 1972.
● RASMUSSEN, KNUD. Intellectual Culture of the Copper Eskimos.Report of the Fifth Thule Expedition, 1921-24, vol. 9, 1932.

CORA

(Mexico) exists as a large, diversified series of groups in the highlands of eastern Nayarit, Mexico; in the deep mountain canyons (especially of the Rio Jesus Maria and Rio San Pedro, with some

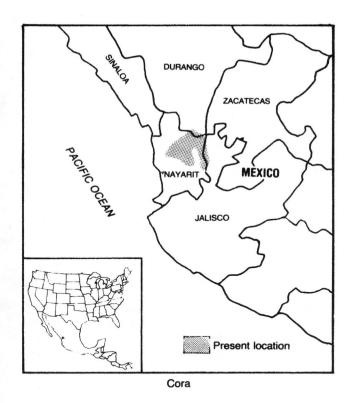

Cora

in the Rio Grande de Santiago Canyon); and in the foothills and coastal zones of the Pacific lateral of Nayarit.

The Cora (pronounced kora) have been known as the "Chora", "Chora Nayalita," and the "Nayarita." "Nayer" is a toponym of a central mesa of population and ceremonial importance. The term "Nayarita," though, was also used to refer to the Huichol, Tequal, and Tepecano. As in the past, most Cora identify themselves by their community of residence.

About half the Cora today live in titled grants of land from the Spanish Crown (comunidades). The other half live in mixed, at times dispersed, communities of peasant farmers or as day-wage workers on the coastal plantations. Aboriginally, there were probably a dozen territorially and culturally distinct groups that merged to form what today is "Cora." Boundaries were fluid.

Confusion exists as to which group should or could be classified as "Cora" at any one time. If "Cora" means the composite mountain-canyon dwellers of eastern Nayarit, then their territory today is less than half what it was at Spanish contact. In addition, fluctuations occurred as the Cora invaded (folk and military) other canyons and the coastal area. Today, Cora territories are receding quickly.

The Cora language belongs to the Huicholan subdivision (i.e. closely related to Huichol, Tequal, Guaynamota, and probably Totorame) of the generalized western Uto-Aztecan branch. Cora and Huichol dialects are mutually intelligible. Dialectation is pronounced among the Cora. This reflects territorial considerations as well as acculturation. East (canyon), west (mesa and foothill), north, and south dialects can be easily recognized, in addition to those from specific comunidades.

As in the past, the Cora today are predominently subsistence agriculturalists. Maize, beans, and squash are the most important crops. Hunting is unimportant, but gathering of wild crops is still an important supplement. Cattle raising is regionally important, but there are difficulties with quality and access to market. Meat is infrequently consumed.

The settlement pattern varies from region to region. In the most traditional areas, farmsteads are dispersed but located within a day's walking distance from a ceremonial center. Many Cora also live permanently in pueblos. The pueblos serve as focal points for most religious and governmental activity. Family social organization is loosely patrilineal. Lineages, however, are no longer very important.

Weaving and bead working are the two best developed crafts. Cora weaving is quite distinctive and very attractive. Regional styles are still preserved. Craft work for the tourist market has become an important income supplement for many Cora.

The Cora are a diversified group both in their culture and social organization. They are not tribal, but rather comunidad oriented peasants, living a colonial rather than strictly indigenous past. Cora diversification is best seen in their religious symbolism. Contemporary religion, in general, is a result of the syncretism of Catholic and native beliefs. The native cycle stressed nature gods and ancestors. Many of these gods now have semi-Catholic characters. For example, Takao (the sun god) is identified with God, Gualu Tetewa (spirit of the underworld) with the Virgin of Guadalupe, and so on. Shamanism is still very important, especially for the agricultural cycle and curing. Most religious activity, whether syncretized or native, is oriented toward agriculture and health. Extremely colorful ceremonies with masked dancers and animal sacrifices used to mark the important events of the yearly cycle. Many of these rites are quickly being modified, changed, and even discontinued.

The comunidad is governed by a large council of church majordomos and civil officers headed by a Tatuan (governor). Each majordomo is in charge of a saint and its yearly festival. The civil officers are responsible for the juridical and fiscal management of the comunidad. The offices are rotated among the qualified members of the *comunidad* , though the rotation is closely supervised by the elders and ex-officers. Government activities are concentrated at the *Casa Fuerte* (government house). Small churches exist in the pueblos and serve as the second focal point of civil-religious activity.

Cora mythology is rich in symbolism and historical content. The entire universe and all its phenomena are explained in detail in the many legends and myths. Only a few men each generation are able to master all this knowledge. They are called *bausi* and are given very special treatment.

Very little archaeology has been accomplished in the Cora zone. Surveys have indicated that there is little complex architecture in the area. This most likely means that the pre-Hispanic Cora were very marginal to the Mesoamerican civilization. Contact with the Spanish began in the late 1520s. Many of the first contacts were violent and, after the Guzman expedition, thousands of neighboring Indians, many in organized groups, took refuge among the Cora. Most of these refugees were from the civilized Totorame area of coastal Nayarit. A long period of merging of refugee and mountain cultural traits began. The Cora became a composite society dedicated to resisting the Spanish and raiding them whenever possible. Their violent raids were accompanied by livestock rustling and kidnappings. Their area continued to function as a refugee area for other Indians and slaves who were disgusted with Spanish rule. The Spanish finally decided to conquer the Nayaritas, but it was not until 1722 that a successful expedition was launched. The zone was at that time theocratically organized around two temples, *Thuacamota* and *Tauta* , each with a priesthood and soldiers. The area after the conquest was reorganized into the Nuevo Reino de Toledo, and it included the Huichol. Jesuits were introduced to missionize the Cora. The zone remained marginal and unstable-a hot-bed for regional revolution and renegade activities. The most widespread revolt in which the Cora participated was that of Lozada's. Lozada was part Cora and understood their problems. He joined the French invaders during the 1860s to fight against the liberal government of Juarez because the French promised to preserve the *comunidad* land tenure system. He even attempted to capture Guadalajara with an Indian army after the French left Mexico.

During and after this period, Cora society developed a defensive stance which was accompanied by cultural conservatism. Relations with outsiders were difficult. This encapsulization lasted through the Mexican Revolution (1910-19) and the Cristero Revolt (1927-29), which continued as vendettas until the 1940s. Recent government activities have stressed economic development rather than military submission, and relations with outsiders have improved. The area is still regarded as volatile, however.

The Cora are currently undergoing an enormous cultural and social transition. As incorporation into the national economy becomes more complete, traditional lifestyles are quickly eroding. Cultural change is at times less obvious than social change among the Cora. Some Coras have become astute regional politicians and are encouraging economic integration into the national network. Various governmental and development bank programs for economic change and education are active within the zone. Many of these programs have been well received. Points of integration into the national economy are cattle raising, contract labor, and craft sales.

Estimates for the pre-Hispanic Cora populations are sheer guesses, but the figure 8-9,000 does not seem too high. By the time of the chartering of the *comunidades* in the late 1700s, the population was c. 2-4,000. Today, there are around 14-16,000 Cora including many thousand that live in the cities and coastal areas.

The Cora are a composite series of diversified societies. They survived as an independent refugee for 200 years after the Spanish had conquered most of the neighboring areas. Today, they live more a colonial lifestyle than a purely Indian one. Their traditions are quickly changing.

(see map page XIX)

BIBLIOGRAPHY –

● HODGE, FREDERICK WEBB. Handbook of American Indians North of Mexico. Washington: Government Printing Office, 2 vols., 1907-10.
● MURDOCK, GEORGE P. Ethnographic Bibliography of North America. New Haven, CT: Human Relations Area Files Press, 1975.
● SWANTON, JOHN R. The Indian Tribes of North America. Washington, DC: U.S. Government Printing Office, 1952.

COREE, or CORANINE.

(U.S.; North Carolina) The significance of the names are unknown. Since the last stages of the Coree existence was passed with an Algonquian tribe, some observers thought that the affiliations of this people were also Algonquian. On the other hand *Lawson, 1860* notes that their language and that of a tribe to the north were mutually intelligible and there is reason for thinking that this northern tribe belonged to the Iroquois Confederacy. At least the Coree were closely associated in many ways with the Iroquoian Tuscarora. They resided on the peninsula south of Neuse River in Carteret and Craven Counties. Their villages were Coranine, Narhantes, and Raruta.

The time and place of the initial meeting between the white settlers and the Coree is unknown, but the tribe appears in the records of the Raleigh colony under the name Cwarennoc. Their numbers were greatly reduced before 1696 in a war with another tribe. They took part with the Tuscarora in their war against the colonists, and in 1715, the remaining members, and what was left of the Machapunga, were assigned to a reservation on Mattamuskeet Lake in Hyde County, where they occupied one village, probably until they became extinct. A few of them appear to have remained with the Tuscarora.

The population of this tribe and the Neusiok was estimated by *Mooney, 1928* at 1,000 in 1600. In 1707, *Lawson* says they had 25 fighting men and were living in two villages. No later enumeration is known. Although some distance from the Coree country, Core Creek Station in Craven County, North Carolina, may perpetuate the name of the Coree.

BIBLIOGRAPHY –

● JOHNSON, ELIAS. Legends, Traditions, and Laws of the Iroquois, or Six Nations, and History of the Tuscarora Indians. Lockport, NY: Union Printing and Publishing, Co., 1881.
● MILLING, CHAPMAN. Red Carolinians. Chapel Hill, NC: University of North Carolina Press, 1940.
● SAMS, CONWAY WHITTLE. The Conquest of Virginia, The First Attempt, Being an Account of Sir Walter Raleigh's Colony on Roanoke Island. Norfolk: Keyser-Doherty Printing Co., 1924.
● SWANTON, JOHN R. The Indian Tribes of North America. Washington, DC: U.S. Government Printing Office, 1952.

COROADO

(South America; Brazil) are closely related linguistically and culturally to the Puri and *Coropo* . Over a hundred years ago the Coroado were a single tribe with the Puri, who later, as the result of a feud between two families, became their enemies.

At the beginning of the 19th century, the Coroado occupied the plain bounded in the east by the Serra de Sao Geraldo (Sao Joze) and in the west by the Serra da Onza in eastern Brazil. They lived mainly along the Xipoto Novo River (Rio dos Coroados). The Corodado were originally divided into three main subgroups: the Maritong, the Cobanipaque, and a third (the name of which had been lost).

During the 17th century, the Coroado were raided by the Paulistas and, as a result they remained bitter enemies by the whites until 1763, when they were induced to make peace. In 1767 they were placed under the authority of special government agents. They were harshly treated by the colonists who exploited them.

In 1813, the Coroado still remained in the Aldea de Pedra on the upper Parahyba River. The popuastion is probably several hundred.

Culture. Subsistence activites. Originally typcial forest nomads, the Coroado subsisted by hunting and collecting fruits and roots, especially the fruits of palm shoots, caratinga, cava, and many other tubers. During the dry season, the Coroado gathered larvae of *bixo da taquara* , which they kept in bamboo receptables, using the fat mainly for preparing corn cakes. Like most forest nomads, they were constantly on the lookout for honey.

The Coroado learned to grow crops and, at the beginning of the 19th century, cultivated maize, gourds, bananas, cara and beans. They were poor farmeers, however, and continued to subsist, in large measure, on the produce of the bush.

The Coroado were skillful stalkers and expert trackers. They lured birds by perfectly imitating calls. Little is known of their other hunting methods except that they caught animals in pitfalls and traps. Birds were captured by means of a noose fixed to the end of a long pole.

The Coroado, who raised some crops, had elaborate cooking techniques and utensils, such as basketry sifters and various earthenware vessels. They prepared mush and maize pounded in cylindrical wooden mortars, boiled game, roasted it on a spit, or smoked it on a babracot.

The Coroado had dogs and fowl which they had acquired from the whites.

Dwellings. The hut of the Coroado was obviously derived from the primitive Puri lean-to. It had the form of a thatched gabled roof resting directly on the ground. Larger huts with wattle-and-daub walls were imitations of the mestizo house.

The main piece of Coroado furniture was the cotton hammock. The Coroado hut contained a platform for storing food and small articles, a wooden mortar, gourds, and various pieces of pottery.

Dress. The aboriginal Puri, Coroado and Coropo went naked; but the men, when first described had already adopted European clothes, while Coroado women wore homemade skirts.

Feather headdresses and feather bracelets were worn by both Puri and Coroado men. Both Puri and Coroado hung around their necks or slung across their chests necklaces composed of animal teeth and of various seeds. Young women wrapped bark strips around their wrists and around their legs, under the knees and around the ankles. These bindings, which served to make the joints slender, were removed after marriage.

All body hair was removed. Both Puri and Coroado painted dots and linear motifs in red (urucu or red clay) and black (genipa) on their persons.

Coroado and Botocudo life

Among the Coroado, both sexes were tattooed by a method not reported elsewhere in South America except for the Tehuelche.

Transporatation. No craft of any kind was used by the Coroado.

Women carried their goods in large baskets. Children were suspended on the hip with a bark sling or carried on their mother's back, supported by a tumpline or hanging in a net.

Social and political organization. The Coroado tribe was split into small groups or bands, each of which comprised one or two extended families totaling some 40 people. Each group lived apart, uniting with others only for defense against enemies or to wage war. Such a group was under the authority of a chief, generally the oldest man of the community.

Within this group there existed a great amount of cooperation. They cultivated their fields in common, hunted together, and enjoyed "commonly the produce of their work." Young people submitted willingly to the authority of older persons and of valiant hunters and warriors. Leaders were distinquished bu beautiful feather diadems.

Rites. When two parties met, one would make a speech and then both would burst into laments for the dead.

Childbirth. The Coroado woman pregnant observed chastity. She and her husband refrained from eating the flesh of certain animals and lived chiefly on fish and fruits. Delivery took place in the forest in a spot protected from moonlight, which was considered harmful to a newborn baby. Soon after the birty, the mother washed herself and resumed her normal activities. A few days later, both she and the baby were fumigated with tobacco smoke by a shaman, an occasion which was celebrated by hearty drinking. Children were nursed until they 4 to 5 years old.

Marriage. Men married at the age of 18, girls when they were about 12. The marriage ceremony consisted of the presentation of game and fruit to the bride's parents. Acceptance of the gift sealed the marriage. The new couple settled with the family of either spouse. Monogamy seems to have prevailed, though chiefs or good hunters had two or more wives. Marital ties were brittle and easily dissolved. Women were often blamed for the separation because of their misconduct.

Death observances. The Coroado placed their dead in large jars, if these were available, after they had broken the limbs of the corpse, lest the ghost return to haunt the living. A person was buried in his hut, his possessions were deposited over the grave, and the house was burned or abandoned. If the deceased had been a chief, the whole settlement was deserted. Relatives cut their hair, and the women painted their bodies black. They uttered funeral laments at dawn, in the evening, and whenever they passed a grave.

Ghosts (which often appeared in the guise of lizards, caimans, jaguars, deer or deer-footed men) were the souls of wicked persons or of people who had not been buried according to prescribed rites.

Shamans. Shamans consulted the souls of th dead about the outcome of important events, such as a war party or an expedition to collect *ipecacuanha* . They also summoned spirits to inquire where abundant game could be found or to ascertain whether they were threatened by a war party. When the Coroado feared an attack by their traditional enemy, the Puri, their shamans conjured up the souls of a dead Puri and asked him the whereabouts of his fellow tribesmen. If the answers were alarming, the shamans advised the people to take defensive measures and to build a fence around the camp.

The Coroado shaman conjured spirits at night while blowing clouds of smoke from his pipe. Spectators could hear the steps of the approaching spirits and their whistled answers to the questions of the shaman. The spirits departed crying "like macuco birds."

The Coroado lived in great fear of sorcerers. If witchcraft were suspected to be the cause of a death, some flesh of skin was cut from the victim's head and countermagic was practiced on it.

Medicine. Sick people were treated by shamans, who sucked them, fumigated them with tobacco smoke, and rubbed them with saliva or with certain herbs.

The Coroado practiced bloodletting with a small bow and an arrow headed with a piece of crystal. This operation was also performed at intervals on healthy persons, especially women. The Coroado incised the skin around the sore spot with a sharp stone or a piece of bamboo. Some men, to improve their marksmanship, cut themselves slightly across the upper arm.

Shamans used various herbs in their massages and put different leaves and grasses on wounds and infections. Most of their drugs were for external use, and like the Chaco, the Coroado showed a strong reluctance to taking internal medicine.

BIBLIOGRAPHY –

● STEWARD, JULIAN H. Handbook of South American Indians. 7 Vols., Washington, DC: U.S. Govt. Printing Office, 1946-59.

COROBICI

(Central America;) are named after a chieftain encountered by Gil Gonzalez Davila during the conquest of Central America by the Spaniards. During the Conquest Period, the Corobici were located along the southern shores of Lake Nicaragua between the Rio Frio and the Cordillera Volcanica. It has been claimed that they inhabited the Solentiname Islands in the lake, as well sa the territory extending westward across the Cordillera de Tilleran and through the valley of the Rio Tenorio to the north shore of the Gulf of Nicoya. Spanish intrusion into the area forced the Corobici to retreat to the plains near San Carlos. Later, known as the Guatuso, they were located in the inaccessible region at the headwaters of the Rio Frio and in the valleys of the Rios Zapote, Guacalito and the Cucaracha to the west. Separate groups of these people, either indigenous or fugitive groups, were found in the region between Bagaces adn Esparata. In the 18th century they raided the countryside until they were eventually driven back north across the mountains. By the 1860s they were relatively isolated occupying areas in the upper Rio Frio Valley. Recent exploration and conquest of the valley has resulted in the decimation of the Guatuso leaving only remnants of these people in the upper sections of the Rio Frio Valley.

The locations of the Corobici or the Guatuso and their relationship to other known tribes in the area is a controversial issue. The tribe may have originally Guetar people but as a result of their social relationships with their neighbors, the Chontal and Chorotega, had become a heterogeneous population and culture. It has also been suggested that the Corobici and the Guatuso are different peoples. The Guatuso, located in the Rio Frio area, may be part of the Rama Indian tribes. The Corobici may have occupied the Nicoya Peninsula proper as well as the lands on the northern side of the bay. Two factors are significant: 1) the tribes in the Central Costa Rican area, including the Corobici, were undergoing considerable intermixing of populations and culture; and 2) the tribes existing in the pre-Hispanic period, as a result of high population densities and consequent warfare, were forced to migrate out of their territories into regions quite different from their original place of habitation. The delimitation of the habitat of the prehistoric, the contact period, and present-day Corobici depends upon the discovery on the coast as well as in the highland areas of social forms and material culture which may be assigned to the Corobici peoples.

The Corobici are classified with the Talamanaca division of cultures of Central America. These were quickly overrun by the Spaniards and a majority of the cultures have long been extinct. Practically all of the people that have survived the Spanish Conquest, as well as subsequent intrusions by black slaves from the Caribbean islands, have been dislocated from their aboriginal habitats.

The archaeological record and the reports of the early chroniclers in comparison to the modern social structure of the Corobici (and other tribes in the area) show drastic changes in the organization of the society. Among modern populations intensive horticulture, dense populations, large villages, class- structured society, the mounds, temples, idols and priests, warfare, cannibalism and human trophies, the elaborate death rites and the technological and esthetic sophistication in metallurgy, weaving, ceramics and stone sculpture are absent. The modern tribes live in small villages, weave simple cloths, make only plain pots. The societies are unstratified and the religious cults are attenuated.

Early chroniclers reported agricultural activities to have been more extensive in the past than in the present. Slash-and- burn agriculture is universally employed. Men clear the fields with their male relatives or friends and simple ceremonies are practiced at this time. Aboriginal foods (maize, beans, yucca, gourds, camote, cacao and others) remain the basis of the diet except where rice, plantains and pigeon peas are grown in large quantities. Game is hunted with the bow and arrow or with the gun. Wild honey and larvae from the hives are collected from the forest and considered a delicacy. Nets, fishhooks, spears and bows and single or multiple-pointed arrows are used to fish. In small cases small fish are caught by hand. There are early references to the presence of domesticated animals including the dog. In modern times people keep dogs, cattle, poultry, tamed parrots and small native mammals. Most food is prepared by boiling. Meat is smoked or salted if ti is not immediately consumed. Maize is boiled and later ground on the metate. It is either eaten fresh or allowed to ferment. It is also formed into cakes, wrapped in husks and steamed.

Early chroniclers report that dwellings were either large or organized in small clusters and were usually fortified by means of a stockade. Unfortified hamlets of several houses were also reported. In modern times the houses are grouped in small communities. Most families live in single structures but larger families have two buildings, the second serving as a kitchen and the home of older people. The modern house lasts about five years; is seldom repaired and the new house is built on an unoccupied site. Round, rectangular or square houses are built, none of which have a specialized function. House sites are usually inherited through the male line. The Guatuso (Corobici?) had houses scattered over a considerable area. The houses were low, pitched-roofed buildings, open at the endes and sides under the eaves.

The aboriginal man's clothing consisted of a breechout, a narrow strip of bark cloth about two meters long which was passes between the legs and wrapped around the waist. Usually it was held up by a belt. The woman's clothing consisted of the breechclout and a knee-length, wrap-around skirt. Both sexes frequently were bare-brested but a short jacket was also worn by both males and females. The Guatuso (Corobici?) were reported to have decorated themselves with paint.

The economy depends on agricultural production but a system of trade for additional items is also carried on. European goods such as cattle, clothing, machetes, fishhooks, and sugar have forced the people to adopt a system of money exchange which is apparently foreign to their traditional trading patterns.

The whole social structure of the Corobici, as well as other tribal groups in the Central Costa Rican area, is now being modified. At the time of the Conquest, the Guetar (Corobici?) were divided into three classes: nobles, commoners, and slaves, the last being women and boys captured in war. Captive men were sacrificed. The modern tribes are less stratified. The basic social unit is the family, a man, his wife or wives, and their children. Land, cattle and all other property is held in the names of the men and the boys although women own some land, cattle and all of the household goods. Evidence fromthe early colonial documents and from more recent sources indicates that the tribes were organized as feudal states. During the wars with the Spaniards, each Indian polity was welded into a strong unit. When these were broken up after the Conquest, realignments were attempted but in modern times the heads of small localized groups hold political power. All of the tribes in the area, including the Corobici, are more or less warlike. The early chroniclers emphasize the fact that the wars were waged for the purpose of acquiring captives for sacrifice but economic, political and territorial competition for control over lands and people also were contributing factors to the incidence of warfare. Early accounts of religious activities are confined to remarks noting that the priests were sacred and secular officials. Only the more important of the many ceremonies reported during the past centuries are still celebrated. Ceremonies from the pre-Conquest period had a religious background and in the modern day involve varying degrees of drunkenness and brawling.

BIBLIOGRAPHY —

● STEWARD, JULIAN H. Handbook of South American Indians. 7 Vols., Washington, DC: U.S. Govt. Printing Office, 1946-59.

COSTANOAN

(U.S.; Calif.) Indians were a comparatively simple people found mainly along the coast of California from the Golden Gate and Susuin and San Pablo bays on the north to the Big Sur River south of Monterey on the south, and extending inland to the crest of the main Coast Range from just north of Mount Diablo in the north to about Santa Rita Peak in the south. The name Costanoan is derived from the Spanish word "Costanos," meaning "Coast Peoples," and has become, by steady usage, the only name generally accepted for this group of small tribes with a similar language.

Social and cultural boundaries and subdivisions. The Costonoans were a part of the Central California Culture Area, which included the Coast Miwok, Pomo, Wintun and Maidu to the north, the Bay, Valley and Hill Miwok, and the Yokuts of the San Joaquin Valley to the east. The Esselen and Salinan peoples to the immediate south had a similar sparce culture, but were more strongly influenced by the culturally complex and creative Chumash and Gabrielino of southern California.

The Costanoans themselves were divided into two main subdivisions, those who dwelt around San Francisco Bay and south to Santa Cruz on the coast, and then inland to the drainage of the Coyote River that empties into the south end of the bay; and those who dwelt farther south in the drainage systems of the lower part of the Salinas River, and all of the river basins of the Carmel and San Benito rivers.

Language. The Penutian Language Family, to which the Costanoans belonged, is a very large family, covering many tribes along the Pacific Coast. Other Penutian-speaking tribes in California besides the Costanoan included the Miwok, Wintun, and Maidu to the north, the Bay, Valley and Hill Miwok, and the Yokuts of the San Joaquin Valley to the east. The Esselen and Salinan peoples to the immediate south had a similar sparce culture, but were more strongly influenced by the culturally complex and creative Chumash and Gabrielino of southern California.

The Costanoans themselves were divided into two main subdivisions, those who dwelt around San Francisco Bay and south to Santa Cruz on the coast, and then inland to the drainage of the Coyote River that empties into the south end of the bay; and those who dwelt farther south in the drainage systems of the lower part of the Salinas River, and all of the river basins of the Carmel and San Benito rivers.

Language. The Penutian Language Family, to which the Costanoans belonged, is a very large family, covering many tribes along the Pacific Coast. Other Penutian-speaking tribes in California besides the Costanoan included the Miwok, Wintum, and Maidu to the north and northeast of the Costanoans, and the widespread and numerous Yokut peoples in the San Joaquin Valley to the east and southeast. The Costanoans themselves had at least seven separate dialects, of which the two most widely different, were the Soledad to the far south, and the Saklan to the far northeast by Susuin Bay, which, by some linguists, is considered more closely related to the Wintun.

Summary of tribal culture. *Subsistence and economy.* Deer was hunted in the usual Pacific coastal way of using a deer head and skin to disguise the hunter when he crept up on the game with bow and arrow. Rabbits were shot with arrows, but also driven in a communal drive aided by fire to a central place where they were killed with clubs. Deadfall traps included one with a heavy board, propped up to fall on mice, rats, etc., and a twig cage with one end propped up to trap quail. A kind of bola, unique for central California, of two bones on a string, was whirled and thrown to catch birds. Large wood rat nests were burned to drive out their occupants for killing with clubs. Dogs were used for hunting, deer, raccoons, etc., something unique on the central coast. A feather fan was used to blow smoke into ground squirrel holes, forcing them out. Bows were either simple self-bows, or very well made and strong sinew-backed bows. Fish spears and nets were used to catch fish, and night fishing, with a bonfire to attract the fish, was unique on the central coast. Soaproot was mashed up and thrown in pools to poison fish.

An important food was acorns, knocked down mainly from live oak trees and later leached with water to take out the poison, either in a sand basin, through fern leaves, or in an open-work basket. Acorns were ground up to a fine meal and often cooked into a very thick mush in water-tight baskets with the help of red-hot stones. Ground seeds were cooked this way, but also by parching them when tossed in a basket over hot coals, so skillfully the basket did not catch fire. Yellow jacket larvae were eaten raw, but grasshoppers were caught and roasted in pits. Seaweed was dried and eaten to provide salt, but salt was also taken after evaporation in ocean rock pools. Roots and bulbs were dug up with digging sticks, while mussels and clams were the main seafood, especially relied upon in winter.

Technology and arts. The domed and circular or conical dwellings were usually small, meant only for one family, and covered with either tule mats or brush over a willow framework. The old was burnt down and a new home was built whenever fleas inside got too numerous. Skins were used for bedding and placed over tule mats on the floor. An earth overn was used for baking acorn or other seed bread. A small conical baking acorn or other seed bread. A small conical sweat house was built, not in a pit as was usual elsewhere, and here men sweated by a hot fire, or held men-only meetings, or otherwise relaxed.

The balsa, or tule raft boat, made of bound-together tules, lashed together in brunches and shaped with a prow was quite expertly navigated with double-bladed paddles on the bay or large rivers. Stone mortars, some in bedrock, others portable, were hollowed out and stone pestles used to grind grain or nuts in them. Special small ones were used to make paint, medicine and tobacco. There were also wooden mortars hollowed out of logs. Household implements included brushes made of soaproot or hair, a paddle-shaped food stirrer, spoons made usually of mussel shell, and bark platters for eating meat. Skin scrapers were made of ribbone or split cobbles.

Hair was worn long or short, often in two braids, but women alone had bangs over the forehead. Beards were plucked with bone tweezers; hair was sometimes doubled back on a woman's head. Men used nose stick ornaments, while both men and women tattooed their face, but women alone on forehead and arms. Men finger-painted their bodies withred and white stripes, while women were likely to wear shell necklaces or ear pendants. Yellow hammer quill bands were used by men on their heads for dances; also bunches of magpie feathers were ited into the hair. Robes and capes of otter skin were used by the well-to-do, while woven rabbitskins were worn by the poor. Women wore a network of plant fibers in front, and a tanned skin behind to make a double dress, but men mostly went naked. The red paint they used came from mecury ore and caused many deaths by poisoning.

Social and political organization. Each tribe was ruled by a hereditary chief and orator. Sometimes the chief uniquely acted as a war leader. Wars were mainly minor skirmishes between tribes.

Very little of this is preserved. Coyote was the great folk hero, who was a hero when he created life, or taught men to hunt or to use acorns, but was a villain when he chased after women or tried to fool the people or other animals and birds. The religion was mainly influenced by shamans who used their powers to make or stop rain, heal the sick, propitiate evil spirits or prevent poisoning or magic by other shamans. There were some women shamans, unique for this part of California. Shamans healed mainly by sucking out supposed evil objects from their patients or by using certain herbs, suchas yerba buena. There was a partial introduction of the elaborate Kuksu Cult healing and initiation ceremonies from the more sophisticated tribes to the north. A bit of quiet humor shines through when we hear that part of the people's astronomical knowledge was calling the Pleiades, "the bunch of little ones shaking!"

Games, such as shinny and kick ball and gambling games, using marked sticks to hide and guess about were the greatest occupiers of leisure time. Rattles, split-stick clappers, whistles, flutes and the musical bow were the main musical instruments, with the split-stick used for the dances.

Life cycle. At birth the baby was usually helped come by a midwife, and both baby and mother were kept warm on leafy branches placed over an oven. At the onset of menstruation the girl was secluded in one corner of the hut for about 3-5 days. Presents were exchanged at the time of marriage, which was more likely to be successful if both parents and the young couple were in favor of it. Chiefs had more than one wife, and some other men in the north married sisters. The dead of the poor were usually buried the same day of death; the better class people usually had cremation.

Summary of tribal history, population and contemporary condition. History began with the coming of the Spaniards in 1774. The missions were established soon after this and at first there was friendliness on both sides, but unfortunately the Padres felt it necessary to use in time the whip, and soldiers to discipline the Indian converts; and disease and inadequate sanitation caused a great many deaths. The Indians, unused to these conditions, became sullen or in despair, so that later visitors to the missions called them spiritless and devoid of intelligence, without understanding the traumatic experiences they had suffered.

The original population of the Costanoans has been estimated by Drs. A. L. Kroeber and Robert Heizer as between 7,000 and 10,000 people. By the mid 20th century it had dropped to zero. Contact with these people wsa lost too quickly and too tragically to have a very true picture of them and their culture today.

BIBLIOGRAPHY —

● HODGE, FREDERICK WEBB. Handbook of American Indians North of Mexico.Washington: Government Printing Office, 2 vols., 1907-10.
● MURDOCK, GEORGE P. Ethnographic Bibliography of North America.New Haven, CT: Human Relations Area Files Press, 1975.

● SWANTON, JOHN R. The Indian Tribes of North America. Washington, DC: U.S. Government Printing Office, 1952.

COSTANOAN FAMILY

(U.S.; Calif.) A linguistic family. In 1877 Powell established a family which he called Mutsun, extending from san San Francisco to Soledad and from the sea inland to the Sierras, and including an area in the Marin county peninsula, North of San Francisco bay, and gave vocabularies from various parts of this territory. In 1891 Powell divided this area between two families. Moquelumnan and Costanoan. The Moquelumnan family occupied the portion of the old Mutsun territory East of San Joaquin River and North of San Francisco bay.

The territory of the Costanoan family extended from the Pacific ocean to San Joaquin River, and from the Golden Gate and Suisun bay on the North to Point Sur on the coast and a point a short distance South of Soledad in the Salinas valley on the South. Farther inland the South boundary is uncertain, though it was probably near Big Panoch Creek. The Costanoan Indians lived mainly on vegetal products, especially acorns and seeds, though they also obtained fish and mussels, and captured deer and smaller game. Their clothing was scant, the men going naked. Their houses were tule or grass huts, their boats balsas or rafts of tules. They made baskets, but no pottery, and appear to have been as primitive as most of the tribes of California. They burned the dead. The Rumsen of Monterey looked upon the eagle, the humming bird, and the coyote as the original inhabitants of the world, and they venerated the redwood. Their languages were simple and harmonious. Seven missions--San Carlos, Soledad, San Juan Baaautista, Santa Cruz, Santa Clara, San Jose, and Dolores (San Francisco)--were established in Costanoan territory by the Franciscans subsequent to 1770, and continued until their confiscation by the Mexican government in 1834, when the Indians were scattered. The surviving individuals of Costanoan blood were mostly "Mexican" in life and manners rather than Indian.

True tribes did not exist in Costanoan territory, the groups mentioned below being small and probably little more than village communities, without political connection or even a name other than that of the locality they inhabited.

BIBLIOGRAPHY –

● HODGE, FREDERICK WEBB. Handbook of American Indians North of Mexico.Washington: Government Printing Office, 2 vols., 1907-10.
● MURDOCK, GEORGE P. Ethnographic Bibliography of North America.New Haven, CT: Human Relations Area Files Press, 1975.
● SWANTON, JOHN R. The Indian Tribes of North America. Washington, DC: U.S. Government Printing Office, 1952.

● WISSLER, CLARK. Indians of the U.S., Four Centuries of Their History and Culture. New York, NY: Doubleday, Doran & Co., 1940.

COSUMNI

(U.S.; Calif.) A tribe, probably Moquelumnan, formerly residing on or near Cosumnes River, San Joaquin county. According to Rice these Indians went almost naked; their houses were of bark, sometimes thatched with grass and covered with earth: the bark was loosened from the trees by repeated blows with stone hatchets, the latter having the head fastened to the handle with deer sinew. Their ordinary weapons were bows and stone-tipped arrows. The women made finely woven conical baskets of grass, the smaller ones of which held water. Their amusements were chiefly dancing and football; the dances, however, were in some degree ceremonial. Their principal deity was the sun, and the women had a ceremony which resembled the sun dance of the tribes of the upper Missouri. Their dead were buried in graves in the earth. The tribe is now practically extinct.

BIBLIOGRAPHY –

● BANCROFT, HUBART HOWE. The Native Races of the Pacific States of North America.San Francisco, CA: 1874.
● HODGE, FREDERICK WEBB. Handbook of American Indians North of Mexico.Washington: Government Printing Office, 2 vols., 1907-10.
● MURDOCK, GEORGE P. Ethnographic Bibliography of North America.New Haven, CT: Human Relations Area Files Press, 1975.
● SWANTON, JOHN R. The Indian Tribes of North America. Washington, DC: U.S. Government Printing Office, 1952.

COTONAM

(U.S.; Tex.) a tribe affiliated with the Carrizos of the Coahuiltecan family and living in their vicinity, though their dialect differs largely from the Comecrudo language. The last of this tribe were at La Noria rancheria, in South Hidalgo county, Texas, in 1886, and one man at Las Prietas was slightly acquainted with the native dialect. They call an Indian *xaima,* and are the Xaimame or Haname of the Texan tribes farther North. The Tonkawa say that the Cotonam were not cannibals and they wore sandals instead of moccasins.

BIBLIOGRAPHY –

● HODGE, FREDERICK WEBB. Handbook of American Indians North of Mexico.Washington: Government Printing Office, 2 vols., 1907-10.
● MURDOCK, GEORGE P. Ethnographic Bibliography of North America.New Haven, CT: Human Relations Area Files Press, 1975.

COUSHATTA

(U.S.; Ala., La., Nebr. Tex.) was a large branch of the Alabama people. They were a Muskhogean speaking people, who also, originally, were called *Soasati* . They adopted Coushatta some time around the 19th century. Their language was such that men and women had differences in their speech patterns.

From 1500 to 1600 they lived along the Tennessee River. Later they moved below the junction of the Coosa and Tallapoosa Rivers.

Like other Muskhogean tribes they relied heavily on hunting, some fishing and agriculture. The Coushattas also made fine baskets and wove cloth, industries the women continue today on the reservations.

They were, in addition, noted for nose decorations.

De Soto was the first white to establish contact with them. In his chronicles he called them *Coste, Acosre, Cotche, and Acosta* . In 1561 they were ready to join with the Creeks and other tribes to prevent Pardo, whose expedition had taken cruel advantage of the Indians, from progressing any further inland. It is not recorded whether they actually fought the Spaniards. Not long after this they began their move to the coosa and Tallapoosa rivers, where they had their greatest contact with the French. The French found them industrious and impeccably honest in all their dealings.

They remained here until the French ceded their power east of the Mississippi in 1763. A large number then went to Tombigee River. They later returned. In 1795 another section crossed the Mississippi to the Red River. Later those in Texas joined the Alabama. Those who stayed moved to Oklahoma, where many lived with the Creeks.

Today there are several hundred (there were more than 500 in 1850), in Texas, Louisiana and Nebraska.

COWLITZ

(U.S.; Wash.) A Salish tribe formerly on the river of the same name. Once numerous and powerful, they were said by Gibbs in 1853 to be insignificant, numbering with the Upper Chehalis, with whom they were mingled, not more than 165. About 1887 there were 127 on Puyallup reservation, Washington. They are no longer known by this name, being evidently officially classed as Chehalis.

BIBLIOGRAPHY –

● BANCROFT, HUBART HOWE. The Native Races of the Pacific States of North America.San Francisco, CA: 1874.
● COAN, CHARLES F. The First Stage of the Federal Indian Policy in the Pacific Northwest, 1849- 1852.Portland, OR: (reprint from vol. XXII, no. 1 of the Quarterly of the Oregon Historical Society.) The Ivy Press, 1921.
● CONGRESS. 66th Congress, 2nd Session, H. Rept. 790.
● MURDOCK, GEORGE P. Ethnographic Bibliography of North America.New Haven, CT: Human Relations Area Files Press, 1975.
● SWANTON, JOHN R. The Indian Tribes of North America. Washington, DC: U.S. Government Printing Office, 1952.

COYOTERO

(U.S.; Ariz.) an earlier term, less used today, applied to a sub- group of the Western Apache tribes, including both the Pinaleno and San Carlos Apache, living in eastern Arizona. The name comes from the old Spanish reference to "wolf men," or "wild men," actually a comment upon their nomadic, aggressive habits. They are included in with the Western Apache population today.

BIBLIOGRAPHY –

● HODGE, FREDERICK WEBB. Handbook of American Indians North of Mexico. Washington: Smithsonian Institution: BAE Bulletin No. 30: U.S. GPO, 1907.
● SWANTON, JOHN R. The Indian Tribes of North America. Washington, DC: U.S. Government Printing Office, 1952.

CREE

(U.S.; Mont., N.Dak.; Canada; Alberta, Ontario) was a huge, diverse tribe of hunters who occupied a large part of Canada. Their lands went as north from the coast of the East Main River nearly to the Churchill River; towards the East they extended to Lakes Mistassini and Nichiheu. Towards the west their boundaries were less certain; in the early 1500s they probably wandered over country west of Lake Winnepeg, and possibly between the Red and Saskatchewan rivers. Once they obtained firearms, however, they made great movements both west and north. By the mid 18th century they controlled northern Manitoba and Saskatchewan as far as the Churchill River, all of northern Alberta, the valley of the Slave River and parts of the land surrounding the Great Slave Lake.

Their name comes from a contraction of *Kristineaux* , which is French form for the name of a Cree branch. The meaning of *Kristineaux* is unknown. The Cree's linguistic stock was Algonquian.

Although a huge tribe numerically, estimates in the 18th century listed 15,000 Crees, there was never any central government. The Crees lived in bands. Like other Athapascan nations Crees took on some characteristics of tribes they contacted. Generally the Cree bands were divided into two types: the plains Cree, living on the Canadian plains, and the woodland or Swampy Cree living in the woodlands.

Some aspects of band life differed from one band to another. For example, dwellings varied. The Southern woodland Cree constructed bark and wooden wigwams. Toward the north, the Cree constructed skin tipis. However, most basic aspects of life, such as hunting and tool construction, were alike. Deer, caribou, and moose were the main source of meat; and rabbits were extensively used both for food and skin blankets. Though the Crees despised fishing, they took it up when other food

Cree chief near Edmonton, Alberta

was scarce. To catch fish they used hooks of sturgeon bones. Other animal bones were used, such as awls made of moose bones. In the north, Crees used an oddly curved knife probably borrowed from the Inuit. Other bands to the south and west used a chiiseled sharp tool similar to other Plains tribes. Flints were used for arrowheads, spear points, and hatchets. Cooking vessels and pottery were made of stone. As contact with whites increased these tools were replaced with European items.

Physically the Cree were copper colored, of medium height and proportion. MacKenzie thought Cree women were the most beautiful of any Indians he had seen. Chastity was not considered a virtue but a wife's infidelity was often severely punished. Polygamy was common and a widower was expected to marry his wife's sister, if she had one.

Tattooing was common until it was prohibited because of white displeasure. Women were content to have simply two lines drawn from the corners of their mouths to their jaws. But many men had lines and patterns drawn all over their bodies.

Government usually consisted of just one chief for each band.

Their religious customs were similar to the Ojibwa's. The major religious group was a secret society which both men and women could join. There were four levels of membership to which one could advance. But few reached the highest levels, for each succeeding level involved heavy payments. Those that were at the highest level were medicine men, and in a position of great power. The Crees believed the great spirits had endowed everything with a soul, so medicine men were those who could appeal to those souls to help cure a sick individual. But Crees also believed that many evil spirits existed, and a medicine amn could use these spirits to harm people. There was great fear of witchcraft. On hunting trips the men would carry little bags of herbs for protection.

Burial places for the dead were covered with stones to protect the bodies from animals. Some items owned by the deceased were placed on the grave.

The tribe always had good relations with the French and the English, who allowed the Crees freedom to pursue their lifestyle. But Crees had difficulty with other tribes. In 1786 a smallpox epidemic struck, reducing the Crees to half their numbers. Other tribes particularly the Blackfeet, had acquired firearms, and used these against the Cree. Then alcohol was introduced into the tribe; and its effects were ruinous. By the 1830s another epidemic struck and the population fell to under 3,000. Today, however, there are more than 20,000 Cree living mostly on reservations in Manitoba.

BIBLIOGRAPHY –

● HODGE, FREDERICK WEBB. Handbook of American Indians North of Mexico. Washington: Smithsonian Institution: BAE Bulletin No. 30: U.S. GPO, 1907.
● MANDELBAUM, DAVID G. The Plains Cree. Anthropological Papers of the American Museum of Natural History, vol. 37, 1940.
● SKINNER, ALANSON. Notes on the Eastern Cree and Northern Saulteaux. Anthropological Papers of the American Museum of Natural History, vol. 9, 1911.
● SWANTON, JOHN R. The Indian Tribes of North America. Washington, DC: U.S. Government Printing Office, 1952.

CREEK

(U.S.; Ala., Ga., Okla.) are important Muskhogean tribe, who, along with the Cherokees, Chickasaws, Choctaws and Seminoles, were one of the "Five Civilized Tribes," so named because they adopted white culture more rapidly than others.

A Muskhogean speaking tribe, they were part of the great Muskhogean confedercy. Interestingly only about half of the tribes forming this confederacy spoke Muskhogean. The Creeks lived in Alabama and Georgia. Like the Chickasaws and Choctaws they migrated there from the north.

As their village life changed, Creeks lived in small wooden houses that were clustered together according to clans. Agriculture and hunting provided the basic staples. Corn was prepared 42 different ways, according to one observer. They ate a variety of fruits and meats and brewed a mildly alcoholic drink called "Hickory Milk." The women spun superb cloth on looms.

As to the social organization, the Creeks, like so many other tribes, were organized into clans. Marriage was only permitted outside the clan. Girls were trained and educated by their oldest maternal aunt; while men handled the young boys.

Adulterous or misbehaving wives could have their ears and noses clipped. Many of these women became prostitutes. Women could start divorce proceedings against husbands, however, by tossing their possessions out of the house. Such men had then to return to their mother's house.

The Creeks were generally a forgiving people. One of the most outstanding characteristics of their religion is that at the annual Green Corn Dance, the most important of Creek ceremonies, every sin or violation, short of murder, was forgiven. The Creek's religious structure was a combination of priests and shamans. Priests had verbatum religious prayers and the individual sought direct contact withthe Gods through dreams. Medicine men were trained in schools, and there were three classes of medicine men.

There were the "knowers," people who had psychic power; the medicine men who could control weather and other0 phenomena; and witches, who were full of lizards and caused murder. If a doctor's patient died he was suspected of witchcraft and was often killed by the deceased'd family.

The dead were usually buried in the bed they occupied in their house. Mothers also buried their dead children in their house to ease their mourning.

One ritual commonly practiced by men before going to war, playing ball, having council meetings, or any auspicious event was the drinking of *Asi* , the Black Drink. This was a mild narcotic which caused nausea. It was taken for spiritual and physical purification.

Every Creek town had its own chief and was autonomous in local government. The chief was his vice-chief were approved by a council. Though the position was not hereditary one clan usually furnished the chief.

The Creeks had no war chiefs; all chiefs were called *Peace Chiefs* . There were three classifications of warriors, each with a certain degree of authority. One went up the ranks according to one's valor in war.

Certain Creek towns called *White Towns* , were designated only for peace ceremonies, and certain others, called *Red Towns* , were designated only for war ceremonies.

The Creeks were first met by De Soto in 1540. In 1559 Tristan de Lunia visited them but all that can be said of the visit is he left the tribe in a deplorable condition. Sometime between then and the alliance with the English, the Muskhogean confederacy was formed between the Creeks and other smaller tribes.

The Creeks came into prominence as English allies in the Apalachee War of 1703-08. They remained friendly to British while hostile to the Spanish in Florida.

Following the American Revolution, certain bands became anti- American while others allied with the Americans. Creek warriors helped Jackson defeat other Creeks at the Battle of Horseshoe Bend in 1812.

Soon after there developed a major split in Creek-American relations, and this resulted in the

Snake Indians of Creek Nation, under arrest at Muskogee, 1901.

Crazy Snake was a Creek chief and leader of the so-called Snake Uprising in Oklahoma in 1901.

Creek Wars of 1813-14. This time they fought Jackson, and the bloody war ended with their total defeat and the loss of many of their lands. Between 1835-43 wsa the Seminole War, a torturous affair which finally secured peace between the Creeks and southern tribes, and ended with most of the Creeks removed to Oklahoma.

In Oklahoma they established a nation based on the U.S. Constitution, with a single executive, a House of Kings-similar to the Senate-and a House of Warriors-similar to the House of Representatives.

The first estimates of Creek population were in the 18th century when they had between 11,000 and 20,000. Today several thousand live on the reservation.

BIBLIOGRAPHY —

● GREEN, DONALD E. The Creek People. Phoenix, AZ: Indian Tribal Series, 1973.
● MANDELBAUM, DAVID G. The Plains Cree. Anthropological Papers of the American Museum of Natural History, vol. 37, 1940.
● SKINNER, ALANSON. Notes on the Eastern Cree and Northern Saulteaux. Anthropological Papers of the American Museum of Natural History, vol. 9, 1911.

● SPENCER, ROBERT F., JESS D. JENNINGS. Native Americans. New York, NY: Harper & Row, Publishers, 1965.

CROATAN

(U.S.; N.C.) are a group of mixed-blood survivors from various eastern tribes, living in Robeson County, North Carolina, of very uncertain ancestry. Originally they seem to have inhabited the island of that name north of Cape Hatteras, today known as Cape Lookout, in North Carolina. Said by some to represent the remnants of the famous "Lost Colony" of Sir Walter Raleigh, they have an almost mythical history. When Raleigh sent his exploring party to "Virginia" in 1585-86, he authorized a party to colonize Roanoke Island. The effort failed, and Sir Richard Greenville assigned 15 men to stay behind to preserve the English claim to the land. In 1587 a second group of 117 persons wea sent over, under John White, who had been instructed to avoid Roanoke due to the earlier failure. Instead, he landed there, found no trace of the 15 occupants, but nevertheless decided to settle. In August of that year, with supplies running low, he returned to England; unfortunately the War with Spain intervened, forcing him to stay until August of 1590, when he returned with the needed provisions, but the colony had vanished. The only indication of their occupancy was the word *Croatoan* carved on a tree; no indication was to be seen of hasty flight or hostile action. Because of the inscription, White felt that the colonists had gone to Croatan Island, or to nearby Hatteras; but their fate has never been accurately determined. This has given rise to the commonly-argued theory that their descendants are the present-day "Croatan Indians" of the region. Certainly the Indian population of Robeson County is a greatly mixed-blood people; some appear obviously Indian, others are apparently half-Indian and half- white, while others demonstrate considerable Negro blood. Of greater interest is their retention of many Shakespearean locutions and 16th century English speech habits, many of English family names, and similar Old World customs. The problem was made even more complicated during the Civil War period, when many Negro slaves escaped from nearby plantations and sought refuge among the Indian population. Although the latter refused intermarriage insofar as was possible, inevitable liaisons occurred to increase the problem of ancestral clarity. To defend their sociological position, the Croatan refused to attend Negro schools; since they were not accepted into white schools; they established their own educational system; eventually a state system of three separate bu equal schools prevailed in North Carolina. On February 10, 1885, under political pressures, the General Assembly of the state designated the Indians of Roberson County as "Croatan Indians," and this status was observed for many years. However, in time this became a label of derision and discrimination, and the Indians sought another term; also, many Indians people themselves opposed the name. Finally, to try to end the quarreling, the term "Cherokee Indians of Roberson County" was applied to them by statute on March 11, 1913. Although even less satisfactory, this held until 1953; but dissident Indians sought other appellations, among them "Siouan Indians of the Lumber River." Meanwhile, one major division had become more active in the effort towards individual definition for social, political and economic reasons, realizing that their state of limbo was a threat to any complete success in American life. In June 7, 1956, they were able to obtain a third legal definition, this time as the "Lumbee Indians of North Carolina"-by which they are known today. The present population numbers some 15,000 persons living in Roberson County and adjacent areas.

CROW

(U.S.; Mt., Wyo.) lived in the northern Great Plains in the neighborhood of the Bighorn Mountains and part of the Yellowstone River Basin of what is now Montana and northern Wyoming. They are a big people, the men often over six feet. As first seen by explorers and mountain men they were said to be friendly as a whole, but often haughty and warlike in demeanor. They had to be brave and good fighters, surrounded as they were by such powerful and warlike tribes as the Dakota to the east, the Cheyenne to the southeast and the Blackfoot to the northeast. They called themselves the *Absaroka* , translated also as the *Apsaruke*.

Social and cultural boundaries and subdivisions. The Plains tribes were so mobile that it is often hard to define their boundaries. The Crow had two main divisions, the River Crow (Minisepere), along the Yellowstone River down to its meeting with the Missouri; and the Mountain Crow (Acaraho) of the Big Horn and Little Big Horn rivers and nearby mountains. But another at least partial division was formed by the people called Kicked-in-Their-Bellies (Erarapio), who joined the Mountain Crow in the spring, but spent the winter in the Wind River Region of the Shoshones in what is now Wyoming at some wonderful hot springs. Though united in language these three divisions generally operated as separate tribes, each under a head-chief. However, the basic social and political unit was more often the extended family or clan, and these did not obey very well any head chief except in especially large hunts or in great danger, such as war.

Language. Crow belonged to the very large Hokan-Siouan language family, which included their greatest enemies the Dakota (Sioux) on their east, their close relatives, the Hidatsa on the North Dakota Missouri, various southeastern tribes such as the Creek and Choctaw, and tribes as far west as California, such as the Pomo and the Chumash.

Summary of tribal culture. *Subsistence and economy.* Perhaps five hundred years or so ago the Crow broke off as a tribe from their close relatives, the Hidatsa, who had developed the cultivation of corn, beans and squash along the Missouri River, and struck out into the Great Plains to become nomadic buffalo hunters. They were noted for their very strong and beautiful bows made from elk and mountain sheep horns, cut and shaped symmetrically by much scraping, bound together with rawhide and sinew-backed. But in the days before they had the horse, death from starvation due to the difficulties in catching the swiftly-running buffalo, elk, and antelope, or attacks by grizzly bears or Indian enemies, must have often been near. With the horse, which probably reached them through the Shoshone to their southwest about 1750, their striking ability and speed greatly increased, and life became easier. However, for some time they still used the ancient method of driving game over a cliff or into stockaded surrounds where the wounded and dying were killed and butchered.

Hunting on horseback was a great adventure, but it had to follow definite rules or game could be lost. Only when the military society that had been given the duty of policemen decided that the hunters were close enough and correctly arranged for attacking a herd of buffalo was the word given to charge. Then silently the hunters raced their horses over a ridge and down upon the herd, each man trying to get up as close as he could to the left shoulder of his victim where he could drive a lance, arrow or bullet into the heart. Buffalo, unlike a modern cow, could turn on a dime and spear a man with its needle-sharp horns in the next second. After flencing off the skin with knives, gutting the carcass and cutting up the meat, pack horses brought up by boys would be loaded with the meat and hides to carry back to the camp. Cooking was done either by roasting or by boiling the meat and wild vegetables in a hide cooking pot, the water heated by red-hot stones. Boys sometimes prankishly dashed up to where the women guarded the meat that was hanging in ranks over the cooking fires and tried to run off with pieces without being caught.

Women and children gathered berries, roots and other wild plant food as the neighborhood allowed, sometimes guarded by men if enemies were thought to be near or grizzly bears around. Boys hunted rabbits, prairie dogs and other small game nearby with bows and arrows, so preparing for manhood. When the best hunters came into camp with game, they usually shared their meat with the sick, the disabled and the old. There was also much trading off or giving away of food at the times of ceremonies, which helped see that everybody had enough to eat.

Technology and arts. The Crow tipi was noted for its very long poles, usually made of cottonwood or pine saplings, and giving an hourglass effect, sometimes 25 feet in height. It was usually erected by women, one holding up the main pole until others could be tied to it, then the sewn skins pulled around it. Before the horse, tipis were much smaller, having to be carried on the top of dog travois of long poles with crossbars. Such a tipi was probably not much more than ten feet high, and made of only 8 to 10 buffalo hides, compared to the 12 to 18 hides of the horse days. Logs for poles had to be stripped of bark and scraped down in the thickness to make them manageable. Tipis were decorated usually rather plainly, but skin screens might be covered with drawings depicting war or hunting exploits. There were no bedsteads, only piles of skins for beds, but backrests of willow strung together with sinew were used.

Clothing and blankets were made of skins, which had usually been kept for several days in water, then scraped of hair and flesh, brains spread on them to soften, and then scraped again with an adz-shaped shoulder blade or other large bone before finally being smoked to tan. Such skins when well-done stayed soft and flexible whether wet or dry. Skins were sewn together to make clothing, which included shirts, hip-high leggings, single- piece moccasins, often decorated with porcupine quills in the old days, later with beads. Also decorated with such quills or later with colored beads were bags, particularly parfleches and the long fringed pipe bags. The Crow used lots of triangles and diamond shapes in their designs, often with a central cross.

Social and religious culture. Crow society was essentially democratic, chiefs leading clans or tribes by virtue of forceful character and kindness and thoughtfulness towards their followers, being soon elected out of office if they proved otherwise. There were several unusual features to Crow society. They had to prove their courage by such acts as stanidng in place without flinching in the face of an enemy attach, but the Crow had certain clubs that engaged in wife stealing. For example, the Foxes and the Lumpwoods would raid each other's families for wives. The man usually had no recourse but to let his wife go, and once gone never take her back. Consequently a husband who really loved his wife often went to extraordinary

Crow lodge of twenty-five buffalo skins

lengths to hide so she would not be stolen.

Though the Crow were noted among Plains tribes for their loose moral standards, there were three unusual features about this. One was that they continued to treat sexually promiscuous men or women with respect so that their lives were not made hard and bitter as in some tribes. A second was that despite the general looseness of sexual relations, the men and women who were most held in respect and given great honors and even riches were the truly virtuous ones. A third was the intense emotional linkage between parents and their children, so strong that when families broke up there were many heartbreaking scenes. Possibly very high standards were once general in this tribe, but became corrupted among the majority in recent centuries.

Vision seeking and colorful dances preceded the sending out of war parties by the military societies, but the societies also often acted as peacemakers when feuds erupted between clans. They tried to stop them by claiming the whole tribe would be weakened by such fights and so made more vulnerable to enemy attack. In war it was more an honor to strike an enemy and get away than actually kill him (called "counting a coup") and, among the Crow, horse stealing from enemies ranked so high that they became probably the most adept and clever of all horse thieves.

Religious life. Religion was closely tied to warfare, as the warrior usually sought a vision before going on a war party to make sure to his success and also to give him courage. Visions by both men and women often determined many actions of life and helped decide whether a man would be a success or a failure. Cutting off a finger joint as a

Crow Indian tobacco planting ceremony, 1934.

sacrifice to induce a good vision was very common. Visions could also be tied in with a religious society, such as the Tobacco Society, determining how the tobacco would be handled or planted. The Tobacco Society had ceremonies using tobacco that could be called the development of sympathetic magic to help the different members of their lives.

Unlike their neighbors, the Crow did not make extensive use of the Sacred Pipe and did not form a society around it. A pipe owner might adopt a "son" or "daughter" to pass on the power of the pipe, and at such a time a dance was held and presents exchanged. It could also be used as a peace pipe when travelling, preventing conflict.

The Sun Dance of the Crow was different in several ways from other tribes. It was usually held much less frequently, mainly because of the difficulty of finding a man to sponsor it who would go through the rigourous fasting and other tests required by the tribe. Nevertheless it was a great occasion every few years and people would come from far to watch its dances and ceremonies. Though ostensibly dedicated to the Sun, it was bound tightly to vengeance and war. The pledger of a Sun Dance was called the *Whistler* , and he chose as *Father* a medicine man who essentially acted as master of ceremonies. The medicine man had to be specifically the *Owner* of a Sacred Sun Dance Doll, which he then used, along with severe fasting and some torture to bring the Whistler into a state of ecstacy that would lead to a vision showing the death of an enemy warrior. Other dancers also went through torture, usually with skewers through the flesh and tied to buffalo

skulls, to aid in the revenge against the enemy. There was a feast also when hundreds of cooked buffalo tongues were given out to all present along with other meat, so all was not grim in the Sun Dance.

Brief history and present condition. The Crow, influneced by leaders such as Plenty Coups and Bell-Rock, felt that the Dakota (Sioux) were a greater menace to their small tribe than the white men, and so cast their lots with the whites, serving as scouts for the U.S. Army (1855-1880). For this loyalty they were given the present large and well-watered and forested Crow Reservation in south central Montana. Their estimated 1830 population of about 3,500 dropped to a low by 1910, but has since come back today to more than equal this 1839 figure. In modern times the old enmity for the Dakota has died out and these and other tribes are invited to the great Crow Fiar which is held every summer and brings many Indians together for dance and drum and other contests. Even the Sun Dance has been revived, though it no longer has the war emphasis it once had. Today the Crow are developing businesses and ranches on their reservations.

(see map page XV)

Plenty Coups

BIBLIOGRAPHY –

● EASTMAN, ELAINE GOODALE. Pratt, The Red Man's Moses. Norman, OK: University of Oklahoma Press, 1935.
● FOREMAN, GRANT. Advancing the Frontier, 1830- 1860. Norman, OK: University of Oklahoma Press, 1933.
----- Pioneer Days in the Early Southwest. Cleveland, OH, The Arthur H. Clark Co., 1926.
----- A Traveler in Indian Territory. The Journal of Ethan Allen Hitchcock. Cedar Rapids, IA: The Torch Press, 1930.
● GABRIEL, RALPH HENRY. The Pageant of America: the Lure of the Frontier. New Haven, CT: Yale University Press, 1929.
● HARMON, GEORGE DEWEY. Sixty Years of Indian Affairs, Political, Economic, and Diplomatic, 1789-1850. Chapel Hill, NC: University of North Carolina Press, 1941.
● HEBARD, GRACE RAYMOND., E. A. BRININSTOOL. The Bozeman Trail; Historical Accounts of the Blazing of the Overland Routes into the Northwest, and the Fights with Red Cloud's Warriors. Cleveland, OH: The Arthur H. Clark Co.
● HODGE, FREDERICK WEBB. Handbook of American Indians North of Mexico. Washington: Government Printing Office, 2 vols., 1907-10.
● HUMFREVILLE, J. LEE. Twenty Years Among Our Hostile Indians. New York, NY: Hunter & Co.
● JAMES, GEN. THOMAS. Three Years Among the Indians and Mexicans. (with notes and biographical sketches) St. Louis, MO: Missouri Historical Society, 1916.
● LOWIE, ROBERT H. The Crow Indians. New York, NY: Farrar and Rinehart, Inc., 1935.
● MURDOCK, GEORGE P. Ethnographic Bibliography of North America. New Haven, CT: Human Relations Area Files Press, 1975.
● POWERS, MABEL. The Indian as Peacemaker. New York, NY: Fleming H. Revell Co., 1932.
● RICHARDSON, RUPERT NORVAL. The Comanche Barrier to South Plains Settlement. Glendale, CA: The A. H. Clark Co., 1933.
● RISTER, CARL COKE. Border Captives, The Traffic in Prisoners by Southern Plains Indians, 1835- 1875. Norman, OK: University of Oklahoma Press, 1940.
● ROYCE, CHARLES C. Indian Land Cessions in the U.S. Washington: 18th Annual Report, Bureau of Ethnology, 1896-97.
● SEYMOUR, FLORA WARREN. Indian Agents of the Old Frontier. New York, NY: and London: D. Appleton-Century Co., Inc., 1941.
● SWANTON, JOHN R. The Indian Tribes of North America. Washington, DC: U.S. Government Printing Office, 1952.
● UNDERHILL, RUTH M. First Penthouse Dwellers of America. New York, NY: J. J. Augustin Publisher, 1938.
● WELLMAN, PAUL I. Death in the Desert. The Fifty Years' War for the Great Southwest. New York, NY: Macmillan Co., 1935.
----- Death on the Prairie, The Thirty Years' Sturggle for the Western Plains. New York, NY: The Macmillan Co., 1934.
● WISSLER, CLARK. Indians of the U.S., Four Centuries of Their History and Culture. New York, NY: Doubleday, Doran & Co., 1940.

CUMANA

(South America; Venezuela) comprise several tribes who live along the northeast coast of Venezuela. Carib-speaking, they are agrarian. Their numbers are not known, but the population is probably several hundred.

Culture. Women do all the work, as the men only clear the land for cultivation. They raise manioc, maize, and fruits. A man, after he marries, works for his wife's family for one year. Chiefs are permitted to have more than one wife. Social classes range from slaves to powerful chiefs. Trading takes place among the Cumana tribes for goods, and with other tribes for gold.

BIBLIOGRAPHY –

● STEWARD, JULIAN H. Handbook of South American Indians. 7 Vols., Washington, DC: U.S. Govt. Printing Office, 1946-59. *(see map page XVIII)*

CUNA

(Central America; Panama) are a people of romantic history noted for their warlike character. Their territory edged on what is now the Panama Canal Zone, and extended eastward and south in both high mountains and valleys to the northern tributaries of the large Tuira River of Darien. Smaller in stature than most neighboring tribes, they made up for this by fierce energy and national pride. The name Cuna means "the people," but those who live on the San Blas Islands off the northeast coast of Panama came to be called the San Blas.

Social and cultural boundaries and subdivisions. The two major divisions of this people are the Island Cuna or San Blas and the mainland Cuna. The Island Cuna had their culture influenced early and changed by their contacts and wars with the Spanish conquistadors, as well as by their collaboration with Dutch, British, and French pirates. The mainland Cuna, protected by high mountains and jungles, maintained a purer original culture, though, but in the last half of the nineteenth century, they too were changing. The Cuna were also vertically stratrified in the old days into the social subdivisions of chiefs, nobles, commoners and slaves. Today there seem to be only two divisions, the rich and poor. To the west of the Cuna were the equally warlike Guaymi, while to the east and south were their near and possibly ancestral relatives the Cueva, plus the more primitive Choco and Catio tribes.

Language. The Cuna belong to the Chibchan-Paezan language family, which includes all their neighbors to their west, east and southeast, as outlined above, plus the more highly-civilized Chibcha, who once dwelt in walled city-states in what is now the country of Columbia in South America.

BIBLIOGRAPHY –

● STEWARD, JULIAN H. Handbook of South American Indians. 7 Vols., Washington, DC: U.S. Govt. Printing Office, 1946-59.